# Accounting
## Theory and Practice

**Pearson Education**

We work with leading authors to develop the
strongest educational materials in Accounting bringing
cutting-edge thinking and best learning practice to
a global market.

Under a range of well-known imprints, including
Financial Times Prentice Hall, we craft high quality
print and electronic publications which help
readers to understand and apply their content,
whether studying or at work.

To find out more about the complete range of our
publishing please visit us on the World Wide Web at:
www.pearsoneduc.com

# Accounting
## Theory and Practice

**SEVENTH EDITION**

M W E Glautier

B Underdown

**FT** Prentice Hall
FINANCIAL TIMES

*An imprint of* **Pearson Education**
Harlow, England • London • New York • Boston • San Francisco • Toronto • Sydney • Singapore • Hong Kong
Tokyo • Seoul • Taipei • New Delhi • Cape Town • Madrid • Mexico City • Amsterdam • Munich • Paris • Milan

**Pearson Education Limited**

Edinburgh Gate
Harlow
Essex CM20 2JE
England

and Associated Companies around the world

*Visit us on the World Wide Web at*
*www.pearsoned.co.uk*

_____

First published in Great Britain in 1976
**Seventh edition published in 2001**

© Guardjust Ltd and B Underdown 2001

ISBN 0273-65161-7

*British Library Cataloguing in Publication Data*
A CIP catalogue record for this book can be obtained from the British Library

10 9 8 7 6 5
06 05 04

Typeset by 30 in 10/12pt Sabon
Printed by Ashford Colour Press Ltd., Gosport

Coventry University

# Contents

# Preface to the seventh edition

The tradition in accounting education has been to focus the teaching of accounting almost entirely upon procedures for processing financial data. The treatment of accounting as a skill, rather than as a body of knowledge, is based on the belief that 'accounting is what accountants do'. Whilst this assertion undoubtedly holds good as a statement of what accountants do, such a view of accounting has serious shortcomings as regards the educational qualities of accounting courses and the education of accountants. First, by restricting the nature and scope of accounting to an exposure of its procedures, it fails to provide an adequate understanding of these procedures in relation to the problems facing accountants. Second, it impedes the recognition of economic and social changes which bear directly on these problems. Third, it supports a conviction widespread among students and practitioners that what they have been taught is in the nature of an everlasting truth, or a collection of everlasting truths.

The most damaging factor as regards the teaching of accounting has been the absence of a theoretical framework to serve as a standard of reference for examining the validity of the assumptions held by accountants. As a result, accounting courses have sometimes tended to be virtually devoid of rigorous analysis, and to be characterized by the uncritical acceptance of the assumptions reflected in accounting procedures. It is not surprising, therefore, that teachers of other subjects tend to regard accounting as being qualitatively inferior in the potential which it offers for the development of the mind and person.

This textbook is committed to a different view of accounting education in a number of important respects. First, as its title *Accounting Theory and Practice* implies, it attempts to provide a theoretical framework for the understanding of the nature of the accounting problem and an appreciation of the purpose of various accounting practices. This approach permits accounting practices to be exposed to critical analysis by means of which their usefulness and relevance may be assessed and their shortcomings exposed. Second, the nature and the scope of accounting is extended beyond accounting procedures by conceiving the essential function of accounting as facilitating socio-economic activities and decisions. Accordingly, we give a global and rounded view of accounting in which the emphasis is appropriately placed on the role of accounting as being the provision of information for decision making.

We have interpreted the broad objectives of accounting as being to provide information for the following purposes:

1 decision making regarding the use of limited resources, including the identification of crucial decision areas, and the determination of objectives and goals;
2 effectively directing and controlling human and material resources;
3 maintaining and reporting on the custodianship of resources;
4 facilitating social functions and controls.

The textbook is divided into five parts (Figure numbers relate to Part numbers), as follows:

Part 1   A theoretical framework
Part 2   Financial accounting – the historical cost approach
Part 3   Financial reporting – alternative valuation approaches
Part 4   Financial reporting – extending the disclosure of information
Part 5   Management accounting

In Part 1 we discuss the nature and the importance of theory covering accounting knowledge and incorporating this knowledge into a unified whole, the purpose of which is the provision of information for decision making.

Part 2 examines the traditional nature of accounting information based on the historical cost approach which illustrates the way of thinking underlying financial accounting practices and looks at the development of financial accounting practice in the context of accounting conventions and standards.

Part 3 examines the problems of financial reporting in terms of alternative valuation methods to those employed in conventional financial accounting, which are based on historical cost.

Part 4 evaluates current financial reporting practices in terms of extending the disclosure of information to investors and employees as well as corporate social reporting.

Part 5 focuses on the role of information for management decision making and examines the needs of management relevant for planning and control.

We would emphasize that although this textbook is divided into five parts, each addressed to a special aspect of accounting, they are nevertheless linked by the provision of a theoretical framework which brings them together and establishes their purposes in the provision of information for decision making.

We believe that this book will be suitable for the following uses:

1  university first- and second-year degree courses in accounting;
2  first-year MBA courses in business schools;
3  professional examinations;
4  practising accountants who wish to acquire a broader viewpoint of the accounting process.

This new edition has been updated to take account of recent events such as developments in financial accounting standards, corporate governance, company taxation, social accounting and the ASB's revised Statement of Principles. Also this edition is more user-friendly. Where possible, the text has been simplified.

A *Lecturer's Guide* is available from Pearson Education free of charge to lecturers adopting this book and gives answers to selected Problems together with a selection of overhead transparency masters.

# Acknowledgements

We wish to place on record our gratitude to colleagues and friends for the advice and help which they have given us in the course of first writing this text. We owe a particular debt to Professor W Rotch and Charles Clark, who were both closely associated with every aspect of the book and who helped us unstintingly, as well as Professor T A Lee, Professor R H Parker, Professor A Hopwood, C P Rickwood, G J Harris, Dr H C Dekker, E C Johnson, C Burke, O A Bello and P J Taylor.

For help with the subsequent editions, thanks are due to: R W Wallis, M H C Lunt, A J Naughton, M Sherer, A Southworth and A Chandiok; to F S Hall, M A Nardone, R A Coates, M Skenfield, R W Wallis, Dr A Goodacre and P Hughes; to C J Jones and J Maltby of the University of Sheffield, and Professor J C Scheid of the Conservatoire Nationale des Arts et Métiers, Paris; and to G L Axelby, M Rimmington, Leslie Chadwick, David Citron, Judy Day, Paul Gordon, Robert Greenhalgh, Gillian Holmes, Peter Miller, Lydia Thompson, Alan Witts and David Welch. For help with the seventh edition, thanks are due to Debbie and Nick Reed, G L Axelby and Anne Underdown.

We have been privileged as authors to have had so much support from our publishers, and this book is indeed the outcome of a close partnership between authors and publishers. We wish to thank all those members of the Pearson staff who have worked with us. We are deeply indebted to Simon Lake, Pat Bond and Elizabeth Tarrant for their assistance in planning previous editions. We are indebted to Catherine Newman and Lyn Roberts for their assistance in planning the seventh edition. The late Dr Ken Watkins of Sheffield University was one of the original instigators of this book, and we owe much to his friendship.

# PART 1

# A theoretical framework

# 1 Scope of accounting

## Setting the scene

Accountants may seem unlikely revolutionaries, but we will see profound transformations in the ways in which they assess and report corporate performance. And the accounting challenge becomes even more urgent now that the sustainability agenda is opening up to embrace not only environmental and economic dimensions, but also social and ethical dimensions. This is why we increasingly talk of the 'triple bottom line' of sustainable development. Simply stated, this means that business people must increasingly recognise that the challenge now is to help to deliver simultaneously economic prosperity, enviromental quality and social equity. Accounting practice must recognise the new challenge.

(Elkington, 1998)

## Learning objectives

After studying this chapter you should be able to:

1 Explain how the changing environment has extended definitions of accounting.

2 Describe how accounting has developed through time.

3 Identify the factors which have caused accounting to be criticized in recent years.

4 Show how accountants have responded to these concerns.

Accounting is in an age of rapid transition; its environment has undergone vast changes in the last two decades and an accelerating rate of change is in prospect for the future. Changing social attitudes combine with developments in information and manufacturing technology, the adoption of new management philosophies and the growing intensity of competition, both local and global, to affect radically the environment in which accounting operates today, thereby creating the need to re-evaluate the objectives of accounting in a wide perspective. Accounting is moving away from its traditional procedural base, encompassing record-keeping and such related work as the preparation of budgets and final accounts, towards a role which emphasizes its social importance.

The changing environment has not only extended the boundaries of accounting but has created a problem in defining the scope of the subject. There is a need for a definition which is broad enough to delineate its boundaries, while at the same time being sufficiently precise as a statement of its essential nature. It is interesting to contrast definitions which were accepted a little time ago with more recent statements. According to a definition made in 1953, 'The central purpose of accounting is to make possible the periodic matching of costs (efforts) and revenues (accomplishments). This concept is the nucleus of accounting theory, and a benchmark that affords a fixed point of reference for accounting discussions' (Littleton, 1953).

The Committee on Terminology of the American Institute of Certified Public Accountants formulated the following definition in 1961: 'Accounting is the art of recording, classifying and summarizing in a significant manner and in terms of money, transactions and events which are, in part at least, of a financial character, and interpreting the result thereof' (AICPA, 1961).

A more recent definition is less restrictive and interprets accounting as the provision of 'information about the reporting entity's financial performance and financial position that is useful to a wide range of users for assessing the stewardship of management and for making economic decisions' (ASB, 1999).

An earlier definition which additionally acknowledges social welfare objectives is closer to our own interpretation of the scope of accounting and the manner in which we should like to treat the subject. We would add the rider that accounting is moving towards a consideration of social welfare objectives. Accordingly the purpose of accounting is to provide information which is potentially useful for making economic decisions and 'aims to assess the impact of an organisation or company on people both inside and outside' (Gonella *et al.*, 1998).

According to this latter viewpoint, the scope of accounting should not be restricted to the private use of information, which has the limited perspective of being concerned with the impact of information on the welfare of individuals as such. The social welfare viewpoint is concerned with improving the allocation of scarce resources. Another aspect of this viewpoint is reflected in the development of social accounting. In the past, the interests of shareholders, investors, creditors and managers have exerted a dominating influence on the development of accounting practices. The social welfare theory of accounting requires that the interests of employees, trade unions and consumers be taken into account, and that the traditional imbalance existing in the supply of information should be corrected. Social accounting draws attention to the gulf existing between the sectarian interests represented in conventional business accounting and its focus on profit, and the need to see the entire social role of business organization in the context of all those affected by its activities.

## The emerging role of accounting

The history of accounting illustrates how accounting is a product of its environment and at the same time a force for changing it. From today's perspective, we may distinguish three phases which may be said to correspond with its developing role.

1 Stewardship accounting has its origins in the function which accounting served from the earliest times in the history of our society of providing the owners of wealth with a means of safeguarding it from embezzlement. Wealthy men employed 'stewards' to manage their property. These stewards rendered periodical accounts of their stewardship, and this notion still lies at the root of financial reporting today. Essentially, stewardship accounting involves the orderly record-

ing of business transactions, and accounting records of this type date back to as early as 4500 BC. Stewardship accounting is associated, therefore, with the need of those in business to keep records of their transactions, the manner in which they invested their wealth and the debts owed to them and by them.

2 Financial reporting has a more recent origin, and dates from the development of large-scale businesses which were made possible by the Industrial Revolution. Indeed, the new technology not only destroyed the existing social framework, but altered completely the method by which business was financed. The industrial expansion in the early part of the nineteenth century necessitated access to large amounts of capital. This led to the advent of the joint stock company, which enables the public to provide capital in return for 'shares' in the assets and the profits of the company. The Joint Stock Companies Act 1844 permitted the incorporation of such companies by registration without the need to obtain a Royal Charter or a special Act of Parliament. In 1855, however, the Limited Liability Act permitted such companies to limit the liability of their members to the nominal value of their shares. This meant that the liability of shareholders for the debts incurred by the company was limited to the amount which they had agreed to subscribe. In effect, by applying for a £1 share, a shareholder agreed to subscribe £1, and, once he had paid that £1, he was not liable to make any further contribution in the event of the company's insolvency. Parliament eventually restated the doctrine of stewardship in a legal form. It made the disclosure of information to shareholders a condition attached to the privilege of joint-stock status and of limited liability. This information was required to be in the form of annual profit and loss accounts and balance sheets. We may say briefly that the former is a statement of the profit or loss made during the year of the report, and the balance sheet indicates the assets held by the firm and how those assets were financed.

The reluctance of company directors to disclose more than the minimum information required by law, along with growing public disquiet as to the usefulness of the information contained in financial accounts culminated in the extension of disclosure requirements in the United Kingdom by means of the Companies Acts 1948 to 1989.

The demand for improvements in corporate governance, i.e. the system by which companies are directed and controlled, has continued this process. For example, the Turnbull Committee's report (ICAEW, 1999) provides guidance to assist companies to implement disclosure requirements in respect of internal controls. This report requires directors to disclose in their annual report that there is an on-going process for identifying, evaluating and managing the significant risks faced by a company.

The legal importance attached to financial accounting statements stems directly from the need of a capitalist society to mobilize savings and direct them into profitable investments. Investors, be they large or small, must be provided with reliable and relevant information in order to be able to make efficient investment decisions.

3 Management accounting is also associated with the advent of industrial capitalism, for the Industrial Revolution of the eighteenth century presented a challenge to the development of accounting as a tool of industrial management. In isolated cases there were some, notably Josiah Wedgwood, who developed costing techniques as guides to management decisions. But the practice of using accounting information as a direct aid to management was not one of the achievements of the Industrial Revolution: this new role for accounting really belongs to the twentieth century.

Certainly, the genesis of modern management with its emphasis on detailed information for decision making provided a tremendous impetus to the development of management accounting in the early decades of this century, and in so doing considerably extended the boundaries of accounting. Management accounting shifted the focus of accounting from recording and analysing financial transactions to using information for decisions affecting the future.

The advent of management accounting demonstrated once more the ability and capacity of accounting to develop and meet changing socio-economic needs. Management accounting has contributed in a most significant way to the success with which modern capitalism has succeeded in expanding the scale of production and raising standards of living.

## Accounting in a changing environment

The process of change has had a dramatic impact on accounting theory and practice in recent years. Rapid changes in the environment have caused much concern and necessitated changes in accounting. The factors which have caused this concern may be identified as follows:

1 The status of the accounting profession has depended to some extent on its monopoly of the auditing and external financial reporting function. However, an important discussion document has attacked the concepts upon which external financial statements are based on the grounds that they are 'neither consistent nor logical and do not lead to a portrayal of economic reality' (ICAS, 1988). Much criticism has been directed at the lack of uniformity in the manner in which periodic profit is measured and the financial position of the enterprise represented. Also severe criticism has been directed at an external financial reporting system that allows management to provide cosmetic improvements to the firm's accounting performance, by the phenomenon of 'creative accounting' (Whelan and McBarnet, 1999). Furthermore, historic cost accounting produces misleadingly high profits in times of inflation.

2 Accounting is shaped by the environment in which it operates. Since this differs from country to country (due to legal, economic, political, cultural, etc. differences) very diverse national financial accounting systems have developed. For example, in some countries financial accounting developed to ensure that the proper amount of income tax is collected by the national government. In an expanding global economy where management and investors are increasingly making cross-border decisions, comparability of international financial information is essential.

3 Since the mid 1980s, following changes in the environment in which many organizations operate, traditional management accounting practices have attracted criticism for lagging behind the times, especially in view of technological developments. The argument has largely centred on the view that managers faced with having to make decisions in fully technology-driven situations are supplied with information by their firm's internal management systems which is inadequate. Johnson and Kaplan (1987) came to the conclusion that, in general, management accounting systems 'are not providing useful, timely information for process control, product costing and performance evaluation of managers'.

4 Increasingly, management is being held responsible not only for the efficient conduct of business as expressed in profitability, but also for what it does about an

endless number of social problems. Hence, with changing attitudes, the time-honoured standards by which performance is measured have fallen into disrepute. There is a growing consensus that the concepts of growth and profit as measured in traditional balance sheets and profit and loss accounts are too narrow to reflect what many companies are trying, or are supposed to be trying, to achieve.

Accountants have responded to these concerns as follows:

1 In the United Kingdom, the need to improve accounting practice was recognized formally by the creation of the Accounting Standards Committee in 1970. More recently, the Dearing Report's (1988) proposals have led to a new administrative structure for accounting standard setting that is designed to improve the quality of accounting standards and to strengthen the enforcement process.

   Much effort has been directed towards developing a theoretical framework for validating external financial reporting practices in terms of their perceived objectives, and to enable future development to take place in accordance with those objectives. In the United States the Financial Accounting Standards Board, since its inception in 1972, has been engaged in developing a series of statements which have established a conceptual framework for financial reporting. More recently, conceptual frameworks have been issued by the Institute of Chartered Accountants of Scotland (*Making Corporate Reports Valuable*, ICAS, 1988), the International Accounting Standards Committee (*Framework for the Preparation and Presentation of Financial Statements*, IASC, 1989), the Institute of Chartered Accountants in England and Wales (*Guidelines for Financial Reporting Standards, the Solomons Report*, ICAEW, 1989) and the Accounting Standards Board (*Statement of Principles for Financial Reporting*, ASB, 1999).

2 In 1973 the International Accounting Standards Committee (IASC) was founded by the accountancy bodies of nine countries with the fundamental aim of increasing comparability of financial information worldwide – or, more formally, 'to formulate and publish, in the public interest, accounting standards to be observed in the presentation of financial statements and to promote their worldwide acceptance and observance'. The IASC has expanded rapidly and now has 128 member bodies in 91 countries.

3 New management accounting systems have emerged in recent years. These systems have prompted the following comments:

   *Management accounting techniques have moved with the times and new techniques and approaches have grown in response to an increasingly competitive market environment for almost all businesses. As a consequence the breadth of activity and the rigour with which it is being monitored and measured within most companies has grown rapidly in the last ten years. (Eccles and Kahn, 1999)*

4 The emergence of social accounting imposes new information objectives for accountants, which will require a new accounting methodology. Latterly, the concept of social accounting has been enlarged to include a concern for ecology in the form of what has become known as 'green accounting'.

## Summary

In this chapter, we have examined the development of accounting from its earliest form as a recording activity to its present importance which stems from the objective of providing socio-economic information for decision making. The history of accounting development reflects the ability to respond to changing social needs.

*References*

Accounting Standards Board (1999). *Statement of Principles for Financial Reporting*.

AICPA (1961). *Committee on Terminology*, American Institute Publishing Co p 9.

Dearing Report (1988). *The Making of Accounting Standards*, Report of the Review Committee.

Eccles, R G and Kahn, H D (1999). *Value Reporting Forecast: 2000*, Price Waterhouse Coopers.

Elkington, J (1998). 'The Sustainability Agenda: Not For The Short Sighted', *Accounting and Business*, September.

Gonella, C, Pilling, A and Zadek, S (1998). *Making Values Count*, ACCA Research Report No 57.

Institute of Chartered Accountants of Scotland (1988). *Making Corporate Reports Valuable*.

Johnson, H T and Kaplan, R (1987). *Relevance Lost*, Harvard Business School.

Littleton, A C (1953). *The Structure of Accounting Theory*, AAA Monograph No 5, p 30.

Solomons, D (1989). *Guidelines for Financial Reporting Standards*, Research Board of the ICAEW.

Whelan, C and McBarnet, D (1999). *Creative Accounting and the Cross-Eyed Javelin Thrower*, John Wiley and Sons.

## Self-assessment questions

1 In what ways have the definitions of accounting changed over time?

2 Discuss the concepts of stewardship, financial and management accounting.

3 Consider the reasons why accounting has attracted criticism in recent years.

4 Describe how accountants have responded to those criticisms.

# 2 Accounting as an information system

**Setting the scene**

The accountants' basic rule as 'informative people' will become increasingly important. To prosper, an information-era company must have even more information and knowledge and use it even more quickly than ever before. The positioning of the accountancy profession is ideal to capitalise on these opportunities.

(R K Elliot, quoted in Fleming, 1999)

**Learning objectives**

After studying this chapter you should be able to:

1 Identify the boundaries between the accounting system and its environment.

2 Analyse the information needs of the groups of people who have vested interests in a business organization.

3 Explain how accounting assists the allocation of resources.

Accountants select raw data relevant to their purposes. The filtering process by which they select accounting data is provided by the conventions of accounting, which play a deterministic role in defining accounting information. This filtering process may be taken as one boundary between the accounting system and its environment: that point at which raw data becomes input data. The data selected forms the input into the processing system which provides accounting information. This information output is used by groups of decision makers, which are identifiable, and it is evident that a decision-oriented information system should produce information which meets the needs of its users. Clearly, these should be specified in accordance with a theory of users' requirements. We may say, therefore, that the other boundary to an accounting information system is established by the specific information needs of its users. We may model these boundaries as in Figure 1.1.

This analysis of accounting as an information system enables us to make some important deductions. First, the goal of the system is to provide information which meets the needs of its users. If we can sufficiently and accurately identify these needs, we can then specify the nature and character of the output of the system. Second, the output requirements should determine the type of data selected as the input for processing into information output. Third, welfare considerations may be taken into account in the selection of data, in accordance with the objectives of accounting stated in Chapter 1.

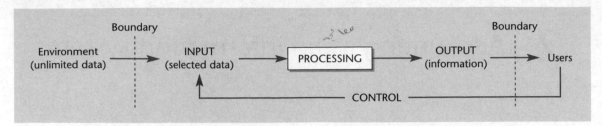

**Figure 1.1**

In this connection, the idea of *control* indicated (in Figure 1.1) shows that users' needs should determine not only the nature of data input but also the extent of the data input which should be determined by a cost-benefit analysis related to these needs and the impact of their decisions on society.

# The output of an information system

The foregoing discussion has served to indicate the importance of the needs of users of accounting information, for such needs determine the objectives of an accounting information system.

There are several groups of people who have vested interests in a business organization – managers, shareholders, employees, customers and creditors. Additionally, the community at large has economic and social interests in the activities of business organizations. This interest is expressed at national level by the concern of government in various aspects of firms' activities, such as their economic well-being, their contribution to welfare, their part in the growth of the national product, to mention but a few obvious examples; and at local level by the concern of local authorities and bodies in the direct socio-economic impact of the activities of local businesses.

According to the decision usefulness approach to accounting, users of accounting information should be regarded as decision makers interested in determining the sacrifices which must be made to obtain the benefits which are expected to flow from the decisions to which they commit themselves. Since all the sacrifices and the benefits necessarily materialize in the future, by reason of the nature of the decision-making process, uncertainty plays a critical role in assessing the sacrifices and benefits associated with particular decisions.

## The information needs of shareholders and investors

Historically, business accounting developed to supply information to those who had invested their wealth in business ventures. As we saw in Chapter 1, financial accounting emerged in the nineteenth century as a result of the need to protect investors in joint stock companies trading under limited liability. It has been evident for a long time that the information needs of investors are not completely met by published balance sheets and profit and loss accounts. In Part 2 we examine the nature of the information disclosed to shareholders and investors, and in Part 4 we subject traditional financial accounting practice considered in Part 2 to a critical analysis based on the question 'What additional information should be provided to investors?'

## The information needs of management

Organizations fall into two broad classes: those having profit objectives, and those having welfare objectives. In this book, we are concerned mainly with business organizations, but it should be remembered that many accounting methods employed in business organizations are also employed by welfare or non-profit organizations. As regards the management of organizations, little difference may exist between the information needs of managers of business organizations and those of managers of welfare organizations.

The management process may be analysed into three major functions – planning, organizing and controlling the activities of the organization. These various management functions have one thing in common: they are all concerned with making decisions, which have their own specific information requirements. Planning decisions, for example, are directed towards realizing broad goals which, in addition to the organization's survival and its profitability, usually include the intention to grow and to capture a large share of the market for its products and services. Other goals include product leadership, increased productivity and improved industrial relations. There is an element of conflict between various organizational objectives, and it is the function of management to reconcile them through the planning process.

## The information needs of employees

It is a popular view that the interests of employees are in direct conflict with those of the firm, and in particular with those of management. Unless employees are able to share in the profits of business organizations, they are effectively dissociated from their activities if we suppose that the objective of business organizations is to maximize profits and maximize returns to shareholders. This classical concept of the objective of business enterprises is being replaced as a result of the social changes taking place in our society, and there is a broadening view of the social and economic responsibilities of management. It is recognized that employees have a vested interest in the outcome of management decisions of every kind. Improvements in industrial democracy through employee participation in management decisions have important implications for the supply of information to employees. Many firms are already investigating this question. As regards the settlement of wage disputes, the question of profit sharing between employees, shareholders and management can only be settled properly on the basis of a full disclosure of the relevant facts. We touch upon these issues in Part 4.

## The information needs of governments

Government agencies, such as central statistical services, ministries of commerce, industry, employment, etc., collect information about the various aspects of the activities of business organizations. Much of this information is a direct output of the accounting system, for example, levels of sales activity, profits, investments, stocks, liquidity, dividend levels, proportion of profits absorbed by taxation, etc. This information is very important in evolving policies for managing the economy.

Governments, in addition, can compel the disclosure of information which is not otherwise made available to the public, such as future investment plans, expected future profits and so on.

By and large, however, governments expect accounting information to be presented in a uniform manner, so that the rules applying to accounting methods and the preparation of accounting reports for government use are the same as those which govern the nature of accounting information disclosed to investors and shareholders. If governments base policy decisions on accounting information which distorts the true position, it is evident that the ill effects of such decisions will be widely felt.

## The information needs of creditors

We define as creditors all those who have provided goods, money or services to business organizations and have accepted a delay in payment or repayment. Creditors may be short-term or long-term lenders. Short-term creditors include suppliers of materials and goods, normally described as trade creditors, credit institutions such as banks and hire-purchase firms which lend money at interest on a relatively short-term basis, and those who have provided services and are awaiting payment, for example, employees, outside contractors who have made repairs or electricity and gas undertakings which have rendered invoices and have not yet been paid. Long-term creditors are those who have lent money for a long period, often in the form of secured loans.

The main concern of creditors is whether or not the enterprise is creditworthy, that is, will it be able to meet its financial obligations? Creditors are interested in the enterprise's profitability only insofar as it affects its ability to pay its debts. On the other hand, creditors are very concerned with the firm's liquidity, that is, those cash or near-cash resources which may be mobilized to pay them, as well as the willingness of banks and other creditors to await payment. Creditors react quickly to changes of opinion about a firm's creditworthiness, and if there is any doubt about a firm's ability to pay, they will press for immediate settlement of debts and probably drive into liquidation a firm whose prospects in the medium and longer term are not necessarily bad. Creditors are interested, therefore, mainly in financial accounting information which affects solvency, liquidity and profitability, that is, with obtaining reports which will describe a firm's financial standing.

## The information needs of other groups

There are two other groups in society interested in the activities of business organizations, and which are pretty well excluded from receiving information: the local community and customers.

### The information needs of the local community

Local communities are very dependent on local industries, not only because they provide employment, but also because they directly affect the entire socio-economic structure of the environment. Firms provide employment, create a demand for local services, cause an expansion in commercial activities, as well as extensions in the provision of welfare services as the economic well-being of the community improves. Large firms, in particular, are able to exert a dominating influence on the local social framework which often is reflected in the corporate personality of the inhabitants. Local industries have both positive and negative influences on the locality. Pollution, despoliation and congestion are all negative aspects of their activities that constitute external direct and indirect social and economic costs, which are borne by the community.

The local community has an interest in the activities of local industries, and requires much more information on social benefits and costs than the public-relations-type information which is presently disclosed. The social audit points to a possible remedy for the lack of objectivity in the information presently disclosed.

### The information needs of customers

In recent years, consumer councils and other bodies have restored in some measure the disproportionate balance of power which has appeared in our society between the large and powerful producers of consumer goods and the voiceless masses of our population who have been at the former's mercy. In a few instances, the Monopolies Commission has acted to protect consumers, but its power to intervene is based upon law.

Customers may well have little influence in markets increasingly dominated by large business organizations, and it is difficult to see how, even if more information were made available, the balance might be redressed. Certainly, customers are interested in information indicating the fairness of pricing policies, such as the relative proportion of unit price which consists of costs, profits and taxes, and in the differential costs between one product and another produced by the same firm at a different price. For example, why should one electric shaver cost £10 more than another, and in what ways is this difference value for money? Clearly, there will be many more social changes in our society before questions of this sort will be recognized and adequately answered.

## Accounting information and the allocation of resources

The various groups of information users just discussed share a common concern, which is to make decisions about the allocation of scarce resources between competing ends. Students of economics will find that such a statement echoes a popular definition of the subject matter of economics. The importance of accounting information is that it makes such an allocation possible in a market economy, where individuals and organizations are largely free to allocate the resources which they control between competing ends. Therefore, one objective of an accounting information system is to enable information users to make decisions which improve the allocation of available resources within their control. Such decision making may be understood only in relation to the objectives of decision makers, so that the various groups of information users whose needs we have just discussed may be said to have very different and occasionally competing decision objectives. Therefore, the objective of accounting information systems is to enable decision makers to improve the allocation of the resources which they control and to assess the actual results of their decisions against the forecast results.

## Behavioural aspects of decision making

The central purpose of accounting is to produce information which will influence behaviour. Unless accounting reports have the potential to influence decisions and actions, it is difficult to justify the cost of preparing such reports. Traditionally, accounting reports have been addressed to shareholders and investors. In Part 4, the behavioural aspects of investor decision making are discussed and the role of accounting information in that context will be examined. In particular, the response of the Stock Exchange to the disclosure of accounting information through the reaction of share prices will be seen to be one way in which the influence of accounting reports of investors may be judged. In Part 5, the behavioural aspects of decision making within organizations are examined and the role of management accounting information as an influence in this respect will be discussed.

Since, from a management point of view, the purpose of accounting information is to enable the organization to attain its goals, it must follow that the effectiveness of accounting information is evidenced in the manner in which it affects behaviour. In this sense, unless accounting information produces the desired action, it has served no purpose at all. Research has shown, for example, that even when managers have all the information which they need, they do not always make good decisions. Hence, the human process which leads managers to recognize or fail to recognize the significance of accounting information deserves a better understanding, and accountants need to be aware of the role of accounting information to enable managers to identify their mistakes and to learn from them. Feedback information plays an important part in this process.

## Summary

We began this chapter with an examination of accounting as an information system consisting of three activities – input, processing and output. It is not sufficient, however, to view accounting purely as an operating system, for its relevance and usefulness may only be judged by the degree with which its output meets the needs of the users of accounting information. By identifying the basic goal of an accounting information system as being the provision of information for decision making, we provide a framework by which to judge the effectiveness of that system.

There are many approaches to the study of decision making – economic, behavioural and quantitative – and the interdisciplinary nature of decision theory has the inevitable consequence that accounting has also become an interdisciplinary subject. The systems approach facilitates an interdisciplinary study of accounting because it requires that it be viewed, not in isolation, but as one element in a broad informational context.

*Reference*   Fleming, P D (1999). 'Steering a Course for the Future', *Journal of Accountancy*, November.

## Self-assessment questions

1 State the groups of persons having vested interests in a business organization and examine the nature of their information needs.

2 Evaluate the role of accounting information in the allocation of resources.

# 3 The role of accounting theory

## Setting the scene

The construction of an accounting theory requires the justification or refutation of existing accounting practices. Under the traditional approach, construction and verification of a theory were considered virtually synonymous. In the past ten years, however, a new approach that employs a distinct verification process has emerged. The underlying objective of both approaches is the same: to develop a conceptual framework for what accountants do or are expected to be doing.          (Belkaoui, 1992)

## Learning objectives

After studying this chapter you should be able to:

1  Appreciate the nature of theories.

2  Explain how theory in accounting differs from that in the natural sciences.

3  Discuss the main features of the descriptive approach.

4  Identify two types of decision usefulness theories.

U nderlying the discussion of accounting as an information system is the important question of the field of knowledge to which accounting information refers. This raises issues about the nature and significance of accounting theory and the relationship between accounting theory and accounting practice.

The purpose of this chapter is to consider these various problems with a view to establishing the role of accounting theory.

## The nature of theories

Essentially, theories are generalizations which serve to organize otherwise meaningless masses of data, and which thereby establish significant relationships in respect of such data. The construction of theories requires a process of reasoning about the problems implicit in the data under observation, as a means of distinguishing the basic relationships. Thus, theory construction is a process of simplification, which requires assumptions that permit the representation of reality by a generalization that is easily understood. The close association of theory and data, or facts, is fundamental to the notion of good theory, for the reliability of a theory is dependent not only upon the facts to which it refers, but also upon an interpretation of those facts requiring validation and continuous reassessment.

Theories are concerned with explanation. Explanation relates a set of observations to a theoretical construction of reality which fits those observations. If no theoretical scheme that does this reasonably well is available, the desire for explanation leads to the creation of a scheme of ideas which provides a definition of the problem observed, as well as an understanding of it, in the form of explanation. In both cases, relating observations to existing theory, and constructing theory to fit observations, have the objective of providing an explanation of those observations.

A misunderstanding of the relationship that exists between facts and theories gives rise to a great deal of misconception about the role of theories. Thus, the complaint that 'it's all right in theory but not in practice' implies that the person making the complaint must hold the belief that an alternative theory provides a different explanation of the facts in question.

The word 'theory' itself gives rise to misunderstanding, and may mean different things to different people. This arises because explanations are made at different levels. At one extreme, explanations are purely speculative, resulting in speculative theories, for example that 'outer-space probes are affecting the weather'. To the

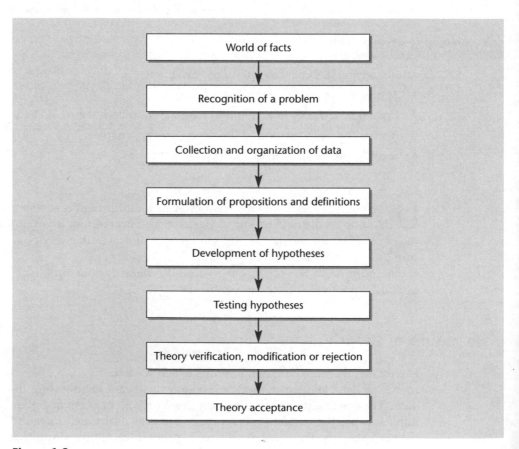

**Figure 1.2**

natural scientist, speculative theories are not really theories at all and explanations have to be conclusive before they are given the status of theories. To this end, their assumptions require verification by the test of experience. At another extreme are to be found explanations which are accepted only when they have been verified. Empirical theories are constructed by the process of verifying assumptions, or hypotheses, through the test of experience. This process is known as the 'scientific method', and is illustrated in Figure 1.2.

Empirical theories assist in making 'predictions', for while they consist of generalizations which explain the present, future occurrences also replicate the same conditions. It is in providing both explanations and predictions that empirical theories have acquired such importance in making decisions about the future which are based on assumptions derived from experience.

## Accounting theory

The word 'theory' is also used at different levels in the literature of accounting. Thus, references to 'accounting theory' may mean purely speculative interpretations or empirical explanations. These references usually do not indicate the level of theory which is implied.

According to Hendriksen,

> *Accounting theory may be defined as logical reasoning in the form of a set of broad principles that (1) provide a general frame of reference by which accounting practice can be evaluated, and (2) guide the development of new practices and procedures. Accounting theory may also be used to explain existing practices to obtain a better understanding of them. But the most important goal of accounting theory should be to provide a coherent set of logical principles that form the general frame of reference for the evaluation and development of sound accounting practices. (Hendriksen, 1992.)*

The relationship between accounting theory and accounting practice is indicated in Figure 1.3, as is the influence of policy makers in relating accounting theory to accounting practice.

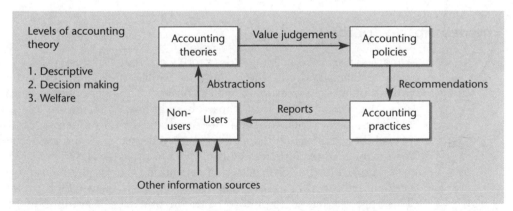

**Figure 1.3**

Figure 1.3 shows that the role played by theory in accounting is very different from that played in the natural sciences, where theories are developed from empirical observations. The converse is the case in accounting, since practice may be changed to accommodate theory. According to Ijiri,

> *Contrary to the fields of linguistics, meteorology or chemistry, accountants can change their practices relatively easily. Therefore, it becomes an essential problem for accountants to know how accounting practices should be developed in the future. The sanctions by which accounting policies have become implemented are quite essential in understanding the field of accounting, since it is possible to change practices to fit theories!! This is unthinkable for scientists in other fields for whom phenomena are almighty. No matter how beautiful and elegant the theory may be, if it does not fit the empirical phenomena, it is replaced by one which fits better. (Ijiri, 1971)*

Figure 1.3 also illustrates how the form of accounting information reported to decision makers depends on the practices adopted. These practices are imposed by accounting policy makers who, having knowledge of accounting theories, have the responsibility of responding to the needs of users of accounting information.

It is evident that deficiencies in four significant areas, namely accounting theory, policy making (by the profession and the government), accounting practice and the use of accounting information, impair the usefulness of an accounting information service. Thus, the failure of policy makers to incorporate research findings in the policies they devise may reduce the potential usefulness of accounting information.

## Approaches to the development of accounting theory

Several approaches to the development of accounting theory have emerged in the last two decades. These approaches may be identified as follows:

1 descriptive;
2 decision usefulness:
  (i) empirical;
  (ii) normative;
3 welfare.

### The descriptive approach

Theories developed using the descriptive approach are essentially concerned with what accountants do. In developing such explanations, descriptive theories rely on a process of inductive reasoning, which consists of making observations and of drawing generalized conclusions from those observations. In effect, the objective of making observations is to look for similarity of instances, and to identify a sufficient number of such instances as will induce the required degree of assurance needed to develop a theory about all the instances which belong to the same class of phenomena.

As applied to the construction of accounting theory, the descriptive approach has emphasized the *practice* of accounting as a basis from which to develop theories. This approach has attempted to relate the practices of accountants to a generalized theory about accounting. In this view, accounting theory is to be discovered by observing the practices of accountants because 'accounting theory is primarily a concentrate distilled from experience . . . it is experience intelligently analysed that produces logical explanation . . . and . . . illuminates the practices from which it springs' (Littleton and Zimmerman, 1962).

The descriptive approach results in descriptive or positive theories of accounting, which explain what accountants do and enable predictions to be made about behaviour, for example, how a particular matter will be treated. Thus, it is possible to predict that the receipt of cash will be entered in the debit side of the cash book.

In effect, the descriptive approach is concerned with observing the functional tasks which accountants have traditionally performed. In 1952, the Institute of Chartered Accountants in England and Wales stated that 'the primary purpose of the annual accounts of a business is to present information to proprietors showing how their funds have been utilized, and the profits derived from such use' (ICAEW, 1952).

Underlying the descriptive approach is the belief that the objective of financial statements is associated with the stewardship concept of the management role, and the need to provide the owners of businesses with information relating to the manner in which their assets have been managed. In this view, company directors occupy a position of responsibility and trust in regard to shareholders, and the discharge of these obligations requires the publication of annual reports to shareholders. With the growth of large corporate enterprises, the weakening of the links between ownership and management created a need for a more elementary notion of stewardship, in which the disclosure of financial information was aimed at protecting shareholders from fraudulent management practices.

As we will see in Part 2 and Part 4 when discussing the work of the Accounting Standards Board in relation to the development of accounting standards, it is evident that the descriptive approach to theory construction in accounting plays an influential role in shaping perceptions of the problems of accounting and the manner in which they should be solved. In effect, the Accounting Standards Board has been concerned with discussing the varied practices used by accountants and reaching a consensus on the most feasible basis on which to reduce the diversity of these practices through the process of standardization.

Figure 1.4 illustrates the framework within which descriptive accounting theory has developed. Elements will be discussed in Chapter 4, concepts in Chapter 5 and accounting procedures in Chapters 6–17.

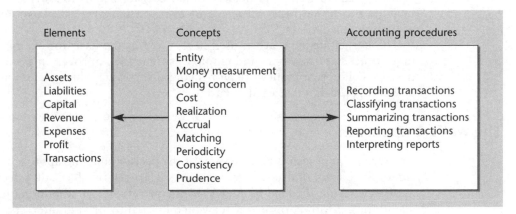

**Figure 1.4**

## Decision usefulness approaches

The expansion of behavioural research into accounting during the 1970s resulted in an interest in decision usefulness theories of accounting. This mood was well captured in the following statement by the American Accounting Association in 1971:

> To state the matter concisely, the principal purpose of accounting reports is to influence action, that is, behaviour. Additionally, it can be hypothesized that the very process of accumulating information, as well as the behaviour of those who do the accounting, will affect the behaviour of others. In short, by its very nature, accounting is a behavioural process. (AAA, 1971.)

Two types of decision usefulness theories of accounting have resulted from this approach, namely, empirical and normative theories.

### Empirical approach

The early 1970s witnessed a substantial increase in empirical research which was designed to make accounting research more rigorous and to improve the reliability of results. Sophisticated statistical techniques became increasingly used for this purpose. Furthermore, the expansion of university courses in accounting increased the number of students with a quantitative background, who could conduct research in this way. The implications of the empirical approach to research in accounting were significant in the development of accounting theory. These implications are discussed further in Part 4.

### Normative approach

Unlike empirical research, which concentrates on how users of accounting information apply this information in decision making, the normative approach to theory construction is concerned with specifying the manner in which decisions ought to be made as a precondition to considering the information requirement.

The normative approach focuses on the decision models which should be used by decision makers seeking to make rational decisions. This focus is seen as providing insights on the information needs of decision makers, as a basis for developing accounting theory.

The normative approach is used in this text as the basis for examining the information needs of investors and employees. It is the approach in recent attempts to develop conceptual frameworks for financial reporting which were noted in Chapter 1. This approach is discussed in Part 4.

## The welfare approach

The welfare approach is an extension of the decision-making approaches, which considers the effects of decision making on social welfare. Basically, decision-making approaches limit the field of interest to the private use of accounting information. If accounting information had a relevance limited to private interests, the decision-making approaches would provide a sufficient analysis of information needs. It is because of the external social effects of decisions made on the basis of accounting information that there is imputed a social-welfare dimension to accounting theory.

The effects of financial information on welfare may be viewed from the standpoint of the vested interests of groups within an organization. The needs of these groups were discussed in Chapter 2. It is evident that the alteration of accounting policies in favour of one group and away from another will affect the distribution of income and wealth within society. In this respect, the movement towards disclosing information to employees and the concept of social accounting, which are discussed in Chapters 24 and 25 respectively, are clearly causing such a change.

## Accounting policy makers

There are two main groups which determine accounting policy. First, the government employs the legislative process to ensure that a minimum level of information is disclosed in company reports. It also acts as a spur to prompt the accountancy profession into action, where there is an apparent urgent need. An example of this influence was the establishment of the Sandilands Committee by the government to consider the problem of accounting under conditions of price level changes. This problem will be discussed in Chapter 20. Another example was the Employment Protection Act 1975, which places a general duty on the employer to disclose information requested by trade union representatives at all stages of collective bargaining. This problem is discussed in Chapter 23.

Second, the accountancy profession itself acts as a regulatory body and deals with the problems of accounting standards implied in financial reports. The influence of the accountancy profession in making accounting policy is introduced in Chapter 6.

## Summary

This chapter has been concerned with an examination of the role of accounting theory in developing knowledge through the construction of theories. The importance of such theory construction for the improvement of accounting practice has also been discussed. The nature of theory was examined in detail in order to establish precisely the significance of theory to knowledge in general, and to accounting in particular. The several approaches to the development of accounting theory were reviewed. Attention was drawn to the successive stages beginning with descriptive theories, and proceeding to normative and to decision-making theories of accounting. The chapter concluded with an introduction to a movement towards welfare-oriented theories of accounting, and a discussion of the role of those responsible for making accounting policies in using the insights produced by research and incorporated in theories of accounting.

*References*    AAA (1971). 'Report of the Committee on the Behavioural Science Content of the Accounting Curriculum', *Accounting Review Supplement*, 46.

Belkaoui, A R (1992). *Accounting Theory*. 3rd edn, Academic Press.

Hendriksen, E S (1992). *Accounting Theory*, 5th edn, Richard D Irwin.

ICAEW (1952). *Accounting in Relation to Changes in the Purchasing Power of Money*, Recommendation No 15, paragraph 1, May.

Ijiri, Y (1971). 'Logic and sanctions in accounting', in Sterling, R R and Bentz, W F (eds), *Accounting in Perspective*, South Western Publishing Co.

Littleton, A C and Zimmerman, V K (1962). *Accounting Theory: Continuity and Change*, Prentice Hall.

## Self-assessment questions

1 Examine the nature of theories.

2 Analyse the relationship between accounting theory, accounting policy and accounting practice. To what extent does the quality of accounting policy and accounting practice depend on accounting theory?

3 Distinguish 'elements', 'concepts' and 'accounting procedures'.

4 Contrast the descriptive and normative approaches to theory construction.

5 Explain how the welfare approach to accounting theory differs from other approaches.

# Introduction to Part 2

Where business firms are concerned, a distinction is normally made between *financial accounting*, which is the activity of recording and analysing the financial results of transactions as a means of arriving at a measure of the firm's success and financial soundness, and *management accounting*, which is the activity of providing information to enable management to make efficient decisions as regards the use and allocation of the firm's resources. Here, the traditional practices of financial accounting based on historical cost valuations are examined. The approach used is based on a descriptive analysis of the practices of accountants, and leads to a descriptive theory of financial accounting. Therefore, we are concerned with *what* accountants do and the conventions and standards by which their activities are regulated.

As we pointed out in Chapter 3, financial reports produced on the basis of financial records may be analysed also in terms of the relevance of the information provided to users for the purposes of decision making. We suggest that such analysis should be conducted in terms of a normative theory. In this part, we restrict ourselves to the discussion of descriptive theories of financial accounting, focusing on accounting practices only; we address the problem of users' needs in Part 4, using normative theories for that purpose.

The purpose here is to examine the nature and the practices of financial accounting which is concerned with the following activities:

1 recording financial transactions;
2 summarizing and presenting financial information in reports.

The nature and methods of financial accounting are determined to a considerable extent by the concepts listed in Chapter 3, which exist among accountants for identifying, evaluating and communicating financial information. This is particularly true of the information which is provided for external users such as shareholders and investors. It is evident that unless accountants obey the same rules as regards selecting, measuring and communicating information to external users, the latter will be at a disadvantage in respect of the reliance which may be attached to the information they receive. The usefulness of accounting concepts lies in the uniformity and comparability of information which is made possible thereby. Accounting concepts secure for external users a greater degree of comparability in the information provided by the same firm over a period of years. Accountants do not in general attempt, however, to meet the specific information needs of external users, and the information which they provide is dictated by the concepts which they have followed for a very long time, rather than by the information needs of external users.

The users of external reports have no direct control over their contents. We may contrast Figure 2.1, which illustrates the boundaries of the financial accounting system for external users, with the user-orientated model shown in Figure 1.1. In this case, there is no direct control by the user over the final output. Hence, it may be suggested that the information system for external decision makers is not user-

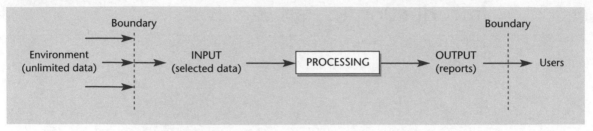

**Figure 2.1**

orientated. The output, and therefore also the input, into this system is determined by concepts embodied in accounting tradition and in law.

A basic assumption underlying communication is that there is a clear separation between the transmitter and the receiver of information. This is acknowledged also in financial reporting by the distinction drawn between the function of the accountant as the transmitter of information and the external user as the receiver of information. External users rely upon accountants to provide them with a significant supply of information for making economic decisions. It is for each user to evaluate and interpret this information when formulating decisions which only he or she may make. It is not the objective of the accountant as the preparer of financial reports to make such evaluations and draw conclusions for the external user. Consequently, it is not the function of the internal accountant to value a firm for the external user: on the contrary, it is for the investor to establish the value of the firm as an investment and to bear the risk involved in acting on such a valuation. The function of the internal accountant is to comply with the legal and other regulations that apply.

In line with this reasoning, we consider in this part the problems associated with the production of financial accounting information. We examine how data is selected from the environment, and the manner in which it becomes an input into the financial accounting system. We discuss also the manner in which the output of the financial accounting system is formulated as financial reports. We examine in Part 4 the relevance of these reports to the decisions which shareholders and investors wish to make.

We have limited our analysis of financial accounting information to those aspects which we consider important and relevant to the textbook as a whole. In Section 1, we examine financial accounting method to gain an understanding of its nature and of the principles underlying its procedures. In Section 2, we analyse the process of periodic measurement, which is one of its main applications. In Section 3, we select for closer analysis the application of financial accounting procedures to the production of financial statements for corporate enterprises.

One important application of financial accounting method relates to the use of accounting records for the day-to-day control of assets and liabilities. These technical aspects of control are treated as a 'background subject' in this text, so as not to detract from the important theoretical and practical aspects of the accountant's role in providing information for decision-making purposes.

# Financial accounting practice

# 4 Financial accounting statements

**Setting the scene**

Without adequate information, users of business reporting cannot judge properly the opportunities and risks of investment opportunities. To make informed decisions, they need a variety of information, including data about the economy, industries, companies and securities. Complete information provided by the best sources enhances the probability that the best decisions will be made. And for company-specific information – which is key because companies are the sources of cash flows that ultimately result in the return on securities or the repayment of loans – management often is the best source . . . In particular, financial statements are viewed as an excellent framework for capturing and organizing financial information.                                    (AICPA, 1994)

**Learning objectives**

After studying this chapter you should be able to:

1  Identify the main elements of a profit and loss account.
2  Explain the structure of a balance sheet, differentiating between fixed and current assets.
3  Appreciate the accrual basis of accounting.
4  Classify the sources and uses of cash flow from business activities.

The descriptive approach was introduced in Chapter 3 where we listed the elements which are contained in its framework – transactions, revenues, expenses, profit, assets, liabilities and capital. This chapter examines these elements and illustrates how they are incorporated in financial statements, which are a summary of all the individual transactions recorded during a period of time. A transaction is financial in nature and is expressed in terms of money. Financial statements are the final product of the accounting function. They give interested readers the opportunity to see what occurred in a neat summary. There are three basic statements, which are inextricably tied together:

1  the profit and loss account;
2  the balance sheet;
3  the cash flow statement.

# The profit and loss account

The measurement of profit is probably the most important function of financial accounting. Investors, managers, bankers and others are interested in knowing how well a business is doing. The profit and loss account shows the results of the 'flow' of activity and transactions and is designed to report the profit performance of a business for a specific period of time, such as a year, quarter or month. Profit represents the difference between revenues and expenses. The profit and loss account reports for a specific period of time the items that comprise the total revenue and total expense and the resulting net profit.

The profit and loss account of Albert Trader is shown below. Note how the heading of the statement specifically identifies the name of the business, the title of the report and the period of time over which the reported net profit was earned.

**Albert Trader**
**Profit and loss account for the year ended 31 December 20X1**

|  | £000 | £000 |
|---|---|---|
| Sales revenue |  | 220 |
| Cost of sales |  | 103 |
| Gross trading profit |  | 117 |
| *Less:* Other expenses |  |  |
| Rent and rates | 6 |  |
| Lighting and heating | 4 |  |
| Wages | 40 |  |
| Depreciation of shop equipment | 8 |  |
|  |  | 58 |
| Profit before interest and tax |  | 59 |
| *Less:* Interest expense |  | 1 |
| Profit before taxation |  | 58 |
| Taxation |  | 20 |
| Net profit |  | 38 |

## Sales revenue

Revenue is earned by a business when it provides goods and services to customers. Whereas a trading business, like that of Albert Trader, will derive revenue mainly from sale of merchandise, a business which renders services, such as a solicitor, will derive revenue as a result of charging for that service. It is not necessary for a business to receive cash before recognizing that revenue has been earned. As we discuss later in this chapter, and more fully in Chapter 5, the accruals concept recognizes revenue which arises from the sale of goods or services on credit.

## Cost of goods sold

This shows the cost of goods sold to produce the revenue. For a trading business like Albert Trader, cost of goods sold equals opening stock, plus purchases, minus closing stock. When calculating business profit for a period, the sales revenue for that period and the costs of earning that revenue must be matched with one another in the profit and loss account.

## Other expenses

In addition to the cost of goods sold, other expenses such as rent and rates, lighting and heating and wages, as shown in Albert Trader's profit and loss account, are incurred in earning revenue. Such expenses may require the immediate payment of cash, or, in the case of credit, the payment of cash some time after the expense is incurred. In some cases, cash is paid before the expense is incurred, as in the case of the payment of office rent in advance of occupancy. For accounting purposes, an expense is recognized in the period in which it is incurred, which is not necessarily the same as the period in which the cash is paid. The period in which an expense is deemed to be incurred is the period in which the goods are used or the services are received.

An expense may represent the cost of using equipment or buildings that were acquired and are being held for use in operating the business rather than for sale. Such items often have a high initial cost at the date of acquisition and, through use, are consumed over an extended period of time known as their useful life. As they are used in operating the business, a portion of their initial cost becomes an expense, known as depreciation. In Albert Trader's profit and loss account £8,000 depreciation of shop equipment is recorded.

## Net profit

Net profit is the excess of total revenues over total expenses. If the total expenses exceed the total revenues, a net loss is reported. Where revenues and expenses are equal for the period, the business is said to break even.

## The balance sheet

The balance sheet, sometimes called the statement of financial position, lists the assets owned by a business, the liabilities owed to others and the accumulated investment of its owners. The balance sheet shows these balances at a specific date. Even though the business is the result of trading over time, the balance sheet is only a 'snapshot' of what the business's resources and obligations are at a stated time. This differs from the profit and loss account which, as we have seen, reports inflows and outflows of resources over a period of time.

The balance sheet may provide helpful information in determining the degree of financial risk. For example, a bank considering a short-term loan to a business would want to know the financial position of the business at the time of the loan.

Albert Trader's balance sheet is shown below. Note how the heading of the balance sheet specifically identifies the name of the business, the title of the report and the specific date of the statement. To assist the preparation of the cash flow statement later in the chapter, we show the balance sheet figures for two years.

**Albert Trader**
**Balance sheet at 31 December 20X1 and 20X0**

| | 31.12.20X1 | | 31.12.20X0 | |
|---|---|---|---|---|
| **Fixed assets** | £000 | £000 | £000 | £000 |
| Store equipment at cost | | 90 | | 60 |
| Accumulated depreciation | | 20 | | 12 |
| Net book value | | 70 | | 48 |
| **Current assets** | | | | |
| Stock | 80 | | 60 | |
| Debtors | 21 | | 10 | |
| Cash | 1 | | 2 | |
| | 102 | | 72 | |
| **Current liabilities** | | | | |
| Trade creditors | 26 | | 32 | |
| **Working capital** | | 76 | | 40 |
| | | 146 | | 88 |
| **Owner's capital** | | | | |
| Opening balance | 88 | | 56 | |
| Net profit for year | 38 | 126 | 32 | 88 |
| **Long-term liability** | | | | |
| Loan | | 20 | | 0 |
| | | 146 | | 88 |

*(handwritten annotations: "long up value", "transferred into cash", "Depreciation –")*

## Assets

Assets are things of value which are possessed by a business. In order to be classified as an asset the money measurement concept, which will be discussed in Chapter 5, demands that a thing must have the quality of being measurable in terms of money. The assets of a business are classified into fixed and current assets, as shown in Albert Trader's balance sheet.

### Fixed assets

Fixed assets are used in the business and are not intended for resale. They include assets having a long life such as buildings, equipment and vehicles. Fixed assets, with the exception of land, are depreciated over time as they are used. Since their productive life is limited, their initial cost is apportioned to expense over their estimated useful life. As we saw earlier, the amount of depreciation for the year is recorded in the profit and loss account as an expense. The cumulative amount of depreciation expense for all past periods since acquisition is deducted on the balance sheet from the cost of the asset to derive the net book value of the asset. This does not represent the current value of the asset. In the case of Albert Trader, the net book value of his fixed assets is shown as £70,000 at 31.12.20X1.

A fixed asset for one business may be a current asset for another. For example, a car is a fixed asset if it is to be driven by a salesman for the next two years, but a current asset if it is held as stock for sale by a car sales company.

### Current assets

Current assets are those which are expected to be transformed during the near future, usually one year, into cash. They include stocks such as materials, supplies, work-in-progress and finished goods as well as debtors. Debtors represent amounts due from customers in respect of past sales on credit. Cash is the amount of cash in the premises, or in the bank, at the balance sheet date.

Assets are reported in the balance sheet in order of increasing liquidity, i.e. the list starts with the items least likely to be turned into cash in the near future.

## Current liabilities

Current liabilities are the amounts owing by the business which will fall due for payment within one year. Most firms find it convenient to buy merchandise and services on credit terms rather than to pay cash. This gives rise to liabilities known as trade creditors – £26,000 at 31.12.20X1 in the case of Albert Trader. The reason why amounts of money owed to the creditors of a business are known as liabilities is that the business is liable to them for the amounts owed.

## Working capital

A business must have sufficient working capital to be able to pay its way and settle its immediate obligations. This implies that there must be funds available for the purchase of stock requirements, for the payment of trade creditors and general running expenses of the business. Working capital (also known as 'net current assets') is the difference between current assets and current liabilities. The working capital of Albert Trader at 31.12.20X1 is:

Current assets – Current liabilities = Working capital
£102,000 £26,000 £76,000

The business has an excess of £76,000 to use in operations after the current assets are converted into cash and the current liabilities are paid. From a banker's viewpoint, a trader with a large amount of working capital may be considered a good credit risk because the business can make its debt payments. Conversely, it may also show that the trader is mismanaging his stocks by holding too many goods or too much cash. The proper amount of working capital depends on the industry concerned.

## Owner's capital

Owner's capital (or owner's equity) represents the owner's investment in the business. Albert Trader's balance sheet shows that the net profit for the year is added to the owner's opening capital.

**Loan**

The loan shown in Albert Trader's balance sheet is classified as a long-term liability. Long-term liabilities, which are due in a period exceeding one year, arise when a firm borrows money as a means of supplementing the funds invested by the owner. In the case of Albert Trader the profit and loss account shows that £1,000 was paid in interest on the loan during the year.

## The accrual basis of accounting

The profit and loss account and balance sheet are based on accrual accounting. As we have explained, profit or loss is measured by matching a period's sales revenue with the expenses incurred in earning those revenues. In accrual accounting cash receipts and payments are replaced by revenues earned and expenses incurred. Any outstanding amounts of cash owed to, or owed by, the business are then recorded as debtors or creditors (as the case may be) in the balance sheet at the end of the period. It is generally agreed that profit measured in this way is a better indicator of a business's economic performance in a period than profit determined on a cash in/out basis.

## The cash flow statement

Cash is the lifeblood of a business. A healthy cash flow (measured as cash inflows minus cash outflows) is fundamental to a business's ability to survive and prosper. Users of financial statements who look merely at the profit and loss account for a measure of financial health can be deceived. Indeed, many businesses with apparently strong profits have foundered through poor control over their cash flow. The cash flow statement can be used by management to avoid such liquidity problems. Its purpose is to show what cash has been generated by a business's operations and where the cash has gone. The importance of cash flow was recognized by the Accounting Standards Board's first standard which came into effect in 1992, and which was revised in 1996. This standard is examined in detail in Chapter 15.

A cash flow statement classifies the sources and uses of cash flow from several types of business activities.

- *Operating activities.* Cash flows from operating activities are the cash effects of transactions relating to operating or trading activities. They are the cash effects of transactions that enter into the determination of operating profit, i.e. profit before interest and tax.
- *Returns on investments and servicing of finance.* These are receipts resulting from the ownership of an investment and payments to providers of finance. They include interest received and interest paid.
- *Taxation.* These are cash flows to and from taxation authorities.
- *Capital expenditure.* These are cash flows associated with the acquisition and disposal of fixed assets.
- *Financing activities.* These comprise receipts from, or repayments to, external providers of finances.

33

These activities are disclosed clearly in cash flow statements as illustrated in the case of Albert Trader below.

**Albert Trader**
**Cash flow statement for the year ended 31 December 20X1**

| Operating activities | £000 | £000 |
|---|---|---|
| Operating profit | | 59 |
| | | |
| Add back non-cash expenses | | |
| Depreciation charges | | 8 |
| | | 67 |
| | | |
| Adjust for changes in working capital | | |
| Stock (increase) | (20) | |
| Debtors (increase) | (11) | |
| Creditors (decrease) | (6) | |
| | | (37) |
| | | |
| Net cash inflow from operating activities | | 30 |
| | | |
| Returns on investment and servicing of finance: | | |
| Interest paid | | (1) |
| Tax paid | | (20) |
| Capital expenditure | | (30) |
| Financing activities: | | |
| Proceeds from loan | | 20 |
| Decrease in cash | | (1) |

## Preparation of the cash flow statement

The preparation of the cash flow statement requires the following information:

1 the profit and loss account for the current period;
2 the balance sheet for the current period;
3 the balance sheet for the prior period.

### Operating activities

In the operating activities section of the cash flow statement accountants calculate the cash generated from the day-to-day operations of a business. The accrual basis net profit is converted to a cash basis by two adjustments:

1 Add back non-cash expenses. For example, depreciation is a 'book item' only and does not represent an outflow of cash. Such an outflow occurs when fixed assets are purchased or disposed of, an occurrence which is included later in the 'Investing activities' section.
2 Adjust net profit for changes in working capital. A comparison of the stock figure in Albert Trader's balance sheet shows that this item increased by £20,000 during the current period (from £60,000 to £80,000). This indicates an increase in cash requirements. Similarly, both Albert Trader's debtors and creditors require an

increase in cash. In total, changes in working capital over the years required the use of £37,000 additional cash.

### Interest paid

Albert Trader paid £1,000 in interest on the loan he took out during the year.

### Tax paid

Albert Trader paid £20,000 in tax.

### Capital expenditure

When a business buys or sells a long-term asset like a building or piece of equipment, the cash relating to the transaction is reflected in the capital expenditure section of the cash flow statement. In the case of Albert Trader, £30,000 was invested in shop equipment between the two balance sheet dates and this is shown on the cash flow statement.

### Financing activities

The two balance sheets show that Albert Trader borrowed £20,000 during the year in order to finance the increase in working capital and the purchase of shop equipment.

### Decrease in cash balance

The reader will note that Albert Trader's cash flow statement explains why the cash balance has decreased by £1,000 despite borrowing £20,000 in the form of a loan and generating £67,000 from operating profit plus depreciation. £37,000 was required to adjust for changes in working capital and £30,000 was required to finance the purchase of fixed assets.

## Summary

This chapter has introduced the three basic statements – the profit and loss account, the balance sheet and the cash flow statement. The profit and loss account reflects only operating activities, the matching of revenues and expenses in earning profit. The balance sheet describes a business's financial position at a point in time. The cash flow statement, unlike the other two statements, is not based on accrual accounting. It reports on cash received and cash payments.

*Reference*  AICPA (1994). *Improving Business Reporting – A Customer Focus* (The Jenkins Report), American Institute of Certified Public Accountants.

## Self-assessment questions

1 What is the purpose of a profit and loss account?

2 What is the purpose of a balance sheet?

3 What is the relationship between the profit and loss account and the balance sheet?

4 Briefly define (a) fixed assets; (b) current assets; (c) current liabilities; (d) working capital.

5 In respect of fixed assets as reported on the balance sheet explain (a) cost; (b) accumulated depreciation; (c) net book value.

6 Explain the difference between a profit and loss account and a cash flow statement.

7 What are the main sections of a cash flow statement?

# 5 Financial accounting concepts

**Setting the scene**

Certain kinds of accounting conventions seem puzzling, even arbitrary, to laymen. Some expenses are accrued as they are incurred, but others are accrued as they are likely to be; some revenue is recognized all at once, other revenue is recognized as time passes. It should be one objective of accounting theory to furnish explanations of seeming inconsistencies in practice, explanations which could be given to laymen if necessary. Perhaps further examination would show that these practices are not, as they might seem, conventional customs that have become coloured with a tinge of arbitrariness. Good and sufficient reasons still control all so-called conventional accounting actions.

(Littleton, 1953)

**Learning objectives**

After studying this chapter you should be able to:

1 Explain how the entity, the money measurement and the going concern concepts affect the basic financial accounting statements.

2 Discuss the assumptions inherent in the cost and realization concepts.

3 Describe the role of the accruals and matching concepts in financial statement preparation.

4 Discuss the periodicity, consistency and prudence concepts.

The concepts of accounting discussed in this chapter may be seen as related to the general problem of developing viable theories of financial accounting. As we shall see, their origin lies in a historical process of development. The on-going nature of this process is discussed in Chapter 6, where the review of the concepts of financial accounting by the accounting profession is seen to focus on the formulation of standard accounting practices.

We mentioned in the Introduction to this part that the nature of financial accounting information is not dictated by the needs of external users, but rather is determined to a considerable extent by the concepts which exist among accountants for identifying, evaluating and communicating financial information. In this chapter, we analyse the nature and the effects of accounting concepts on the manner in which accountants generate financial information. The need for these concepts is discussed, as well as the problems which they pose.

## The nature of financial accounting concepts

Accounting concepts define the assumptions on which the financial accounts of a business are prepared. Financial transactions are interpreted in the light of the concepts which govern accounting methods. In effect, the concepts of financial accounting largely determine the interpretations given in financial reports of the events and results which they portray. For example, the concept relating to the recognition of revenue determines the dimension of the profit reported to shareholders and the value of the enterprise as judged from the balance sheet.

Figure 2.2 illustrates the manner in which financial accounting concepts act as filters in selecting data as input into the processing system and as output of information for users.

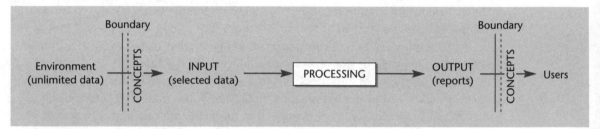

**Figure 2.2**

## Financial accounting concepts

Financial accounting is founded on the following principal concepts:

1  entity
2  money measurement
3  going concern
4  cost
5  realization
6  accruals
7  matching
8  periodicity
9  consistency
10  prudence/conservatism.

### The entity concept

The practice of distinguishing the affairs of the business from the personal affairs of its owner originated in the early days of double-entry bookkeeping some 400 years ago. Accounting has a history which reaches back to the beginning of civilization, and archaeologists have found accounting records which date as far back as 4000 BC, well before the invention of money. Nevertheless, it was not until the fifteenth century that the separation of the owner's wealth from the wealth invested in a business venture was recognized as necessary. This arose from the use of paid managers or stewards to run a business who were required to render accounts of their stewardship of the funds and assets. Consequently, the 'capital' invested in the business represented not only the initial assets of the business but a measure of its indebtedness to the owner. This principle remains enshrined in modern financial accounting, and the owner is shown as entitled to both the 'capital' which s/he has invested in the business, and also the profits which have been made during the year. The accounting and legal relationship between the business and its owner is shown on the balance sheet, which states the firm's assets and liabilities and hence indicates its financial position and well-being.

**Example 1**  J Soap recently inherited £30,000 and decides that the moment is opportune for him to realize his lifetime ambition and open a hairdressing salon. Accordingly, he makes all the necessary arrangements to begin on 1 April 20X0, under the name 'J Soap – Ladies' Hairdresser', and commits £10,000 of his money to that business. He therefore opens an account at his bank under the name 'J Soap – Ladies' Hairdresser'.

As a result, the financial position of the firm on 1 April 20X0, from an accounting point of view, will appear as follows:

**J Soap – Ladies' Hairdresser**
**Balance sheet at 1 April 20X0**

| Capital | £10,000 | Bank balance | £10,000 |
|---|---|---|---|

The business is shown as having £10,000 as its asset at that date, and as owing J Soap £10,000, that is, recognizing its indebtedness to him in respect of the capital he has invested therein.

The accounting effect of the entity concept is to make a clear distinction between J Soap's private affairs and his business affairs: what he does with his remaining £20,000 is of no concern to the accountant, but what happens to the £10,000 invested in the business is the subject matter of accounting.

The interesting aspect of the entity concept is that it establishes a fictional distinction between J Soap and the business which is not recognized in law: he remains legally liable for the debts of the business, and should the business fail, he will have to pay the creditors out of his private funds.

In the case of corporations, there is a legal distinction between the owners, that is the shareholders, and the business, so that the shareholders are not liable for the corporation's debts beyond the capital which they have agreed to invest. The accounting treatment of the relationship between the shareholders and the corporation is no different from that accorded to the sole trader and his business, except of course that the capital of the corporation is divided into a number of shares.

**Example 2**  Multiform Toys plc was registered on 1 April 20X0 as a public limited company, the objective being to manufacture a wide range of children's toys. The promoters need £100,000 to launch the company. They offer for sale 100,000 £1 ordinary shares to the public, and agree themselves to subscribe for 25,000 shares.

If we assume that all the shares have been issued and paid for on 1 May 20X0, the balance sheet will be as follows:

### Multiform Toys plc  Balance sheet at 1 May 20X0

| | | | |
|---|---|---|---|
| Share capital | £100,000 | Bank balance | £100,000 |

The promoters are now shareholders, together with those members of the public who have subscribed for the shares. The liability of the company to the shareholders amounts to £100,000, and the company has £100,000 cash to pursue its objectives.

The effect of the entity concept in the case of an incorporated business is to recognize the separate identity of the company from that of its shareholders. The shareholders themselves are not liable for the debts of the company, and their liability is limited to the £100,000 which they have subscribed. We shall discuss the full implications of incorporation from an accounting point of view in Chapter 13.

## The money measurement concept

Both trade and accounting existed before the invention of money, which we know began to circulate in the sixth century BC. Its role as a common denominator, by which the value of assets of different kinds could be compared, encouraged the extension of trade. By Roman times, money had become the language of commerce, and accounts were kept in money terms. Hence, there is an accounting tradition which dates back some 2,000 years of keeping the records of valuable assets and of transactions in monetary terms. It is not surprising, therefore, that accounting information today reflects the time-hallowed practice of dealing only with matters capable of expression in money.

The money measurement concept sets an absolute limit to the type of information which may be selected and measured by accountants, and hence limits the type of information which accountants may communicate about a business enterprise.

**Example 3**  The Solidex Engineering Co Ltd is a long-established company which specializes in the production of a single component used in the manufacture of mining gear. The balance sheet at 31 December 20X0 reveals the following position:

### The Solidex Engineering Co Ltd
### Balance sheet at 31 December 20X0

| | £ | £ |
|---|---|---|
| **Fixed assets** | | |
| Land and buildings | 30,000 | |
| Equipment | 25,000 | |
| | | 55,000 |
| **Current assets** | | |
| Stocks | 30,000 | |
| Bank balance | 15,000 | |
| | | 45,000 |
| | | 100,000 |
| **Share capital** | | 100,000 |
| | | 100,000 |

For some time, it has been known that a competitor has developed a better product, and that the company is likely to lose its market. The managing director is ill, the production manager and the accountant are not on speaking terms and the labour force is resentful about the deterioration in working conditions in the factory. The buildings are dilapidated, but the land itself is valuable. The equipment is old and needs a great deal of maintenance, and as a result, there is a considerable wastage of labour hours because of machinery breakdowns.

It is clear from the foregoing example that the most significant information of interest to shareholders is not what is contained in the balance sheet but the information which is left out of it, which is much more relevant to an understanding of the firm's position. Yet, the accountant is unable to measure and communicate that information to shareholders directly in money terms, although all these facts may explain poor profit figures. The reader of a financial accounting report should not expect, therefore, that all or perhaps even the most important facts about the business will be disclosed, and this is why there is such a premium on 'inside' information in order to make correct assessments of a firm's true position. One of the major problems of accounting today is to find means of solving the measurement problem: how to extend the quality and the coverage of information in a way which is meaningful. The advantage of money terms is that the layman is able to grasp the meaning of facts which are stated in money, and it remains the obvious standard of measurement.

There are further problems associated with the practice of using money as a standard of measurement in accounting. Money does not have a constant value through time, nor does the value of specific assets remain the same in relation to money. Until recently, accountants turned a blind eye to this problem by assuming that the money standard did have a constant value. The rising rates of inflation in the 1960s and 1970s destroyed this fiction.

Financial accounting records serve two distinct and important purposes. First, they provide evidence of the financial dimensions of rights and obligations resulting from legal contracts. For this purpose these records must be kept in the form of unadjusted money measurements. Second, they are used as a basis for providing financial information for shareholders, investors and a variety of users who need such information for decision making. For this purpose, money measurements must reflect the economic reality of business transactions and for this reason must be adjusted for changes in price levels. In this part we discuss the first purpose of financial accounting records, and in Parts 3 and 4 we discuss the second.

## The going concern concept

The valuation of assets used in a business is based on the assumption that the business is a continuing one, not on the verge of cessation. This concept is important: many assets derive their value from their employment in the firm, and should the firm cease to operate the value which could be obtained for these assets on a closing-down sale would probably be much less than their book value.

**Example 4**  The Zimbabwe Gold Mining Company Ltd has been mining gold for many years. Its assets consist of a mineshaft half a mile deep which enables the company to reach the gold reef, small-gauge railway tracks and trucks within the mine, lifting gear, conveyor belts, crushing plant and sundry equipment. The balance sheet at 1 April 20X0 shows the following position:

**The Zimbabwe Gold Mining Company Ltd**
**Balance sheet at 1 April 20X0**

| Fixed assets | £ | £ |
|---|---|---|
| | | |
| Mineshaft | 500,000 | |
| Land and buildings | 25,000 | |
| Plant and equipment | 200,000 | |
| | | 725,000 |
| **Current assets** | | |
| Tools | 15,000 | |
| Gold in transit | 50,000 | |
| Bank balance | 10,000 | |
| | | 75,000 |
| | | 800,000 |
| | | |
| **Owners' capital** | | |
| Share capital | | 500,000 |
| Retained profit | | 300,000 |
| | | 800,000 |

The mineshaft was sunk originally with the money raised by the issue of shares, and the other assets were financed out of loans which were repaid out of profits, which were not distributed to shareholders. In terms of the entity convention the total indebtedness of the company to shareholders is, therefore, £800,000 – which is the amount they might expect to receive if the company ceased to operate. For the time being, apart from £60,000 in gold or cash, their interest is substantially the mineshaft and the plant and equipment amounting to £700,000. If the gold reef ceased to be economically workable and the mine had to be abandoned, the mineshaft, being purely a hole in the ground, would become valueless, as would much of the plant. Hence, it is unlikely that shareholders would get back even a fraction of their investment.

The going concern concept underpins the historical cost values shown in the balance sheet. To abandon this concept would imply that assets should be valued on a realizable value basis. In recent years, as we will see in Chapter 6, the concept has been extended to include the survival of the enterprise for the 'foreseeable future'.

# The cost concept

Accountants calculate the value of an asset by reference to the cost of acquisition, and not by reference to the value of the returns which are expected to be realized. Hence, the 'value in use' of assets which the going concern concept maintains is the cost of acquisition. To the accountant, the difference between the value in use and the cost of acquisition of an asset is profit:

$$\text{Value in use} - \text{Cost of acquisition} = \text{Profit}$$

**Example 5**   W E Audent & Son is a firm of chartered accountants with a large audit practice. Its major asset is the staff of audit clerks. The value in use of the staff may be calculated by reference to the hourly rate at which their services are charged out to clients; the cost of securing their services to the firm is represented by their salaries; and the annual profit of the firm is the difference, less, of course, the administrative expenses of running the firm.

In accounting, cost is used as a measure of the financial 'effort' exerted in gaining access to the resources which will be deployed in earning revenues. Since these resources are secured through financial transactions, the financial effort is measured at the time of acquisition, which coincides, of course, with the legal obligation to pay for those resources in money. The cost concept raises the following problems:

1 The historical cost of acquisition of assets is not a dependable guide to their current value because it fails to reflect:
   (a) changes in the general purchasing power of money;
   (b) changes in the specific value of individual assets in relation to money.
2 The historical cost of acquisition of assets used up in the activity of earning profit does not form a dependable basis for calculating profit.

**Example 6**   John Smith is a dealer in hides. He obtains his yearly supplies from Canada in the autumn, and sells them in the United Kingdom during the ensuing 12 months. In October 20X0 he bought 2,000 hides at an average cost of $20 Canadian, equivalent to, let us say, £10, and by September 20X1 had sold them all at an average price of £20, making a profit of £20,000. Meanwhile, the price of Canadian hides has increased by 50 per cent so that to replace stock he has sold during the year he will now have to pay an average of £15 a hide. Hence, the profit of £20,000 is overstated by £10,000 because the hides sold have been valued at £10 instead of £15 each – which is their current value in Canada.

3 The accounting practice of writing off the cost of certain assets as depreciation against revenue means that it is possible to remove the cost of these assets from the accounts altogether. For a long time, for example, it was the practice of banks to reduce the value of land and buildings to £1 and so create secret reserves.
4 Since incurring a cost depends upon a financial transaction, there are assets which create profits for the firm which can never appear as such in the accounts. Often the major asset of a highly successful firm is the knowledge and the skill created as a result of teamwork and good organization. This asset will not appear in the accounts, since the firm has paid nothing for it, except in terms of salaries which have been written off against yearly profits. Allied to this problem is the failure to make any mention in the balance sheet of the value of the human assets of the firm. Long ago, the economist Alfred Marshall stated that 'the most valuable of all capital is that invested in human beings' (Marshall, 1964), and it is universally recognized that the firm's human assets are its chief source of wealth. Yet, it is only recently that accountants have begun to recognize this fact, and efforts are now being made to find ways in which information on the value of human assets may be most appropriately presented. Other important assets of which no mention is made in financial accounting statements are, for example, the value to the firm of its hold on the market, which may be a very valuable asset if the firm enjoys a monopoly position, and the value of the firm's own information system, which will affect the quality of its decisions.

Many of the most controversial issues in financial accounting theory and practice revolve around the cost concept. External users of financial statements basically wish to have information on the current worth of the firm on the basis of which they may make investment decisions. In order to make their balance sheets more realistic many companies carry some fixed assets, especially properties, in their accounts at revalued amounts.

## The realization concept

The realization concept is also closely related to the cost concept, for as the recorded value of an asset to the firm is determined by the transaction which was necessary to acquire it, so any change in its value may only be recognized at the moment the firm realizes or disposes of that asset. The realization concept reflects totally the historical origin of accounting as a method for recording the results of transactions. To an accountant there is no certainty of profit until a sale has been made: hence, increases in value which have not been realized are not recorded as profit.

The realization concept is strongly criticized by economists. They argue that if an asset has increased in value then it is irrelevant that it has not been sold. For economists, it is sufficient that the gain in value could be realized for that gain to be recognized. The realization concept, it is true, may lead to absurd conclusions.

| Example 7 | William James and George Lloyd have bought a pair of dilapidated cottages in Gwynedd for £50,000. They spend £20,000 on restoring the cottages, so that their total cost amounts to £70,000. Both cottages are identical and form part of one unit, that is, they are semidetached. The cottages were bought as part of a speculative venture to make profit out of the popularity of Welsh cottages as holiday homes. A businessman from Manchester offers to buy both cottages for £100,000 each, but the partners decide to sell only one of the cottages and to retain the other for sale at a higher price in the future. |

From an accounting point of view, the cottage which is sold is recognized as being worth £100,000, and the difference of £65,000 between the accounting cost and the sale price is the realized profit. The second cottage, which could also have been sold for £100,000 to the same man, is recorded as being worth only £35,000 – being the costs associated with acquiring and restoring it.

Unrealized gains in value are widely recognized by non-accountants. Bankers, who are perhaps the most cautious of people, are prepared to lend money on unrealized values: business people reckon as gains increases in the value of assets even though they are unsold – yet accountants will not do so unless and until a contract of sale has taken place which creates a legal right to receive the agreed value of the asset sold.

As a result of the realization concept, two classes of gains may be distinguished – 'holding gains', which are increases in value resulting from holding an asset; and 'trading or operating gains', which are gains realized as a result of selling assets. 'Holding gains' are not recorded, but 'operating gains' are reported. The realization concept means, in effect, that the reported profit of a business is only a part of the total increases in value which accrue to a firm during an accounting period.

The realization concept does not require the accountant to await the receipt of cash before recording a transaction. Indeed, in many cases the delivery of goods and the receipt of cash occur after the legal agreement which determines the timing of the transaction.

**Example 8**  On 1 January 20X0, Midlands Motor Engineers receive an order from one of their accredited dealers for five tractor engines each costing £400. The engines are despatched on 10 January, and on 5 February a cheque for £2,000 is received in payment.

From a legal point of view, the acceptance of the order on 1 January marks the timing of the sale, and the creation of the contractual obligation to deliver the engines as well as the contractual right to receive payment. Accounting follows the law in this respect, and it is common practice to write to confirm the receipt of an order and its acceptance, so as to leave no doubt as to the legal and accounting position.

On occasions, however, when a contract is for work which cannot be completed for a long period of time, the contract may stipulate when rights to payment arise. This is particularly the case as regards large civil-engineering contracts, shipbuilding contracts and large government contracts. In these situations, accounting practices once more follow the law, and the timing of the right to receive cash is determined by the contract.

**Example 9**  Westlands Civil Engineering Co Ltd is awarded a government contract for the building of a fifty-mile section of a motorway. The work is required to be completed in three years. Payments are to be made by the government on the basis of work completed in each three-monthly period. It is agreed that an independent firm of quantity surveyors will certify the cost of work completed in each period, and that these certificates will form the basis for calculating the period payments to the company on the 'percentage-of-completion' method.

In accordance with this contract, the timing of the realizations will depend upon the issue of the certificates by the quantity surveyors.

# The accruals concept

The realization concept asserts that gains in value may not be recognized until the occurrence of a transaction is reinforced by the accruals concept, which applies equally to revenues and expenses.

The accruals concept makes the distinction between the receipt of cash and the right to receive cash, and the payment of cash and the legal obligation to pay cash, because in practice there is usually no coincidence in time between cash movements and the legal obligations to which they relate.

Let us examine first the manner in which the accruals concept applies to revenue. Revenue may be defined as the right to receive cash, and accountants are concerned with recording these rights. Cash receipts may occur as follows:

1 concurrently with the sale;
2 before a right to receive arises;
3 after the right to receive has been created;
4 in error.

The accruals concept provides a guideline as to how to treat these cash receipts and the rights related thereto.

**Example 10**   Mrs Smith is an old lady who occupies a flat owned by Mereworth Properties Ltd. The rent is payable monthly in advance on the first day of each month, and amounts to £250 a month. She is very forgetful, and rarely does a month pass without some complication in the payment of her rent.

On 1 January she sends her cheque for £250 for the rent due for January. This rent is due and payable to the company, and must be included as revenue for that month. On 10 January Mrs Smith sends another cheque for £250, thinking that she had not paid her rent for January. This is a cash receipt to which the company is not presently entitled, and it must either be returned to Mrs Smith, or kept on her behalf as a payment in advance of her February rent. The company returns her cheque saying that she has already paid her rent for January, and she receives this letter on 20 January. She forgets to pay her rent on 1 February. The accountant is obliged to include the rent due in February in the revenue for that month, even though it is only ultimately paid on 15 March. Until Mrs Smith has paid her rent for February, she will be a debtor of the company for the rent owing.

Similar rules apply to the treatment of expenses incurred by the firm. Expenses may be defined as legal obligations incurred by the firm to pay in money or money's worth for the benefit of goods or services which it has received. Cash payments may occur as follows:

1  at the time of purchase;
2  before they are due for payment;
3  after due date for payment;
4  in error.

The accruals concept requires the company to treat as expenses only those sums which are due and payable. If a payment is made in advance, it must not be treated as an expense, and the recipient is a debtor until his/her right to receive the cash matures. Cash paid in error is never an expense, and until it is recovered the person to whom it was paid is also a debtor. Where an expense had been incurred, however, and no payment has been made, the expense must be recorded, and the person to whom the payment should have been made is shown as a creditor.

We will see in Chapter 9 the importance of the accruals concept as regards record-keeping and the presentation of financial accounting statements.

## The matching concept

One of the important purposes of financial accounting is to calculate profit resulting from transactions. This means identifying the gains resulting from transactions and setting off against those gains the expenses which are related to those transactions. The realization concept identifies the timing of gains, and the accruals concept enables the accountant properly to record revenues and expenses; neither, however, helps the accountant to calculate profit. The matching concept links revenues with their relevant expenses.

**Example 11**   On 1 April Cash and Carry Ltd purchase for resale 2,000 tins of beans at a cost of 5p a tin. The selling price is 8p a tin. During the month of April 1,000 tins are sold. What is the profit for the month which is attributable to this line of goods?

We know that the expenses are 2,000 × 5p = £100, and that the revenues are 1,000 × 8p = £80. On the face of it, therefore, Cash and Carry Ltd have made a loss of £100 less £80, that is, £20. This conclusion is nonsense, because we are setting off against the sale proceeds of 1,000 tins the cost of acquiring 2,000 tins.

In accordance with the matching concept, the accountant establishes the profit for the month of April by calculating the cost of purchasing 1,000 tins of beans and setting this expense against the revenue realized from the sale of these tins:

| | |
|---|---|
| Sales revenue | 1,000 tins @ 8p = £80 |
| Cost of sales | 1,000 tins @ 5p = £50 |
| Profit | £30 |

The 1,000 tins remaining unsold remain in the accounting records as assets, and when they are eventually sold the profit from sales will be calculated by deducting the cost of acquisition from the sales revenue realized.

The matching of revenues and expenses is sometimes a most difficult problem in accounting, because many types of expense are not easily identifiable with revenues.

**Example 12**   Bloxwich Pharmaceutical Co Ltd manufactures and sells pharmaceutical products. Its major activity is the manufacture of antibiotics, which accounts for 80 per cent of its sales revenue. The remaining 20 per cent of its sales is derived from beauty creams. Its expenses for the year 20X0 are as follows:

| | |
|---|---|
| Manufacturing costs of antibiotics | £500,000 |
| Manufacturing costs of beauty creams | 20,000 |
| Administrative costs | 100,000 |
| Selling and financial costs | 50,000 |
| Research and development costs | 150,000 |
| Total expenses for the year | £820,000 |

In the same year, the total revenue from sales of both antibiotics and beauty creams amounts to £1,000,000. Calculate the profit on the antibiotics side of the business.

We can begin to answer this problem as follows:

| | |
|---|---|
| Sales revenue from antibiotics (80% of total) | £800,000 |
| Manufacturing costs of antibiotics | 500,000 |
| | 300,000 |
| Other expenses | ? |
| Profit on antibiotics | ? |

Clearly, we need more information in order to allocate the administrative, selling and financial costs between antibiotics and beauty creams. It is unlikely that an exact allocation could be made, and in the end, an estimate would be made.

*est- a que tu as lu foi ?*

The research and development costs of new antibiotics and beauty creams are a more difficult problem. Strictly speaking, we should not set these costs against the revenues of the year, since the benefit will not occur in this year. Much of it, however, may not lead to new products. Therefore, if we ignore this expenditure, the company's reported profit will be inflated and unrealistic.

From the foregoing example, it is seen that the exact matching of revenues and expenses is often impossible. Nevertheless, the computation of periodic profit requires that expenses be allocated, where necessary, in order that the financial results may be stated in a consistent manner.

## The concept of periodicity

The custom of making periodic reports to the owner of a business dates from the time when wealthy men employed servants to manage and oversee their affairs. Periodic accounting has its origin in the idea of control, and company law sees the role of financial reports as being essentially the communication of information from the managers of the business, that is the directors, to the owners of the business, that is the shareholders. However much we may disagree with this view of the relationship of directors and shareholders as being unrealistic, we must accept that there is an element of shareholder control over directors which stems from the legal duty laid on the latter to issue reports on their stewardship of the firm's assets.

The concept of periodicity is now established by law as regards certain types of reports such as balance sheets and profit and loss accounts. The Companies Act requires yearly reports to shareholders, and the Income Tax Acts require accounts for all businesses to be submitted annually. However, there is nothing to prevent companies from providing information at more frequent intervals to investors, if they so wish.

Annual reports have grown out of custom, and many would question the wisdom of selecting an arbitrary period of twelve months as a basis for reporting upon the activities of a business. The idea of annual reports is deeply entrenched, and even the government runs its business on a yearly basis and budgets for one year, although many of its activities are continuing ones which cannot be seen correctly in the perspective of twelve months. This is also true for all large companies, and many smaller businesses.

**Example 13** Universal Chemicals Ltd manufactures a wide range of chemical products and has factories throughout the country. Owing to unusually difficult labour relations, rising raw material costs and stiffening competition, its reported profit for the year ended 31 December 20X0 has decreased by 10 per cent from that of the previous year. Its borrowings, however, have increased by 20 per cent owing to an enlarged capital investment programme which is designed to add substantially to profit in about five years' time.

Clearly, in this case the reader of the report for the year 20X0 should consider the report in context, and look to the long-term trend of profits and to the better financial position which is expected in the future.

The concept of periodicity as expressed in yearly accounting fails to make the important distinction between the long-term trend and the short-term position. Hence, it limits the usefulness of the information communicated to shareholders and investors.

The matching and periodicity concepts seek to relate the transactions of one particular year with the expenses attributable to those transactions. From a practical point of view, accountants carry forward expenses until they can be identified with the revenues of a particular year, and carry forward receipts until they can be regarded as the revenue of a particular year in accordance with the realization convention. Since all assets become 'costs' in accounting, the convention of periodicity creates difficulties with regard to the allocation of fixed assets as expenses of particular years. We examine this matter when we discuss depreciation in Chapter 10.

So far we have mentioned the effect of the concept of periodicity on the usefulness of information communicated to external users; we now comment on its effect on profit measurement. The majority of economists treat accounting profit as the 'income' of a business, and hence as a measure of the income which investors and shareholders derive from their investment in the firm. As a result, they impose the economic criteria appropriate to the measurement of economic income to accounting profit and disapprove of the shortcomings of accounting profit which they see as stemming from accounting concepts for calculating periodic income. Ideally, an accurate measurement of the profit or loss of a business can be made only after the business has ceased operating, sold off all its assets and paid off all its liabilities. The net profit accruing to investors would then be the difference between the sum total of all their receipts, either as dividends or capital repayments, and their initial investment. It is clear, however, that accounting profit is merely the result of completed transactions during a stated period: the concept of periodicity is a statement of this view.

# The concept of consistency

The usefulness of financial information lies to a considerable extent in the conclusions which may be drawn from the comparison of the financial statements of one year with those of a preceding year, and the financial reports of one company with those of another company. It is in this way that we may deduce some of the most important information for decision making, such as an indication that there has been an improvement in profit since last year and that therefore it is worth buying more shares, or the profit of Company A is better than that of Company B and given current share prices one should switch from holding shares in Company B and buy those of Company A.

The comparability of financial statements depends largely upon the choice of accounting methods and the consistency with which they are applied. A change in the basis on which a firm values stocks, for example, may result in a profit figure different from that which would have been computed had the accountant adhered to a consistent basis of valuation. If firms wish to change their method for treating a particular problem, such as the valuation of stocks or the value attached to a particular asset, they may do so, but they should mention the effect on the profit of the change in accounting methods.

Comparing the accounts of different companies is much more difficult, and unfortunately the accounting methods of individual firms are not always the same. There is no uniformity of accounting methods which would provide the consistency of treatment of information necessary for the comparison of the accounts of different companies. Whereas the accounting concept of consistency is generally followed by individual firms, there is no agreement at all that different firms should use the same accounting methods. Hence, the needs of investors for greater comparability of information between companies is frustrated by accounting concepts which insist on consistency, but allow different methods of measurement and treatment which cannot yield comparable results. The Accounting Standards Board is charged with the task of trying to secure agreement on appropriate accounting methods which will ensure a higher degree of comparability of accounting information, and in this book we examine some of its achievements so far.

## The concept of prudence/conservatism

Prudence reflects accountants' view of their social role and their responsibilities towards those for whom they provide information. It is seen at work in some of the concepts which we have examined in this chapter, for example the realization concept which requires the realization of a gain before it may be recognized, and the cost convention which holds that the value of an asset is the cost of acquisition.

There are two principal rules which stem directly from the concept of prudence:

1 the accountant should not anticipate profit and should provide for all possible losses;
2 faced with two or more methods of valuing an asset, the accountant should choose that which leads to the lesser value.

These two rules contravene some accounting concepts, for example the cost concept, for if the market value of trading stocks has fallen below the cost of acquisition it must be valued at the market value. Equally, the logic which underlies the realization concept as regards gains, that there is no certainty of a gain until there is a sale, does not extend to the treatment of anticipated losses. Thus, accountants provide for losses in value which are sufficiently foreseeable to make them a present reality, on the basis that to ignore such losses might mislead the user of accounting information. One of the clearest explanations of the policy of prudence was made by G O May as long ago as 1946, as follows:

> The great majority of ventures fail, and the fact that enterprises nevertheless continue is attributable to the incurable optimism (often dissociated from experience) as well as to the courage of mankind. In my experience, also, losses from unsound accounting have most commonly resulted from the hopes rather than the achievements of management being allowed to influence accounting dispositions. To me, conservatism is still the first virtue of accounting, and I am wholly unable to agree with those who would bar it from the books of accounts and statements prepared therefrom and would relegate it to footnotes. (May, 1946)

The caution of the accountant may well be a foil for the optimism of business people but, although it may be desirable for the accountant to be prudent in the estimates which are made, the selection of accounting methods for recording and presenting information on the basis that they deliberately understate assets of earning should not be an overriding principle. Investors and shareholders need reliable and useful information: to understate is as bad as to overstate – investment in a business may be discouraged if it appears to be less valuable than it really is. Users of accounting information, like others who are faced with making decisions, look for guidance to the lowest value, the highest value and the probable value. In restricting accounting information to the statement of the lowest value, the accountant is not fulfilling the social role expected of a supplier of comprehensive financial information.

## Summary

Accounting concepts serve as guideposts, but tend to emphasize the reliability of information rather than its usefulness. The conflict between reliability and usefulness is controversial. At one extreme, some accountants contend that if a measurement is useful, further justification is unnecessary. At the other extreme, others hold that the reliability of accounting information is the most important criterion, and will ultimately determine the extent to which external users accept accounting statements for making investment decisions.

**References**   Littleton, A C (1953). *Structure of Accounting Theory*, American Accounting Association.

Marshall, Alfred (1964). *Principles of Economics*, 8th edn, Macmillan (London).

May, G O (1946). *Financial Accounting: A Distillation of Experience*, Macmillan (New York).

## Self-assessment question

1 Examine the role of so-called concepts in the analysis of accounting transactions and the preparation of financial statements.

## Problems  *(* indicates that a solution is to be found in the Lecturer's Guide)*

1 Consultat Inc is a firm of consulting engineers, newly established to advise on a large project taking three years to complete. Their fee for this work is a percentage of the total project costs, payable on completion of the project. In the interim, advances on the final fee are made at six-monthly intervals. The total project costs will not be known until the project is completed. The following advances were received by Consultat Inc during the three-year period:

year ended 31 December 20X0   £25,000
year ended 31 December 20X1   £30,000
year ended 31 December 20X2   £30,000

When the total costs were computed during the year ended 31 December 20X0, it was found that a further sum of £50,000 was due to Consultat Inc.

*Required:*
(a) Explain how Consultat Inc would show the payments made during the periods covered by the project. Justify your explanation in terms of the concepts of accounting which you consider apply to this situation.
(b) Would you change your reasoning at all in the light of the following information?
    (i)   the advance payments are not contractual but discretionary on the part of the paying company;
    (ii)  a clause in the consulting agreement requires Consultat Inc. to undertake – free of charge – extra work to remedy defects appearing within three years of the completion of the project.

Suggest how you would treat these problems by reference to accounting concepts.

2     Bloxwich Engineers Ltd borrows £100,000 at a fixed interest rate of 10 per cent for a period of five years for the purpose of acquiring a stamping press of advanced design. Suggest how you would treat the accounting aspects of the transactions associated with the acquisition and the financing of the stamping press in the following circumstances:

     (a)  by the end of the third year of use, the stamping press has been depreciated to £70,000, but due to a new design having appeared, its market value is only £30,000. The stamping press, nevertheless, continues to generate the same level of revenue as it did in the first year of use;

     (b)  during the fourth year, the stamping press generates only £8,000 of revenues, and the Managing Director of Bloxwich Engineers Ltd has written an instruction to the effect that 'since the press is now making a loss of £2,000 when interest is taken into account', it should be sold forthwith. The market value has now fallen to £15,000. The monies realized are to be applied to the acquisition of further plant, and the interest charge remains to be paid during the following and final year of the loan.

    Support your discussion of the accounting problems you have identified by reference to the conventions which justify your reasoning.

3*     Lewis, Jones and Peers, newly qualified as architects, decide to form a partnership on 1 January 20X0. During their first year of business, a substantial operating loss is realized, amounting to £20,000. They had anticipated such a loss and had provided sufficient funds to cover it when they first formed the partnership. 'After all', said Peers, 'it is well known that the first year of practice for architects always produces a loss, since they are really establishing the business. They do, in fact, earn little money as they build up contacts which will earn future revenues'. 'That's right', continued Lewis, as he was explaining to the accountant, who has prepared the profit and loss account showing the loss of £20,000, 'you can't show the £20,000 as a loss, when it is the cost of setting up the business. To be consistent with the facts, you have to show the £20,000 as an asset on the balance sheet.' 'Yes, I agree,' concluded Jones, 'that is the most conservative way of looking at the situation. Then, we recognize the creation of an asset we can write off over several years and match against the future revenues which are really the result of this year's efforts.'

    How would you deal with the arguments of your clients if you were the accountant in this situation? Refer the problems you see to such accounting concepts as are applicable to them, and in particular, explain how you would deal with the terms 'consistent' and 'prudence' used by the partners in their discussion with you.

# 6 Financial accounting standards

## Setting the scene

People in every walk of life are affected by business reporting, the cornerstone on which our process of capital allocation is built. An effective allocation process is critical to a healthy economy that promotes productivity, encourages innovation, and provides an efficient and liquid market for buying and selling securities and obtaining and granting credit. Conversely, a flawed allocation process supports unproductive practices, denies cost-effective capital to companies that may offer innovative products and services that add value, and undermines the securities market. . . . Reporting standards play an important role in helping the market mechanism work effectively for the benefit of companies, users, and the public.

(AICPA, 1994)

## Learning objectives

**After studying this chapter you should be able to:**

1  **Discuss the purpose underlying the issue of UK accounting standards.**

2  **Identify four 'fundamental concepts' mentioned in SSAP 2 and compare them with the corresponding concepts discussed in Chapter 5.**

3  **Explain the meaning and role of 'accounting bases'.**

The financial accounting concepts discussed in Chapter 5 were seen as core elements in the development of a descriptive theory of financial accounting. The review of the concepts of financial accounting which was conducted by the accounting profession in the 1970s, and which has resulted in the publication of a series of financial accounting standards, is part of the on-going process of developing accounting practice by seeking consensus among practitioners.

The concepts allow a variety of alternative practices to coexist. As a result, the financial results of different companies cannot be compared and evaluated unless full information is available about the accounting methods which have been used. Not only have the variety of accounting practices permitted by the conventions of financial accounting made it difficult to compare the financial results of different companies, but the application of alternative accounting methods to the preparation of the financial reports of the same company have enabled entirely different results to be reported to shareholders.

The need for the imposition of standards arose because of the lack of uniformity existing as to the manner in which periodic profit was measured and the financial position of the enterprise represented. The purpose of this chapter is to examine the significance of the development of accounting standards for a descriptive theory of financial accounting based on concepts and consensus.

## The importance of comparability

The information contained in published financial statements is especially important to external users, such as shareholders and investors, for without such information they would have to take decisions about their investments under a considerable degree of uncertainty. A major problem is that there are no formal channels for communicating to companies the type and nature of the financial information which external users believe they require, and the manner in which such information ought to be presented. Traditionally, Parliament has assumed the responsibility for legislation specifying the type and the minimum level of information which companies should disclose, and the accounting profession has assumed the responsibility for ensuring the proper presentation of such information. In this respect, it is evident that the concepts applied to the presentation of financial information should not permit too much discretion, and that the manner in which financial information is treated in financial statements should conform to carefully considered standards.

The function of accounting standards may best be examined by reference to the basic purpose of financial statements, which may be stated as being concerned with the communication of information affecting the allocation of resources. Ideally, such information should make it possible for investors to evaluate the investment opportunities offered by different firms and to allocate scarce resources to the most efficient. In theory, this process should result in the optimal distribution of resources within the economy, and should maximize their potential benefit to society.

In this analysis of the purpose of financial statements, it is apparent that one of the most important criteria for the presentation of financial information is that which ensures an appropriate standard of comparison between different firms. The accounting methods used by different firms for presenting information should allow appropriate comparisons to be made. For example, they should not enable a company to report profits which result simply from a change in accounting methods, rather than from increased efficiency. If companies were free to choose their accounting methods in this way, the consequence might well be that deliberate distortions would be introduced in the pricing of shares on the Stock Exchange, leading eventually to a misallocation of resources in the economy. This would occur because relatively less efficient companies would be able to report fictitious profits, and as a result divert capital to themselves on more favourable terms than those available to the more efficient companies which have adopted rigorous accounting methods.

## Reasons for concern about standards

In the United Kingdom, the Institute of Chartered Accountants in England and Wales began to make recommendations about accounting practices as early as 1942.

Ultimately, a series of 29 recommendations on accounting practices were issued with the objective of codifying the best practices which ought to be used in particular circumstances. However, there were several disadvantages to this procedure:

1 The recommendations were not mandatory, and were issued for the guidance of members of the Institute.
2 The recommendations did not result from fundamental research into the objectives of accounting, but merely codified existing practices.
3 The recommendations did not reduce the diversity of accounting methods. For example, Recommendation No 22, 1960, which was concerned with stock valuation, advocated five different methods of computing the cost of stock. Furthermore, four of these methods could be computed differently for partly and fully finished stocks. To complicate matters further, Recommendation 22 stated that cost could be defined in three different ways!

In the late 1960s, there was a spate of public criticism of financial reporting methods, which arose from the publicity accorded to aspects of the financial statements of a number of companies. These included Pergamon Press, General Electric Company and Vehicle and General Company. The manner in which these cases jolted the accounting profession may be judged from the example of the General Electric Company.

In 1967, the General Electric Company (GEC) made a takeover bid for Associated Electric Industries (AEI). AEI produced a profit forecast for that year of £10 million, which was based on ten months' actual profit and two months' budgeted profit. The GEC takeover bid was successful, and afterwards GEC reported that, in fact, AEI had made a loss of £4.5 million for that year. According to GEC auditors, £9.5 million of the £14.5 million difference between the two calculations of profit for 1967 was due to a difference in judgement about such matters as the amounts written off stock and the provision for estimated losses.

The angry reaction of the press to the disclosure of the amended figures for 1967 centred on the fact that two accounting firms could justifiably produce such widely differing results for the same year. One observer commented that it appeared that accounting was really an art form, and that it seemed that two firms of accountants looking at the same figures were capable of producing profit figures as far apart as a Rubens is from a Rembrandt.

## The Accounting Standards Committee

The response of the accounting profession to this criticism was to establish the Accounting Standards Committee. This was replaced in 1990 by the Accounting Standards Board.

The prime objective of the Accounting Standards Committee was to narrow the areas of difference and variety in accounting practice. The procedure used for this purpose was initiated by the issue of an 'Exposure Draft' on a specific topic for discussion by accountants and the public at large. Comments made on the Exposure Draft were taken into consideration when drawing up a formal statement of the accounting method to be applied when dealing with that specific topic. This formal statement was known as a Statement of Standard Accounting Practice (SSAP). Once the Statement of Standard Accounting Practice had been adopted by the accounting profession, any material departure from the standard used in presenting a financial report was to be disclosed in that report.

The following Statements of Standard Accounting Practice were issued:

SSAP 1  'Accounting for the Results of Associated Companies'
SSAP 2  'Disclosure of Accounting Policies'
SSAP 3  'Earnings per Share'
SSAP 4  'The Accounting Treatment of Government Grants'
SSAP 5  'Accounting for Value Added Tax'
SSAP 6  'Extraordinary Items and Prior Year Adjustments'
SSAP 8  'The Treatment of Taxation under the Imputation System in the Accounts of Companies'
SSAP 9  'Stocks and Long-Term Contracts'
SSAP 10 'Statements of Source and Application of Funds'
SSAP 12 'Accounting for Depreciation'
SSAP 13 'Accounting for Research and Development'
SSAP 14 'Group Accounts'
SSAP 15 'Accounting for Deferred Taxation'
SSAP 16 'Current Cost Accounting' (*abandoned in 1988*)
SSAP 17 'Accounting for Post Balance Sheet Events'
SSAP 18 'Accounting for Contingencies'
SSAP 19 'Accounting for Investment Properties'
SSAP 20 'Foreign Currency Translation'
SSAP 21 'Accounting for Leases and Hire Purchase Contracts'
SSAP 22 'Accounting for Goodwill'
SSAP 23 'Accounting for Acquisitions and Mergers'
SSAP 24 'Accounting for Pension Costs'
SSAP 25 'Segmental Reporting'

The list of topics on which Statements of Standard Accounting Practice were issued shows that the work of the Accounting Standards Committee profoundly affected the development of accounting theory and methods. Individual Statements of Standard Accounting Practice will be referred to in later chapters, where the topics covered by these documents themselves are analysed.

The earlier discussion in this chapter of the relationship between accounting concepts and accounting methods implies matters of accounting policy. For this reason SSAP 2, which deals with the disclosure of accounting policies, is highly significant to the central issues to which this chapter is directed and its provisions will now be examined in detail.

## SSAP 2 'Disclosure of Accounting Policies'

SSAP 2 is addressed to the relationship between accounting concepts, accounting methods and accounting policies. The relationship is illustrated in Figure 2.3, where it is seen that accounting concepts provide the foundations to both accounting methods and policies. These are defined by SSAP 2 as follows:

● *Fundamental accounting concepts* are broad general assumptions which underlie the periodic financial accounts of business enterprises.

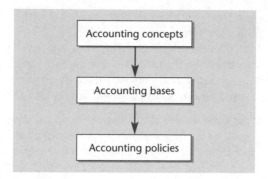

**Figure 2.3**

- *Accounting bases* are the methods which have been developed for expressing or applying fundamental accounting concepts to financial transactions and items. By their nature, accounting bases are more diverse and numerous than fundamental concepts, since they have evolved in response to the variety and complexity of types of business and business transactions and, for this reason, there may justifiably exist more than one recognized accounting basis for dealing with particular items.
- *Accounting policies* are the specific accounting bases judged by business enterprises to be most appropriate to their circumstances and adopted by them for the purpose of preparing their financial accounts.

SSAP 2 states that there are four fundamental accounting concepts which should be regarded as established standard concepts. They are as follows:

- The *going concern concept*, which implies that the enterprise will continue in operational existence for the foreseeable future. This means, in particular, that the profit and loss account and balance sheet assume no intention or necessity to liquidate or reduce significantly the scale of operation.
- The *accruals concept*, which requires that revenue and costs are accrued, matched with one another so far as their relationship can be established or justifiably assumed, and dealt with in the profit and loss account of the period to which they relate, provided, generally, that where the accruals concept is inconsistent with the prudence concept (see below), the latter prevails. The accruals concept implies that the profit and loss account reflects changes in the amount of net assets that arise out of the transactions of the relevant period, other than distributions or subscriptions of capital. Revenue and profits dealt with in the profit and loss account are matched with associated costs by including in the same account the costs incurred in earning them, so far as these are material and identifiable.
- The *consistency concept*, which requires that there should be consistency of accounting treatment of like items within each accounting period and from one period to the next.
- The *concept of prudence*, which requires that revenue and profits are not anticipated, but recognized by inclusion in the profit and loss account only when realized in the form either of cash or of assets (usually legally enforceable debts), the ultimate cash realization of which can be assessed with reasonable certainty; provision should be made for all known liabilities (expenses and losses) whether the amount of these is known with certainty or is a best estimate in the light of the information available.

In December 1999, the Accounting Standards Board issued an Exposure Draft which is intended to replace SSAP 2. The most significant proposed change is that the Exposure Draft emphasises comparability rather than consistency and links prudence to reliability rather than realization.

SSAP 2 is concerned with ensuring that accounting bases are disclosed in financial reports, whenever significant items are shown which have their significance in value judgements, estimated outcome of future events or uncompleted transactions, rather than ascertained amounts. In the words of SSAP 2,

> *In circumstances where more than one accounting basis is acceptable in principle, the accounting policy followed can significantly affect a company's reported results and financial position, and the view presented can be properly appreciated only if the principal policies followed are also described. For this reason, adequate disclosure of the accounting policies should be regarded as essential to the fair presentation of financial accounts.*

Concern that the public receive further information about the risks of business failure led the Cadbury Committee, in 1992, to recommend additional disclosures relating to the going concern concept. These are examined in Chapter 13. Furthermore, the Auditing Practices Board, in 1994, issued a statement of Auditing Standards (SAS 130) which provides guidance for auditors in respect of their consideration of the going concern basis. According to this standard, auditors should perform procedures specifically designed to identify indications that the going concern concept basis may not be valid. They should also obtain a statement from the directors confirming their considered view that the company is a going concern. In forming an opinion on whether the company is a going concern, the auditors should look ahead one year from the date of the directors' approval of the accounts.

## The Accounting Standards Board

The Accounting Standards Board (ASB) replaced the Accounting Standards Committee in 1990, following the review of the standard-setting process under the chairmanship of Sir Ron Dearing (1988). This report suggested wide-ranging changes to the formulation of accounting standards.

At its first meeting the ASB unanimously agreed to adopt the 22 extant SSAPs issued by the ASC. However, they made it plain that they were going to work from principles which, in due course, may make some of these SSAPs in need of substantial change. The ASB's consultative process includes: first, the issue of Working Drafts for Discussion (DDs); these then become Financial Reporting Exposure Drafts (FREDs); and result in the publication of Financial Reporting Standards (FRSs). The following Financial Reporting Standards have been published to date:

FRS 1    'Cash Flow Statements' (supersedes SSAP 10)
FRS 2    'Accounting for Subsidiary Undertakings' (supersedes SSAP 14)
FRS 3    'Reporting Financial Performance' (supersedes SSAP 6 and SSAP 3)
FRS 4    'Accounting for Capital Instruments'
FRS 5    'Reporting the Substance of Transactions'
FRS 6    'Acquisitions and Mergers' (supersedes SSAP 23)
FRS 7    'Fair Values in Acquisition Accounting'
FRS 8    'Related Party Disclosures'
FRS 9    'Associates and Joint Ventures' (supersedes SSAP 1)

FRS 10    'Goodwill and Intangible Assets' (supersedes SSAP 22)
FRS 11    'Impairment of Fixed Assets and Goodwill'
FRS 12    'Provisions, Contingent Liabilities and Contingent Assets' (supersedes SSAP 18)
FRS 13    'Derivatives and Other Financial Instruments: Disclosure'
FRS 14    'Earnings Per Share' (supersedes SSAP 3)
FRS 15    'Tangible Fixed Assets' (supersedes SSAP 12)
FRS 16    'Current Tax' (supersedes SSAP 8)
FRSSE    'Financial Reporting Standard for Smaller Entities'

As we saw in Chapter 1, in the area of accounting standard setting, there is an increasing demand for uniform standards that apply internationally. Consequently, the international dimension plays a prominent part in shaping the Board's agenda.

*The ASB has accepted the argument that there should really be only one way of accounting for similar transactions throughout the world ... Unless we disagree with the international trend we try to align our standards closely to those of the International Accounting Standards Committee. (Tweedie, 1999).*

Almost all the Board's recent work on new standards has been concerned with international harmonization.

## Standards and the Companies Acts

In Chapter 13 we examine the legal requirements which apply to the financial reporting procedures of companies and the manner in which financial accounting information must be disclosed in the profit and loss accounts and balance sheets. Two aspects of these requirements are directly related to the accounting concepts and standards considered in this chapter.

First, the four fundamental accounting concepts of SSAP 2 have become enshrined in law by the Companies Act 1981. Final accounts prepared within the terms of this Act must follow these concepts. Second, since 1948 all final accounts prepared for the purpose of compliance with the Companies Acts have been required to give a 'true and fair view', an obligation described as 'overriding'. This implies that if the final accounts are to contain information which is sufficient in quantity and quality to satisfy the reasonable expectations of users then they should be prepared in accordance with the concepts and standards formulated by the accountancy profession. Third, the Companies Act 1989 introduced a requirement to state whether the accounts have been prepared in accordance with applicable accounting standards and give details of, and reason for, any material departures.

## Summary

The concepts of financial accounting and the accounting standards issued by the standard setting boards represent a theory of accounting which has evolved by descriptions of the practices of accountants.

The concepts of accounting have resulted in the evolution of a variety of practices. Consequently, the lack of uniformity has made it difficult for users of financial reports to compare the results of different companies. The need for comparability has been judged to be one of the most important criteria for the presentation of financial reports. The reasons for concern about the quality of accounting information based on concepts were discussed, and were seen to relate to the different results which could be drawn from the same set of data. The work of the standard setting boards has resulted in the reduction of variety of accounting practice.

**References**

AICPA (1994). *Improving Business Reporting – A Customer Focus* (The Jenkins Report), American Institute of Certified Public Accountants.

Dearing, Sir Ron (Chairman) (1988). *The Making of Accounting Standards*, Report of the Review Committee, ICAEW.

Tweedie, D (1999). *The 1998 Annual Review of the Financial Reporting Council.*

## Self-assessment questions

1 Discuss the purpose underlying the issue of UK accounting standards.

2 Identify the four 'fundamental accounting concepts' mentioned in SSAP 2 and compare them with the corresponding concepts discussed in Chapter 5.

3 Explain the meaning of an 'accounting base'. State why accounting bases are more diverse than fundamental concepts.

# 7 The generation of financial accounting data

**Setting the scene**

We have a duty to present timely and accurate information to decision makers from the information systems we direct. Over the past ten years, our ability to extract information from raw data has undergone something of a transformation. One of the fundamental skills required of an accountant is to excel at defining what information is and placing it in context. So it follows that we must have a good understanding of the different ways to extract data and be familiar with the tools available for such an exercise. It also follows that we must have a really good understanding of what constitutes data – how data are gathered, stored and used. (Williams, 1999)

**Learning objectives**

After studying this chapter you should be able to:

1 Explain the meaning and importance of 'source documents' in the financial accounting process.

2 Discuss the role of the journal, day books and cash book in the recording of financial accounting data.

3 Describe the development of data-processing systems.

Earlier we examined the nature and the boundaries of the financial accounting system. We noted that the concepts of financial accounting constituted one of the boundaries in so far as they act as a filtering process for the data which is fed into the financial accounting system. We concluded that these concepts played a crucial role in determining the nature of financial accounting information.

This chapter examines the processes involved in the generation of financial accounting data prior to its transformation into accounting information.

## An outline of the information generation process

The output of financial accounting information is the result of a process involving the following stages:

1  the preparation of source documents;
2  the entry of basic data into source records;
3  the posting of data from the source records into the ledger, which is a permanent record of data.

The production of financial accounting information in the form of reports is illustrated in Figure 2.4.

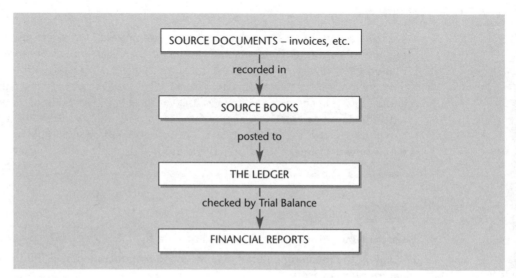

**Figure 2.4**

Although the principles underlying the financial accounting system remain unchanged, its processes have undergone and are continually undergoing modification and improvement. In particular, technological change has dramatically affected these processes. The advent of the computer has considerably speeded up and streamlined the data recording process, and indeed, as we shall see, has permitted the integration of several stages of this process into a single operation.

In this chapter we are concerned with an analysis of the traditional data recording practices relating to source documents and source books, and we examine the impact of the computer on these practices. We will examine the process of preparing financial reports in subsequent chapters.

## Source documents

As we explained in Chapter 5, financial accounting data originates in transactions. Source documents capture the details of these accounting events. They also have a very important functional purpose as regards the activities of an enterprise.

Data flows are generated by a business and classified according to their sources.

1 Financial accounting data flows are generated from activities conducted between the firm and external groups such as customers and suppliers of materials, goods, services and finance.

2 Data flows generated internally constitute a substantial volume of the total information flows.

These flows are generated and channelled through a management information system (MIS) the function of which is to meet the needs of management for the purposes of planning and control. The relationship between external and internal data flows and the documentation involved in facilitating these flows are illustrated in Figure 2.5. This shows the focal role played by accounting data in relation to the firm's basic operations as well as the nature of the source documents involved in the generation of financial accounting data.

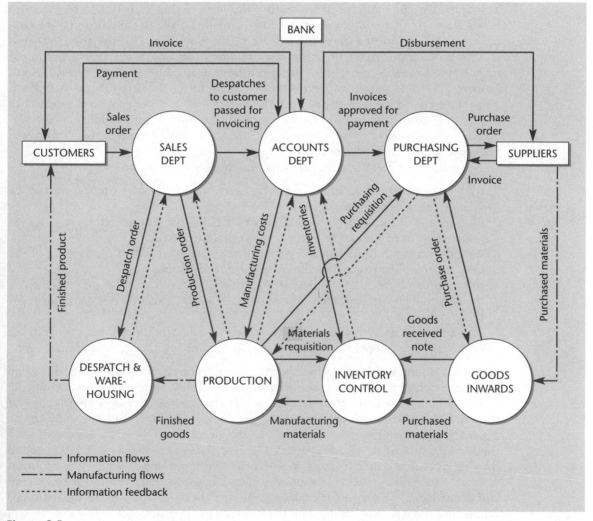

**Figure 2.5**

## Source documents related to sales

The function of the sales department is to encourage the sales of the firm's products. Once a salesperson has concluded a sale with a customer, s/he completes a sales order form. The original is sent to the customer as an acknowledgement of the order, and in the case of a credit sale, one copy of the sales order form goes to the credit control department for approval. If the goods are in stock, the credit control department will pass the authenticated sales order form to the stock control department so that the release and despatch of the goods may be effected. An advice note is sent to the customer when the goods are despatched advising the date of despatch and mode of delivery. The goods are normally accompanied by a delivery note stating the description of the goods and the quantity involved though not the price. The customer acknowledges receipt of the goods by signing the delivery note.

When the goods have been released by the stock control department for despatch, a further copy of the sales order stating the date of despatch is sent to the sales invoice section of the accounts department, so that the sales invoice may be prepared. The sales invoice states the nature, quantity and price of the goods ordered and the amount due to the firm from the customer. Customers are normally required to pay within one or more months, depending on the agreed credit terms. Often, however, customers are required to pay on receipt of the invoice, though some firms issue statements each month showing the number of invoices sent to the customer during the month and the total sum due in respect of the month's orders.

The copy sales invoice is the source document which provides the data which will be recorded in the financial accounting system.

The sales order form is used, therefore, for the following purposes:

1  As a record and confirmation of a sale. One copy of the sales order form will be kept by the sales department.
2  As a means of initiating a procedure for checking the creditworthiness of a customer prior to proceeding with the completion of the order.
3  As a document authorizing the release of the goods from stock. One copy of the sales order will be retained by the stock control department.
4  As a means of checking and despatching the right goods to the right customer by the despatch department. One copy of the sales order is kept by this department for this purpose.
5  As a means of preparing the sales invoice which will state the amount due from the customer. One copy of the sales order will be retained by the accounts department.

Where goods are not kept in stock but are manufactured to order, the receipt of an order puts the production process in motion. We examine the cost accounting process in Part 5, but for the purposes of this chapter, we may note that a copy of the production order will be sent to the production manager and one copy to the accounts department, which is responsible for collecting all the costs associated with the manufacture of the goods ordered. Figure 2.5 shows that the materials required may be obtained either from existing stocks or by purchase. Where the required materials are held in stock, the issue of a materials requisition form to the stock control department will procure the release of these materials. One copy of the materials requisition form will be retained by the stock control department and one copy will be sent to the accounts department for costing purposes. Where the required materials have to be purchased, the production department issues a purchase requisition form to the purchasing department.

## Source documents related to purchases

The purchasing department obtains the raw materials, equipment and supplies needed by the firm. Each request is made on a requisition form stating the nature and the quantity required, which is signed by an authorized person. The purchasing department selects a suitable supplier and sends a purchase order form setting out the description, quantity and required delivery date of the goods, together with instructions as regards despatch and invoicing. The purchase order will refer to the quoted price of the goods according to the supplier's catalogue or other statements of the supply price, although quoted prices in advertisements are not binding on suppliers. In effect, the purchase order form is an offer to purchase and when accepted by the supplier constitutes a legal contract between buyer and seller. Copies of the purchase order are distributed to the several departments concerned, namely the receiving department which needs to know the details and the date of receipt of the goods, the stock control department to advise of the pending arrival of goods and to serve as a check on the receiving department, the accounts department for checking that the price quoted compares with the price list, and the ordering department, to confirm that the order has been placed.

## Source documents related to the receipt of goods

Upon delivery of the goods, the receiving department verifies that the goods delivered compare in every detail to the copy purchase order. When they agree, a goods received note is prepared which details the description of the goods received, their quantity, quality and condition. A copy of the goods received note is sent to the department concerned with the audit of the receipt of goods, which is usually the purchasing department. A copy is also sent to the accounts department and the department responsible for the order. The stock control department is also notified because it is responsible for the storage, distribution and control of stocks. The stock control department maintains records of stocks, and ensures that adequate stock levels are maintained.

In due course, the supplier sends an invoice stating the description, quantity and price of the goods ordered, the date of acceptance of the order, which is usually shown as the date of despatch of the goods, and the amount now owing. The invoice is checked by the accounts department against the goods received note, and if there are no queries then the invoice is cleared for payment in due course. Normally, invoices are paid monthly. This permits the workflow in the accounting department to be efficiently organized and allows the payment procedure to be properly supervised.

## The entry of basic data in the source books

The accounting record of the events described in the source documents begins with the issue or receipt of invoices. Although legal obligations are created with the acceptance of an order, either by the firm or its suppliers, for practical reasons, these obligations are not recorded until they are formally stated. Should there be any dispute, however, about the existence of an order, the appropriate source document provides evidence of that order.

The practice of keeping daily records of accounting events in a diary or rough-book dates from the early history of accounting. The practice of keeping a daily journal was recommended by Paciolo in 1494 for the purpose of enabling the businessman to check daily the records kept by his clerk. Once agreed, they could be entered into the ledger. It became a golden rule in accounting that no entry should appear in the ledger which has not first been entered in the journal.

At first, the journal was used to record all commercial transactions. They were entered chronologically and showed the details of these transactions as well as the ledger account to which the entry was ultimately posted, as shown below.

The data entered in the journal consisted of:

1 the date of the transaction;
2 the name of the purchaser or the asset purchased;
3 the name of the seller or the asset sold;
4 the sum involved;
5 a short narrative describing the transaction.

| Date | Journal description | Folio | Dr £ | Cr £ |
|---|---|---|---|---|
| 5 Jan | Goods Dr | L5 | 100 | |
| | To A Smith | L7 | | 100 |
| | Being 100 shirts | | | |
| | bought for resale | | | |
| 5 Jan | B Jones Dr | L10 | 5 | |
| | To Cash | | | 5 |
| | Being wages due to the | | | |
| | week ending 5 January | | | |

Periodically, the entries in the journal were transferred to the main record, described as the ledger, by a procedure known as posting. The folio references in the journal indicated the pages in the ledger to which the postings were made.

As trade expanded and the number of transactions increased, it became the practice to group the entries to be made in the journal into the following classes:

1 purchases of trading goods on credit;
2 sales of trading goods on credit;
3 cash receipts and payments;
4 all other transactions.

This classification enabled entries of like nature to be kept together, and facilitated the operation of entering data into the source books. It led to the division of the journal into four parts, which were renamed as follows:

1 the purchases day book, in which were entered credit purchases;
2 the sales day book, in which were recorded credit sales;
3 the cash book, in which were recorded all cash transactions;
4 the journal proper, in which were recorded transactions which could not be recorded in the other source books. The journal proper has been retained as a book of original entry for such transactions.

## The day books

Since the bulk of source documents relate to the purchase or sale of goods, the function of the purchases and sales day books is to allow such data to be collected and posted to the ledger. An example of a purchases day book is given below.

**Purchases day book**

| Date | Name | Invoice No | Folio | £ |
|---|---|---|---|---|
| 1 June | S Smith | 101 | L15 | 50 |
| 2 | W Wright and Co | 113 | L20 | 35 |
| 2 | J James | 148 | L10 | 140 |
| 3 | T Tennant | 184 | L16 | 20 |
| 3 | Transferred to purchases account | | L50 | 245 |

The posting of the purchases day book to the ledger is effected by crediting the account of each supplier with the value of the goods supplied and transferring the total value of all purchases in the period to the purchases account. The details entered in the day books are obtained from the invoices which are filed and kept.

The sales day book is written up in the same manner as the purchases day book, except that the source document is a copy of the invoice sent to the customer.

## The cash book

Only cash transactions are entered in the cash book, the purpose of which is to record all receipts and payments of cash. As we will see, the cash book has a dual role, being a journal and a ledger account.

As the practice grew of using cheques for the settlement of business debts, so the cash book came to reflect this practice, and to record all payments out of and into the firm's bank account.

Unlike the day books, the cash book records receipts and payments side by side, so that flows in and out are seen together and their impact on the balance may be readily seen. At the end of the accounting period, the cash book is reconciled with the bank statement by means of a bank reconciliation statement which explains any difference between the balance recorded in the cash book and that recorded by the bank. This difference is due to the time-lag between the posting of a cheque to a creditor and its clearing through the bank, delays in clearing cheques paid in, bank charges and direct payments into and out of the bank.

Where transactions take place in cash as well as by cheques, and cash discounts are given and allowed, the cash book is given extra columns, and becomes known as a 'three-column cash book'. The transfer of cash in and out of the bank account is recorded as well as the receipts and payments by cheques, as follows:

**Cash book**

| Date | Details | Folio | Discounts allowed £ | Cash £ | Bank £ | Date | Details | Folio | Discounts received £ | Cash £ | Bank £ |
|---|---|---|---|---|---|---|---|---|---|---|---|
| 1 Jan | Balance | J1 | | 50 | 800 | 1 Jan | B Brown | L3 | 7 | | 103 |
| 1 | Sales | L15 | | 60 | | 1 | Purchases | L14 | | 20 | |
| 1 | W White | L9 | 5 | | 95 | 1 | Cash | | | | 20 |
| 1 | Bank | | | 20 | | | | | | | |

The explanation of some of these entries is as follows:

1 Jan   B Brown – this represents the payment of an account owing to Brown amounting to £110 which was settled by the payment of £103, the balance being in the form of a discount which was received.

1 Jan   W White – this represents the receipt of a cheque for £95 in settlement of an amount owing of £100, a discount of £5 being allowed.

1 Jan   Bank – this represents a cash cheque drawn on the bank for £20. The corresponding payment of cash by the bank is shown on the other side of the cash book.

For security reasons, few firms like to keep large sums in cash about their premises and cash takings are banked daily. Moreover, it is sound practice to use cheques for the settlement of debts, so that there is generally no need to keep cash on hand beyond relatively small sums. All firms, therefore, tend to have a petty cash box to meet any immediate need for cash, for example enabling a secretary or porter to take a taxi to deliver a document, or to buy a small article which is urgently required.

The cashier is usually entrusted with the petty cash box and any payments must be claimed by means of a petty cash voucher signed by an authorized person, who is usually a head of department. The cashier is given a petty cash float which may be, say, £50 and pays out petty cash only against petty cash vouchers, which are retained. As the petty cash float decreases, so petty cash vouchers of an equivalent value accumulate in the petty cash box. In due course, the vouchers are checked or audited and the petty cash paid out is refunded to the cashier, thereby restoring the petty cash float to its original sum.

## Division of the ledger

A firm large enough to divide its journal into day books and cash books will probably also need to divide its ledger. The sales ledger (or debtors ledger) contains all the personal accounts of the firm's customers. The purchases ledger (or creditors ledger) contains all the personal accounts of the firm's suppliers. The nominal ledger (also general ledger or private ledger) contains the rest of the firm's accounts. The main reason for dividing the ledger is that it allows several people to be engaged in the recording process and permits sectionalization of the work around these groups of accounts.

## The development of data-processing systems

Although the system of source documents remains today much as we have described, the system for processing the data they contain has been improved dramatically by developments in computer technology. These developments have reduced the size of computers available and they enable most businesses, no matter how small, to take advantage of advanced technology. Indeed, the distinction between mini- and micro-computers has become increasingly blurred as technology has developed. New chips have vastly increased the speed and processing power of microcomputers. A typical computer now runs much faster than earlier PCs. Internal hard disks with a capacity exceeding 200 megabytes are now available and micros are ideal for use as file servers at the centre of a network of other micros and peripheral devices such as printers. This allows more than one person at a time to access and modify the company's data, thus allowing, for example, one person to process sales at the same time as someone else processes purchases or receipts. Furthermore, a 486 based machine with 4+ megabytes of Random Access Memory (processing space) and a storage capacity of 100 megabytes and more (enough for quite a large business) is inexpensive, while the minimum configuration suitable for a business, including a printer, is quite cheap to buy.

At the same time as hardware has developed, so has software. These 'off the peg' packages of programs have become more 'user-friendly' in approach, except that as they develop and become capable of performing more functions they tend to become more complex.

## The application of computer systems

Computer systems can be seen as falling into two main areas for our purposes: special accounting packages and more general packages which may have accounting implications.

### Accounting applications

1 stock recording and control;
2 sales ledger;
3 purchase ledger;
4 nominal ledger;
5 payroll;
6 job costing;
7 invoicing.

It makes sense for these applications to be integrated because every sale will eventually be reflected in the sales ledger and nominal ledger and there are many other interrelationships as illustrated below.

Integrated accounting packages should not be seen as mere straightforward replacements for similar manual systems. The careful design of coding systems allows a considerable amount of useful information to be produced, almost without cost, as a by-product of the recording system. This might include information such as the amount of sales generated by individual sales representatives, or the amount of sales in a particular region as an aid to marketing decisions. The way the coding system is designed is of particular importance and is derived from an analysis of the information needs of the business.

69

## More general applications

1 *Planning and control through the use of spreadsheets.* This might include budgeting, financial modelling, etc. It is common for data to be exported from the accounting system described above into a spreadsheet for further manipulation.
2 *Word processing.* This will allow for more effective communication with customers, suppliers and other business contacts. Mail merge facilities allow for 'personalized' mailshots. It is also possible to link a word processing package with other applications such as spreadsheets or accounting packages to produce letters and reports including up-to-date financial information as either numbers or graphs.
3 *Databases.* These allow for more effective recording of business contacts which can be used, for example, as a way of identifying specific 'targets' for promotions, etc.
4 *Communications.* This is an area which is expanding rapidly and where the computer is, yet again, demonstrating its usefulness. For example, it is possible to use the computer to send data to another computer or a fax machine at times when that machine would otherwise be inactive, or to take advantage of cheaper rates for phone calls (e.g. the middle of the night).

## Electronic data storage and retrieval

Earlier in this chapter we considered the role of source documents for capturing details of accounting events. In a manually operated system, each stage in processing data is a source of potential error, and each involves a labour cost. For example, the manually operated ledger system of a wholesale warehouse on the receipt of an order could involve:

1 noting the order in a sales order day book;
2 writing a sales order form;
3 typing a despatch note;
4 calculating an invoice value involving quantity, price discounts and VAT;
5 typing the invoice;
6 posting the invoice to the sales ledger;
7 typing monthly statements;
8 analysing the age structure of the customer's account balances in order to ascertain how long they have remained unpaid;
9 updating stock records for the goods despatched;
10 typing purchase orders to replenish stock.

Computers may be programmed to make decisions automatically and the implications of this characteristic for data processing are featured in the following example.

**Example 1**

Figure 2.6 illustrates the facilities available in an integrated computer system for processing a sales order. The sales order is fed into the computer, which then accesses information from the debtor's ledger and up-to-date information from stock records.

First, the computer provides information on the outstanding customer's balance and shows whether the customer is creditworthy. Credit limits are established in advance for each customer. The computer adds the value of the order to the balance outstanding on the customer's account in the sales ledger, and compares the total with the credit limit. If the credit limit has not been reached, the order is cleared for further processing. If the credit limit has been reached, the operative will need to confirm that the order will or will not be processed. This procedure allows the company to exercise a meaningful credit control check and to avoid processing any orders for customers with an excessive debt.

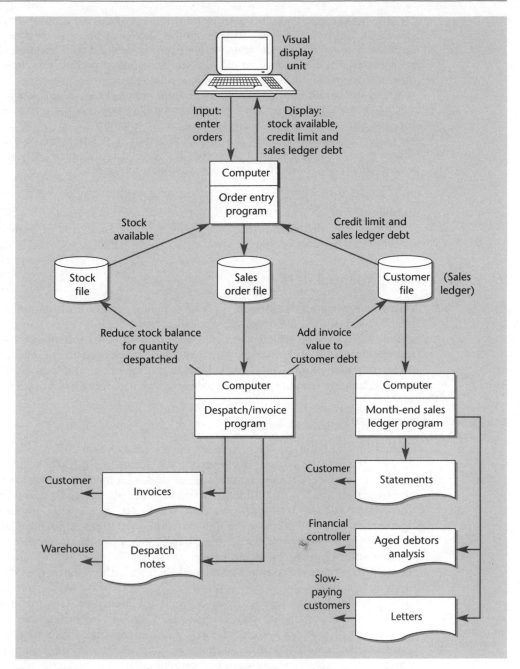

**Figure 2.6**

Second, the computer provides details of the stock available and allows the firm to identify immediately which items can be despatched. For these items, the computer's despatch/invoice program would automatically produce a despatch note (to send to the warehouse) and an invoice (to send to the customer).

Third, the invoice is automatically posted to the customer's account in the sales ledger and, via the sales day book, to the sales account in the nominal ledger.

Fourth, the computer adjusts the stock records in respect of the order and calculates a new balance. It compares the new balance with the balance in stock which is required for each particular item. A 'reorder point' will have been determined for each item of stock. If the stock level falls below the reorder point, then the computer produces a purchase requisition in order to replenish the stock to the designated level.

Fifth, at the month end, statements of account are produced automatically showing how much customers owe the firm at a given date and an analysis of the age structure of debts. Also, the system will automatically produce letters to customers detailing the amount and age of their debt and requesting payment. The text of these letters can be modified in order to create the impression that they are not just computer output. This type of facility has proved extremely valuable in speeding up payments by customers.

This example illustrates how an integrated computer system reduces drastically the number of manual operations performed.

Furthermore, the level of information provision is improved in terms of speed and accuracy and the cost of data processing is greatly reduced.

## Ways of reducing manual data input

Many enterprises are looking at ways of reducing the input of manual data even further. Typical of these developments are the point-of-sale terminals in shops using bar codes and light pens which identify the items sold. This information is fed directly into the computer and updates the stock level. Stock monitoring and control procedures are thereby improved. Fewer items of more lines can be kept on the shop floor, thereby enabling retailers to make more effective use of the available space.

## Data transfer systems

There are two main types of system for the transfer of data collected by the terminals. On-line or real-time systems are permanently connected directly to the central computer and produce virtually instantaneous updating of the computer's records. This type of system is used by building societies and banks for their own customers. The other system is batch transfer where data is collected by a small computer, is grouped together, and then sent down the line to the main computer. Such a system might be used by a bank for customers of other banks. Also, it is being used increasingly as a way for sales representatives to process orders. The sales representative will enter details into a portable computer and will then send the data to the company's main computer for processing, either by reporting in to a location with a company computer terminal or by sending the data down a public telephone line. Great care must be taken over security for systems which can be accessed through public telephone lines.

The type of transfer system selected will depend on circumstances. A real-time system will generally be more expensive than a batch system but it will update records more quickly and may well be more secure.

## Computer systems

The type of computer system a firm requires may be considered from the overall model illustrated in Figure 2.7.

*Data storage* incorporates all the data storage files, e.g. sales and purchase ledgers and stock records. The firm has to decide the number of records it requires to maintain in order to determine the size of storage to be supported by the computer system. Storage devices can be floppy disks (for use in microcomputers), hard disks (used in all categories of computers) or tapes and cartridges (used mainly for keeping security copies of data held on disk storage).

A *terminal* is the name given to an input–output device which is at the end of a communication line. Terminals can be printers or visual display units (VDUs). The number of terminals will be determined by:

1 the volume of input and output data required;
2 the number of different locations which require access to the enterprise's records to be displayed on either VDUs or printed reports (statements, invoices, etc.).

The *computer memory* will determine:

1 the size of computer programs that can be used: for example, some very sophisticated modelling packages require a large computer memory for their operation.
2 whether more than one program can be run at the same time. Where it can, this is often referred to as a multi-user system. This allows one person to have access to the sales ledger, say, on one VDU while another person has access to the stock records on another VDU.

The *central processing unit* (CPU) is the device that accesses data storage and executes instructions. The capability of the CPU used will determine:

1 the number of terminals it will support;
2 the size of the data storage that can be attached;
3 whether a multi-user system can be operated.

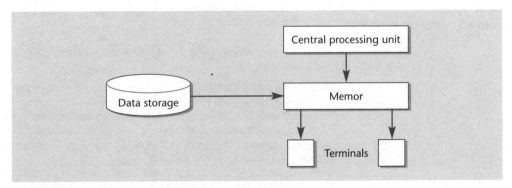

**Figure 2.7**

## Summary

The generation of financial accounting information is a process involving the following stages:

1 the generation of data through the preparation of source documents;
2 the entry of basic data into source books;
3 the posting of data from source books into the ledger;
4 the production of financial reports converting financial information data into financial information.

By making data processing more cost-effective, developments in computers have enabled smaller firms to take advantage of computer techniques. User-friendly systems can be operated by people who have no previous computer experience. Integrated computer systems reduce overall clerical requirements and improve the accuracy and speed of processing data.

*Reference*   Williams, (1999). 'Reporting with a Purpose', Ca *(Canada) Magazine*, March.

## Self-assessment question

1   What do you understand by a 'source document'? Give three examples of source documents, and explain their importance to the accounting process.

## Problems   *(\* indicates that a solution is to be found in the Lecturer's Guide)*

1   Name the books of original entry to be used for recording the following transactions, and state the accounts to be debited and credited:

Transaction (a)  Purchase of equipment on credit.
Transaction (b)  Payment of cash to a creditor.
Transaction (c)  Bank charges paid.
Transaction (d)  Receipt of cash from a customer.
Transaction (e)  Sale to a customer on credit.
Transaction (f)  Goods returned by a customer.

2   Prepare journal entries for the following transactions and indicate the journal in which they would normally appear.

| | |
|---|---|
| 1 April | Received invoice for £400 being equipment purchased from Equipment Supplies Ltd. |
| 2 April | Received invoice for £700 for goods supplied by Jones Ltd. |
| 4 April | Received cheque for £50 from J Brown for goods supplied. Sent cheque to S Supplier for £250 in payment of purchases effected in March. |
| 5 April | Received an invoice from Standfast Supplies Ltd for goods supplied £800. |
| 6 April | Invoiced J Shepherd for goods sold £98. |
| 7 April | Received a cheque for £70 from W Smith in settlement of his account for goods sold. |
| 8 April | Received rates statement showing rates due £500. |
| 9 April | Banked weekly cash takings of £700. |

3\*   Show the following entries as they would appear in a three-column cash book:

| | |
|---|---|
| 1 May | Credit balance (on bank statement) at bank £700, cash in hand £5. Cash drawn from bank for the till £30. Cheque sent to Brown for £67 in settlement of amount due of £70, discount being received for prompt payment. |
| 2 May | Received cheque from Jones for £45 in payment of invoiced amount of £47, less cash discount. |
| 3 May | Cash sales for the day £190 |
| 4 May | Banked cash sales of previous day £190. |
| 5 May | Sent cheque to Blewett £100 being instalment due on loan repayment. |
| 6 May | Took £10 out of till for taxi fares. |

# 8 Data processing and double-entry bookkeeping

## Setting the scene

The resources that come into the company are equal to the resources that are recognized as going out, whether at the present time or at some future date. This equality between the resources that come into a company and those that go out forms a vital part of the accountant's view of the company. It reflects the fact that a company only owns assets on behalf of third parties. These third parties are shareholders and others who are financing the company's operations. The company never really owns assets on its own behalf, but only holds them prior to passing the benefit of ownership on to another party. This means that, whenever the company acquires assets, it must also acquire the finance to hold those assets. This gives rise to the double-entry system which records this twofold aspect of each transaction.          (Chopping and Skerratt, 1995)

## Learning objectives

**After studying this chapter you should be able to:**

1  **Show the effects of transactions on the accounting equation.**

2  **Describe the nature of double-entry bookkeeping.**

3  **Enter transactions in accounting records and take out a trial balance.**

4  **Identify errors which are not revealed by the trial balance.**

We saw in the preceding chapter that financial accounting data has its source in original records of financial transactions. We noted two very important aspects of data generation. First, when reporting to external users, accounting information is presented usually in a form which is concerned with the monetary aspect of a firm's activities. Second, we noted that accounting conventions play a determining role as regards the nature and the quality of the data which is processed.

The purpose of this chapter is to examine the structure which has evolved for handling financial accounting data.

# The accounting equation

Financial accounting is based on a simple notion known as the accounting equation. The accounting equation depicts the equality which exists between the resources owned by the enterprise and the claims against the enterprise in relation to those resources.

One side of the accounting equation expresses, in monetary terms, the resources held by the enterprise. These resources are known as 'assets'. The acquisition of assets by the enterprise will have been financed by funds provided either by the owner(s) or from borrowings. The funds provided by the owner(s) constitute the 'capital' of the enterprise. The funds borrowed constitute liabilities and are known as such. Therefore, the other side of the accounting equation describes how the acquisition of assets has been financed and the claims which exist against the business as a result.

The accounting equation may be stated as follows:

$$\text{capital} + \text{liabilities} = \text{assets}$$

The concept underlying the accounting equation is that the enterprise itself is a vehicle through which assets are held and utilized, and that claims exist against those assets to their full monetary value. Given that liabilities arising from borrowings are stated as legal debts of determined monetary sums, the owners of the enterprise are entitled to the balance of the assets after liabilities have been settled. Accordingly, the accounting equation may be used to express capital as follows:

$$\text{capital} = \text{assets} - \text{liabilities}$$

It follows from our discussion in Chapter 5 that the balance sheet is founded on the accounting equation, for it is a list of the assets held by the enterprise against which is set a list of the claims existing against the enterprise. Both lists are equal in total.

# Transactions and the accounting equation

Given that the balance sheet indicates the financial position of an enterprise at a given point in time, successive transactions would maintain the accounting equation on which the balance sheet rests, though its dimensions and its constituent elements would vary. It is possible to record the effects of successive transactions on the balance sheet equation.

### Transaction 1

Returning to the example cited earlier (see page 39), where J Soap invested £10,000 on 1 April 20X0 in a ladies' hairdressing business, on 1 April 20X0 the opening transaction would be shown as follows:

**Balance sheet 1**

|  | £ |  | £ |
|---|---|---|---|
| Capital | 10,000 | Assets: Bank balance | 10,000 |

The manner in which the subsequent transactions affect the balance sheet through the accounting equation may be seen from the following examples.

## Transaction 2

J Soap paid the monthly rent for the business amounting to £500. This is an expense of the month which will ultimately have to be taken into account in determining the profit or loss for the period. Since the profit made, or loss suffered, in effect augments or diminishes the funds contributed to the business by the proprietor, the expense may be interpreted as a temporary reduction in proprietorship equity which must be offset against revenue earned in order to measure the net increase or reduction in proprietorship equity resulting from trading operations. From the point of view of the accounting equation, therefore, the effect of the transaction on the balance sheet is to reduce cash by £500, and at the same time reduce the capital by the same amount. The balance sheet after this transaction would appear as:

**Balance sheet 2**

|  | £ |  | £ |
|---|---|---|---|
| Capital | 9,500 | Assets: Bank balance | 9,500 |

## Transaction 3

J Soap purchased equipment for £2,000 from Hairdressers' Supplies Ltd on credit. As a result, a new asset appears on the balance sheet as the equipment, and a liability of £2,000 appears in respect of the amount owing. The balance sheet now appears as follows:

**Balance sheet 3**

|  | £ |  |  | £ |
|---|---|---|---|---|
| Capital | 9,500 | Assets: | Equipment | 2,000 |
| Liability: |  |  |  |  |
| Creditor | 2,000 |  | Bank balance | 9,500 |
|  | 11,500 |  |  | 11,500 |

It will be noted that, although the balance sheet totals increase by £2,000, there is no change in the capital of the business. Instead, the balance sheet shows that the equipment purchased has been financed by a liability of exactly that amount.

## Transaction 4

J Soap paid wages amounting to £200 in cash for part-time assistance. This is an expense of the month, and its effect on the balance sheet is to reduce cash by £200 and the capital by the same amount. The balance sheet now appears as follows:

**Balance sheet 4**

|  | £ |  |  | £ |
|---|---|---|---|---|
| Capital | 9,300 | Assets: | Equipment | 2,000 |
| Liability: |  |  |  |  |
| Creditor | 2,000 |  | Bank balance | 9,300 |
|  | 11,300 |  |  | 11,300 |

## Transaction 5

J Soap's revenue from clients for April amounted to £1,500, of which £1,400 was received in cash. Revenue earned from sales will ultimately be compared with costs and expenses incurred in order to ascertain the change in proprietorship equity resulting from operations in the period. Therefore, the effect of these transactions is to increase the capital by £1,500 and to increase cash at bank by £1,400. The amount outstanding of £100 requires a new asset account to be opened – Debtors – in the sum of £100. The balance sheet now appears as follows:

**Balance sheet 5**

|  | £ |  |  | £ |
|---|---|---|---|---|
| Capital | 10,800 | Assets: | Equipment | 2,000 |
| Liability: |  |  | Debtor | 100 |
| Creditor | 2,000 |  | Bank balance | 10,700 |
|  | 12,800 |  |  | 12,800 |

## Transaction 6

J Soap withdraws the sum of £400 in cash for his own use. The effect of this withdrawal is to reduce capital by £400 and cash by the same amount. The withdrawal of cash from the business is the reverse of the first transaction in which J Soap invested in the business. Consequently, the capital account is reduced by the amount of the withdrawal. The balance sheet now stands as follows:

**Balance sheet 6**

|  | £ |  |  | £ |
|---|---|---|---|---|
| Capital | 10,400 | Assets: | Equipment | 2,000 |
| Liability: |  |  | Debtor | 100 |
| Creditor | 2,000 |  | Bank balance | 10,300 |
|  | 12,400 |  |  | 12,400 |

# Simplifying the recording of transactions

The process of drawing up a new balance sheet after each transaction would be extremely cumbersome in practice, given the large number of transactions which an enterprise may conduct daily. The problems are threefold. First, how to calculate the effects of successive transactions in terms of the profit they have generated? Such a calculation would explain why there occurred an increase in the capital from an original amount of £10,000 to £10,800, prior to the withdrawal made by J Soap. Second, how to reflect the investment of the owner, J Soap, in a convenient manner? Such a calculation would involve summarizing the effects of transactions on the capital account as it stands at the end of the accounting period. Third, how to devise a system of recording transactions which avoids the necessity of drawing up successive balance sheets?

The first problem is resolved by summarizing all transactions associated with the profit-earning process during the period in a statement known as the profit and loss account. Unlike the balance sheet, which states the financial position of the enterprise at different points in time, the profit and loss account seeks to establish the success or failure of the enterprise as the result of transactions over a period of time. The preparation of the profit and loss account involves identifying the revenues of the period, and the expenses which may properly be charged against those revenues. In the example of J Soap above, the successive balance sheets for the month of April, which resulted in the increase in the capital account from £10,000 to £10,800 by balance sheet 5, may be summarized by a profit and loss account for April 20X0 as follows:

**J Soap – Ladies' Hairdresser**
**Profit and loss account for April 20X0**

|  | £ | £ |
| --- | --- | --- |
| Revenue |  | 1,500 |
| Expenses: |  |  |
| Rent | 500 |  |
| Salaries | 200 | 700 |
| Net profit for April |  | 800 |

The second problem, namely portraying the investment of the owner of the business at the close of the accounting period, involves using both the profit and loss account of the period and the balance sheet at the close of the period. In this respect, the profit and loss account and the balance sheet complement each other. The profit and loss account summarizes the operating results between successive balance sheets, and these results are reflected in the capital shown on the closing balance sheet. The factors which have affected the amount of the owner's capital at the date of the closing balance sheet may be summarized in a detailed statement of the capital account. As regards the example of J Soap given above, the analysis of the capital account would be shown on the closing balance sheet as follows:

**J Soap – Ladies' Hairdresser**
**Capital account as at 30 April 20X0**

|  | £ | £ |
|---|---|---|
| Balance, 1 April 20X0 |  | 10,000 |
| Net profit for April | 800 |  |
| *Less*: Drawings | 400 | 400 |
| Balance, 30 April 20X0 |  | 10,400 |

The third problem, that of devising a system of recording transactions which avoids drawing up successive balance sheets, was resolved several centuries ago by the invention of the system of double-entry bookkeeping.

## The nature of double-entry bookkeeping

The collection and recording of data is known as bookkeeping. The practice of recording financial data in 'books' dates from a very long time ago. These books were usually 'bound books' – bound so as to prevent the possibility of fraud by either the insertion or the removal of pages. Nowadays, mechanical and electronic data processing have frequently removed the bookkeeper as a person concerned with entering the results of financial transactions into the books.

The double-entry system of bookkeeping, however, remains the basis for record keeping regardless of whether or not a firm employs advanced data-processing techniques, mechanical or manual methods. It is, therefore, the logical method for recording financial information, and as such the basis of financial accounting practice.

The term 'double-entry' adds a special meaning to the process of bookkeeping. It is a method of recording financial data as transactions involving flows of money or money value between different accounts. It involves a network of integrated accounts, in which an account is designated for each accounting item. The entries recorded on the successive balance sheets of J Soap for April 20X0 would appear in a double-entry bookkeeping system.

### Transaction 1

The initial investment of £10,000 cash by J Soap in the ladies' hairdressing business is shown as a flow of money from the capital account to the cash book, as follows:

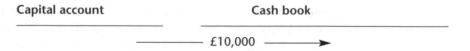

**Capital account**          **Cash book**

———— £10,000 ————→

Business transactions are represented in double-entry bookkeeping as flows of money or money value between the various accounts concerned, but clearly any one transaction involves only one flow, as shown above. In order to identify the direction of any one flow, all accounts are divided into two parts. A flow out of the account is recorded on the right-hand side, and a flow into an account is recorded on the left-hand side. Hence, the transaction shown above would appear as follows:

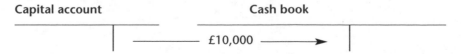

**Capital account**          **Cash book**

———— £10,000 ————→

Flows out could conveniently be described by a minus sign, but the accounting convention which dates from the Italian origins of bookkeeping utilizes the term *Credit* (Cr), which means 'to give'. Likewise, flows in could be described by a positive sign, but the accounting appellation is *Debit* (Dr), which means 'to owe'. Hence, this additional information may be inserted in the accounts to identify the direction of the flow, and replacing the arrow which we have used up to now.

| Capital account | Cash book |
|---|---|
| Cr £10,000 | Dr £10,000 |

There are now only two additional items of information which are required to identify the transaction flow, namely the point of origin and the point of destination. These, too, are made easy in bookkeeping by the simple expedient of describing in the credited account where the flow has gone, and by inserting in the debited account the source of the flow.

| Capital account | Cash book |
|---|---|
| Cr Cash £10,000 | Dr Capital £10,000 |

In practice, accountants know very well that the left-hand side of an account is the debit side, and vice versa for the right-hand side, so that they do not head up the accounts with Dr or Cr. In the old days, they used to add the word *By* on the narration of credit entries, and *To* on the narration of debit entries – but this too is unnecessary, and most accountants have abandoned the practice. The reader will occasionally find entries recorded as follows:

**Capital account**

| | By cash | £10,000 |
|---|---|---|

**Cash book**

| To capital | £10,000 | |
|---|---|---|

We will not, however, use these superfluous terms.

Lastly, the date of the transaction must be recorded, and it is done as follows:

**Capital account**

| | 20X0 1 April | Cash £10,000 |
|---|---|---|

**Cash book**

| 20X0 1 April | Capital £10,000 | |
|---|---|---|

To simplify the exposition of the double-entry bookkeeping system in the examples which follow, the dates will be omitted.

In the manner in which transactions are recorded under this method, the reader will have been quick to notice an important feature – the flow has remained constant in value as it has moved from the credited account to the debited account. As a result, double-entry bookkeeping possesses a mathematical foundation which has its logic in the simple proposition that as regards any one transaction the credit must be equal to the debit. At any time, therefore, the arithmetical precision of the bookkeeping process may be checked by adding up all the debit entries and all the credit entries. If the total debit entries do not equal, that is balance with, the credit entries, there has been an error in the recording process. As we see on page 89, the trial balance is the means whereby accountants check for arithmetical errors in recording transactions. If the trial balance shows a difference as little as 1p between the total debits and the total credits, the error must be found. This is because accountants know that the result of a great many cumulative errors may boil down to a difference of only 1p.

Double-entry bookkeeping is a logical and precise system for recording financial transactions as flows of money or money value. It is easy to operate, and simple to adapt to modern computer methods by using positive and negative electric charges to signal whether an account should be debited or credited.

## Transaction 2

The payment of £500 rent by J Soap is interpreted as a flow of money from the cash book to the rent account. It reduces cash by £500 and appears as an increase in the balance shown in the rent account by £500. The rent account is an 'expense' account which will be transferred later for the purposes of calculating the net profit for April. The entries will appear as follows:

| Cash book | | | Rent account | | |
| --- | --- | --- | --- | --- | --- |
| | | £ | | £ | |
| | Rent | 500 | Cash | 500 | |

## Transaction 3

The purchase of equipment on credit for £2,000 by J Soap from Hairdressers' Supplies Ltd does not yet involve the payment of cash, but requires the debt owing to Hairdressers' Supplies Ltd to be shown. This is effected by crediting the account of Hairdressers' Supplies Ltd with £2,000. Therefore the firm acquires a liability in order to acquire an asset. The entries would be as follows:

**Hairdressers' Supplies Ltd account**

| | | £ |
| --- | --- | --- |
| | Equipment | 2,000 |

**Equipment account**

| | £ | |
| --- | --- | --- |
| Hairdressers' Supplies Ltd | 2,000 | |

## Transaction 4

The payment of £200 as wages is another example of an expense account. Note that in the case of such accounts, the persons receiving payment are not named on the accounts themselves. Separate records would be kept in the form of a wages book, rent book, etc. This transaction decreases cash by £200 and increases wages by the same amount. The entries would be as follows:

| Cash book | | | Wages account | | |
|---|---|---|---|---|---|
| | | £ | | | £ |
| | Wages | 200 | Cash | | 200 |

## Transaction 5

The treatment of the revenue generated from the sale of hairdressing services involves two problems. First, the cash sales involving the receipt of cash amounting to £1,400 are entered directly as follows:

| Sales book | | | Cash book | | |
|---|---|---|---|---|---|
| | | £ | | | £ |
| | Cash | 1,400 | Sales | | 1,400 |

The treatment of credit customers is rather more complex. First, the individuals concerned are shown in the debtors' ledger. The total amount of credit sales during the month of £100 appears in a summary account known as the debtors account. The entries are as follows:

| Sales account | | | Debtors account | | |
|---|---|---|---|---|---|
| | | £ | | | £ |
| | Debtors | 100 | Sales | | 100 |

The payments made by debtors during the month totalled £1,400, leaving an amount outstanding of £100 at the end of April and shown as follows:

**Debtors account**

| | £ | | £ |
|---|---|---|---|
| Sales | 1,500 | Cash | 1,400 |
| | | Balance | 100 |
| | 1,500 | | 1,500 |

### Transaction 6

J Soap withdrew £400 for his personal use. This transaction, which reduces his capital account by £400, could be entered directly as follows:

| Capital account | | | | Cash book | | |
|---|---|---|---|---|---|---|
| | | | £ | | | £ |
| | | £ | | | | |
| Cash | 400 | Cash | 10,000 | | Capital | 400 |

The effect of this transaction would be to reduce the capital account by £400 to £9,600. This reduction could be shown as follows:

**Capital account**

| | £ | | £ |
|---|---|---|---|
| Cash | 400 | | |
| Balance c/d | 9,600 | Cash | 10,000 |
| | 10,000 | | 10,000 |
| | | Balance b/d | 10,000 |

In order to minimize entries in the capital account in respect of regular withdrawals by the owner of a business, the normal practice is to show them in a separate drawings account. At the end of the accounting period, the drawings account is transferred to the capital account, so that only one entry is made in respect of drawings. Using the drawings account, the withdrawal of £400 would be shown as follows:

| Drawings account | | | Cash book | | |
|---|---|---|---|---|---|
| | £ | | | | £ |
| Cash | 400 | | | Drawings | 400 |

The capital account illustrates a technical operation known as balancing an account. Where there is more than one entry in an account the net effect of transactions affecting that account may be determined by calculating the balance of the account. This is the difference between the sum of the credit entries and the sum of the debit entries. In the case of the capital account the sum of the credit entries exceeds the sum of the debit entries. The balance is described as a credit balance. A debit entry is made in the account for the balance, which is said to be carried down (c/d); a credit entry is made on the next line to record the amount of the balance brought down (b/d) and to preserve the principle of double entry.

## Double-entry bookkeeping as a 'closed' system

The term 'system' is commonly used to mean any unit which may be identified as an independent whole, having its own objectives and its own internal functions. An 'open' system is one whose behaviour is affected by external factors. The British economy, for example, is an 'open system' because it is affected by its trading relationships with the rest of the world. A 'closed' system is one in which all the functions are internalized in the system, and are not affected by outside factors. Double-entry bookkeeping has the characteristics of a closed system in that all the transactions recorded take place within the accounts system. By this we mean that all flows resulting from transactions are depicted as having their origin in an account which is found in the system, and they have their destination in another account in the system. It is impossible for a flow to originate from an account outside the accounts system. Likewise, it is impossible for a flow of money or of money value to go to an account outside the accounts system.

**Example 1**  Let us go back to the example given above. J Soap opens up a business under the name of 'J Soap – Ladies' Hairdresser'. He invests £10,000 in cash into the business. The effect of the entity convention is that J Soap opens and keeps separate books for the business of J Soap – Ladies' Hairdresser, which is regarded as a separate entity from J Soap himself. Double-entry bookkeeping gives expression to the entity convention since all the accounts of J Soap – Ladies' Hairdresser relate only to the financial transactions of that business. J Soap himself is an external party as far as the business is concerned.

The question is – how can we depict the flow of £10,000 from J Soap into the business? Now, we have said that no flow may originate from outside the accounts system. Hence, we must have an account within the accounts system whence it has originated. That account is the account of J Soap himself in his capacity as owner of the business, which we described above as the capital account. The source of the flow of £10,000 is therefore found in the capital account, and its destination is the cash account.

**Capital account**

|  |  | £ |
|---|---|---|
|  | 20X0 |  |
|  | 1 April | 10,000 |

**Cash book**

|  | £ |  |
|---|---|---|
| 20X0 |  |  |
| 1 April | 10,000 |  |

Let us suppose for a moment that on 2 April J Soap decides that he has put too much money in the business and wishes to take out £3,000. In the accounts system, the transaction could be shown as follows:

**Capital account**

|  | £ |  | £ |
|---|---|---|---|
| 20X0 |  | 20X0 |  |
| 2 April   Cash | 3,000 | 1 April   Cash | 10,000 |

85

**Cash book**

|  |  | £ |  |  | £ |
|---|---|---:|---|---|---:|
| 20X0 |  |  | 20X0 |  |  |
| 1 April | Capital | 10,000 | 2 April | Capital | 3,000 |

The significance of these entries reflects the fact that accounting is not concerned with the ultimate destination of the actual sums of money, but simply with portraying the full transaction as a *record* of the flow of money. Successive entries are made in accounts which have been opened, and where a transaction involves a new account then that account is opened. Likewise, if an account is no longer needed, it is closed.

The implications of these statements as far as bookkeeping being a closed system of accounts are:

1 The bookkeeping system of any firm is infinitely elastic in size. As many accounts are opened as are necessary to record in full the transactions which have taken place. It is not surprising, therefore, that large businesses have many thousands of accounts.

2 All the accounting flows of money or of money value take place between the various accounts found in the system. The accounts system, therefore, consists of a set of 'interlocking accounts'.

3 The accounts themselves represent 'realities' – whether they are persons or assets involved in transactions.

4 Firms are continually involved in transactions: this activity is mirrored in the constant flow of money and of money value in the accounts system.

5 Since all the flows have both their source and their destination in the accounts to be found in the system, the total debits and the total credits remain equal at all times. If this is not so, there are one or more errors.

## Accounts as descriptions of transactions

We have already noted that the accounts system is used to describe the direction of a flow of money or of money value, as well as the timing of the flow. Business transactions affect a firm in different ways: some are concerned with the acquisition of assets to be used in earning profits, others concern the supply of finance to the firm, either by the owner or by lenders, others relate to goods purchased or sold to persons so that the exchange of goods expressed as money value creates rights or liabilities in money terms, and others yet relate to revenues and costs.

If a firm is to make any sense of the large number of accounts kept, some grouping is necessary, so that accounts of the same business nature are kept together. The integration of accounts into groupings enables the accountant to extract information with much greater ease. For example, to find out how much is owed to persons by the business, the accountant has merely to go to the accounts of the creditors. This term means that such persons have been the source of a flow of money, or of money value to the firm, and have not been repaid. Likewise, the debtors accounts are referred to to find out how much is owing to the business by those people who have received money or money value and have not settled their accounts.

Transactions frequently involve two or more different classes of accounts.

**Example 2**  J Soap supplies hairdressing services to Mrs B Brown to the value of £20 on 1 April 20X0. In the accounts of J Soap, the transaction will be shown as a flow of money value (goods) from the sales account, which is a nominal account, to Mrs B Brown's account, which is a personal account. Nominal accounts contain all of the items that are transferred to the profit and loss account and so include items such as sales, purchases, wages and expenses.

**Sales account**

| | | £ |
|---|---|---|
| | 20X0 | |
| | 1 April    Mrs B Brown | 20 |

**Mrs B Brown account**

| | £ | |
|---|---|---|
| 20X0 | | |
| 1 April    Sales | 20 | |

Since Mrs Brown has received services from J Soap she is a debtor to the amount of £20. At the end of the month, J Soap will send her a statement showing that £20 is due for payment. Mrs B Brown sends her cheque for £20, which will be banked on 1 May. This is shown as another transaction, the settlement of a debt, as follows:

**Mrs B Brown account**

| | £ | | £ |
|---|---|---|---|
| 20X0 | | 20X0 | |
| 1 April    Sales | 20 | 1 May    Cash | 20 |

**Cash book**

| | £ | |
|---|---|---|
| 20X0 | | |
| 1 May    Mrs B Brown | 20 | |

Thus, this transaction is one between a personal account and a real account. At this point, we may make two interesting observations:

1  A 'credit' transaction is a flow of money value to or from a personal account, and involves the creation of a debt towards the business, or a liability against the business. Hence, the use of the terms debtor and creditor respectively to denote the nature of such legal rights and obligations.
2  The payment of any liability involves another accounting transaction which records the flow of money from or to the appropriate personal account to or from the cash book. In this connection, the cash book records all the money flows through the firm's bank account.

## The mathematical implications of double-entry bookkeeping

We have already noted that the arithmetical accuracy of the entries made in the accounts may be verified by means of a trial balance which involves comparing the total debits with the total credits.

During any accounting period, there may have been several entries in an account, so that several debits and several credits may be shown. A simple calculation may be made to calculate the net balance, for the purpose of the trial balance itself, and to ascertain the net state of the account.

**Example 3** In the foregoing example several cash transactions took place during the month of April, as follows:

**Cash book**

|         | £      |          | £   |
|---------|--------|----------|-----|
| Capital | 10,000 | Rent     | 500 |
| Sales   | 400    | Wages    | 200 |
| Debtors | 1,000  | Drawings | 400 |

If we wish to ascertain the balance on the cash book, the procedure for so doing is simply to add up both sides of the account and to calculate the difference. This difference is the balance.

**Cash book**

|         | £      |          | £      |
|---------|--------|----------|--------|
| Capital | 10,000 | Rent     | 500    |
| Sales   | 400    | Wages    | 200    |
| Debtors | 1,000  | Drawings | 400    |
|         |        | Balance  | 10,300 |
|         | 11,400 |          | 11,400 |

This balance represents the excess of the debits over the credits and it indicates that the bank balance is £10,300 in hand. In order to show this fact in the account after it has been balanced, the balance is brought down as a debit balance.

**Cash book**

|             | £      |             | £      |
|-------------|--------|-------------|--------|
| Capital     | 10,000 | Rent        | 500    |
| Sales       | 400    | Wages       | 200    |
| Debtors     | 1,000  | Drawings    | 400    |
|             |        | Balance c/d | 10,300 |
|             | 11,400 |             | 11,400 |
| Balance b/d | 10,300 |             |        |

Balancing the accounts is the first stage in preparing the trial balance. Some accounts will have debit balances and others will have credit balances. When we compare the total balances, they should be equal.

# The trial balance

The trial balance is a list of balances extracted from all the accounts arranged in such a way that the debit balances are listed on one side and the credit balances on the other side.

*Example 4*  The following trial balance was extracted on 30 April 20X0 from the books of J Soap – Ladies Hairdresser:

**Trial balance as on 30 April 20X0**

|  | Debit balances £ | Credit balances £ |
|---|---|---|
| Capital account on 1 April 20X0 |  | 10,000 |
| Drawings | 400 |  |
| Cash | 10,300 |  |
| Rent | 500 |  |
| Wages | 200 |  |
| Equipment | 2,000 |  |
| Sales |  | 1,500 |
| Debtors | 100 |  |
| Creditors |  | 2,000 |
|  | 13,500 | 13,500 |

The trial balance not only serves to act as a check on the arithmetical accuracy of the bookkeeping process, but is a summary of the balances of all the accounts, which, as we shall see in the next chapter, serves as a working paper in the course of preparing financial statements. We note that in the process of summarizing information for the purpose of the trial balance, the personal accounts of the debtors and the creditors have been totalled.

The trial balance will not reveal the following types of errors:

1  errors of omission, where a transaction has been completely overlooked;
2  errors of principle, where an amount is correctly recorded but is placed in the wrong class of account – for example, where the purchase of equipment is shown under purchases rather than under equipment;
3  errors of commission, where an amount is correctly recorded in the correct class of account, but is entered in the wrong account – for example, where a sale of £50 to Mr B Brown is entered in Mrs B Brown's account;
4  errors of original entry, where the transaction is recorded in the wrong amount – for example, where a sale to Mrs B Brown of goods to the value of £20 is recorded as £2 in the sales journal;
5  errors in recording the direction of the flow, although the correct account is recorded – for example, instead of being shown as a debit to the cash book and a credit to Mrs B Brown's account it is shown the other way round;
6  compensating errors which cancel each other out will not be revealed. Thus, an error in adding up the trade debtors which is cancelled out by a similar error in adding up the trade creditors will not be revealed.

**Example 5**  Fairburn is a retailer and on 1 January 20X0 his assets were:

|  | £ |
|---|---|
| Cash in bank | 686 |
| Stock in trade | 916 |
| Furniture and fittings | 396 |
| Sundry debtors –  Grime | 36 |
| Spear | 78 |
| Murta | 52 |

His only liabilities were to the following suppliers:

|  | £ |
|---|---|
| Windle | 24 |
| Naik | 42 |

The following transactions took place during January:

| Event | January |  | £ |
|---|---|---|---|
| 1 | 1 | Sold goods to Spear on credit | 248 |
| 2 | 5 | Paid wages | 24 |
| 3 | 6 | Bought goods on credit from Windle | 300 |
| 4 | 8 | Grime settled his account |  |
| 5 | 9 | Paid the amount owing Naik |  |
| 6 | 10 | Cash sales | 128 |
| 7 | 13 | Paid wages | 28 |
| 8 | 17 | Bought goods for cash | 150 |
| 9 | 18 | Paid Windle the balance on his account |  |
| 10 | 19 | Bought a new office desk for cash | 64 |
| 11 | 20 | Paid wages | 34 |
| 12 | 23 | Cash sales | 220 |
| 13 | 24 | Paid office expenses | 6 |
| 14 | 25 | Spear paid on account | 50 |
| 15 | 26 | Cash sales | 168 |
| 16 | 27 | Paid wages | 30 |
| 17 | 30 | Cash sales | 60 |

*Required:*
Enter these transactions in Fairburn's accounting records and test the arithmetical accuracy of your work by preparing a trial balance at 31 January 20X0.

**Bank account**

|  |  | £ |  |  | £ |
|---|---|---|---|---|---|
|  | Balance b/d | 686 | (2) | Wages | 24 |
| (4) | Grime | 36 | (5) | Naik | 42 |
| (6) | Sales | 128 | (7) | Wages | 28 |
| (12) | Sales | 220 | (8) | Purchases | 150 |
| (14) | Spear | 50 | (9) | Windle | 324 |
| (15) | Sales | 168 | (10) | Fixtures and fittings | 64 |
| (17) | Sales | 60 | (11) | Wages | 34 |
|  |  |  | (13) | Office expenses | 6 |
|  |  |  | (16) | Wages | 30 |
|  |  |  |  | Balance c/d | 646 |
|  |  | 1,348 |  |  | 1,348 |
|  | Balance b/d | 646 |  |  |  |

**Capital account**

|  | £ |  | £ |
|---|---|---|---|
| Balance c/d | 2,098 | Balance b/d | 2,098 |
|  |  | Balance b/d | 2,098 |

**Fixtures and fittings account**

|  |  | £ |  | £ |
|---|---|---|---|---|
|  | Balance b/d | 396 |  |  |
| (10) | Bank | 64 | Balance c/d | 460 |
|  |  | 460 |  | 460 |
|  | Balance b/d | 460 |  |  |

**Sales account**

|  | £ |  |  | £ |
|---|---|---|---|---|
|  |  | (1) | Spear | 248 |
|  |  | (6) | Bank | 128 |
|  |  | (12) | Bank | 220 |
|  |  | (15) | Bank | 168 |
| Balance c/d | 824 | (17) | Bank | 60 |
|  | 824 |  |  | 824 |
|  |  |  | Balance b/d | 824 |

**Wages account**

|  |  | £ |  | £ |
|---|---|---|---|---|
| (2) | Bank | 24 |  |  |
| (7) | Bank | 28 |  |  |
| (11) | Bank | 34 |  |  |
| (16) | Bank | 30 | Balance c/d | 116 |
|  |  | 116 |  | 116 |
|  | Balance b/d | 116 |  |  |

**Purchases account**

|  | £ |  | £ |
|---|---|---|---|
| (3) Windle | 300 |  |  |
| (8) Bank | 150 | Balance c/d | 450 |
|  | 450 |  | 450 |
| Balance b/d | 450 |  |  |

**Office expenses account**

|  | £ |  | £ |
|---|---|---|---|
| (13) Bank | 6 | Balance c/d | 6 |
|  | 6 |  | 6 |
| Balance b/d | 6 |  |  |

**Grime's account**

|  | £ |  | £ |
|---|---|---|---|
| Balance b/d | 36 | (4) Bank | 36 |

**Spear's account**

|  | £ |  | £ |
|---|---|---|---|
| Balance b/d | 78 | (14) Bank | 50 |
| (1) Sales | 248 | Balance c/d | 276 |
|  | 326 |  | 326 |
| Balance c/d | 276 |  |  |

**Murta's account**

|  | £ |  | £ |
|---|---|---|---|
| Balance b/d | 52 | Balance c/d | 52 |
| Balance b/d | 52 |  |  |

**Windle's account**

|  | £ |  | £ |
|---|---|---|---|
| (9) Bank | 324 | Balance b/d | 24 |
|  |  | (3) Purchases | 300 |
|  | 324 |  | 324 |

**Naik's account**

|  | £ |  | £ |
|---|---|---|---|
| (5) Bank | 42 | Balance b/d | 42 |

**Fairburn trial balance 31.1.20X0**

|  | £ Dr | £ Cr |
|---|---|---|
| Bank | 646 | |
| Capital | | 2,098 |
| Stock | 916 | |
| Fixtures and fittings | 460 | |
| Sales | | 824 |
| Wages | 116 | |
| Purchases | 450 | |
| Office expenses | 6 | |
| Debtors – Spear | 276 | |
| Murta | 52 | |
| | 2,922 | 2,922 |

## Summary

The evolution of double-entry bookkeeping has provided accountants with a method of processing data in a systematic manner, and with a means of checking the accuracy of accounting records which was built into its processes by virtue of the interlocking nature of the accounts system. At the end of an accounting period, it is axiomatic that the total debit entries must be equal to the total credit entries and vice versa.

With the advent of the computer the usefulness of the double-entry method as a check on the accuracy of record-keeping has largely disappeared. Nevertheless, double-entry bookkeeping remains the basis for recording financial transactions as flows of money, or of money value from one account to another, whether or not the accounts system is computerized.

Far more significant, however, as regards the usefulness of the data recorded in the double-entry system are the effects of accounting conventions, which require in particular that the values recorded should be determined by transactions.

*Reference*  Chopping, D and Skerratt, L (1995). *Applying GAAP 1995/96*, Accountancy Books.

## Problems *(*indicates that a solution is to be found in the Lecturer's Guide)*

1   Show the effects of the following transactions on the accounting equation. For this purpose, enter these transactions in columns as under:

| Col 1 | | Col 2 | | Col 3 |
|---|---|---|---|---|
| Capital | + | Liabilities | = | Assets |
| .............. | | .............. | | .............. |
| .............. | | .............. | | .............. |

Transaction (a)   J Johnson opens a garage by investing £20,000 in cash in the business.
Transaction (b)   He borrows £5,000 from the bank.
Transaction (c)   He purchases petrol for £1,000 and pays in cash.
Transaction (d)   He buys equipment to the value of £10,000 and agrees to pay that amount within four weeks.
Transaction (e)   He purchases second-hand cars from Middleton Motors and pays £15,000, being the agreed amount.
Transaction (f)   Customers pay £2,000 for services rendered.
Transaction (g)   Wages paid amount to £1,000.

2   Show the accounting effects of the following transactions by reference to the balance sheet and the profit and loss account. (Example: cash sale £200 would add £200 to revenue on the profit and loss account and £200 to the asset cash on the balance sheet.)

| | Accounting effects | |
|---|---|---|
| Transaction | Balance sheet | P & L a/c |
| Cash sales £400 | .................... | .................... |
| Cash purchases £75 | .................... | .................... |
| Received from trade debtor £35 | .................... | .................... |
| Equipment purchased on credit terms £345 | .................... | .................... |
| Invoice received for repairs to machinery £67 | .................... | .................... |
| Wages paid £78 | .................... | .................... |
| Payment of rent due last month £90 | .................... | .................... |
| Equipment sold as scrap £20 (book value £10) | .................... | .................... |
| Loan received £600 | .................... | .................... |
| Bank interest charged £49 | .................... | .................... |

3   Bill Cashing sets up practice as an architect, investing £10,000 of his own money into the business and effecting a transfer of that sum from his personal account to his business account at Barclays Bank Ltd. The transfer is effected on 1 January 20X0, the date on which he formally commenced. The following transactions took place in the following month:

| Event | | |
|---|---|---|
| 1 | 1 January | Paid office rent for January £200. |
| 2 | 1 January | Purchased office equipment on account from Equipit Ltd £1,000. |
| 3 | 1 January | Purchased office supplies on account from W Brown for £150. |
| 4 | 3 January | Hired a junior out of school. |
| 5 | 4 January | Surveyed a property for A Bond and sent out an invoice of £50. |

| 6  | 7 January  | Decided to transfer his own car to the business at a value of £2,000. |
|----|------------|-----------------------------------------------------------------------|
| 7  | 10 January | Bought petrol for £10, paid by cheque. |
| 8  | 11 January | Took a client to lunch at a cost of £20, and was asked to prepare plans for a new factory for which work he estimated he would earn £1,200. |
| 9  | 17 January | Conducted another property survey for A Bond and invoiced him for £60. |
| 10 | 20 January | Took another prospective client to lunch at a cost of £30, and found that he would not be able to undertake work for that client. |
| 11 | 30 January | Paid the office junior his monthly wage of £70. |
| 12 | 30 January | Sent a cheque to Equipit Ltd for £1,000. |
| 13 | 30 January | Sent a cheque to W Brown for office supplies £150. |
| 14 | 30 January | Banked a cheque received from A Bond for £50. |

*Required:*
Enter these transactions in Bill Cashing's accounting records, and test the arithmetical accuracy of your work by preparing a trial balance when you have completed the entries needed to be made.

4   As at 31 December 20X0, the accountant of AB Ltd extracted a trial balance from the firm's accounting records and, there being a difference, inserted a balancing figure in a suspense account.

Later, it was found that:

(a) a payment of £150 for stationery in the cash book had been posted in the ledger as £50;
(b) a total of £637 in the sales day book had been carried forward as £673;
(c) an amount of £60 paid to S Jones on 2 January 20X1 had been included in the purchase ledger balances shown in the trial balance;
(d) goods which cost £75 had been returned to R Brown and, while a correct entry had been made in the purchases returns book, £175 had been posted to the credit of R Brown's account in the sales ledger;
(e) at the beginning and end of the accounting period stocks were valued at £1,250 and £2,250 respectively. In error, the latter figure had been shown in the trial balance;
(f) discounts allowed amounting to £325 had been credited to the appropriate nominal ledger account;
(g) £256, being the amount of discounts received, had been debited to the nominal ledger as £265;
(h) cash at bank was shown in the trial balance as £350. In fact this was the balance shown by the bank statement which on 31 December 20X0 was £20 in excess of the bank balance correctly recorded in the cash book.

After rectification of the above discrepancies the books balanced.

*Required:*
Show journal entries necessary to correct the above errors and set out the suspense account as it would finally appear in the books.

5*  (a) Harold Davies is the proprietor of a small building firm. He does not understand the term 'balance sheet' and asks you to explain to him whether the following items should be on his balance sheet. Indicate the nature of the items (e.g. current asset, long-term liability, not applicable, etc.) and give the reason for your answer.

   (i)   stock of sand and cement;
   (ii)  air compressor purchased for cash;
   (iii) air compressor hired for three weeks;
   (iv)  wages paid to labourer;

(v)   lorry used for transporting materials;

(vi)   diesel fuel in lorry fuel tank;

(vii)  washing machine bought for Mrs Davies;

(viii) bank overdraft;

(ix)   petty cash in hand;

(x)    £2,000 owing to an uncle who says Harold need not pay until five years have elapsed.

(b)   Explain what effect the following transactions will have on a balance sheet to which they relate:

(i)    Shareholders invest a further £20,000 in the company.

(ii)   The company buys raw material for cash £1,200.

(iii)  The company buys raw material on credit £4,000.

(iv)   The company pays £5,000 to its creditors.

(v)    The wages payable are paid £2,000.

6   Oliver commenced business on 1 June 20X0. The following transactions took place during the month of June.

| Event | June | |
|---|---|---|
| 1 | 1 | Introduced cash of £4,000 and car valued at £1,750. |
| 2 | 2 | Bought goods for cash at a cost of £1,130. |
| 3 | 8 | Paid wages of £13 and sundry expenses of £2. |
| 4 | 9 | Sold goods on credit to Victor for £190. |
| 5 | 14 | Sold goods on credit to Susan for £240. |
| 6 | 18 | Bought goods on credit from William for £85. |
| 7 | 22 | Bought fixtures and fittings at a cost of £350. |
| 8 | 25 | Paid wages of £38. |
| 9 | 26 | Paid drawings to himself of £80. |
| 10 | 30 | Victor paid the full amount owing. |
| 11 | 30 | Paid rent of £500. |

*Required:*
Enter these transactions in Oliver's accounting records and take out a trial balance at 30 June 20X0.

7   Richard started up a business as a butcher on 1 March 20X0. His transactions during March were:

1    Borrowed £10,000 from his father and paid the money into a business bank account.

2    Made cash purchases totalling £6,000.

3    Made cash sales totalling £8,000.

4    Bought a delivery bicycle for £140 cash.

5    Paid rent for one month £240.

6    Made credit purchases totalling £4,000 and by the end of the month had paid all but £1,000 of this amount.

7    Made credit sales totalling £7,600 and at the end of the month debtors still owed £3,400 of this amount.

8    Received a legacy of £2,000 and paid this into the business.

9    Paid for electricity for one month £180.

10   Drew £240 for his personal expenses.

*Required:*
Enter the transactions in Richard's accounting records and take out a trial balance at 31 March 20X0.

8* Simon is a retailer and on 1 June 20X0 his balance sheet was as follows:

|  | £ | £ |  | £ | £ |
|---|---|---|---|---|---|
| **Capital** |  | 14,000 | **Fixed assets** |  |  |
|  |  |  | Premises | 10,000 |  |
|  |  |  | Fixtures | 2,000 | 12,000 |
| **Current liabilities** |  |  | **Current assets** |  |  |
| William | 2,000 |  | Stock | 5,000 |  |
| Paul | 3,000 | 5,000 | Debtor – Sam | 600 |  |
|  |  |  | Bank | 1,400 | 7,000 |
|  |  | 19,000 |  |  | 19,000 |

His transactions during June were:

*June*

1  Purchased goods on credit from William for £1,000.
2  Cash sales £2,000.
3  Sold items £600 on credit to Clare.
4  Paid William £600 on account.
5  Sam paid £560 in full settlement, which allowed him a discount of £40.
8  Cash sales £1,800.
9  Purchased fixtures £700 cash.
10  Sold goods on credit to Sam for £800.
11  Sold goods to Ann for £300.
16  Purchased goods on credit from Paul for £4,000.
17  Purchased items from William on credit for £2,000.
19  Paid Paul £6,600 in full settlement.
21  Returned goods cost £200 to William.
23  Returns received from Ann selling price £200.
26  Ann paid £90 in full settlement.
28  Cash sales £4,600.
30  Paid William £1,800 on account.

*Required:*
Enter these transactions in Simon's accounting records and take out a trial balance at 30 June 20X0.

# 2 Periodic measurement

# 9 Double-entry bookkeeping and periodic measurement

## Learning objectives

After studying this chapter you should be able to:

1 Distinguish between revenue and capital expenses.

2 Explain how revenue and expenses are attributed to the accounting period.

3 Calculate accruals and prepayments and enter them in the accounting records.

In Chapter 8, we examined the double-entry method as a means of recording financial transactions as flows of money or of money value. We said that firms are continually involved in transactions, and that this activity is mirrored in the double-entry bookkeeping process by the constant flow through the accounts system of the money or money values involved in those transactions.

The accounts system is merely a repository of financial data about transactions. To be meaningful, this data must be extracted from the accounts system and organized in such a way that it is useful to those who need information for decision making. The concept of periodicity which we mentioned in Chapter 5 represents the view that, although the activities of a firm continue through time so that the decisions taken at one point in time cannot be separated from their effects whenever they materialize, those activities should nevertheless be regularly reported on. In other words, the financial health of a business should be tested at periodic intervals. The concept of periodicity poses problems in adapting the data recorded in the accounts system so that it will correctly reflect the result of the transactions concluded in the selected period, and the financial health of the firm at the end of that period. The two accounting statements employed for this purpose are the profit and loss account for the year, and the balance sheet as at the end of the year.

The purpose of this chapter is to examine the preliminary stages in the preparation of these statements.

## Problems in periodic measurement

The reader will recall that when we discussed the concept of periodicity in Chapter 5, we noted not only that the transactions of a period should be identified, but also that the expenses attributable to those transactions should be matched with the revenues derived from them in accordance with the matching concept.

The first major problem, therefore, in adapting the information recorded in the accounts system has a twofold aspect, i.e. to identify:

1 the revenues attributable to transactions during the year;
2 the expenses related to those revenues.

The second major problem concerns adjustments which must be made in order to arrive at a measure of the surplus or deficit of revenues over expenses. These adjustments involve an element of judgement, for example, how much to provide for depreciation and bad debts, and what adjustments to make in respect of expected losses. Such adjustments are made because the end product is a statement of the profit or loss made in the accounting period. We consider these problems in the next chapter.

## Identifying the revenues and expenses of the period

The data recorded in the accounts system provides the basis for identifying the revenues and expenses of an accounting period. First, we need to extract from the accounts system the data recorded in respect of all the transactions concluded in the period. We saw in Chapter 8 that the summary of all the transactions is obtainable by means of a trial balance drawn up on the last day of the accounting period.

**Example 1**    The following trial balance was extracted from the books of John Smith on 31 December 20X0, being the end of the first year of trading.

|  | £ Dr | £ Cr |
|---|---|---|
| Capital |  | 25,000 |
| Motor vehicles | 10,000 |  |
| Furniture and fittings | 2,500 |  |
| Purchases | 31,000 |  |
| Bank balance | 6,000 |  |
| Sales |  | 70,000 |
| Debtors | 18,000 |  |
| Creditors |  | 3,500 |
| Rent | 4,500 |  |
| Salaries | 22,800 |  |
| Insurances | 400 |  |
| Motor expenses | 2,000 |  |
| Light and heat | 1,000 |  |
| General expenses | 300 |  |
|  | 98,500 | 98,500 |

## The meaning of revenue and expense

The trial balance does not distinguish between flows of profit and flows of capital, neither does it make a distinction between expenditure incurred to earn revenue and expenditure on the acquisition of assets. The first problem is to identify the revenues of the year, and this is a matter of definition. By revenue we mean the flows of funds, that is money or rights to money, which have resulted from the trading activities of the business, as distinct from funds (capital) invested by the owner or loans made by creditors and others. In this case, the only revenue item shown on the trial balance is from sales amounting to £70,000. The second problem is to identify the expenses. We define revenue expenses as the costs of running the business during the accounting period. In contrast, capital expenses are the costs incurred in acquiring fixed assets or adding to the profit-earning structure of the firm. The calculation of periodic profit is by means of a formula which deducts expenses from revenues:

**periodic profit = revenues – expenses**

Looking at the trial balance, the expenses of the year, as defined, are as follows:

|                  | £      |
| ---------------- | ------ |
| Purchases        | 31,000 |
| Rent             | 4,500  |
| Salaries         | 22,800 |
| Insurances       | 400    |
| Motor expenses   | 2,000  |
| Light and heat   | 1,000  |
| General expenses | 300    |

An alternative definition of expenses is that adopted by accountants, who treat as expenses all those costs the benefit of which has been used up during the year. Looking at the expenses which we have identified in the trial balance, it is clear that the benefit derived by the firm from expenditure on these items is limited to the accounting period. The only exception is the goods purchased which have not been sold by the end of the year, and we discuss this problem in Chapter 11.

We have completed, therefore, the first stage in periodic measurement by identifying the revenue and expenses attributable to the 'profit-earning' transactions of the firm during the year, which we may list as follows:

|                  | £      |       | £      |
| ---------------- | ------ | ----- | ------ |
| Purchases        | 31,000 | Sales | 70,000 |
| Rent             | 4,500  |       |        |
| Salaries         | 22,800 |       |        |
| Insurance        | 400    |       |        |
| Motor expenses   | 2,000  |       |        |
| Light and heat   | 1,000  |       |        |
| General expenses | 300    |       |        |

## Periodic measurement and the accruals concept

The next task of the accountant is to ensure that the revenues and expenses are attributable to the accounting period. It is the normal practice to record in the expense accounts only those amounts actually paid during the period. As a result, at the end of the period, these accounts may be understated or overstated. Likewise, it is possible that there may be some outstanding revenue due to the business, other than sales revenue, which must be brought into the year's profit.

The governing principle which affects these adjustments is the accruals concept discussed in Chapter 5. The accruals concept, it will be recalled, makes a distinction between the receipt of cash and the right to receive cash, and the payment of cash and the legal obligation to pay cash. As there is often no coincidence in time between the creation of legal rights and obligations and the transfer of cash, it follows that the accountant must scrutinize the revenue and expenses accounts to make sure that amounts due and payable are accrued. Similarly, payments made in advance must be excluded and carried forward to the next accounting period. The adjustments are effected in the accounts themselves.

An accrued expense is a cost that has expired during the accounting period but has not been recognized in the accounts. Accrued expenses often include salaries, interest, business rent, taxes and other expenses. In the case of an accrued expense, both an expense and a liability exist at the end of the accounting period without having been recorded in the books. The nature of the problem becomes clear when we look at some examples.

## The accrual of income

At the end of an accounting period, the total sales revenue will have been recorded in the accounts system, and the amounts unpaid by customers in respect of these sales will have been included under sundry debtors. The outstanding income which may not already have been recorded is limited, therefore, to income other than sales, such as rent receivable, commissions receivable, etc. The accountant must adjust his end-of-year figures so as to include all the income to which the business is legally entitled, even though it has not been received.

**Example 2**  On 1 December 20X0, John Smith had sublet a portion of his premises which had never been utilized for a monthly rent of £60 payable in advance on the first of each month. By 31 December 20X0, the date on which the trial balance was extracted, the rent receivable had not yet been received. To accrue the rent receivable, the accountant must enter the amount accrued in the rent receivable account as follows:

**Rent receivable account**

|  |  |  |
|---|---|---|
|  | 20X0 | £ |
|  | 31 Dec   Accrued | 60 |

This amount is taken to the profit and loss account as profit for the year 20X0:

**Rent receivable account**

| 20X0 |  | £ | 20X0 |  | £ |
|---|---|---|---|---|---|
| 13 Dec  Profit & loss account |  | 60 | 31 Dec  Accrued c/d |  | 60 |
|  |  | 60 |  |  | 60 |
| 20X1 |  |  |  |  |  |
| 1 Jan  Accrued b/d |  | 60 |  |  |  |

Students are often puzzled that rent receivable should be a credit. The reason is that the rent receivable account is used to denote the source of a flow of funds so that there is a flow out from the rent receivable account into the cash account. Let us assume that on 1 January 20X1, the rent outstanding is paid. The entries would be as follows:

**Rent receivable account**

| 20X1 | | £ | 20X1 | | £ |
|---|---|---|---|---|---|
| 1 Jan | Accrued b/d | 60 | 1 Jan | Cash | 60 |

**Cash book**

| 20X1 | | £ | | |
|---|---|---|---|---|
| 1 Jan | Rent receivable | 60 | | |

In adjusting the receipts for the year so that they will correctly show the income of the year, the accountant accrues income not yet received, as we have seen above, but also carries forward to the following year any receipts of the current year which are the income of the following year.

If, however, there had been an omission of income from the accounts of the preceding year, and this income is received in the current year, it would not be practical to go back and adjust the accounts of the previous year. Those accounts will have been closed at the end of that accounting period. The accountant will include last year's income in the current year's account, and indicate that it was an omission from last year, or explain how this income arose. Adjustments of this nature often arise out of the settlement of legal disputes or compensation claims.

## The accrual of expenses

The accrual of expenses occurs much more frequently than the accrual of income, for it is the nature of things that firms delay the payment of expenses. As a result, nominal accounts such as rent, insurance, wages, light and heat, etc. have to be adjusted to show the total payments due and payable in respect of the accounting year. Occasionally, however, firms are obliged to pay in advance for services, so that there is a possibility that a portion of the payment relates to the next accounting period. Accordingly, the accrual of expenses involves two types of adjustments:

1 an accrual in respect of expenses of the year which have not yet been paid;
2 an exclusion from the recorded expenses of that part which relates to the next year.

*Example 3*  Let us return to the trial balance extracted from John Smith's books. We are informed that:

1 The yearly rent is £6,000 payable quarterly. The rent of £1,500 payable on 1 December had not been paid.
2 Insurance premiums paid amounting to £400 included a payment of £50 in respect of a new policy taken out on 31 December 20X0.

It is clear, therefore, that the legal obligation in respect of the rent is understated in the rent account by £1,500. Equally, the insurance premiums applicable to the year ended 31 December 20X0 amount to £350 and not £400. It is necessary to adjust these accounts as follows:

1  to increase the rent chargeable as an expense by £1,500;
2  to decrease the insurance chargeable as an expense by £50.

## Underpayment of rent

Let us assume that the rent payments were made on due date as follows:

**Rent account**

| 20X0 | | £ |
|---|---|---|
| 1 Feb | Cash | 1,500 |
| 1 May | Cash | 1,500 |
| 1 Aug | Cash | 1,500 |

The amount which should be charged against the income for the year ended 31 December 20X0 is £6,000. The rent unpaid at 31 December 20X0 may be accrued as follows:

**Rent account**

| 20X0 | | £ |
|---|---|---|
| 1 Feb | Cash | 1,500 |
| 1 May | Cash | 1,500 |
| 1 Aug | Cash | 1,500 |
| 31 Dec | Accrued | 1,500 |

Having made this adjustment, the rent account for the year ended 31 December 20X0 may be closed by transferring the rent of £6,000 to the profit and loss account for the year ended 31 December 20X0. The rent unpaid is, of course, a liability of the firm on 31 December 20X0, and is shown by bringing down the amount accrued as a credit balance on the rent account. The adjusted rent account will appear as follows:

**Rent account**

| 20X0 | | £ | 20X0 | | £ |
|---|---|---|---|---|---|
| 1 Feb | Cash | 1,500 | 31 Dec | Profit & loss a/c | 6,000 |
| 1 May | Cash | 1,500 | | | |
| 1 Aug | Cash | 1,500 | | | |
| 31 Dec | Accrued c/d | 1,500 | | | |
| | | 6,000 | | | 6,000 |
| | | | 20X1 | | |
| | | | 1 Jan | Accrued b/d | 1,500 |

We note the rent outstanding at 31 December 20X0 is £1,500, and we have brought this amount down to show:

1  that there is a credit balance outstanding at 31 December 20X0;
2  that on 1 January 20X1 there is an outstanding liability in respect of the previous year, so that the firm will have to pay £7,500 during the year ended 31 December 20X1.

The trial balance on 31 December 20X0 may now be adjusted as follows:

|  | £ | £ |
|---|---|---|
| Rent | 6,000 | |
| Rent accrued | | 1,500 |

If the firm pays the rent outstanding on 2 January 20X1, and thereafter pays the rent on due date, the rent account for the year 20X1 will appear as follows:

**Rent account**

| 20X1 | | £ | 20X1 | | £ |
|---|---|---|---|---|---|
| 2 Jan | Cash | 1,500 | 1 Jan | Accrued b/d | 1,500 |
| 1 Feb | Cash | 1,500 | 31 Dec | Profit & loss a/c | 6,000 |
| 1 May | Cash | 1,500 | | | |
| 1 Aug | Cash | 1,500 | | | |
| 1 Dec | Cash | 1,500 | | | |
| | | 7,500 | | | 7,500 |

## Prepayment of insurance

For certain services, payments are made before the associated benefits are received, i.e. the payment is made in advance. In these cases an arithmetic apportionment of the amount paid must be made between the two consecutive accounting periods.

Let us assume that the insurance premiums were paid in advance as follows:

| 1 January 20X0 | £350 |
|---|---|
| 31 December 20X0 | 50 |
| | £400 |

These transactions will be shown in the insurance account as follows:

**Insurance account**

| 20X0 | | £ | |
|---|---|---|---|
| 1 Jan | Cash | 350 | |
| 31 Dec | Cash | 50 | |

The premium paid on 31 December 20X0 is the prepayment of an expense for the year ending 31 December 20X1. Hence, it cannot be shown as an expense for the year ended 31 December 20X0. Thus the purpose of the adjustment is:

1 to measure the expense applicable to the year ended 31 December 20X0, and to transfer this amount to the profit and loss account for that year;
2 to carry forward the premium paid in advance to the following year.

The adjusted account will appear as follows:

**Insurance account**

| 20X0 | | £ | 20X0 | | £ |
|---|---|---|---|---|---|
| 1 Jan | Cash | 350 | 31 Dec | Profit & loss a/c | 350 |
| 31 Dec | Cash | 50 | 31 Dec | Prepaid c/d | 50 |
| | | 400 | | | 400 |
| 20X1 | | | | | |
| 1 Jan | Prepaid b/d | 50 | | | |

We may note that the insurance prepaid at 31 December 20X0 is brought down as a debit balance on 1 January 20X1, and as a result:

1  there is a debit balance in favour of the firm on 31 December 20X0;
2  the firm will not have to pay the premium of £50 in the subsequent year, if the yearly premium is only due and payable on 1 January each year.

The trial balance on 31 December 20X0 may now be adjusted to read as follows:

| | £ | £ |
|---|---|---|
| Insurance | 350 | |
| Insurance prepaid | 50 | |

Assuming that the firm pays the insurance premium in the following year on the due date, the insurance account for that year will be as follows:

**Insurance account**

| 20X1 | | £ | 20X1 | | £ |
|---|---|---|---|---|---|
| 1 Jan | Prepaid b/d | 50 | 31 Dec | Profit & loss a/c | 400 |
| 1 Jan | Cash | 350 | | | |
| | | 400 | | | 400 |

The reader will observe how easily the accounts system permits the adjustments made in respect of the accruals of revenue and expenses to be reconciled with the subsequent receipts and payment of cash. Although we have interfered with the recording process in order to adjust the accounts so as to reflect the true picture at the end of the accounting period, the double-entry system continues to record the accounting flows and is not itself affected by the adjustments which have been made.

# The results of the accrual adjustments

The reader will recall that the trial balance is merely a working paper which the accountant uses to extract the information which he requires from the accounts system, and to check its accuracy. We may alter the original details shown on the first trial balance to reflect the adjustments which we have so far made.

**Example 4** The adjusted trial balance for John Smith's business as at 31 December 20X0 may be set out as follows:

|  | £ Dr | £ Cr |
|---|---|---|
| Capital |  | 25,000 |
| Motor vehicles | 10,000 |  |
| Furniture and fittings | 2,500 |  |
| Purchases | 31,000 |  |
| Bank balance | 6,000 |  |
| Sales |  | 70,000 |
| Debtors | 18,060 |  |
| Creditors |  | 3,500 |
| Rent | 6,000 |  |
| Rent accrued |  | 1,500 |
| Insurance | 350 |  |
| Insurance prepaid | 50 |  |
| Salaries | 22,800 |  |
| Motor expenses | 2,000 |  |
| Light and heat | 1,000 |  |
| General expenses | 300 |  |
| Rent receivable |  | 60 |
|  | 100,060 | 100,060 |

The effect of these adjustments on the revenues and expenses for the year ended 31 December 20X0 may be summarized as follows:

|  | £ |  | £ |
|---|---|---|---|
| Purchases | 31,000 | Sales | 70,000 |
| Rent | 6,000 | Rent receivable | 60 |
| Salaries | 22,800 |  |  |
| Insurance | 350 |  |  |
| Motor expenses | 2,000 |  |  |
| Light and heat | 1,000 |  |  |
| General expenses | 300 |  |  |

It will be noted also that the adjustments have given rise to the following balances on the accounts:

|  | £ Dr | £ Cr |
|---|---|---|
| Rent accrued |  | 1,500 |
| Insurance prepaid | 50 |  |
| Rent receivable | 60 |  |

As these balances represent sums owing by the business and debts due to the business, they will be shown, as we shall see in Chapter 11, as liabilities and assets respectively at the end of the accounting period.

## The matching of revenues and expenses

The purpose underlying the accountant's efforts to identify and correctly measure the revenues and expenses of an accounting period is to attempt to match them so as to obtain a measure of the 'financial effort' of earning the revenues of that period. The matching of expenses and revenues is far more complicated than appears at first sight. So far, we have assumed that by correctly measuring the revenues and expenses attributable to the accounting year they have been correctly matched. In other words, we have made the assumption that the expenses of the accounting period are the expenses related to the revenues of that period. The realization concept permits the accountant to recognize only financial results in the form of sales revenues. It is well known, of course, that there is a time-lag between buying or manufacturing goods for sale and selling them. At the end of an accounting period, therefore, there will always be goods awaiting sale and raw materials unused. The expenses attributable to unsold goods and unused materials, usually described as stocks, must be excluded from the expenses of the period and carried forward to the next accounting period, when the goods will have been sold and the materials used. The importance of stock adjustments to the correct measurement of periodic profit is crucial.

**Example 5**    Mr Hancock's trial balance at 31 December 20X0 included the following debits:

|                    | £     |
|--------------------|-------|
| Rent               | 1,800 |
| Business rates     | 760   |
| Light and heating  | 1,180 |
| Insurance          | 520   |

Rent of £600 for the last three months of 20X0 had not been paid and no entry had been made in the books. Of the rates, £560 was for the year ended 31 March 20X1. The remaining £200 was for the three months ended 31 March 20X0. In accordance with the matching concept the rates included in the profit and loss account would be £200 + (£560 × $\frac{3}{4}$) = £620.

Fuel had been delivered on 10 December 20X0 at a cost of £30 and had been consumed before the end of 20X0. The invoice had been received for this fuel in 20X0; however, no entry had been made in the records of the business. £70 of the insurance paid was in respect of insurance cover for the year 20X1.

The above information would be recorded in the following accounts which show transfers to the profit and loss account for the year ended 31 December 20X0.

**Rent account**

|  | £ |  | £ |
|---|---|---|---|
| 31 Dec  Balance b/d | 1,800 | 31 Dec  Profit & loss account | 2,400 |
| 31 Dec  Balance c/d | 600 |  |  |
|  | 2,400 |  | 2,400 |
|  |  | 1 Jan      Balance b/d | 600 |

**Rates account**

|  | £ |  | £ |
|---|---|---|---|
| 31 Dec  Balance b/d | 760 | 31 Dec  Profit & loss account | 620 |
|  |  | 31 Dec  Balance c/d | 140 |
|  | 760 |  | 760 |
| 1 Jan      Balance b/d | 140 |  |  |

**Light and heating account**

|  | £ |  | £ |
|---|---|---|---|
| 31 Dec  Balance b/d | 1,180 | 31 Dec  Profit & loss account | 1,210 |
| 31 Dec  Balance b/d | 30 |  |  |
|  | 1,210 |  | 1,210 |
|  |  | Balance b/d | 30 |

**Insurance account**

|  | £ |  | £ |
|---|---|---|---|
| 31 Dec  Balance b/d | 520 | 31 Dec  Profit & loss account | 450 |
|  |  | 31 Dec  Balance c/d | 70 |
|  | 520 |  | 520 |
| 1 Jan      Balance b/d | 70 |  |  |

## Stock adjustments

By definition, the closing stock at the end of an accounting period is the residue of the purchases of that period which remains unsold or unused.

*Example 6*

John Smith's purchases account includes all goods purchased during the year ended 31 December 20X0. At the end of the year, the stock of materials unused is quantified, and its cost price is valued at £3,000. The accounting problems relating to this stock are as follows:

1  Since the business has to pay for all goods purchased, it would be imprudent to reduce the purchases account by the amount of stock at the end of the year. Hence, the purchases account must not be adjusted and the total purchases must be charged as expenses.
2  By charging all purchases against sales, however, the profit for the year would be understated by £3,000. Means must be found, therefore, to take the closing stock out of the profit calculation. This is effected by opening a stock account on 31 December 20X0 and posting the stock to it.

**Stock account**

| 20X0 | £ | |
|---|---|---|
| 31 Dec | 3,000 | |

As soon as an account is opened for the purpose of recording a flow of value it is necessary to describe the source of the flow and its destination. We know that the purchases account is not the source of the flow of stocks to the stock account, because we have deliberately refused to adjust the purchases account. We need to value stocks in order to calculate the profit or loss for the period. The accountant states that the stock adjustment comes from the profit and loss account which is employed to measure profit. The full accounting entries are, therefore, as follows:

**Profit and loss account for the year ended 31 December 20X0**

| | | 20X0 | £ |
|---|---|---|---|
| | | 31 Dec   Stock | 3,000 |

**Stock account**

| 20X0 | £ | |
|---|---|---|
| 31 Dec   Profit & loss a/c | 3,000 | |

The effect of these entries is to solve the problem of profit measurement, because the *credit* flow from the profit and loss account is taken into the calculation of profit, as follows:

| | £ | | £ |
|---|---|---|---|
| Purchases | 31,000 | Sales | 70,000 |
| | | Closing stocks | 3,000 |

The stock account is an interesting account because it exists to measure profit and since that is done on the last day of the accounting year, the stock account only exists for one day. In fact, the closing stock on the last day of the year is the opening stock on the first day of the next accounting year. Hence, on the first day of the next accounting period, the stock must be posted to the profit and loss account of the next period, as follows:

**Profit and loss account for the year ended 31 December 20X1**

| 20X1 | £ | |
|---|---|---|
| 1 Jan  Stock | 3,000 | |

**Stock account**

| 20X0 | £ | 20X1 | £ |
|---|---|---|---|
| 31 Dec  Profit & loss a/c | 3,000 | 1 Jan  Profit & loss a/c | 3,000 |

The reader will now observe that the stock account has served its purpose and may be closed. This is done by drawing a double line beneath the entries.

**Stock account**

| 20X0 | £ | 20X1 | £ |
|------|---|------|---|
| 31 Dec  Profit & loss a/c | 3,000 | 1 Jan  Profit & loss a/c | 3,000 |

In practice, the accountant will not reverse the stock into the profit and loss account of the year 20X1 until 31 December 20X1 when s/he prepares that account. As a result, the trial balance for the year ended 31 December 20X1 will include a debit balance in respect of the stock account in the amount of £3,000. As the trial balance is always extracted before the stock adjustment is made, the opening stock always appears on the trial balance but the closing stock is never shown.

## Summary

In this section of Part 2, we consider the procedural problems involved in periodic measurement. This chapter deals with the problems of adapting the financial accounting data lodged in the data-processing system to the objective of measuring periodic profit.

The first stages in the measurement of periodic profit are:

1 the identification of the revenues attributable to transactions concluded in the accounting period;
2 the identification of the expenses related to those revenues.

The accruals concept requires the inclusion of amounts receivable and payable, as well as amounts received and paid, in the measurement of revenues and expenses. We examined the accounting procedures involved in accruing revenue and expenses.

The objective of periodic measurement is the matching of revenues and expenses to establish accounting profit. The exclusion of stocks unsold at the end of the accounting period is a further problem in periodic measurement considered in this chapter.

## Self-assessment question

1 State the concepts which apply to the manner in which periodic revenues and expenses are identified and related. Illustrate your answer.

## Problems  (* indicates that a solution is to be found in the Lecturer's Guide)

1 If goods which cost £10,000 were in stock on 1 January, goods purchased during the year amounted to £40,000 and goods costing £15,000 were in stock at 31 December, state the cost of the goods which were sold during the year.

2 From the following information construct the combined Rent and Rates Account for the year ended 30 June 20X1 showing the figures that would appear for rent and rates in the profit and loss account and the figures that would appear in the balance sheet as at 30 June 20X1.

The property of the business was rented at £1,600 per annum payable quarterly in arrears on the usual quarter days. The rates were £600 per annum payable half yearly in advance on

1 October and 1 April in each year. The rent was one quarter in arrears on 30 June 20X0 and the rates for the half year to 30 September 20X0 had not been paid.

The following transactions took place during the year to 30 June 20X1:

20X0
July 2    Cash – One quarter's rent to 24 June 20X0
July 2    Cash – Half year's rates to 30 September 20X0
Oct 10   Cash – Half year's rates to 31 March 20X1
Oct 10   Cash – One quarter's rent to 29 September 20X0

20X1
Jan 4    Cash – One quarter's rent to 25 December 20X0
April 6   Cash – Half year's rates to 30 September 20X1
April 6   Cash – One quarter's rent to 25 March 20X1

3*    Star Enterprises Ltd is a company formed to manage the affairs of a successful pop group. All the group's revenue and expenses are recorded in the company's books. The group's recording contract with IME Records stipulates a payment of advance royalties of £50,000 on the recording of a record. Actual royalties are 50p per record. Any sales in excess of 100,000 copies will result in additional royalties being paid. If sales are less than 100,000, then any excess advance is recouped from future payments.

During the year ended 31 March 20X1 the company received the following royalties:

|  | £ | £ |
|---|---|---|
| Advance Record 1 |  | 50,000 |
| Advance Record 2 | 50,000 |  |
| *Less*: Shortfall on Record 1 | 17,000 | 33,000 |
| Additional royalties Record 2 |  | 44,000 |
| Advance Record 3 |  | 50,000 |

Record 3 was recorded and released shortly before the year end. No sales figures are yet available.

The company has also incurred advance expenditure of £35,000 on promoting a tour the group will undertake during April 20X1.

*Required:*
(a)  State the accounting principles which are used in revenue and expense recognition.
(b)  Write a report to the management of the company advising on the treatment of royalties and advance expenditure, and showing how these items will be treated in the accounts to 31 March 20X1.

(Problem supplied by A J Naughton)

4    Norman is preparing a profit and loss account for the year ended 31 December 20X0.
The following payments and income appear as balances on their individual ledger accounts:

|  | £ |  |
|---|---|---|
| Rent | 300 | Rent is payable £100 per quarter in arrears. |
| Telephone | 60 | The last quarter's bill is outstanding. |
| Rates | 400 | Rates of £200 were paid for a half-year from 1 October 20X0. |
| Insurance | 100 | Premium paid for year from 31 March 20X0. |
| Electricity | 80 | Last bill paid on 31 October 20X0. |
| Rent receivable | 500 | Rent receivable £100 per quarter in advance. |
| Commission receivable | 300 | Commission of £200 due from September to 31 December 20X0 not yet received. |

113

*Required:*
Prepare ledger accounts and balance off all relevant debtors and creditors. Assume no opening debtors and creditors; all adjustments to be calculated on a time basis. The rateable year runs from 6 April to 5 April (i.e. for accounts purposes April to March).

5* Alistair rents three shops and maintains one account for rent and rates for all three premises. The rents are fixed for each year and increases take effect as from 1 January.

At 1 January 20X0, he had paid all of the rent up to date, but there was a prepayment in relation to rates of £1,100.

During the year ended 31 December 20X0 he made the following payments:

| Date | Shop | £ | |
|------|------|------|---|
| 10 January | A | 540 | Rent for January 20X0–June 20X0 |
| 10 April | A | 800 | Rates for April 20X0–March 20X1 |
| 3 July | A | 540 | Rent for July 20X0–December 20X0 |
| 29 December | A | 600 | Rent for January 20X1–June 20X1 |
| | | | |
| 3 February | B | 1,200 | Rent for January 20X0–December 20X0 |
| 28 March | B | 1,060 | Rates for April 20X0–March 20X1 |
| | | | |
| 6 January | C | 350 | Rent for January 20X0–March 20X0 |
| 24 March | C | 1,600 | Rates for April 20X0–March 20X1 |
| 15 May | C | 350 | Rent for April 20X0–June 20X0 |
| 10 September | C | 350 | Rent for July 20X0–September 20X0 |

*Required:*
Write up the rent and rates account for 20X0 showing the total profit and loss account charge.

# 10 Losses in asset values and periodic measurement

## Setting the scene

High-tech hearing aid supplier Hidden Hearing has suffered a sharp setback, with news that an accounting 'error' will drag its interim results into the red. Directors expect to report a loss up to £100,000 for the half year, after providing for auditor's costs and also a £200,000 termination payment for its finance director. The accounting 'error', which was the use of a lower depreciation rate than required on computer equipment, also saw the restatement of 1999 annual pre-tax profit from £2.03m to £1.43m.

The company sells advanced and unobtrusive hearing aids which are designed and fitted for customers at between £700 and £2,400 a pair.

(*The Daily Telegraph*, 27 December 1999)

## Learning objectives

**After studying this chapter you should be able to:**

1 **Explain the nature of depreciation.**

2 **Calculate depreciation and incorporate the figures in the accounting records.**

3 **Account for the disposal of fixed assets.**

4 **Make adjustments for bad and doubtful debts.**

In the previous chapter, we discussed the various adjustments to the data in the double-entry bookkeeping system, so that this data might correctly reflect the income and expenses appropriate to the activities conducted during the accounting period in question. The accrual of revenues and expenses involved, as we saw, the exclusion of payments and receipts for other periods.

In this chapter, we discuss adjustments which are made in respect of losses in asset values. The first which we will examine concerns the depreciation of fixed assets. The second is the loss in the value of debtors caused by the recognition that a portion of the debtor balances will not be paid and must be recognized as bad debts, and that a further portion may ultimately prove to be bad so that a provision for doubtful debts must also be made.

## The treatment of losses in asset values

The concept of prudence requires that losses should be recognized as soon as they become evident, so as to ensure that profit and capital values are not overstated in financial reports. Losses in asset values appear under a variety of guises. Losses of cash and stock by theft, embezzlement or accidental damage are written off immediately against income, insurance recoveries being treated as a separate matter. Losses to fixed assets due to accidental damage, theft or other causes are also written off against income, as are losses arising on the sale of fixed assets which result from a difference between the sale price and the book value of the assets sold. (The book value means the value according to the accounting records.) Most fixed assets also diminish in value as their usefulness is exhausted over a period of years. Finally, losses in asset values also result from the exercise of judgement, as in the case of bad debts when accountants have to decide whether a recorded value does exist at all.

## Losses in the value of fixed assets

Losses in the value of fixed assets arising through sale, accidental loss or theft present no difficulties from an accounting viewpoint, for such losses are written off immediately against income. By contrast, the diminution in value described as depreciation has been the subject of much controversy. Depreciation is of a complex nature and now occupies an important role in three different areas of the subject. First, it is related to the problem of cost allocation, both as regards the matching of revenues and expenses in the process of profit measurement, and as regards product costing in management accounting. Second, it is related to the concept of capital maintenance in income theory. Third, it is central to decision making as regards the life and the replacement of fixed assets. The notion of depreciation has varied and multiplied in such a way that its analysis is not an easy matter. In this chapter, we take a limited view of depreciation, and concern ourselves solely with its financial accounting implications.

## The nature of depreciation

The term 'depreciation' is susceptible to four different meanings:

1 a fall in price;
2 physical deterioration;
3 a fall in value;
4 an allocation of fixed-asset costs.

### Depreciation as a fall in price

A fall in the price of an asset is one aspect of depreciation, but it is not a reliable guide to a valid accounting concept of depreciation. A fall in price may occur independently of any decrease in the usefulness of an asset, for example the immediate fall in price occurring on the purchase of a new asset.

## Depreciation as physical deterioration

Depreciation in this sense means impaired utility arising directly through deterioration or indirectly through obsolescence. It is implied in much of the discussion of this concept of depreciation that an asset is 'used up', so that the 'use' of an asset is the extent to which it has been used up. It is evident that these ideas are represented in the rates of depreciation which are attached to depreciable assets. It should be noted, however, that an asset is not necessarily 'used up' through use, because adequate maintenance may prevent deterioration in some cases. Thus, for example, if irrigation ditches are well maintained, they will not deteriorate through use.

The concept of depreciation as deferred maintenance has not been properly investigated, although it is a concept of depreciation which may be more relevant than conventional concepts as regards certain types of assets.

## Depreciation as a fall in value

There are problems associated with the use of the term 'value' and the relationship of depreciation to the concept of value. Value may mean 'cost value', 'exchange value', 'use value' (utility) or 'esteem value'. Clearly, 'cost value' is not affected by events occurring after acquisition, so that it is not meaningful to relate depreciation in this sense to a fall in cost value. 'Exchange value' changes only twice in the experience of the owner of an asset – at the point of purchase and at the point of sale. In this sense, depreciation may mean only a fall in price between two points, and we have already discussed this concept of depreciation. Depreciation as a decrease in utility is also already covered by the concept of physical deterioration, while the notion of the esteem value of an asset is entirely subjective and not amenable to an objective concept of measurement.

If one attempts to relate the notion of depreciation to economic income, however, one would have the basis of an accounting concept of particular usefulness for decision making. The economic value of an asset is regarded as the discounted value of expected future cash flows associated with that asset in a particular use. Hence, depreciation may be conceptualized and measured as the progressive decrease in the net cash flows yielded by the asset as its economic utility declines through time, for whatever reason. Normally, of course, its income-earning capacity falls due to increasing inefficiency arising from physical deterioration. As regards certain classes of assets, for example computers, falls in economic value have occurred more rapidly from obsolescence.

## Depreciation as cost allocation

The orthodox view of accountants is that depreciation represents that part of the cost of a fixed asset which is not recoverable when the asset is finally put out of use. Provision for this loss of capital is an integral cost of conducting the business during the effective commercial life of the asset and is not dependent upon the amount of profit earned.

The practice of treating depreciation as an allocation of historical cost is based on two assumptions:

1 that the expected benefit to be derived from an asset is proportional to an estimated usage rate;
2 that it is possible to measure that benefit.

Hence, the current practice is part of the procedure of matching periodic revenues with the cost of earning those revenues. The essential difference between fixed assets and current operating expenses is that the former are regarded as costs which yield benefits over a period of years, and hence must be allocated as expenses against the revenues of those years, whereas the latter yield all their benefits in the current year, so that they may be treated as the expenses of that year and matched against the revenues which they have created.

The practice of treating depreciation as an allocation of costs presents a number of serious theoretical problems. The known objective facts about an asset are few, and adequate records are not usually kept of the various incidents in the life in use of an asset apart from its purchase price. Repair and maintenance costs, for example, are charged separately, as are running costs. Other unresolved problems concern the selection of appropriate bases for allocating the cost of depreciable assets, for example should depreciation be calculated by reference to units of actual use rather than time use? Finally, should the residual value of an asset be regarded as a windfall gain or should it be set off against the replacement cost of the asset rather than used as a point of reference for calculating the proportion of the cost of fixed assets which should be allocated as depreciation?

## The accounting concept of depreciation

According to the AICPA, depreciation accounting is 'a system of accounting which aims to distribute the cost . . . of tangible capital assets, less salvage (if any), over the estimated useful life of the unit . . . in a systematic and rational manner. It is a process of allocation, not of valuation' (AICPA, 1953).

From the foregoing definition, two important points may be made:

1 Depreciation accounting is not concerned with any attempt to measure the value of an asset at any point of time. One is trying to measure the value of the benefit the asset has provided during a given accounting period, and that benefit is valued as a portion of the cost of the asset. Hence, the balance sheet value of depreciable assets is that portion of the original cost which has not yet been allocated as a periodic expense in the process of profit measurement. It does not purport to represent the current value of those assets.
2 Depreciation accounting does not itself provide funds for the replacement of depreciable assets, but the charging of depreciation ensures the maintenance intact of the original money capital of the entity. Indeed, a provision for depreciation is not identified with cash or any specific asset or assets.

### Factors in the measurement of depreciation

Four factors are important in the process of measuring depreciation from an accounting viewpoint, as follows:

1 identifying the cost of the asset;
2 ascertaining its useful life;

3 determining the expected residual value;
4 selecting an appropriate method of depreciation which must be systematic and rational.

## Identifying the cost of the asset

Depreciation is calculated on historical cost values, which include acquisition costs and all incidental costs involved in bringing an asset into use. In the case of buildings, for example, cost includes any commissions, survey, legal and other charges involved in the purchase, together with the costs incurred in preparing and modifying buildings for a particular use. In the case of plant and machinery, all freight, insurance and installation costs should be capitalized.

Problems occur where a firm manufactures assets, for example, if an engineering firm constructs a foundry. In such cases, the cost of labour, materials, etc. associated with the activity of construction should be segregated from those associated with the normal trading activities, and capitalized. There are costing problems involved in ascertaining such costs. Moreover, improvements effected to existing assets should be capitalized. The distinction between a repair and an improvement is not always easy to establish. In some circumstances, the intention may be to repair but the cheaper solution is a replacement. An old boiler, for example, may be replaced more cheaply than repaired. The cost of repairs is chargeable as a current expense: the cost of replacement should be capitalized.

## Ascertaining the useful life of an asset

The useful life of an asset is defined as that period during which it is expected to be useful in the profit-earning operations of the firm. In most cases, the useful life is determined by two factors:

1 the rate of deterioration;
2 obsolescence.

The rate of deterioration is a function of the type of use to which the asset is put, and the extent of that use. A lorry used by civil engineering contractors may have a shorter life expectancy than a lorry employed by cartage contractors, for the former may operate in rough terrain, whereas the latter is used on roads. It is not unusual to find that the estimated useful life of a lorry in the first case may be two years or less, whereas the estimated life in the second may well be four years. Moreover, an asset used intensively will have a shorter life than one used for shorter periods. In this respect, assets are built to certain specifications which determine to some extent their durability in use. The useful life is determined on the basis of past experience, which is a good indicator of the probable life of a particular asset.

It should be pointed out, however, that the estimated useful life of an asset is also a question of policy and may be determined accordingly. Thus, a car-hire firm may decide to renew its fleet each year, and in this case the useful life of its fleet of cars is one year for the purpose of calculating depreciation.

The problem of taking obsolescence into account in assessing the useful life of an asset is altogether more complex, for obsolescence occurs with the appearance of an asset incorporating the result of technological developments. In respect of certain assets, such as cars, each year may see the introduction of an improved model, so

119

that owners of fleets of cars may decide that obsolescence, or assumed obsolescence, is a more important factor in the useful life of cars than depreciation. Relying on new models or improved versions each year, a firm may decide to renew its fleet each year. However, it is hard to distinguish the extent to which such decisions are influenced by the need to have the latest product or to avoid excessive repair bills stemming from large mileages. It would seem, therefore, that obsolescence is one factor which affects the useful life of fixed assets and accelerates their progress towards the scrapheap. Accordingly, the estimated useful life of an asset is determined by that length of time for which, as a matter of policy, it is wished to employ an asset. That length of time will be a function of a number of factors, but the most important will be the increasing cost of employing that asset due to higher yearly maintenance cost and possible declining revenues.

From a theoretical point of view, there is a point at which the net cash inflows associated with an asset are equal to the costs of operating that asset. Those costs may be expressed as the opportunity costs represented by revenues forgone as a result of using that asset rather than replacing it, or the opportunity costs represented by alternative returns which may be derived from cash outlays committed to repairs and maintenance. These two measures of opportunity cost are not necessarily equivalent. In terms of this analysis, the length of useful life of an asset would be determined as in Figure 2.8.

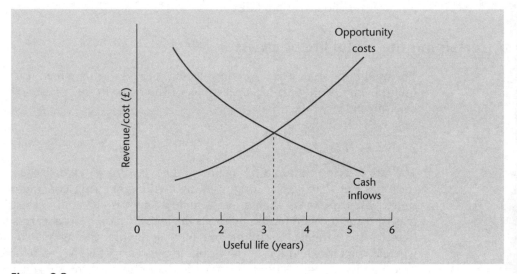

**Figure 2.8**

## Determining the expected residual value

The residual value of an asset is estimated at the time of acquisition so that the net cost may be allocated to the accounting periods during which the asset is usefully employed. The residual value is the expected realizable value of the asset at the end of its useful life. Hence, the residual value will depend on the manner and on the length of time that the asset is to be used. Where, for example, it is intended to use an asset until it is completely worn out or obsolete, its residual value will be negligible. Where, as in the case of the replacement of fleets of cars, the length of useful life is shortened to one year, the residual value will be higher.

Where it is intended to extract the maximum use from an asset, the residual value should be nominal: where it is intended to replace the asset when it still has some useful life, its residual value should be estimated on a conservative basis so as to minimize the effect of variations in the price of second-hand assets. The cost allocated against the revenues of the accounting periods involved are calculated as follows:

| | |
|---|---|
| Cost of acquisition (say) | £2,000 |
| Residual value (say) | 200 |
| Cost to be allocated as depreciation | 1,800 |

## Selecting the method of depreciation

There are several methods of depreciation but the most common are the straight-line method and the decreasing-balance method.

The matching convention requires that 'the choice of the method of allocating the cost of a long-term asset over its effective working life should depend upon the pattern of expected benefits obtainable in each period from its use' (Barton, 1984).

### The straight-line method

The formula for calculating the annual depreciation provision under the straight-line method is as follows:

$$\text{annual depreciation provision} = \frac{\text{acquisition cost} - \text{estimated residual value}}{\text{expected useful life in years}}$$

**Example 1**  A lorry is acquired at a cost of £3,000. Its estimated useful life is three years, and its residual value is estimated at £600.

$$\text{annual depreciation provision} = \frac{£3,000 - £600}{3 \text{ years}}$$

$$= £800 \text{ per annum}$$

The straight-line method allocates the net cost equally to each year of the useful life of an asset. It is particularly applicable to assets such as patents and leases where time is the key factor in the effluxion of the benefits to be derived from the use of an asset. Although it is in general use for other fixed assets, it suffers from the following disadvantages:

1  it does not reflect the fact that the greatest loss in the market value occurs in the first year of use;
2  it does not reflect the unevenness of the loss in the market value over several years;
3  it does not reflect the diminishing losses in value which occur in later years, as the asset approaches the end of its useful life.

For these reasons, the straight-line method of depreciation does not provide an accurate measure of the cost of the service potential allocated to the respective accounting periods during which an asset is employed.

## The decreasing-balance method

To calculate the annual depreciation provision under this method, a fixed percentage is applied to the balance of the net costs not yet allocated as an expense at the end of the previous accounting period. The balance of unallocated costs decreases each year, and, theoretically, the balance of the unallocated costs at the end of the estimated useful life should equal the estimated residual value. The formula used to calculate the fixed percentage to be applied to the allocation of net costs as depreciation is:

$$r = 1 - n\sqrt{\frac{s}{c}}$$

where   $n =$   the expected useful life in years
$s =$   the residual value (this value must be significant or the depreciation rate will be nearly one)
$c =$   the acquisition cost
$r =$   the rate of depreciation to be applied.

**Example 2**   Calculate the rate of depreciation to be applied to a lorry acquired at a cost of £3,000, having an expected useful life of three years and an estimated residual value of £600.

$$r = 1 - 3\sqrt{\frac{£600}{£3,000}}$$

$$= 0.4152 \text{ or } 41.52\%$$

The depreciation calculation for each of the three years would be as follows:

|  |  | £ |
|---|---|---|
|  | Cost | 3,000 |
| Year 1 | Depreciation at 41.52% of £3,000 | 1,246 |
|  | Unallocated costs end of year 1 | 1,754 |
| Year 2 | Depreciation at 41.52% of £1,754 | 728 |
|  | Unallocated costs end of year 2 | 1,026 |
| Year 3 | Depreciation at 41.52% of £1,026 | 426 |
|  | Residual value at end of year 3 | 600 |

In practice, the annual percentage rate of depreciation is not calculated so precisely. A rate is selected which approximates to the estimated useful life, for example an estimated useful life of three years would imply a $33\frac{1}{3}$ per cent rate of depreciation. The advantage of the decreasing-balance method is that it approximates reality in respect of certain assets, for example motor vehicles, where the depreciation calculated in the first year is greatest, thereby reflecting the greater loss in market value at this stage of a vehicle's life.

## Depreciation and total asset costs

The total costs associated with the benefits derived from fixed assets consist of depreciation and the costs of repairs and maintenance. It follows, therefore, that the proper application of the matching convention to the allocation of total asset costs requires that depreciation and repairs and maintenance be considered jointly as regards the selection of an appropriate method for allocating total asset costs to the accounting periods benefiting from their use. The depreciation calculated under the two methods which have been examined may be compared in Figures 2.9 and 2.10.

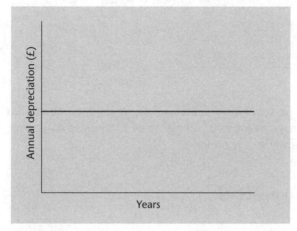

**Figure 2.9**

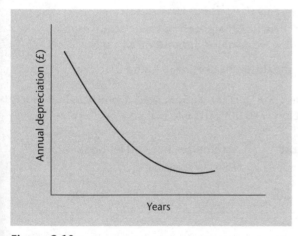

**Figure 2.10**

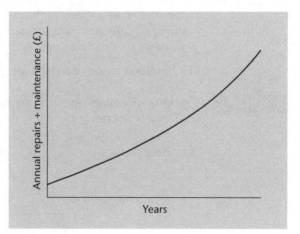

**Figure 2.11**

The cost of repairs and maintenance may be assumed to increase through time, as the asset deteriorates through use. This is reflected in real life by the expectancy that the first year in use should be relatively trouble free. The pattern of repair and maintenance cost is illustrated in Figure 2.11. The total annual assets costs under the straight-line and decreasing-balance methods of depreciation may be compared as in Figures 2.12 and 2.13.

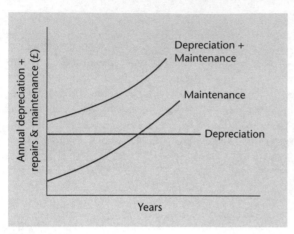

**Figure 2.12**

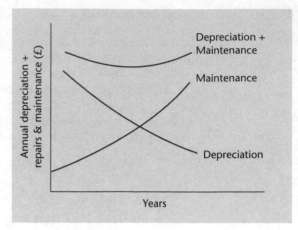

**Figure 2.13**

From the foregoing illustrations, it may be seen that the decreasing-balance method provides a better allocation of total asset costs over the useful life of an asset than the straight-line method.

## Accounting for depreciation

There are several methods for providing for depreciation. Legislation requires that the following information in respect of fixed assets be shown on the balance sheet:

1 the cost or valuation, as the case may be;
2 the aggregate amount provided or written off since the date of acquisition or valuation, as the case may be, for depreciation or diminution in value.

The net book value of fixed assets is the difference between 1 and 2 above.

*Example 3* | The historical cost of plant and machinery is £100,000. Accumulated depreciation to date is £60,000 and the net book value is, therefore, £40,000. This information is disclosed as follows:

| Fixed assets | Cost | Accumulated depreciation | Net book value |
|---|---|---|---|
| | £ | £ | £ |
| Plant and machinery | 100,000 | 60,000 | 40,000 |

The accounting procedure required to generate this information is to debit the acquisition cost, or valuation as the case may be, in the asset account, and to accumulate depreciation yearly in a provision for depreciation account. The annual provision for depreciation is charged to the profit and loss account.

**Example 4**

Assume that the plant and machinery shown in the previous example was acquired on 1 January 20X0 for £100,000, that its estimated useful life is five years, the expected residual value is nil, and that depreciation is calculated on a straight-line basis at the rate of £20,000 a year. The appropriate accounts would record the following data by the end of the year 20X2.

**Plant and machinery account**

| 20X0 | £ | 20X0 | £ |
|---|---|---|---|
| 1 Jan  Cash | 100,000 | 31 Dec  Balance c/d | 100,000 |
| | 100,000 | | 100,000 |
| 20X1 | | 20X1 | |
| 1 Jan  Balance b/d | 100,000 | 31 Dec  Balance c/d | 100,000 |
| 20X2 | | 20X2 | |
| 1 Jan  Balance b/d | 100,000 | 31 Dec  Balance c/d | 100,000 |
| 20X3 | | | |
| 1 Jan  Balance b/d | 100,000 | | |

**Provision for depreciation account**

| 20X0 | £ | 20X0 | £ |
|---|---|---|---|
| 31 Dec  Balance c/d | 20,000 | 31 Dec  Profit & loss a/c | 20,000 |
| | 20,000 | | 20,000 |
| 20X1 | | 20X1 | |
| | | 1 Jan    Balance b/d | 20,000 |
| 31 Dec  Balance c/d | 40,000 | 31 Dec  Profit & loss a/c | 20,000 |
| | 40,000 | | 40,000 |
| 20X2 | | 20X2 | |
| | | 1 Jan    Balance b/d | 40,000 |
| 31 Dec  Balance c/d | 60,000 | 31 Dec  Profit & loss a/c | 20,000 |
| | 60,000 | | 60,000 |
| | | 20X3 | |
| | | 1 Jan    Balance b/d | 60,000 |

**Profit and loss account for the year ended 31 December 20X0**

| | £ | |
|---|---|---|
| Provision for depreciation | 20,000 | |

**Profit and loss account for the year ended 31 December 20X1**

| | £ | |
|---|---|---|
| Provision for depreciation | 20,000 | |

**Profit and loss account for the year ended 31 December 20X2**

|  | £ |
|---|---|
| Provision for depreciation | 20,000 |

# Accounting for the disposal of assets

The cost of the benefits derived from the use of assets cannot be ascertained until the assets have completed their useful life and have been sold or otherwise disposed of. In the meantime, the annual provision for depreciation is merely an estimate of that actual cost. The practice is to make an adjustment to the profit for the year of sale in respect of any difference between the book value and the realized value of the asset. It is not the practice, therefore, to attempt to reopen previous years to make a correction for the actual depreciation suffered.

The method is to open an asset realization account, often called a 'disposal account', and to reverse the existing entries in the asset realization account and the provision for depreciation account in respect of the asset sold or disposed of, recording directly in the asset realization account the sale price, if any, obtained.

*Example 5*    On 31 December 20X0, plant and machinery acquired at a cost of £100,000 three years ago was sold for £30,000. The accumulated depreciation to date was £60,000. The accounting procedure for dealing with this event is as follows:

**Plant and machinery account**

| 20X0 | | £ | 20X0 | | £ |
|---|---|---|---|---|---|
| 1 Jan | Balance b/d | 100,000 | 31 Dec | Asset realization | 100,000 |
| | | 100,000 | | | 100,000 |

**Provision for depreciation account**

| 20X0 | | £ | 20X0 | | £ |
|---|---|---|---|---|---|
| 31 Dec | Asset realization | 60,000 | 1 Jan | Balance b/d | 60,000 |
| | | 60,000 | | | 60,000 |

**Cash book**

| 20X0 | | £ | | |
|---|---|---|---|---|
| 31 Dec | Asset realization | 30,000 | | |

**Asset realization account**

| 20X0 | | £ | 20X0 | | £ |
|---|---|---|---|---|---|
| 31 Dec | Plant & machinery | 100,000 | 31 Dec | Cash | 30,000 |
| | | | 31 Dec | Provision for depreciation | 60,000 |
| | | | 31 Dec | Profit & loss a/c | 10,000 |
| | | 100,000 | | | 100,000 |

**Profit and loss account for the year ended 31 December 20X0**

| | £ | |
|---|---|---|
| Loss on sale of plant and machinery | 10,000 | |

Therefore the gain or loss on disposal of fixed assets would be reported on the profit and loss account, and the machinery would no longer be reported on the balance sheet.

## Narrowing accounting differences

In Chapter 6 we discussed the problems created in the financial reporting process by the existence of a variety of practices permitted by the concepts of accounting. These problems appear in the lack of comparability between the financial reports of different companies, and in the consequent inability of users of financial reports to make informed judgements about different enterprises. The former Accounting Standards Committee was established with the purpose of narrowing the areas of difference and variety.

Depreciation is one area where substantial differences exist between accounting methods permitted by the concepts of accounting. In common with other controversial topics in accounting, many of the differences have their origins in the means adopted for allocating costs. As it is impossible to devise cost allocation methods which are entirely objective, accountants resort to methods which are more or less arbitrary. For example, the straight-line method of depreciation assumes that asset costs should be allocated to successive periods in uniform amounts, whereas the decreasing-balance method of depreciation assumes that rate of allocation should be constant through time. The assumptions underlying these alternative methods are defensible in the context of the circumstances which they also assume. In effect, 'for each situation in which allocation is contemplated, there is a variety of possible allocation methods, each of which could be defended. The allocation problem arises because there is no conclusive way to choose one method in preference to all others, except arbitrarily' (Thomas, 1974, p 2).

Although there is no solution to the problems posed by the existence of competing methods of allocating fixed asset costs through depreciation to successive accounting periods, users of financial reports may be assisted in evaluating the financial results reported, and making the adjustments necessary when comparing different companies. It was for this reason that the Accounting Standards Committee issued SSAP 12 'Accounting for Depreciation', which was later superseded by FRS 15 'Tangible Fixed Assets'. These reinforce the requirement in the Companies Act 1985 that tangible fixed assets must be depreciated.

Depreciation is defined in FRS 15 as the 'measure of the cost of the economic benefits of the fixed asset that have been consumed during the period. Consumption includes the wearing out, using up or other reduction in the useful economic life of a fixed asset whether arising from use, effluxion of time or obsolescence through either changes in technology or demand for the goods and services produced by the asset.' Freehold land need not normally be depreciated but all other tangible fixed assets should be. However, the FRS acknowledges that there may be exceptional circumstances where a long useful economic life or high residual value can be justified, giving rise to immaterial depreciation. But annual impairment reviews must be performed on such assets in accordance with FRS 11, 'Impairment of Fixed Assets and Goodwill', a complicated procedure, and for all assets with lives greater than fifty years.

Depreciation should represent a fair allocation of the asset's value over the useful life of the asset. To determine a fair allocation requires consideration of the cost or valuation of the asset, its nature and expected useful life and its estimated residual value. Cost less residual value should then be allocated over the periods which benefit from the asset's use throughout its expected useful life.

The standard requires that provision for depreciation of fixed assets having a finite useful life be made by allocating the cost or revalued amount less estimated residual values of the assets as fairly as possible to the periods expected to benefit from their use. On a revision of the estimated useful life of an asset, the undepreciated cost should be charged over the revised remaining useful life. Where the method of depreciation is changed, which is permissible only where the new method will give a fairer presentation of the results and financial position, the undepreciated cost should be written off over the remaining useful life on the new basis, commencing with the period in which the change is made, and the effect, if material, disclosed in the year of change. Where assets are revalued, depreciation should be based on the revalued amount and current estimate of remaining useful life with the effect, if material, disclosed in the year of change.

The following should be disclosed in the financial statements for each major class of depreciable asset:

1  the depreciation methods used;
2  the useful lives or the depreciation rates used;
3  total depreciation allocated for the period;
4  the gross amount of depreciable assets and the related accumulated depreciation.

No specific method of depreciation is laid down in the standard, this being the responsibility of the management of the business, i.e. to select a method most appropriate to the asset in question. Freehold land need not normally be depreciated but buildings with a limited life should be. This latter requirement was a major innovation. Prior to SSAP 12, it was common practice for depreciation not to be provided for buildings on the ground that market values tended to exceed net book values shown on the balance sheet. SSAP 12 took the view, reiterated by FRS 15, that because buildings have a limited life, they should be depreciated using the same criteria applied to other fixed assets. This requirement provoked strong objection from property investment companies. SSAP 19 'Accounting for Investment Properties' (1981) allows companies not to provide for depreciation in respect of investment properties. An investment property is defined as an interest in land and/or buildings, where construction work and development are completed and which is held for its investment potential.

## Losses arising from the default of debtors

The necessity to give credit to customers results in the investment of substantial funds in what are in effect short-term loans. There are three important financial aspects as regards debtors which are of interest to both management and investors. First, there is the problem of working capital management in respect of the balance of claims in favour of and against the firm, and its implications in respect of liquidity and solvency. Second, there is the problem of the overall level of debtors in relation to other assets, and the need for the firm to have sufficient funds to invest in the maintenance and expansion of its profit-earning structure. This has implications for present and future profitability. Third, there is the risk associated with the recovery of amounts due from debtors. This is a problem of credit control and the prevention of losses due to default by debtors.

The valuation of amounts due from debtors at the end of an accounting period presents no difficulty as regards determining debtor balances in an objective manner. Provided that accounting records have been kept properly, the objectivity of the valuation of debtors is founded in the law of contract and is a claim enforceable at law against debtors. The recoverability of debts, however, is a question to which the accountant must address himself, since the concept of prudence requires that losses be recognized when they arise. The recoverability of debts for financial reporting purposes is a question of law in some cases and of judgement in others. Thus, where a debtor has been declared bankrupt the recoverability of the debt is subject to the law of bankruptcy, and where no dividend is likely, the loss must be recognized and the amount written off as bad. When, however, a debtor cannot be traced or is unable to pay owing to personal circumstances and the sum involved does not warrant legal action, then the decision to recognize the loss is a matter of judgement. By and large, accountants examine the debtors ledger at the end of the financial year and identify those debts likely to be bad debts by reference to the delay in payment and the attempts made to secure payment. Debts considered irrecoverable are written off by debiting the profit and loss account and crediting debtors, and if they should be recovered subsequently, then the debt is restored in the debtors ledger.

Failure to deal adequately with the problem of defaulting debtors will distort the measurement of profit and asset values in the following respects:

1 The measurement of profit for an accounting period will be overstated to the extent that any credit sales taken into profit have created debts which are not recoverable.
2 The measurement of profit for the subsequent accounting period will be understated to the extent that debts created in the previous accounting period are recognized belatedly as bad and written off against the profit of the subsequent accounting year.
3 The balance sheet statement of the value of debtors includes debts which, though legally enforceable, are irrecoverable. It is not possible, for example, to recover debts from bankrupt persons, or persons who cannot be traced.

Accordingly:

1 bad debts should be recognized as soon as they arise;
2 the risk of further possible losses should be anticipated in accordance with the concept of prudence.

Accounting practice is to deal separately with the problem of debts which are recognized as bad, and to anticipate further losses in the future. In effect, three types of debts are distinguished:

1 good debts;
2 bad debts;
3 doubtful debts.

# The treatment of bad debts

Careful supervision of debtors' accounts will minimize bad debts. The enforcement of time limits for settlement of accounts helps in the prevention of a build-up of arrears and in identifying doubtful debts. Once a debt is recognized as bad, it should be written off immediately, so that the list of debtor accounts represents only good debts, that is, those expected to be paid in full.

**Example 6**  H Smith Ltd, a firm of building contractors, had been regular customers of Hervey Building Supplies Ltd and enjoyed a credit limit of £1,000. On 1 January 20X0 the balance on its account in the books of Hervey was £900, and purchases in January 20X0 totalled £150. H Smith informed Hervey on 5 February of its inability to pay its account. Hervey stopped further credit to H Smith until the position was clarified. Shortly thereafter, it was discovered that H Smith was insolvent, and that it was unlikely that any of the debt of £1,050 would be paid. On 1 March, it was decided to treat the debt as a bad debt.

The accounting entries in the books of Hervey would be as follows:

**H Smith Ltd account**

| 20X0 | | £ | 20X0 | | £ |
|---|---|---|---|---|---|
| 1 Jan | Balance | 900 | 1 Mar | Bad debt | 1,050 |
| 31 Jan | Sales | 150 | | | |
| | | 1,050 | | | 1,050 |

**Bad debts account**

| 20X0 | | £ | | |
|---|---|---|---|---|
| 1 Mar | H Smith Ltd | 1,050 | | |

At the end of the accounting period, the total on the bad debts account is debited to the profit and loss account.

**Example 7**  Assume that the only bad debt suffered by Hervey Building Supplies Ltd was in respect of H Smith Ltd in the sum of £1,050, as above. The bad debts account for the year ended 31 December 20X0 would be closed as follows:

**Bad debts account**

| 20X0 | | £ | 20X0 | | £ |
|---|---|---|---|---|---|
| 1 Mar | H Smith Ltd | 1,050 | 31 Dec | Profit & loss a/c | 1,050 |
| | | 1,050 | | | 1,050 |

**Profit and loss account for the year ended 31 December 20X0**

| 20X0 | £ | | |
|---|---|---|---|
| Bad debts | 1,050 | | |

# The treatment of doubtful debts

The question of doubtful debts, as distinct from bad debts, is examined only at the end of each accounting period. A final scrutiny of the debtors account will eliminate all those accounts considered to be bad and the necessary transfers will be made to the bad debts account. Of the remaining debtors, some may ultimately prove to be bad but there may be reasonable grounds for hoping that all remaining debtors will settle their accounts. The concept of prudence requires that the risk should be discounted of further debts proving to be bad. The normal practice is to create a provision for doubtful debts out of the current year's profit, without seeking to identify particular debts as being doubtful of recovery. There are several methods of estimating doubtful debts. The most common method is to allow past experience to establish the percentage of debtors which has proved to be bad, and to calculate the provision for doubtful debts by applying this percentage to the debtors outstanding at the end of the accounting period. A more accurate method is to classify debtor balances in terms of their age, and to apply to the several groups of debts the loss rates established by experience.

**Example 8** The sales ledger balances existing in the books of the Bumpa Trading Company at the end of the financial year are as follows:

| Duration of debts | Amount | Loss rate % | Provision |
|---|---|---|---|
| | £ | | £ |
| Less than 1 month | 10,000 | 1 | 100 |
| 1–2 months | 3,000 | 3 | 90 |
| 2–3 months | 1,000 | 5 | 50 |
| 3–4 months | 500 | 10 | 50 |
| Over 4 months | 100 | 20 | 20 |
| | 14,600 | | 310 |

One of the advantages of this method of creating a provision for doubtful debts is that it enables management to understand the relationship between the slow collection of debts and the financial losses caused by defaulting debtors.

The accounting entries would be as follows:

**Profit and loss account for the year ended 31 December 20X0**

| | £ | |
|---|---|---|
| Provision for doubtful debts | 310 | |

**Provision for doubtful debts account**

| | | £ |
|---|---|---|
| | 20X0 | |
| | Profit & loss y/e 31 Dec | 310 |

The provision for doubtful debts is not identified with any individual debtors. It is carried forward as an estimated liability, and may be shown on the balance sheet as follows:

131

**Balance sheet as at 31 December 20X0**

|  | £ | £ |
|---|---|---|
| Debtors | 14,600 | |
| *less* Provision for doubtful debts | 310 | |
| | | 14,290 |

In this manner, the objective of presenting a realistic valuation of trade debts is achieved.

**Example 9**  During 20X0 J Snow had to write off the debts of C Wild and J Hope who owed £80 and £260 respectively. At 31 December 20X0 the total of sundry debtors was £2,880. Snow made a provision for doubtful debts of 5 per cent.

On 3 March 20X1 J Hope unexpectedly paid his debt. At 31 December 20X1 the total of sundry debtors, other than Wild and Hope, was £2,520 and the provision was maintained at 5 per cent.

J Snow's accounting entries would be as follows:

**Bad debts account**

| 20X0 | | £ | 20X0 | £ |
|---|---|---|---|---|
| 31 Dec | C Wild | 80 | 31 Dec Profit and loss account | 484 |
| | J Hope | 260 | | |
| | Provision for doubtful debts | 144 | | |
| | | 484 | | 484 |

**Profit and loss account for the year ended 31 December 20X0**

| | £ | |
|---|---|---|
| Bad debts | 340 | |
| Provision for bad debts | 144 | |

**Balance sheet as at 31 December 20X0**

| | £ | £ |
|---|---|---|
| Debtors | 2,880 | |
| *Less* Provision | 144 | 2,736 |

**C Wild**

| 20X0 | | £ | 20X0 | £ |
|---|---|---|---|---|
| 1 Jan | Balance b/d | 80 | 31 Dec Bad debts | 80 |

**J Hope**

| 20X0 | | £ | 20X0 | £ |
|---|---|---|---|---|
| 1 Jan | Balance b/d | 260 | 31 Dec Bad debts | 260 |

**Provision for doubtful debts account**

| 20X1 | | £ | 20X0 | | £ |
|---|---|---|---|---|---|
| 31 Dec | Bad debts (excess | | 31 Dec | Bad debts | 144 |
| | provision) | 18 | | | |
| | Balance c/d | 126 | | | |
| | | 144 | | | 144 |
| | | | 20X1 | | |
| | | | 1 Jan | Balance b/d | 126 |

**Bad debts recovered**

| 20X1 | | £ | 20X1 | | £ |
|---|---|---|---|---|---|
| 31 Dec | Profit & loss account | 260 | 3 Mar | J Hope | 260 |

**Profit and loss account for the year ended 31 December 20X1**

| | | £ |
|---|---|---|
| | Bad debts recovered | 260 |
| | Excess provision for | |
| | doubtful debts | 18 |

**Balance sheet as at 31 December 20X1**

| | | £ | £ |
|---|---|---|---|
| | Debtors | 2,520 | |
| | *Less* Provision | 126 | 2,394 |

The decrease in sundry debtors from £2,880 to £2,520 reduces the provision for doubtful debts by £18 (5% of £360) at 31 December 20X1.

## Summary

This chapter examined two important items in the measurement of periodic profit, namely, depreciation and financial losses resulting from bad debts. Both are concerned with the manner in which losses in asset values should be recognized. Depreciation is a difficult problem from a theoretical viewpoint, and its treatment in accounting as an allocation of historical costs is a limited view of this problem. Nevertheless, such treatment is compatible with the matching concept for the allocation of asset costs to the revenues derived from their use. Not all assets are depreciable, and depreciation should take into account all the relevant costs of acquisition as well as the useful life of assets.

Two methods of depreciation were examined, and their implications discussed. The adjustments required on the sale or disposal of assets were also examined.

Losses caused by defaulting debtors were analysed and their impact on the measurement of periodic profit was discussed. Accounting adopts a two-stage approach to this problem, namely the recognition of losses actually incurred by declaring certain debts as *bad*, and the provision against the risk of loss through creating provisions for doubtful debts.

**References**    AICPA (1953). *Accounting Research Bulletin No 43*.

Barton, A D (1984). *The Anatomy of Accounting*, University of Queensland Press.

Thomas, A L (1974). 'The allocation problem: Part 2', *Studies in Accounting Research*, AAA.

## Self-assessment questions

1 Analyse the main factors which should be considered when selecting a policy for depreciating fixed assets.

2 Explain the main provisions of FRS 15.

## Problems   *(\* indicates that a solution is to be found in the Lecturer's Guide)*

1 Lodgemoor Company acquired a machine on 1 July 20X0 for £48,000 and immediately spent a further £2,000 on its installation. The machine was estimated to have a useful life of eight years and a scrap value of £4,000 at the end of this time.

*Required:*
Compute the depreciation provision for the year ended 30 June 20X1 and 20X2 if the company chooses to use:

(a) the straight-line method;
(b) the reducing-balance method.

2 Beale Company purchased a machine on 1 January 19X9, at an invoice price of £142,600. Transportation charges amounted to £2,000, and £3,400 was spent to install the machine. Costs of removing an old machine to make room for the new one amounted to £1,200, and £200 was received for the scrap value of the old machine.

*Required:*
(a) State the amounts of depreciation which would be provided on the machine for the first year on a straight-line basis and on a decreasing-balance basis, assuming an estimated life of eight years and no salvage value expected at the end of that time.
(b) Compute the depreciation provision for the year ended 31 December 20X1, assuming a revised total life expectancy for the machine of 12 years; assume that depreciation has been recorded through 31 December 20X0 on a straight-line basis.

3 From the following information relating to the fixed assets of a business prepare the following accounts as they should appear in the ledger:

(a)    plant and machinery;
(b)    motor vehicles;
(c)    plant and machinery provision for depreciation;
(d)    motor vehicles provision for depreciation;
(e)    asset realization.

The plant and machinery was acquired on 1 January 19X6, at a cost of £7,500, and the motor vehicles were acquired on 1 July 19X8, at a cost of £3,500.

It has been the practice of the business to depreciate assets using the straight-line method and they estimate the life of the plant to be ten years and that of the motor vehicles to be five years.

The accounts of the business are made up to 31 December in each year and it is usual to calculate depreciation for a full year on the assets in the possession of the business at balance sheet date.

During the year to 31 December 20X0, a new machine costing £1,000 was acquired and a machine bought on 1 January 19X6 for £500 was sold for £325; and a car costing £750 on 1 July 19X8 was sold for £400.

4* The year-end balance on the debtors account amounted to £100,000. Net sales for the year totalled £1,200,000. Explain how you would deal with the following information.

(a) An analysis of the sales ledger indicates that irrecoverable debts amount to £11,400.
(b) Past trends suggest that 5 per cent of debts eventually should be provided as doubtful.
(c) The existing provision for doubtful debts is £3,000.

5 A business maintains in its ledger a combined bad debts and provision for doubtful debts account. The provision was created in the accounts for the year ended 31 March 19X9 by calculating an amount equal to 5 per cent of the £10,000 outstanding debts at that date. During the year ended 31 March 20X0 bad debts of £250 were incurred and at the balance sheet date the outstanding debts amounted to £12,500. It was decided to maintain the provision for doubtful debts at 5 per cent of the outstanding debts. During the year to 31 March 20X1, bad debts of £270 were incurred and the debts outstanding at balance sheet date amounted to £10,000. It was decided to adjust the doubtful debts provision to an amount equal to 4 per cent of the debts outstanding at 31 March 20X1.

Required:
(a) Record the above in the ledger of the business.
(b) Show the entries that would appear in the profit and loss account for each of the years to 31 March 19X9, 20X0 and 20X1 and on each of the three balance sheets made up to those dates.

6 An airline company purchased and put into operation a jet aircraft on 1 February 19X7 for £7,000,000. The expectation then was that the aircraft would be flown for a total of 10,000 hours over a period of 4 years and then traded in for a new model. The trade-in value was expected to be £1,500,000 at the end of January 20X1. The number of flying hours actually logged by the aircraft was as follows:

| 1 February 19X1–31 January 19X8 | 3,000 |
| 1 February 19X2–31 January 19X9 | 2,800 |
| 1 February 19X3–31 January 20X0 | 2,300 |
| 1 February 19X4–31 January 20X1 | 500 |

The aircraft had a serious accident in June 20X0 and was a total write-off – although an insurance company agreed to pay £1,200,000 in settlement.

Required:
(a) Calculate the depreciation charges for each of the four financial years to 31 January 20X1
    (i) using the straight-line method (applied on a full-year basis), and
    (ii) on a basis of flying hours logged.
(b) Show the appropriate ledger accounts for the year ended 31 January 20X1 for the two methods.

7    A Mayberry Ltd, a company with a turnover of £30,000 per year, acquired a machine on 1 January 20X0 for £8,000. It was company policy to depreciate machinery on a straight-line basis at 20 per cent per year. During 20X0, a modification was made to the machine to improve its technical reliability at a cost of £800 which it was considered would extend the useful life of the machine by two years. At the same time, an important component of the machine was replaced at a cost of £500, because of excessive wear and tear. Routine mainte-nance during the year cost £250.

*Required:*
Show the asset account, the provision for depreciation account, and the charge to profit and loss account in respect of the machine for the year ended 31 December 20X0.

8*   Brannan own plant and equipment which is used on their construction sites. The deprecia-tion policy of the company is to charge a full year's depreciation in the year of acquisition but none in the year of disposal.
     During the year ended 31 March 20X1 the following changes took place:

**Purchases 20X0/1**

| Date | Cost |
| --- | --- |
| | £ |
| 1 July | 8,200 |
| 31 August | 6,800 |
| 1 December | 12,600 |
| 28 February | 7,500 |

**Sales 20X0/1**

| Date | Cost | Date of purchase | Receipts |
| --- | --- | --- | --- |
| | £ | | £ |
| 15 August | 4,200 | 15 May 19X6 | 250 |
| 30 September | 5,800 | 1 December 19X4 | 100 |
| 29 December | 9,000 | 1 February 19X8 | 510 |
| 1 March | 11,000 | 31 March 19X9 | 3,000 |

All the remaining assets had been owned for less than four years. Depreciation is charged on a straight-line basis using a rate of 25 per cent per annum. The balance on the plant and equipment account at 1 April 20X0 was £187,600 and on the provision for depreciation account £62,100.

*Required:*
Prepare the following accounts:

(a)  A plant and equipment account.
(b)  A plant and equipment provision for depreciation account.
(c)  A disposal account.

# 11 Preparing a profit and loss account and a balance sheet

*Setting the scene*

Financial statements are at the centre of business reporting. They represent the financial picture of a company, both at a point in time and over a period of time, translating into financial terms many, but not all, of the events and activities that affect it . . . Many investment decisions – such as whether to lend money, whether to buy, hold or sell securities – are based, in large part, on the information in financial statements.

(AICPA, 1994)

*Learning objectives*

**After studying this chapter you should be able to:**

1 **Prepare a profit and loss account after making adjustments for accruals, stocks and depreciation.**

2 **Prepare a balance sheet.**

3 **Reconcile the balance on the bank account in the ledger with the balance shown on the bank statement.**

In Chapter 10, we examined the role of the trial balance as a working paper which enables the accountant not only to check the arithmetical accuracy of the entries recorded during an accounting period, but which also serves as a basis for considering adjustments to be made for the purpose of measuring periodic profit. The extraction of a trial balance at the close of the accounting period is the first step, therefore, in the preparation of a profit and loss account and a balance sheet.

We examined in Chapter 9 how the trial balance is adjusted in respect of the accrual into the accounting period of revenues and expenses, and we analysed in Chapter 10 the nature of the losses in asset values which have to be taken into consideration in the measurement of periodic profit.

The purpose of this chapter is to summarize the various adjustments which must be made to the trial balance, and the manner in which these adjustments are incorporated into the process of preparing a profit and loss account and a balance sheet.

## Preparing a profit and loss account

The preparation of a profit and loss account is a two-stage exercise. The first stage is an informal one and consists of using the trial balance as a worksheet for accumulating all the data which incorporate the various adjustments we referred to earlier. The adjustments are then entered in the appropriate accounts, and the profit and loss account is formally included in the accounts system. It is important to remember that the profit and loss account is an account to which the revenue and expense accounts for the accounting period are transferred as summarized totals, and which exists solely for the purpose of measuring the accounting profit for that period.

The following example illustrates the nature of the profit and loss account.

*Example 1*  Let us return to the trial balance given on page 101, which listed the balances extracted from the books of John Smith on 31 December 20X0 at the end of the first year of trading:

|  | £ Dr | £ Cr |
|---|---|---|
| Capital |  | 25,000 |
| Motor vehicles | 10,000 |  |
| Furniture and fittings | 2,500 |  |
| Purchases | 31,000 |  |
| Bank balance | 6,000 |  |
| Sales |  | 70,000 |
| Debtors | 18,000 |  |
| Creditors |  | 3,500 |
| Rent | 4,500 |  |
| Salaries | 22,800 |  |
| Insurances | 400 |  |
| Motor expenses | 2,000 |  |
| Light and heat | 1,000 |  |
| General expenses | 300 |  |
|  | 98,500 | 98,500 |

We noted in Chapter 9 that the following adjustments were required:

1  Rent unpaid at the end of the year was £1,500.
2  Insurance paid in advance amounted to £50.
3  Rent receivable, but not recorded in the account, amounted to £60.
4  Closing stock at 31 December 20X0 was valued at £3,000.

We are now given the following additional information:

1  Depreciation is to be provided on the undermentioned assets and calculated on the reducing-balance method. Their estimated residual values are shown in brackets.

| Motor vehicles | 20% | (£1,000) |
| Furniture and fittings | 10% | (£250) |

2  Bad debts to be written off amount to £180, and a provision for doubtful debts is to be made of £178.

# Adjusting for accruals

We saw also that the adjustments for accruals and prepayments resulted in the following revisions of balances in the trial balance:

|  | Original balance | Adjustment | New balance |
|---|---|---|---|
|  | £ | £ | £ |
| 1  Rent | 4,500 | 1,500 | 6,000 |
| 2  Insurance | 400 | 50 | 350 |
| 3  Insurance prepaid | – | 50 | 50 |
| 4  Rent receivable | – | 60 | 60 |

We explained in Chapter 9 that items 1, 2 and 3 represented adjustments to the revenues and expenses of the year and affected the profit and loss account. The following resulting balances of the accounts affect the balance sheet and we shall see later in this chapter how they are incorporated in that statement:

|  | £ Dr | £ Cr |
|---|---|---|
| Rent accrued |  | 1,500 |
| Insurance prepaid | 50 |  |
| Rent receivable | 60 |  |

The corrected total revenues and expenses may now be listed on a worksheet used in the preparation of the profit and loss account:

**Draft profit and loss account for the year ended 31 December 20X0**

|  | £ |  | £ |
|---|---|---|---|
| Purchases | 31,000 | Sales | 70,000 |
| Rent | 6,000 | Rent receivable | 60 |
| Salaries | 22,800 |  |  |
| Insurance | 350 |  |  |
| Motor expenses | 2,000 |  |  |
| Light and heat | 1,000 |  |  |
| General expenses | 300 |  |  |

# Adjusting for stocks

We noted in Chapter 9 that periodic measurement involved valuing the stocks of goods unsold at the end of the accounting period. The closing stock is valued in accordance with the cost concept, and represents the residue of the purchases of the year which have not been sold at the year end, though they may be sold in the next accounting period. Opening stocks are shown, therefore, as a *debit balance* in the trial balance, whereas closing stocks do not appear, since they are valued after the close of the accounting period. It is for this reason that the appropriate entries must be made in the stock account to make possible the measurement of periodic profit. In the example in question, there is no opening stock because it is the first year of trading.

We saw in Chapter 9 that the adjustment for closing stock had a twofold effect. First, it is effected by means of a credit to the profit and loss account and a debit to the stock account. Second, it results in a debit balance in the stock account which must be incorporated in the balance sheet.

The closing stock is entered on the draft profit and loss account as follows:

### Draft profit and loss account for the year ended 31 December 20X0

| | £ | | £ |
|---|---|---|---|
| Purchases | 31,000 | Sales | 70,000 |
| Rent | 6,000 | Rent receivable | 60 |
| Salaries | 22,800 | Closing stock | |
| Insurance | 350 | 31 December 20X0 | 3,000 |
| Motor expenses | 2,000 | | |
| Light and heat | 1,000 | | |
| General expenses | 300 | | |

## Adjusting for the loss in asset values

We mentioned in Chapter 10 the most important losses in asset values which the accountant has to recognize in the measurement of periodic profit. We do not propose to deal here with the variety of gains and losses in asset values which may occur, since we are concerned only with the process of periodic measurement and with the most significant losses in asset values which enter into that process.

In the example, we are required to deal with depreciation, bad and doubtful debts.

### Calculation of depreciation

It is the usual practice to detail in the profit and loss account the component elements of the provision for depreciation, and as we shall see later fixed assets are also described in their categories on the balance sheet. The provision for depreciation in respect of the different fixed assets may be reconciled, therefore, with the yearly provision for depreciation shown on the balance sheet.

| | £ | £ |
|---|---|---|
| **1  Motor vehicles** | | |
| Cost | 10,000 | |
| Estimated residual value | 1,000 | |
| Net cost for depreciation purposes | 9,000 | |
| Depreciation for the year 20X0 at 20% | 1,800 | 1,800 |
| Residual balance for depreciation in following years | 7,200 | |

| | £ | £ |
|---|---|---|
| **2  Furniture and fittings** | | |
| Cost | 2,500 | |
| Estimated residual value | 250 | |
| Net cost for depreciation purposes | 2,250 | |
| Depreciation for the year 20X0 at 10% | 225 | 225 |
| Residual balance for depreciation in following years | 2,025 | |
| | | |
| Total depreciation for the year | | 2,025 |

## Calculation of the provision for doubtful debts

| Duration of debt | Balance £ | Loss rate, % | Provision £ |
|---|---|---|---|
| Less than 1 month | 15,960 | $\frac{1}{2}$ | 80 |
| 1–2 months | 1,800 | 5 | 90 |
| 2–3 months | 40 | 10 | 4 |
| over 3 months | 20 | 20 | 4 |
| | 17,820 | | 178 |

These adjustments may be included in the draft profit and loss account as shown below:

**Draft profit and loss account for the year ended 31 December 20X0**

| | £ | | £ |
|---|---|---|---|
| Purchases | 31,000 | Sales | 70,000 |
| Rent | 6,000 | Rent receivable | 60 |
| Salaries | 22,800 | Closing stock at | |
| Insurance | 350 | 31 December 20X0 | 3,000 |
| Motor expenses | 2,000 | | |
| Light and heat | 1,000 | | |
| General expenses | 300 | | |
| Depreciation | | | |
| Motor vehicles | 1,800 | | |
| Furniture and fittings | 225 | | |
| | 2,025 | | |
| Bad debts | 180 | | |
| Provision for doubtful debts | 178 | | |

# Calculating the periodic profit

The details shown on the draft profit and loss account above are sufficient to permit the calculation of the profit for the year ended 31 December 20X0. The profit and loss account is set out, however, so as to enable significant information to be immediately apparent. In this respect, a distinction is made between *gross* profit and *net* profit, the former being the profit resulting after the deduction from the gross sales revenue of expenses directly connected with the production or purchase of the goods sold, while the latter reflects the deduction of overhead expenses from gross profit. Although the net profit is the most important result, dividing the profit and loss account into two parts highlights the burden of overhead expenses, as well as focusing attention on important aspects of business activity.

## Calculating gross profit

In the case of a trading business – as is the case in the example quoted – the gross profit from trading may be shown as follows:

|  | £ |  | £ |
|---|---|---|---|
| Purchases | 31,000 | Sales | 70,000 |
| *Less:* Closing stock at |  |  |  |
| 31 December 20X0 | 3,000 |  |  |
| Cost of sales | 28,000 |  |  |
| Gross trading profit | 42,000 |  |  |
|  | 70,000 |  | 70,000 |

This arrangement shows the following points:

1 Although purchases amounted to £31,000, the cost of goods actually sold amounted to only £28,000. Hence, the gross trading profit expressed as a percentage of sales is:

$$\frac{42,000}{70,000} \times 100 = 60\%$$

This percentage is often referred to as the gross profit ratio. Expressed as a percentage of cost of sales, the gross trading profit is:

$$\frac{42,000}{28,000} \times 100 = 150\%$$

2 The level of trading activity may also be judged from the average length of time stock is held. The rate of stock turnover may be calculated as follows:

$$\frac{\text{cost of sales}}{\text{average stock}}$$

The average stock is obtained by the arithmetic mean of the opening and closing stock. In the example under consideration, the rate of stock turnover for the year was as follows:

$$\frac{28,000}{3,000} = 9.3 \text{ times}$$

so that stock was held for approximately 39 days (365 days ÷ 9.3), or replaced approximately 9.3 times in the year.

The segregation of the gross trading profit in the process of calculating periodic profit provides useful ratios for the analysis of trading performance, and for indicating areas of trading where efficiency might be improved.

It is the practice for firms to identify the nature of gross profit. Thus manufacturing firms show manufacturing gross profit, contracting firms show contracting gross profit and so on.

The problem of deciding which expenses to include in the calculation of the gross profit lies in defining direct as distinct from indirect operating expenses. Direct expenses, such as purchases, freight and other expenses associated with the acquisition of goods for resale, for example, are included in the calculation of gross profit.

## Calculating the net profit

The calculation of the net profit is affected by charging against the gross profit the indirect expenses accumulated in the trial balance, and other expenses such as depreciation, bad debts and provisions for the year ended 31 December 20X0 may be calculated as shown:

**Net profit for year ended 31 December 20X0**

| | £ | | £ |
|---|---|---|---|
| Rent | 6,000 | Gross trading profit | 42,000 |
| Salaries | 22,800 | Rent receivable | 60 |
| Insurance | 350 | | |
| Motor expenses | 2,000 | | |
| Light and heat | 1,000 | | |
| General expenses | 300 | | |
| Depreciation | | | |
|    Motor vehicles 1,800 | | | |
|    Furniture and fittings 225 | | | |
| | 2,025 | | |
| Bad debts | 180 | | |
| Provision for doubtful debts | 178 | | |
| | 34,833 | | |
| Net profit | 7,227 | | |
| | 42,060 | | 42,060 |

Miscellaneous income, such as interest, rents and dividends, which forms a minor element in the business profit, is usually shown in the calculation of the net profit rather than in the calculation of the gross profit.

The segregation of the net profit calculation also affords a clearer view of significant ratios. The net profit is itself the most significant performance result, and its dimensions may be assessed not only in relation to the gross trading profit, but also to gross revenue. The net profit as a percentage of sales indicates the level of activity required to produce £1 of net profit, and may be calculated as follows:

$$\frac{\text{net profit before interest and tax}}{\text{sales}}$$

Thus, whereas the percentage of gross profit to sales was 60 per cent, the percentage of net profit to sales was only 13 per cent, indicating thereby not only the relative burden of direct and indirect expenses but also the relative efficiency of the business.

# The formal presentation of the profit and loss account

Although the profit and loss account is part of the accounts system, and may be shown in an account form, its formal presentation has been influenced by its use as a financial reporting statement. This influence has encouraged the further classification of indirect expenses into selling, administration and financial expenses, and the presentation of the profit and loss account in a vertical form as follows:

**John Smith trading as general dealer**
**Profit and loss account for the year ended 31 December 20X0**

|  | £ | £ | £ |
|---|---|---|---|
| **Sales** |  |  | 70,000 |
| **Cost of sales** |  |  |  |
| Purchases |  | 31,000 |  |
| *Less:* Closing stock |  | 3,000 |  |
|  |  |  | 28,000 |
| **Gross trading profit** |  |  | 42,000 |
| **Other income** |  |  |  |
| Rent |  |  | 60 |
|  |  |  |  |
| **Total profit** |  |  | 42,060 |
| **Selling and distribution expenses** |  |  |  |
| Sales representatives' salaries | 12,000 |  |  |
| Motor expenses | 2,000 |  |  |
| Depreciation – motor vehicles | 1,800 | 15,800 |  |
|  |  |  |  |
| **Administrative expenses** |  |  |  |
| Rent | 6,000 |  |  |
| Office salaries | 10,800 |  |  |
| Insurance | 350 |  |  |
| Light and heat | 1,000 |  |  |
| General expenses | 300 |  |  |
| Depreciation – furniture and fittings | 225 |  |  |
|  |  | 18,675 |  |
| **Financial expenses** |  |  |  |
| Bad debts | 180 |  |  |
| Provision for doubtful debts | 178 | 358 |  |
|  |  |  |  |
| **Total overhead expenses** |  |  | 34,833 |
| **Net profit** |  |  | 7,227 |

## Preparing a balance sheet

The preparation of the balance sheet is a two-stage process, and, in this sense, it follows the same pattern as the preparation of the profit and loss account, that is, an informal stage based on a worksheet, and a formal stage represented by the balance sheet presented as a financial report. There are, however, a number of important differences between a profit and loss account and a balance sheet. First, from a procedural point of view, the profit and loss account is part of the accounts system and, as we explained earlier, it is itself an account. By contrast, the balance sheet is not an account, but a list showing the balances of the accounts which remain following the preparation of the profit and loss account. Second, the profit and loss account is the effective instrument of periodic measurement in accounting, whereas the balance sheet does not do other than state residual balances. Third, residual debit balances are shown on the balance sheet as assets, but there are problems stemming from this description which we discuss in Chapter 12. Fourth, by attaching accounting measurements to debit and credit balances described as assets and liabilities respectively, the balance sheet is often interpreted as indicating the net worth of the business. This is a misconception, and in the case of corporations has led to much controversy. We explore these problems further in Part 3.

## Collecting and classifying balances

The preparation of the balance sheet need not await the entry of all the adjustments into the individual accounts following the preparation of the profit and loss account. It may be prepared in draft form from the trial balance and the finalized draft of the profit and loss account.

Debit balances are either assets, losses or expenses. The preparation of the profit and loss account involves the removal from the trial balance of all expenses in respect of the year, so that any debit balances remaining are treated as assets. These assets, as defined, are classified as follows:

1 Long-term assets representing an enduring benefit to the enterprise. Long-term assets, described as fixed assets, for example plant and machinery, are subject to depreciation. Other long-term assets, such as land and intangible assets, may or may not be subject to depreciation or other changes in their book value. We examine these problems in Chapter 12.
2 Short-term assets, described as current assets, include the following:
   (a) closing stocks at the end of the accounting period;
   (b) trade debtors;
   (c) prepayments on expense accounts, for example, insurance paid in advance;
   (d) bank balance and cash.

The measurement of closing stocks presents particular problems, which we discuss in Chapter 12. We have already examined the accounting problems relating to trade debtors which arise from the writing-off of bad debts and the making of provisions for doubtful debts. We shall deal presently with the verification of bank balances and overdrafts.

By contrast, credit balances are either liabilities, revenues or investments in the firm in the form of capital and long-term loans. The removal of periodic revenues from the trial balance means that the remaining credit balances are either liabilities or investments. The provision for depreciation is one of a number of exceptions to this rule. These exceptions, as in the case of prepayments shown as debit balances, arise from accounting procedures. Credit balances are collected and classified as follows:

1 capital account, representing the owner's original investment in the firm and accumulated profits less drawings;
2 long-term borrowings;
3 short-term liabilities, described as current liabilities, which include such credit balances as sundry creditors, accrued expenses, payments received in advance, provisions for taxation and bank overdrafts.

## Verifying balances

Accounts are usually subjected to yearly audits, that is, they are checked by a firm of professional accountants. The purpose of the audit is not only to check the accuracy of the records, but also to ensure that the statements contained in those records are correct. Thus, the physical existence of the assets in the assets accounts is verified, as is the existence of liabilities in various creditors' accounts. In the case of large corporations, audits are obligatory and auditors are appointed by shareholders. In this connection, they are required to report that both the profit and loss account and the balance sheet reflect a true and fair view of the information they are legally required to convey.

## Bank reconciliation statement

It is unlikely that on any specific day the bank balance shown in the cash book will correspond with the statement of the balance in the bank account issued by the bank. This is due not only to the normal delays occurring in the process of clearing cheques, but also to delays in lodging and presenting cheques for payment. Moreover, payments and receipts may be effected directly through the bank. For example, dividends and interest receivable may be paid directly into the bank account, and routine payments may be effected by standing orders and direct debit procedures. The bank also charges commission, fees and interest directly to the account, and the bank statement is used to convey these details to the client.

The bank reconciliation statement reconciles the balance at the bank as per the bank statement with the bank balance as per the cash book, whenever a bank statement is received.

When preparing a balance sheet, the bank balance as shown in the cash book must be supported by a bank statement stating the balance on the last day of the accounting period, and the bank reconciliation statement explains any differences which have not been already adjusted in the cash book. Thus, any charges such as bank commission and interest will be entered in the cash book and will be shown as expenses in the profit and loss account. In effect, therefore, the bank reconciliation statement explains the nature of the unadjusted differences between the cash book and the bank statement.

**Example 2** The bank balance according to the cash book was £6,000 on 31 December 20X0. The bank statement balance was £6,500. The difference is explained as follows:

1. cheques received from debtors on 31 December 20X0 which were not banked until after 1 January 20X1 amounted to £250;
2. cheques sent to creditors on 31 December 20X0 and not presented for payment until after 1 January 20X1 amounted to £750.

### Bank reconciliation statement as on 31 December 20X0

|  | £ |
|---|---|
| Balance at bank as per bank statement | 6,500 |
| *Add:* Cheques received but not credited | 250 |
|  | 6,750 |
| *Less:* Cheques issued but not presented | 750 |
| Balance at bank per cash book | 6,000 |

# The formal presentation of the balance sheet

In the case of corporations, legislation provides rules for the presentation of both the profit and loss account and the balance sheet. As we see in Chapter 13, these rules apply to published financial reports. The rules reflect the practices of the accounting profession, and are designed not only to secure sufficient disclosure but also to permit salient features to be quickly recognized.

It is usual, therefore, to classify assets and liabilities in groupings as we mentioned earlier, and to rank them according to liquidity. Thus, asset groupings are shown from the most fixed to the most liquid, and liabilities from the long-term to the most current.

The importance of the balance sheet, together with the profit and loss account for the purpose of financial reporting and investment decision making, has focused attention on the arrangement of particular groupings to assist the interpretation and the analysis of results. We deal with this analysis in Chapter 16, but we may mention at this stage that the relationship between long-term finance and long-term investment needs of the firm (long-term capital as defined in finance) and short-term finance and short-term financial needs (working capital) is important to financial analysts. Other areas of interest are the return on capital employed which is the ratio of net profit to equity capital (owner's investment in the firm), liquidity and solvency.

The vertical form of presentation of the balance sheet is illustrated below.

### John Smith  Balance sheet at 31 December 20X0

| Fixed assets | Cost | Depreciation to date | Net | | |
|---|---|---|---|---|---|
| | £ | £ | £ | £ | £ |
| Motor vehicles | 10,000 | 1,800 | 8,200 | | |
| Furniture and fittings | 2,500 | 225 | 2,275 | | |
| | 12,500 | 2,025 | 10,475 | 10,475 | |
| | | | | | |
| **Current assets** | | | | | |
| Stocks at cost | | | 3,000 | | |
| Debtors | | 17,820 | | | |
| *Less:* Provision for doubtful debts | | 178 | 17,642 | | |
| Accruals and prepayments | | | 110 | | |
| Bank balance | | | 6,000 | | |
| | | | 26,752 | | |
| **Current liabilities** | | | | | |
| Creditors | | 3,500 | | | |
| Accruals | | 1,500 | 5,000 | | |
| Net current assets | | | | 21,752 | |
| | | | | | 32,227 |
| **Capital employed** | | | | | |
| Capital account | | | | 25,000 | |
| Net profit for the year | | | | 7,227 | |
| | | | | | 32,227 |

**Example 3** The following trial balance was extracted from the books of Peter Ardron as at 31 December 20X0:

|  | £ | £ |
|---|---:|---:|
| Purchases | 54,520 | |
| Sales | | 79,060 |
| Salaries | 8,760 | |
| Rates | 1,170 | |
| Office expenses | 3,950 | |
| Motor expenses | 3,790 | |
| Capital account, 1 January 20X0 | | 13,640 |
| Freehold properties at cost | 7,500 | |
| Furniture and fittings at cost | 2,000 | |
| Motor cars at cost | 6,300 | |
| Accumulated depreciation | | |
|     Freehold properties | | 450 |
|     Furniture and fittings | | 800 |
|     Motor cars | | 2,370 |
| Stock 1 January 20X0 | 6,740 | |
| Drawings | 4,800 | |
| Provision for doubtful debts 1 January 20X0 | | 600 |
| Loan | | 4,000 |
| Debtors | 9,240 | |
| Creditors | | 10,040 |
| Bank balance | 2,190 | |
| | 110,960 | 110,960 |

The following matters are to be taken into account:

1  Stock at 31 December £7,330.
2  Rates paid in advance 31 December £250.
3  Provision for doubtful debts to be made equal to 5 per cent of debtors at 31 December.
4  Provide depreciation for the year at the following annual rates calculated on cost, assuming no scrap value:

    freehold properties        1%
    furniture and fittings     10%
    motor cars           20%

5  Provide for interest on the loan at 5 per cent per annum.

Peter Ardron's profit and loss account for the year ended 31 December 20X0 and a balance sheet at that date appear as follows:

**Peter Ardron**
**Profit and loss account for the year ended 31 December 20X0**

|  | £ | £ | £ |
|---|---|---|---|
| Sales |  |  | 79,060 |
| Cost of sales |  |  |  |
| Opening stock |  | 6,740 |  |
| Purchases |  | 54,520 |  |
|  |  | 61,260 |  |
| *Less* Closing stock |  | 7,330 | 53,930 |
| **Gross profit** |  |  | 25,130 |
| **Expenses** |  |  |  |
| Salaries |  | 8,760 |  |
| Rates £(1,170 – 250) |  | 920 |  |
| Office expenses |  | 3,950 |  |
| Motor expenses |  | 3,790 |  |
| Doubtful debts provision not required |  | (138) |  |
| Loan interest |  | 200 |  |
| Depreciation: Freehold properties | 75 |  |  |
| Fixtures and fittings | 200 |  |  |
| Motor cars | 1,260 | 1,535 | 19,017 |
| **Net profit** |  |  | 6,113 |

**Balance sheet at 31 December 20X0**

|  | £ (Cost) | £ (Dep'n) | £ (NBV) |
|---|---|---|---|
| **Fixed assets** |  |  |  |
| Freehold properties | 7,500 | 525 | 6,975 |
| Furniture and fittings | 2,000 | 1,000 | 1,000 |
| Motor cars | 6,300 | 3,630 | 2,670 |
|  | 15,800 | 5,155 | 10,645 |
| **Current assets** |  |  |  |
| Stock |  | 7,330 |  |
| Debtors | 9,240 |  |  |
| *Less* Provision for doubtful debts | 462 |  |  |
|  |  | 8,778 |  |
| Prepayments |  | 250 |  |
| Bank balance |  | 2,190 |  |
|  |  | 18,548 |  |
| **Current liabilities** |  |  |  |
| Creditors | 10,040 |  |  |
| Accruals | 200 | 10,240 | 8,308 |
| **Net current assets** |  |  | 18,953 |
|  |  |  |  |
| **Capital account** |  |  |  |
| Balance b/d |  | 13,640 |  |
| Profit for year |  | 6,113 |  |
|  |  | 19,753 |  |
| Drawings |  | 4,800 | 14,953 |
| Loan |  |  | 4,000 |
|  |  |  | 18,953 |

**Workings**
**Provision for doubtful debts account**

| | £ | | £ |
|---|---|---|---|
| Balance c/d (5% × £9,240) | 462 | Balance b/d | 600 |
| Profit & loss account | | | |
|    (provision no longer required) | 138 | | |
| | 600 | | 600 |

## Summary

This chapter has been concerned with the accounting procedures for preparing and presenting the two main financial reports, namely the profit and loss account and the balance sheet.

The extraction of the trial balance at the close of the accounting period marks the first stage in the preparation of these reports. Earlier chapters have examined the adjustments required for the purposes of periodic measurement. These include accruals, depreciation and adjustments in respect of bad and doubtful debts. All these adjustments are effected informally on working sheets, and once they have been verified and confirmed, the final accounts are drawn up.

The importance of the profit and loss account lies not only in the fact that it is the main vehicle of periodic measurement and provides the measurement of periodic profit, but also in that it is part of the accounts system. The objective purpose underlying the preparation of the profit and loss account is the measurement of net profit, which is used as a basis for measuring business efficiency. The distinction between gross profit and net profit facilitates the analysis of the financial results, as does the classification of expenses under various categories.

By contrast, the balance sheet is a list of residual balances following the preparation of the profit and loss account. It forms no part of the accounts system. The balance sheet is used in conjunction with the profit and loss account in the analysis of the financial performance of the business, and the treatment and classification of assets and liabilities are important to this analysis. Consequently, particular attention is paid to the manner in which important financial aspects of the business are highlighted in the presentation of the balance sheet.

Reference     AICPA (1994). *Improving Business Reporting – A Customer Focus* (The Jenkins Report), American Institute of Certified Public Accountants.

## Problems *(\* indicates that a solution is to be found in the Lecturer's Guide)*

1   Jack Daw has prepared the following balance sheet as at 30 June 20X1:

|  | £ |  | £ | £ |
|---|---|---|---|---|
| Capital account |  | Plant at cost | 8,000 |  |
| Balance, 1 July 20X0 | 10,000 | *Less:* Depreciation | 2,000 | 6,000 |
| Profit for the year | 2,050 | Vehicles at cost | 3,000 |  |
|  | 12,050 | *Less:* Depreciation | 1,000 |  |
|  |  |  |  | 2,000 |
| Creditors and provisions | 5,000 | Stock |  | 7,000 |
| Bank overdraft | 1,000 | Debtors | 3,200 |  |
|  |  | *Less:* Provision for |  |  |
|  |  | doubtful debts | 200 | 3,000 |
|  |  | Cash | – | 50 |
|  | 18,050 |  |  | 18,050 |

Daw asks you to audit his accounts and in the course of your examination you find the following:

(a)  A dividend of £100 has been paid direct to the bank and no entry has been made in the books.
(b)  A debt of £100 is irrecoverable and you agree with Daw that the provision for doubtful debts should be fixed at 10 per cent of the remaining debtors.
(c)  A purchase of plant, costing £500, has been charged to repairs. It was agreed that this should be depreciated by 10 per cent on cost.
(d)  The stock on 30 June 20X1 was overvalued by £250.
(e)  On counting the petty cash you find there is only £10 in the box. It seems likely that the balance has been stolen by an employee.

*Required:*
(a)  A statement showing the necessary adjustments to the profit for the year to 30 June 20X1.
(b)  The amended balance sheet as at 30 June 20X1.

2   The balances in the books of account for John Reeve at 31 March 20X1 are given below:

|  | £ |
|---|---|
| Sales | 50,000 |
| Purchases | 30,000 |
| Stock, 1 April 20X0 | 35,000 |
| Administration expenses | 5,000 |
| Selling expenses | 5,000 |
| Trade creditors | 27,000 |
| Bank overdraft | 32,000 |
| Trade debtors | 55,000 |
| Debentures | 50,000 |
| Plant and machinery, at cost | 80,000 |
| Plant and machinery, depreciation provision, 1 April 20X0 | 30,000 |
| Fixtures and equipment, at cost | 40,000 |
| Fixtures and equipment, depreciation provision, 1 April 20X0 | 10,000 |
| Capital account, 1 April 20X0 | 51,000 |

You are also given the following information:

(a) On 31 March 20X1, the stock was valued at £40,000.

(b) Depreciation of plant and machinery and fixtures and fittings is to be calculated at the rate of 20 per cent of cost.

*Required:*

Using the vertical form of presentation, prepare the profit and loss account for the year ended 31 March 20X1 and a balance sheet as at that date.

3* The following trial balance was extracted from the books of T Bone as at 31 December 20X0.

| | £ | £ |
|---|---|---|
| Capital account | | 20,500 |
| Purchases | 46,500 | |
| Sales | | 60,900 |
| Repairs | 848 | |
| Motor car (cost) | 950 | |
| Car expenses | 318 | |
| Freehold land and buildings | 10,000 | |
| Bank balance | 540 | |
| Furniture and fittings (cost) | 1,460 | |
| Wages and salaries | 8,606 | |
| Discounts allowed | 1,061 | |
| Discounts received | | 814 |
| Drawings | 2,400 | |
| Rates and insurances | 248 | |
| Bad debts | 359 | |
| Provision for bad debts, 1 Jan 20X0 | | 140 |
| Trade debtors | 5,213 | |
| Trade creditors | | 4,035 |
| General expenses | 1,586 | |
| Stock, 1 Jan 20X0 | 6,300 | |
| | 86,389 | 86,389 |

The following matters are to be taken into account:

(a) Stock at 31 December 20X0 was £8,800.

(b) Wages and salaries outstanding at 31 December 20X0 were £318.

(c) Rates and insurances paid in advance at 31 December 20X0 amounted to £45.

(d) During the year, Bone took goods ex-stock valued at £200 for his own use. No entry has been made in the books in this respect.

(e) Depreciation is to be provided at the rate of 20 per cent on the motor and at 10 per cent on furniture and fittings.

(f) The provision for bad debts is to be reduced to £100.

*Required:*

Prepare a profit and loss account for the year ended 31 December 20X0, and a balance sheet as at that date.

4   Matt Spode is a china wholesaler. A trial balance extracted from his books on 31 December 20X0 revealed the following balances:

|  | £ | £ |
|---|---|---|
| Capital account | | 112,000 |
| ✓ Purchases | 92,400 | |
| ✓ Sales | | 157,240 |
| Premises at cost | 64,000 | |
| ✓ Motor vehicles at cost | 30,000 | |
| ✓ Accumulated depreciation of motors | | 8,200 |
| ✓ Fixtures and fittings at cost | 6,500 | |
| ✓ Accumulated depreciation – fixtures & fittings | | 1,100 |
| ✓ Motor expenses | 7,300 | |
| ✓ Rates | 2,300 | |
| Balance at bank | 4,200 | |
| ✓ Wages and salaries | 42,000 +1,200 = 43,200 | |
| Drawings | 9,600 | |
| Insurance | 2,000 – 1,200 = 800 | |
| ✓ Trade debtors | 18,000 +800 = 18,800 | |
| ✓ Provision for doubtful debts | | 560 +1,200 = |
| Trade creditors | | 15,000   1,760 |
| ✓ Sundry expenses | 16,200 | |
| Long-term loan | | 20,000 (-2000) |
| ✓ Stock at 1 Jan 20X0 | 19,250 | |
| ✓ Cash in hand | 350 | |
| | 314,100 | 314,100 |

The following information was available at 31 December 20X0:

(a)  Stock at 31 December was £22,400.
✓ (b)  There were wages and salaries of £1,200 owing.
✓ (c)  There was a payment of £1,200 on 30 September to cover 12 months' insurance.
✓ (d)  On reviewing debtors, it was discovered that a debt of £800 would not be recovered and that a further £1,200 was doubtful.
✓ (e)  Depreciation is 25 per cent reducing-balance on motors and 10 per cent straight-line on fixtures and fittings.
(f)  Loan interest at 10 per cent has not been allowed for.

*Required:*
Prepare a profit and loss account and balance sheet for Matt Spode to cover the period in question.

6,000 – m@
650 – f3f@

5    The following trial balance was drawn up from the books of A Merchant at 31 December 20X0:

| | £ | £ |
|---|---|---|
| Capital account: A Merchant | | |
| Capital account at 1 January 20X0: | | 90,000 |
| Introduced by A Merchant during the year | | 1,500 |
| Drawings during the year | 8,000 | |
| Gross profit for the year | | 27,000 |
| Stock, 31 December 20X0 | 23,600 | |
| Selling and distribution expenses | 4,500 | |
| Motor vehicles at cost | 20,000 | |
| Freehold premises at cost | 30,000 | |
| Provision for depreciation of motor | | |
| vehicles at 1 January 20X0 | | 4,000 |
| Debtors and creditors | 52,000 | 31,100 |
| Bank balance | 8,750 | |
| Rates and insurances | 6,000 | |
| Office salaries | 3,000 | |
| Office expenses | 1,250 | |
| Doubtful debts provision | | 2,500 |
| Bad debts written off | 500 | |
| Discounts | 1,500 | 3,000 |
| | 159,100 | 159,100 |

*Required:*
Prepare a profit and loss account for the year ending 31 December 20X0, and a balance sheet as at that date, taking into account the following:

(a)  Provision is to be made for depreciation of motor vehicles for the year at the rate of 20 per cent per annum on the cost of the vehicles.
(b)  The doubtful debts provision is to be adjusted to an amount equal to 5 per cent of the outstanding debtors.
(c)  The rates are £4,000 per annum and have been paid to 31 March 20X1.

6    Jackson owns a retail shop. From the few records he keeps the following information is available for the beginning and end of 20X0:

| | 1 January £ | 31 December £ |
|---|---|---|
| Cash in shop till | 350 | 250 |
| Bank overdraft | 800 | 300 |
| Stock | 2,600 | 3,300 |
| Owed by customers | 4,500 | 5,100 |
| Owed to suppliers | 1,450 | 1,900 |
| Loan from wife | 4,000 | 2,500 |

*Notes:*
(a) Jackson tells you that during 20X0 he took from the till, before making the weekly bankings:
    (i)   £200 a week for his personal expenses, and
    (ii)  £80 a week for his assistant's wages.
(b) Returned cheques show that all payments out of the bank account were to suppliers except:
    (i)   a payment of £250 to an insurance company, being £150 for the insurance of the shop's contents and £100 for the insurance of Jackson's own house, and
    (ii)  a payment of £600 for furniture for Jackson's own house.
(c) During the year Jackson had paid business expenses of £3,100 through his private bank account.
(d) Although no record of it is kept, Jackson owned the shop purchased on 1 January 19X6 for £40,000 and shop fittings and fixtures purchased on the same date for £6,000. It is agreed that fair rates of depreciation are 5 per cent per annum on cost for the shop and 10 per cent per annum on cost for the fittings and fixtures.

*Required:*
(a) Calculate Jackson's profit for 20X0.
(b) Compile a statement of the financial position of this business on 31 December 20X0.

7\* A businessman has no double-entry records of his transactions but has a cash book from which the following summary for the year ended 31 December 20X1 has been prepared:

|  | £ |
|---|---|
| Bank overdraft, 31 December 20X0 | 7,500 |
| Receipts from trade debtors | 90,000 |
| Further capital introduced | 30,000 |
| Loan from X on 31 March on which interest is payable | |
| at the rate of 5 per cent a year | 20,000 |
| Payments to trade creditors | 35,000 |
| General expenses | 9,000 |
| Wages | 12,000 |
| Drawings | 22,000 |
| On 3 December 20X0, the business had | |
| trade debtors for | 70,000 |
| trade creditors for | 50,000 |
| stocks valued at | 30,000 |
| sundry fixed assets which had cost | 60,000 |
| provision for depreciation | 10,000 |
| On 31 December 20X1 there were | |
| trade debtors for | 85,000 |
| trade creditors for | 65,000 |
| stocks valued at | 27,000 |
| sundry fixed assets which had cost | 68,000 |

Draft a profit and loss account for the year ended 31 December 20X1, and a balance sheet as at that date, providing for 5 per cent depreciation of the fixed assets on a straight-line basis.

8  From the following information relating to Snailsby, a village shopkeeper who keeps no proper books of account, prepare accounts for the year ended 30 June 20X1.

### Summary of banking account

| | £ | | £ |
|---|---|---|---|
| Opening balance | 2,600 | Payments for goods bought | |
| Shop takings paid in | 98,740 | for stock | 57,180 |
| Sale of motor van, 1 Jan 20X1 | 3,600 | Payments of business expenses | 6,720 |
| | | Private items | 5,400 |
| | | Purchase of new motor van, | |
| | | 1 Jan 20X1 | 8,500 |
| | | Closing balance | 27,140 |
| | 104,940 | | 104,940 |

| | 30 June 20X0 | 30 June 20X1 |
|---|---|---|
| | £ | £ |
| Stock in trade | 24,000 | 29,000 |
| Amount owing for goods sold | 800 | 1,250 |
| Amount owing for goods bought | 7,640 | 18,400 |
| Amount owing for business expenses | 1,320 | 730 |
| Furniture, fixtures and fittings | 6,000 | 6,000 |
| Motor van | 4,500 | 8,500 |
| Cash in hand | 800 | 350 |

Of shop takings of £6,000 which were not banked, £1,500 were used to pay various business expenses.

Estimated annual depreciation on written-down values: furniture, fixtures and fittings, 5 per cent; motor van, 20 per cent.

The cost of the van sold during the year was £5,625.

9  On 30 June 20X1 the bank column of John Smith's cash book showed a debit balance of £12,600. On examination of the cash book and bank statement the following was revealed:

(a)  Cheques amounting to £935 which were issued to creditors and entered in the cash book before 30 June were not presented for payment until after that date.

(b)  Cheques amounting to £230 had been recorded in the cash book as having been paid into the bank on 30 June, but were entered on the bank statement on 1 July.

(c)  A cheque for £70 had been dishonoured prior to 30 June, but no record of this fact appeared in the cash book.

(d)  A dividend of £340 paid direct to the bank had not been recorded in the cash book.

(e)  Bank interest and charges of £60 had been charged in the bank statement but not entered in the cash book.

(f)  No entry had been made in the cash book for a trade subscription of £15 paid by banker's order in January 20X1.

*Required:*

(a)  To make appropriate adjustments in the cash book bringing down the correct balance.

(b)  To prepare a statement reconciling the adjusted balance in the cash book with the balance shown in the bank statement for 30 June 20X1 which was a credit balance of £13,500.

10* The following balances were extracted from the books of D Stowe at 31 December 20X0:

| | £ |
|---|---|
| Sales | 15,620 |
| Purchases | 10,400 |
| Stock at 1 January 20X0 | 4,140 |
| Motor vehicles | 16,400 |
| Provision for depreciation at 1 January 20X0 | 7,900 |
| Debtors | 12,300 |
| Creditors | 15,600 |
| Cash at bank | 3,215 |
| Motor expenses | 620 |
| Rent and rates | 1,160 |
| Insurance | 185 |
| Electricity | 120 |
| Postage and telephone | 250 |
| Drawings | 4,100 |
| Sundry expenses | 270 |
| Capital at 1 January 20X0 | 14,040 |

The following matters are to be taken into account:

(i)  Stocks at 31 December 20X0 were £7,350.
(ii)  Depreciation of £1,200 is to be charged.
(iii)  Expenses accrued at 31 December 20X0 were electricity £45, telephone £65 and sundry expenses £24.
(iv)  Expenses prepaid at 31 December 20X0 were rent and rates £240, insurance £40.

*Required:*
Prepare a profit and loss account for the year ended 31 December 20X0, and a balance sheet at that date.

11  The following trial balance was extracted from the books of Tim Russell at 31 December 20X0.

| | £ | £ |
|---|---|---|
| Sales | | 105,560 |
| Purchases | 71,224 | |
| Discounts allowed and received | 1,206 | 684 |
| Carriage | 2,588 | |
| Drawings | 431 | |
| Rent, rates and insurance | 5,973 | |
| Postage and stationery | 1,213 | |
| Advertising | 1,852 | |
| Salaries and wages | 13,076 | |
| Bad debts | 1,234 | |
| Debtors | 13,170 | |
| Creditors | | 11,640 |
| Cash in hand | 312 | |
| Cash at bank | 3,054 | |
| Stock as at 1 January | 7,154 | |
| Equipment – | | |
| at cost | 48,700 | |
| accumulated depreciation | | 21,650 |
| Capital | | 31,653 |
| | 171,187 | 171,187 |

157

The following additional information as at 31 December 20X0 is available:

1 £588 of the carriage represents carriage inwards on purchases.
2 Equipment is to be depreciated at 10 per cent per annum using the straight-line method.
3 Rates have been prepaid by £213.
4 Advertising is accrued by £177.
5 Salaries and wages includes £5,500 which was paid on a weekly basis to Tim.
6 Stock at the close of business was valued at £8,221.

*Required:*
Prepare a trading and profit and loss account for the year ended 31 December 20X0 and a balance sheet as at that date.

# 12 Reporting recorded assets and liabilities

## Learning objectives

After studying this chapter you should be able to:

1  Identify the general rules for valuing fixed assets.

2  Demonstrate how the various methods used for valuing stocks affect profit measurement.

3  Explain the problem of recognizing profit or loss on long-term contracts.

4  Discuss the problems inherent in valuing intangible assets.

5  Explain how liabilities are valued in the financial statements.

In this chapter we examine further the logic and the methodology which underlie the traditional manner in which assets and liabilities are recorded and depicted on the balance sheet. First, we discuss the conventional historical cost valuation of assets and the implications of this method of valuation for balance sheet purposes. Second, we discuss the adjustments to historical cost values which are made at the stage of preparing the balance sheet. Third, we review the implications of the variety of different results obtained from traditional accounting practices. In this chapter, therefore, the concern is with historical cost valuation. The discussion of alternative valuation bases is deferred to Part 3.

The financial accounting concepts we examined in Chapter 5 may be said to have their origin in the concept of stewardship accounting. A number of these concepts have a determining influence on valuation for financial reporting purposes, and reflect the stewardship concept of financial reporting as regards the manner in which boards of directors should communicate information to shareholders about the way in which their funds have been handled. For example, when a transaction occurs, it is said that both parties to the transaction are agreed as to the exchange value of the asset involved: that value may be verified at that point, that is, it is an objective measure of value for accounting purposes. It follows, therefore, that the cost of acquiring assets has traditionally been thought to provide the best method of valuing assets for financial reporting purposes on the assumption that the objective of financial reporting is to explain to shareholders how their funds have been utilized.

Since the stewardship concept of financial reporting has its roots also in the prevention of frauds, it is interesting to note that one of the major arguments in favour of historical cost valuation is the prevention of fraud. Accountants feel that to depart from this basis of valuation would open the way to fraudulent practices since other measures of value are essentially in the nature of opinions and judgement.

Note that the concept of prudence leads to a modification of the cost concept in certain cases, and to reporting to shareholders the lowest likely value. If the net realizable value of stocks, for example, is lower than its historical cost value, the concept of prudence requires that the net realizable value be adopted.

The concept of consistency requires that once a basis of valuation has been adopted, it should not be changed except for valid reasons.

Finally, it should be noted that company law stipulates the manner in which values should be reported. In the United Kingdom, the law reflects the concepts of accounting, and in this respect we may say that in developing legal rules for financial reporting, the law has followed its tradition of codifying concepts existing among practitioners.

## The valuation of assets

The key to an understanding of the manner in which the accountant approaches the problem of valuation is to be found in the classification of assets. Fixed assets are long-term assets whose usefulness in the operations of the firm is likely to extend beyond one accounting period. They are not intended for resale, so that their economic value depends upon the expected future cash flows they are intended to generate. By contrast, current assets are those intended to be exhausted in the profit-earning operations of the next accounting period, and this includes their availability for meeting current liabilities.

There are three general rules for valuing fixed assets:

1 The enterprise should be considered as a going concern, unless the facts indicate the contrary. Thus the valuation of fixed assets should reflect the continued expectation of their usefulness to the enterprise. For this reason, their realizable value is inappropriate, and their historical cost is regarded as the most objective measure of value. Historical cost includes the original purchase price and, in addition, all other costs incurred in rendering the asset ready for use.

2 Changes in the market value of fixed assets have traditionally been ignored in the valuation process, although, as we shall see, this position has changed in recent years.

3 Losses in value attributable to wear and tear should always be recognized.

## The valuation of fixed assets

In accordance with FRS 15 'Tangible Fixed Assets', a fixed asset should initially be recorded at cost. 'Cost' here includes those costs that are directly attributable to bringing the asset into working condition for its intended use.

### The valuation of land

Land has traditionally been valued at cost despite rises or falls in market value. Cost includes broker's commission, surveying and legal fees and insurance charges. In addition, draining, levelling and landscaping costs and other improvements such as fencing, sewerage and water mains should be included, though it is quite common in the case of farm accounts for these improvements to be shown separately because of the different tax allowances which they occasionally enjoy. Land is not generally regarded as susceptible to depreciation.

# The valuation of buildings

Buildings have traditionally been valued on a historical cost basis – whether they have been acquired or constructed. Construction costs include such incidental expenses as architects' fees, inspection fees and insurance costs applicable to a construction project. Where an existing building is purchased, the costs of rendering the building suitable for its intended purpose should be added to the purchase price in arriving at its historical cost value.

The valuation process for buildings differs from that of land in two ways:

1 A cost of maintenance is involved in the repairs which have to be made from time to time in the upkeep of the building. Such maintenance expenses are charged as they are incurred to the profit and loss account. Additions and improvements to the building, which are distinguished from repairs, must be capitalized and added to the value of the building.
2 Buildings depreciate with age. The accounts value should be shown at cost less the accumulated depreciation to date.

# The valuation of plant and machinery and other fixed assets

Plant and machinery, furniture and fittings, motor vehicles, tools and sundry equipment are usually valued at historical cost with proper allowance for depreciation. Cost includes purchase price, freight charges, insurance in transit and all installation costs. As we saw in Chapter 10, the purpose of depreciation in accounting is to allocate the cost of fixed assets to the several years of their useful life to the firm.

# The revaluation of fixed assets

During the 1960s the practice of historical cost accounting for fixed assets was modified in an attempt to deal with the problems created by changing prices. Increasingly, companies adopted the practice of revaluing fixed assets, and reporting the revalued figures in the balance sheet.

The practice of revaluing assets was recognized by legislation in the United Kingdom in 1948, when the Companies Act of that year stipulated that fixed assets should be shown at cost, or, if it stands in the company's books at a valuation, the amount of the valuation. However, no guidance was given by the Act as to when a valuation should be made, except in the case of property where a 'substantial difference' between cost and market value should be indicated in the balance sheet.

Before FRS 15 was issued, companies could freely pick and choose which of their assets they wished to revalue and when, enabling them to manipulate their published results. FRS 15 does not require companies to revalue assets but it does stipulate that, where a revaluation policy is adopted, it should be applied consistently to individual classes of assets and the revaluations must be kept up-to-date. FRS 15 ensures some internal consistency in a company's accounting, but it does not directly provide for comparability between companies. Analysts of financial statements will still need to make allowances for different accounting policies on tangible fixed asset valuation.

Revaluation gains and losses should be reported in the profit and loss account.

## The valuation of current assets

Current assets consist of cash and other assets, such as debtors and stocks, which are expected to be converted into cash or to be used in the operations of the enterprise within one year. The most complex problems lie in the valuation of the three different types of stocks – raw materials, work-in-progress and finished goods. The production process may be viewed as adding value to successive categories of stocks, that is, from raw material to finished goods. Furthermore, stock values affect the profit and loss account as well as the balance sheet. Since they are an important constituent of the expenses chargeable against sales revenue, they occupy a key position in the determination of periodic profit.

## Stocks

Stocks are valued at the lower of cost and net realizable value. SSAP 9 'Stocks and Long-Term Contracts' requires that the cost of stocks 'should comprise that expenditure which has been incurred in the normal course of business in bringing the product or service to its present location and condition'. Acquisition costs reflected in stock values should be added to the costs of purchasing, of packaging and of transport. Where applicable, trade discounts should be deducted from the purchase price. There are, however, many different methods for determining the cost value of stocks, and these methods produce valuations which differ markedly from each other. A simple example serves to illustrate how three different valuation methods lead to divergent values.

**Example 1**

A firm has an opening stock of 100 items valued at £1.00 each. During the accounting period, 100 units were purchased for £1.20 each and a further 100 units were purchased for £1.30 each. There remained 100 units in stock at the end of the accounting period, that is, after 200 units had been sold for £300.

The firm is considering the effects of the undermentioned three methods of stock valuation:

1  first in, first out (FIFO);
2  last in, first out (LIFO);
3  weighted average cost.

The effects of these alternative methods may be seen from the tabulation of stock data below:

|  | Unit | Unit cost (£) | Value (£) |
| --- | --- | --- | --- |
| Opening stock | 100 | 1.00 | 100 |
| First purchase | 100 | 1.20 | 120 |
| Second purchase | 100 | 1.30 | 130 |

1 The FIFO method assumes that the oldest items in stock are used first, so that the items in stock are assumed to be the remnants of more recent purchases. The result of the application of FIFO to the given data is that the cost of goods sold during the year is taken to be £220, and the value of the closing stock is £130.

Advocates of the FIFO method argue that its underlying assumption is in accordance with conventional practice that goods purchased first are sold first, and that this method eliminates the opportunities for management to manipulate profit and stock values by selecting out of the existing stock the values which serve their purposes best. Under conditions of rising prices, FIFO requires that the stock of the earliest date and prices be deemed sold first, with the effect that the profit and loss account reflects a higher level of profit than would have been the case if current replacement costs had been used. Closing stock values are shown at the more recent acquisition prices and thus approximate current replacement costs.

2 The LIFO method assumes that the most recently purchased stocks are used first, so that the items remaining in stock at the end of the year are assumed to be the remnants of earlier purchases. Under this method, the cost of goods sold during the year is taken to be £250, and the value of the closing stock is £100. The LIFO method has the opposite effect, therefore, to that of FIFO on the measurement of profit and the valuation of closing stock.

Though LIFO approximates the replacement cost basis of valuation as regards the input of resources to the profit-earning process, it does not necessarily correspond with replacement cost valuation. LIFO reflects the latest cost price of the specific commodity, which may or may not be the actual replacement cost. In the case of seasonal buying, for example, the cost of the last purchase may not be equivalent to the current replacement cost. As a result, LIFO eliminates only an indeterminate part of the effects of specific price changes. Indeed, when sales exceed purchases, that is, when stocks are being depleted, the gap between replacement cost and LIFO may become very great. A classic example of this situation arose in the United States during the Korean War, which resulted in stock reduction on such a scale that Congressional approval was given for next-in-first-out stock valuation as a relief for taxpayers who were on the LIFO basis! A further disadvantage of the LIFO method of stock valuation is that it leads to distortions in balance sheet valuations. If the quantity in stock remains stable or increases LIFO can result in an asset balance that is substantially out of line with current costs.

3 The weighted average cost method requires the calculation of the unit cost of closing stock by means of a formula which divides the total cost of all stock available for sale during the accounting period by the physical units of stock available for sale.

The weighted average cost of the 300 units available for sale may be calculated as follows:

$$\frac{\text{Total cost of annual stock}}{\text{Total annual units of stock}} = \frac{£350}{300} = £1.167 \text{ per unit}$$

Hence, the cost of goods sold during the year is £233, while the value of the closing stock is £117. The weighted average cost method is a compromise, therefore, between the extreme points established by FIFO and LIFO respectively.

**Example 2**  The effects of different methods of stock valuation on the calculation of profit may be seen in the example given below. For simplicity, it is assumed that the business is considering a change in the method of valuation which gave an opening stock value of £100.

|  | FIFO | LIFO | Weighted average |
| --- | --- | --- | --- |
|  | £ | £ | £ |
| Purchases | 250 | 250 | 250 |
| *Add:* Opening stock | 100 | 100 | 100 |
|  | 350 | 350 | 350 |
| *Less:* Closing stock | 130 | 100 | 117 |
| Cost of goods sold | 220 | 250 | 233 |
| Sales | 300 | 300 | 300 |
| Net profit | 80 | 50 | 67 |

This simple example shows that the closing stock may be valued at £130, £100 or £117, depending on the assumptions made about the flow of costs. Three different profit figures result from using different stock valuation methods, namely £80, £50 and £67. It should be remembered that the closing stock for one year becomes the opening stock of the following year. Therefore, in the long term, there will be no difference in the calculation of the net profit of the business. It is in the short term that different stock valuation methods give different results. This fact emphasizes the significance of any changes in the stock valuation method used. Although the Companies Act 1985 allows the use of LIFO, SSAP 9 states that the LIFO method does not usually bear a reasonable relationship to actual cost where balance sheet values are concerned, and so at present LIFO is not usually appropriate as a method of stock valuation.

## Long-term contracts

Construction contracts, such as those for dams, roads, ships and industrial plants, may take years to complete. At the end of a given accounting period, a contracting company has to determine the extent to which a profit or loss should be recognized as arising only on the completion of the contract. Profit realization rests on a factual basis. On completion date, all revenues and costs are known, and the profit earned on the contract may be determined readily. If the contract covers several accounting periods, this method of accounting for profit will result in wide profit fluctuations over these periods. SSAP 9 'Stocks and Long-Term Contracts' states that 'where the business carries out long-term contracts and it is considered that their outcomes can be assessed with reasonable certainty before their conclusion, the attributable profit should be calculated on a prudent basis and included in the accounts for the period under review'. Attributable profit may be calculated as follows:

$$\text{accrued profit} = [\text{total contract price} - (\text{costs to date} + \text{estimated costs of completion})] \times \frac{\text{work certified to date}}{\text{total contract price}}$$

It is the normal practice in long-term contracts to have stages certified as completed for the purpose of determining progress payments. The issue of a work-completed certificate justifies the calculation of the profit or loss to be taken at that point. No profit should be recognized until it may be predicted with reasonable certainty. As soon as it becomes evident that a loss on completion is likely, the entire loss and not merely the accrued proportion must be recognized immediately.

**Example 3**

J Nicholl, contractor, had undertaken to extend a factory building for I McClure at a contract price of £100,000, estimating the work would take 18 months to complete. At the financial year end he estimated that costs to date were £30,000 and that a further £50,000 would be involved in completing the project. The value of work certified was £25,000. J Nicholl would estimate attributable profit as follows:

|  | £ | £ |
|---|---|---|
| Contract price |  | 100,000 |
| Costs to financial year end | 30,000 |  |
| Estimated costs to complete | 50,000 |  |
|  |  | 80,000 |
| Estimated total profit |  | 20,000 |

$$\text{attributable profit} = \frac{\text{work certified to date}}{\text{total contract price}} \times \text{estimated total profit}$$

$$= \frac{£25,000}{£100,000} \times £20,000 = £5,000$$

## Debtors

The problems associated with the valuation of debtors were discussed in Chapter 10.

## The valuation of other assets

### Investments

In financial accounting, investments are defined as shares and other legal rights acquired by a firm through the investment of its funds. Investments may be long-term or short-term, depending upon the intention of the firm at the time of acquisition. Where investments are intended to be held for a period of more than one year, they are in the nature of fixed assets: where they are held for a shorter period, they are in the nature of current assets. Shares in subsidiary and associated companies are usually not held for resale, and hence would be classified as being of the nature of fixed assets. Short-dated government stocks, for example, may provide a convenient vehicle for the investment of excess funds not immediately needed. Such short-term holdings would be classified as current assets in the balance sheet.

Investments, therefore can be found in two places on the balance sheet – fixed assets or current assets. Like any other fixed asset, long-term investments must be shown at cost less any necessary provisions. If the net realizable value falls below the cost/valuation, a provision will have to be made to cover 'diminution value'. As an alternative to showing fixed asset investments at their cost, a market valuation may be used.

Current asset investments are normally stated at the lower of their purchase price and net realizable value. Where a current asset investment has been written down to its net realizable value, but the provision which has been made proves not to have been required, then the provision must be eliminated or reduced, as appropriate. Current asset investments may also be stated at their current cost.

# Intangible assets

Intangible assets do not have any physical features, rather they represent legal rights and relationships beneficial to their owner. The most important single characteristic of intangible assets is the high degree of uncertainty regarding the value and existence of the future benefits to be received. The most common examples are:

1 patents, copyrights, and trade marks;
2 research and development costs;
3 goodwill.

## Patents

A patent is a legal right to exploit a new invention, and is obtained following the registration of its specification with the Designs Registry of the Patent Office. Patents are recorded at cost and are amortized (written off) over their effective life, usually on a straight-line basis. A similar treatment is applied to other such exclusive rights which are granted by government authority, for example copyrights and trade marks.

## Research and development costs

SSAP 13 defines research and development under three main headings:

1 *pure research:* experimental or theoretical work undertaken primarily to acquire new scientific knowledge or technical knowledge for its own sake;
2 *applied research:* original or critical investigation undertaken in order to gain new scientific or technical knowledge and directed towards a specific practical aim or objective;
3 *development:* use of scientific or technical knowledge in order to produce new or substantially improved materials, devices, products or services, to install new processes or systems prior to the commencement of commercial production or commercial applications, or to improving substantially those already produced or installed.

As regards expenditure falling within the first two categories, which may be regarded as part of a continuing operation required to maintain a company's business and its competitive position, this should be written off against revenue in the year in which expenditure is incurred. This excludes the cost of fixed assets acquired or constructed for research and development activities over a period of time which should be capitalized and written off over the useful life of the assets. Expenditure on development should be written off in the year of expenditure except in the following circumstances, where it may be deferred to future periods:

1 there is a clearly defined project;
2 the related expenditure is separately identifiable;
3 the outcome of such a project has been assessed with reasonable certainty as to its technical feasibility, and its ultimate commercial viability;
4 if further development costs are to be incurred on the same project, the aggregate of such costs, together with related production, selling and administration costs are reasonably expected to be more than covered by related future revenues; and
5 adequate resources exist, or are reasonably expected to be available, to enable the project to be completed and to provide any consequential increases in working capital.

In the circumstances defined above, development expenditure may be deferred to subsequent years, and shown on the balance sheet as an asset to the extent that its recovery can be regarded as reasonably assured. Such expenditure will be subsequently amortized against revenue. Deferred development expenditure should be reviewed at the end of each accounting period, and when the circumstances which have justified the deferral of the expenditure no longer apply then the expenditure to the extent considered irrecoverable should be written off immediately.

It is interesting to compare SSAP 13 with the US standard FASB Statement No 2, which prescribes that all expenditure on research and development should be written off in the year incurred rather than capitalized as intangible assets. The American approach is inconsistent with the accruals and matching concepts, and therefore cannot be justified in accordance with descriptive accounting theory. However, the standard has greatly simplified accounting practice in this area and has eliminated the manipulation of research and development expenditure for the purpose of adjusting reported profit.

## Goodwill

Goodwill may be described as the sum of those intangible attributes of a business which contribute to its success, such as a favourable location, a good reputation, the ability and skill of its employees and management, and its long-standing relationships with creditors, suppliers and customers. The valuation of goodwill is a controversial topic in accounting because of its vague nature and the difficulty of arriving at a valuation which is verifiable. Hence, in view of its lack of accounting objectivity, it is generally excluded from the balance sheet. Goodwill only enters the accounting system in connection with a valuation ascribed to it in the acquisition price of a business. In such a case, that portion of the purchase price which exceeds the total value of the assets, less the liabilities taken over, represents the amount paid for goodwill. At this point, therefore, there is no objective measure of the value of goodwill.

The principal objective of FRS 10 'Goodwill and Intangible Assets' is 'to ensure that purchased goodwill and intangible assets are charged to the profit and loss account in the period in which they are depleted'. Therefore, the standard is based on the matching concept which links revenues with their relevant expenses. The option of writing off goodwill immediately against reserves, which was available and almost exclusively adopted by UK companies in the era of SSAP 22, has been ruled out completely. Purchased goodwill, according to FRS 10, should be capitalized and amortized (i.e. depreciated) over its expected useful economic life, which in general will not exceed twenty years.

However, FRS 10 allows a company to amortize more slowly, or indeed not at all, if it can demonstrate that such a policy is justifiable. But if a company either amortizes goodwill over more than twenty years, or does not amortize it at all, it has to carry out an impairment test in accordance with FRS 11 'Impairment of Fixed Assets and Goodwill', which is a complex exercise.

Since the requirements of FRS 10 impact adversely on company profit and loss accounts, it is not surprising that most companies are choosing to amortize their goodwill over the maximum useful economic life generally acceptable to standard setters. Twenty years is likely to be regarded as a norm to be departed from comparatively rarely by most companies.

### Brands

There has been considerable controversy in the UK recently regarding accounting for brands. This originated from the decision of several large companies to attribute values to their brand names and include the values in their balance sheets. The objectives of these companies were to add strength to their balance sheets, improve their share prices, diminish their vulnerability to takeover and increase their borrowing power. Certainly, the balance sheets of these companies were transformed by their decision on brands. Two major issues relate to these decisions. First, there is no generally accepted method of objectively valuing brands. The uncertainties surrounding the calculations of brand values cast doubts on their usefulness to users. Second, as stated in the Introduction to this part, it is not the objective of the balance sheet to place a value on a company.

In their report to the ICAEW's Research Board, Barwise *et al.* (1989) concluded that the issue of brand accounting is 'inseparable from the accounting treatment of goodwill'. The Accounting Standards Committee adopted the same view in a technical release (TR 780) which was published in 1990:

*The ASC's analysis leads it to conclude that whatever definition is adopted the term 'brand' describes what is generally regarded for accounting purposes as goodwill. It is concluded that for such purposes brands are subsumed within goodwill and this should be accounted for in accordance with the requirements for accounting for goodwill.*

## Leases

A lease is a contract which grants the right to operate or use property for a specified period of time. The lessor retains the ownership of the asset, but conveys to the lessee the right of use in consideration of the payment of a specified rent.

The traditional approach to accounting for leases has been to record the transactions in their legal form. Thus, the lessee merely debits the rent due and payable to the profit and loss account. Since the lessee has no ownership right, no asset is shown on the balance sheet. The lessor, on the other hand, remains the owner of the asset leased, which is recorded as an asset on the lessor's balance sheet. At the same time, the rent receivable is recorded as revenue in the lessor's profit and loss account. Seen from a business viewpoint, the lessee acquires the use of an asset without needing to buy it, therefore avoiding the necessity of raising finance for its acquisition. Had the lessee acquired the asset, and borrowed money to that end, both the assets and the debt would have been recorded on the balance sheet. For this reason, leasing is frequently referred to as 'off-balance-sheet financing'. The leasing of assets is a practice which is increasing. The traditional treatment of leases in accounting may be misleading to users of financial statements wishing to assess a company's state of affairs.

SSAP 21 'Accounting for Leases and Hire Purchase Contracts' prescribes an alternative treatment, which seeks to reflect the economic nature of a leasing transaction by bringing leases on to balance sheets.

The standard's principal requirement is for lessees to capitalize finance leases, i.e. those which transfer substantially all the risks and rewards of ownership of a leased asset to the lessee. A capitalized asset is then depreciated over its useful life. A corresponding liability for future lease payments is recorded at the net present value of the future payments. The interest rate applied to find net present value is the rate 'implicit in the lease'. Part of each lease payment is treated as being payment of interest on the outstanding liability: the balance is debited against the liability. Therefore, instead of charging the full amount of lease payments against profits, the lessee charges depreciation and interest. In any one year, the sum of these two charges may exceed or fall short of the lease payment but over the period of the life of the asset the total of depreciation and interest will equal total lease payments.

In the lessor's accounts, the lease transaction is treated as though it were an outright sale. A deferred receivable is recorded which is the counterpart of the lessee's liability.

**Example 4**  A lessee enters into a lease for an item of plant. The following details apply:

| | |
|---|---|
| Fair value of asset | £100,000 |
| Residual value of asset | nil after 5 years |
| Lease terms | £25,000 for 5 years commencing 1 Jan 20X0 |

The implicit rate of return which equates five payments of £25,000 annually in advance to the purchase price of £100,000 is approximately 12.5 per cent. The lessee's profit and loss account will reflect both the finance charge and depreciation on the asset as follows:

**Profit and loss accounts**

| Year | Average amount outstanding | Charge to interest at 12.5% | Depreciation, 20% straight line | Total |
|---|---|---|---|---|
| | £ | £ | £ | £ |
| 20X0 | 75,000 | 9,375 | 20,000 | 29,375 |
| 20X1 | 59,375 | 7,422 | 20,000 | 27,422 |
| 20X2 | 41,797 | 5,225 | 20,000 | 25,225 |
| 20X3 | 22,022 | 2,978 | 20,000 | 22,978 |
| 20X4 | | | 20,000 | 20,000 |
| | | 25,000 | 100,000 | 125,000 |

The balance sheets would record the net book value of the asset and the obligations show the outstanding principal of the loan together with the accrued interest for the year. The amount of principal outstanding is apportioned to show the amount falling due within one year and that which falls due after more than one year of the balance sheet date.

**Balance sheets**

| Year | 20X0 | 20X1 | 20X2 | 20X3 | 20X4 |
|---|---|---|---|---|---|
| Cost | 100,000 | 100,000 | 100,000 | 100,000 | 100,000 |
| Depreciation | 20,000 | 40,000 | 60,000 | 80,000 | 100,000 |
| | 80,000 | 60,000 | 40,000 | 20,000 | – |
| | | | | | |
| **Current liabilities** | | | | | |
| Obligations under | | | | | |
| finance lease | 15,625 | 17,578 | 19,775 | 22,022 | – |
| Accrued interest | 9,375 | 7,422 | 5,225 | 2,978 | – |
| | 25,000 | 25,000 | 25,000 | 25,000 | – |
| **Deferred liabilities** | | | | | |
| Obligations under | | | | | |
| finance lease | 59,375 | 41,797 | 22,022 | – | – |
| | 84,375 | 66,797 | 47,022 | 25,000 | – |

In our example we have used the actuarial approach for capitalizing the finance lease. SSAP 21 states that the rule-of-78/sum-of-digits method may normally be regarded as an acceptable method. The calculations using the rule of 78 are shown below.

| Year | Rental (£) | Interest charge (£) |
|---|---|---|
| 20X0 | 25,000 × 4/10 | 10,000 |
| 20X1 | 25,000 × 3/10 | 7,500 |
| 20X2 | 25,000 × 2/10 | 5,000 |
| 20X3 | 25,000 × 1/10 | 2,500 |
| 20X4 | – | – |
| | | 25,000 |

# Provisions, contingent liabilities and contingent assets

The basic objective of FRS 12, which was promulagted in 1999, is to try to ensure that provisions, contingent liabilities and contingent assets are recognized and measured on a consistent basis.

## Provisions

Before FRS 12, provisions were often used to smooth the trend of reported profits. For example, a company could establish a general provision for future reorganization expenses in a year of very good profitability without having any actual obligation to carry out the reorganization. The decision to reorganize could then be subsequently reversed, with the effect that the provision would then be released to a future profit and loss account to improve otherwise poor results.

The changes which were introduced by FRS 12 stem from the new definition of a liability as an 'obligation of an entity to transfer economic benefits as a result of past transactions or events'. For there to be a liability there has to be a past event that has given rise to present obligations. A provision, which is in fact a liability, requires two further conditions relating to outflow of benefits and reliable measurement. Provisions should only be made when:

1  there is a present obligation arising from a past event;
2  there will be a probable outflow of economic benefits;
3  the amount can be reliably measured.

The reference to 'past event' means that there must be a condition at the balance sheet date. A decision or intention to do things in the future is not enough.

## Contingent liabilities

FRS 12 defines a contingent liability as 'a possible obligation that arises from past events and whose existence will be confirmed only by the occurence of one or more uncertain future events not wholly within the entity's control'. Under the old standard, SSAP 18 'Accounting for Contingencies', a probable liability was accrued in the financial statements. Under FRS 12 there is no such item. A probable contingent liability is instead defined as a provision. A contingent liability, under FRS 12, must never be accrued but instead should be disclosed in the notes to the accounts unless it is unlikely to be incurred.

## Contingent assets

Contingent assets usually arise from unplanned or other unexpected events that give rise to the possibility of an inflow of economic benefits to the entity. Contingent assets are not recognized in financial statements because to do so could result in the recognition of profit that may never be realized. However, when the realization of the profit is virtually certain, the related asset is not a contingent asset and its recognition is appropriate.

## Summary

It is necessary to understand the logic and methodology which underlie the recorded values of assets and liabilities in order to appreciate the nature of financial accounting information. A number of concepts surround the problem of valuation of assets and liabilities shown on profit and loss accounts and balance sheets.

This chapter examines the accounting approach to the valuation of fixed and current assets, and considers the effects of inflation in modifying the historical cost concept for fixed asset valuation. The chapter also illustrates the effects of traditional accounting practices in creating variety in the accounting treatment of different items. We also saw how FRS 12 aims to ensure that provisions, contingent liabilities and contingent assets are recognized and measured on a consistent basis.

*Reference*  Barwise, P, Higson, C, Likierman, A and Marsh, P (1989). *Accounting for Brands*, ICAEW and London Business School.

## Self-assessment question

1  Examine the problems of accounting for research and development expenditure, and explain the requirements of SSAP 13.

## Problems  *(\* indicates that a solution is to be found in the Lecturer's Guide)*

1\*  You are the Chief Accountant of a retailing company which operates from a number of department stores throughout the country. You are approached early in 20X1 by a member of your staff who is preparing the annual accounts for the Barnsley store for the year ended 31 December 20X0. He seeks your advice on the following matters:

(a)  how to treat the goodwill arising on the acquisition of a local bakery during 20X0. The Barnsley store acquired the bakery for the purpose of securing its own supply of bread. The cost was £85,000 including goodwill of £20,000;

(b)  whether to depreciate the cost of the freehold of the furniture department's warehouse which was purchased during the year. The cost was £44,000 split between land £10,000 and buildings £34,000. Legal fees of £800 were incurred;

(c)  how to value two items of stock about which he is unsure. These are:
  (i)   a large stock of over-ordered Christmas cards costing £780;
  (ii)  a stock of skateboards purchased in 19X9 for £1,000;

(d)  whether to treat an advertising campaign as an expense in 20X0 or to carry it forward to 20X1. The campaign costing £1,700 involved a series of advertisements in the *Barnsley Sun* newspaper in December 20X0 informing readers of the January sale. The sale was not as popular as it has been in recent years.

*Required:*
Draft a memorandum to your staff setting out the accounting principles to be followed in each of the above cases and give advice on the most appropriate treatment in the circumstances given.

(Problem supplied by A J Naughton)

2  The summarized balance sheet of Demiwood Ltd for 31 December 20X0 is shown below.

|  | £ | £ |
|---|---|---|
| Share capital |  | 250,000 |
| Revenue reserves |  | 95,000 |
|  |  | 345,000 |
| 10% debentures |  | 86,000 |
|  |  | 431,000 |
| Fixed assets (all tangible) |  | 295,000 |
| Current assets | 221,000 |  |
| Current liabilities | (85,000) |  |
| Net current assets |  | 136,000 |
|  |  | 431,000 |

On 1 January 20X1 Demiwood Ltd bought out the McMaltby Company which was a private company with a summarized balance sheet at 31 December 20X0 as follows:

|  | £ | £ |
|---|---|---|
| Capital |  | 62,000 |
| Represented by: |  |  |
| Tangible fixed assets |  |  |
| Freehold premises |  | 25,000 |
| Plant |  | 20,000 |
|  |  | 45,000 |
| Current assets | 32,000 |  |
| Current liabilities | (15,000) |  |
| Net current assets |  | 17,000 |
|  |  | 62,000 |

An independent valuer estimated that McMaltby's premises were worth £60,000 and its plant was worth £25,000 at replacement cost. It was also estimated that stock was undervalued by £5,000 but that debtors were overvalued by £3,000.

The agreed price for McMaltby was £120,000 which was made up of cash from a new loan of £100,000 and £20,000 in liquid assets that Demiwood already owned. The McMaltby Company ceased to exist on 1 January 20X1 and all its assets and business activities became part of Demiwood Ltd.

*Required:*

(a) Calculate the goodwill arising on the takeover of the McMaltby Company.

(b) Explain how goodwill should be treated in Demiwood's books.

(c) Prepare a summarized balance sheet for Demiwood immediately following the takeover.

3 A fire completely destroyed Arthur's timber yard and all his accounting records, during the night of 31 December 20X0.

From duplicate bank statements and circularization of his debtors and creditors, Arthur was able to ascertain the following figures.

|  | £ |
|---|---|
| Debtors, 1 January 20X0 | 5,130 |
| Creditors, 1 January 20X0 | 1,790 |
| Cash paid to creditors during the year | 22,220 |
| Cash received from debtors during the year | 30,080 |
| Creditors, 31 December 20X0 | 1,870 |
| Debtors, 31 December 20X0 | 6,050 |

Arthur's trading accounts for the two years ended 31 December 19X9 were as follows:

| | Year ended Dec 19X8 | Year ended Dec 19X9 | Year ended Dec 19X8 | Year ended Dec 19X9 |
|---|---|---|---|---|
| | £ | £ | £ | £ |
| Opening stock | 1,235 | 1,700 | Sales 18,850 | 25,740 |
| Purchases | 13,660 | 17,718 | | |
| | 14,895 | 19,418 | | |
| Less: Closing stock | 1,700 | 1,400 | | |
| | 13,195 | 18,018 | | |
| Gross profit | 5,655 | 7,722 | | |
| | 18,850 | 25,740 | 18,850 | 25,740 |

Assuming that the ratio of gross profit to sales was the same in 20X0 as in previous years, calculate the value of the stocks destroyed by fire. Submit your workings.

4* Viva Ltd does not keep records of stock movements. A physical stocktaking is made at the end of each quarter and priced at cost. This figure is used for compiling quarterly accounts. Draft accounts have been prepared for the year ended 31 March 20X0, but have not been completed as the details of the stock count on 31 March 20X0 have been mislaid and cannot be found. The company operates on a gross-profit markup of $33\frac{1}{3}$ per cent of cost.
You have ascertained the following facts:

(a) the total of sales invoiced to customers during January, February and March 20X1 was £53,764. This figure includes £4,028 relating to goods despatched on or before 31 December 20X0. The total of the goods despatched to customers before 31 March 20X1 but invoiced in the following month was £5,512;

(b) the total of purchase invoices entered in the purchase day book during January, February and March 20X1 was £40,580 and this figure includes £2,940 in respect of goods received on or before 31 December 20X0. Invoices relating to goods received in March 20X1 but which were not entered in the purchase day book until April 20X1 totalled £3,880;

(c) the value of the stock at cost on 31 December 20X0 was £42,640;

(d) in the stock sheets at that date;
  (i) the total of one page was over-cast by £85;
  (ii) 120 items, the cost of which was £2 each, had been priced at 40p each;
  (iii) the total of the stock in one section, which was £5,260, had been included in the summary as £5,620.

*Required:*
Show how you would arrive at the figure for the stock at cost as on 31 March 20X1.

(Problem supplied by A J Naughton)

5   Purchases and sales data for the first three years of a firm's operation were as follows (purchases are listed in order of acquisition):

|            | 19X8              | 19X9              | 20X0              |
|------------|-------------------|-------------------|-------------------|
|            | £                 | £                 | £                 |
| Sales      | 12,000 units @ 50 | 15,000 units @ 60 | 18,000 units @ 65 |
| Purchases  | 4,000 units @ 22  | 5,500 units @ 32  | 7,000 units @ 40  |
|            | 6,000 units @ 25  | 6,000 units @ 34  | 4,500 units @ 43  |
|            | 5,000 units @ 30  | 4,000 units @ 37  | 5,000 units @ 45  |

*Required:*
(a)  Prepare a schedule showing the number of units on hand at the end of each year.
(b)  Compute the year-end stocks for each of the three years using (i) FIFO, (ii) LIFO, (iii) average cost.
(c)  Calculate the gross profit for each of the three years based on (i) FIFO, (ii) LIFO and (iii) weighted average.
(d)  Which method of stock valuation do you consider the most appropriate? Why?

6   Z Ltd is engaged upon a contract the price of which is £250,000. At 31 December 20X0 the expenditure on the contract is as follows:

|                                                      | £      |
|------------------------------------------------------|--------|
| Materials issued from store                          | 42,000 |
| Wages                                                | 39,820 |
| Expenses directly chargeable to the contract         | 12,130 |
| Materials purchased and delivered direct to the site | 4,910  |
| Plant in use on site valued at                       | 6,840  |
| Proportion of overhead charges                       | 790    |

The amount of work completed to date as certified by the architect after 20 per cent retention money was £100,000. Materials in stock at the site were valued at £970 and depreciation is to be charged at 5 per cent. Prepare the contract account showing the proportion of profit you would advise should be taken to the profit and loss account.

7   Builders Ltd commenced work on 1 July 20X0 on a contract the agreed price of which was £250,000. Expenditure incurred during the year to 30 June 20X1 was as follows:

Wages £60,000; plant £17,500; materials £42,500; sundry expenses £4,000; and head office charges allocated to the contract amounted to £5,500. Part of the plant which had cost £1,300 was sold for £1,500.

Of the contract price £100,000 representing 80 per cent of the work certified had been received by 30 June 20X1 and on that date the value of the plant on the site was deemed to be £4,500 and that of the unused materials £1,250. Work costing £12,500 had been completed but not certified at 30 June 20X1.

It was decided to estimate what further expenditure would be incurred in completing the contract for the purpose of computing the estimated total profit that would be made on the contract and to take to the credit of the profit and loss account for the year a proper proportion thereof.

The estimate of additional expenditure that would be required, based on the assumption that the contract would be finished in six months' time, was as follows:

(a) Wages to complete £52,800.
(b) Materials in addition to those in stock on 30 June 20X1 would cost £35,000.
(c) Sundry expenses would amount to £1,800.
(d) Plant in addition to plant in hand at 30 June 20X1 would cost £6,500 and the residual value of plant at 31 December 20X1 would be £3,750.
(e) Contingencies would require a further £3,500.

Prepare a contract account at 30 June 20X1.

8* Rover Company leases certain heavy equipment from the London Leasing Company under an eight-year lease. The economic life of the equipment is ten years. No residual value will remain at the end of that period. The lease agreement calls for eight annual payments of £150,000 beginning at the inception of the lease. The first payment is to be made on 1 January 20X1. Each payment thereafter falls to be made on the first day of the year. The fair value of the equipment is £1 million. Rover Company depreciates similar assets by the straight-line method.

*Required:*
Show how the transaction would be recorded in Rover Company's final accounts.

# 3 The application of financial accounting method to corporate enterprises

# 13 Companies: their nature and regulation

### Setting the scene

KPMG, the accounting firm appointed to investigate accounting irregularities at Versailles, the troubled finance group, has stopped working for the company. It is understood Versailles terminated the relationship after KPMG indicated it was unlikely to endorse its accounting policies. A person close to KPMG said 'It came down to an issue of whether their accounting policies were appropriate for the product on the market. We didn't think they were.' The company, valued at £631 million on suspension, provided complex bridge financing to small companies importing goods.

*(Financial Times, 5 January 2000)*

### Learning objectives

After studying this chapter you should be able to:

1 Distinguish between share capital and loan capital.

2 Explain 'gearing' and illustrate its significance for ordinary shareholders.

3 Discuss the various means by which financial reporting is regulated in the UK.

4 Describe Chapters 1 and 3 of the ASB's Statement of Principles for Financial Reporting.

Companies are created and regulated by law. By a legal fiction, the legal personality of a business enterprise established as a company is separate from the legal personalities of the various individuals having an interest therein, whether as owners, managers or employees. This means, for example, that although a company has no physical life, it may nevertheless own property, enter into contracts, sue and be sued in a court of law and undertake any activity consistent with the objectives envisaged at the time of its creation. It acts through its directors with whom it enters into contracts of employment.

The proprietors of a company are recognized in law as being those persons owning its capital. The capital is divided into shares or stock, and by acquiring shares, investors become shareholders. As evidence of their legal title to the shares they own, shareholders are issued with share certificates. Shares are transferable property rights, and may be negotiated either privately or through a stock exchange. Stock exchanges have rules for granting permission for the shares of individual companies to be traded on them, or to be 'listed on the Stock Exchange', which is the term given to such permission.

Companies are usually established by the formal registration of documents with a Public Registrar charged with enforcing statutory provisions in respect of enterprises operating as companies. In the United Kingdom, for example, individuals wishing to incorporate themselves for the purpose of carrying on trade are called promoters, and it is their responsibility to arrange for the process of incorporation. This involves lodging a number of documents with the Registrar of Companies and paying the required fees. The two most important documents are the memorandum of association, which defines the powers and objectives of the companies, and the articles of association which contain the rules for its internal regulation. The name, objectives and the capital clauses are found in the memorandum of association. For our purposes, the capital clause is the most important, for it states the number, classes and nominal value of the shares which the company has power to issue. The authorized capital is stated in the capital clause, and it is the maximum capital which the company may raise. The capital clause may be altered, however, by a formal process.

A company obtains capital by the issue of shares. Investors are invited to apply for shares. They usually have to pay a portion of the purchase price on application and the balance when the shares have been formally allotted to them. The capital clause states the value of each share as a nominal figure. Thus, the authorized capital may be stated to consist of 1 million shares of £1 each, giving the company an authorized capital of £1 million. When a company offers shares for sale, however, it may set a price which is higher than the nominal value, and it need not offer for sale all the shares which it is authorized to sell. That portion of the authorized capital which is sold is called the issued capital.

Once shares have been issued, they become the property of the individual investors who have acquired them, and these investors are free to sell their shares to anyone. The sale price is negotiated between buyer and seller, and the deal may be effected through a Stock Exchange if the shares are quoted shares. The seller transfers shares formally to the buyer by notice to the company, and the buyer is registered in the register of shareholders as the new shareholder. Shares transferred in this way are known as registered shares. An alternative type of shareholding, which is restricted by law in some countries, is known as a bearer share. A bearer share is more easily transferred than a registered share since the share certificate does not detail the name of the shareholder who is not registered in the register of shareholders. Consequently, bearer shares are transferable by hand.

A company receives only the issue price of a share. The legal effect of shareholding is to grant ownership rights in respect of the fraction of capital represented by the share, and a right to receive the appropriate portion of corporate net profit distributed in the form of a dividend. Companies usually retain a portion of net profit for reinvestment, and distribute the balance as dividends. We will consider shortly the accounting consequences of the distinction made between retained profit and distributable profit.

The distinction between ownership and management is one of the most distinctive features of corporate activity. As owners, shareholders may be considered as having ultimate control over the activities of the company through their right to appoint directors. The rights of shareholders to exercise control over the affairs of companies are defined by legislation. Once appointed, directors exercise day-to-day control of the company's affairs, and although they are accountable to shareholders, the diffusion of shares among many shareholders usually places directors in a very strong position *vis-à-vis* shareholders. Although they are treated as stewards of corporate assets on behalf of shareholders, the effective power to make decisions of major importance in respect of those assets lies almost entirely in their hands.

Social change is affecting the traditional method of regulating corporate enterprise in a number of ways. First, the recognition of the right of employees to share managerial responsibility is an important feature of the democratization of corporate control. Some European countries have already legislated for two-tier boards of directors, and this feature has been included in the *Societas Europea SE*, the European Company which is formed by registration in the European Commercial Register kept by the Court of the European Communities in Luxembourg. Employee participation in the management of companies is an explicit admission that the interests of employees are as important as those of shareholders. Second, the concept of social accounting, which we discuss in Part 4, further broadens the classical notion of stewardship as a definition of the function of directors to include a responsibility to all sections of society having an interest in the activities of corporate enterprises. Thus, consumers, as well as the local community, are included in the group of those having a vested interest in the nature of corporate activity.

## Financial accounting implications of corporate status

Corporate status, as distinct from the one-person type of business which we examined in Section 2, implies a distinctive treatment of the capital structure and of the allocation of the net profit as between dividends and retained profit.

The normal procedure for dealing with the financial accounting implications of corporate status is to establish a separation of functions between the accountant and the company secretary. The former is usually concerned with the financial accounting procedures directed at recording business transactions: the latter usually maintains the register of shareholders, including such details as the record of shareholders' names and addresses, class and number of shares held, instructions regarding correspondence and payment of dividends. Much of the routine work of the secretary's department in this respect involves recording the transfer of shares and the payment of yearly dividends to shareholders. The specialized nature of share transfer work, as well as its sheer volume in some corporations, often requires a separate department under a share transfer registrar. In such cases, the share transfer registrar is a senior official of the company.

The financial accounting aspects of the share capital with which the accountant is concerned consist of the ledger records associated with shareholders, that is, the share capital account, the dividend account, and those accounts retaining profit in the form of capital or current reserves. We will deal with the nature of these accounts shortly. These accounts are concerned with aggregate figures.

**Example 1**   Excel plc is a public company having a share capital of one million £1 shares held in different proportions by 20,000 individual shareholders. The detailed records of the individual shareholding are kept by the registrar, and the accountant will keep the following ledger record:

**Share capital account**

|  |  |  |
|---|---|---|
|  | Sundry shareholders | £1,000,000 |

# The capital structure

The capital structure may consist of both share capital and loan capital, and represents the long-term finance available to the company, as distinct from the short-term finance represented by the credit facilities offered by trade creditors and bank overdrafts. Shareholders are regarded at law as owners. The share capital is at risk, and in the event of business failure shareholders may lose all the capital invested since they rank last as claimants on the residual assets of the corporation. By contrast, loan capital is made available by creditors on a long-term basis. Thus, a company may invite the public to supply loan capital for a period of, say, five years at a rate of interest of, say, 10 per cent. Individuals may offer varying sums, and receive from the company a debenture certificate. Debentures frequently involve the mortgage of specific corporate assets to the body of debenture-holders represented by a trustee for debenture-holders, and in the event of the company defaulting in any way on the conditions of the debenture instrument, the specified assets may be seized and sold on behalf of the debenture-holders. The charge on the corporate assets may be fixed, as we have mentioned, or floating, that is, not be specific as regards any particular assets but applying to all corporate assets. Debenture-holders are guaranteed, therefore, both repayment of loan capital and interest as specified in the conditions of issue. It is the duty of the trustee for the debenture-holders to act before any loss threatens debenture-holders. Very large and financially strong companies may be able to raise long-term loans without mortgaging their assets to lenders. They issue certificates of indebtedness described as unsecured notes, which also carry an obligation to pay interest and to redeem at the end of the stated period. Holders of unsecured notes rank as ordinary creditors in liquidation.

Shares, debentures and unsecured notes may all be quoted on the Stock Exchange and transacted between buyers and sellers. Appropriate registers of debenture-holders and holders of unsecured notes must be kept by the company.

The share capital may consist of different classes of shares, but the two most common classes of shares are preference shares and ordinary shares.

Preference shares give preferential rights as regards dividends, and often as regards the repayment of capital on winding-up. Preference shares may be issued as redeemable preference shares, that is, they may be redeemed and cancelled by the company. Preference shares may also be issued as cumulative preference shares, which means that if the net profit of any particular year is insufficient to pay a dividend to preference shareholders of this class, the right to receive a dividend for that year is carried forward to the following year, and so on, until such time as the accumulated dividend entitlement may be declared and paid out of profits. Preference shareholders are usually entitled to a fixed dividend expressed as a percentage of the nominal value of the share. Thus, a holder of 100 preference shares of £1 each carrying a fixed dividend rate of 8 per cent will be entitled to a total yearly dividend of £8. However, preference shares may also be issued as participating preference shares, meaning that in addition to the fixed-dividend-rate entitlement, they participate in the remainder of the net profit with ordinary shareholders. It is common for conditions to be imposed limiting the participating rights of such shares to allow for a minimum level of dividend for ordinary shareholders. Thus, a participating preference share may carry a right to a fixed dividend of 8 per cent and a right to participate in the remaining net profit after the ordinary shareholders have received their dividend.

181

Ordinary shares provide the bulk of the share capital. In return for bearing the risk involved in financing corporate activities, ordinary shareholders enjoy the right to the whole of the net profit – either as dividends or, if retained, as the increased value of net corporate assets – subject to the rights of preference shareholders. Some companies obtain the whole of the share capital in the form of ordinary shares. The reason for issuing a variety of shares – preference shares of different classes and ordinary shares – is to tap the funds held by investors with differing investment needs. A young person with money to invest will be looking for growth in the value of their capital and will be attracted to buying ordinary shares in a company having good prospects of expansion. A retired person, looking for a safe investment providing a steady income, may wish to hold some preference shares. Institutional buyers, such as pension funds and insurance companies, also have a wish to hold shares of different classes. Deferred shares are a separate class of shares to both preference and ordinary shares, and may be issued in restricted numbers to managers of the company. In such a case, deferred shares carry an entitlement to dividend only after the ordinary shareholders have received a specified dividend rate.

## Gearing and the capital structure

The nature of the capital structure has important implications for financial management purposes, and in this respect, the gearing is an important consideration.

The gearing expresses the relationship between the proportion of fixed interest (loan capital) and fixed dividend (preference share capital) to ordinary shares. A company with a large proportion of fixed-interest- and fixed-dividend-bearing capital to ordinary capital is said to be highly geared.

**Example 2**  Companies Alpha, Beta and Gamma have the same total capital which is issued as follows:

|  | Alpha | Beta | Gamma |
|---|---|---|---|
|  | £ | £ | £ |
| **Share capital** |  |  |  |
| 8% Preference shares of £1 each | 40,000 | 10,000 | – |
| Ordinary shares of £1 each | 20,000 | 80,000 | 100,000 |
| **Loan capital** |  |  |  |
| 7% Debentures of £100 each | 40,000 | 10,000 | – |
|  | 100,000 | 100,000 | 100,000 |

The gearing of these three companies may be calculated as follows:

| 1 | Alpha | (40,000 + 40,000) : | 20,000 | or | 4 : 1 |
|---|---|---|---|---|---|
| 2 | Beta | (10,000 + 10,000) : | 80,000 | or | 0.25 : 1 |
| 3 | Gamma | : | 100,000 | or | 0 |

Alpha is, therefore, the most highly geared company.

The importance of the gearing is that fluctuations in net profit may have dispropor-tionate effects upon the return accruing to ordinary shareholders in the case of a highly geared company, and hence on the pricing of ordinary shares on the Stock Exchange. Directors looking for stability in the price of the company's ordinary shares will be swayed by this consideration when faced with raising further capital. The net cost of debenture interest may be lower than the net cost in dividends of fur-ther issues of ordinary shares. Similarly, fixed dividend preference shares may also cost less than issuing ordinary shares. The following example shows the effects of fluctuating net profit levels on the return to ordinary shareholders, assuming that the available net profit is wholly distributed.

**Example 3** The consequence of fluctuations in net distributable profit on ordinary shareholders in Alpha Company, Beta Company and Gamma Company geared in the ratios established in the example above may be judged as follows:

| | Alpha | | Beta | | Gamma | |
|---|---|---|---|---|---|---|
| | £ | £ | £ | £ | £ | £ |
| **Assuming net profit of £15,000** | | | | | | |
| Net profit | | 15,000 | | 15,000 | | 15,000 |
| 8% Preference shares | 3,200 | | 800 | | – | |
| 7% Debentures | 2,800 | | 700 | | – | – |
| | | 6,000 | | 1,500 | | |
| Available for ordinary shares | | 9,000 | | 13,500 | | 15,000 |
| | | | | | | |
| Maximum dividend for ordinary shareholders | $\frac{9,000}{20,000}$ | = 45% | $\frac{13,500}{80,000}$ | = 16.875% | $\frac{15,000}{100,000}$ | = 15% |
| | | | | | | |
| **Assuming net profit of £10,000** | | | | | | |
| Net profit | | 10,000 | | 10,000 | | 10,000 |
| 8% Preference shares | 3,200 | | 800 | | – | |
| 7% Debentures | 2,800 | | 700 | | – | – |
| | | 6,000 | | 1,500 | | |
| Available for ordinary shares | | 4,000 | | 8,500 | | 10,000 |
| | | | | | | |
| Maximum dividend for ordinary shareholders | $\frac{4,000}{20,000}$ | = 20% | $\frac{8,500}{80,000}$ | = 10.625% | $\frac{10,000}{100,000}$ | = 10% |

Hence, in a highly geared company such as Alpha, a fall of $33\frac{1}{3}$ per cent in net profit has produced a fall of 56 per cent in the maximum dividend payable to ordinary shareholders, and in Gamma, a $33\frac{1}{3}$ per cent fall in profits has produced a $33\frac{1}{3}$ per cent fall in dividends.

## Accounting procedures applied to the capital structure

### The share capital

We mentioned earlier that a distinction exists between the authorized capital and the issued capital. The former is the maximum limit in the total value of shares of different classes which a company is permitted to issue under the conditions of its registration; the latter is the nominal value of shares of different classes which have been issued. The reason why companies do not establish the value of the authorized capital greatly in excess of their anticipated requirement lies in the taxes imposed on the value of the authorized capital, which deter promoters from incurring unnecessary expenses.

The financial accounting procedures applied to the treatment of the share capital may be said to have two main objectives:

1 recording the issue of shares and the consideration received in respect of such shares;
2 providing information about the share capital in the balance sheet.

We do not propose to deal with the procedures applied to the redemption of redeemable preference shares, or those applied to the issue of bonus shares, since these procedures are not essential to the thesis of this book. It may be mentioned, however, that bonus shares are commonly issued free of cost to existing shareholders in proportion to their shareholdings by way of distribution of accumulated profits.

### Recording the issue of shares

It has become the practice for companies seeking to make an issue of shares to the public to employ the services of merchant bankers not only to act as advisers but also to deal with the details of the issue, such as issuing the prospectus advertising the offer of the shares for sale, recording the applications from investors and the monies received with the applications, the allotment of shares to individual shareholders where an offer has been oversubscribed, and arranging for the shares undersubscribed to be taken up by the underwriters who have acted as insurers in respect of the issue of the shares in return for a commission. The detailed accounting procedures for dealing with the issue of shares need not detain us, for they have become part and parcel of a rather specialized aspect of work.

The central financial problems relating to the issue of shares concern the nature of the shares to be issued, that is, whether to issue preference or ordinary, how many to issue and the price to be attached to such shares. All these are problems in respect of which a company will seek expert advice. The financial accounting procedures which we shall consider reflect merely the outcome of the decisions taken.

We mentioned earlier that shares are described in the memorandum of association as having a nominal value. This practice applies in the United Kingdom, although in United States, for example, it is the practice for shares not to have a nominal value, and they are issued as 'shares of no par value'. This means that the recorded issue value of the share capital reflects the price determined at the time of issue.

In the United Kingdom, the practice of attaching a nominal value to shares makes it possible for an issue of shares to be made:

1  *at par* – that is, a share having a nominal value of £1 is issued at a price of £1;
2  *at a premium* – that is, a share having a nominal value of £1 is issued at a price higher than £1;
3  *at a discount* – that is, a share having a nominal value of £1 may be issued at a price which is less than £1. In practice, legislation attaches very strict conditions to the issue of shares at a discount.

A number of considerations affect share issues, not the least of which is that the issue should be a financial success. This means that the company should receive a realistic price for the shares offered and that the issue should be wholly subscribed.

The following examples show the accounting procedures applied to the issue of ordinary shares at par and at a premium.

### The issue of ordinary shares at par

The Omega Co Ltd has issued 2 million £1 ordinary shares at par. The purchase price has been paid on application and allotment and the company's cash book has been debited with the amount received. The entries in the company's accounts are as follows:

**Ordinary share capital account**

|  |  | Sundry ordinary shareholders | £2,000,000 |
|---|---|---|---|

**Sundry ordinary shareholders**

| Ordinary share capital | £2,000,000 | Cash | £2,000,000 |
|---|---|---|---|

**Cash book**

| Sundry ordinary shareholders | £2,000,000 |  |  |
|---|---|---|---|

The detailed list of individual shareholdings does not form part of the financial accounting system, but rather of the register of shareholders. Hence, the sundry ordinary shareholders account does not exist as such: it is represented by the register of shareholders. From a financial accounting viewpoint, only the ordinary share capital account and the cash book are significant.

### The issue of ordinary shares at a premium

The Onedin Co Ltd has issued two million £1 ordinary shares at a premium of 50 pence, that is, at £1.50 a share. The purchase price has been paid on application and allotment and the company's cash book has been debited. The practice in the United Kingdom is to separate the par value of the shares from the share premium. Legislation permits adjustments to the share premium account, for example in redeeming preference shares at a premium.

The accounting entries are as follows:

**Ordinary share capital account**

|  |  | Sundry ordinary shareholders | £2,000,000 |
|---|---|---|---|

**Share premium account**

|  |  | Sundry ordinary shareholders | £1,000,000 |
|---|---|---|---|

**Sundry ordinary shareholders**

| Ordinary share capital | £2,000,000 | Cash | £3,000,000 |
|---|---|---|---|
| Share premium | 1,000,000 |  |  |
|  | £3,000,000 |  | £3,000,000 |

**Cash book**

| Sundry ordinary shareholders | £3,000,000 |  |  |
|---|---|---|---|

As we explained earlier, the sundry ordinary shareholders do not exist as a formal account, but are found in the register of shareholders. Consequently, the only accounts of significance are the ordinary share capital account, the share premium account and the cash book.

In the United States and Canada, the practice for the last fifty years has been to issue shares of no par value. This simplifies the accounting process, for there is no need to have a share premium account and the share capital account shows the amount actually received from the sale of shares. The case against shares of fixed nominal value is that they bear no relation to the real value of the issued shares, and hence the nominal value is virtually meaningless except as a measure of growth.

The procedures outlined above apply equally to the treatment of other classes of shares.

# Loan capital

There is very little difference in the accounting treatment of loan and share capital. Registers of debenture-holders and of holders of unsecured notes are kept, and the method of issue is identical to that of shares in so far as the issuing process tends to be conducted on behalf of the company by merchant bankers. Debentures may be issued at par, at a premium or at a discount. Premiums received on the issue of debentures are regarded as capital profits, and are usually transferred to a capital reserve account. Discounts allowed on the issue of debentures are treated as finance costs, as required by FRS 4, 'Accounting for Capital Instruments'.

**Example 4**  Hightrust Investment Company offers for sale 10,000 9 per cent debentures in units of £10 at a premium of 5 per cent. The debentures are repayable on 31 December 20X8. The accounting entries are as follows:

**9% Debentures 20X8 account**

| | |
|---|---|
| | Sundry debenture holders £100,000 |

**Capital reserve account**

| | |
|---|---|
| | Sundry debenture holders £5,000 |

**Cash book**

| | |
|---|---|
| Sundry debenture holders £105,000 | |

As in the case of the issue of shares, details of individual debenture-holders would be found in the register of debenture-holders.

## Distributable profits

The important difference between a limited company and a sole trader lies in the manner in which periodic profit is appropriated. In the case of the sole trader, the net profit belongs to the owner and is transferred to the capital account at the end of the accounting period. By contrast, once the net profit of a company has been ascertained, the board of directors have to decide the proportion which should be paid out to shareholders as dividends and the proportion which should be retained. The amount of dividend declared from time to time should be determined by sound financial principles that ensure that the profits calculated as available for distribution have been established in accordance with accepted accounting principles and the relevant company law.

In considering the manner in which the net profit should be appropriated, the following factors are important:

1 Adequate provision should be made in respect of corporation tax payable on the net profit for the year. In this connection, under- or overprovisions in respect of previous years have to be taken into account.
2 Adequate provision should be made for anticipated expenditure on the replacement of fixed assets. During periods of inflation, in particular, the cost of replacing fixed assets exceeds amounts provided for depreciation.
3 Adequate provision should be made for capital expenditure which is to be financed out of earnings.

The Companies Act 1980 introduced complex provisions that deal with distributed profits. The Act provided that no company may make a distribution except out of accumulated realized profits less accumulated realized losses. There is one exception to this rule. If a company has revalued a fixed asset, and subsequently calculates depreciation on the higher revalued figure, the depreciation attributable to the excess may be counted as a realized profit.

It is quite common for companies to distribute only about half their after-tax profit to shareholders. Usually an interim dividend is declared during the account

187

period in anticipation of a final dividend, which is declared after the final results for the year have been ascertained.

# The regulation of financial reporting

Financial reporting in the UK is regulated by three major means: company law, accounting standards and the Listing Agreement of the Stock Exchange. Company law provides a broad framework of legal regulations which is supplemented by the accounting standards provided by the accounting profession. The Listing Agreement augments disclosure requirements for companies whose shares are listed on the Stock Exchange. Other influences on financial reporting are three reports on corporate governance which appeared in the 1990s, and international considerations which are playing an increasing part in the setting of UK standards.

## Legal regulations

Since the first general legislation on companies was enacted in 1844, numerous Companies Acts have introduced varying amounts of change into the legal require-ments for accounting disclosure. The current framework is the result of legislation over a period of over forty years beginning with the Companies Act 1948 which was added to by subsequent acts in 1967, 1976, 1980 and 1981, as consolidated in the Companies Act 1985 and the Companies Act 1989.

The introduction of the Companies Act 1948 marked a radical departure from the approach adopted in previous legislation. For the first time emphasis was placed on the importance of providing information in financial reports to assist in investment deci-sions. Amongst the major provisions of the Act were: the subjection of the profit and loss account to audit; the requirement for group accounts; a considerable extension in the requirements regarding individual items of information which should be disclosed; and, most importantly for subsequent developments in company financial reporting, the requirement that auditors report whether financial statements present a 'true and fair view' of the company's financial position and profitability. The criterion of a 'true and fair view' superseded that of a 'true and correct view' which first appeared in 1844. The Companies Act 1948 provided that the 'true and fair view' shall override all other requirements for the Companies Act as to matters to be included in a company's financial reports. This means that information not specifically required by law must be provided in order to give a true and fair view. Despite its overriding importance, the interpretation of the 'true and fair view' has not been without its difficulties.

In 1983 the Accounting Standards Committee (ASC) obtained a written opinion from counsel on the meaning of 'true and fair' with particular reference to the role of accounting standards. The ASC intended to take account of the opinion in all its future work. The opinion states that financial statements will not be true and fair unless the information they contain is sufficient in quantity and quality to satisfy the reasonable expectations of the readers to whom they are addressed. But the expecta-tions of the readers will have been moulded by the practices of accountants because, by and large, they will expect to get what they ordinarily get and that, in turn, will depend upon the normal practices of accountants. Therefore, the courts will treat compliance with accepted accounting principles as prima-facie evidence that the financial statements are true and fair.

The opinion also states that since the function of the ASC was to formulate what it considered should be generally accepted accounting principles, the value of a Statement of Standard Accounting Practice to a court is:

1 as a statement of professional opinion as to what readers may expect in financial statements which are true and fair;
2 that readers expect financial statements to comply with standards.

The opinion concludes, therefore, that financial statements which depart from standards may be held not to be true and fair, unless a strong body of professional opinion opts out of applying the standard. The Companies Act 1989 introduced a requirement to state whether the accounts have been prepared in accordance with applicable accounting standards and to give details of, and the reason for, any material departures. According to a more recent legal opinion, the effect of the 1989 Act is to 'increase the likelihood that the courts will hold that in general compliance with accounting standards is necessary to meet the true and fair view requirement' (Arden, 1993).

## Regulation by the accountancy profession

We saw in Chapter 6 that the Accounting Standards Board (ASB) replaced the Accounting Standards Committee in 1990. The ASB has the power to issue accounting standards (Financial Reporting Standards or FRSs) on its own authority and is part of a larger structure as shown in Figure 2.14.

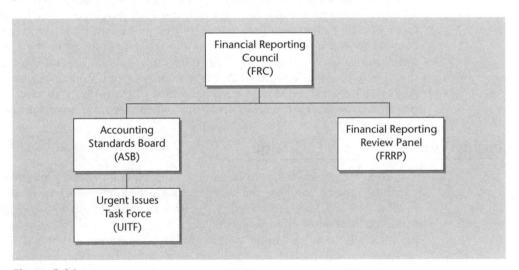

**Figure 2.14**

The Financial Reporting Council gives guidance to the ASB on priorities, work programme and issues of public concern, and acts as an instrument for promoting good accounting practice.

The Financial Reporting Review Panel examines accounts, either on its own initiative or in response to outside representations, in cases where departures from standard accounting practice have occurred, and an issue of principle is involved or the accounts do not give a true and fair view. The Review Panel may invite the company's auditors and directors to give evidence. If it concludes that the accounts need revision in order to give a true and fair view, it will notify the Stock Exchange and any other relevant professional body, and may publish its findings. In the last resort, the Review Panel may bring civil proceedings against a company which will not revise its accounts in order to give a true and fair view. This power is effectively delegated by the Companies Act 1989.

The aims of the ASB are as follows: to establish and improve standards of financial accounting and reporting, for the benefit of users, preparers and auditors of financial information. The ASB intends to achieve its aims by:

1  developing principles to guide it in establishing standards and to provide a framework within which others can exercise judgement in resolving accounting issues (these principles will be examined later in this chapter);
2  issuing new accounting standards, or amending existing ones, in response to evolving business practices, new economic developments and deficiencies being identified in current practice;
3  addressing urgent issues promptly.

As we saw in Chapter 6, the ASB's consultative process includes, first, the issue of Working Drafts for discussion (DDs); these then become Financial Reporting Exposure Drafts (FREDs); this process results in the publication of Financial Reporting Standards (FRSs).

The way in which the ASB addresses urgent issues promptly is through the UITF, which is a committee of the ASB. The UITF's main role is to assist the ASB in areas where an accounting standard or a Companies Act provision exists, but where unsatisfactory or conflicting interpretations have developed or seem likely to develop. In such circumstances it operates by seeking a voluntary consensus as to the accounting treatment that should be adopted. The UITF operates within the framework of the law and the principles established in accounting standards and other pronouncements of the ASB. UITF pronouncements, which are issued in the form of abstracts, are therefore intended to be complied with by companies when preparing financial statements.

## Regulation by the Stock Exchange

Any company which wishes to obtain a full listing and hence a quotation on the Stock Exchange must comply with the listing requirements in the rules issued under the authority of the Stock Exchange Council. These impose additional disclosure requirements such as the publication of interim reports and a statement that shows how much of a company's bank loans and other borrowings are repayable within one and two years, between two and five years and in excess of five years. Listed companies are also expected to comply with the provisions of accounting standards and companies are required to give reasons for any significant departures from standard accounting practice.

## Corporate governance

The Combined Code on Corporate Governance (1998) was an important step in improving company reporting. It brought together the work of three committees which were set up because of the low level of confidence in financial reporting and auditing. A series of spectacular failures coupled with criticism of board accountability over matters such as directors' pay suggested that corporate governance required improvement.

The code establishes principles of good corporate governance related to a well-balanced board of directors and the information it receives from management, relations with shareholders, internal audit, and control and risk management. With regard to the last item, the board is required to disclose that there is an on-going process for identifying, evaluating and managing the significant risks faced by the company; that this process has been in place for the year under review and up to the annual report approval date; and that it is regularly reviewed by the board.

The London Stock Exchange requires UK listed companies to make a statement of compliance with the Combined Code in their annual report.

## International influences

Two international bodies which have influenced accounting regulations in the UK are the European Union (EU) and the International Accounting Standards Committee (IASC).

The EU has a broad commitment to economic and policitical union and harmonization of laws. To encourage capital movement and capital formation, the EU is harmonizing the generally accepted accounting principles of member countries. The accounting harmonization effort is a part of a broader programme by the EU to harmonize the many types of policies related to economic activities. In order to achieve its harmonization objectives the EU has issued various Directives which are EU laws that member states are obliged to incorporate into their own national laws. The Directives most relevant to financial accounting are the Fourth, Seventh and Eighth. These Directives are considered in Chapters 14 and 18.

The International Accounting Standards Committee was formed in 1973 to coordinate the development of accounting standards internationally. Compliance with IASC standards is voluntary, since the IASC has no power to enforce them. Nevertheless, its standards influence the financial reporting practices of many countries, either by being adopted where no national standard-setting body exists, or by being incorporated into domestic standards. Through membership of the IASC, the UK profession is expected to promote the application of International Accounting Standards. As we saw in Chapter 6, almost all the ASB's recent work on new standards has been concerned with international harmonization.

## The development of a conceptual framework

The main criticism levelled against the programme adopted by the Accounting Standards Committee was that it failed to establish objectives for financial reports. This resulted from the failure to develop the accounting standards programme within a framework which would have allowed that programme to proceed in a coherent manner. The ASB has aimed to remedy this defect by developing a clear Statement of Principles from which work on individual standards will derive, and providing a framework for the standards themselves. The ASB's intention is that accounting standards should be based on principles backed up by examples rather than on detailed *ad hoc* rules. The seven chapters making up the Statement were published as Discussion Drafts or Exposure Drafts in the period 1991 to 1994. In 1999 the ASB issued a new Exposure Draft which presented all the chapters together with minor changes. Two chapters which are most relevant to this introductory text are summarized below.

# Chapter 1: the objective of financial statements

The Statement of Principles begins with the proposition that:

*The objective of financial statements is to provide information about the reporting entity's financial performance and financial position that is useful to a wide range of users for assessing the stewardship of management and for making economic decisions.*

The statement emphasizes that financial statements cannot provide all the information that users may need to make economic decisions, because they largely portray the financial effects of past events and do not necessarily provide non-financial information. Also, the information presented in financial statements is subject to various limitations. It is subject to uncertainty because it incorporates estimates, and because the effects of transactions are allocated to discrete reporting periods. Information that cannot be expressed in monetary terms cannot be reflected in the primary financial statements. Moreover, the information in financial statements is largely historical, in that it relates to the position at a point in time and performance for a prior period.

Seven potential user groups are identified.

1 Investors are interested in information that is useful in assessing the stewardship of management and in taking decisions about their investment or potential investment in the entity. They are, as a result, concerned with the risk inherent in, and return provided by, their investments, and need information on the entity's financial performance and financial position that helps them to assess its cash-generation abilities and its financial adaptability.
2 Lenders wish to determine whether their loans and the attached interest will be paid when due.
3 Suppliers wish to determine whether amounts owing to them will be paid when due.
4 Employees are concerned with their employer's stability and profitability, and with assessing the ability of the enterprise to provide the remuneration and retirement benefits.
5 Customers are concerned with the continuance of an enterprise.
6 Governments require information enabling them to regulate firms' activities, determine taxation policies and compile national statistics.
7 The public may be affected by enterprises in different ways. For instance, an enterprise may have a major effect on the local economy. Local residents will want information about the prosperity of the enterprise.

Some, but not all, information needs are common to all users. The Statement concludes that the provision of information meeting the needs of investors will satisfy most of the needs of other user groups.

The Statement identifies three different information requirements among users of financial statements; these are for information about the financial position of an enterprise, its performance and its financial adaptability.

## ┼Financial position

The financial position of an enterprise encompasses the economic resources it controls, its financial structure, its liquidity and solvency, and its capacity to adapt to changes in the environment in which it operates. Information on financial position is provided in the balance sheet.

## ⅄ Performance

The performance of an enterprise comprises the return obtained by the enterprise and the resources it controls, including the cost of its financing. Information on performance is provided in the profit and loss account and in the statement of total recognized gains and losses.

## ⅄ Financial adaptability

Financial adaptability consists of the ability of an enterprise to take effective action to alter the amount and timing of its cash flows so that it can respond to unexpected events and opportunities. All the primary financial statements provide information that is useful in evaluating the financial adaptability of the enterprise.

# Chapter 3: The qualitative characteristics of financial information

Qualitative characteristics are the characteristics that make the information provided in financial statements useful to users for assessing the financial position, performance and financial adaptability of an enterprise.

Some qualitative characteristics relate to the content of the information contained in financial statements; others relate to how that information is presented. The primary qualitative characteristics relating to content are relevance, reliability, comparability and understandability.

Figure 2.15, reproduced from the statement, summarizes the points dealt with in Chapter 3 of the Statement. Each of the numbered items in the figure is briefly explained below.

1 *Materiality*. Information is material if it could influence users' decisions taken on the basis of the financial statements.
2 *Relevance*. To be useful, information must be relevant to the decision-making needs of users. Information that is relevant has predictive value or confirmatory value.
   (a) *Predictive value* helps users to evaluate or assess past, present, or future events.
   (b) *Confirmatory value* helps users to confirm or correct their past evaluations and assessments.
   Information may have both predictive value and confirmatory value. For example, information about the current level and structure of asset holdings helps users to assess the entity's ability to exploit opportunities and react to adverse situations. The same information helps to confirm past assessments about the structure of the entity and the outcome of operations.
3 *Reliability*. To be useful, information must also be reliable. Information is reliable when it possesses the following characteristics:
   (a) *Freedom from material error*.
   (b) *Faithful representation*. Information must represent faithfully the effect of the transactions and other events it either purports to represent or could reasonably be expected to represent.
   (c) *Neutrality*. The information contained in financial statements must be neutral, i.e. free from bias. Financial statements are not neutral if they include information that has been selected or presented in such a way as to influence the making of a decision or judgement in order to achieve a predetermined result or outcome.

193

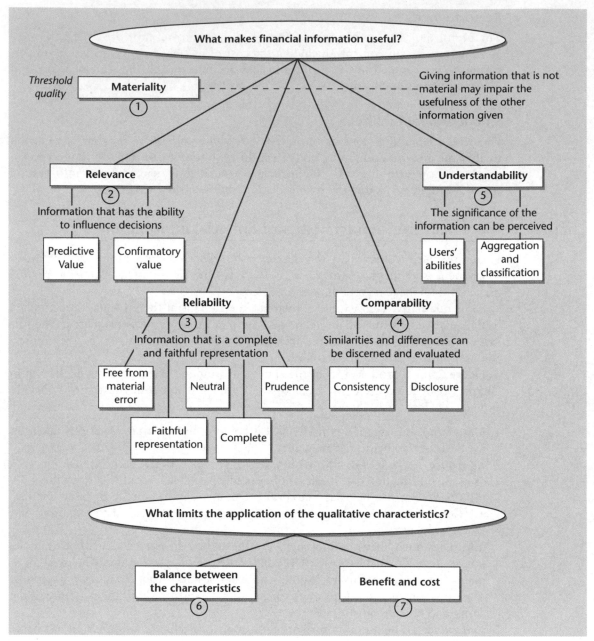

**Figure 2.15**    The qualitative characteristics of financial information.

(d) *Prudence*. The prudence concept is an essential feature in preparing financial statements. Caution needs to be exercised when estimating the outcome of uncertain events. However, the exercise of prudence does not allow, for example, the creation of hidden reserves or excessive provisions or the deliberate understatement of assets, income or expenses, because the financial statements would not be neutral and, therefore, not have the quality of reliability.

4 *Comparability*. Users must be able to compare the financial statements of an enterprise over time to identify trends in its financial position and performance. Users must also be able to compare the financial statements of different enterprises to evaluate their relative financial position, performance and financial adaptability. It is therefore necessary for similar events and states of affairs to be represented in a similar manner.

Compliance with accounting standards helps to achieve comparability by ensuring that different entities account for similar transactions and events in a similar way.

(a) *Consistency*. Comparability requires the measurement and display of the financial effect of like transactions and other events to be carried out in a consistent way within each accounting period and from one period to the next, and also in a consistent way by different entities. Although consistency is necessary to attain comparability, it is not in itself always sufficient. For example, if assets are consistently measured on a historical cost basis during a period of inflation, two entities with precisely similar economic conditions and performance will report different results if they aquired their assets at different times.

(b) *Disclosure*. A prerequisite of comparability is disclosure of the accounting policies employed in the preparation of the financial statement, and also any changes in those policies and the effects of such changes. Users need to be able to identify differences between the accounting policies for like transactions and other events used by the same enterprise from period to period and by different enterprises.

5 *Understandability*. An essential quality of the information provided in financial statements is that it should be readily understandable by users. Whether information is understandable will depend on:

(a) *Users' abilities*. Those preparing financial statements are entitled to assume that users have a reasonable knowledge of business and economic activities and accounting and a willingness to study with reasonable diligence the information provided.

(b) *Aggregation and classification*. An understandable presentation requires that items are aggregated and classified in an appropriate way.

6 *Balance between characteristics*. One constraint is that a balancing, or trade-off, between qualitative characteristics is often necessary. For example, information that is more reliable is frequently less relevant and vice versa. Generally the aim is to achieve an appropriate balance among the characteristics in order to meet the objective of financial statements. The relative importance of the characteristics in different cases is a matter of judgement.

7 *Benefit and cost*. As a general principle, the benefits derived from the provision of information should exceed the cost of providing it.

## Summary

In this chapter, we have examined the nature of limited companies and the financial accounting implications of incorporation. These implications stem from the manner in which companies are capitalized and from the manner in which the net profit is appropriated. We discussed particular financial problems such as gearing. The accounting procedures relating to the share capital are concerned principally with recording the issue of share capital, and with providing information about the share capital in financial accounting reports.

The accounting procedures applicable to periodic profit are concerned with the manner in which the profit is appropriated to various purposes. The size of the dividend is a matter of financial policy which directors have to consider in relation to capital requirements, its effect on the share price and the availability of other sources of finance.

We considered also the regulation of financial reporting in the UK and its three major means: company law, accounting standards and the Listing Agreement of the Stock Exchange. Also we considered the influence of international bodies. Finally, we examined two chapters of the ASB's Statement of Principles for Financial Reporting.

*Reference*    Arden, M (1993) 'The True and Fair View Requirement', Appendix to Foreword to *Accounting Standards*, Accounting Standards Board.

## Self-assessment questions

1 Distinguish between share capital and loan capital.

2 Explain 'gearing'. Why is it significant for ordinary shareholders?

3 What is meant by issuing shares at a premium? How is this recorded in the accounts?

4 Explain the importance of a 'true and fair view'.

5 Distinguish between the roles of:
   (a) the Financial Reporting Council;
   (b) the Accounting Standards Board;
   (c) the Financial Reporting Review Panel;
   (d) the Urgent Issues Task Force.

6 How is financial reporting practice in the UK affected by international influences?

7 Explain the role of a conceptual framework. Distinguish between financial position, performance and financial adaptability.

8 What are qualitative characteristics?

9 Explain 'relevance' and 'reliability'. What makes information relevant and reliable?

# 14 Published financial statements

## Setting the scene

Although companies utilise a wide variety of media to disseminate information to the investment community such as in-person briefing, interim publications and the Internet, financial reports have historically been the primary vehicle by which public companies communicate with shareholders, customers and a host of other stakeholders. Since the financial report supplements historical financial detail with information about a company's strategy, its management, current position and future prospects, it is not surprising that it should be relied on so heavily by investors and analysts to assess value.

(Price Waterhouse Coopers, 1999)

## Learning objectives

After studying this chapter you should be able to:

1 Prepare the financial statements of a limited company for publication.

2 Explain how taxation is dealt with in the financial statements.

3 Describe additional disclosure requirements.

The purpose of this chapter is to examine the financial reporting implications of incorporation, and the procedures applied to the financial reporting problems peculiar to public as distinct from private companies. We define public companies as those private-sector companies in which the public at large may become shareholders, and private companies as those private-sector companies which have a restricted and selected number of individuals as shareholders.

The statutory requirements relating to the disclosure of financial information are governed by the Companies Acts 1948, 1967, 1976, 1980 and 1981, as consolidated in the Companies Act 1985, which, as amended by the Companies Act 1989, contains the overall legal framework. As we saw in the previous chapter, many of the statutory requirements contained in these Acts have been enlarged as the result of the issue of accounting standards, and a company listed on a stock exchange in Great Britain or Ireland must observe certain additional requirements.

## The Companies Act 1981

The Companies Act 1981 (CA81) implemented the European Economic Community's Fourth Directive, aimed at harmonizing the accounts of member countries. This directive applies only to the accounts of individual companies in European Union member states; group company accounts are dealt with in the Seventh Directive. However, the Companies Act 1981 requires that group accounts shall be prepared as far as possible to comply with the accounting rules laid down for individual companies. Accounting for groups of companies is considered in Chapters 17 and 18.

The Companies Act 1981 introduced major changes in British company legislation:

1 Precise formats for the profit and loss account and balance sheet are prescribed for the first time in United Kingdom law and they require disclosure of considerably more detail than was previously the case.

2 Fundamental principles (concepts) for the preparation of published accounts are prescribed. First, the company is to be presumed to be carrying on its business as a going concern. Second, all accounting principles are to be applied consistently from one financial year to the next. Third, the amount of any item is to be determined on a prudent basis and in particular only profit realized at the balance sheet date is to be included in the profit and loss account. Fourth, revenues and expenses are to be accounted for on an accruals basis. Fifth, in determining the aggregate amount to be shown in respect of any item in the accounts the amount of each individual component asset or liability must be determined separately. Sixth, amounts in respect of items representing assets or income may not be set off against amounts in respect of items representing liabilities or expenditure. The first four of these principles are the fundamental accounting concepts discussed in Chapter 5.

   If it appears to the directors of a company that there are special reasons for departing from any of these six principles in preparing the company's accounts then the particulars of the departure, the reasons for it and its effects must be given in a note to the accounts.

3 Historical cost and alternative accounting rules are prescribed. These rules do not differ from those generally followed in practice; they merely represent a shift from non-statutory to statutory regulation. They will be detailed later in this chapter. The alternative accounting rules allow assets to be valued at their current cost.

4 A distinction is drawn between the publicity and filing requirements of different companies according to their size. Small and medium-sized companies must present a full set of accounts to their shareholders. However, they may file modified reports with the Registrar of Companies. Details of the qualifying conditions and exemptions are considered later in this chapter.

The Companies Act 1989 introduced a requirement to state whether the accounts have been prepared in accordance with applicable accounting standards and to give details of, and the reasons for, any material departures. Small and medium-sized companies are exempt from this disclosure requirement.

Company accounts contain five financial statements. These consist of:

1 a profit and loss account;
2 a statement of total recognized gains and losses;
3 a balance sheet;
4 reconciliation of movements of shareholders' funds;
5 a cash flow statement.

These statements are examined in the remainder of this chapter and in Chapter 15.

## The profit and loss account

The Companies Acts provide two horizontal and two vertical formats for the presentation of the profit and loss account. Essentially, the two formats may be distinguished by the way in which costs are analysed. Format 1 analyses costs by type of operation, while Format 2 analyses costs by type of expenditure. The vertical formats of these two different types of analyses are:

**Profit and loss account – Format 1**

1   Turnover
2   Cost of sales
3   Gross profit or loss
4   Distribution costs
5   Administrative expenses
6   Other operating income
7   Income from shares in group companies
8   Income from shares in related companies
9   Income from other fixed-asset investments
10   Other interest receivable and similar income
11   Amounts written off investments
12   Interest payable and similar charges
13   Tax on profit or loss on ordinary activities
14   Profit or loss on ordinary activities after taxation
15   Extraordinary income
16   Extraordinary charges
17   Extraordinary profit or loss
18   Tax on extraordinary profit or loss
19   Other taxes not shown under the above items
20   Profit or loss for the financial year

**Profit and loss account – Format 2**

1   Turnover
2   Change in stocks of finished goods and in work in progress
3   Own work capitalized
4   Other operating income
5   (a) Raw materials and consumables
   (b) Other external charges
6   Staff costs:
   (a) wages and salaries
   (b) social security costs
   (c) other pension costs
7   (a) Depreciation and other amounts written off tangible and intangible fixed assets
   (b) Exceptional amounts written off current assets
8   Other operating charges

| | |
|---|---|
| 9 | Income from shares in group companies |
| 10 | Income from shares in related companies |
| 11 | Income from other fixed-asset investments |
| 12 | Other interest receivable and similar income |
| 13 | Amounts written off investments |
| 14 | Interest payable and similar charges |
| 15 | Tax on profit or loss on ordinary activities |
| 16 | Profit or loss on ordinary activities after taxation |
| 17 | Extraordinary income |
| 18 | Extraordinary charges |
| 19 | Extraordinary profit or loss |
| 20 | Tax on extraordinary profit or loss |
| 21 | Other taxes not shown under the above items |
| 22 | Profit or loss for the financial year |

The Acts require disclosure of the following items on the face of the profit and loss account although they do not appear in the formats:

1 profit or loss on ordinary activities before taxation;
2 transfers and proposed transfers to and from reserves;
3 the aggregate amount of dividends paid and proposed.

A company must adhere to the format it has chosen in subsequent accounting years, unless in the opinion of the board of directors there are special reasons for a change. Details of any decision to change the format must be given in the note to the accounts.

The profit and loss account must be prepared in the order and under the headings given in the formats. Each item in the format is prefixed by an arabic number, which need not be shown in the published accounts. It is permissible to amalgamate certain items if the amount involved is not material, or if such an amalgamation facilitates the assessment of the company's affairs. It is also possible to adapt the title or to rearrange the position of certain items where the special nature of the company's business requires such alteration.

In addition to the items shown in the formats, and those noted above, the Companies Acts specify certain items of information which must be shown on the face of the profit and loss account or in notes to the accounts. In particular,

1 corresponding amounts for the preceding financial year must be shown for every item in the profit and loss account and the notes thereon – where a corresponding amount would not be comparable with the current-year item, an adjusted corresponding amount must be shown, particulars of the adjustment and the reasons for it being included;
2 the accounting policies followed by a company in determining the amount of profit or loss must be stated.

## Turnover

Turnover means any amount derived by the company from the provision of goods and services in the context of its ordinary activities. The term turnover replaces the term sales previously used. It includes all receipts from these activities after deduction of traded discounts, value added tax and any other sales-based tax (e.g. excise duty).

Additionally, there must be disclosed in notes to the accounts the following information relating to the analysis of the turnover:

1 where the company carries on two or more classes of business which differ substantially from each other, the amount of the turnover attributable to each class;
2 where the company has traded in different 'markets' (defined by geographical boundaries), the amount of the turnover attributable to each market must be stated.

## Expenditure

In calculating the cost of sales, distribution costs and administrative expenses (Format 1), the following must be included:

1 Provisions for depreciation or diminution in value of assets. Amounts written off investments must be shown separately.
2 Directors' and employees' emoluments. Additionally, notes to the accounts must show the following information:
   In respect of directors, distinguishing between directors' fees and directors' salaries:
   (a) aggregate emoluments, including fees and percentages, expense allowances charged to United Kingdom tax, pension contributions paid in respect of them and benefits in kind;
   (b) aggregate of directors' and past directors' pensions, excluding pensions from schemes maintained by contributions;
   (c) aggregate of compensation paid to directors or past directors for loss of office;
   (d) prior-year adjustments arising from expense allowances being disallowed for tax purposes, or a director retaining emoluments for which he or she was previously accountable.
   In respect of employees:
   (e) the average number of employees, calculated by dividing the annual number of employees by the number of weeks in the accounting year. Where format 1 is used, there must be shown in respect of all employees taken into account in determining the relevant annual numbers:
      (i) wages and salaries paid to employees,
      (ii) social security costs (being contributions by the company towards any state social security or pension scheme),
      (iii) other pensions costs (being contributions to company pension schemes and pensions paid);
   (f) the average number of employees for each category of employees, such category being defined by the directors having regard to the manner in which the company's activities are organized.
3 Sums payable for the hire of plant and machinery, the sums so payable being shown in the notes to the accounts.
4 Auditors' remuneration, the total payable being shown in the notes to the accounts.
5 Sums paid in respect of any exceptional transactions, being defined as transactions falling outside the ordinary activities of the company.

## Other operating income

Other operating income includes income from normal operations which does not fall under any other headings, e.g. royalties and rent received. Income from rents of land and buildings (net of outgoings) must be shown separately if this is a substantial part of a company's revenue.

## Other investment income

The four formats require income from other fixed-asset investments and other interest receivable and similar income to be shown separately. Income from listed investments must be separately identified in the notes if not in the profit and loss account.

## Amounts written off investments

This item is required to be shown on the face of the profit and loss account. Where a fixed-asset investment has diminished in value a provision for the diminution in its value may be made. However, where the reduction in value of any fixed asset (including investments) is expected to be permanent, a provision for the diminution in value must be made. Consequently, no asset may be stated at a net value in excess of its estimated recoverable amount. Where the reasons for any provision for diminution in value no longer apply, the provision must be written back to the extent that it is no longer necessary.

## Interest payable and similar charges

There must be shown in the notes to the accounts information relating to the interest charged in respect of the following:

1 Bank loans and overdraft and other loans made to the company which are either repayable otherwise than by instalment and fall due for repayment within five years from the end of the accounting year, or repayable by instalment, the last of which falls due for payment before the end of that period.
2 Loans of any other kind made to the company, i.e. those repayable wholly or in part after more than five years.

## Profit or loss on ordinary activities before taxation

As previously stated, this item must be shown on the face of the profit and loss account. The figure reported must represent the balance of all previously mentioned items including exceptional items (see below) that relate to the ordinary activities of the company, but excluding taxation and extraordinary items (see below).

## Extraordinary items, exceptional items and prior year adjustments

The required formats for the presentation of the profit and loss account provide headings for extraordinary income, extraordinary charges and tax on extraordinary profit or loss. The Companies Acts do not define extraordinary items. They were interpreted in the light of SSAP 6 'Extraordinary Items and Prior Year Adjustments' as 'those items which derive from events or transactions outside the ordinary activities of the business and which are both material and expected not to recur frequently or regularly. They do not include items which, though exceptional on account of size or incidence, derive from the ordinary activities of the business.' The importance of extraordinary items arose from the effect of their treatment on a company's earnings per share (EPS) which was defined in SSAP 3 as the 'profit in pence attributable to each equity share before taking into account extraordinary items'. SSAP 6 attracted much criticism. The facility it allowed for extraordinary items was much abused by companies which increasingly created such items to boost EPS.

FRS 3 'Reporting Financial Performance' (1992) supersedes SSAP 6 and amends SSAP 3. This standard made extraordinary items virtually extinct and reduced the emphasis on EPS as a single measure of performance. Much of this was achieved not by forcing companies to reveal new information but by altering the presentation of what was already disclosed. The standard requires all profit and loss items down to operating profit to be analysed between amounts attributable to continuing and discontinued operations, with new acquisitions being shown as a sub-category of continuing operations. Where an activity both starts and ceases in a period, it should be treated as discontinued. An illustrative example, which is a simplified version of the example in FRS 3, is given below.

**Profit and loss account**

| | Continuing operations Existing | New acquisitions | Discontinued operations | Total |
|---|---|---|---|---|
| | £m | £m | £m | £m |
| Turnover | 550 | 50 | 175 | 775 |
| Cost of sales | 415 | 40 | 165 | 620 |
| Gross profit | 135 | 10 | 10 | 155 |
| Distribution and administrative expenses | 85 | 4 | 25 | 114 |
| Operating profit | 50 | 6 | (15) | 41 |
| Profit on sale of properties | 29 | | | 29 |
| Loss on sale of discontinued operations | | | (7) | (7) |
| | 79 | 6 | (22) | 63 |
| Interest payable | | | | 18 |
| Profit on ordinary activities before taxation | | | | 45 |
| Taxation | | | | 16 |
| Profit on ordinary activities after taxation | | | | 29 |
| Extraordinary items | | | | – |
| Profit for financial year | | | | 29 |
| Dividends | | | | 8 |
| Retained profit for the financial year | | | | 21 |

The logic behind the distinction between continuing and discontinued operations is that where financial statements are used to assess the likely future performance of a company, then the results from those operations that the company no longer owns need to be excluded, because it is only the continuing operations that will affect the future. Similarly, if the actual results of a period are to be sensibly compared with forecasts made for that period, then the contributions from any operations acquired during the year need to be eliminated so that like can be compared with like. All exceptional items should be credited or charged in arriving at the profit or loss on ordinary activities and should be attributed to continuing or discontinued operations as appropriate. Where other exceptional items are involved (e.g. a large bad debt or stock write-offs,) these should be included within one of the statutory headings in the profit and loss account and disclosed in the notes to the accounts.

Prior period adjustments are those 'material adjustments applicable to prior periods arising from changes in accounting policies or from the correction of fundamental errors'. Such adjustments may be made through reserves.

## Taxation

The requirements of the Companies Acts are twofold. First, the profit and loss account must disclose the net profit or loss on ordinary activities before taxation, and the taxation charge on those activities should be deducted to give the net profit or loss on ordinary activities after taxation. Second, the notes to the accounts must contain the following additional information:

1 the amount of the charge for United Kingdom corporation tax;
2 if that amount would have been greater but for double taxation relief, the amount it would have been but for such relief;
3 the amount of the charge for United Kingdom income tax;
4 the amount of the charge for taxation imposed outside the United Kingdom on profits, income and (so far as charged on revenue) capital gains.

These notes must also specify the base on which the charge to United Kingdom corporation tax and income tax is calculated, and give details of any circumstances affecting the liability to corporation tax, income tax and capital gains in the current and succeeding years.

## Appropriation of profit

The following items must be disclosed separately:

1 any amounts set aside for the redemption of share capital or the redemption of loans;
2 any amount set aside or withdrawn, or that is proposed to be set aside or withdrawn from reserves;
3 the aggregate amount of any dividends paid and proposed.

## The statement of total recognized gains and losses

This primary statement, which was introduced in 1993 as part of FRS 3, must appear alongside the profit and loss account, the balance sheet and the cash flow statement. The ASB argued that such a statement is necessary because not all components of a company's financial performance are reflected in the profit and loss account. As we saw in Chapter 5, the realization convention requires that the profit and loss account include only realized profits which are determined by transactions resulting from sales that have been made. However, a company can make substantial profits or losses through the revaluation of fixed assets. These are recognized by increasing the value of the assets in the balance sheet, the double entry being to a revaluation reserve included in shareholders' funds.

The objective of the statement is to show the extent to which shareholders' funds have increased from any gains that the company has included in its accounts and, therefore, have been recognized in the period. Although such information has always been found in the accounts, in the note on reserves, it may not have been included by non-professional readers in their attempts to determine the company's financial performance during the period. FRS 3 puts the argument as follows:

*Statements of total recognised gains and losses contribute further to the purposes of financial reporting by:*
*(a) combining information about operating and related performance with other aspects of a reporting entity's financial performance; and*
*(b) providing information (jointly with the other primary statements) that is useful for assessing the return on investment in a reporting entity.*

If a company has no recognized gains or losses other than a profit or loss for the period a statement to this effect should be shown immediately below the profit and loss account.

An illustrative example, which is a simplified version of the example in FRS 3, is given below.

**Statement of total recognized gains and losses**

|  | £m |
|---|---|
| Profit for the financial year (this is the profit shown in the profit and loss account after charging tax and after allowing for extraordinary items if any) | 29 |
| Unrealized surplus on revaluation of properties | 4 |
| Unrealized loss on trade investment | (3) |
| Total gains and losses recognized since last annual report | 30 |

This statement brings together information from the profit and loss account and balance sheet. Its aim is to give the information a greater prominence and reduce the likelihood of misinterpretation.

## The balance sheet

The Companies Acts provide two formats for the balance sheet presentations, one vertical, the other horizontal. Once a company has chosen which format it intends to adopt, it may not alter that choice without giving an explanation to shareholders in a note to the accounts.

Note from the vertical format shown hereunder that the Acts provide for the classification of broad headings by a letter prefix. Major subdivisions are identified by roman numerals, minor subdivisions by arabic. These prefixes do not have to be shown on the published balance sheet, but are used to set out the manner in which accounting items have to be aggregated on the balance sheet, and the extent to which information has to be disclosed. In this regard, note particularly that any item shown on the format which is preceded by a letter or roman-numeral prefix must be disclosed in a company's published balance sheet.

A company's balance sheet may include any item not otherwise shown on the proposed format, and indeed may show any item in greater detail than is required by the Companies Acts. The following items may not, however, be treated as assets in any company's balance sheet:

1 preliminary expenses;
2 expenses and commissions relating to the issue of shares or debentures;
3 research costs.

With regard to the arrangement of items, it is provided that items preceded by arabic numerals on the format may be amalgamated if they are not material or if the amalgamation facilitates the assessment of the company's state of affairs. In the latter case, the individual items amalgamated must be disclosed by note. Furthermore, these items may be shown in a different order or may have their title adapted where the special nature of the company's business requires such alteration.

### Balance sheet – Format 1

A  Called-up share capital not paid
B  Fixed assets
   I   Intangible assets
      1  Development costs
      2  Concessions, patents, licences, trade marks and similar rights and assets
      3  Goodwill
      4  Payments on account
   II  Tangible assets
      1  Land and buildings
      2  Plant and machinery
      3  Fixtures, fittings, tools and equipment
      4  Payments on account and assets in course of construction
   III  Investments
      1  Shares in group companies
      2  Loans to group companies
      3  Shares in related companies
      4  Loans to related companies
      5  Other investments other than loans
      6  Other loans
      7  Own shares
C  Current assets
   I   Stocks
      1  Raw materials and consumables
      2  Work–in–progress
      3  Finished goods and goods for resale
      4  Payments on account
   II  Debtors
      1  Trade debtors
      2  Amounts owed by group companies
      3  Amounts owed by related companies
      4  Other debtors
      5  Called-up share capital not paid
      6  Prepayments and accrued income
   III  Investments
      1  Shares in group companies
      2  Own shares

3   Other investments
IV   Cash at bank and in hand
D   Prepayments and accrued income
E   Creditors: amounts falling due within one year
   1   Debenture loans
   2   Bank loans and overdrafts
   3   Payments received on account
   4   Trade creditors
   5   Bills of exchange payable
   6   Amounts owed to group companies
   7   Amounts owed to related companies
   8   Other creditors including taxation and social security
   9   Accruals and deferred income
F   Net current assets (liabilities)
G   Total assets less current liabilities
H   Creditors: amounts falling due after more than one year
   1   Debenture loans
   2   Bank loans and overdrafts
   3   Payments received on account
   4   Trade creditors
   5   Bills of exchange payable
   6   Amounts owed to group companies
   7   Amounts owed to related companies
   8   Other creditors including taxation and social security
   9   Accruals and deferred income
I   Provisions for liabilities and charges
   1   Pensions and similar obligations
   2   Taxation, including deferred taxation
   3   Other provisions
J   Accruals and deferred income
K   Capital and reserves
   I   Called-up share capital
   II   Share premium account
   III   Revaluation reserve
   IV   Other reserves
      1   Capital redemption reserve
      2   Reserve for own shares
      3   Reserves provided for by the articles of association
      4   Other reserves
   V   Profit and loss account

As with the profit and loss account, general disclosure rules for establishing the comparability of accounting numbers are provided. Thus, corresponding amounts for the previous year must be shown for all balance sheet items, and where, for example, due to a change of accounting policy the numbers are not comparable, adjustments must be made to the previous year to establish comparability. Equally, corresponding amounts must be given, and they must likewise be adjusted if necessary, in respect of every item stated in the notes to the balance sheet (other than amounts relating to the movements on fixed assets, reserves and provisions). Full amounts must be disclosed, and there should be no setoff of items representing assets against items representing liabilities.

As stated previously, the Companies Acts prescribe historical cost and alternative accounting rules. The Acts acknowledge that the historical cost of purchase or production is the primary method of valuing assets. Purchase price is defined to include expenses incidental to acquisition. Production cost is defined to include all costs directly attributable to the production of the asset and may also include a reasonable proportion of indirect costs as well as any interest paid on money borrowed to finance the asset in question. The inclusion of distribution cost is specifically prohibited.

# Fixed assets

Subject to any provision for depreciation or diminution in value, fixed assets are to be shown at purchase price or production cost, as the case may be. Fixed assets with limited useful economic life must be depreciated.

A provision for the diminution in value of a fixed-asset investment may be made, and must be made in respect of any fixed asset where the reduction in value is expected to be permanent. The fixed assets so reduced are shown at their reduced amount on the balance sheet, and the provision for reduction in value is disclosed in a note to the accounts or shown on the profit and loss account.

While maintaining historic cost valuations as the normal basis for balance sheet purposes, the Companies Acts allow alternative valuation bases provided that the items affected and the basis of valuation are shown in a note to the accounts. This permits companies to revalue assets or to use current cost valuations. The amount of profit or loss arising from the adoption of an alternative accounting valuation must be credited or debited, as the case may be, to the revaluation reserve.

The Companies Acts require the following information to be disclosed in respect of each fixed asset item:

1 the aggregate purchase price, production cost or alternative accounting valuation at the beginning and end of the accounting reference period, showing the effect of acquisitions, disposals or transfers or any revaluation during this period;

2 the cumulative provision for depreciation, or diminution of value as at the beginning and end of the accounting reference period, showing the annual provision arising from the disposal of any asset and any other adjustment to the provision.

**Example 1**  The requirements of the Companies Acts would be satisfied by the following presentation:

| | Freehold land and buildings | Plant and machinery | Total |
|---|---|---|---|
| | £000 | £000 | £000 |
| Cost: | | | |
| At 1 January | 1,000 | 200 | 1,200 |
| Additions | 30 | 40 | 70 |
| Disposals | – | (20) | (20) |
| | 1,030 | 220 | 1,250 |
| **Accumulated depreciation** | £ | £ | £ |
| At 1 January | 200 | 50 | 250 |
| Depreciation for the year | 20 | 24 | 44 |
| Disposals | – | (19) | (19) |
| At 31 December | 220 | 55 | 275 |
| **Net book values** | £ | £ | £ |
| At 31 December | 810 | 165 | 975 |

With regard to *intangible assets*, these must be included on the face of the balance sheet under this main heading, with the following subheadings included either on the face of the balance sheet or in a note: development costs; concessions, patents, licences, trade marks and similar rights and assets; goodwill; and payments on account. The Acts make the following provisions:

1 *Development costs* (but not research costs) may be capitalized, but only in 'special circumstances'. In practice, this treatment must be read in conjunction with SSAP 13 'Accounting for Research and Development', discussed in Chapter 12, which defines the special circumstances that must exist before development costs may be capitalized. Where development costs are capitalized and shown on the balance sheet, the Companies Acts require that notes must be appended disclosing (a) the period over which the costs are being written off and (b) the reason for capitalizing the development costs.

2 *Concessions, patents, licences, trade marks, etc.* may be shown on the balance sheet only if they have been acquired by purchase and are not required to be shown under goodwill, or if they were created by the company itself.

3 *Goodwill* may be shown as an asset on the balance sheet only if it was acquired by purchase. In such a case, it must be written off over a period which does not exceed its useful economic life.

## Investments

The formats show that investments may be reported either in the category of fixed assets or of current assets. Investments intended to be retained by a company on a continuing basis should be treated as fixed assets, while any other investments should be listed under current assets. When investments are of a long-term nature then they must be classified under the following headings:

1 Shares held in group companies, where the company is a member company in a group of companies.

2 Loans to group companies. Group companies are discussed in Chapter 17.

3 Shares in related companies, where the company is related to another company in which the relationship involves at least 20 per cent shareholding by one company in another.

4 Loans to related companies.

5 Other investments other than loans, for example shares in companies which are neither group nor related companies.

6 Other loans.

7 Own shares, where – as allowed by the Companies Acts – a company is allowed to purchase its own shares.

The valuation of investments poses particular problems, where there is no stock exchange quotation for shares or debentures. The Companies Acts do not require unquoted investments to be valued, and the requirements would be satisfied by the conventional historical cost of such investments.

Where investments are listed on a recognized stock exchange, the aggregate market value must be disclosed where this value differs from the value at which they were stated on the balance sheet.

## Current assets

The value to be placed on any current asset is the lower of the purchase price or production cost and the net realizable value. With regard to stocks, the Companies Acts require stocks to be subdivided into the following categories:

1 raw materials and consumables;
2 work-in-progress;
3 finished goods and goods for resale;
4 payments on account.

Stocks may be valued using any of the recognized valuation methods, namely FIFO (first in first out), LIFO (last in first out), or weighted average cost.

As noted in Chapter 12, SSAP 9 'Stocks and Long-Term Contracts' does not recommend the use of LIFO. Any material difference between the value of the stock shown on the balance sheet and its replacement cost, or, if more appropriate, the most recent purchase price, must be disclosed for each category of stocks.

Debtors must be disclosed as a main heading on the balance sheet and the following items must be disclosed either on the face of the balance sheet or in the notes thereto: trade debtors; amounts owed by group companies; amounts owed by related companies; other debtors; called-up share capital not paid; prepayments and accrued income. Additionally, the amounts falling due after more than one year must be shown separately for each item.

## Creditors

The Companies Acts require creditors to be shown under the following subheadings either on the face of the balance sheet or in the notes thereto: debenture loans, bank loans and overdrafts; payments received on account; trade creditors; bills of exchange payable; amounts owed to group companies; other creditors including taxation and social security; and accruals and deferred income. The amounts falling due after more than one year must be shown separately for each item.

## Provisions for liabilities and charges

FRS 12, discussed in Chapter 12, defines provisions as 'liabilities of uncertain timing or amount' and lays down the conditions that must be fulfilled before a provision can be included in the financial statement totals.

## Share capital

The share capital issued and the amount called up must be shown separately. Where the company has issued shares of different classes, the number and aggregate nominal value of each class must be given by name on the balance sheet. Where redeemable shares have been issued, the following information must be given:

1 the earliest and latest dates on which the company has power to redeem the shares;
2 whether those shares must be redeemed in any event, or are liable to be redeemed at the option of the company;
3 whether any premium (and if so, what) is payable on redemption.

Moreover, if there has been an issue of shares during the financial year, the following information must also be given:

1 the reason for the issue;
2 the class of shares issued;
3 in respect of each class of shares issued, the number issued, their aggregate nominal value and the consideration received by the company.

## Reserves

The Companies Acts do not give a general definition of a 'reserve' but it is generally accepted that the term 'reserve' does not include the following:

1 a provision for depreciation, renewal or diminution in value of assets;
2 a provision for a known liability;
3 a provision for undue fluctuations in charges for taxation.

Any share premium account and any revaluation reserve must be shown separately under 'reserves', and any other reserve built up by the company must be shown under an appropriate heading. The profit and loss account balance must be shown separately.

In the event that there has been any transfer to or from the reserves shown as separate items during the accounting period, there must be shown by way of note to the balance sheet the following information:

1 the amount of reserves at the beginning of the year;
2 the amounts transferred either in or out, and the source and application of such amounts;
3 the amounts of reserves at the end of the year.

## Guarantees and financial commitments

The following information, if not included in the accounts, must be given in the notes:

1 particulars of any charge on the assets of the company to secure the liabilities of any person, indicating where practicable, the amount secured;
2 the estimated amount of future capital expenditure;
3 pension commitments, both provided for and not provided for;
4 particulars of other financial commitments which are not provided for in the accounts but which are relevant to assessing the company's state of affairs.

## Other disclosure requirements

Among other disclosure requirements to be noted are the following:

1 there must be disclosed in a note to the accounts the accounting policies used by the company in determining the amounts shown as items in these accounts;
2 the basis of translation of any item originally denominated in foreign currencies and translated into sterling must be shown.

Three additional requirements are examined below. These are:

1 reconciliation of movements in shareholders' funds;
2 note of historical cost profits and losses;
3 segmental information.

## Reconciliation of movements in shareholders' funds

The profit and loss account and the statement of total recognized gains and losses are intended to measure the performance of the company during the period. However, there might be other changes in the shareholders' funds (for example, movements on share capital) which are important to understanding the changes in the company's financial position. Shareholders' funds consist of the share capital plus all the various reserves that may exist. Examples of reserves are:

1 the share premium account, which represents the extra premium paid, over the nominal value, for the shares that have been issued by the company;
2 the revaluation reserve, which represents the amount by which shareholders' interest in a company rises when assets are revalued upwards;
3 the profit and loss account, which shows the balance of the retained profit at the balance sheet date. This is the only distributable reserve.

FRS 3 requires that a reconciliation of the movement in shareholders' funds be given where there have been any such changes which are not included in the statement of total recognized gains and losses. Items that would appear in such a reconciliation include:

1 dividends for the period;
2 capital contributions from shareholders or repaid to shareholders during the period;
3 goodwill that has been written off during the period.

An illustrative example is given below.

### Reconciliation of movements in shareholders' funds

|  | £m |
|---|---|
| Profit for the financial year | 29 |
| Dividends paid and proposed | (8) |
|  | 21 |
| Other recognized gains and losses (net) | (1) |
| New share capital subscribed (total received) | 20 |
| Goodwill written off | (25) |
| Net addition for shareholders' funds | 15 |
| Opening shareholders' funds as at beginning of year | 365 |
| Closing shareholders' funds | 380 |

## Note of historical cost profits and losses

As we saw at the beginning of this chapter, the Companies Act 1981 allows companies to draw up their accounts on either a historical cost basis or one of the alternative bases. An alternative basis that is widely used by companies which wish to make their accounts more realistic is historical cost modified by the revaluation of certain assets. Where a company produces financial statements on any basis other than historical cost, then FRS 3 requires that they include a note showing the historical cost profit, and reconciling this amount to the actual profit if the difference is material.

Two reasons for disclosing the profit or loss for a period on the unmodified historical cost basis of accounting are commonly cited. The first of these is to report profits or losses of different companies on a more comparable basis. Where a company revalues an asset, depreciation is based on that increased value. Therefore, the reported profit is less than it would have been if the revaluation had not taken place. The second reason is the wish of some users to assess the profit or loss on the sale of assets that is based on the historical cost of the assets sold rather than on the revalued amount. An illustrative example, adapted from FRS 3, is given below.

### Note of historical cost profits and losses

|  | £m |
| --- | --- |
| Reported profit on ordinary activities before taxation | 45 |
| Realization of property revaluation gains of previous years | 9 |
| Difference between a historical cost depreciation charge and the actual depreciation charge of the period calculated on revalued amounts | 5 |
| Historical cost profit on ordinary activities before taxation | 59 |

It is necessary to point out that since many of the fixed assets that are commonly revalued are those with long useful economic lives the effect of the cost convention is usually immaterial with regard to reported profits (although it may be material with regard to the balance sheet).

## Segmental information

A feature of business development that began in the 1960s has been the growth of diversified companies in which different segments of the operations are subject to significantly different notes of profitability, degrees of risk and opportunities for growth. The disclosure of segmental information for diversified companies is necessary in order to provide the user with a better basis for the assessment of the enterprise's past performance and future prospects.

The statutory requirements for disclosure of segmental information are contained in the Companies Act 1985. These were alluded to earlier in this chapter when we examined the disclosure requirements for turnover. These requirements were extended by SSAP 25 ' Segmental Reporting' which was issued in 1990. Two types of segment are recognized:

1 class of business, the identification and designation of which is entirely a matter on which the directors must exercise their judgement;
2 geographical segments. Such a segment may consist of a single country or a group of countries in which the business operates or to which it supplies products or services.

SSAP 25 requires the segmental disclosure of:

1 turnover;
2 profit before interest and tax;
3 net assets.

213

The purpose of the net assets disclosure requirement is that it enables the turnover and profit/loss of each segment to be related to the net assets which generate them.

**Example 2** | **Sloan Products plc**
**Report and accounts for the year ended 31 December 20X0**

The following illustration conforms with the requirements of the Companies Acts for the publication of profit and loss accounts and balance sheets except that comparative figures are omitted for the sake of clarity. The illustration does not take account of the supplementary disclosures required by accounting standards such as earnings per share information nor of the Stock Exchange Listing Agreement. In the illustration the profit and loss account and the balance sheet follow Format 1.

**Sloan Products plc**
**Profit and loss account for the year ended 31 December 20X0**

| Notes | | £000 |
|---|---|---|
| 2 | Turnover | 22,340 |
| | Cost of sales | (15,782) |
| | Gross profit | 6,558 |
| | Distribution costs | (1,801) |
| | Administrative expenses | (1,972) |
| 3 | Operating profit | 2,785 |
| 6 | Investment income | 18 |
| | Interest payable and similar charges | (210) |
| | Profit on ordinary activities before taxation | 2,593 |
| 7 | Tax on profit on ordinary activities | (808) |
| | Profit for the financial year | 1,785 |
| 8 | Dividends paid and proposed | (900) |
| | Retained profit for the year | 885 |

**Sloan Products plc**
**Balance sheet at 31 December 20X0**

| Notes | | £000 | £000 |
|---|---|---|---|
| | **Fixed assets** | | |
| 9 | Intangible assets | | 30 |
| 10 | Tangible assets | | 7,828 |
| 11 | Investments | | 150 |
| | | | 8,008 |
| | **Current assets** | | |
| 12 | Stocks | 1,574 | |
| 13 | Debtors | 1,436 | |
| 14 | Investments | 68 | |
| | Cash at bank and in hand | 63 | |
| | | 3,141 | |
| 15 | **Creditors:** amounts falling due within one year | (1,840) | |
| | Net current assets | | 1,301 |
| | Total assets *less* current liabilities | | 9,309 |

| | | |
|---|---:|---:|
| 16 **Creditors:** amounts falling due after more than one year | 360 | |
| 17 **Provisions for liabilities and charges** | 134 | (494) |
| | | 8,815 |

**Capital and reserves**

| | |
|---|---:|
| 18 Called-up share capital | 6,000 |
| Share premium account | 123 |
| 19 Revaluation reserve | 104 |
| 20 Profit and loss account | 2,588 |
| | 8,815 |

**Sloan Products plc**
**Statement of total recognized gains and losses**

| | £000 |
|---|---:|
| Profit for the financial year | 1,785 |
| Unrealized surplus on revaluation of properties | 104 |
| Total gains and losses recognized since last annual report | 1,889 |

**Sloan Products plc**
**Reconciliation of movements in shareholders' funds**

| | £000 |
|---|---:|
| Profit for the financial year | 1,785 |
| Dividends paid and proposed | (900) |
| | 885 |
| New capital subscribed (total received) | 200 |
| Goodwill written off | (10) |
| Net addition to shareholders' funds | 1,075 |
| Opening shareholders' funds at the beginning of year | 7,740 |
| Closing shareholders' funds | 8,815 |

**Sloan Products plc**
**Notes to the accounts at 31 December 20X0**

1   **Accounting policies**
    **(a) Basis of accounting**
    The accounts have been prepared under the historical cost convention, modified by the revaluation of properties.
    **(b) Depreciation**
    Depreciation is provided on all tangible fixed assets, other than freehold land, at rates calculated to write off the cost or valuation, less estimated residual value, of each asset evenly over its expected useful life, as follows:
    Freehold buildings             40 years
    Plant and machinery          10 years
    **(c) Goodwill**
    Goodwill acquired for cash relating to a business purchased by the company is amortized over five years. In the opinion of the directors this represents a prudent estimate of the period over which the company will derive a direct economic benefit from the products acquired as part of the business.

215

**(d) Research and development expenditure**

This is written off in the year in which it is incurred.

**(e) Stocks and work-in-progress**

These are stated at the lower of cost and net realizable value. In general, cost is determined on a first in, first out basis and includes transport and handling costs; in the case of manufactured products cost includes all direct expenditure and production overheads based on the normal level of activity. Net realizable value is based on estimated selling price less further costs expected to be incurred to completion and disposal.

**(f) Foreign currencies**

Assets and liabilities in foreign currencies are translated into sterling at the rates of exchange ruling at the balance sheet date.

**(g) Pensions**

Retirement benefits to the present employees of the company are funded by contributions from the company and employees. Payments are made to pension trusts, which are financially separate from the company, in accordance with calculations made periodically by consulting actuaries. The cost of these contributions and of providing pensions to some former employees is charged against the profits of the period.

**2  Segmental information**

|  | Turnover £000 | Profit £000 | Net assets £000 |
|---|---|---|---|
| **Class of business** | | | |
| Domestic appliances | 16,004 | 2,053 | 7,300 |
| Water sports | 6,336 | 732 | 1,515 |
|  | 22,340 | 2,785 | 8,815 |
| **Geographical analysis** | | | |
| United Kingdom | 7,673 | 756 | 2,715 |
| United States | 2,342 | 359 | 864 |
| Europe | 12,325 | 1,670 | 5,236 |
|  | 22,340 | 2,785 | 8,815 |

**3  Operating profit**

| Operating profit is stated after charging: | £000 |
|---|---|
| Depreciation | 1,052 |
| Amortization of goodwill | 10 |
| Hire of plant and machinery | 43 |
| Auditors' remuneration | 11 |
| Exceptional bad debt | 7 |

**4  Employee information**

**(a) Number employed**

The average number of employees during the year was as follows:

| | |
|---|---|
| Office and management | 70 |
| Domestic appliances | 231 |
| Water sports | 68 |
|  | 369 |

**(b) Payroll costs**

|  | £000 |
|---|---|
| The aggregate payroll costs were: | |
| Wages and salaries | 3,912 |
| Social security costs | 455 |
| Other pension costs | 188 |
|  | 4,555 |

**5 Directors' emoluments**

|  | £000 |
|---|---|
| Fee | 37 |
| Other emoluments | 282 |
| Pensions to past directors | 16 |
|  | 335 |

The chairman received emoluments of £42,000 and the highest-paid director £46,000. The emoluments of the other directors were within the ranges:

| | |
|---|---|
| £15,001 – £20,000 | 2 |
| £20,001 – £25,000 | 4 |
| £30,001 – £35,000 | 7 |

**6 Investment income and interest payable**

|  | £000 |
|---|---|
| Income from listed investments | 18 |
| Interest payable on bank loans, overdrafts and loans: | |
| repayable within five years | 17 |
| on other loans | 141 |
|  | 158 |

**7 Tax on profit on ordinary activities**

|  | £000 |
|---|---|
| Corporation tax at 30% on taxable profit for the year | 756 |
| Deferred taxation | 52 |
|  | 808 |

**8 Dividends**

|  |  | £000 |
|---|---|---|
| Ordinary dividend: | | |
| interim (paid) | 5.0p per share | 300 |
| final (proposed) | 10.0p per share | 600 |
|  | 15.0p | 900 |

**9 Intangible fixed assets**

|  | £000 | £000 |
|---|---|---|
| Goodwill | | |
| Cost | | 50 |
| Accumulated amortization at 1 January 20X0 | 10 | |
| Provision for the year to 31 December 20X0 | 10 | 20 |
| Net book value at 31 December 20X0 | | 30 |

**10 Tangible assets**

| Cost or valuation | Freehold Land £000 | Buildings £000 | Plant and machinery £000 | Total £000 |
|---|---|---|---|---|
| Cost: | | | | |
| At 1 January 20X0 | 204 | 1,146 | 9,250 | 10,600 |
| Revaluation surplus | – | 104 | – | 104 |
| Additions | 32 | 87 | 800 | 919 |
| Disposals | (15) | (100) | (280) | (395) |
| At 31 December 20X0 | 221 | 1,237 | 9,770 | 11,228 |

**Depreciation:**

|                      |   |        |         |         |
| -------------------- | - | -----: | ------: | ------: |
| At 1 January 20X0    | – | 480    | 2,083   | 2,563   |
| Provision for year   | – | 32     | 1,020   | 1,052   |
| Disposals            | – | (75)   | (140)   | (215)   |
| At 31 December 20X0  | – | 437    | 2,963   | 3,400   |

**Net book values:**

|                      |     |     |       |       |
| -------------------- | --: | --: | ----: | ----: |
| At 31 December 20X0  | 221 | 800 | 6,807 | 7,828 |

Part of the buildings were revalued on 1 June 20X0 by Wheeler and Wright, chartered surveyors and valuers. It was valued on 'an open-market existing-use basis' and resulted in a revaluation surplus of £104,000. This has been credited to a revaluation reserve in the balance sheet.

## 11  Investments

| Cost:               | £000 |
| ------------------- | ---: |
| At 1 January 20X0   | 125  |
| Additions           | 25   |
| Disposals           | –    |
| At 31 December 20X0 | 150  |

|                       | £000 |
| --------------------- | ---: |
| Listed investments    | 140  |
| Unlisted investments  | 10   |
|                       | 150  |

| **Valuation:**                     | £000 |
| ---------------------------------- | ---: |
| Listed investment at market value  | 210  |

The unlisted investment comprises £10,000 ordinary shares in Vesta plc, representing 15 per cent of the issued share capital of that company. Vesta plc was incorporated in Great Britain which is the principal country of operation. Taxation of £7,500 would be payable if the investments were sold at valuation.

## 12  Stocks

|                    | £000  |
| ------------------ | ----: |
| Raw materials      | 407   |
| Work-in-progress   | 283   |
| Finished goods     | 884   |
|                    | 1,574 |

Current replacement costs exceed costs of the above items as follows:

|                    | £000 |
| ------------------ | ---: |
| Raw materials      | 6    |
| Work-in-progress   | 4    |
| Finished goods     | 12   |
|                    | 22   |

## 13  Debtors

|                               | £000  |
| ----------------------------- | ----: |
| Trade debtors                 | 1,082 |
| Other debtors                 | 298   |
| Prepayments and accrued income| 56    |
|                               | 1,436 |

## 14  Investments

|                     | £000 |
| ------------------- | ---: |
| Short-term deposits | 68   |

| 15 Creditors: amounts falling due within one year | £000 |
|---|---|
| Bank loans and overdrafts | 42 |
| Trade creditors | 286 |
| Taxation and social security | 1,105 |
| Accruals | 7 |
| Proposed dividends | 400 |
| | 1,840 |

| 16 Creditors: amounts falling due after more than one year | £000 |
|---|---|
| 11% debentures | 360 |

The debentures are secured by a floating charge over the company's assets. They are repayable at the company's option between 20X4 and 20X9 with a final redemption date of 31 December 20X9.

| 17 Provisions for liabilities and charges | £000 |
|---|---|
| Pensions and similar obligations | 55 |
| Taxation, including deferred taxation | 79 |
| | 134 |

| 18 Called-up share capital | £000 |
|---|---|
| Allotted, issued and fully paid: | |
| Ordinary shares of £1 each | 6,000 |
| Authorized 8m ordinary shares of £1 each | 8,000 |

| 19 Revaluation reserve | £000 |
|---|---|
| At 1 January 20X0 | – |
| Revaluation of buildings | 104 |
| Balance at 31 December 20X0 | 104 |

| 20 Profit and loss account | £000 |
|---|---|
| At 1 January 20X0 | 1,703 |
| Retained for year | 885 |
| | 2,588 |

| 21 Capital commitments | £000 |
|---|---|
| Contracted for but not yet provided | 72 |
| Authorized by directors but not yet contracted for | 230 |
| | 302 |

# Additional disclosures

In addition to the financial statements and notes to the financial statements, certain other information is disclosed in a corporate report. The nature of this information has been affected, in recent years, by two events. The first was the publication of 'a statement of best practice', called *Operating and Financial Review,* by the ASB in 1993. This aimed to provide a framework for directors to discuss and analyse the business's performance and the factors underlying its results and financial position, in order to assist users to assess for themselves the future potential of the business. The second event was developments in corporate governance. As we saw earlier in this chapter, good corporate governance informs financial report users how the directors are running an organization to ensure its resilience. The Combined Code encourages companies to review the effectiveness of their governance procedures and to provide sufficient disclosure so that investors and others can assess company performance and governance practice and respond in an informed way.

In summary form, 'best practice' would include the following disclosures:

## Chairman's statement

This statement comments on the overall financial results and the dividend recommended. Praise is normally heaped on the hard work of the staff which made the results possible. The outlook for the business is examined.

## Operating review

The principle aim of the operating review is to enable the user to understand the dynamics of the various lines of business undertaken – that is, the main influences on the overall results, and how they interrelate. In particular, it should explain:

1 the dynamics of the business;
2 investment for the future;
3 profit for the financial year, total recognized gains and losses, dividends and earnings per share;
4 accounting policies.

## Financial review

This should explain:

1 the capital structure of the business and treasury policy;
2 taxation;
3 cash flows from operating activities;
4 current liquidity;
5 company resources and strengths not reflected in the balance sheet.

## Board of directors

This report gives a brief biography of each director – their age, qualifications, date they were appointed, previous jobs and other directorships.

## Report of directors

The directors' report normally deals with the following matters in particular:

1 principal activities of the company during the period and any significant changes in those activities;
2 significant developments during the year, e.g. acquisitions;
3 research and development, giving an indication of activities in this area;
4 significant changes in fixed assets;
5 post balance sheet events, particularly important events affecting the company which have occured since the end of the year;
6 major shareholders, disclosing companies which hold 3 per cent or more of the company's share capital, in accordance with the Companies Act 1985;
7 charitable and political contributions;
8 employment policies;
9 employee participation.

## Corporate governance

This statement outlines how the company has applied the principles set out in the Combined Code on Corporate Governance:

1 the board of directors – the structure of the board, directors' responsibilities, the provision of information to them;
2 board committees – the role of the audit, remuneration and personnel committees;
3 internal financial control;
4 risk management;
5 relations with shareholders.

## Remuneration report

The aim of the Remuneration Committee is to determine the company's policy on remuneration, and in particular:

1 to consider and make recommendations to the board on remuneration arrangements including bonuses, share options, pension rights, service contracts and compensation payments;
2 to review employee share schemes;
3 to disclose the remuneration received by each director during the year;
4 to disclose directors' interests in ordinary shares and share options.

## Statement of directors' responsibilities

Company law requires directors to prepare accounts for each financial year which give a true and fair view of the state of affairs and the profit and loss for the company. This statement confirms that the directors have:

1 used appropriate accounting policies, consistently applied;
2 made judgements and estimates that are reasonable and prudent;
3 ensured that all applicable accounting standards have been followed; and
4 prepared the financial statements on the going concern basis.

## Report of auditors

The auditor give an opinion on whether the accounts give a true and fair view of the state of affairs of the company and of the profit and loss and cash flows for the year.

## Notice of meeting

This statement gives notice of the location, time and agenda for the Annual General Meeting.

# Small and medium-sized companies

We noted earlier that the Companies Acts allow small and medium-sized companies to file modified accounts with the Registrar of Companies, although they must still prepare accounts in full form for presentation to their members. A company qualifies to be treated as small or medium-sized for a financial year if, both for that year and the preceding year, it satisfies any two or more of the following conditions:

|  | Small | Medium |
|---|---|---|
| Turnover not exceeding | £2.8m | £11.2m |
| Balance sheet total not exceeding | £1.4m | £5.6m |
| Employees less than | 50 | 250 |

Until recently, all companies were required to follow accounting standards, with a few exceptions, in spite of the fact that most have been developed particularly with the needs of large listed companies in mind. The FRSSE (Financial Reporting Standard for Small Entities), issued in 1997 and amended in 1999, is an optional standard which collects together in a simplified form the requirements from other accounting standards that are applicable to smaller entities.

## Taxation in company accounts

There have been several changes to the UK tax system over the last few years, the most important of which were the abolition of repayment of tax credits to pension schemes and UK companies in 1997 and the abolition of advance corporation tax (ACT) in 1999. These changes made a significant proportion of SSAP 8 'The Treatment of Taxation under the Imputation System in the Accounts of Companies' redundant. SSAP 8 has been superseded by FRS 16 'Current Tax', which is applicable to accounting periods ending on or after 23 March 2000, although earlier application is encouraged.

The main principles under FRS 16 are:

(a) Current tax should be recognized in the profit and loss account for the period. The only exception is where a gain or loss is recognized directly in the statement of total recognized gains and losses. In these cases the related tax should also be recognized in that statement.

(b) Dividends, interest and any other payables or receivables should be recognized –
   (i) net of any available tax credit or other taxes not payable wholly on behalf of the recipient;
   (ii) grossed up for any withholding taxes payable wholly on behalf of the recipient. Such taxes normally arise on overseas dividends.

This inclusion of dividends net of any tax credit, i.e. recording the income at the actual dividend received, is a significant departure from the old SSAP 8, provisions. Under SSAP 8, dividends received from UK companies were grossed up for ACT tax credits. The net effect of the abolition of ACT, and of the consequential introduction of FRS16, is that pre-tax profits for a company that receives UK dividend income will be reduced.

*Example 3*  A company with taxable profits of £80,000 declares a dividend of £21,000. The rate of corporation tax is assumed to be 30 per cent.

|  | £ |
|---|---|
| Profits before tax | 80,000 |
| Corporation tax at 30% | 24,000 |
|  | 56,000 |
| Dividend | 21,000 |
| Retained profit | 35,000 |

## Computing taxable profit

Financial accounting, which is governed by a 'true and fair' presentation of financial position and the results of operations, does not share in all respects the principles which govern the computation of taxable profits. Differences between 'book' and tax accounting originate from the following:

1 Some items which appear in the profit and loss account are not allowed for tax purposes. These include entertaining expenses and certain types of donations and subscriptions.
2 Dividends received from other companies resident in the UK do not incur corporation tax.
3 Timing differences. The first two categories give rise to permanent differences where, because of legislation, particular revenues or expenses are omitted from the computation of taxable profit. A timing difference, on the other hand, arises when an item is includable or deductible from profit for tax purposes in one period, but in profit for general reporting purposes in another. The different treatment of fixed assets creates timing differences because depreciation is not an allowance deductible for tax purposes, capital allowances being granted instead.

**Example 4**   A company has accounting profit of £150,000, depreciation of £50,000, entertaining expenses and donations of £10,000, dividend received of £10,000 and capital allowances of £100,000. Taxable profit is calculated as follows:

|  | £ | £ |
|---|---|---|
| Accounting profit |  | 150,000 |
| *Add:* Depreciation |  | 50,000 |
| *Add:* Entertaining, etc. |  | 10,000 |
|  |  | 210,00 |
| *Less:* Capital allowances | 100,000 |  |
| *Less:* Dividend received | 10,000 | 110,000 |
| Taxable profit |  | 100,000 |

## Deferred taxation

The provision for deferred taxation originates from the timing differences which we discussed above. Deferred tax arises because certain types of income and expenditure are not included in the calculation of taxable profits at the same time as they are reflected in accounting profits. When such timing differences arise, the tax assessed for the year is not regarded as the full liability for that year. Deferred tax is recorded to adjust the tax charge for the year to the amount that will be payable over time on the profits shown in the accounts.

SSAP 15 requires deferred tax to be provided for using the 'partial provision' method. Provision is made only to the extent that the timing differences at the balance sheet date are expected to reverse without being replaced in the future.

**Example 5**  A company buys a machine for £50,000 which it intends to use for five years. Using the straight-line depreciation method, £10,000 would be written off each year. Although this is not currently available, we make the simplistic assumption that the system of capital allowances for tax purposes allows the entire cost of the machine to be written off in the first year. We assume accounting profit is £200,000. Deferred taxation for the year is calculated as follows:

|  | £ |
|---|---|
| Accounting profit | 200,000 |
| *Add:* Depreciation | 10,000 |
|  | 210,000 |
| *Less:* Capital allowances | 50,000 |
| Taxable profit | 160,000 |
| Tax on accounting profit (30% of £200,000) | 60,000 |
| Tax on taxable profit (30% of £160,000) | 48,000 |
| Deferred taxation | 12,000 |

The profit and loss account would be debited with the full amount of tax of £60,000 described as follows:

| | |
|---|---|
| Corporation tax (including £12,000 credited to deferred taxation account) | £60,000 |

The deferred taxation account balance of £12,000 would be shown as a separate item in the balance sheet.

The 'partial provision' method required by SSAP 15 is criticized primarily because of its subjectivity (relying heavily on management expectations about future events) and is inconsistent with other areas of accounting. For these reasons, it has lost favour internationally. Other major standard setters and the International Accounting Standard IAS 12 now require deferred tax to be provided in full. In 1999, the ASB published an Exposure Draft of a new accounting standard for deferred tax which would require entities applying accounting standards to account for deferred tax on a 'full provision' basis, thereby bringing the UK more into line with international practice.

## Summary

A public company that is listed on the stock exchange is required to present an annual report to its shareholders. The annual report consists of a number of statements. We have considered four financial statements, namely the profit and loss account, the statement of total recognized gains and losses, the reconciliation of movements of shareholders' funds and the balance sheet and, in addition, certain other information which is disclosed in a corporate report. These disclosure requirements have been determined mainly by company law, accounting standards and the Listing Agreement. They have developed in an *ad hoc* fashion with no obvious, overriding rationale for the disclosure of information. We return to this topic in Part 4.

**Reference**  PriceWaterhouseCoopers (1999). *Value Reporting Forecast 2000.*

1* The partnership of Black, White and Grey are considering forming a limited company to obtain the benefits of limited liability. However, they are uncertain as to whether the capital of the company should be in shares or debentures and are also unsure of the method of appropriating profit.

At 31 December 20X0 the capital accounts of the partners were:

|  | £ |
|---|---|
| Black | 44,000 |
| White | 36,000 |
| Grey | 48,000 |

Interest of 10 per cent per annum is allowed on the capital accounts.

Black is the managing partner and receives a salary of £20,000 p.a. White works part-time but does not receive a salary. Grey takes no active part in the business. The balance of profits is shared equally.

The budgeted profit for 20X1 is £260,000 before any appropriation to the partners.

*Required:*
(a) Advise the partners on the difference between debentures and ordinary shares and suggest the most appropriate capital structure for the new company.
(b) Advise the partners on a suitable method of rewarding themselves when the company is formed. Prepare a profit and loss appropriation account for year ended 31 December 20X1 on the assumption that the company is formed on I January 20X1, and your recommendations are accepted. Assume a corporation tax rate of 30 per cent.

(Problem supplied by A J Naughton)

2 Scheid and Sons Ltd are considering expanding their operations. Several alternative strategies are being discussed for financing this expansion. The latest balance sheet of the company as at 31 December 20X0 is as follows:

**Scheid and Sons Ltd**
**Balance sheet at 31 December 20X0**

|  | £ | £ |
|---|---|---|
| **Fixed assets** | | |
| Land and buildings | | 40,000 |
| Plant and equipment | | 90,000 |
| | | 130,000 |
| **Current assets** | | |
| Stocks | 50,000 | |
| Debtors | 40,000 | |
| Cash | 5,000 | |
| | 95,000 | |
| Creditors: amounts falling due within one year | 25,000 | |
| Net current assets | | 70,000 |
| Total assets *less* current liabilities | | 200,000 |
| Creditors: amounts falling due within one year: | | |
| 12% loan repayable 20X6 | | 90,000 |
| | | 110,000 |

| Share capital and reserves | £ |
|---|---|
| 8% cumulative preference shares of £1 each | 30,000 |
| Ordinary shares of £1 each | 50,000 |
| Profit and loss account | 30,000 |
| | 110,000 |

The board of directors has identified the following possible alternative ways of obtaining the additional £50,000 required during the following year:

(a)  Issue additional ordinary shares
(b)  Issue additional 8 per cent preference shares
(c)  Raise an additional long-term loan at 12 per cent.

Discuss the company's existing capital structure in terms of its gearing, and examine the advantages and disadvantages of each alternative method of financing the expansion plan.

3   The Huby Haulage Company Ltd produced the following trial balance at the end of December 20X0. Using this and the additional information following prepare a profit and loss account, appropriation account and balance sheet for the year ended 31 December 20X0.

| | £ | £ |
|---|---|---|
| £1 ordinary shares fully paid | | 200,000 |
| Retained profit | | 70,000 |
| 10% Debenture | | 50,000 |
| Sales | | 365,000 |
| Bank and cash | 20,000 | |
| Motor lorries – at cost | 360,000 | |
|            – accumulated depreciation | | 110,000 |
| Freehold property | 165,000 | |
| Repairs and renewals | 22,000 | |
| Drivers' wages | 60,000 | |
| Maintenance wages | 15,000 | |
| Parts and consumables | 70,000 | |
| Licences and insurance | 20,000 | |
| Administration salaries | 20,000 | |
| Sundry administrative expenses | 12,000 | |
| Drivers' overnight expenses | 6,000 | |
| Directors' salaries | 25,000 | |
| | 795,000 | 795,000 |

(a)  Drivers' claims for £150 relating to overnight expenses had not been taken into account.
(b)  The parts and consumables account included parts valued at 1 January 20X0 at £15,000. A stocktake at 31 December revealed that parts valued at £18,000 were held at that date.
(c)  It was estimated that there was a prepayment of £4,000 with regard to licences and insurance at the end of 20X0.
(d)  Depreciation of £62,500 is to be charged on vehicles for the year to 31 December 20X0.
(e)  Tax is estimated at £22,400.
(f)  There is a proposed dividend of £20,000.

4   Nether Edge plc, a retailing company, has an authorized share capital of 700,000 ordinary shares of £1 each. The following trial balance was extracted from the books of account as at 31 December 20X0.

|  | Dr £000 | Cr £000 |
|---|---|---|
| Issued share capital |  | 560 |
| Share premium account |  | 140 |
| Profit and loss account |  | 180 |
| 10% Debentures |  | 100 |
| Furniture and fittings at cost | 400 |  |
| Depreciation to 1 January 20X0 |  | 200 |
| Cash balances | 118 |  |
| Trade creditors |  | 120 |
| Trade debtors | 500 |  |
| Stock at 1 January 20X0 | 400 |  |
| Hire charges (distribution, vehicles, etc.) | 680 |  |
| Purchases | 1,000 |  |
| Administrative expenses | 300 |  |
| Deferred taxation |  | 80 |
| Distribution costs | 200 |  |
| Accrued expenses |  | 50 |
| Auditors' remuneration | 40 |  |
| Interim dividend (paid on 1 July 20X0) | 14 |  |
| Trade investments at cost (market value £170,000) | 140 |  |
| Debenture interest (gross) | 10 |  |
| Dividends received (on 1 December 20X0) |  | 30 |
| Turnover |  | 2,400 |
| Prepaid expenses | 58 |  |
|  | 3,860 | 3,860 |

You are also given the following information:

(a)  Turnover excludes value added tax.
(b)  Stock at 31 December 20X0 was valued at £600,000.
(c)  Depreciation of £80,000 is to be charged on the furniture and fittings for the year to 31 December 20X0.
(d)  Administration includes directors' emoluments of £110,000.
(e)  The corporation tax payable (based on the profits for the year to 31 December 20X0 at a rate of 30 per cent) is estimated to amount to £100,000.
(f)  The company proposes to pay a final ordinary dividend of 10 per cent.

*Required:*
Prepare financial statements for publication, together with relevant notes. (Work to the nearest £1,000.)

5*  The following data has been extracted from the records of Purple plc at 31 March 20X1:

|  | £ |
|---|---|
| Turnover | 18,108,488 |
| Cost of sales | 16,471,616 |
| Distribution costs | 864,531 |
| Administrative expenses | 1,494,228 |
| Surplus on sale of fixed assets | 11,054 |
| Interest receivable | 21,721 |
| Losses due to seizure of imported sugar | 351,890 |
| Overdraft interest | 139,001 |
| Loan interest (loan repayable 31 March 20X9) | 162,299 |
| Corporation tax for the year | 8,101 |
| Dividends (interim 0.25p per share) | 17,292 |
| Transfer from reserves | 1,389,105 |

You are also .given the following information:

(a)  Number of ordinary shares in issue during the year: 7,192,380.
(b)  Turnover excludes value added tax.
(c)  Distribution costs and administrative expenses given above include the following items:

|  | £ |
|---|---|
| Depreciation | 365,928 |
| Directors' emoluments | 105,773 |
| Auditors' remuneration | 26,020 |
| Hire of plant and machinery | 3,084 |

You are required to prepare a profit and loss account for publication, together with any notes required. It should comply with the Companies Acts.

# 15 Cash flow statements

**Setting the scene**

As the value of intangible assets such as intellectual property or bonds increases as a proportion of the company's total value, while conversely the amount of long-term (i.e. non liquid) assets decreases, the correlation between book value and market value lessens. This increases the importance of cash flow as a key metric for judging company performance. If the company provides sufficient cash to shareholders through dividends or if management invests it in ways that investors approve, markets typically show their gratitude by increasing the company's share price.

(PricewaterhouseCoopers, 1999)

**Learning objectives**

After studying this chapter you should be able to:

1 Appreciate the advantages of cash flow statements.

2 Prepare cash flow statements for publication.

3 Identify the factors that cause a company's cash flow position to change.

As we saw in Chapter 4, the purpose of cash flow statements is to report the cash receipts and payments of an accounting period. This chapter elaborates further on the nature and preparation of cash flow statements.

In 1991 the Accounting Standards Board's first standard, FRS 1 'Cash Flow Statements', introduced the requirement for medium and large companies to prepare a cash flow statement as part of their general financial statements. This standard superseded SSAP 10 'Statements of Source and Application of Funds' which was introduced in the United Kingdom in 1975. FRS 1 was revised in 1996.

## Advantages of cash flow statements

As with all financial reporting systems a consideration of cash flow statements must contain reference to the importance of user needs. The major report user groups were identified in Chapter 2. The purpose of financial reporting is to enable users to make decisions about the reporting entity. Financial theory postulates that those interested in an entity will base their economic decisions about that entity on their assessment of its future cash flows. Historical cash flows give relevant information about future cash flow because they illustrate how the entity generates cash and how it is spent. An entity may be considered as a cash-generating machine: cash flow information should help to show how the machine works (Lee, 1984; Lawson, 1978; Heath, 1978).

Historical cash flow information may assist users of financial statements in making judgements on the amount, timing and degree of certainty of future cash flows; it gives an indication of the relationship between profitability and cash-generating ability, and thus of the quality of the profit earned. Additionally, users of financial information often develop models to assess and compare the present value of the future cash flows of entities. Historical cash flow information could be useful to assess the accuracy of their previous predictions for that period.

A cash flow statement in conjunction with a balance sheet provides information on liquidity, viability and financial adaptability. The balance sheet provides information about an entity's financial position at a particular point in time including assets, liabilities and equity and their relationship with each other at the balance sheet date. The balance sheet is often used to obtain information on liquidity, but the information is incomplete for this purpose as the balance sheet is drawn up at a particular point in time. Cash flow statements should normally be used in conjunction with profit and loss accounts and balance sheets when making an assessment of future cash flows. This is because a cash flow statement provides incomplete information for assessing future cash flows. Some cash flows result from transactions that took place in an earlier period and some cash flows are expected to result in further cash flows in a future period.

## Understanding changes in cash

In Chapter 4 we explained how cash flows are inextricably linked with the profit and loss account and balance sheet. In Chapter 8 we examined the accounting equation (Capital + Liabilities = Assets) and explained how successive transactions maintain the accounting equation on which the balance sheet rests, though its constituent elements would vary. The accounting equation can be expanded in order to include both the short-term (less than one year) and long-term (more than one year) elements:

fixed assets + current assets = long-term creditors + short-term creditors + capital and reserves

We can disaggregate current assets and isolate cash, and rewrite the equation as follows:

cash = long-term creditors + short-term creditors + capital and reserves − fixed assets − stocks − debtors

This equation may be used to illustrate how changes in the various elements on the right-hand side of the equation affect changes in cash.

Cash inflows (i.e. increases in cash) result from:

1  increases in long-term creditors, short-term creditors and capital and reserves; and
2  decreases in fixed assets, stocks and debtors.

Cash outflows (i.e. decreases in cash) result from:

1  decreases in long-term creditors, short-term creditors and capital and reserves; and
2  increases in fixed assets, stocks and debtors.

For example, if short-term creditors (say, trade creditors) increase, cash increases because less cash is required to finance short-term creditors and this cash can be used for other purposes. Conversely, an increase in stocks causes an outflow (or a decrease)

in cash because more cash is required to pay for these extra stocks. Similarily, an increase in debtors is financed by an outflow of cash.

# Reporting cash flows

FRS 1 (revised) states that cash flows are increases or decreases in amounts of cash, and cash is cash in hand and deposits repayable on demand at any bank less overdrafts from any bank repayable on demand. A company's cash flow statement should list its cash flows for the period classified under the following standard headings:

1 operating activities;
2 returns on investments and servicing of finance;
3 taxation;
4 capital expenditure ;
5 acquisitions and disposals;
6 dividends paid;
7 management of liquid resources;
8 financing.

Individual categories of inflows and outflows under the standard headings should be disclosed separately either in the cash flow statement or in a note to it.

An example of a cash flow statement, based on FRS 1, is given below.

Example 1

**XYZ Limited**
**Cash flow statement for the year ended 31 March 20X1**

|  | £000 |
|---|---|
| Net cash inflow from operating activities | 6,889 |
| Returns on investments and servicing of finance (note 3) | 2,999 |
| Corporation tax paid | (2,922) |
| Capital expenditure | (1,525) |
|  | 5,441 |
| Equity dividends paid | (2,417) |
|  | 3,024 |
| Management of liquid resources (note 1) | (450) |
| Financing (note 1) | 57 |
| Increase in cash | 2,631 |

**Notes to the cash flow statement**

**1 Reconciliation of operating profit to net cash inflow from operating activities**

|  | £000 | £000 |
|---|---|---|
| Operating profit |  | 6,022 |
| Depreciation charges |  | 893 |
| Loss on sale of tangible fixed assets |  | 6 |
| Increase in stocks |  | (194) |
| Increase in debtors |  | (72) |
| Increase in creditors |  | 234 |

231

|  | £000 | £000 |
|---|---|---|
| **2 Net cash inflow from operating activities** | | 6,889 |
| **3 Returns on investments and servicing of finance** | | |
| Interest received | 3,011 | |
| Interest paid | (12) | |
| | | 2,999 |
| **4 Capital expenditure** | | |
| Payments to acquire intangible fixed assets | (71) | |
| Payments to acquire tangible fixed assets | (1,496) | |
| Receipts from sales of tangible fixed assets | 42 | |
| | | (1,525) |
| **5 Management of liquid resources** | | |
| Purchase of treasury bills | (650) | |
| Sale of treasury bills | 200 | |
| | | (450) |
| **6 Financing** | | |
| Issue of ordinary share capital | 211 | |
| Repurchase of debenture loan | (149) | |
| Expenses paid in connection with share issues | (5) | |
| | | 57 |

**Reconciliation of net cash flow to movement in net debt** (note 7)

| | | |
|---|---|---|
| **Increase in cash in the period** | 2,631 | |
| Cash repaying debenture | 149 | |
| Cash paid to increase liquid resources | 450 | |
| **Change in net debt*** | | 3,230 |
| **Net debt at 1 April 20X0** | | (2,903) |
| **Net cash at 31 March 20X1** | | 327 |

* In this example all changes in net debt are cash flows.

**7 Analysis of changes in net debt**

| | At 1 April 20X0 | Cash flows | At 31 March 20X1 |
|---|---|---|---|
| | £000 | £000 | £000 |
| Cash in hand, at bank | 42 | 847 | 889 |
| Overdrafts | (1,784) | 1,784 | |
| | | | 2,631 |
| Debt due within one year | (149) | 149 | |
| Debt due after one year | (1,262) | | (1,262) |
| Current asset investments | 250 | 450 | 700 |
| Total | (2,903) | 3,230 | 327 |

## Operating activities

Cash flows from operating activities are in general the cash effects of transactions and other events relating to operating or trading activities. Net cash flow from operating activities represents the net increase or decrease in cash resulting from the operations shown in the profit and loss account in arriving at operating profit. Cash flows in respect of any provision for operating items such as the costs or redundancy or reorganization should also be included in this section.

A reconciliation between the operating profit (for non-financial companies normally profit before interest) reported in the profit and loss account and the net cash flow from operating activities should be given either introducing the cash flow statement or as a note. The reconciliation should disclose separately the movements in stocks, debtors and creditors related to operating activities and other differences between cash flows and results.

## Returns on investments and servicing of finance

These are receipts resulting from the ownership of an investment and payments to providers of finance. They include: interest received, including any related tax recovered; dividends received (disclosing separately dividends received from equity accounted entities), net of any credits; interest paid (whether or not the charge is capitalized), including any tax deducted and paid to the relevant tax authority; the interest element of finance lease rental payments.

## Taxation

The cash flows included under the heading taxation are cash flows to or from taxation authorities in respect of the reporting entity's revenue and capital profits. Taxation cash inflows include cash receipts from the relevant tax authority of tax rebates, claims or returns of overpayments. Taxation cash outflows are cash payments to the relevant tax authority of tax.

## Capital expenditure

The cash flows included in 'capital expenditure' are those related to the acquisition or disposal of any fixed asset, and any current asset investment not included in liquid resources.

Cash inflows from 'capital expenditure' include receipts from sales or disposals of fixed assets other than trades, businesses or entities, and receipts from sales of investments in other entities. Cash outflows from capital expenditure include payments to acquire fixed assets and payments to acquire investments in other entities.

## Dividends paid

The cash outflows included in 'dividends paid' are those related to dividends paid on shares.

## Management of liquid resources

To assist users to assess the liquidity and financial adaptability of companies, cash flow statements reflect the way that liquid resources are managed to ensure the availability of cash to carry on or expand the business. Each company has a particular policy on which current asset investments it uses as a store of liquid resources, although an investment must be a readily disposable current asset to qualify (debtors, therefore, do not qualify). The 'management of liquid resources' section could, therefore, include cash flows related to a wide range of investments and each company should explain its policy on liquid resources and any changes to it.

Cash inflows in management of liquid resources include sales of government securities, debt instruments of other entities held as current assets, derivative instruments held as liquid resources and highly liquid equity investments held as liquid resources. Cash outflows in management of liquid resources include purchases of government securities, debt instruments of other entities held as current assets, derivative instruments held as liquid resources and highly liquid equity investments held as liquid resources.

## Financing

Financing cash flows comprise receipts from or repayments to external providers of finance of amounts in respect of principal amounts of finance.

Financing cash inflows include: receipts from issuing shares or other equity instruments; receipts from issuing debentures, loans, notes and bonds and from other long- and short-term borrowings (other than overdrafts).

Financing cash outflows include: repayments of amounts borrowed (other than overdrafts); the capital element of finance lease rental payments; payments to re-acquire or redeem the entity's shares; payments of expenses or commissions on any issue of shares.

The amounts of any finance cash flows received from or paid to equity accounted entities should be disclosed separately.

## Reconciliation of net debt

A note reconciling the movement of cash in the period with the movement in net debt should be included either at the end of the cash flow statement or in a note. The reconciliation is not part of the cash flow statement: if included at the end of the cash flow statement, it should be clearly labelled and kept separate.

The objective of the reconciliation of cash flows to the movement in net debt is to provide information that assists in the assessment of liquidity, solvency and financial adaptability. Net debt is defined to include liabilities in relation to borrowings less assets comprising the entity's store of liquidity because movements of net debt so defined are widely used as indicating changes in liquidity, and therefore assist in assessments of the financial strength of the entity. The definition excludes non-equity shares of the entity because, although these have features that may be similar to those of liabilities in relation to borrowings, they are not actually liabilities of the entity. The definition also excludes debtors and creditors because, while these are sources of finance to the entity, their main role is as part of the entity's trading activities.

This reconciliation will enable users to assess the cash flows of the entity in the wider context of the information given in the other financial statements.

## Exceptional and extraordinary items

Where cash flows relate to items that are classed as exceptional items in the profit and loss account these exceptional cash flows should be shown under the appropriate standard headings, according to the nature of each item. Sufficient disclosure of the nature of cash flows relating to exceptional items should be given in a note to the cash flow statement to allow a user of the financial statement to gain an understanding of the effect on the reporting entity's cash flows of the underlying transactions.

Where cash flows relate to items that are classed as extraordinary items in the profit and loss account, these extraordinary cash flows should be shown separately under the appropriate standard headings, according to the nature of each item. In the extremely rare circumstances where it is inappropriate to include a cash flow relating to an extraordinary item under one or more of the standard headings within the cash flow statement the cash flows should be shown within a separate section in the cash flow statement. Sufficient disclosure of the nature of cash flows relating to extraordinary items should be given in a note to the cash flow statement, to allow a user of the financial statements to gain an understanding of the effect on the reporting entity's cash flows of the underlying transactions.

## Reporting on operating activities

FRS 1 allows a choice between two methods of presenting operating cash flows: the indirect and direct methods. The indirect method, as illustrated in Example 1, starts from profit before tax and adjusts it for non-cash charges and credits to reconcile it to the net cash flow from operating activities.

The direct method shows operating cash receipts and payments (including, in particular, cash receipts from customers, cash payments to suppliers and cash payments to and on behalf of employees), aggregating to the net cash flow from operating activities. Had Example 1 chosen the direct method the net cash inflow from operating activities might have appeared as follows:

|  | £000 | £000 |
|---|---|---|
| Cash received from customers | 98,524 | |
| Cash payments to suppliers | (53,673) | |
| Cash paid to employees | (37,962) | |
| Cash flow from operating activities | | 6,889 |

The principal advantage of this method is that information about operating cash receipts and payments may be useful in assessing future cash flows. In the United States, where a similar choice between the indirect and direct methods is allowed, the vast majority of companies use the indirect method (Kronquist and Newman-Limata, 1990).

**Example 2**   The draft balance sheets of Stannington plc as at 31 December 20X0 and 31 December 20X1 are as follows:

|  | 20X0 | | 20X1 | |
|---|---|---|---|---|
|  | £000 | £000 | £000 | £000 |
| **Fixed assets** |  |  |  |  |
| Land and buildings at cost |  | 2,400 |  | 3,000 |
| Aggregate depreciation on buildings |  | (450) |  | (525) |
| Plant and equipment at cost |  | 3,000 |  | 5,100 |
| Aggregate depreciation on plant |  | (1,350) |  | (1,875) |
|  |  | 3,600 |  | 5,700 |
| **Current assets** |  |  |  |  |
| Stock | 900 |  | 1,125 |  |
| Debtors | 450 |  | 675 |  |
| Cash | 300 |  | – |  |
|  | 1,650 |  | 1,800 |  |
| **Current liabilities** |  |  |  |  |
| Creditors | 300 |  | 450 |  |
| Taxation | 375 |  | 450 |  |
| Dividends | 225 |  | 225 |  |
| Overdraft | – |  | 75 |  |
|  | 900 |  | 1,200 |  |
| **Net current assets** |  | 750 |  | 600 |
|  |  | 4,350 |  | 6,300 |
| **Capital and reserves** |  |  |  |  |
| Ordinary share capital |  | 3,000 |  | 4,500 |
| Share premium |  | 300 |  | 600 |
| Retained profits |  | 750 |  | 1,200 |
| 10% debentures repayable 31/12/20X1 |  | 300 |  | – |
|  |  | 4,350 |  | 6,300 |

Extracts from the profit and loss account for the year ended 31 December 20X1 are as follows:

|  | £000 | £000 |
|---|---|---|
| Profit before taxation |  | 1,350 |
| Taxation for the year |  | 525 |
|  |  | 825 |
| Dividends for the year |  |  |
| Interim dividends paid | 150 |  |
| Final dividend proposed | 225 | 375 |
| Retained profit for the year |  | 450 |
| Retained profits at 1 January 20X1 |  | 750 |
| Retained profits at 31 December 20X1 |  | 1,200 |

*Further information*

1  Depreciation charge for the year amounted to £900,000.

2  An item of plant was disposed of during the year for £225,000. It had cost £450,000 when new and had a depreciated value of £150,000.

**Stannington plc**
**Cash flow statement for the year ended 31 December 20X1**

|  | £000 | £000 |
|---|---|---|
| **Net cash inflow from operating activities** |  | 1,905 |
| **Returns on investment and servicing of finance** |  |  |
| Interest paid (W1) |  | (30) |
|  |  |  |
| **Corporation tax paid** (W2) |  | (450) |
| **Capital expenditure** |  |  |
| Payments to acquire fixed assets (W3) | (3,150) |  |
| Receipts from sales of fixed assets | 225 |  |
| Net cash outflow from the capital expenditure |  | (2,925) |
|  |  | (1,500) |
| **Dividends paid** |  | (375) |
|  |  | (1,875) |
|  |  |  |
| **Financing** |  |  |
| Issue of ordinary share capital (W4) | 1,800 |  |
| Repurchase of debenture loan | (300) |  |
| Net cash inflow from financing |  | 1,500 |
| **Decrease in cash** |  | (375) |

**Notes to the cash flow statement**

**1  Reconciliation of operating profit to net cash inflow from operating activities**

|  | £000 |
|---|---|
| Operating profit (1,350 + 30) | 1,380 |
| Depreciation charges | 900 |
| Profit on sale of fixed assets | (75) |
| Increase in stocks | (225) |
| Increase in debtors | (225) |
| Increase in creditors | 150 |
| Net cash inflow from operating activities | 1,905 |

**2  Reconciliation of net cash flow to movement in net debt**

|  | £000 |
|---|---|
| Decrease in cash in period | £375 |
| Cash repaying debenture | £300 |
| Change in net debt | (75) |
| Net debt at 1.1.20X1 | – |
| Net cash at 31.12.20X1 | (75) |

237

**Workings**

**1 Interest paid**
10% × £300,000 = £30,000

**2 Tax and dividends payable**

|  | Tax<br>£000 | Dividends<br>£000 |
|---|---|---|
| Opening balances | 375 | 225 |
| Appropriations for year | 525 | 375 |
| Total liability for the year | 900 | 600 |
| Closing balances | 450 | 225 |
|  | 450 | 375 |

**3 Fixed asset acquisitions**

|  | Land/<br>buildings<br>£000 | Equipment<br>£000 |
|---|---|---|
| Opening balances | 2,400 | 3,000 |
| *Less:* cost of disposals | – | 450 |
|  | 2,400 | 2,550 |
| Closing balances | 3,000 | 5,100 |
| Acquisitions during year | 600 | 2,550 |

**4 Share issues**

|  | £000 |
|---|---|
| Increase in share capital | 1,500 |
| Increase in share premium account | 300 |
| Total cash received | 1,800 |

## Summary

It is the ability to generate cash that determines the success of an entity. Therefore the major user groups of financial statements use an assessment of future cash flows on which to base their economic decisions about entities.

Historical cash flow information may assist users of financial statements in making judgements on the amount, timing and uncertainty of future cash flows. It gives an indication of the relationship between profitability and cash generating ability and thus of the quality of the profit earned.

Cash flow statements are important for financial planning purposes. In this context, they are associated with budget forecasts. The particular importance of the cash flow budget is to highlight the financial consequence of budget plans and predict the cash surpluses and deficits which will occur periodically through the planning period. This function of cash flow statements is examined in Part 5.

**References**

Heath, L C (1978). *Financial Reporting and the Evaluation of Solvency*, Accounting Research Monograph 3, American Institute of Certified Public Accountants.

Kronquist, S L and Newman-Limata, N (1990). 'Corporate cash flows', *Management Accounting (USA)*, July.

Lawson, G H (1978). 'The rationale of cash flow accounting', in C van Dam (ed), *Trends in Managerial and Financial Accounting*, Martinus Nijhoff.

Lee, T A (1984). *Cash Flow Accounting*, Van Nostrand Reinhold.

PricewaterhouseCoopers (1999). *Value Reporting Forecast 2000*.

1   The following information relates to South Ltd for the year ended 31 December 20X0:

|  | £000 |
|---|---|
| Cash and cash equivalents | |
|     at 1 January 20X0 | 8,952 |
|     at 31 December 20X0 | 10,043 |
| Operating profit | 4,100 |
| Depreciation charges | 1,080 |
| Increase in working capital | 165 |
| Proceeds of sale of tangible assets (book value £116,000) | 96 |
| Issue of ordinary share capital | 400 |
| Expenses in connection with share issue | 10 |
| Purchase of intangible fixed assets | 150 |
| Purchase of tangible fixed assets | 2,540 |
| Corporation tax paid | 2,460 |
| Dividends paid | 1,570 |
| Interest received | 2,290 |

*Required:*
Prepare a cash flow statement for the year ended 31 December 20X0.

2   Set out below are the condensed balance sheets for Walkley Ltd for 20X0 and 20X1, and a profit and loss account for the year ended 31 December 20X1.

**Balance sheets**

|  | 20X0 £000 | 20X1 £000 |
|---|---|---|
| Ordinary share capital (£1 shares) | 740 | 940 |
| Revenue reserves | 531 | 864 |
| Share premium account | – | 100 |
| Loans | 320 | 150 |
| Trade creditors | 152 | 141 |
| Proposed dividends | 140 | 170 |
| Current taxation | 470 | 602 |
| Bank overdraft | – | 766 |
|  | 2,353 | 3,733 |
| Plant and machinery | | |
|   Cost | 2,700 | 3,831 |
|   Accumulated depreciation | 748 | 1,125 |
|  | 1,952 | 2,706 |
|   Stock | 203 | 843 |
|   Debtors | 147 | 184 |
|   Cash at bank | 51 | – |
|  | 2,353 | 3,733 |

### Profit and loss account for the year ended 31 December 20X1

|  | £000 | £000 |
|---|---|---|
| Profit before tax |  | 1,195 |
| Corporation tax |  | 602 |
| Profit after tax |  | 593 |
| Ordinary dividends |  |  |
| Paid | 90 |  |
| Proposed | 170 | 260 |
|  |  | 333 |

*Notes:*
1  The only new loan raised during the year was a five-year bank loan amounting to £65,000.
2  Depreciation charged during the year amounted to £401,000.
3  During the year, plant which originally cost £69,000 was disposed of for proceeds of £41,000.
4  During the year, the company offered 200,000 shares by way of rights to existing shareholders.

*Required:*
Prepare a cash flow statement for 20X1.

3*  The balance sheets for Jobin & Co Ltd for the years ended 20X0, 20X1 and 20X2 are as follows:

### Jobin & Co Ltd
### Balance sheets at 31 December

|  | 20X0 £000 | 20X1 £000 | 20X2 £000 |
|---|---|---|---|
| **Fixed assets** |  |  |  |
| Plant and equipment | 13,200 | 16,110 | 16,410 |
| **Current assets** |  |  |  |
| Stocks | 2,190 | 2,280 | 2,490 |
| Trade debtors | 2,040 | 2,100 | 2,430 |
| Short-term investments | 4,200 | 1,800 | 1,290 |
| Cash at bank and in hand | 1,920 | 1,650 | 2,160 |
| Creditors: amounts falling due within one year |  |  |  |
| Short-term loans | (2,340) | (2,580) | (2,550) |
| Trade creditors | (2,760) | (2,610) | (2,670) |
| Taxation | (360) | (420) | (530) |
| Net current assets | 5,460 | 5,610 | 5,750 |
| Net current assets | 4,890 | 2,220 | 2,620 |
| Total assets *less* current liabilities | 18,090 | 18,330 | 19,030 |
| **Capital and reserves** |  |  |  |
| Called-up share capital | 4,500 | 4,500 | 4,500 |
| Share premium account | 9,000 | 9,000 | 9,000 |
| Other reserves | 3,280 | 4,060 | 4,570 |
| Profit and loss account | 1,310 | 770 | 960 |
|  | 18,090 | 18,330 | 19,030 |
| **Other data** |  |  |  |
| Profit before tax | 960 | 1,020 | 1,590 |
| Tax on annual profit | 360 | 420 | 530 |
| Tax paid during the year | 300 | 360 | 420 |
| Annual depreciation | 645 | 780 | 900 |
| Dividends declared and paid | 360 | 360 | 360 |

In 20X1, equipment was sold at a loss of £210,000. New plant in 20X1 cost £5,100,000 and in 20X2 cost £1,200,000. Profit transferred to other reserves in 20X1 and 20X2 amounted to £780 and £510 respectively.

*Required:*
Prepare a cash flow statement for 20X1 and 20X2.

4   Set out below are the condensed balance sheets for Zepf and Co Ltd for 20X0 and 20X1, and a profit and loss account for the year ended 31 December 20X1.

**Comparative balance sheets at 31 December 20X0 and 20X1**

|  | 20X0 | | 20X1 | |
|---|---|---|---|---|
|  | £000 | £000 | £000 | £000 |
| **Fixed assets** | | | | |
| Land and buildings at cost | 240 | | 240 | |
| Accumulated depreciation | 30 | | 40 | |
|  | | 210 | | 200 |
| Plant and machinery at cost | 262 | | 694 | |
| Accumulated depreciation | 42 | | 84 | |
|  | | 220 | | 610 |
| Motor vehicles | 60 | | 60 | |
| Accumulated depreciation | 30 | | 34 | |
|  | | 30 | | 26 |
|  | | 460 | | 836 |
| **Current assets** | | | | |
| Stocks | 204 | | 234 | |
| Trade debtors | 360 | | 432 | |
| Cash at bank and in hand | 276 | | 10 | |
|  | 840 | | 676 | |
| Creditors: amounts falling due within one year: | | | | |
| Trade creditors | (144) | | (192) | |
| Taxation | (60) | | (80) | |
| Proposed dividend | (16) | | (20) | |
|  | (220) | | (292) | |
| Net current assets | | 620 | | 384 |
| Total assets *less* current liabilities | | 1,080 | | 1,220 |
| Creditors: amounts falling due after one year: | | | | |
| 7% debenture loans | | 140 | | 200 |
|  | | 940 | | 1,020 |
| **Capital and reserves** | | | | |
| Called-up share capital | | 600 | | 600 |
| Share premium account | | 100 | | 100 |
| Other reserves | | 80 | | 100 |
| Profit and loss account | | 160 | | 220 |
|  | | 940 | | 1,020 |

**Summarized profit and loss account for the year ended 31 December 20X1**

|  | £000 | £000 |
|---|---|---|
| Turnover |  | 1,324 |
| Cost of sales |  | 936 |
| Gross profit |  | 388 |
| Distribution costs | 98 |  |
| Administrative expenses | 100 |  |
|  |  | 198 |
| Profit on ordinary activities |  | 190 |
| Taxation on ordinary activities |  | 80 |
|  |  | 110 |
| Loss on the sale of assets |  | 10 |
| Profit for the financial year |  | 100 |
| Ordinary dividend proposed |  | (20) |
| Transfer to reserves |  | (20) |
| Retained profit for the financial year |  | 60 |

Plant and machinery recorded at cost of £28,000 and at written-down value of £16,000 was sold for £6,000.

*Required:*
Prepare a cash flow statement for the year ended 31 December 20X1.

5* Kashvlow Limited has the following balance sheets for the years ended 31 December 20X0 and 31 December 20X1.

**Kashvlow Limited**
**Balance sheet as at 31 December 20X0**

|  | £ | £ |  | £ | £ | £ |
|---|---|---|---|---|---|---|
|  |  |  |  |  | Accumulated |  |
| **Capital** |  |  | **Fixed assets** | Cost | depreciation |  |
| Ordinary shares |  | 350,000 | Buildings | 310,000 |  | 310,000 |
| Redeemable preference shares |  | 150,000 | Plant | 431,000 | 195,000 | 236,000 |
| Profit and loss account |  | 210,000 | Vehicles | 196,000 | 85,000 | 111,000 |
|  |  | 710,000 |  | 937,000 | 280,000 | 657,000 |
|  |  |  |  |  |  |  |
| **Long-term liabilities** |  |  |  |  |  |  |
| Debentures |  | 50,000 | Investment in associate |  |  | 120,000 |
|  |  |  |  |  |  |  |
| **Current liabilities** |  |  | **Current assets** |  |  |  |
| Taxation | 70,000 |  | Stock |  | 100,000 |  |
| Dividend | 40,000 |  | Debtors |  | 120,000 |  |
| Creditors | 110,000 |  | Bills receivable |  | 20,000 |  |
| Bank overdraft | 40,000 |  | Cash in hand |  | 3,000 |  |
|  |  | 260,000 |  |  |  | 243,000 |
|  |  | 1,020,000 |  |  |  | 1,020,000 |

**Kashvlow Limited**
**Balance sheet as at 31 December 20X1**

| | £ | £ | | £ | £ | £ |
|---|---|---|---|---|---|---|
| | | | | | Accumulated | |
| **Capital** | | **Fixed assets** | | Cost | depreciation | |
| Ordinary shares | | 350,000 | Buildings | 250,000 | | 250,000 |
| Capital redemption reserve fund | | 150,000 | Plant | 460,000 | 287,000 | 173,000 |
| Profit and loss account | | 139,000 | Vehicles | 220,000 | 100,000 | 120,000 |
| | | 639,000 | | 930,000 | 387,000 | 543,000 |
| | | | | | | |
| **Long-term liabilities** | | | | | | |
| Debentures | | 100,000 | Investment in associate | | | 140,000 |
| | | | Loan to associate | | | 40,000 |
| | | | | | | |
| **Current liabilities** | | | **Current assets** | | | |
| Taxation | 80,000 | | Stock | | 120,000 | |
| Dividend | 60,000 | | Debtors | | 170,000 | |
| Creditors | 140,000 | | Bank balance | | 5,000 | |
| | | | Cash in hand | | 1,000 | |
| | | 280,000 | | | | 296,000 |
| | | 1,019,000 | | | | 1,019,000 |

*Notes:*
1  During the year a building was sold for £90,000 and motor vehicles costing £90,000 were sold for £40,000, a book loss of £10,000. New vehicles were bought for £114,000.
2  Depreciation is 20 per cent straight-line for plant, and 25 per cent straight-line for vehicles.
3  A £15,000 premium on the redemption of preference shares was written off to P & L in the year.

*Required:*
(a)  Reconstruct the company's profit and loss account for 20X1.
(b)  Prepare a cash flow statement.

# 16 Interpreting and comparing financial reports

**Setting the scene**

Financial statements generally provide users with essential information that heavily influences their decisions. They are an excellent model for capturing and organising financial information. They package information in a structured fashion that permits analysis of a wide range of trends and relationships among the data. These trends and relationships, in turn, provide considerable insight into a company's opportunities and risks, including growth and market acceptance, costs, productivity, profitability, liquidity and many others.

(AICPA, 1994)

**Learning objectives**

After studying this chapter you should be able to:

1 Conduct a ratio analysis using the contents of the financial statements of a commercial organization.

2 Discuss the limitations of the analytical techniques used.

3 Examine the ability of published financial statements to predict business failure.

Financial reports combine facts and personal judgements, both of which are influenced in the manner of presentation to users by accounting concepts. In attempting to interpret the information disclosed, it is necessary to be aware of the limitations imposed by accounting concepts and methods of valuation which, as we have noted in previous chapters, may seriously distort the basic underlying events of importance to investors.

Ratio analysis is the most widely used technique for interpreting and comparing financial reports. Ratios are useful because they can be used to summarize briefly relationships and results that are significant to an appreciation of critical business indicators of performance, for example, the ratio of net profit to assets employed. Moreover, ratios are particularly useful for the purpose of comparing performance from year to year, and the performance of different companies, given that aggregate figures are always of differing orders of magnitude. However, it must be emphasized that companies differ one from another in many ways and also may change from year to year in terms of strategy. Ratios, on their own, will not be sufficient providers of information about a company. Information of a non-financial nature will generally be required before a meaningful analysis is possible.

The collection of ratios on a systematic basis allows trends to emerge, and throws into relief the significance of changes indicated by the analysis of current events. Since the future is uncertain, the analyst has to rely substantially on past behaviour for predicting future changes. In this respect, the trends indicated by ratios are very useful for making predictions. For example, it is not known which soccer team will win the championship next season. Hence, in making any predictions in this respect, one has to rely on the performance of all the clubs in previous seasons.

The function of ratio analysis, therefore, is to allow comparisons to be made which assist in predicting the future. In this connection, it should be stressed that the fact that Ada Ltd has a ratio of net profit to assets employed of 10 per cent in the year 20X0 is meaningless by itself. To be meaningful, that ratio must be compared with the ratios obtained from the results of previous years, and may be made even more meaningful by comparing it with those of its competitors. In this respect, inter-firm comparisons were facilitated in the United Kingdom when the Centre for Inter-Firm Comparisons Ltd, a non-profit-making organization, was established in 1959 by the British Institute of Management in association with the British Productivity Council. This organization collects a large amount of management accounting information from its subscribers. Then, maintaining a high level of confidentiality, it computes a whole range of ratios which are reported back to subscribers together with the best, worst and average ratios. By contrast, the external analyst is confined to the information disclosed in published reports, and tends to rely on such other information as he is able to obtain from other sources in assessing the performance and prospects of individual firms.

## The nature of ratio analysis

Numerous ratios may be computed from financial reports and from other sources, notably stock exchange share prices. In this chapter, we limit our discussion to a number of important ratios which focus on two critical areas – namely, the ability of the firm to survive and grow, and the efficiency of its financial performance.

From the investor's viewpoint, these particular ratios are related directly to the two central issues, which we postulated in Chapter 1 to be the focal points of a normative theory of financial reporting. We argued that the maintenance and increase of the value of the capital invested was the first consideration, and that the second consideration was the level of income which investors expected to derive from the invested capital. Clearly both these considerations are interrelated and interdependent.

The maintenance of the value of the capital invested depends on the ability of the firm to survive, for shareholders, and particularly ordinary shareholders, bear most of the costs if the company fails. Solvency is the most important criterion of the firm's ability to survive. Solvency is the ability of the firm to meet its debts as they fall due for payment, and it is a matter of both fact and law. If a creditor presses a claim for payment of the amount due, and the firm is unable to pay, its inability so to do is a fact. The firm may have substantial assets which may not be realizable at a fair value if they are sold, especially if that sale is pressurized. Its prospects may not necessarily be bad in terms of its future or even its present ability to generate profits

– what is crucial, however, is that it has insufficient liquid resources, that is, cash or near cash, to meet an individual claim, and, moreover, has no further credit facilities available. Solvency becomes a question of law by the formal process in which the creditor seeks the recovery of a debt through a court of law, and upon a direction by the judge that the firm has defaulted upon a payment of a debt ordered by the court, the firm is declared insolvent. The legal procedure for the firm's liquidation by winding-up ensues under a liquidator appointed by the court. Solvency is related, therefore, to the problem of liquidity in relation to the size of current obligations in favour of creditors, and to available credit facilities.

The level of income which investors expect to derive from their investment is related in the first instance to the firm's current financial performance, and in the next instance to its future growth prospects.

The income of shareholders may be seen as consisting of a stream of dividend flows. Over the long term, dividends are related to the level of earnings, that is, realized profit, and this in turn is reflected in the market value of the shares. Ratio analysis enables views to be formulated about the efficiency of current financial performance by relating net profit to such indicators as net assets or share prices, and as far as the investor is concerned by relating dividends to corporate net profit and to share prices. So far as companies with a market quotation are concerned, reported financial performance is a major factor in the determination of share price and hence the wealth of the shareholder. Ratios of financial performance are one way that the market assesses the performance and prospects of a company.

We use the accounts of Ada Ltd which appear below for demonstrating the calculations involved in ratio analysis.

The current stock market price of the ordinary share is £2

**Ada Ltd**
**Profit and loss account for the year ended 31 December 20X0**

|  | £ |
|---|---:|
| Turnover | 350,000 |
| Cost of sales | 208,000 |
| Gross profit | 142,000 |
| Distribution costs | 80,000 |
| Administrative expenses | 30,000 |
| Interest on long-term loan | 4,000 |
| Profit on ordinary activities | 28,000 |
| Tax on profit on ordinary activities | 14,000 |
| Profit on ordinary activities after taxation | 14,000 |
| Preference dividend | 2,000 |
| Profit for the financial year | 12,000 |
| Ordinary dividend | 5,000 |
| Retained profit | 7,000 |

**Ada Ltd**
**Balance sheet at 31 December 20X0**

| | | £ |
|---|---|---|
| **Fixed assets** | | |
| Tangible assets at cost less depreciation | | 130,000 |
| | | |
| **Current assets** | £ | |
| Stock (opening £35,000) | 45,000 | |
| Debtors | 40,000 | |
| Cash | 7,000 | |
| | 92,000 | |
| Creditors: amounts falling due within one year: | | |
| Trade creditors | 23,000 | |
| Other liabilities | 28,000 | |
| | 51,000 | |
| Net current assets | | 41,000 |
| Total assets *less* current liabilities | | 171,000 |
| Creditors: amounts falling due after more than one year: | | |
| Debenture loans | | 40,000 |
| | | 131,000 |
| **Capital and reserves** | | |
| 80,000 £1 ordinary shares | | 80,000 |
| 20,000 10% preference shares | | 20,000 |
| Profit and loss account | | 31,000 |
| | | 131,000 |

## The analysis of solvency

We mentioned earlier that solvency was a question of fact in the first instance. Given the nature of financial reports, it follows that ratio analysis may make only a limited contribution to assessing solvency for the following reasons:

1 The firm's total current liabilities and total current assets at the end of the last accounting period may indicate that its financial stability is precarious, but solvency happens in the present and not in the past. In this respect, a firm may be perfectly solvent on the last day of the accounting period, and may now be insolvent by reason of the sudden withdrawal of a credit facility upon which it relied.
2 The balance sheet does not reveal sources of credit which the firm may tap, nor the willingness of creditors and investors to see the firm through a difficult period.
3 The accounts do not disclose the complete nature of a company. It is important to have a good idea of a company's receipts and payments pattern in interpreting solvency. For example, a supermarket will be able to generate funds from inventories much more quickly than a manufacturing company.

### Short-term solvency

Although shareholders risk losing their investment in the event of insolvency, unsecured creditors risk financial losses. In the face of a deteriorating financial situation,

247

long-term creditors, such as debenture-holders, may either attempt to realize their security by selling specific assets mortgaged under the debenture instrument, or they may be willing to hold their hand if a viable rescue operation is mounted. Short-term creditors such as trade creditors are generally not willing to allow credit to a firm which is running into financial difficulties, and action from creditors is usually the precipitating cause of insolvency.

Small firms in difficulties perish quickly: large firms, however, bring losses to many around them, not only to short-term creditors but to financial institutions which have supported capital expenditure programmes and granted credits. Indicators of short-term financial stability are particularly important, therefore, in respect of larger firms whose shares are listed, for if action is needed to prevent losses early indicators are required to enable such action to be taken. There are two classes of ratios which are useful in this respect:

1 Ratios which relate current assets to current liabilities, and indicate an imbalance between the burden of immediate debts in relation to the firm's ability to meet such debts.
2 Ratios which indicate the rate at which short-term assets are utilized, thereby affording a measure of the elasticity with which they are transformed into cash.

## Ratios of current assets to current liabilities

Two ratios in common use are:

1 the current ratio;
2 the acid test (or quick) ratio.

The current ratio is the ratio of current assets to current liabilities expressed as follows:

$$\frac{\text{current assets}}{\text{current liabilities}}$$

Because Ada Ltd has current assets valued at £92,000 and current liabilities amounting to £51,000 the current ratio is 1.8:1. It will be recalled that the surplus of current assets over current liabilities also measures working capital, that is, the funds conventionally regarded as being available to finance current operations.

A number of problems stem from the use of the current ratio as a predictor of financial stability. First, since current assets include stock and trade debtors as well as cash, an element of subjectivity is introduced into this ratio by methods of valuing stocks and by the assessment of the likelihood of bad debts. Second, an efficient business may be able to reduce stocks and debtor levels without affecting its financial stability, which is secured by a high rate of funds flowing from current operations. Hence, its current ratio may conceivably be relatively low, and it will still be a viable concern. It will be noted also that some businesses, such as cash retailers, will have a rapid stock turnover and few debtors. In such a case we might expect a very low current ratio to represent the norm. By contrast, a firm with a high current ratio represented by high levels of stocks, debtors and cash may be a very inefficient firm, and the current ratio may conceal a poor rate of funds generation, and hence a very unstable situation. For this reason, Glautier (1971) has argued that the current ratio is not a useful indicator of solvency from a theoretical viewpoint. Nevertheless, it should be said that what is a normal current ratio is peculiar to given industries, and financial analysts tend to look for current ratios falling within acceptable limits for the company's particular sector.

The acid test ratio is particularly easy to misinterpret and this stems partly from the traditional definition of this ratio as follows:

$$\frac{\text{current assets} - \text{stocks}}{\text{current liabilities}}$$

An implication of accepting this definition is that stocks will always be unavailable as providers of short-term funds to meet pressing liabilities. A more flexible definition is required of this ratio which attempts to compare potential sources of short-term funds with potential needs for short-term funds. The traditional definition of the acid test ratio would be entirely inappropriate as a measure of the solvency of a business such as a supermarket chain. It might be entirely appropriate to exclude stock when considering a manufacturing company selling on credit to other commercial concerns, but there will be many other companies where much care will need to be exercised. However, we might argue in general terms that if a company does not have sufficient assets which will be converted into cash during the normal credit period, then there is likely to be some risk of insolvency. If we assume that Ada Ltd will have to find £51,000 to meet current liabilities out of its short-term resources of debtors and cash, we find that it has only £47,000 to meet those requirements. This is a ratio of 0.92 to 1 and indicates a potential shortfall. But it would be incorrect to place too much emphasis on a single ratio unless we have something against which to compare it.

While the acid test ratio is a stricter indicator of solvency, it suffers from the same disadvantages which affect the current ratio, that is, it ignores the importance of cash flows from current operations and by emphasizing cash and debtors tends to put the less efficient firm in a more favourable light. It should also be emphasized that there is no such thing as a universally desirable ratio and, therefore, 'rules of thumb' like 2:1 current ratios and 1:1 acid test ratios might be very misleading.

## Ratios of the cash elasticity of current assets (i.e. activity ratios)

Given that current assets normally consist of cash, debtors and stocks, the firm's ability to meet current liabilities depends upon the rate at which cash flows into the firm from current operations. Since sales is the critical event in this respect, the rate at which stocks are sold is clearly crucial. Where a substantial proportion of sales are on credit terms, the rate at which debtors settle their accounts is also crucial. For these reasons, the following ratios are good indicators of the cash elasticity of current assets:

1 average stock turnover;
2 collection period of trade debts.

### *Average stock turnover*
The average stock turnover is calculated by the following formula:

$$\frac{\text{cost of goods sold during the period}}{\text{average stock held}}$$

For Ada Ltd the average stock turnover is as follows:

$$\frac{£208,000}{(£35,000 + £45,000)/2} = 5.2 \text{ times}$$

This ratio means that the average length of time that stocks are held before being sold is 365 days/5.2, that is, 70 days.

The average stock turnover ratio is only a crude measure of the rate at which stocks are sold for the purpose of comparing the cash elasticity of stocks of different enterprises. Different marketing situations face different industries and trades. A butchery will clearly have a much higher stock turnover rate than a firm selling luxury goods. Methods of stock valuation also distort the significance of inter-firm comparisons. It is also important to recognize that average stock as calculated above is only an approximation and that seasonal fluctuations, or increased sales and stockholdings during the year, may seriously distort this figure. A company with major sales at one time of the year such as a fireworks manufacturer could produce wildly differing average stock figures if they are calculated at different times of the year on the above basis.

Nevertheless, the average stock turnover may give a useful indication of trading difficulties facing a particular firm by comparing it with the average stock turnover for previous periods. A fall in the average stock turnover may indicate stiffening competition, adverse marketing circumstances or a degree of obsolescence in the firm's products. At the same time, firms operating in similar markets may be expected to have roughly similar average stock turnover ratios, so that even as a crude ratio of comparability, it may be a useful indicator for investors.

### Collection period of trade debts

An important measure of the cash elasticity of debtor balances may be obtained from the average collection period of trade debtors by using the following formula:

$$\frac{\text{trade debtors} \times 365}{\text{credit sales}}$$

If we assume that Ada Ltd sells all its goods on credit, we calculate the average collection period as follows:

$$\frac{£40,000 \times 365}{£350,000} = 42 \text{ days}$$

These calculations show that 42 days is the approximate time required to collect trade debts outstanding at 31 December 20X0. By applying this ratio, analysts establish if the average collection period for debtors is too slow. A rough rule of thumb which is sometimes used by credit agencies is that the average age of trade debts should not exceed $1\frac{1}{3}$ times the net credit period. If a firm gives 30 days' credit for the settlement of debtor accounts, the average collection period should not exceed approximately 40 days. However, information about credit terms is not included in a company's accounts. Again, it must be recognized that the calculation of days' sales in debtors is an approximation which assumes more or less consistent sales levels during the year. If a company experienced relatively high sales in the period immediately before the accounting date, this would have the effect of increasing the collection period, since a high current sales level would be compared to a lower average level for the year. Companies will have accurate information available internally through analysis of the sales day book or, more likely, computerized analysis of the average collection period for debtors plus detailed aged debtors lists.

## Other factors affecting short-term solvency

In addition to the ratios mentioned above, other factors which should be taken into account when evaluating short-term solvency include:

1 *The size of operating costs.* Neither the profit and loss account nor the balance sheet reveal the cash required to meet current operating costs such as payroll, rent and other expenses. Where a firm has very few liquid assets in its balance sheet, and it is faced, for example, with very large payroll obligations, it may be extremely short of cash.
2 *Bank credit.* A firm which has sufficient credit facility at the bank may, as we mentioned earlier, have lower current and acid test ratios.
3 *Seasonal patterns of trade.* Where firms normally expect seasonal patterns of trade, there will be distortions in the solvency ratios arising from seasonal build-up of stocks, trade debtors and cash depletions during the time interval across the peak season as mentioned above. Where such seasonal patterns of trade exist, they must be taken into account when making inter-firm comparisons.

# Long-term solvency

We defined solvency as the ability to meet current liabilities as they fall due for payment. The long-term financial stability of the firm may be considered as dependent upon its ability to meet all liabilities, including those not currently payable.

Two ratios which are considered important in this respect are:

1 the shareholders' equity ratio;
2 the interest coverage ratio.

## Shareholders' equity ratio

This ratio is considered by many analysts to be equal in importance to the current ratio as an indicator of financial stability. It is computed as follows:

$$\text{shareholders' equity ratio} = \frac{\text{shareholders' equity}}{\text{total assets}} \times 100$$

Substituting figures from Ada's accounts:

$$\frac{£111,000}{£222,000} \times 100 = 50\%$$

It is generally felt that the larger the proportion of the shareholders' equity, the stronger is the financial position of the firm. This is related to the notion of 'gearing' which we discussed in Chapter 13. By increasing long-term borrowing, the firm may increase its current assets, thereby creating a more favourable current ratio. At the same time, however, it reduces the shareholders' equity, signalling a possible over-dependence on outside sources for long-term financial needs. This creates a problem associated with high levels of gearing, namely that where net profit tends to fluctuate, a high level of fixed interest payments may greatly impair the ability of the company to make dividend payments and will certainly magnify the variations in earnings attributable to shareholders and hence share prices.

Although no explicit rules of thumb exist regarding desirable shareholders' equity ratios, financial analysts may have a general idea of the appropriate financial structure of a particular company by considering the stability of its profit. The less variable a company's underlying business activities and profits, the more safely it can use long-term debt. The total risk of a company is made up of business risk (i.e. risk inherent in the type of business) and financial risk (i.e. through borrowing) and, therefore, if a company has low business risk it will generally be able to absorb more financial risk.

### Interest coverage ratio

The ability of a firm to meet its debt service costs out of current earnings is a rough indicator of its long-term solvency. Long-term loans which are usually in the form of debentures carry interest charges which must be paid regularly. The inability to meet such interest charges places the firm's solvency into jeopardy. The interest cover ratio is calculated as follows:

$$\text{interest coverage ratio} = \frac{\text{profit before interest and tax}}{\text{periodic interest charges}}$$

$$= \frac{£32,000}{£4,000} = 8 \text{ times}$$

Generally speaking, a firm which can cover its debt service costs several times over by its operating profit even in a poor year would be regarded as a satisfactory risk by long-term creditors. The level of safety required would, however, depend on the company's level of business (inherent) risk.

## The analysis of financial performance

There are two aspects of a company's financial performance of interest to investors. First, its financial performance may be assessed by reference to its ability to generate profit. Ratios of financial efficiency in this respect focus on the relationships between profit and sales and profit and assets employed. Second, the company's financial performance may be assessed in terms of the value of its shares to investors. In this sense, ratios of financial performance focus on earnings per share, dividend yield and price/earnings ratios.

## The analysis of earning power

The overall measure of earnings performance for purposes of comparison is the return on capital employed. This ratio is made up of several components, two of the most important of which are the asset turnover ratio and the return-on-sales ratio.

### Return on capital employed

There are several ways of expressing this ratio, and care must be taken in making inter-firm comparisons that the basis used is the same. The return on capital employed may be expressed as follows:

$$\text{return on net assets} = \frac{\text{operating profit (before interest and tax)}}{\text{total assets less current liabilities}}$$

$$\text{return on shareholders' equity} = \frac{\text{profit (after interest and tax)}}{\text{shareholders' equity}}$$

In these ratios interest is added back to profit so as to make comparisons between firms with different gearing more comparable.

Return on net assets indicates the efficiency with which management used the resources to earn profit. For Ada Ltd it is computed as follows:

$$\frac{£32,000}{£171,000} \times 100 = 18.7\%$$

Return on shareholders' equity measures the return which accrues to the shareholders after interest payments to creditors and taxes are deducted. It does not measure the efficiency with which available resources were used, but rather the residual return to the owners on their investment in the business. For Ada Ltd the return on shareholders' equity is calculated as follows:

$$\frac{£12,000}{£111,000} \times 100 = 10.8\%$$

When comparing the ratios of different companies it is necessary to adjust the data for any differences in accounting policies. However, it will be difficult for an outsider to assess the effects of such differences. Also, the inherent weaknesses of the historic cost accounting system might be especially significant when considering these ratios because the true value of corporate assets may be difficult to assess.

The factors which affect the return on capital employed may be broken down into the following ratios:

These ratios may be further subdivided, for example, by a closer analysis of the components of current assets, that is, stocks and debtors, and the elements of direct and overhead expenses.

The ratio of return on capital employed (ROCE) is generally expressed as follows:

$$ROCE = \frac{sales}{capital\ employed} \times \frac{net\ profit}{sales} \times 100$$

## Asset turnover ratios

The first component of the formula for calculating the ROCE is an asset utilization ratio. It is intended to reflect the intensity with which assets are employed. Thus, if the firm has a low ratio of sales to assets, it is implied that some substantial underutilization of assets is occurring, or alternatively that assets are not being efficiently employed. This ratio focuses, therefore, on the use of assets made by management. Because it is a measure of past managerial efficiency in this respect, it is thought to provide a reasonable basis for forecasting management's future efficiency. It is considered to be a prime determinant of the level of future profit flows.

The following ratios may be used and the data for their calculation is derived from the accounts of Ada Ltd.

$$\text{total assets turnover} = \frac{\text{turnover}}{\text{total assets}}$$

$$= \frac{£350,000}{£222,000} = 1.6 \text{ times}$$

$$\text{fixed assets turnover} = \frac{\text{turnover}}{\text{fixed assets}}$$

$$= \frac{£350,000}{£13,000} = 2.7 \text{ times}$$

$$\text{working capital turnover} = \frac{\text{turnover}}{\text{net current assets}}$$

$$= \frac{£350,000}{£41,000} = 8.5 \text{ times}$$

### The ratio of net profit on sales

This is the second component of the formula for calculating the ROCE. It seeks to assess the profitability of sales, that is, the efficiency of sales as a critical event in generating profit.

The ratio of net profit on sales varies widely from industry to industry, so that it should be used solely for comparing similar companies in the same industry, or in assessing the performance of the same company over a period of time. Some companies may operate in an industry characterized by low profit margins and high levels of turnover, for example, the manufacture and distribution of foodstuffs. It is also possible that a company might make a strategy decision to move up or down market.

In considering the relevance of ratios of performance, conventional accounting measurements introduce limitations. Current value accounting removes at least two basic difficulties. First, the effect of the timing differences in the acquisition of assets, which results in the aggregation of assets of differing money value being removed, and similar values are added together. Second, the use of historical cost measurements results in arbitrary allocations, e.g. LIFO and FIFO allocations of stocks to the cost of sales. Replacement cost accounting increases the usefulness of ratio analysis by providing uniformity in cost allocations, since all costs are allocated at their replacement price.

For Ada Ltd the ratio is calculated as follows:

$$\frac{£32,000}{£350,000} \times 100 = 9.1\%$$

## The analysis of investment decisions

In buying the shares of a particular company, investors are seeking to make the best allocation of their investment funds. Although the earnings efficiency of that company is very important to the investors, it has to be related to its shares. For this reason, several ratios are used by investors to appraise the performance of companies in terms of share prices and yields.

## Earnings per share

FRS 14, which superseded SSAP 3, requires that all companies listed on a recognized stock exchange show in their published accounts the earnings per share (EPS) for the accounting period and for the previous period. EPS is the profit in pence attributable to each equity share after deducting preference dividend and extraordinary items, divided by the weighted average number of ordinary shares outstanding during the period. The EPS for Ada Ltd is calculated as follows:

$$\text{EPS} = \frac{£12,000}{80,000} = 15 \text{ pence per share}$$

The Institute of Investment Management and Research (1993) sets out a 'headline' definition of earnings which states:

1 All the trading profits and losses of the company for the year (including abnormal items) should be included in the earnings number.
2 Profits and losses arising in operations discontinued at some point during the year, or in operations acquired at some point during the year, should remain in the earnings figure. The profit or loss on the sale or termination of a discontinued operation should be excluded.
3 Profits and losses on the sale of fixed assets or of businesses, or on their permanent diminution in value or write-off, should be excluded.

EPS is an important ratio for two reasons. First, the trend in EPS is a useful indicator to investors in the company of the profitable use of their money. Second, EPS is related by investment analysts to the market price of the shares to derive the price/earnings ratio. (See below.) For these reasons, it is important that EPS should be calculated and disclosed on a comparable basis from year to year and between one company and another.

## Price/earnings ratio

This ratio indicates the number of years it would take to recover the share price out of the current earnings of the company. It is calculated by dividing the market price of the ordinary shares of a company by the EPS figure described above. For Ada Ltd the price/earnings ratio is calculated as follows:

$$\text{price/earnings ratio} = \frac{£2}{15 \text{ pence}} = 13.3$$

What this means is that if £2 is paid for these shares, then 13.3 years of current earnings of 15 pence per share are being bought. Because the current market value of a share reflects the expectations of investors concerning the future profits of a company, the ratio is effectively measuring the market's anticipations for future earnings compared to the current performance of the company. Therefore, the price/earnings ratio is an indicator of the confidence that the stock market has in the company. A low price/earnings ratio suggests a lack of confidence in the company's ability to maintain earnings, while a high price/earnings ratio suggests a belief that the company is expected to increase earnings in the future. However, as with all ratios, interpretation must allow for differences between companies. A highly risky company will be expected to generate higher returns than a 'safe' one and this will be reflected by a relatively lower price/earnings ratio.

### Dividend yield

The dividend yield focuses closely on the value of the declared dividends to an investor. It is calculated as follows:

$$\text{dividend yield} = \frac{\text{dividend per ordinary share}}{\text{market price per ordinary share}}$$

In the case of Ada Ltd the dividend per ordinary share is:

$$\frac{£5,000}{80,000} = 6.25 \text{ pence}$$

The dividend yield is:

$$\frac{6.25 \text{ pence}}{£2} = 3.1\%$$

The dividend yield shows the return currently earned in the form of dividends from an investment in shares. Future returns will be affected by changes in the rate of dividend and movement in the share price.

### Dividend cover ratio (or payout ratio)

The ability of a company to continue to pay current dividend levels in the future may be forecast by the dividend cover ratio, which may be calculated as follows:

$$\text{dividend cover} = \frac{\text{net profit after taxation and preference dividend}}{\text{ordinary dividend}}$$

The dividend cover ratio indicates the proportion of earnings retained by the company and the level of risk in future years, should earnings decline, for the company to be able to maintain the same dividend payments. Interpretation of dividend ratios is difficult because some investors will prefer low payout (dividend) companies and others high payout companies. Other things being equal, a lower payout leads to greater growth in the value of the company which can then be realized by investors in the form of capital gains through the sale of shares. It is not at all clear whether high or low payout policies will have any effect on share prices and returns, but it is likely that investors will prefer companies to adopt a consistent policy.

## Cash flow ratios

In Chapter 15 we argued that the cash flow statement is designed to aid users in making judgements on the amount, timing and degree of certainty of future cash flows. It has a further purpose: it enables ratios to be developed which relate the cash flow statement to items in the profit and loss account and balance sheet. Two such ratios are explained below.

## Cash return on capital employed

This ratio is expressed as a percentage and is calculated as follows:

$$\frac{\text{net cash flow from operating activities}}{\text{capital employed}} \times 100$$

To many users of financial statements it is cash return on investment rather than the profit-based return on investment that is of greater meaning and value.

## Operating cash flow/total debt

This ratio indicates a firm's ability to cover total debt with the yearly cash flow. The higher the ratio, the better the firm's ability to carry its total debt.

## Ratios as predictors of business failure: empirical studies

Empirical studies have been undertaken to determine the extent to which financial ratios may be used to predict business failure. The ability to predict company failure is particularly important from both the private investor's viewpoint and the social viewpoint, as it is an obvious indication of resource misallocation. An early warning signal of probable failure would enable both management and investors to take preventive measures.

In a study using more powerful statistical techniques than used by his predecessors, Beaver (1966) found that financial ratios proved to be useful in the prediction of failure in that such failure could be predicted at least five years before the event. He concluded that ratios could be used to distinguish correctly firms which would fail from those which would not, with much more success than would be possible by random prediction. One of his significant conclusions was that the most effective predictor of failure was the ratio of both short-term and long-term cash flow to total debt. The next best ratio was the ratio of net profit to total assets. One of Beaver's most surprising findings was that the current ratio was among the worst predictors of failure. Turnover ratios were found to be at the bottom of the list of effective predictors. Generally, Beaver found that 'mixed ratios', which had profit or cash flows compared to assets or liabilities, outperformed short-term solvency ratios which had been believed traditionally to be the best predictors of failure.

In a later study, Beaver (1968) suggested that business failure tends to be determined by permanent factors. He argued that if the basic financial position of a company was sound and profit prospects were good, it would recover from a temporary shortage of liquid assets, but that if the long-term prospects in these areas were not good, business failure could not be prevented by a good liquid position.

Altman (1968, 1983) extended Beaver's univariate (single-variable) analysis to allow for multiple predictors of business failure. He used a multiple discriminant analysis for the purpose of developing a linear function of a number of explanatory variables to predict failure. Altman used twenty-two financial ratios based on data obtained one year before failure, and selected five financial ratios for the purposes of establishing his final discriminant function. These five financial ratios were:

1 working capital/total assets as an indicator of liquidity;
2 retained earnings/total assets as an indicator of the age of the firm and its cumulative profitability;
3 earnings before interest and tax/total assets as an indicator of profitability;
4 market value of the equity/book value of debt as an indicator of financial structure;
5 sales/total assets as an indicator of capital turnover.

Altman's five-variable model correctly identified 95 per cent of the total sample of companies tested for bankruptcy. This percentage rate of success in predicting failure fell to 72 per cent when the data used was obtained two years prior to failure. As earlier data was used in testing the model, so its predictive ability became more unreliable.

Taffler and Tisshaw (1977; Taffler, 1983) applied Altman's multiple discriminant analysis to companies in the United Kingdom. They tested the predictive value of eighty different ratios in a variety of combinations. The best results were found when four ratios were combined in accordance with weighting which reflected their significance to the analysis of business failure.

The ratios used by Taffler and Tisshaw and the weightings which they were given were as follows:

1 Profit before tax/current liabilities (53 per cent), which 'is a profitability measure indicating the ability of an enterprise to cover its current liabilities through its earning power. If it has a low or negative value, its downside risk is clearly greater than that for the average company.'
2 Current assets/total liabilities (13 per cent), which 'is related to the conventional current ratio, and is a measure of the working capital position of the firm. The greater the ratio, the sounder the enterprise.'
3 Current liabilities/total assets (18 per cent), 'which measures the company's current liabilities position and is a financial leverage ratio. The greater its magnitude, the more serious the problems the company has to face in financing the cost of its debt and the acquisition of new debt.'
4 Immediate assets minus current liabilities/operating costs minus depreciation (16 per cent), which 'calculates the time for which the company can finance its continuing operations from its immediate assets, if all other sources of short-time finance are cut off, and is a ratio relatively new to the accounting literature . . . and is akin to the acid test.'

All these empirical studies present evidence to support the conclusion that firms which avoided failure had stronger ratios in areas of significant analysis than firms which failed. The measures used by Altman and Taffler and Tisshaw are expressed by a number known as a 'Z score'. Scores such as these are now available through on-line data services such as 'Datastream'.

Morris (1998) has drawn attention to the limitations of financial ratio analysis which restrict the usefulness of financial ratios for predicting business failure. In particular, he argues that most failure prediction models probably tell potential users little they don't already know. Furthermore, case study research shows that corporate failure is usually the result of an unfortunate and unforeseeable conjunction of events, and the underlying causes of financial distress differ at varying stages of the economic cycle. However, it seems likely that decision makers will continue to refer to failure prediction models.

# Summary

Ratio analysis provides the most commonly used indicators to assess and compare the financial performance of companies, both over time and as between different companies. However, unless ratios are collected in a systematic and uniform manner, comparisons may be very misleading. For this reason, they are most useful when collected and developed by such organizations as the Centre for Inter-Firm Comparisons.

It is very important that external users of financial reports should understand the limitations of ratios based on conventional accounting measurements; otherwise, their analyses will not be sound nor their interpretations valid. The conclusion which may be drawn from our examination of ratio analysis is that its general usefulness and relevance to investors would be enhanced by increasing the uniformity of financial reporting practices and adopting current value accounting.

Considerable interest exists in the possibility of using financial ratios as predictors of business failure. Several studies have been conducted that show that there exist ratios and combinations of ratios which are significant in this regard. Nevertheless, caution is required in accepting the conclusions suggested by financial ratios as regards business failure.

**References**

AICPA (1994). *Improving Business Reporting*, American Institute of Certified Public Accountants.

Altman, E I (1968). 'Financial ratios, discriminant analysis and the prediction of corporate bankruptcy', *Journal of Finance*, No 7.

Altman, E I (1983). *Corporate Financial Distress*, Wiley.

Beaver, W H (1966). 'Financial ratios as predictors of failure', *Journal of Accounting Research*, No 4.

Beaver, W H (1968). 'Alternative accounting measures as predictors of failure', *The Accounting Review*, January.

Glautier, M W E (1971). 'Towards a reformulation of the theory of working capital', *Journal of Business Finance*, Spring.

Institute of Investment Management and Research (1993). *The Definition of Headline Earnings*, Statement of Investment Practice No 1.

Morris, R. (1998). 'Forecasting bankruptcy: how useful are failure prediction models?', *Management Accounting*, May.

Taffler, R J (1983). 'The assessment of company solvency and performance using a statistical model – a comparative UK-based study', *Accounting and Business Research*, Autumn.

Taffler, R J and Tisshaw, H (1977). 'Going, going, gone – four factors which predict', *Accountancy*, March.

**Problems** *(\* indicates that a solution is to be found in the Lecturer's Guide)*

1   The following information relates to the operations of the East Lancashire Trading Company for the three-year period ended 31 December 20X2:

### Profit and loss accounts

|  | 20X2 | 20X1 | 20X0 |
|---|---|---|---|
|  | £ | £ | £ |
| Net sales | 1,000,000 | 900,000 | 800,000 |
| Cost of goods sold | 600,000 | 550,000 | 545,000 |
| Gross profit | 400,000 | 350,000 | 255,000 |
| Selling and administrative expenses | 300,000 | 275,000 | 220,000 |
| Net profit before tax | 100,000 | 75,000 | 35,000 |
| Tax at 50% | 50,000 | 37,500 | 17,500 |
| Net profit after tax | 50,000 | 37,500 | 17,500 |
| Dividends | 30,000 | 25,000 | 10,000 |
| Net increase in retained earnings | 20,000 | 12,500 | 7,500 |

### Balance sheets

|  | 20X2 | 20X1 | 20X0 |
|---|---|---|---|
|  | £ | £ | £ |
| **Assets** |  |  |  |
| Land and buildings | 500,000 | 450,000 | 425,000 |
| Plant and equipment (net) | 450,000 | 500,000 | 410,000 |
| Stocks (at cost) | 635,000 | 600,000 | 520,000 |
| Debtors | 425,000 | 410,000 | 440,000 |
| Bank balance | 40,000 | 55,000 | 63,000 |
|  | 2,050,000 | 2,015,000 | 1,858,000 |
| **Shareholders' equity and liabilities** | £ | £ | £ |
| Ordinary share capital £1 shares fully paid | 600,000 | 600,000 | 600,000 |
| Share premium account | 125,000 | 125,000 | 125,000 |
| Retained earnings | 532,000 | 512,000 | 500,000 |
| 12% debentures 20X9 | 200,000 | 200,000 | 200,000 |
| Creditors | 496,000 | 493,000 | 390,000 |
| Accrued expenses | 15,000 | 17,000 | 9,000 |
| Taxation | 52,000 | 43,000 | 24,000 |
| Provision for dividends | 30,000 | 25,000 | 10,000 |
|  | 2,050,000 | 2,015,000 | 1,858,000 |

*Required:*
From the foregoing information, calculate the following ratios for the years 20X1 and 20X2 (assume that all sales are on a credit basis and the year is 360 days):

(a)  The current ratio
(b)  The acid test ratio
(c)  The average stock turnover
(d)  The average collection period for debtors
(e)  The shareholders' equity ratio
(f)   The return on capital employed
(g)  The earnings per share.

Evaluate the liquidity position of the company at the end of 20X2 as compared with 20X1.

2*   Evaluate the usefulness of financial ratio analysis in assessing the financial state of an enterprise. Use the case below to illustrate your answer.

*Case*
A summary of the results of Sandygate Enterprises Limited for the last three years is as follows:

|  | Year ended 31 December | | |
|  | 20X0 | 20X1 | 20X2 |
| --- | --- | --- | --- |
|  | £ | £ | £ |
| Sales | 480,000 | 560,000 | 690,000 |
| Profits before tax | 63,000 | 70,000 | 74,000 |
| Tax | 23,000 | 25,000 | 28,000 |
| Profits after tax | 40,000 | 45,000 | 46,000 |
| Dividends | 30,000 | 30,000 | 36,000 |
| Retained profit for year | 10,000 | 15,000 | 10,000 |
|  | £ | £ | £ |
| Share capital (600,000 £0.25 shares) | 150,000 | 150,000 | 150,000 |
| Retained profit | 85,000 | 100,000 | 110,000 |
| Shareholders' funds | 235,000 | 250,000 | 260,000 |
| 10% debentures | 65,000 | 150,000 | 150,000 |
| Capital employed | 300,000 | 400,000 | 410,000 |
| Market price per share at 31 December | £1 | £1.50 | £1.25 |
| Debt interest | £6,500 | £15,000 | £15,000 |

3   Jack and Jill each carry on business as wholesalers of the same product. Their respective accounts for the year ended 31 December 20X0 are as follows:

**Profit and loss accounts**

|  | Jack | | Jill | |
|---|---|---|---|---|
|  | £ | £ | £ | £ |
| Sales |  | 144,000 |  | 140,000 |
| Cost of sales: |  |  |  |  |
|   Opening stocks | 28,000 |  | 3,200 |  |
|   Purchases | 124,000 |  | 121,600 |  |
|  | 152,000 |  | 124,800 |  |
| Closing stocks | 32,000 | 120,000 | 4,800 | 120,000 |
| Gross profit |  | 24,000 |  | 20,000 |
| Selling expenses | 7,200 |  | 2,800 |  |
| Admin expenses | 8,160 | 15,360 | 9,500 | 12,300 |
| Net profit |  | 8,640 |  | 7,700 |

**Balance sheets at 31 December 20X0**

|  | Jack | Jill |
|---|---|---|
|  | £ | £ |
| Freehold property | 20,000 | 14,000 |
| Fixtures and fittings | 21,750 | 13,840 |
| Motor vehicles | 12,000 | 6,000 |
|  | 53,750 | 33,840 |
| Stocks | 32,000 | 4,800 |
| Debtors | 28,800 | 11,200 |
| Bank | 8,950 | 11,360 |
|  | 123,500 | 61,200 |
| Capital | 108,000 | 30,800 |
| Creditors | 15,500 | 30,400 |
|  | 123,500 | 61,200 |

*Notes:*
(a)  All sales are on credit.
(b)  The amounts of debtors and creditors have not changed significantly over the year.
(c)  All fixed assets are at written-down value.

*Required:*
Compare the profitability and financial position of the two businesses by:

(a)  calculating suitable ratios for each business;
(b)  commenting on the significance of the results of your calculations.

4   You are financial adviser to a retailing company, Us Ltd. You obtain the accounts of its main competitor operating in the same market, Them Ltd, and extract the comparison shown below:

**Balance sheets as at 31 March 20X0**

| | Us Ltd £000 | Us Ltd £000 | Us Ltd £000 | Them Ltd £000 | Them Ltd £000 | Them Ltd £000 |
|---|---|---|---|---|---|---|
| **Fixed assets** | | | | | | |
| Land and buildings | | 381 | | | 286 | |
| Fixtures and fittings | | 342 | | | 218 | |
| Vehicles | | 62 | | | 59 | |
| | | | 785 | | | 563 |
| **Current assets** | | | | | | |
| Stocks | 96 | | | 122 | | |
| Trade debtors | 166 | | | 124 | | |
| Cash | 9 | | | 6 | | |
| | | 271 | | | 252 | |
| **Current liabilities** | | | | | | |
| Overdraft | 20 | | | 21 | | |
| Trade creditors | 132 | | | 97 | | |
| Accruals | 48 | | | 42 | | |
| | 200 | | | 160 | | |
| | | | 71 | | | 92 |
| | | | 856 | | | 655 |
| **Shareholders' funds** | | | | | | |
| Share capital | | 470 | | | 350 | |
| Capital reserves | | 35 | | | 65 | |
| Profit and loss account | | 287 | | | 185 | |
| | | | 792 | | | 600 |
| 10% Debentures | | | 64 | | | 55 |
| | | | 856 | | | 655 |

**Profit and loss accounts for the year ended 31 March 20X0**

| | Us Ltd £000 | Us Ltd £000 | Them Ltd £000 | Them Ltd £000 |
|---|---|---|---|---|
| Sales (on credit) | | 570 | | 747 |
| Cost of sales | | | | |
| Opening stock | 92 | | 102 | |
| Purchases (on credit) | 381 | | 588 | |
| | 473 | | 690 | |
| Closing stock | 96 | | 122 | |
| | | 377 | | 568 |
| Gross profit | | 193 | | 179 |
| Distribution costs | 60 | | 64 | |
| Administration costs | 29 | | 31 | |
| | | 89 | | 95 |
| | | 104 | | 84 |
| Interest charges | | 8 | | 9 |
| Net profit | | 96 | | 75 |
| Taxation | | 45 | | 37 |
| | | 51 | | 38 |
| Dividend | | 37 | | 24 |
| Retained profit for the year | | 14 | | 14 |

263

Upon analysing this information, you observe that it reveals significant differences between the companies.

*Required:*
(a) Calculate and identify the key differences in profitability and in working capital management as between the two companies.
(b) Based upon the analysis at (a) above, recommend actions which the management of Us Ltd should consider in order to improve their financial performance.
(c) State any reservations you may have about drawing conclusions from the comparative analysis of the two companies.

# 17 Financial accounting for groups of companies

## Learning objectives

After studying this chapter you should be able to:

1 Define a group of companies.

2 Give examples of internal transactions requiring elimination on consolidation.

3 Prepare consolidated accounts.

Corporate growth has manifested itself in several ways. By the process of horizontal integration, firms engaged in the production or sale of comparable goods have combined to create monopoly or semi-monopoly situations. Similarly, the process of vertical integration has been important in the historical process by which the giant corporation has emerged. Vertical integration is the combination of firms having a supplier–customer relationship. Finally, the conglomerate is a group of companies having diversified activities, which has been brought under centralized control. The process of corporate growth has continued unabated for several decades. The multinational corporation has emerged, with activities straddling many nations, creating thereby special managerial and accounting problems. Through these processes groups of companies have emerged as a major feature of modern industrial and commercial organization.

There are many reasons why this external expansion by the process of 'acquiring' or 'merging with' another company is preferred to investing in internal expansion. External expansion provides a growing company with immediate access to productive capacity, distribution networks and suppliers, thereby avoiding startup delays which could be lengthy and costly. Also, by acquiring an existing company, the growing company obtains an existing experience of its problems, profitability and other factors relevant to the new management, indicating the success factors and the pitfalls associated with a new business venture. Similarly, the easiest way of entering a competitive market may be by acquiring an existing company, thereby avoiding the risks and problems which a new entrant to that market would face.

This chapter is concerned with setting out the framework within which the accounting problems of 'groups' of companies may be discussed. These revolve around two principal issues:

1 How should a group be defined?
2 How should consolidated accounts be prepared?

## The regulatory framework

United Kingdom law and practice is defined in the Companies Acts 1985 and 1989, which contain detailed requirements governing consolidation, and FRS 2 'Accounting for Subsidiary Undertakings' (1992). Although the standard operates within and in accordance with these requirements, it makes significant improvements to these provisions by reducing alternatives and by making definitions and requirements more precise. In addition, FRS9 'Associates and Joint Ventures' deals with companies which are closely related to a group, but do not fall within it for the purpose of consolidation.

## Definition of a group

If two separate companies operate independently of each other, they will maintain separate accounting records and prepare separate financial statements. However, if one company controls the other, a group is said to exist which consists of the controlling or parent company and the controlled or subsidiary company. Both companies will retain their separate legal identity and operations and separate accounting records. Equally, they will remain responsible in law for all their actions and liable to tax on their own profits. However, the objective of preparing financial statements in the form of balance sheets and profit and loss accounts assumes an additional dimension. If the shareholders of the parent company are to be fully informed of its activities, they will need to be informed about the substance of the controlling interest it has in the subsidiary company. This information need is met by the preparation of consolidated accounts for the group, in the form of a consolidated balance sheet and a consolidated profit and loss account, created by aggregating the separate balance sheets and profit and loss accounts of the parent and subsidiary companies.

The initial problem to be resolved is how to determine when an obligation to produce consolidated accounts exists. United Kingdom law and practice, as reflected in the Companies Acts and FRS 2, is based on the legal control concept. According to the Companies Act 1989 an undertaking is a parent undertaking in relation to another undertaking, a subsidiary, if:

1 it holds a majority of the voting rights in the undertaking; or
2 it is a member of the undertaking and has the right to appoint or remove a majority of its board of directors; or
3 it has the right to exercise dominant influence over the undertaking
  (a) by virtue of provisions contained in the undertaking's memorandum or articles; or
  (b) by virtue of a control contract; or
4 it is a member of the undertaking and controls alone, pursuant to an agreement with other shareholders or members, a majority of the voting rights in the undertaking.

The main change introduced by the Act is that the definition of a subsidiary is based on a company's ability to exercise control over another, rather than on the ownership of a majority of a particular class of shares. Accordingly, a group is said to exist whenever legal entities which are independent of each other are brought under central management, regardless of the situation of the equity ownership. In addition to implementing the EC Seventh Directive, this change to the definition of a subsidiary should curb the use of off-balance-sheet finance vehicles used, for example, to reduce the apparent level of group borrowing through special purpose vehicles controlled by the parent company but structured to fall outside the pre-1989 Companies Act definition. Some companies which were not subsidiaries under the previous definition have been consolidated by the requirements of the Act. Vehicles other than companies, including certain partnerships and joint ventures, can also come within the consolidation requirement.

Finally, as far as definitions are concerned, it is appropriate at this stage to note the existence of the concept of an associated company. FRS 9 defines an associate as an investor who holds a participating interest and exercises a significant influence in the direction of its investee through participation in policy decisions. An associated company is not part of the group and its accounts are, therefore, not consolidated with those of other group companies. Instead, the concept of equity accounting is applied, the principles of which are dealt with in Chapter 18.

## Preparation of consolidated accounts

The purpose of preparing consolidated accounts is to present the financial results and position of the companies in the group as though they were a single enterprise. Generally, all companies within a group adopt the same accounting year. When the final accounts of all the separate companies in the group have been prepared, the process of preparing group accounts is begun. To put it very simply, consolidated accounts are prepared by aggregating all the individual balance sheets and profit and loss accounts. The balance sheet and profit and loss account of the parent company are used as the basis for compiling the group balance sheet and profit and loss account. Thus, the shareholders of the parent company receive a group balance sheet and group profit and loss account which are expansions of those of the parent company, resulting from adding to the parent company's accounts those of its subsidiaries.

The objective of consolidation is to present the accounts of the group as if it were a single business. This objective requires that all internal group transactions are eliminated and that only the transactions external to the group are recorded in the consolidated accounts. Examples of internal transactions requiring elimination on consolidation include:

1 inter-company income and expenditure, such as sales, purchases, rents, royalties, interest or dividends;
2 inter-company profits and losses included in the assets of the group. Typically, this will affect closing stocks resulting from inter-company purchases and comprising the selling company's profit margin on sales. Accordingly, this profit margin must be excluded from the valuation of closing stock and a corresponding adjustment made to net profit (this is discussed further below);
3 inter-company debts and claims, whether short-term trading accounts or long-term advances;
4 the investment in the subsidiary recorded in the books of the parent company is cancelled with the issued share capital of the subsidiary.

In a simple situation, the above elimination followed by aggregation of the remaining balances is all that is required to produce a consolidated balance sheet and profit and loss account. However, two further adjustment areas should be recognized and will frequently be encountered.

First, if the parent company owns less than 100 per cent of the total issued capital of the subsidiary, a minority interest is said to exist in that subsidiary. These non-group shareholders have an interest in the profits and net assets of the subsidiary which must be reflected in the consolidation process. United Kingdom practice effects the consolidation on a control rather than an ownership basis and then separately recognizes any minority interest. Thus, even if less than 100 per cent of the issued capital of the subsidiary is owned by the parent company, the whole of the assets, liabilities and profit and loss account items of the subsidiary are aggregated with those of the holding company, and the minority interest is then shown separately in the consolidated financial statements. As far as the balance sheet is concerned, it is necessary to compute the non-group shareholders' interest in the net assets (share capital and reserves) of the subsidiary at the balance sheet date. For profit and loss account purposes, the minority shareholders' interest in the post-tax profits for the year of the subsidiary is calculated and deducted in the consolidated profit and loss account.

Reference was made above to the fact that inter-company profits reflected in the assets of the group must be eliminated on consolidation, with an effect on the net profit of the group. The question arises as to how the adjustment to profit should be effected. While a number of possible methods may be encountered (some of which are discussed in Chapter 18), the general approach adopted in this book for illustration purposes is to treat all inter-company profit adjustments as being adjustments to the reserves of the group as a whole without any effect on the reserves of profits of any individual group company. Thus minority interests in subsidiaries are, through this approach, unaffected by the inter-company profit eliminated.

The second additional adjustment area will arise where the parent company purchased shares in an existing, operating subsidiary and paid a price for the shares which differed from their par (or nominal) value. This difference would arise because the parent company perceived that the accumulated profits (or losses) of the subsidiary at acquisition rendered the shares worth more than (or less than) their par value. Such profits or losses existing at the date the parent company purchased its interest in the subsidiary are known as pre-acquisition profits (or losses) and are capitalized as part of the consolidation process, i.e. they are removed from the group's reserves figures and, together with the par value of the shares purchased, are compared with the cost of the investment to the parent company.

If the cost of the investment exceeds the total of share capital plus pre-acquisition reserves purchased, then goodwill arises on consolidation. Should the cost of the investment be less than the total of share capital plus pre-acquisition reserves purchased, then negative goodwill arises. The current UK accounting practice applicable to goodwill and negative goodwill is discussed in Chapter 18.

There now follows a comprehensive example, together with worked solution, on the preparation of consolidated financial statements. Further practice questions are included at the end of the chapter.

**Example 1**  P plc is the parent company of S plc, the only subsidiary in the P Group. The following are their respective balance sheets and profit and loss accounts as at 31 December 20X0.

### Balance sheets at 31 December 20X0

| | | P plc | | | | S plc | |
|---|---|---|---|---|---|---|---|
| **Fixed assets** | £ | £ | £ | £ | £ | £ | £ |
| Tangible assets | | 210,000 | | | | 180,000 | |
| Investments | | | | | | | |
| Shares in S plc at cost | | 210,000 | | | | – | |
| Other shares | | 100,000 | | | | – | |
| Loan to S plc | | 50,000 | | | | | |
| | | 570,000 | | | | 180,000 | |
| **Current assets** | | | | | | | |
| Stocks | 220,000 | | | | 80,000 | | |
| Debtors | | | | | | | |
| Trade debtors | 420,000 | | | | 260,000 | | |
| Owed by S plc | 60,000 | | | | – | | |
| Cash | 130,000 | | | | 80,000 | | |
| | 830,000 | | | | 420,000 | | |
| Creditors: amounts falling due within one year: | | | | | | | |
| Trade creditors | (480,000) | | | | (79,000) | | |
| Owed to P plc | – | | | | (60,000) | | |
| Net current assets | | 350,000 | | | | 281,000 | |
| Total assets *less* current liabilities | | 920,000 | | | | 461,000 | |
| Creditors: amounts falling due after one year: | | | | | | | |
| Debenture loan | | (100,000) | | | | – | |
| Owed to P plc | | – | | | | (50,000) | |
| | | 820,000 | | | | 411,000 | |
| **Capital and reserves** | | | | | | | |
| Called-up share capital | | 500,000 | | | | 300,000 | |
| Retained profits brought forward for 20X0 | | 270,000 | | | | 90,000 | |
| Profit and loss account | | 50,000 | | | | 21,000 | |
| | | 820,000 | | | | 411,000 | |

The following additional information is available:

1  P plc holds two-thirds of the issued share capital of S plc.
2  P plc has an issued capital of £50,000 shares of £10 each.
3  P plc also holds 10,000 shares in N plc acquired at £10 each. This holding represents 2 per cent of the equity of N plc.

4   P plc has made an interest-free loan of £50,000 to S plc, which is repayable in five years.
5   P plc is owed £60,000 by S plc in respect of sales made to the latter by the former. P plc has no outstanding debts towards S plc at the year end.
6   P plc's closing stock comprised £30,000 purchased from S plc. S plc's profit margin on sales is 10 per cent. The opening stocks did not include any stocks acquired from S plc.
7   S plc's closing stock comprised £20,000 purchased from P plc. P plc's profit margin on sales is 20 per cent. The opening stock also included £20,000 purchased from P plc before it became the parent company of S plc.
8   Inter-company trading transactions were as follows:
    P plc purchases from S plc amounted to £200,000 during the year.
    S plc purchases from P plc amounted to £100,000 during the year.
9   P plc leased a building to S plc at an annual rent of £80,000.
10  S plc has paid a dividend of £30,000, being the dividend declared out of the previous year's profits.
11  P plc purchased its interest in S plc on 1 January 20X0.

### Profit and loss account for the year ended 31 December 20X0

|  | P plc £ | S plc £ |
|---|---|---|
| Turnover | 2,320,000 | 1,000,000 |
| Cost of sales | 1,070,000 | 500,000 |
| Gross profit | 1,250,000 | 500,000 |
| | | |
| Expenses | 1,250,000 | 450,000 |
| | 0 | 50,000 |
| Other operating income: | | |
| Rent from S plc | 80,000 | – |
| | 80,000 | 50,000 |
| Income from shares in group companies: dividend S plc | 20,000 | – |
| Profit on ordinary activities | 100,000 | 50,000 |
| Tax on ordinary activities | 50,000 | 29,000 |
| Profit for the year after tax | 50,000 | 21,000 |

## Consolidated balance sheet as at 31 December 20X0 – worksheet

| | P plc | S plc | P+S plc | Cancellation of inter-company debts and claims | Cancellation of parent company's investments in subsidiary and subsidiary's capital and reserves | Cancellation of inter-company profit/losses | Consolidated balance sheet |
|---|---|---|---|---|---|---|---|
| | £000 | £000 | £000 | £000 | £000 | £000 | £000 |
| **Fixed assets** | | | | | | | |
| Tangible assets | 210 | 180 | 390 | | | | 390 |
| Investments | | | | | | | |
|   Shares in S plc | 210 | – | 210 | | $-210^{(c)}$ | | – |
|   Other shares | 100 | – | 100 | | | | 100 |
|   Loan to S plc | 50 | | 50 | $-50^{(a)}$ | | | |
| | 570 | 180 | 750 | –50 | –210 | – | 490 |
| **Current assets** | | | | | | | |
| Stocks | 220 | 80 | 300 | | | $-7^{(e)}$ | 293 |
| Debtors | | | | | | | |
|   Trade debtors | 420 | 260 | 680 | | | | 680 |
|   Owed by S plc | 60 | – | 60 | –60 | | | – |
| Cash | 130 | 80 | 210 | | | | 210 |
| | 830 | 420 | 1,250 | $-60^{(b)}$ | | $-7^{(e)}$ | 1,183 |
| Creditors: amounts falling due within one year: | | | | | | | |
|   Trade creditors | (480) | (79) | (559) | | | | (559) |
|   Owed to P plc | | (60) | (60) | –(60) | | | – |
| | (480) | (139) | (619) | $-(60)^{(b)}$ | | | (559) |
| Net current assets | 350 | 281 | 631 | $-^{(b)}$ | – | $-7^{(e)}$ | (624) |
| Total assets *less* current liabilities | 920 | 461 | 1,381 | $-50^{(a)}$ | $-210^{(c)}$ | $-7^{(e)}$ | 1,114 |
| Creditors: amounts falling due after one year: | | | | | | | |
|   Debenture loan | (100) | – | (100) | | | | (100) |
|   Owed to P plc | | (50) | (50) | (–50) | | | – |
| | 820 | 411 | 1,231 | $-^{(a)}$ | $-210^{(c)}$ | $-7^{(e)}$ | 1,014 |
| **Capital and reserves** | | | | | | | |
| Called-up share capital | 500 | 300 | 800 | | $-300^{(c)}$ | | 500 |
| Retained profits brought forward | 270 | 90 | 360 | | $-90^{(c)}$ | | 270 |
| Difference on consolidation (non-distributable reserve) | | | | | $50^{(c)}$ | $+20^{(f)}$ | 70 |
| Consolidated profit and loss account (20X0) | 50 | 21 | 71 | | | $-34^{(g)}$ | 37 |
| Minority interests | | | | | $130^{(d)}$ | $+7^{(e)}$ | $137^{(h)}$ |
| | 820 | 411 | 1,231 | | –210 | –7 | 1,014 |

(*a*), (*b*), (*c*), etc. refer to the accompanying explanatory notes.

**Consolidated profit and loss account for year ended 31 December 20X0 – worksheet**

| | P plc | S plc | P+S plc | Cancellation of inter-company income and expenses | Consolidation of profit on inter-company closing stock | Cancellation of inter-company distributions | Consolidated profit and loss a/c |
|---|---|---|---|---|---|---|---|
| | £000 | £000 | £000 | £000 | £000 | £000 | £000 |
| Turnover | 2,320 | 1,000 | 3,320 | $-300^{(i)}$ | | | 3,020 |
| Cost of sales | (1,070) | (500) | (1,570) | $+300^{(i)}$ | $(-7)^{(k)}$ | | (1,277) |
| Gross profit | 1,250 | 500 | 1,750 | – | $(-7)^{(k)}$ | | 1,743 |
| Expenses | (1,250) | (450) | (1,700) | $+80^{(j)}$ | | | (1,620) |
| Operating profit | 0 | 50 | 50 | +80 | (–7) | | 123 |
| Other operating income: | | | | | | | |
| Rent from S plc | 80 | – | 80 | $-80^{(j)}$ | | | – |
| Total operating profit | 80 | 50 | 130 | – | (–7) | | 123 |
| Income from shares in group companies: | | | | | | | |
| Dividend S plc | 20 | – | 20 | | | $(20)^{(l)}$ | – |
| Profit on ordinary activities | 100 | 50 | 150 | – | (–7) | (20) | 123 |
| Tax on ordinary activities | (50) | (29) | (79) | | | | (79) |
| Profit for year after tax | 50 | 21 | 71 | – | $(-7)(k)$ | $(20)^{(l)}$ | 44 |

| | |
|---|---|
| Minority interest in S plc's profit after tax for the year ($\frac{1}{3} \times 21$) | $(7)^{(m)}$ |
| Consolidated profit for the year | 37 |

# Explanatory notes: consolidated balance sheet as at 31 December 20X0

## 1 Cancellation of inter-company debts and claims

The rule requiring the cancellation of inter-company debts and claims is applied as follows:

(a) The cancellation of the loan of £50,000 by P plc to S plc. Therefore, it is eliminated from total group assets and total group liabilities, the net effect on the consolidated balance sheet being zero.

(b) The cancellation of the balance of £60,000 owed by S plc to P plc arising from inter-company sales. Therefore, it is eliminated from total group trade debtors and total group trade creditors, the net effect on the consolidated balance sheet being zero.

## 2 Cancellation of the parent company's investment in the subsidiary company and the cancellation of the subsidiary company's capital and reserves

The rule requiring the cancellation of the parent company's investment in the subsidiary company and the subsidiary company's capital and pre-acquisition reserves is applied as follows:

(c) The cancellation from total group assets of the shares acquired by P plc in S plc at their cost of £210,000.

The cancellation from total group capital and reserves of the called-up share capital and pre-acquisition reserves of S plc amounting to £390,000.

The substitution in the consolidated capital and reserves of a sum representing the difference between the value of the group's interest in the net worth of the subsidiary as against the cost at which this interest was acquired by the parent company. It is calculated as shown on p. 290.

The negative goodwill is added to reserves on the consolidated balance sheet. (For the effect of the dividend paid by S plc on this figure, see (f) below.)

|  | £ |
|---|---|
| S plc: Called-up share capital | 300,000 |
| Reserves | 90,000 |
| | 390,000 |
| | £ |
| P plc: Two-thirds interest therein | 260,000 |
| *Less:* Cost of acquisition | 210,000 |
| Difference on consolidation ('negative goodwill') | 50,000 |

(d) Where the subsidiary company is not wholly owned, the interest of minority shareholders has to be recognized on consolidation. It is shown as an external liability of the group, and is calculated as follows:

|  | £ |
|---|---|
| S plc: Called-up share capital | 300,000 |
| Pre-acquisition reserves | 90,000 |
| | 390,000 |
| | £ |
| Share of minority interests one-third thereof | 130,000 |

This is subject to further adjustment for 20X0 profits – see (h) below.

## 3 Cancellation of inter-company profit/losses

The rule requiring the cancellation of inter-company profits/losses is applied as follows:

(e) The closing stocks held by P plc and S plc resulting from inter-company transactions contain an inter-company profit element which has to be eliminated from the valuation of closing stocks calculated as follows:

|  | £ | £ |
|---|---|---|
| P plc closing stocks purchased from S plc | 30,000 | |
| Inter-company profits thereon being S plc's gross profit margin of 10 per cent | | 3,000 |
| | £ | |
| S plc closing stock purchased from P plc | 20,000 | |
| Inter-company profits thereon, being P plc's gross profit margin of 20 per cent | | 4,000 |
| Inter-company profit included in closing stocks | | 7,000 |

(f)  The dividend of £30,000 paid by S plc was in respect of the previous year's profits, i.e. a year before S plc became a subsidiary of P plc. The £20,000 of the dividend received by P plc is a dividend received out of pre-acquisition profits and as such must be capitalized on consolidation.

In the books of P plc this £20,000 should have been credited to the investment account not to profit, since it represents a return to P plc of part of the cost of its investment in S plc. Since this has not been done in the books of P plc, the adjustment must be effected on consolidation.

In the light of this, the negative goodwill arising on consolidation per note (c) above requires adjustment as follows:

|  | £ | £ |
|---|---|---|
| Two-thirds interest in the capital and pre-acquisition reserves of S plc ($\frac{2}{3} \times$ £390,000) |  | 260,000 |
| Cost of investment | 210,000 |  |
| Less: Pre-acquisition dividend | (20,000) | 190,000 |
| Difference on consolidation (negative goodwill) |  | £70,000 |

(g)  The group's consolidated profits for 20X0 have to be calculated, and since no dividends were paid, the sum calculated will be shown on the balance sheet as at 31 December 20X0 as the profit and loss account balance for the year. It is calculated as shown below.

|  | £ | £ |
|---|---|---|
| Total profits of P plc and S plc as shown |  | 71,000 |
| Less: Cancellation of inter-company profits on consolidation: |  |  |
| Cancellation effected in respect of P plc: |  |  |
| Dividends received from S plc | 20,000 |  |
| Cancellation of profit element on closing stock held by S plc and sold by P plc (note (e)) | 4,000 |  |
| Cancellation effected in respect of S plc: |  |  |
| Cancellation of profit element on closing stocks held by P plc and sold by S plc (note (e)) | 3,000 | 27,000 |
| Less: Share of minority interests in S plc's profit – |  | 44,000 |
| $\frac{1}{3}$ of £21,000 |  | 7,000 |
|  |  | 37,000 |

In accordance with the approach outlined earlier in this chapter, the minority interest in the 20X0 profits of S plc is unaffected by the inter-company profit elimination.

(h)  It remains to show total amounts relating to minority interest, i.e.

|  | £ |
|---|---|
| Share of S plc's profits, calculated as above | 7,000 |
| Share of capital and pre-acquisition reserves (note (d)) | 130,000 |
|  | 137,000 |

# Explanatory notes: consolidated profit and loss account for the year to 31 December 20X0

## 1 Cancellation of inter-company income and expenses

The rule requiring the cancellation of inter-company income and expenses is applied as follows:

(*i*) Inter-company sales and purchases are cancelled, as follows:

|  | £ |
|---|---|
| P plc sales to S plc | 100,000 |
| S plc sales to P plc | 200,000 |
| – | 300,000 |
| P plc purchases from S plc | 200,000 |
| S plc purchases from P plc | 100,000 |
| – | 300,000 |

It will be noted that these are, at this stage, self-cancelling adjustments as regards the consolidated gross profit.

(*j*) Other inter-company income and expenses are cancelled, as follows:

|  | £ |
|---|---|
| S plc rent paid to P plc | 80,000 |
|  | £ |
| P plc rent income received from P plc | 80,000 |

It will be noted that these are likewise self-cancelling adjustments as regards consolidated operating profits.

## 2 Cancellation of inter-company profits on closing stocks resulting from inter-company transactions

The rule requiring the cancellation of inter-company profits on closing stocks resulting from inter-company transactions is applied as follows:

(*k*) The inter-company profits on closing stocks amounting to £7,000, as calculated above (see (g)), have to be eliminated from the consolidated profits. This is most conveniently effected by increasing cost of sales by £7,000, the amount of the profit to be eliminated.

## 3 Cancellation of inter-company distributions

The rule requiring cancellation of inter-company distributions is applied as follows:

(*l*) The cancellation of inter-company distributions from group profits on consolidation means that the dividends received by P plc from S plc must be eliminated from the consolidated profits. Accordingly, the dividends amounting to £20,000 are eliminated from group revenues. Note (f) above pointed out that this is a pre-acquisition dividend, capitalized on consolidation.

## 4 Minority interest

The outside shareholders' interest in the subsidiary's net profit after tax for the year is calculated and deducted in the consolidated profit and loss account: $\frac{1}{3} \times £21,000 = £7,000$.

## Problems  (* indicates that a solution is to be found in the Lecturer's Guide)

1   Set out below are the balance sheets for Macro plc and Micro plc as at 31 December 20X0.

### Balance sheets as at 31 December 20X0

| | Macro plc | | | Micro plc | | |
|---|---|---|---|---|---|---|
| | £000 | £000 | £000 | £000 | £000 | £000 |
| **Fixed assets** | | | | | | |
| Tangible assets | | 5,121 | | | 1,230 | |
| Investments | | | | | | |
| Shares in Micro plc | | 962 | | | – | |
| | | 6,083 | | | 1,230 | |
| **Current assets** | | | | | | |
| Stocks | 1,244 | | | 514 | | |
| Debtors | | | | | | |
| Trade debtors | 2,048 | | | 390 | | |
| Owed by Micro plc | 57 | | | – | | |
| Cash at bank | 960 | | | 46 | | |
| | 4,309 | | | 950 | | |
| Creditors: amounts falling due within one year | | | | | | |
| Trade creditors | (2,825) | | | (634) | | |
| Owed to P plc | – | | | (40) | | |
| Taxation | (315) | | | (60) | | |
| Net current assets | | 1,169 | | | 216 | |
| Total assets *less*: current liabilities | | | 7,252 | | | 1,446 |
| Creditors: amounts falling due after one year | | | | | | |
| Debenture loan | | | (750) | | | – |
| | | | 6,502 | | | 1,446 |
| | | | £000 | | | £000 |
| **Capital and reserves** | | | | | | |
| Called-up share capital | | | 1,800 | | | 600 |
| Reserves brought forward | | | 4,050 | | | 702 |
| Profit and loss account – 20X0 | | | 652 | | | 144 |
| | | | 6,502 | | | 1,446 |

Macro plc bought its holding of 400,000 ordinary shares in Micro plc when the latter's reserves stood at £312,000.

During the year ended 31 December 20X0, Macro plc regularly sold products to Micro plc at a selling price of cost plus 33⅓ per cent. At 31 December 20X0, Micro plc's closing stock included £208,000 purchased from Macro plc.

The difference between the Micro plc's current account of £57,000 shown under debtors on Macro plc's balance sheet and Macro plc's current account of £40,000 shown under creditors on Micro plc's balance sheet is due to the fact that a cheque of £17,000 mailed by Micro plc on 31 December 20X0 was not received by Macro plc until 5 January 20X1.

*Required:*
Prepare a consolidated balance sheet for the Macro Group as at 31 December 20X0.

2  P plc is the parent company of S plc, the only subsidiary in the P Group. The following are their respective balance sheets and profit and loss accounts as at 31 December 20X0:

**Balance sheets at 31 December 20X0**

|  | P plc | | | | S plc | |
|---|---|---|---|---|---|---|
|  | £000 | £000 | £000 | £000 | £000 | £000 |
| **Fixed assets** | | | | | | |
| Tangible assets | | 40,000 | | | 20,000 | |
| Investments | | | | | | |
| Shares in S plc | | 12,000 | | | – | |
| Other shares | | 3,000 | | | – | |
| | | 55,000 | | | 20,000 | |
| **Current assets** | | | | | | |
| Stocks | 7,100 | | | 6,600 | | |
| Debtors | | | | | | |
| Trade debtors | 8,000 | | | 4,000 | | |
| Owed by S plc | 3,500 | | | – | | |
| Cash | 3,400 | | | 2,400 | | |
| | 22,000 | | | 13,000 | | |
| Creditors: amounts falling due within one year | | | | | | |
| Trade creditors | (12,000) | | | (10,250) | | |
| Owed to P plc | – | | | (3,500) | | |
| Net current assets | | 10,000 | | | (750) | |
| Total assets *less* current liabilities | | 65,000 | | | 19,250 | |
| Creditors: amounts falling due after one year | | | | | | |
| Debenture loan | | (23,000) | | | | |
| | | 42,000 | | | 19,250 | |
| | | £000 | | | £000 | |
| **Capital and reserves** | | | | | | |
| Called-up share capital | | 30,000 | | | 15,000 | |
| Reserves brought forward | | 10,000 | | | 4,000 | |
| Profit and loss account for 20X0 | | 2,000 | | | 250 | |
| | | 42,000 | | | 19,250 | |

277

### Profit and loss accounts for the year ended 31 December 20X0

| | P plc £000 | S plc £000 |
|---|---|---|
| Turnover | 300,800 | 150,500 |
| Cost of sales | 116,900 | 59,400 |
| Gross profit | 183,900 | 91,100 |
| Expenses | 180,400 | 88,600 |
| Operating income | 3,500 | 2,500 |
| Income from shares in group companies: | | |
| Dividend S plc | 500 | – |
| Profit on ordinary activities | 4,000 | 2,500 |
| Tax on ordinary activities | 2,000 | 1,500 |
| Profit for the year after tax | 2,000 | 1,000 |
| Dividend | – | 750 |
| | 2,000 | 250 |

The following additional information is also available:

1  P plc holds two-thirds of the issued share capital of S plc, comprising 1,000,000 shares of £10 acquired at £12 each.
2  P plc also holds 200,000 shares of £10 in N plc acquired for £3,000,000 representing 10 per cent of the called-up capital of N plc.
3  P plc is owed £3,500,000 by S plc in respect of sales made to the latter by the former. P plc has no outstanding debts towards S plc at the year end, and does not purchase stock from S plc.
4  S plc's closing stock included £5,000,000 purchased from P plc. P plc's profit margin on sales is 20 per cent. S plc's opening stock did not include any stock purchased from P plc. Total sales from P to S during the year were £15,000,000.
5  P plc purchased its shares in S plc on 1 January 20X0.
6  The dividend received by P plc from S plc is a distribution in respect of the year 20X0 profits of S plc.

*Required:*
Prepare consolidated accounts for the group.

3 The balance sheets of Expanding plc and its two subsidiaries Growing plc and Declining plc as at 31 December 20X0 were as follows:

**Balance sheets at 31 December 20X0**

| | Expanding plc £000 | Growing plc £000 | Declining plc £000 |
|---|---|---|---|
| **Fixed assets** | | | |
| Tangible assets | 525 | 210 | 60 |
| Investments | | | |
| 100,000 shares Growing plc | 140 | – | – |
| 40,000 shares Declining plc | 32 | – | – |
| | 697 | 210 | 60 |
| **Current assets** | | | |
| Stocks | 63 | 83 | 28 |
| Debtors | | | |
| Trade debtors | 60 | 36 | 15 |
| Growing plc | 24 | – | – |
| Declining plc | 16 | 9 | – |
| Cash at bank | 10 | 7 | 2 |
| Creditors: amounts falling due within one year | | | |
| Trade creditors | (120) | (68) | (46) |
| Expanding plc | – | (22) | (16) |
| Growing plc | – | – | (8) |
| Net current assets | 53 | 45 | (25) |
| Total assets *less* current liabilities | 750 | 255 | 35 |
| **Capital and reserves** | | | |
| Called-up share capital (£1 shares) | 400 | 150 | 50 |
| Reserves brought forward | 200 | 45 | – |
| Profit and loss account for 20X0 | 150 | 60 | (15) |
| | 750 | 255 | 35 |

The following additional information is available:

1 At 31 December 20X0, goods transferred at cost £2,000 were in transit between Expanding plc and Growing plc. A cheque for £1,000 was in transit between Declining plc and Growing plc.
2 The closing stock of Expanding plc included goods supplied by Growing plc at an invoiced value of £3,600. Growing plc had priced these goods at cost plus 20 per cent, the standard group markup.
3 Expanding plc purchased all its investments in its subsidiaries on 1 January 20X0.

*Required:*
Prepare a consolidated balance sheet for the Expanding Group as at 31 December 20X0.

4* The balance sheets of Pip plc and its two subsidiaries Squeak plc and Wilfred plc as at 31 March 20X1 were as follows:

**Balance sheets at 31 March 20X1**

| | Pip plc £000 | Squeak plc £000 | Wilfred plc £000 |
|---|---|---|---|
| **Fixed assets** | | | |
| Tangible assets | 315 | 120 | 77 |
| Investments | | | |
|    80,000 shares in Squeak plc | 110 | – | – |
|    50,000 shares in Wilfred plc | 45 | – | – |
|    Debentures in Squeak plc | 5 | – | – |
| | 475 | 120 | 77 |
| **Current assets** | 250 | 70 | 41 |
| Creditors: amounts falling due within one year | | | |
|    Trade creditors | (100) | (20) | (30) |
|    Proposed dividends | | | |
|      Ordinary | (50) | (10) | – |
|      Preference | – | (1) | – |
| Net current assets | 100 | 39 | 11 |
| Total assets *less* current liabilities | 575 | 159 | 88 |
| Creditors: amounts falling due after more than one year | | | |
|    Debenture loan | – | (20) | – |
| | 575 | 139 | 88 |
| **Capital and reserves** | | | |
| Called-up share capital | | | |
|    Ordinary shares of £1 | 500 | 100 | 80 |
|    10% Preference shares | – | 10 | – |
| General reserves | – | 10 | – |
| Profit and loss account | 75 | 19 | 8 |
| | 575 | 139 | 88 |

**Profit and loss accounts for the year ended 31 March 20X1**

| | Pip plc £000 | Squeak plc £000 | Wilfred plc £000 |
|---|---|---|---|
| Balance at 31.3.X0 | 50 | 10 | (2.4) |
| Dividend received from Squeak plc | 2 | – | – |
| Net profit for year | 73 | 32.5 | 10.4 |
| | 125 | 42.5 | 8 |
| Transfer to general reserves | – | (10) | – |
| Dividends paid, ordinary shares | | (2.5) | |
| Proposed dividends | | | |
|    Ordinary shares | (50) | (10) | – |
|    Preferrence shares | – | (1) | – |
| Balance at 31.3.X1 | 75 | 19 | 8 |

The following additional information is given:

1  The parent company purchased all its shares in its subsidiaries on 1 April 20X0.
2  There is no intra-group trading.
3  The parent company has recorded only dividend income received from its subsidiaries.

*Required:*
Prepare a consolidated balance sheet for the year ended 31 March 20X1.

# 18 Understanding consolidated financial statements

After studying this chapter you should be able to:

1   Appreciate the problems of accounting for minority interests in consolidated accounts.

2   Explain the accountancy treatment of associated companies.

3   Distinguish between merger and acquisition accounting.

4   Discuss the problems of accounting for multinational groups.

Accounting for groups of companies is an important area of financial accounting by reason of the tendency of companies to grow by forming or acquiring subsidiary companies. Financial reporting for groups of companies by means of consolidated year-end accounting reports is complicated by a number of problems, which fall into two classes. First, there are technical problems of dealing with the complexity of data to be treated when preparing consolidated accounts. These problems have been explained in outline form in the previous chapter. Second, there are problems of understanding the nature of the consolidation process as it affects the meaning of the information which the accounts contain. This chapter deals with the following topics which are central to understanding consolidated financial statements:

1   minority interests present in subsidiaries that are less than 100 per cent owned;

2   the accounting treatment of associated companies;

3   mergers and acquisitions;

4   multinational groups.

The purpose of this chapter is to provide an introductory overview of the theory and practice of accounting for these complexities.

## Accounting for minority interests

In this section, we discuss the problems of accounting for minority interests in consolidated accounts, where a parent–subsidiary relationship exists requiring the full consolidation of the balance sheets and profit and loss accounts of companies so defined.

The assets, liabilities, revenues and expenses of the subsidiary must be consolidated in full with those of the parent company. The procedure for consolidation requires the elimination of inter-company transactions. The minority interests are represented as a separate item on the consolidated balance sheet and the consolidated profit and loss account.

The problems relating to the recognition of minority interests in consolidated financial statements will be considered under the following headings:

1 the nature of the minority interest;
2 calculations required to quantify the minority interest;
3 the treatment of the elimination of extra group profits as far as the minority interest is concerned.

## The nature of the minority interest

The question to be addressed here is: what is the nature of the minority interest, as reflected on a consolidated balance sheet? Two principal views exist. One view (the parent company concept) recognizes the parent company as being dominant in its relationship with the minority interest. The minority interest as depicted on the consolidated balance sheet is viewed as a liability of the group rather than a co-owner of the group. One result of this is that no attempt is made under this concept to attribute any goodwill relating to the holding company's acquisition of the subsidiary to the minority interest.

*Example 1*

H plc purchased 90 per cent of the issued capital of S plc for £90,000 when the net assets of S plc (at fair value) amounted to £80,000.

On consolidation, goodwill of £18,000 arises (i.e. £90,000 – 90 per cent of £80,000). Under the parent company concept, no attempt is made to attribute goodwill to the other 10 per cent of the capital held by the minority interest. (Any goodwill which was so attributed could be quantified as:

$$\frac{£18,000}{9} = £2,000$$

This could be added to goodwill and to minority interest on consolidation.)

FRS 2 states that the minority interest on a consolidated balance sheet should not be classified as part of shareholders' funds, thus indicating that UK standard practice adopts a parent company approach to the minority interest.

The alternative view is expressed in the entity concept which treats the parent company and the minority as partners or co-owners in the subsidiary. Under this concept, the minority interest is classified as part of shareholders' funds, and in quantifying the amount of that interest, parent company and minority would both be treated alike. Thus, referring back to Example 1, goodwill would be treated as being £20,000 (not £18,000) with £2,000 of that goodwill being added to the minority interest as shown on the consolidated balance sheet.

## The calculation of minority interests

The objective of calculating minority interests on consolidation can be summarized as follows:

- for balance sheet purposes: to show the interest of the non-group shareholders in the net assets of the group as at the relevant balance sheet date;
- for profit and loss account purposes: to show the non-group shareholders' interest in the profit after tax for the year of the subsidiary.

As far as the calculations are concerned, care is needed whenever there is more than one class of capital in the subsidiary, especially if the minority interest differs between the classes.

**Example 2**   Extracts from the financial statements of S plc for the year to 31 March 20X0 show the following:

| Balance sheet | | Profit and loss account | |
|---|---|---|---|
| **Called-up capital:** | | | |
| £1 ordinary shares | £500,000 | **Profit after tax** | £65,000 |
| £1 8% preference shares | 50,000 | **Preference dividend:** | |
| | 550,000 | Paid | (20,000) |
| | | Proposed | (20,000) |
| **Reserves:** | | | |
| Retained profits | 160,000 | **Ordinary dividend:** | |
| | £710,000 | Proposed | (15,000) |
| Net assets | £710,000 | Retained for the year | £10,000 |

It is known that H plc owns 80 per cent of the issued ordinary capital of S plc and 50 per cent of the issued 8 per cent preference shares.

The calculation of the relevant minority interest figures is as follows:

**Profit and loss account**

| | | Minority interest |
|---|---|---|
| Profit after tax | £65,000 | |
| *Less:* Preference dividends | (40,000) × 50% | £20,000 |
| Equity profits | £25,000 × 20% | £5,000 |
| | | |
| Total minority interest for the consolidated profit and loss account | | £25,000 |

**Balance sheet**

| | Minority interest |
|---|---|
| Called-up share capital: | |
| Ordinary: £500,000 × 20% | £100,000 |
| Preference: £50,000 × 50% | 25,000 |
| Reserves (all preference dividends have been paid or proposed | |
| – so consider equity interest only) £160,000 × 20% | 32,000 |
| Minority interest for the consolidated balance sheet | £157,000 |

## Intra-group profit elimination

As mentioned in Chapter 17, a number of differing views exist as to how adjustments to eliminate unrealized intra-group profits should be effected on consolidation. In some circumstances, the minority interest in the subsidiary may be affected by the choice of elimination method.

One view (as adopted for illustrative purposes in this book) is that the elimination of unrealized intra-group profits is purely a 'consolidation' adjustment and is therefore dealt with in total group profits or reserves, without allocating the adjustment to any specific company. On this view, where a subsidiary sells to a parent company and the goods remain in stock, the calculation of any minority interest in that subsidiary is unaffected by the profit elimination.

A second approach is to allocate the profit adjustment to the accounts of the group company which sold the stock in question. Here, if S plc sells to P plc and the stock remains in the parent company's balance sheet, any profit recorded by S plc on the transaction could be removed from its profit figure. Consequently, the calculation of any minority interest in S plc will be based on the adjusted (reduced) profit figure.

A third approach would, as in the first, treat any adjustment as a group adjustment but limit the adjustment to an amount equal to the parent company's percentage interest in the profits of the selling subsidiary.

**Example 3** H plc has owned 80 per cent of the issued capital of S plc since the incorporation of that company. During the year to 31 December 20X0, S plc sold goods to H plc at a profit of £10,000, these goods were unsold by H plc at 31 December. The retained profits per the accounts of the two companies at 31 December 20X0 were H plc £100,000, S plc £50,000. The issued capital of S plc was £60,000 in £1 ordinary shares. The stocks in the balance sheets of the separate companies were H plc £250,000; S plc £170,000.

The three methods outlined above give the following results:

| | Method one | Method two | Method three |
|---|---|---|---|
| **Profit adjustment** | £ | £ | £ |
| Group reserves | 10,000 | | |
| S plc reserves | | 10,000 | |
| Group reserves | | | |
| (80% × 10,000) | | | 8,000 |
| | | | |
| **Consolidated reserves** | £ | £ | £ |
| H plc | 100,000 | 100,000 | 100,000 |
| S plc (80% of £50,000) | 40,000 | | 40,000 |
| Profit adjustment | (10,000) | (80% × 10,000) | (8,000) |
| S plc (80% × 50,000 – 10,000) | 130,000 | 32,000 | 132,000 |
| | | 132,000 | |
| | | | |
| **Minority interest for balance sheet** | £ | £ | £ |
| Subsidiary's capital | 60,000 | 60,000 | 60,000 |
| Subsidiary's reserves | 50,000 | | 50,000 |
| (50,000 – 10,000) | | 40,000 | |
| | 110,000 | 100,000 | 110,000 |
| Minority interest (20%) | 22,000 | 20,000 | 22,000 |
| | | | |
| **Consolidated stocks** | £ | £ | £ |
| H plc | 250,000 | 250,000 | 250,000 |
| S plc | 170,000 | 170,000 | 170,000 |
| | 420,000 | 420,000 | 420,000 |
| *Less:* adjustment | (10,000) | (10,000) | (8,000) |
| | 410,000 | 410,000 | 412,000 |

All these methods will be found in practice (together with others not covered here). It should be appreciated that no one method is viewed as being correct and often the amounts involved are immaterial in relation to the group's results and net assets.

## Accounting for associated companies

The definition of an associated company was dealt with in Chapter 17. Here it is necessary to consider in detail the accounting treatment required by FRS 9 in the group accounts.

It will be recalled that an associated company holds a participating interest and excersises a significant influence on policy decisions. The associate is not consolidated in the group accounts, but instead is dealt with under the equity method of accounting for investments.

This method sets out to state the investment in the associate on the consolidated balance sheet, not at cost but at a figure approximating to the value of the equity interest in the associate. Also, because of the existence of participating interest, the profit and loss account includes the investing company's share of profits of the associate, not just dividend income.

Table 2.1 summarizes and compares the equity accounting method with the consolidation method, and Example 4 then shows the FRS 9 balance sheet presentation of an investment in an associated company.

**Table 2.1  Summary and comparison of equity, accounting and consolidation**

|  | Consolidation | Equity accounting |
|---|---|---|
| **Profit and loss account** | The dividend from the subsidiary is eliminated. | The dividend from the associate is eliminated. |
|  | The profit and loss account captions of the subsidiary are aggregated with those of the parent company. | The consolidated profit and loss account includes as a separate item the group's share of the operating profit associate. |
|  | A separate minority interest is calculated and disclosed. | No separate minority interest adjustment is necessary. |
| **Balance sheet** | The separate assets and liabilities of the subsidiary are aggregated with those of the parent company. | The investment account is retained, but stated at its equity value (per SSAP 1) i.e: |
|  | The investment account and other internal items are cancelled. | Share of net assets of the associate (less goodwill)    x<br>Share of the associate's goodwill    x<br>Premium/discount on acquisition    <u>x</u>  <u>x</u><br>                                 <u>x</u> |

**Example 4**

Octopus plc acquired a block of shares in Guppy plc for £100,000 on 1 January 20X0, giving it 25 per cent of the called-up capital. At that date the called-up capital and reserves of Guppy plc amounted to £360,000. In the balance sheet of Octopus plc, these shares would be shown at their historic cost of £100,000. On consolidation, Guppy plc would be defined as an associated company. Guppy plc's capital and reserves amount to £600,000 at 31 December 20X0, the net profit for the year being £240,000. Applying the equity method, the interest of the Octopus Group in Guppy plc will be shown as follows:

**Consolidated balance sheet 31 December 20X0**

| | £ |
|---|---:|
| **Fixed assets** | |
| Investments: | |
| Shares in related company: | |
| 25% of net assets (25% × £600,000) | 150,000 |
| Premium on acquisition (£100,000 – 25% × £360,000) | 10,000 |
| | 160,000 |

The premium on acquisition above is, of course, purchased goodwill, the treatment of which is described below.

# Mergers and acquisitions

Groups of companies may be formed in two ways. First, a parent company may form a subsidiary company. This is often the case with 100-per-cent-owned subsidiary companies. Second, a company may purchase shares in another company, that company becoming a subsidiary through a business combination.

Business combinations are a frequent topic of discussion in the financial press. They may result from discussions between two companies on the benefits which would flow from a merger of their business. On the other hand, negotiations between two companies may involve the acquisition of one company by the other. This is frequently a case of a big company acquiring a small successful company. Acquisitions may also result from aggressive expansionist policies of a company seeking to take over another company. In this case, the takeover will take the form of an acquisition of its shares by bidding up a price which will induce shareholders to sell them to the bidding company.

Current practice recognizes these differing situations by employing two different methods of recording business combinations in consolidated accounts:

1 acquisition accounting (also called the purchase method);
2 merger accounting (also called the pooling of interests).

## Acquisition accounting

Under this, the consolidated balance sheet includes the assets and liabilities of the subsidiary at their cost to the group rather than at the values at which they are shown in the subsidiary's balance sheet.

The purchase method requires first the acquisition cost of the subsidiary to be established as a total by reference to the amount of cash paid and the value of shares exchanged for its shares. The second stage is to allocate the acquisition cost to the particular assets and liabilities of the subsidiary. The EC Seventh Directive gives little by way of guidelines on how this difficult task is to be performed, except to say that the acquisition cost should be allocated as much as possible to all identifiable assets and liabilities. FRS 2 includes a similar requirement, stating that allocation should be on the basis of the 'fair value' of the assets to the buying company. Any difference between the value of the subsidiary's net assets and the purchase consideration represents goodwill – positive or negative.

## Merger accounting

Here, the business combination is treated as a merger which forms a new business as the result of the pooling of the assets and liabilities of two previously separate and independent businesses. The merger of two companies does not necessarily imply that one company disappears by liquidation. Frequently, mergers are implemented by the formation of a holding company to which the shares of the merging companies are transferred in exchange for shares in the holding company.

If the merging companies remain in business, but operate in the context of a group, then year-end consolidated accounts will have to be prepared. Accounting for mergers recognizes the on-going nature of the business by the pooling of the interests of the two companies. The assets and liabilities of both companies are therefore simply added together at the value at which they appear in the separate balance sheets, without 'fair value' adjustments arising.

The key profit and loss account differences between merger and acquisition accounting is that the former consolidates for an entire year in the year of the merger and requires the prior year figures to be shown on a merged basis, while acquisition accounting does not. Acquisition accounting leads to the creation of goodwill, while merger accounting avoids it completely. Merger accounting was formally recognized in the Companies Act 1981, and the Accounting Standards Board issued FRS 6 'Acquisitions and Mergers' in 1995.

## When is a combination a merger?

A business combination *may* be treated as a merger rather than as an acquisition in the following circumstances only:

1 if it results from an offer to all equity holders (and all holders of other voting shares), and
2 if the offer is accepted by at least 90 per cent of the equity shareholders (by value and by votes), and
3 if the new parent company did not hold more than 20 per cent of the equity or votes immediately before the merger, and
4 if at least 90 per cent of the fair value of the purchase consideration is in the form of equity shares.

Note that if the above four conditions are satisfied, the business combination *may* be accounted for on a merger basis, but it is not compulsory to do so. However, if the above four conditions are not satisfied, the combination *must* be accounted for as an acquisition. FRS 6 'Acquisitions and Mergers' seeks to introduce a new set of criteria for defining a merger, based on the guiding principle that the combining companies should be substantially equal partners with neither of them being identifiable as the acquirer or acquiree. The detailed conditions to be satisfied are all of the following:

1 neither party sees itself as acquirer or acquiree;
2 neither party dominates the management of the combined entity;
3 the equity shareholders of neither party have, or could have, disposed of a material part of their shareholdings, directly or indirectly, for shares carrying reduced rights in the combined enterprise or any non-equity consideration. (This would prevent transactions involving vendor placings from qualifying, as well as deals involving straight cash consideration);
4 no minority interests of more than 10 per cent of the equity remain in any of the enterprises to whom an offer is made;
5 neither of the combining parties is more than 50 per cent larger than the other, unless special circumstances (which could include voting and share agreements) prevent the larger from dominating the other; and
6 the share of the equity in the combination allocated to any party to it does not depend on the post-combination performance of the business previously controlled by that party. (This rules out deals involving earn-out clauses.)

The proposed rules are extremely restrictive and very few transactions would qualify for merger accounting.

## Merger accounting: main principles

The principles of consolidated accounts outlined in Chapter 17 followed acquisition principles. It is now necessary to summarize the main points of merger accounting.

FRS 6 recommends the following accounting method for mergers. The shares transferred to the holding company as part of a merger should be recorded in the books of the holding company at the nominal value of the shares issued in exchange. No share premium is recognized or necessary on the new shares issued by the holding company. As a consequence of using the nominal value the only difference to be dealt with on consolidation will be the difference between the nominal value of the shares issued as consideration by the holding company and the nominal value of the shares transferred by the shareholders of the new subsidiary company to the holding company. Where the nominal value of the shares issued is less than that of the shares transferred the differences should be treated as a reserve (non-distributable) arising on consolidation. If the nominal value of the shares issued is greater than that of the shares received in exchange, the difference is the extent to which the reserves of the subsidiary have in effect been capitalized consequent on the merger, and this difference should therefore be treated on consolidation primarily as a reduction of the existing reserves; it should be applied first against any unrealized surplus and second against revenue income or realized surpluses. Essentially, this indicates that to the extent that reserves are regarded as capitalized, non-distributable reserves are capitalized before distributable reserves.

Where there is some additional consideration in some form other than equity shares, for example cash or loan stock, the value of such additional consideration should be included by adding it to the nominal value of the shares issued by the holding company, so as to arrive at the total consideration paid for the shares in the merged subsidiary, and this total of the consideration would be debited to the investment in the subsidiary account. By following these procedures the reserves in the consolidated accounts will thus be either:

1 the total of the reserves of the constituent companies increased by any reserve arising on consolidation; or

2 the total of the reserves of the constituent companies reduced by any part of the reserves of subsidiaries which have been in effect capitalized as a result of the merger.

**Example 5**

In this example the reserves of the constituent companies are increased by a reserve arising on consolidation.

P Ltd has just increased its share capital by issuing 70,000 ordinary shares of £1 each plus a cash payment of £10,000 to gain 90 per cent control of the issued share capital of S Ltd. The separate balance sheets of the two companies immediately after the merger are as follows.

|  | P Ltd | S Ltd |
|---|---|---|
|  | £ | £ |
| Ordinary shares of £1 each | 270,000 | 100,000 |
| Revaluation reserve |  | 20,000 |
| Revenue reserves | 50,000 | 30,000 |
|  | 320,000 | 150,000 |
|  | £ | £ |
| Fixed and current assets less liabilities | 240,000 | 150,000 |
| Investment – shares in S Ltd | 80,000 |  |
|  | 320,000 | 150,000 |

Note that the cost of the shares in S Ltd is recorded in the books of P Ltd at the nominal value of the shares issued in exchange (£70,000) plus the value of any additional consideration (£10,000 in cash). The 70,000 ordinary shares of £1 each will have been issued at a premium (they must have been to comply with condition (4) above that 90 per cent in *value* of the offer is in equity voting capital) but such premium is not recognized when using the merger or pooling-of-interest method. In preparing the consolidated balance sheet the investment account in P's books is set against the nominal value of the shares purchased in S Ltd, thus:

|  | £ | £ |
|---|---|---|
| Nominal value of shares in S Ltd pooled by P Ltd |  | 90,000 |
| Cost of investment in S Ltd: |  |  |
| Shares at nominal value | 70,000 |  |
| Cash | 10,000 |  |
|  |  | 80,000 |
| Capital reserve arising on consolidation |  | 10,000 |

and the full consolidated balance sheet appears as follows:

**Consolidated balance sheet after merger**

|  | £ |
|---|---|
| Ordinary shares of £1 each | 270,000 |
| Capital reserve arising on consolidation | 10,000 |
| Revaluation reserve (90% × 20,000) | 18,000 |
| Revenue reserves (50,000 + 90% × 30,000) | 77,000 |
| Minority interest (10% × 150,000) | 15,000 |
|  | 390,000 |
| Fixed and current assets *less* liabilities | 390,000 |

The minority interest is calculated in the same manner in a merger as in an acquisition.

**Example 6**   In this example the nominal value of the shares issued by P Ltd exceeds the nominal value of the shares purchased in S Ltd, and the excess is treated as a capitalization of reserves of the subsidiary. The facts are as in the previous example, but P Ltd issues 110,000 £1 ordinary shares plus cash of £10,000 to gain control of a 90 per cent shareholding in S Ltd. In this case the separate balance sheets of the two companies immediately after the merger are as follows:

|  | P Ltd | S Ltd |
|---|---|---|
|  | £ | £ |
| Ordinary shares of £1 each | 310,000 | 100,000 |
| Revaluation reserve |  | 20,000 |
| Revenue reserves | 50,000 | 30,000 |
|  | 360,000 | 150,000 |
|  | £ | £ |
| Fixed and current assets *less* liabilities | 240,000 | 150,000 |
| Investment – shares in S Ltd | 120,000 |  |
|  | 360,000 | 150,000 |

The book value of the shares held by P Ltd in S Ltd is compared with the par value of the shares acquired, thus:

|  | £ |
|---|---|
| Cost of investment | 120,000 |
| Nominal value acquired (90%) | 90,000 |
| Excess | £30,000 |

This excess is to be offset against group reserves, unrealized first, then realized. Thus:

|  | £ |
| --- | --- |
| Offset against revaluation reserve (90% × £20,000) | £18,000 |
| Offset against revenue reserves (balance) | 12,000 |
|  | £30,000 |

The consolidated balance sheet will be as follows:

**Consolidated balance sheet after merger**

|  | £ |
| --- | --- |
| Ordinary shares of £1 each | 310,000 |
| (Capital reserves – nil) |  |
| Revenue reserves (50,000 + 27,000 – 12,000) | 65,000 |
| Minority interest | 15,000 |
|  | 390,000 |
| Fixed and current assets less liabilities | £390,000 |

The above examples illustrate that one of the major differences between acquisition and merger accounting lies in the treatment of the reserves of the subsidiary at the date of acquisition. The acquisition (purchase) approach regards these as capitalized at the date of the takeover against the purchase price. The purchase price is based on a realistic assessment of the current values of the shares issued by the parent company. So where the purchase price exceeds the value placed on the proportion of the net assets acquired in the subsidiary, a difference, or figure for goodwill, will arise. The merger or pooling method regards the situation as being one where previously independent companies have merged as voluntary partners and that consolidation should be the mere amalgamation of balance sheets. Taking the valuation of the shares exchanged at face or par value is a mere bookkeeping device to cancel out the shares issued by P Ltd against those of S Ltd on consolidation, with any resulting difference being treated as an increase in reserves (as in Example 5) or as a capitalization of existing reserves (as in Example 6).

# Multinational groups

Multinational groups face a number of complex accounting problems, which result from the economic, legal, organizational, managerial and fiscal environment in which they operate. Given that nation states see problems at a national level and set up rules for the conduct of business that reflect national interests, and that multi-nationals see problems at a global level, it follows that the resolution of conflict is a major preoccupation of multinational groups.

## Conflict of accounting principles and procedures

A number of countries have codified accounting systems for business in the form of uniform charts of accounts, to which companies must adhere. In France, for example, the *Plan Comptable Révisé* is a nationalized accounting system setting out classes of accounts, detailing for each class the names of accounts and ascribing to them a number. In accordance with French commercial law, accounts are properly kept only if they accord with the *Plan Comptable Révisé*. A French subsidiary of a US multinational is required to keep its accounts in accordance with the *Plan Comptable Révisé*. At the same time, it must report year-end results for consolidation purposes to the US in the form which fits US practice, which is based upon US GAAP (generally accepted accounting principles). This means that the same accounting data must be rehashed again before it is suitable for consolidation. Moreover, French tax law regulates such items as depreciation charges and provisions, and in this way they regulate the extent to which amounts may be charged as expenses. In effect, the accounting profit and the taxable profit correspond closely as a result. When consolidating the accounts of the French subsidiary with the US parent, they must be redrafted to conform with US tax laws. The resolution of these conflicts of accounting and tax rules imposes a heavy burden of work on the French subsidiary.

The International Accounting Standards Board has produced a number of standards to help reduce these problems. It is also the objective of the EC Fourth and Seventh Directives to increase uniformity of accounting principles and methods, but the extent to which harmonization is possible is limited by fundamental differences in the institutions of nations.

## The currency problem

The currency problem has two aspects. The financial aspect is the most important and complex one, for it involves the management of corporate resources across different currencies which fluctuate daily on world currency markets. Financial management decisions, the evaluation of investment and of corporate performance, the management of international cash balances and the avoidance of exchange risks are all part of this management problem. Generally, multinationals adopt a base currency as the functional currency for worldwide operations. For US multinationals, this currency is evidently the US dollar. Some non-US multinationals have found it useful also to adopt the US dollar as the functional currency. Some Dutch multinationals have adopted this option and prepare consolidated accounts in US dollars. This means that budgets are set in one base currency, but local activities involve the use of the local currency. It is possible, therefore, for a subsidiary of a US multinational to have a flexible budget as a result simply of currency movements rather than activity variances.

## The currency translation problem

Multinational groups experience the currency translation problem in three different ways:

1 Inter-company transactions across currency borders are realized transactions which are translated at the rate of exchange ruling at the transaction date. It was noted in the previous chapter that these transactions are eliminated on consolidation. Therefore, they would be eliminated at the rate of exchange ruling on the transaction date. In practice, this requirement means that inter-company transactions have to be recorded separately from external transactions to facilitate consolidation at year end.

2 Inter-group dividends are also realized transactions involving the movement of funds through remittances. They crystallize on the due date of payment and are translated

at the rate of exchange ruling on that date. Again, inter-group dividends are eliminated on consolidation at the rate of exchange ruling on the due date of payment.

The transactions falling under 1 and 2 above do not involve a problem of choice as to which exchange rate to apply. Moreover, they are eliminated on consolidation, and do not influence the overall presentation of group consolidated accounts.

3 The preparation of consolidated accounts involves the consolidation of all remaining assets, liabilities, revenues and expenses in order to show to shareholders the financial status and the net profit of the group as a single unit. It requires the translation of the profit and loss accounts and balance sheets of all companies within a group into one currency, which is the base currency for the group.

The rate of exchange which should be applied for that purpose has been the subject of much controversy for two reasons:

(a) The assets, liabilities, expenses and revenues to be translated are not the subject of remittances to the parent company. In the case of assets and liabilities, they remain legal rights and obligations expressed in the local currency of the foreign subsidiary. Moreover, non-current items on the foreign subsidiary's balance sheet such as fixed assets, issued capital and reserves are not considered as involving any currency movements in the short term. In the case of current assets and liabilities, they form the substance of the foreign subsidiary's working capital. Given that inter-company items fall to be eliminated on consolidation, the items consolidated also are unlikely to involve currency movements. The expenses and revenue items on the subsidiary's profit and loss account have been transacted across the accounting period, and to translate them with precise accuracy would mean tracking each transaction at a daily exchange rate, thereby imposing an impossible burden of accounting work. Also, they do not involve currency movements.

(b) The purpose of translating the accounts of foreign subsidiaries into the base currency of the group is to place all companies on to a uniform unit of measurement without infringing the historical cost rule of valuation. The problem lies in defining how the historical cost rule should be applied to the assets, liabilities, expenses and revenues of foreign subsidiaries at the close of each accounting period.

The currency translation debate is centred, therefore, on the issue of applying the historical cost principle in the process of consolidating the accounts of foreign subsidiaries, when the items to be translated do not imply any currency movements at balance sheet date.

Although a large number of translation methods have been put forward and used across the years, much of the debate has been resolved by the issue of SSAP 20 'Foreign Currency Translation' which sets out two permitted translation methods together with their uses and the accounting treatment of any resulting translation gain or loss. The two methods of translation permitted by the SSAP are known as the temporal method and the closing rate/net investment method. Table 2.2 provides a summary of the main points of each method as outlined in SSAP 20.

Table 2.2  SSAP 20 translation methods

|  | Temporal | Closing rate/net investment |
|---|---|---|
| 1  Uses of method | Where the foreign currency transaction has a direct effect on the cash flows of the UK company, i.e.<br>(a)  'individual company stage' (e.g. the UK parent company buying/selling overseas or receiving dividends from the overseas subsidiary);<br>(b)  'consolidation stage' of the overseas entity is seen as being merely an extension of the UK company (e.g. overseas subsidiaries which are:<br>– selling agencies<br>– group finance<br>– companies<br>– group suppliers) | Used at the consolidation stage only, where the overseas entity is seen to be 'semi-independent' of the UK company.<br><br>It is envisaged that this method would apply to the translation of the accounts of most subsidiaries for consolidation purposes. |
| 2  Mechanics of method | Items are translated at the rate ruling when the amount was established in the accounts, *but* items on the balance sheet at 'current value' are translated at closing rate.<br>Thus:<br>(a)  B/S items are:<br>Fixed assets<br> at cost – acquisition rate<br> at valuation – valuation rate<br>Stocks<br> at cost – acquisition rate<br> at NRV – closing rate<br> all monetary items –<br> closing rate;<br>(b)  P/L items are:<br>All except stocks and<br> depreciation – at average<br> rate for the period<br>Stocks – as for balance sheet<br>Depreciation – as for the<br> related fixed asset | All balance sheet assets and liabilities are translated at closing rate.<br><br><br><br><br><br><br><br><br><br><br><br><br>All profit and loss account items may be translated at *either* closing rates or average for the period. |
| 3  Accounting for the translation gain/loss | Viewed as a normal risk/benefit of trading overseas and therefore included in the 'profit on ordinary activities' before taxation. | Viewed as a revaluation in sterling of the net investment in an overseas entity and therefore presented as part of the movement for the period period of group reserves, profits being unaffected. |

# The inflation problem

Meaningful comparisons of balance sheets and profit and loss accounts from year to year are rendered impossible under inflationary conditions, when the money unit of measurement becomes unstable. This problem had been recognized in the United Kingdom and in many other countries. Some countries, such as the United Kingdom and the United States, have required companies to disclose the effects of inflation in accounts. There is, however, no international standard for dealing with this problem, nor indeed is there a consensus as to how it should be treated. Multinationals are particularly affected because of the variety of inflation rates to which their business is exposed worldwide.

Moreover, although there is no connection in the short term between speculative changes in exchange rates and levels of domestic inflation, some assert that such a connection may be established in the long term. From an accounting viewpoint, financial statements deal with short-term periods of one year, and consequently fluctuations in exchange rates and changes in rates of domestic inflation may both affect the meaning of consolidated accounts involving foreign subsidiaries.

# Problems

1   Consider the following draft data relating to the year ended 31 December 20X0 of Royal plc and Butler plc.

| Balance sheets | Royal plc £000 | Butler plc £000 |
|---|---|---|
| Fixed assets (net) – tangible | 6,500 | 4,000 |
| Investment in Butler plc – cost | 2,000 | |
| Current assets | 3,500 | 3,000 |
| Current liabilities | (4,550) | (2,500) |
| Debentures (20X9) | (2,000) | (1,500) |
| | 5,450 | 3,000 |
| Issued ordinary share capital | 2,000 | 1,000 |
| Reserves | 3,450 | 2,000 |
| | 5,450 | 3,000 |
| Profit and loss accounts | | |
| Operating profit before tax | 1,100 | 500 |
| Dividend from Butler plc including tax credit | 143 | – |
| Taxation | (433) | (200) |
| Profit after tax | 810 | 300 |
| Dividends paid | (300) | (200) |
| | 510 | 100 |

Royal plc acquired 50 per cent of the ordinary share capital of Butler plc on 1 January 20X0 for £2,000,000 when its reserves were £1,900,000 and sold this holding on 3 January 20X1 for £2,050,000.

*Required:*
(a)  prepare the 'group' profit and loss account and balance sheet on three bases: when Butler is treated as (i) a subsidiary; (ii) an associated company; and (iii) an investment.
(b)  comment on the validity of these three alternatives.

2   On 3 July 20X0 Expo plc acquired 95 per cent of the issued share capital of Sition Ltd.
     The terms of the merger were as follows:
   For every 10 shares held in Sition, the shareholder received 8 shares in Expo at an agreed
   value of £1.90 per share plus £1.50 unsecured 15 per cent loan stock dated 20X0.
     The draft accounts for the two companies at 31 December 20X0 were as follows:

|  | Expo plc (£000) | Sition Ltd (£000) |
|---|---|---|
| **Balance sheet** | | |
| Fixed assets | 18,650 | 10,200 |
| Goodwill at cost | | 1,000 |
| Investments | 9,025 | |
| Current assets | 3,550 | 6,650 |
| Current liabilities | (2,850) | (3,200) |
| | 28,375 | 14,650 |
| Share capital | | |
| £1 ordinary shares | 21,600 | 10,000 |
| Profit and loss | 5,350 | 4,650 |
| 15% loan stock | 1,425 | |
| | 28,375 | 14,650 |
| **Profit and loss account** | | |
| Turnover | 12,850 | 8,500 |
| Profit before tax | 3,250 | 1,300 |
| Taxation | 590 | 30 |
| | 2,660 | 1,270 |
| Dividends | 1,200 | |
| Retained profits | 1,460 | 1,270 |

*Notes:*
(i)   It is Expo's policy to write off goodwill over five years. Sition has not, to date, written off
      any goodwill and the balance in their accounts relates to a business bought in 19X9.
(ii)  At the date of the takeover, the estimated profit of Sition for the year to date was
      £600,000.

*Required:*
1  Prepare a consolidated balance sheet and profit and loss account in summary form for
   Expo group, adopting the merger accounting method in line with SSAP 23.
2  Explain the major differences between your statement and the way in which the same
   information would have been presented using traditional group accounting practices.
3  Assess the relative strengths and weaknesses of merger and group accounting. Explain
   why merger accounting has only been applied in the UK since 1981.

# Financial reporting – alternative valuation approaches

# Introduction to Part 3

The process of attaching money measurements to accounting events and items is essentially a process of valuation. Valuation enters into accounting measurements in two senses. First, the money standard of measurement is itself unstable through time. One pound today does not have the same value as one pound yesterday, or one pound tomorrow, since the purchasing power of money over goods and services changes. Second, the use of money measurements in accounting implies a choice between one of several different valuation bases. It is possible to represent the original cost of acquisition of an asset by the enterprise as a representation of a past financial effort. Equally, it is possible to represent the value of an asset to the enterprise in terms of the future net benefits it represents.

Accounting for changes in the value of money is a subject which has long occupied the attention of accounting researchers. It was not until 1975, however, with the publication of the Sandilands Report, that the subject received attention from accountants generally. The ensuing lively debate illustrated the problem of producing a consensus regarding the best method of dealing with price level changes. One reason for the controversy which characterized the inflation accounting debate was due to the failure of accountants to reach agreement on the objectives of financial reports.

The importance of understanding the interaction and interdependence between valuation and measurement is apparent in such important areas of accounting as income determination and asset valuation. In this sense, the notions of capital and income are largely dependent on valuation concepts.

In this part, six valuation concepts are discussed:

1 *Historical cost*, as we saw in Part 2, is the conventional valuation concept used in accounting. Resources are valued in accordance with their cost of acquisition by the enterprise. The historical cost valuation concept poses many difficulties under price level changes.
2 *Present value* is a concept which relates the value of an asset to the decision to hold it and to derive its utility from using it in the production of income. It is defined as the sum of the future expected net cash flows associated with the use of the asset, discounted to their present value.
3 *Current purchasing power* is basically an adjusted historical cost concept, in which adjustments are made to recorded historical cost values for changes in the purchasing power of money by means of a consumer price index.
4 *Current replacement cost* is where the value of an asset is determined by the current cost of replacing it, and using the replacement to maintain the same service to the enterprise. It requires current market price data as a basis for preparing financial reports.
5 *Net realizable value* estimates the value of an asset to the enterprise as the amount which would be realized from its sale, after adjusting for selling expenses.

6 *Current value accounting* is a valuation concept which combines the concept of current replacement cost and net realizable value in determining whether selling (exit) or buying (entry) prices should be used for the purposes of establishing the value of an asset to the business.

Chapter 19, 'Capital, value, income', deals with the conceptual problems involved in the valuation of the enterprise and the measurement of income. Chapter 20, 'Accounting and economic concepts of income and value', considers two different approaches to income measurement and valuation. Chapter 21, 'Accounting for changing prices', examines alternatives to the traditional historical cost accounting model.

# 19 Capital, value, income

**Setting the scene**

Current financial reporting suffers from a number of deficiencies. It concentrates on the legal form of transactions more than on their economic substance and frequently does not reflect economic reality, it concentrates on the past rather than the future, it concentrates on cost rather than value and it leads to too much attention being paid to 'profit' and not enough to wealth and changes in it. (ICAS Research Committee, 1988)

**Learning objectives**

After studying this chapter you should be able to:

1 Discuss the significance of capital maintenance and describe the different concepts that have been postulated.

2 Explain the relationship between capital and income.

3 Identify the purposes for which businesses require income measurements.

We stated in Chapter 2 that the objectives of financial reporting to investors should be found in the decisions which investors have to make about their investment in companies. Hence, we argued, financial reporting should be concerned with the provision of such information as is required for making those decisions. We assumed, also, that investors were principally concerned with the worth of their investments in two senses. First, they are concerned with maintaining and increasing the value of their capital. Second, they are concerned with maintaining and increasing the income which is derived from that capital. Financial reporting ought to be concerned, therefore, with the valuation of shareholders' capital and income. In accordance with the stewardship concept of financial reporting, feedback information is required in order that investors may ascertain the current value of share capital and income. The decision-making concept of financial reporting asserts that financial reports should contain information which is useful in assisting investors to predict future changes in capital and income.

Three main concepts involved in financial reporting are capital, value and income. Together they provide the focus for this part. The purpose of this chapter is to introduce and explain the nature of these three concepts.

# Capital

To the economist, the term 'capital' relates to those assets which are used in the production of goods and services. The capital of the firm is represented by the firm's stock of assets, and investment by the firm occurs when the stock is increased. From the point of view of society, the term 'capital' is restricted similarly to those assets which produce goods and services. Capital includes, therefore, physical assets in the form of buildings, plant and machinery, housing, hospitals, schools, etc. as well as intangible assets such as technology, human skills (human capital), etc.

In accounting theory, a person's capital is increased by the amount of his periodic income which he has not consumed. Financial accounting procedure effects this transfer by crediting the net profit to the capital account, and if the level of consumption, or drawings, is less than that profit, the capital is increased by the difference. In the case of companies, dividends are analogous to drawings, and retained profit is added to the total of the shareholders' equity. One of the important implications of profit measurement in the case of companies lies in calculating what may be safely distributed as dividends.

Early writers on bookkeeping recommended, as a first step in the record-keeping process, the preparation of an inventory or statement of capital showing all the personal and real property, as well as debts due and owing on the first day of business. Paciolo in 1494 advised the businessman to prepare his inventory in the following way:

> First of all, he must write on a sheet of paper or in a separate book all his worldly belongings, that is, his personal or real property. He should always begin with the things that are more valuable and easier to lose. . . . He must then record all other things in proper order in the Inventory. (Gene Brown and Johnston, 1963, p 27)

It is evident that at this stage of development, accounting made no distinction between personal capital and business capital. In the course of subsequent developments, however, a distinction emerged between total wealth and wealth committed to business activities. Whereas in Paciolo's time capital was taken to mean the entire amount of what was owned, the capital account became ultimately a device which described and quantified that portion of private wealth invested in a business enterprise.

The development of the entity theory of accounting, as distinct from the proprietory theory, which culminated in the appearance of the joint stock company, gave expression to two important notions. First, as we saw in Part 2, an enterprise could be separated from its owner by a legal fiction and used by the owner as a vehicle for conducting business. Second, the fictional life granted to the enterprise by accounting practice, and additionally in the case of corporations by law, was to serve limited purposes. The capital account was to remain the umbilical cord linking the enterprise to its owner or owners. In line with this view, the enterprise continued to be regarded as an asset and this view has important implications for the valuation of capital and income.

From the foregoing, it is evident that there are some fundamental differences between economists and accountants in the manner in which the notion of capital is conceptualized. As Littleton (1961, p 244) points out, the balance sheet presentation of 'capital' emphasizes its legal rather than its economic aspect, for capital is shown as a liability, whereas in economics, capital refers to assets. The assets held by a business and actively employed by it are usually greater in value than the so-called 'capital'. In the light of modern interests, we may say that the terminology of financial reports in this respect is misleading. However, supposing that the total assets employed by an enterprise were to be redefined as its 'capital', there remain a number of problems:

1 the valuation of business capital;
2 the valuation of investors' financial interests, that is, personal capital;
3 the methods selected for these valuations;
4 the manner in which these valuations are to be communicated.

From our previous discussion of the objectives of financial reporting, we may say that investors are interested primarily in the valuation of their shareholding and this valuation is dependent on the valuation of business capital.

# Capital maintenance

We stated earlier in this chapter that investors are concerned with maintaining the value of their capital. The concept of capital maintenance is central to discussions regarding price level adjustments. There is general agreement that profit is a residue available for distribution once provision has been made for maintaining the value of capital intact. Difficulties begin to emerge when discussion turns to the consideration of the meaning of 'capital maintenance'. Several alternative interpretations of this concept have been offered and are considered below.

## The money amount concept

The aim of this concept is to maintain financial capital in money terms. Consequently, the measurement of periodic profit should ensure that the monetary value of the shareholders' equity is maintained intact. In effect, the profit of the period amounts to the increase in monetary terms in the shareholders' equity measured between the beginning and the end of the period. It is this amount which may be distributed to ensure that the money capital is maintained intact. The money amount maintenance concept is reflected in historical cost accounting.

## The financial capital concept

The objective of this concept is to maintain the financial capital of an enterprise in real terms by constantly updating the historical cost of assets for changes in the value of money. The translation of historical asset cost is effected by a retail price index, and results in the representation of asset values in common units of purchasing power. This concept of capital maintenance purports to show to shareholders that their company kept pace with general inflationary pressures during the accounting period, by measuring profit in such a way as to take into account changes in the price levels. In effect, it intends to maintain the shareholders' capital in terms of monetary units of constant purchasing power. The use of a retail price index based on a range of goods and services restricts adjustments for changes in the purchasing power of money to those changes which would be experienced by consumers.

## The operating capability concept

The financial capital concept of capital maintenance views the capital of the enterprise from the standpoint of the shareholders as owners. Hence, it reflects the proprietorship concept of the enterprise as regards both income and capital, and seeks valuation systems which fit this view. By contrast, the operating capability concept of capital maintenance views the problem of capital maintenance from the perspective of the enterprise itself, thereby reflecting the entity concept of the enterprise.

The operating concept states that the productive (operating) capacity of the enterprise should be maintained as a prime objective in the course of profit measurement. The operating capability concept of capital maintenance asserts that profit is a residue after provision has been made for replacing the resources exhausted in the course of operations. In this view, 'there can be no recognition of profit for a period unless the capital employed in the business at the beginning of the period has been maintained. . . . The starting point will be the various items making up the capital' (Goudeket, 1960). The criteria imposed on profit measurement by the operating concept are reflected by the system of replacement cost accounting, in which assets are valued at their replacement cost to the firm. Replacement cost accounting takes into account changes in the prices of commodities specific to the enterprise, either directly or by using specific price indices to measure changes in the prices of similar commodities.

## The disposable wealth concept

Whereas all previous concepts of capital maintenance envisage the enterprise as a going concern, the disposable wealth concept suggests that the maintenance of capital should be viewed from the perspective of the realizable value of the assets of the enterprise. Accordingly, the measurement of periodic profit is required to take into account changes in the realizable value of the net assets attributable to the shareholders' equity. At the beginning of the accounting period, the shareholders' equity, defined as the capital of the enterprise, is valued by reference to the realizable value of assets, after deducting realization expenses. A similar valuation of the net amount which would accrue to shareholders from the realization of assets is made at the end of the accounting period.

The disposable wealth concept of capital maintenance is based on the proprietorship theory of the enterprise. However, it interprets this theory in terms of the 'exit' rather than the 'entry' values of enterprise assets.

## Income

The concepts of capital and income are closely related. Irving Fisher expressed their relationship in 1919 as follows: 'A stock of wealth existing at a given instant of time is called capital; a flow of benefit from wealth through a given period of time is called income' (Fisher, 1919, p 38).

An analogy may be found in the relationship between a tree and its fruit – it is the tree which produces the fruit, and it is the fruit which may be consumed. Destroy the tree, and there will be no more fruit: tend the tree with care and feed its roots and it will yield more fruit in the future.

Once the concept of value is introduced into the relationship between capital and income, however, the exact nature of this relationship becomes clearer. According to Fisher (1969, p 40),

*It would seem . . . that income must be derived from capital; and, in a sense, this is true. Income is derived from capital goods, but the value of the income is not derived from the value of the capital goods. On the contrary, the value of the capital is derived from the value of the income. . . . Not until we know how much income an item will probably bring us can we set any valuation on that capital at all. It is true that the wheat crop depends on the land which yields it. But the value of the crop does not depend on the land. On the contrary, the value of the land depends in its crop.*

Economic and accounting theory are both concerned with the relationship between capital and income and the implications of this relationship. There is agreement between accountants and economists on a number of aspects of the relationship and considerable disagreement as regards the valuation of capital and income. There is agreement, for example, that only income should be available for consumption, and that in arriving at a measure of income, it is necessary to maintain the value of capital intact. Since the ultimate aim of economic activity is the satisfaction of wants, it follows that income is identified as a surplus which is available for consumption. The valuation of income in this analysis is subject to a fairly conservative criterion which Hicks expressed as follows: 'The purpose of income calculations in practical affairs is to give people an indication of the amount which they can consume without impoverishing themselves' (Hicks, 1946).

Income plays a central role in many business and personal decisions, since it is based essentially on the notion of spending capacity. As Hicks pointed out, income should be an operational concept providing guidelines to spending. As applied to business corporations, Hicks's definition of income has been interpreted as the 'amount the corporation can distribute to the owners of equity in the corporation and be as well off at the end of the year as at the beginning' (Alexander, 1962, p 139). It is evident, however, that income is used for other purposes as well. For this reason, we examine the objectives of income measurements before proceeding to the analysis and selection of appropriate concepts.

## The objectives of income measurement

### Income as a measure of efficiency

Income is used as a measure of efficiency in two senses. First, the overall efficiency of a business is assessed in terms of income generated. Hence, income tends to provide the basic standard by which success is measured. There are clearly problems in focusing upon financial efficiency to the detriment of other concepts of business efficiency – such as the effectiveness of the business as a social unit and its efficiency in developing and using new ideas and processes. Nevertheless, those who support the use of income as a measure of business efficiency argue that in the last analysis all other aspects of efficiency converge on income. Second, shareholders assess the efficiency of their investments by reference to reported income. Hence, the allocation of investment funds, the selection of portfolios and the operations of the financial system depend upon income as a standard by which decisions are taken.

### Income as a guide to future investment

As we see in Part 5, the selection of investment projects is made on the basis of estimates of future cash flows. These estimates are self-sufficient to the extent that risk and uncertainty have been sufficiently discounted in the decision-making process. In a more general way, however, current income acts to influence expectations about the future. This is particularly so as regards investors who have to rely on financial reports and whose willingness to hold and to subscribe for further shares will be affected by reported income.

## Income as an indicator of managerial effectiveness

Management is particularly sensitive about the income which is reported to shareholders since the effectiveness of managers both as decision makers and as stewards of resources is judged by reference to reported income. It is in this respect that auditors play a key role in ensuring that the statements placed before shareholders reflect a 'true and fair' view of the financial results. What is 'true and fair' is a contentious problem for accountants. Nevertheless, what is evidently neither true nor fair rarely avoids comment.

## Income as a tax base

The tendency of most governments to take a substantial share of corporate income in the form of taxation means that the basis on which corporate tax is assessed is critically important to shareholders and management. Although taxation legislation does not define 'income', it does specify what is taxable and what is deductible in arriving at a measure of taxable income. Much litigation in this area has revolved around the meaning of words, but the taxation authorities accept accounting profit as the base from which to assess taxable profit.

## Income as a guide to creditworthiness

A firm's ability to obtain credit finance depends on its financial status and its current and future income prospects. For this reason, credit institutions and banks require assurances of a firm's ability to repay loans out of future income and look upon current income levels as a guide in this respect.

## Income as a guide to socio-economic decisions

A wide range of decisions take into account the levels of corporate income. Thus, price increases tend increasingly to be justified in terms of income levels, and wage-bargaining procedures usually involve appeals by both sides to their effects on corporate income. Government economic policies are guided by levels of corporate income as one of the key economic indicators.

## Income as a guide to dividend policy

The distinction between capital and income is central to the problem of deciding how much may be distributed to shareholders as dividends. A series of important legal cases have been concerned with the concept of capital maintenance, and rules have been established for the measurement of distributable income with a view to protecting the interests of creditors. Thus, there is a rule which provides that losses in the value of current assets should be made good, whereas in arriving at the measure of distributable income, there is no need to make good losses in the value of fixed assets.

Nowadays, however, dividend policy is directed towards establishing the proportion of current income which should be retained and the proportion which should be distributed. This is because companies expect to finance part of their investment needs from retained income.

## Income concepts for financial reporting

The application of different accounting valuation concepts to asset valuation and income measurement offers a variety of alternative bases for drawing up financial reports. In this part, we examine the implications of reporting to shareholders on the basis of the six alternative accounting valuation concepts listed in the introduction to this part, namely historical cost, present value, current purchasing power, replacement cost, net realizable value and current value.

Two criteria – relevance and feasibility – are highly significant in this regard. The stewardship concept of financial reporting is identified with historical cost accounting. This concept focuses on safeguarding assets rather than on presenting measurements useful for decision making. Clearly, financial reports should provide some safeguards against the misuse of assets by management, but they should also provide measurements to shareholders indicative of the efficiency with which assets have been employed. The latter type of measurement is relevent for decision making by shareholders and investors. It has become apparent that when applying the criterion of relevance to users' information needs, historical cost measurements fail to satisfy those needs. Feasibility embraces such aspects of the measurement problem as objectivity and ease of understanding, as well as considerations of costs of implementation.

Unfortunately, the selection of accounting measurements on the basis of the two criteria of relevance and feasibility does not rely on a simple set of accept/reject decision rules. To some extent each measurement currently available meets both criteria, but meets them at different levels of quality. For example, an accounting method which utilizes a measurement which scores highly for relevance may not score well for feasibility.

A second problem which will be examined in this part stems from alternative definitions of capital maintenance. Thus, there is some controversy about the manner in which concepts of capital maintenance may be made operational for financial reporting purposes. For example, the debate which followed the Sandilands Report illustrates that the operating capacity concept of capital maintenance does not immediately suggest agreement about the choice of an accounting valuation system which would satisfy the objectives of such a concept.

## Summary

The purpose of this chapter was to examine the implications for financial reporting of three concepts – capital, value and income. Two meanings may be attached to the concept of capital. First, capital may be seen as the totality of enterprise assets which give rise to income. Second, capital may be seen as the investment made by shareholders in the equity of the enterprise and from which they expect to derive income in the form of dividends. Investors are concerned not only with the interdependence of the value of their shareholdings and the value of enterprise assets, but also with maintaining the value of that capital. The value of capital and the measurement of income are also interdependent in the sense that income is the difference between the value of capital at two points in time. Therefore, a central issue in the measurement of periodic income is the notion of capital maintenance. Difficulties arise in reporting income due to the different concepts of capital maintenance discussed in this chapter.

Further problems arise in financial reporting from the application of different valuation concepts to asset valuations. The combination of different capital maintenance and asset valuation concepts lies at the heart of much of the controversy in financial reporting. The problem of selecting a financial reporting framework requires the evaluation of alternative accounting valuation systems in terms of criteria of relevance and feasibility.

**References**   Alexander, S S (1962), revised by Solomons, D. 'Income measurement in a dynamic economy', in Baxter, W T and Davidson, S (eds), *Studies in Accounting Theory*, Sweet & Maxwell.

Fisher, I (1919). *Elementary principles of economics*.

Fisher, I (1969). 'Income and capital', in Parker, R H and Harcourt, G C (eds), *Readings in the Concept and Measurement of Income*, Cambridge University Press.

Gene Brown, R and Johnston, K S (1963). *Paciolo on Accounting*, McGraw-Hill.

Goudeket, A (1960). 'An application of replacement value theory', *Journal of Accountancy*, July.

Hicks, J R (1946). *Value and Capital*, 2nd edn, Oxford University Press.

ICAS Research Committee (1988). *Making Corporate Reports Valuable*, Kogan Page.

Littleton, A C (1961). *Essays on Accounting*, University of Illinois Press.

## Self-assessment questions

1 How do accountants define capital?

2 Compare the accountants' definition of capital with the definition used by economists.

3 Discuss the significance of the concept of 'capital maintenance'.

4 Explain briefly the different concepts of capital maintenance that have been postulated.

5 Identify which of these concepts of capital maintenance would be most appropriate to the following two groups of decision makers, with brief explanations of your reasons:

   (a) corporate shareholders;
   (b) management.

6 Explain briefly how accountants measure business income.

7 Review the various purposes for which businesses require income measurement.

8 Explain what you understand as 'value'.

9 'Valuation is a process by which value is established. However, since there are different approaches to valuation, it follows that there are different values.' Comment on this statement.

10 In the light of Question 9, consider the significance of alternative values to the measurement of capital and income.

# 20 Accounting and economic concepts of income and value

## Setting the scene

The adoption of a value basis of accounting would remove many of the difficulties which we have identified in relation to the present profit and loss account. It would obviate the need for a depreciation charge when assets were gaining in value, although assets which were losing value would still need to be written down to their current value. There will be those who think that revenue should bear a charge for the consumption of assets used in earning it: this would mean, under our suggestion, the results of the period including the write-up for any increase in the worth of an asset and a write-down to provide for consumption. This makes sense if one accepts the matching concept of measuring profit, but it is rather cumbersome. If the comparison of financial wealth from period to period is accepted as the basis for judging results, we are of the opinion that the double step is unnecessary.

(ICAS Research Committee, 1988)

## Learning objectives

**After studying this chapter you should be able to:**

1 **Appreciate the effects of the cost and realization conventions on the measurement of income.**

2 **Explain the essential differences between the accounting and economic approaches to income measurement.**

3 **Describe the relation between income and value in the measurement of economic income.**

4 **Discuss the difficulties of applying economic concepts of income and value to accounting measurements.**

## Accounting concepts

Accounting concepts of income and value have been influenced mainly by two con-ventions – the cost convention and the realization convention. These conventions have received much criticism in recent years on the ground that they restrict the use-fulness of financial accounting reports for decision-making purposes.

## The effects of the cost convention

The historical cost method of valuation seriously distorts the measurement of income when the value of money is changing. This distortion results from the difference between the historical cost and the current cost which, as we shall see later, is a function of the time gap between the acquisition and the utilization of assets committed to earning periodic revenues. For items such as wages and other current expenses, this difference may be very small, but for such assets as stocks and fixed assets there may be a substantial difference between the acquisition cost and the current cost when those assets are charged against revenue under the matching rule. Under conditions of rising prices, the historical cost may bear no resemblance to the current cost of assets, with the result that income is overstated. Conservative asset values on the balance sheet are contrasted by over-optimistic profit measurements in the profit and loss account.

The historical cost method of valuation creates a particular problem in periods of inflation when money units of different values are brought together in the accounting process as though they were money units of the same value. Such arithmetic is quite incorrect, for it involves adding together amounts expressed in different measurement scales. Accordingly, historical cost values are not additive during periods of changing money values.

**Example 1**    A firm constructed a building at a cost of £100,000. Ten years later, a similar building was constructed at a cost of £200,000. In accordance with the conventions of historical cost accounting, these two items were added together in the balance sheet to show a total historical cost of £300,000. Clearly, the two buildings are not comparable in the sense that the second building is a building which is either twice as large as the first or more costly, in real terms, to build. In effect, no such conclusions could be drawn. Adding together pounds which represent units of different purchasing power is similar in nature to adding together pints, quarts and gallons without converting them to a common denominator. Consider what would be the effect of such arithmetic on the depreciation provision for the buildings. If we assume that the buildings are in fact identical, an annual rate of depreciation of 5 per cent would provide depreciation at the rate of £5,000 for the first building, and £10,000 for the second building. Therefore, it may be concluded that the entire arithmetic underlying the balance sheet representation of asset values would be incorrect under inflation, when asset values purchased at different times are added together in asset totals.

The main advantage which is claimed for historical cost valuation is that it is verifiable. The stewardship approach to financial reporting theory is the major factor which supports this method of valuation. It may be argued, however, that if it is objectivity which accountants are seeking, they should restrict themselves purely to counting cash, since this asset is virtually the only one in respect of which complete objectivity is possible. As soon as accountants move away from cash, they are dealing with subjective factors. For example, there are many alternative measures available for valuing stocks, calculating depreciation, allocating overheads and providing for bad debts. Consequently, 'true' objectivity under historical cost valuation is not possible.

## The effects of the realization convention

In accordance with the realization convention, the accountant does not recognize changes in value until they have crystallized following a transaction. Until a right enforceable at law comes into existence, gains in book values are ignored for the purpose of income measurement.

It has been suggested that there are two principal reasons which favour the practice of measuring income on realization rather than on value added. The first is that a sale affords an objective measure of a change in value, and the second is that the sale is generally considered to be the most decisive and significant event in the chain of transactions and conditions making up the stream of business activity.

By focusing on realized gains and ignoring unrealized gains, the realization convention can lead to absurd results.

**Example 2**   Two investors each have £1,000 to invest. Each invests £1,000 in the shares of Texton plc. The shares of Texton plc double in value by the end of the accounting period. On the last day of the accounting period, the first investor sells his shares for £2,000 and places this sum in the Homestead Building Society. Hence, one investor has £2,000 in the building society and the other holds shares in Texton valued at £2,000. They are both equally well-off, yet, under the realization convention, the investor who has sold his shares is seen as having realized income of £1,000, whereas the investor who has held on to his shares is shown as having no income from this source.

## Economic concepts

The process of valuation is central to all aspects of decision making. As we will see in Part 5, capital budgeting decisions require forecasts to be made about the present value of streams of future net cash receipts associated with investment projects.[1] Similarly, investors may also be regarded as exchanging current assets, namely cash or cash equivalents, for a stream of future dividends in the form of cash dividends or increments in the value of their shares.

In this analysis, capital is valued on the basis of discounted future net receipts. Therefore, it is directly relevant to the information needs of shareholders and investors. The value of the firm to the shareholder is computed in such a way as to facilitate the investment decision, which is to seek that investment which will yield the highest value.

In economics, the value of capital is derived from the value of income. The economic concept of income relies on Hicks's definition of income as the amount which a man can consume during a period and still remain as well off at the end of the period as he was at the beginning (Hicks, 1946, p 172). This concept of income was adopted by Alexander to define the income of a company as the amount the company can distribute to shareholders and be as well off at the end of the year as it was at the beginning (Alexander, 1962). It is measured by comparing the value of the company at two points in time in terms of the present value of expected future net receipts at each of those two points.

The economic concept of income treats assets of all kinds as representing future receipts expected to flow from them to the firm. The main measurement problem lies in comparing the capitalized value of the future net receipts expected both at the beginning and at the end of the accounting period, for the difference represents income, that is, what may be consumed under the Hicksian criterion. Hicks himself recognized the problems of measurement involved in his criterion in the following terms:

> At the beginning of the week the individual possesses a stock of consumption goods, and expects a stream of receipts which will enable him to acquire in the future other consumption goods. . . . Call this Prospect I. At the end of the week

*he knows that one week out of that prospect will have disappeared; the new prospect which he expects to emerge will have a new first week which is the old second week. . . . Call this Prospect II. Now if Prospect II were available on the first Monday, we may assume that the individual would know whether he preferred I to II at that date: similarly, if Prospect I were available on the second Monday he would know if he preferred I to II then. But to enquire whether I on the first Monday is preferred to II on the second Monday is a nonsense question; the choice between them could never be actual at all; the terms of comparison are not in pari materia. (Hicks, 1946)*

Hicks was making a very crucial point regarding the measurement problem of his criterion, for comparative states of well-offness at Prospect I and Prospect II must be established in order to know how much may be spent. Neither points nor prospects are comparable in reality, for they exist at different times.

The economic concept of income based on Hicks's criterion is an estimate since, in deciding how much may be spent, Prospect II must be estimated from the standpoint of Prospect I. In view of this problem two concepts of economic income have evolved. The first concept is called ex-ante income, and compares Prospect II with Prospect I from the time perspective of Prospect I. The second concept is called ex-post income, and compares Prospect II with Prospect I from the time perspective of Prospect II. Neither concept overcomes the fundamental difficulty which Hicks pointed out, that is, that one cannot compare alternatives which are not available together at the same time in making decisions requiring a concept of income. Despite this difficulty, income ex-ante and income ex-post have become established as central concepts in the theory of economic income.

It is important always to remember that both income ex-ante and income ex-post are based on estimates of future expected net receipts both at Prospect I and Prospect II. The valuation of income is inseparable, therefore, from the valuation of assets, since assets are valued in terms of the present value of the sum of future expected net receipts associated with their use by the firm. The valuation of income and capital in economics is therefore based on predictions.

## Estimation of ex-ante income

The nature of ex-ante income may be seen from the following example.

**Example 3**  Seeking to maximize the return on its funds, Excel Ltd plans to invest those funds in the purchase of assets, which at 1 January 20X0 are expected to produce the following future net receipts:

| Year | Amount |
| --- | --- |
| | £ |
| 20X0 | 10,000 |
| 20X1 | 10,000 |
| 20X2 | 10,000 |
| 20X3 | 10,000 |

This stream of expected future net receipts represents a return on investment of 10 per cent, which may be assumed to be the best return obtainable by Excel Ltd. Accordingly, the present value of those future net receipts discounted at 10 per cent may be calculated as follows:

| Year | Expected net receipts at end of year | Present value on 1 January 20X0 | |
|------|------|------|------|
| | £ | | £ |
| 20X0 | 10,000 | 10,000/1.10 | = 9,091 |
| 20X1 | 10,000 | $10,000/(1.10)^2$ | = 8,264 |
| 20X2 | 10,000 | $10,000/(1.10)^3$ | = 7,513 |
| 20X3 | 10,000 | $10,000/(1.10)^4$ | = 6,831 |
| Present value of expected future net receipts at 1 January 20X0 | | | 31,699 |

Since the present value of expected future net receipts associated with the purchase of those assets is £31,699, Excel Ltd would be unwilling to pay more than this sum for those assets. Hence, we may say that the economic value of those assets is £31,699 at 1 January 20X0.

The present value of the expected future net receipts on 1 January 20X1 may be calculated as follows:

| | £ |
|------|------|
| Cash received at end of year 20X0 | 10,000 |
| Present value of future new receipts: | |
| End of year 20X1 | 9,091 |
| End of year 20X2 | 8,264 |
| End of year 20X3 | 7,513 |
| Present value of the assets in terms of actual and future expected net receipts on 1 January 20X1 | 34,868 |

The two valuations of the present value of the assets enable us to calculate ex-ante income as follows:

| | | £ |
|------|------|------|
| Present value of assets at 1 January | 20X1 | 34,868 |
| | 20X0 | 31,699 |
| Ex-ante income for the year | 20X0 | 3,169 |

Note that since the income of £3,169 represents the expected increase in the value of the assets during the year, given an expected rate of return on investment of 10 per cent, it also represents 10 per cent of the initial value of those assets estimated at £31,699 on 1 January 20X0.

## Estimation of ex-post income

In the foregoing example, the income for the year 20X0 has been calculated on the basis that the expected future net receipts at the end of the year 20X0 remained the same as those at the beginning of the year. Under such conditions, ex-ante and ex-post income would be the same.

If, however, the present value of expected future net receipts at the end of the year 20X0 is different from the present value of those expected receipts at the beginning of the year, we may say that the ex-post income is different from the ex-ante income. The ex-ante income refers, therefore, to the estimated income derived from the time perspective of the beginning of the year, and the ex-post income refers to the estimated income derived from the time perspective at the end of the year.

**Example 4**    Let it be assumed that the revised estimates of the present value of future net receipts on 1 January 20X1 are as follows (the estimates at 1 January 20X0 are in brackets):

| Year | Expected net receipts at end of year as at 1 January 20X1 | | Present value of expected receipts as at 1 January 20X1 | | |
|---|---|---|---|---|---|
| | £ | £ | £ | £ | £ |
| 20X0 | 10,000 | (10,000) | 10,000 | | (9,091) |
| 20X1 | 9,000 | (10,000) | 8,182 | (9,000/1.10) | (8,264) |
| 20X2 | 9,000 | (10,000) | 7,438 | (9,000/(1.10)$^2$) | (7,513) |
| 20X3 | 9,000 | (10,000) | 6,762 | (9,000/(1.10)$^3$) | (6,831) |
| Present value of expected future net receipts on 1 January 20X1 | | | 32,382 | | (31,699) |

Ex-post income for the year 20X0, based on the revised estimates established on 1 January 20X1, is as follows:

| | | £ |
|---|---|---|
| Estimated present value on 1 January | 20X1 | 32,382 |
| | 20X0 | 31,699 |
| Ex-post income for the year | 20X0 | 683 |

The ex-post income for the year 20X0 is made up of the following components:

| | £ |
|---|---|
| Ex-ante income | 3,169 |
| Ex-post adjustment | 2,486 |
| Ex-post income | 683 |

# The subjective nature of economic income

The net present value method of valuation presents measurement problems in a number of ways. Accuracy of measurement depends upon the degree of certainty under which the forecasts of expected future cash flows are made. Ideally, the size of the net future cash flows should be estimated with reasonable accuracy as should the time profile of these future cash flows. This is because a sum of money in two years' time is worth more than the sum of money in three years' time. We discuss the problems further in Chapter 32 when we examine capital budgeting decisions.

The net present value concept also requires that the discount rate selected for reducing the future cash flows to their present value should reflect accurately the time value of money. If interest rates are going to fluctuate during the time period considered for using the asset, it follows that the present value of the asset will be distorted because the correct discount rate has not been applied.

Because the future cash flows and discount rate cannot be determined with certainty, Edwards and Bell (1961) call economic income 'subject income', and dismiss the concept on the grounds that it cannot be satisfactorily applied on an operational basis. They echo, therefore, Hicks's own dissatisfaction with the concept, which we mentioned earlier in this chapter.

We mentioned in Part 2 that because of uncertainty surrounding the valuation of a firm, it is not the accountant's function to value the firm for the shareholder or investor. On the contrary, it is for the investor to establish the firm's value as an investment and to bear the risk implied in such a valuation. The role of the accountant is to furnish information which is useful for this purpose. The usefulness and relevance of the information provided in financial reports lies in the effectiveness with which it allows the investor to formulate valuations with some degree of accuracy. In the face of uncertainty, accuracy can never be guaranteed, but information about past and current performance may be used as a basis of developing projections and estimates of likely future trends. The adequacy of the accountant's presentation of information for this purpose and the clarity and sufficiency of disclosure are the central problems, therefore, facing the accounting profession in this area. Investors should use the information provided to make their own estimates of future net receipts, and taking into account their assessment of the degree of uncertainty involved in those estimates, they should discount those estimated net receipts by an appropriate discount rate to arrive at a valuation of the firm. This valuation will retain a high degree of subjectivity, for the discount rate will vary from individual to individual depending upon their respective risk preferences. Therefore, the concept of well-offness is really a matter of an individual's personal preferences. For all these reasons, the concept of economic income has little applicability to the practical problems of financial reporting.

However, it has uses in focusing our attention on aspects of financial reporting that will be of interest to investors, and on the problems that require attention (e.g. future cash flows and the risks of those cash flows).

## Summary

Conventional accounting concepts of income and value possess a limited usefulness for decision making, because of the limitations inherent in the conventions of historical cost and realization which govern the measurement of accounting income. Under conditions of inflation, conservative asset values on the balance sheet contrast with over-optimistic profit measurement in the profit and loss account. Changes in value are not reported as they occur. Changing money values also undermine the stability of the unit of measurement in accounting.

Under conditions of certainty, economic income provides an ideal concept for financial reporting purposes. The value of the firm's future net receipts may be capitalized, thereby providing the investor with a basis for decision making.

The presence of uncertainty, which is the general rule, precludes the use of economic income because of its essentially subjective nature. Future cash flows and discount rates cannot be estimated with certainty. For this reason, the accountant does not attempt to value the firm. Instead, financial reports are concerned with past performance, and investors are required to make their own valuations from the information made available.

Despite these practical limitations, the importance of economic concepts of income and value lies in the emphasis they place on value and value changes rather than on historical costs. Moreover, they stress the limitations of accounting conventions such as the realization convention for financial reporting purpose, and emphasize the importance of the concept of capital maintenance to income measurement.

**References**   Alexander, S S (1962), revised by Solomons, D. 'Income measurement in a dynamic economy', in Baxter, W T and Davidson, S (eds), *Studies in Accounting Theory*, Sweet & Maxwell.

Edwards, E O and Bell, P W (1961). *The Theory and Measurement of Business Income*, University of California Press.

Hicks, J R (1946). Value and Capital, 2nd edn, Oxford University Press.

ICAS Research Committee (1988). *Making Corporate Reports Valuable*, Kogan Page.

## Self-assessment questions

1 Analyse the effects of the cost convention on the measurement of accounting income.

2 Analyse the effects of the cost convention on accounting valuations.

3 Discuss the modifications that could be made to historic cost accounting that would improve the quality of accounting information for financial reporting purposes.

4 Explain the significance of the realization convention with respect to accounting information. Are accountants justified in their commitment to the realization convention?

5 Explain the essential differences between the accounting and economic approaches to income measurement.

6 Comment briefly on Hicks's definition of income.

7 Comment briefly on Alexander's definition of business income.

8 Explain briefly the relation between income and value in the measurement of economic income.

9 Explain the difference between 'ex-ante' and 'ex-post' income. What are the implications of these two approaches for the measurement of economic income?

10 Comment briefly on the difficulties that could be found in applying economic concepts of income and value to accounting measurements.

# 21 Accounting for changing prices

## Setting the scene

Too much attention has been devoted to the theoretical differences in the various valuation models which have been advanced as alternatives to the historical cost model. The provision of useful information should take precedence over adherence to any single measurement model, none of which may be able consistently to provide the best information content. The greater relevance of current values in providing such useful information suggests that they should be the preferred model in all cases where they can be employed to produce meaningful figures. As no single valuation method can meet every valuation need, it will be necessary to create an eclectic system which employs the methods best suited to the specific properties of individual categories of assets.

(Arnold *et al.*, 1991)

## Learning objectives

After studying this chapter you should be able to:

1 Convert money measurements recorded at historical cost into their current purchasing power equivalent in calculating periodic profit or loss and financial position.

2 Appreciate the objectives of asset value accounting and explain its different forms.

3 Explain the concept of 'value to the business'.

Accounting measurements are based on a monetary standard which hitherto has been assumed to be stable. However, experience of recent history has proved this assumption to be unrealistic with the result that the measurement of corporate profit during periods of changing price levels has become a controversial issue.

Price changes may be seen as having general and specific effects. General price changes reflect increases or decreases in the value of the monetary unit. In this case, general price changes are measured by an index, so that the value of a currency in relation to goods and services is different through time. For example, if £15 can only buy today what £10 would have bought on an earlier date, we may say that the price level has increased, the purchasing power of money has fallen and the economy is in a period of inflation. By contrast, specific price changes occur for several reasons. Changes in consumer tastes, technological improvements and speculation by buyers are all reasons found at the root of specific price changes.

Adjusting for the effects of price changes may take the following forms:

1 general adjustments: based on current purchasing power accounting;
2 specific adjustments based on current values:
   – replacement cost accounting – which is based on the current acquisition value of assets, so that in affect they are valued at their current entry price;
   – realizable value accounting – which is based on the current realizable value of assets – that is, their current exit price;
   – current value accounting – which is concerned with the value to the business of assets. While, in many cases, this value would, in fact, be the replacement cost, in some circumstances it would be the net present value of the future income from the asset or its net realizable value;
3 a combination of (1) and (2).

## Current purchasing power accounting

In 1974, the professional accounting bodies in the United Kingdom recommended that a supplementary statement should be attached to the financial reports of companies showing the conversion of the figures in the financial reports in terms of their current purchasing power (CPP) at the closing day of the accounting period. They recommended that the Retail Price Index (RPI) should be used to effect the conversion of historical cost values into current purchasing power equivalents (SSAP 7, 1974, withdrawn 1978).

CPP adjustments are limited to dealing with changes in the general purchasing power of money which occur during periods of inflation or deflation. Accordingly, the view is taken that the purpose of price level adjustments is to express each item in the financial report in terms of a common monetary unit, that is, in terms of pounds of the same purchasing power. The RPI is assumed to reflect the general movement in price of all goods and services. Thus, the doubling of the RPI from 100 to 200 between two points in time would mean that the purchasing power of money had fallen by half during that time interval.

Historical cost accounting is based essentially on the maintenance of financial capital in money terms. Such a concept asserts that all funds available to the firm in excess of the original contribution of funds by shareholders make the firm better off. High levels of inflation experienced in recent years have undermined the validity of this assertion. CPP accounting attempts to deal with this problem by adjusting historical cost measurements for the effects of inflation. As a result, the purchasing power held by the firm is maintained. The profit which results from CPP adjustments may be defined as those gains arising during the accounting period which may be distributed to shareholders, so that the purchasing power of the shareholders' interest in the company is the same at the end of the year as it was at the beginning. However, as we shall see in this chapter, the adjustment of historical cost for the effects of inflation cannot of itself ensure the maintenance of the productive capacity of the assets held by the company. The price level correction alone ignores the fact that capital may be dispersed through changes in individual prices if those relevant to the individual firm rise at a rate faster than the rate of change in the price level. Also, real capital will increase if the relationship is reversed.

## Monetary and non-monetary items

For the purpose of CPP accounting it is necessary to distinguish between two classes of items – monetary and non-monetary items.

*Monetary items* may be defined as those fixed by contract or by their nature and are expressed in pounds regardless of changes in the price level. They include monetary assets such as cash, debtors and loans, and exist as money or as claims to specified sums of money. Holders of monetary assets suffer a loss in the general purchasing power of their assets during periods of inflation. Thus, if one holds money in the form of a bank deposit and the yearly rate of inflation is 25 per cent, the loss in the purchasing power of that money by the end of the period will be 25 per cent.

Monetary items include monetary liabilities such as creditors, bank overdrafts and long-term loans. As the value of money falls during a period of inflation, it follows that the value of such liabilities in current pounds will fall similarly, and this fall represents a purchasing power gain to the debtor. Consequently, those who incur monetary liabilities gain at the expense of creditors during periods of inflation, since they will settle these liabilities with pounds possessing less purchasing power than those they have previously received – directly or indirectly at the time the liabilities were incurred.

*Non-monetary* items are assets and liabilities such as fixed assets, stocks and shareholders' equity, which are assumed neither to lose nor to gain in value by reason of inflation or deflation. This is because price changes for these items will tend to compensate for changes in the value of money. For example, if stocks on hand at the beginning of the year remain unsold at the end of the year, there will be no purchasing power loss since one assumes the sale price when they are sold would be adjusted upwards to take account of the fall in the value of money.

If £100,000 was used to purchase land on a date when the RPI stood at 100, and it now stands at 150, the assumption underlying this movement in prices is that £150,000 in today's money has the same purchasing power as £100,000 when the RPI stood at 100. Hence, to report on the purchasing power invested in the land, its acquisition cost should be stated as £150,000. This value does not say anything about the present market value of that particular piece of land. Property values may have increased more or less than the general movement in prices indicated by the RPI. The particular piece of land mentioned in this example may now be worth £300,000 or only £90,000. Hence, the figure of £150,000 represents only the historical cost of acquisition adjusted for the decrease in the general value of the pound.

Nevertheless, the acceptance of the need to adjust accounting measurements for inflation is a recognition of a fundamental proposition in income theory, namely that provision should be made for maintaining the value of capital intact. Hence, there can be no recognition of income for a period unless it has been established that the purchasing power of the capital employed in a firm is the same at the end of the accounting period as it was in the beginning.

A simple example serves to explain the nature of adjustments which are required to financial reports based on historical cost measurements in order to remove the effects of general price level changes.

**Example 1**   Bangored Supplies plc was formed on 1 January 20X0, with a share capital of £75,000 which was fully subscribed in cash on that date. On the same day, equipment was purchased for £45,000, of which £20,000 was paid immediately, the balance of £25,000 being payable two years thence. The price level index was 100 on 1 January 20X0.

Goods were purchased in two instalments prior to commencing business as follows:

1st purchase in the sum of £44,000, when the price level index was 110;
2nd purchase in the sum of £45,000, when the price level index was 120.

All sales were made when the price level index was 130, and expenses of £16,000 were also incurred at the same index level. Stocks were valued on the FIFO method and the closing stock was valued at £29,000. The price level index at 31 December 20X0 was 130.

The profit and loss account and balance sheet in respect of this year, prepared on a historical cost basis, were as follows:

### Balance sheet as at 31 December 20X0

|  | £ | £ |
|---|---|---|
| **Fixed assets** | | 45,000 |
| *Less:* Accumulated depreciation | | 4,500 |
| | | 40,500 |
| **Current assets** | | |
| Stock | 29,000 | |
| Debtors | 19,000 | |
| Bank balance | 39,500 | |
| | 87,500 | |
| *Less:* Current liabilities | 33,500 | |
| Net current assets | | 54,000 |
| | | 94,500 |
| Share capital | | 75,000 |
| Profit and loss account | | 19,500 |
| | | 94,500 |

### Profit and loss account for the year ended 31 December 20X0

|  | £ | £ |
|---|---|---|
| Sales | | 100,000 |
| Cost of goods sold | | 60,000 |
| Gross operating income | | 40,000 |
| Expenses | 16,000 | |
| Depreciation (10% of £45,000) | 4,500 | |
| | | 20,500 |
| Net operating profit | | 19,500 |

*Required:*
(a) Calculate the purchasing power gain or loss on the monetary items.
(b) Prepare an inflation-adjusted profit and loss account for the year ended 31 December 20X0.
(c) Prepare an inflation-adjusted balance sheet as at 31 December 20X0 when the price level index was 130.

(a) **Calculation of purchasing power gain or loss on short-term monetary items during the year ended 31 December 20X0**

|  | Unadjusted monetary items | Conversion factor | Adjusted monetary items |
|---|---|---|---|
|  | £ |  | £ |
| Net current monetary items on 1 January 20X0 (cash invested) | 75,000 | 130/100 | 97,500 |
| Add: Sales | 100,000 | 130/130 | 100,000 |
|  | 175,000 |  | 197,500 |
| *Less:* |  |  |  |
| Purchases of equipment | 20,000 | 130/100 | 26,000 |
| Purchase of goods |  |  |  |
| (i) index at 110 | 44,000 | 130/110 | 52,000 |
| (ii) index at 120 | 45,000 | 130/120 | 48,750 |
| Expenses | 16,000 | 130/130 | 16,000 |
|  | 125,000 |  | 142,750 |
| Net current monetary items on 31 December 20X0 | 50,000 |  | 54,750 |
| Unadjusted net current monetary items on 31 December 20X0 |  |  | 50,000 |
| Purchasing power loss for the year ended 31 December 20X0 |  |  | 4,750 |

(b) **Preparation of inflation-adjusted profit and loss account for the year ended 31 December 20X0**

|  | Unadjusted | Conversion factor | Adjusted |
|---|---|---|---|
|  | £ |  | £ |
| Sales | 100,000 | 130/130 | 100,000 |
| Cost of goods sold |  |  |  |
| At index 110 | 44,000 | 130/110 | 52,000 |
| At index 120 | 16,000 | 130/120 | 17,333 |
| Expenses | 16,000 | 130/130 | 16,000 |
| Depreciation | 4,500 | 130/100 | 5,850 |
|  | 80,500 |  | 91,183 |
| Net profit | 19,500 |  | 8,817 |

## (c) Preparation of inflation-adjusted balance sheet as at 31 December 20X0

| | Unadjusted | Conversion factor | Adjusted |
|---|---|---|---|
| | £ | | £ |
| Fixed assets | 45,000 | 130/100 | 58,500 |
| Less: Accumulated depreciation | 4,500 | 130/100 | 5,850 |
| | 40,500 | | 52,650 |
| | | | |
| Current assets | | | |
| Stock | 29,000 | 130/120 | 31,417 |
| Debtors | 19,000 | 130/130 | 19,000 |
| Bank balance | 39,500 | 130/130 | 39,500 |
| | 87,500 | | 89,917 |
| Less: Current liabilities | 33,500 | 130/130 | 33,500 |
| | | | |
| Net current assets | 54,000 | | 56,417 |
| Total assets | 94,500 | | 109,067 |
| | | | |
| Share capital | 75,000 | 130/100 | 97,500 |
| Profit and loss account | 19,500 | – | 8,817 |
| Accumulated purchasing power gain | | | 2,750 |
| | 94,500 | | 109,067 |

### Calculation of accumulated purchasing power gain

Gain on unpaid balance of purchase price of equipment

| | |
|---|---|
| Adjusted balance (£25,000 × 130/100) | 32,500 |
| Unadjusted balance | 25,000 |
| | 7,500 |
| Less: Loss as computed on short-term monetary items | 4,750 |
| | |
| Net accumulated purchasing power gain | 2,750 |

# An appraisal of CPP accounting

CPP can be applied with a high degree of objectivity, required of accounting valuation, as it does not depart in principle from historical-cost-based measurement. Price level adjustments are verifiable by reference to the index used to measure changes in the purchasing power of money, and result in alterations to historical cost measurements which are themselves objective. Therefore, both criteria of objectivity and verifiability are satisfied in CPP accounting.

An objection to CPP accounting is raised by some authorities who believe that there is no such thing as generalized purchasing power (Gynther, 1974). Organizations and people do not see themselves as holding general purchasing power when they hold money; rather, they see themselves as holding specific purchasing power in respect of those relatively few items which they wish to purchase. Hence, the purchasing power of money should be related to those items on which money is intended to be spent. A unit of measurement which relies for its validity on the purchasing power of money assessed by reference to a set of goods and services will not be equally useful to all individuals and entities.

Moreover, the concept of income on which these adjustments are based is not one which maintains the service potential of capital. A general price index, particularly a consumer price index, is a weighted average of the price change occurring in a wide variety of goods and services available in the economy. Therefore, adjusting financial data for the effects of inflation is not the same as reporting current values. Price-adjusted data still represents costs, or funds, committed to non-monetary items: these costs are merely translated into the equivalent costs in terms of today's pounds.

General price indices assume that the movements in the price of all goods correspond with each other. However, only by coincidence will a change in the general price index correspond with the change in the price of any particular good or service during the same period. Indeed, there is no reason why they may not move in opposite directions. Thus, a general price index will not be relevant to any business entity which needs to make adjustments to asset valuations in order to maintain the value of its capital in the long term.

Controversy surrounds the treatment of gains and losses arising on monetary items. By our approach in Example 1, the gain or loss on net monetary items is disclosed separately and is not included in income from continuing operations. It is treated as a capital adjustment. The 'gains' resulting from these adjustments do not increase sums available for distribution as dividends to shareholders, since they are purely accounting adjustments. They could be distributed only by drawing on existing cash resources or by borrowing. Hence, if the net 'gains' on monetary items are regarded as available for distribution, the users of adjusted financial reports could be seriously misled.

Although CPP accounting has serious limitations, many writers have argued the need to adjust accounting income for general inflation. According to Baxter (1984):

*Hitherto we have found little fault with statistical tables (e.g. of national income) in constant prices; we do not decry the indexing of tax allowances; most of us would accept indexed investments as a godsend. Admittedly the retail price index does not reflect precisely the consumption patterns of wealthy shareholders; but the divergence does not seem to be big. No system of inflation accounting will be perfect, and correction of income by a general index seems the least bad of the possibilities.*

## Replacement cost accounting

The basic concept underlying replacement cost accounting is that the firm is a going concern, which is continuously replacing its assets. Therefore, the cost of consuming such assets in the profit generation process should be equivalent to the cost of their replacement. Replacement cost accounting differs from current purchasing power accounting in that it is concerned with the manner in which price changes affect the individual firm. It focuses on the specific commodities and assets employed by the firm taking into account changes in the price of such commodities and assets reflected in specific price indices or price indices of groups of similar commodities and assets.

Replacement cost accounting is addressed to the concept of capital maintenance, interpreted as maintaining the operating capacity of the firm, and involves:

1 calculating current operating profit by matching current revenues with the current cost of resources exhausted in earning those revenues;
2 calculating holding gains and losses;
3 presenting the balance sheet in current value terms.

## Components of replacement cost profit (RCP)

The treatment of the two components of replacement cost profit (RCP), namely current operating profit and holding gains and losses, is a controversial matter in the literature of accounting.

Current operating profit results from operating activities and is calculated by matching revenues with the current cost of resources exhausted in these activities. Holding gains and losses result from holding rather than operating activities.

According to the method of replacement cost accounting suggested by Edwards and Bell (1961), holding gains and losses should be reported together with current operating profit in the measurement of RCP. In identifying holding gains as they arise, thereby distinguishing these gains from gains occurring on realization, the pattern of profit recognition differs under replacement cost accounting from that associated with conventional accounting profit, as may be seen from the following example.

**Example 2** During the year ended 31 December 20X0, an asset was acquired at a cost of £40. By 31 December 20X0 its replacement cost had risen to £60. It was sold during the year ended 31 December 20X1 for £100, and at the time of sale its replacement cost was £65.

For the purpose of measuring accounting profit, the profit arising from the sale of the asset (assuming no depreciation) would accrue in the year ended 31 December 20X1 and would be calculated as follows:

$$\text{accounting profits} = \text{revenue} - \text{historical cost}$$
$$= £100 - £40$$
$$= £60$$

For the purpose of measuring RCP, three distinct gains are recognized which occur as follows:

1 A holding gain in the year ended 31 December 20X0, measured as the difference between the replacement cost at 31 December 20X0 and the acquisition cost during the year, that is, £60 − £40 = £20.
2 A holding gain in the year ended 31 December 20X1, measured as the difference between the replacement cost at 31 December 20X0 and the replacement cost on the date of sale, that is, £65 − £60 = £5.
3 An operating gain resulting directly from the activity of selling, measured as the difference between the realized sale price and the replacement cost at the date of sale, that is, £100 − £65 = £35.

These differing timings of profit recognition may be compared as follows:

| Year ended 21 December | 20X0 | 20X1 |
|---|---|---|
| | £ | £ |
| Accounting profit | – | 60 |
| Replacement cost profit | | |
| Holding gains | 20 | 5 |
| Current operating gain | – | 35 |

It is clear from this example that the RCP concept provides more detailed information than the accounting profit concept for the purpose of evaluating the results of activities. Moreover, RCP indicates whether the sales proceeds are sufficient to cover the replacement cost of the resources sold, that is, whether the activity of selling itself is efficient. Where the goods sold are manufactured by the firm, current operating profit indicates whether the manufacturing process is profitable, for the input factors of production are valued at their current replacement cost. Hence, from a long-term point of view, it affords a means of evaluating the firm as a going concern.

## Profit measurement by historical cost and replacement cost compared

The extent of the differences between these two concepts of profit are revealed by a more comprehensive example.

*Example 3*  The financial position of Preifat Ltd, as revealed by the balance sheet as at 31 December 20X0 using historical cost measurements, is as follows:

| | £ | | £ |
|---|---|---|---|
| Share capital | 1,400 | Fixed asset | 1,000 |
| | | Stock | 400 |
| | 1,400 | | 1,400 |

The fixed asset shown on the balance sheet was acquired on 31 December 20X0 and has an estimated life of five years, with no scrap value.

Data recorded in respect of the year ended 31 December 20X1 is as follows:

| | £ |
|---|---|
| Sales | 2,000 |
| Purchases at historical cost | 700 |
| Closing stock: at historical cost | 200 |
| at replacement cost | 250 |
| Cost of goods sold at replacement cost | 1,000 |

It was also estimated that the replacement cost of the fixed asset had risen to £1,200 by 31 December 20X1.

On the basis of this information, the accounting profit for the year 20X1 may be computed as follows:

## Accounting profit for the year ended 31 December 20X1

|  | £ | £ |
|---|---:|---:|
| Sales |  | 2,000 |
| Cost of goods sold: |  |  |
|   Opening stock | 400 |  |
|   Purchases | 700 |  |
|  | 1,100 |  |
|   Closing stock | 200 |  |
|  |  | 900 |
|  |  | 1,100 |
| Depreciation (£1,000 ÷ 5) |  | 200 |
|   Accounting profit |  | 900 |

By contrast, the calculation of the components of replacement cost profit gives a more comprehensive analysis of the nature of operating and holding gains, as follows:

## Replacement cost profit for the year ended 31 December 20X1

|  | £ | £ | £ |
|---|---:|---:|---:|
| Sales |  |  | 2,000 |
| Cost of goods sold (at replacement cost) |  |  | 1,000 |
|  |  |  | 1,000 |
| Depreciation (£1,200 ÷ 5) |  |  | 240 |
| **Current operating profit** |  |  | 760 |
| **Holding gains** |  |  |  |
|   Realized through use during the year |  |  |  |
|     Fixed assets | 40 |  |  |
|     Stocks | 100 |  |  |
|  |  | 140 |  |
|   Unrealized at the end of the year |  |  |  |
|     Fixed assets | 160 |  |  |
|     Stocks | 50 |  |  |
|  |  | 210 |  |
| Total holding gains |  |  | 350 |
| Current operating profit plus holding gains |  |  | 1,100 |

Notes:

1 Depreciation is calculated on the replacement cost of the fixed assets (£1,200) rather than on the historical acquisition cost (£1,000). By this means, the depreciation provision is more realistic in relation to the current cost of resource utilization.

2 Stocks are charged against sales at their current replacement cost at the time of sale.

3 Holding gains are of two kinds:

  (a) Realized holding gains which result from the application of replacement cost values to the input of resources to the profit generation process. In the example, depreciation charged under replacement cost accounting is £40 greater than that charged under historical cost accounting. Similarly, the cost of goods sold under replacement cost is £100 greater than that charged under historical cost accounting. Both amounts represent holding gains realized by reason of the use or the sale of assets.

(b) Unrealized holding gains which result from the increased value of assets held by the firm and remaining unused or unsold at the end of the accounting period. In the example, the unrealized holding gains are calculated as follows:

(i) Fixed assets: unallocated value at the end of the accounting period:

| | |
|---|---:|
| Under replacement cost | £1,200 – 240 = £960 |
| Under historic cost | £1,000 – 200 = 800 |
| *Unrealized holding gain* | 160 |

(ii) Stock: stock unsold at the end of the accounting period:

| | |
|---|---:|
| Under replacement cost | £250 |
| Under historical cost | 200 |
| *Unrealized holding gain* | 50 |

## Historical cost and replacement cost balance sheets compared

The effect of applying historical cost and replacement cost valuations to balance sheets is seen in the following balance sheet drawn from data given in the example.

**Balance sheet as at 31 December 20X1**
**(assuming that all sales and purchases were paid in cash)**

| | Historical cost | Replacement cost |
|---|---:|---:|
| | £ | £ |
| **Fixed assets** | 1,000 | 1,200 |
| *Less:* Accumulated depreciation | 200 | 240 |
| | 800 | 960 |
| Current assets | | |
| Stock | 200 | 250 |
| Cash | 1,300 | 1,300 |
| | 2,300 | 2,510 |
| **Share capital** | 1,400 | 1,400 |
| **Retained profit** | | |
| Accounting profit | 900 | |
| Current operating profit | | 760 |
| Revaluation reserve | | 350 |
| | 2,300 | 2,510 |

*Note:*
Cash balance is calculated as follows:

Sales £2,000 – Purchases £700 = Cash £1,300

As may be observed, the application of replacement cost values attempts to reflect economic reality by maintaining the value of asset balances in line with changes in the value of money and changes in the specific value of the assets concerned.

## The treatment of holding gains

One of the controversial issues in the debate about replacement cost accounting is whether holding gains constitute profit. There is little doubt that current operating profit satisfies the accounting convention relating to realization, and at the same time is directed to the maintenance of capital, which is a basic principle in the measurement of economic income.

How holding gains are treated depends on one's view of capital maintenance. Proponents of the maintenance of financial capital in money terms (i.e. the original amount of money invested in the assets of the entity) view the holding gains as an item of profit. Profit is considered to be the total gain arising during the period which could be distributed in full while still maintaining capital, in the sense of the original financial investment, at the level which existed at the beginning of the period. Advocates of the operating capability concept, however, argue that increases in the price of items that a firm must have if it is to continue in business are not an element of profit, but a capital maintenance adjustment to be placed directly in the owners' equity. This amount is that which is necessary for replacing assets. This is the view taken in the above example.

## An evaluation of replacement cost accounting

As a method of financial reporting, replacement cost accounting provides a concept of profit which can be assessed against the criteria of relevance and feasibility which were discussed earlier.

Replacement cost profit is more relevant to investors than accounting profit for the purpose of decision making. First, it provides for the maintenance of the service potential of capital by charging against revenue the cost of replacing the assets exhausted in earning revenue. Second, an important distinction is made between operating profit and holding gains, thereby allowing investors to appraise the firm as a going concern. Third, it recognizes changes in the value of assets, since they are related to current market prices. For these reasons, investors are provided with information which is more relevant than accounting profit for evaluating the business, and they are placed in a better position to predict the future. By providing more accurate valuations of assets in use, replacement cost accounting is likely to lead to a more efficient allocation of financial resources than that afforded by conventional accounting methods. A further argument in favour of replacement cost accounting lies in the diversity of values found in conventional accounting due to the employment of a variety of valuation methods, such as LIFO, FIFO or average cost. With replacement cost accounting, however, values are uniformly derived from the current replacement cost of specific assets, so that comparisons are much more meaningful.

Criticisms are sometimes advanced against replacement cost accounting on the ground that the measurements involved are subjective. There exist, however, government indices which relate to fixed assets of various kinds which may be employed for the purpose of calculating the replacement cost of specific fixed assets. The Sandilands Committee recommended that the Government Statistical Service should publish as soon as possible a new series of price indices specific to particular industries for capital expenditure on plant and machinery. Such a series of indices should be designed to provide a 'standard reference basis' for making reasonable approximations of current replacement costs. The derivation of replacement costs for stocks could present problems. However, when the various different methods of valuing stocks at the present time are considered, it appears that replacement cost provides a more objective measure.

A major problem arises during periods of rapid technological change. Most authorities argue that since a measure of the profitability of existing operations is required, current replacement costs should be measured in terms of the market prices prevailing for the actual fixed assets which are exhausted in producing profit. Some authorities are opposed to this view, since it seemingly ignores the effect of technological change. They argue that the replacement cost of new-generation assets should be used, because 'the primary interest is in the long-run prospects of the firm, and there seems to be no particular reason why these long-run prospects would be indicated by the prospects of the present mode of production, when becoming obsolete'. Accordingly, if the firm is using a second-generation computer made obsolete by the development of third-generation computers, they argue that the current replacement cost should be based on the current market price of third-generation rather than second-generation computers.

## Realizable value accounting

Both historical cost and replacement cost accounting employ entry values, that is, they are based on the acquisition cost of assets. By contrast, realizable value accounting employs exit values, that is, it is based on the realizable price of assets.

The distinction between entry and exit values leads to two different concepts of profit – realized and realizable income. Realized profit arises only upon sale, so that unsold assets are valued at cost. By contrast, realizable profit is based on the current selling price of the assets, thereby indicating the revenue which could be obtained should the assets be sold. As a result, unsold assets are valued not at cost, but at realizable value.

### The case for realizable value accounting

The realizable value model is based on the concept of opportunity cost, that is, value is expressed in terms of the benefit lost in holding assets in their present form rather than in the next-best alternative form. For example, as regards closing stocks, the next best alternative to holding stocks is selling them, so that on an opportunity cost basis, the value of closing stocks is what they would realize if sold.

Chambers and Sterling have argued in favour of realizable value accounting. According to Chambers, for example, the most important characteristic of the firm is its capacity to adapt to a changing environment, and in this way, to ensure its survival. The survival of the firm depends, therefore, on its ability to acquire goods and services, which is related to the realizable value of its existing assets. Chambers coined the term 'current cash equivalent' to indicate the realizable value of the firm's currently held assets, that is, the cash represented by those assets and available, if sold, for investing in market alternatives and consequently redeploying its resources (Chambers, 1966; Sterling, 1970).

By contrast, replacement cost accounting reflects a relatively static situation, and does not inform investors about the economic sacrifice made in holding resources in their current form.

Another argument in favour of realizable value accounting is that realizable value profit is an acceptable surrogate for economic income, for it indicates minimum future cash flows which may result from the realization of currently held assets. As argued in Chapter 19, the present value of future cash flows associated with the holding of assets is the most relevant concept of value from the point of view of investors. Backward-looking concepts, such as historical cost and replacement cost values, are poor surrogates as predictors of future cash flows. Finally, a further argument in favour of realizable value lies in its relevance to the needs of creditors for information about the market value of the assets held by a company to which they have extended credit facilities, particularly if the security for loans and other forms of credit is represented by liens or mortgages over such assets.

## Components of realizable profit

Realizable profit reflects the periodic change in the value of enterprise capital measured in terms of resale price. It consists of two components:

1 realized gains resulting from the sale of assets during the accounting period, which are measured as the difference between the actual realized revenue from sale and the realizable value estimated at the beginning of the period;
2 unrealized gains resulting from changes in the realizable value of assets which have remained unsold at the end of the accounting period.

**Example 4** During the year ended 31 December 20X0 an asset was acquired for £40. At 31 December 20X0, its estimated realizable value was £85, and it was sold during the year ended 31 December 20X1 for £100. The realizable profit for the years ended 31 December 20X0 and 20X1 is as follows:

|  | 20X0 | 20X1 |
|---|---|---|
| **Realizable profit** |  |  |
| Unrealized gain | £85 – 40 = £45 |  |
| Realized gain |  | £100 – 85 = £15 |

We noted in our earlier discussion of holding gains arising under replacement cost accounting that such gains could not be treated as part of replacement income. The reason for this view is to be found in the capital maintenance criterion to which replacement cost profit is directed. By contrast, the realizable value concept of profit is directed towards measuring the firm's ability to adapt to a changing environment, and for this purpose profit is required to measure changes in the firm's command over goods and services. This may be measured by reference to both realized gains and unrealized gains which result, as we mentioned earlier, from changes in the realizable value of assets during the year. Hence, under realizable value profit, no distinction is maintained between current operating profit and holding gains. Assets are shown on the balance sheet at their realizable value.

## Limitations of exit values

Exit values imply a short-run approach to the analysis of business operations because they entail disposition and liquidation values being shown on the balance sheet. Hence, business operations resulting in realizable profit only indicate that it is worth staying in business in the short run, not that it is worth replacing assets and staying in business in the long term. Realizable value accounting values all assets at exit prices even though many assets are not held for resale.

It has been argued that the crucial test of the usefulness of exit values in financial reports lies in the treatment of highly specific assets, which may have very little value for anyone except the present owner for whom they were constructed. The most extreme example of such assets are mineshafts, which, being large holes in the ground, have no exit value. Such assets may be presumed to have been worth as much to the firm as their acquisition or construction costs. Otherwise, it is clear that they would not have been acquired or constructed. The question is, what would be the sense of writing such assets down to their current realizable value?

Another limitation of exit values lies in their anticipation of operating profit, before the critical event giving rise to revenue has occurred. It has been argued, for example, that:

> If profit is to be recognized at a moment of time, we must select that moment. The economist gives a clue in the formulation of entrepreneurship as the function of directing a business, bearing the risks and reaping the rewards of the business. This suggests that profit is earned at the moment of making the most crucial decision or of performing the most difficult task in the cycle of a complete transaction. (Myers, 1973)

Where production is the critical event and sale presents no problem, the valuation of products at net realizable value gives a better indication of managerial performance than does replacement cost. Where selling is the main difficulty, the sale is the critical event which must occur before managerial performance may be correctly evaluated, for without a contract of sale or an active quoted market for the product, the accountant has little evidence of managerial accomplishment. The accountant must assume, in these circumstances, that the product will be sold for at least the break-even price, so that replacement cost is the most suitable measurement of value in these circumstances.

## Current value accounting

Current value accounting is a modification to historical cost profit to arrive at the surplus after allowing for the impact of price changes on the funds needed to continue the existing business and to maintain its operating capability, whether financed by shares or borrowings.

Current value accounting utilizes two important theoretical concepts:

1 operating capability, and
2 value to the business.

## Operating capability

Operating capability is assumed to be represented by net operating assets that include not only physical assets, such as fixed assets and stocks, but also the net monetary working capital.

## Value to the business

The concept of 'value to the business' should determine whether exit or entry values should be used in the valuation process. One way of determining 'value to the business' is to reverse the opportunity cost concept, and to define opportunity value as the least costly sacrifice avoided by owning the asset. This approach to the valuation of an asset to the business has been adopted by a number of economists. Bonbright (1937, p 71), for example, defined opportunity value in the following terms: 'The value of a property to its owner is identical in amount with the adverse value of the entire loss, direct and indirect, that the owner might expect to suffer if he were deprived of the property.'

In no sense may historical cost be measured as the value of an asset to the business because it is not related to the amount which would have to be paid for the asset, the amount that might be gained from disposing of it or the amount to be gained by holding it. It remains to consider, therefore, the other three bases of valuation which were listed in the introduction:

1 the current purchase price (replacement cost) of the asset (RC);
2 the net realizable value of the asset (NRV);
3 the present value of expected future earnings from the asset (PV).

It has been argued (Parker and Harcourt, 1969, p 17) that six hypothetical relationships exist between these three values:

|  | Correct valuation basis |
| --- | --- |
| (a)  NRV > PV > RC | RC |
| (b)  NRV > RC > PV | RC |
| (c)  PV > RC > NRV | RC |
| (d)  PV > NRV > RC | RC |
| (e)  RC > PV > NRV | PV |
| (f)  RC > NRV > PV | NRV |

In (a) and (b) above, NRV is greater than PV. Hence, the firm would be better off selling rather than using the asset. The sale of the asset necessitates its replacement, if the NRV is to be restored. We may say, therefore, that the maximum loss the firm would suffer by being deprived of the asset is RC. In (c) and (d) above, PV is greater than NRV, so that the firm would be better off using the asset rather than selling it. The firm must replace the asset in order to maintain PV, so that the maximum loss the firm would suffer by being deprived of the asset is again RC.

The general statement which may be made, therefore, in respect of the first four cases (a) to (d) is that, where either NRV or PV, or both, are higher than RC, RC is the appropriate value of the asset to the business. As regards a current asset such as stocks, RC will be the current purchase price (entry value). In the case of a fixed asset, RC will be the written-down current purchase price (replacement cost), since the value of such an asset will be the cost of replacing it in its existing condition, having regard to wear and tear.

As regards cases (e) and (f), RC does not represent the value of the asset to the business, for if the firm were to be deprived of the asset then the loss incurred would be less than RC. Case (e) is most likely to arise in industries where assets are highly specific, where NRV tends to zero and where RC is greater than PV, so that it would not be worth replacing the asset if it were destroyed, but it is worth using it rather than attempting to dispose of it. The conclusion which may be reached as regards fixed assets is that except in the rare occurrence of case (e) fixed assets which are held for use should be valued at RC if such assets are to represent their value to the business.

Case (f) applies to assets held for resale, that is, where NRV must be greater than PV. If RC should prove to be greater than NRV, such assets would not be replaced. Hence, it implies that they should be valued at NRV or RC, whichever is the lower. This recommendation, despite its superficial resemblance to the lower of cost or market value which we argued to be illogical in Part 2, is not a concession to the convention of conservatism, but represents an attempt to measure the value of assets to the business. If RC exceeds NRV, stocks will not be replaced, so that NRV represents their value to the firm. Conversely, where NRV exceeds RC, stocks are worth replacing, so that their value to the firm is determined by RC.

## Recent developments

The Accounting Standards Committee issued in 1988 a document *Accounting for the Effects of Changing Prices: A Handbook*. The objective was to specify the limitations of historical cost accounting and examine various remedies. Although the debate hitherto had often been expressed as a straight choice between CCA and CPP, the *Handbook* embraces more than one model of financial reporting. It argues that both the operating and financial capital maintenance concepts can provide useful information about the effects of changing prices. The *Handbook* considers the case for combining these concepts, so that both may be included in the reporting system. The *Handbook* argues for current costs as the method of valuing assets, combined with a financial capital maintenance system (based on CPP type measurements) which maintains shareholders' funds in 'real terms'.

More recently, the Accounting Standards Board published a Discussion Paper, *The Role of Valuation in Financial Reporting,* in 1993, and considers valuation issues in Chapters 4 and 5 of its *Statement of Principles for Financial Reporting* which appeared in 1995. The ASB acknowledges the superiority of a current value approach over a historical costing approach. According to the *Statement*,

> *The current value based on the value to the business model . . . allows users to observe current operating margins and gives a better guide to future potential performance than the historical cost profit which combines operating margins and any gains or losses from holding assets. Thus, the use of current values for both assets and liabilities provides the information that is most relevant to the decisions of users.*

However, the Board is not anxious to repeat the SSAP 16 fiasco. The approach, it argues, should be evolutionary rather than revolutionary. The ASB's Revised

Exposure Draft Statement of Principles which was issued in 1999 does not advocate radical changes in the basis of measurement. It envisages that 'the approach now adopted by the majority of the larger UK listed companies will continue to be used'. This approach involves carrying some categories of balance sheet items at historical cost and others at current value.

## Summary

If the value of money is changing, it is clear that the money standard of measurement ceases to be efficient. Financial reports should be adjusted, therefore, for the effects of changes in the value of money for the following reasons:

1 to provide a more accurate basis for assessing the value of a shareholder's investment in a company;
2 to enable more meaningful comparisons to be made between the reported results of successive years;
3 to enable more meaningful inter-company comparisons to be effected.

The unsatisfactory nature of historical cost as a basis for financial reporting is reflected in the fact that companies have been increasingly incorporating partial adjustments for inflation in their reported values. The revaluation of fixed assets by firms in the United Kingdom, and the adoption of LIFO by companies in the United States, are examples of this phenomenon.

CPP accounting allows adjusted historical costs to be matched against current revenues. It computes losses arising through holding monetary items during periods of inflation.

Current value accounting combines the best characteristics of economic and accounting income by associating value and changes in value with transactions.

In recent years, the case for combining the characteristics of CCA and CCP in the same reporting system has received increasing support.

References

Arnold, J, Boyle, P, Carey, A, Cooper, M and Wild, K (1991). *The Future Shape of Financial Reports*, ICAEW.

Baxter, W T (1984). *Inflation Accounting*, Philip Allen.

Bonbright, J C (1937). *The Valuation of Property*, McGraw-Hill.

Chambers, R J (1966). *Accounting, Evaluation and Economic Behaviour*, Prentice Hall.

Edwards, E O and Bell, P W (1961). *The Theory and Measurement of Business Income*, University of California Press.

Gynther, R S (1974). 'Why use general purchasing power?' *Accounting and Business Research*, Spring.

Myers, J H (1973). 'The critical event and recognition of net profit', in Zeff, S A and Keller, T F (eds), *Financial Accounting Theory*, McGraw-Hill.

Parker, R H and Harcourt, G C (1969). *Readings in the Concept and Measurement of Income*, Cambridge University Press.

SSAP 7 'Accounting for Changes in the Purchasing Power of Money', London, 1974, withdrawn 1978.

Sterling, R R (1970). *Theory and Measurement of Enterprise Income*, University of Kansas Press.

# Self-assessment questions

1 Review briefly the possible effects of changes in price levels on accounting data.

2 State what is meant by current purchasing power accounting.

3 Describe how you would convert money measurements recorded at historic cost into their current purchasing power equivalent in calculating periodic profit or loss.

4 Describe how you would convert money measurements accumulated on balance sheets into their current purchasing power equivalent for preparing a year-end balance sheet.

5 State the objectives of current value accounting, and explain its different forms.

6 Explain the significance of the distinction made under replacement cost accounting between current operating profit and losses and holding gains and losses.

7 Comment briefly on the concept of 'value to the business', used in connection with current value accounting.

# Problems  *(\* indicates that a solution is to be found in the Lecturer's Guide)*

1 Vitex plc was created on 1 January 20X0 with a share capital of £150,000, fully paid in cash on that date. The price level index at that date was 100. The following transactions were recorded:

Purchased equipment for £90,000, £40,000 paid when the index was 100, and payment of the balance being deferred for 18 months.

Purchased goods for £88,000 when the index was 100.

Purchased goods for £90,000 when the index was 110.

Sold goods for £200,000 when the index was 120, the cost of sales amounting to £120,000.

Cash expenses amounted to £32,000, and a depreciation provision of 10 per cent on historic cost of equipment was made at year end.

Additional information as at 31 December 20X0 was as follows:

| | |
|---|---|
| Trade debtors | £36,000 |
| Bank balance | £81,000 |
| Creditors | £67,000 |

Closing stock was valued at £58,000 on a FIFO basis.

The index at year end was 120.

*Required:*
(a) Calculate the purchasing power gain or loss on the monetary items.
(b) Prepare an inflation-adjusted profit and loss account for the year ended 31 December 20X0.
(c) Prepare an inflation-adjusted balance sheet as at 31 December 20X0 when the price level index was 130.

**2\*** ABC Ltd has traded for several years. Its accounts are kept on a conventional historical cost basis.

**Balance Sheet**

|  | 31.12.X0 | 31.12.X1 |  | 31.12.X0 | 31.12.X1 |
|---|---|---|---|---|---|
|  | £ | £ |  | £ | £ |
| Capital | 38,100 | 38,100 | Plant | 100,800 | 100,800 |
| Retained profit | 8,490 | 19,260 | *Less:* Depn | 37,800 | 44,800 |
|  | 46, 590 | 57,360 |  | 63,000 | 56,000 |
| Loan | 27,000 | 27,000 | Stocks | 4,290 | 7,560 |
| Creditors | 3,600 | 8,600 | Debtors | 9,000 | 24,000 |
| Cash |  |  |  | 900 | 5,400 |
|  | 77,190 | 92,960 |  | 77,190 | 92,960 |

| Indices | General | Stock | Plant |
|---|---|---|---|
|  | £ | £ | £ |
| Date capital acquired | 50 |  |  |
| Date plant acquired | 80 |  | 70 |
| Date opening stocks acquired | 85.8 | 110 |  |
| 1 January 20X1 | 90 | 120 | 100 |
| 30 June 20X1 | 100 | 130 | 115 |
| 30 September 20X1 | 105 | 135 | 122 |
| 31 December 20X1 | 110 | 140 | 130 |

No purchases or sales of plant took place during the year. No dividends have been paid or proposed. Ignore taxation.

Closing stock was valued at 30 September prices.

*Required:*
Prepare a balance sheet as at 31 December 20X1 on a CPP basis and on an RC basis.

**3\*** Keaton Ltd started business 1 January Year 1. Set out below is the balance sheet on a historical cost basis as at 31 December:

|  |  | Year 1 |  | Year 2 |
|---|---|---|---|---|
|  |  | £000 |  | £000 |
| Land |  | 110 |  | 110 |
| Plant cost | 40 |  | 40 |  |
| Depreciation | 4 | 36 | 8 | 32 |
| Stocks |  | 90 |  | 120 |
| Debtors |  | 30 |  | 50 |
| Bank |  | 60 |  | 50 |
|  |  | 326 |  | 362 |
| Creditors |  | 50 |  | 80 |
|  |  | 276 |  | 282 |
|  |  | £ |  | £ |
| Share capital |  | 250 |  | 250 |
| Retained earnings |  | 26 |  | 32 |
|  |  | 276 |  | 282 |

The realizable value of the assets is as follows:

|  | £ | £ |
|---|---|---|
| Land | 150 | 160 |
| Plant | 25 | 22 |
| Stocks | 130 | 170 |

The profit and loss account for Year 2 on a historical cost basis is:

|  | £ |
|---|---|
| Sales | 130 |
| Cost of sales | 90 |
|  | 40 |
| Depreciation | 4 |
|  | 36 |
| Dividend | 30 |
| Retained earnings | 6 |

*Required:*
Prepare balance sheets at the end of Years 1 and 2 on the basis of realizable value accounting.

(Problem supplied by A J Naughton)

## PART 4

# Financial reporting – extending the disclosure of information

# Introduction to Part 4

The scope of accounting was defined in Part 1 as being 'to provide information which is potentially useful for making economic decisions and aims to assess the impact of an organization or company on people both inside and outside'. This definition of the scope of accounting was followed by a discussion of the development of accounting theory, where several approaches to accounting theory (e.g. descriptive, decision-usefulness, normative and empirical, welfare) were discussed. It was seen, in particular, that the current state of accounting knowledge depended substantially on a descriptive approach to accounting theory. This emphasized observations of the practices of accountants as a major source of accounting knowledge. It was for this reason that Part 2 was devoted to an analysis of the knowledge provided by a descriptive approach to accounting theory. Part 3 was seen as necessary in the context of the adjustments considered necessary to historical cost accounting by reason of the instability of the monetary standard of measurement. This instability affects not only the measurement of periodic profit but also the valuations which are significant in financial reports.

The problem which must be posed is the relevance of accounting information in the context of the needs of users for decision making. This problem, which was posed in the definition of accounting given in Part 1, was only dealt with partly in Part 3. In Chapter 13 we saw that the ASB's Statement of Principles, which adopts a decision usefulness approach, forms a framework for the future development of financial reporting. The ASB's intention is that accounting standards should be based on principles rather than *ad hoc* rules. In this part we consider how such principles may be applied in practice.

*Tomorrow's Company*, a study by The Royal Society for the Arts (1996), examined the kinds of companies likely to succeed in tomorrow's business climate. The study concluded that tomorrow's company would form deeper relationships with key stakeholders as a means of achieving financial success. These key stakeholders are the groups of people with an interest in a business organization, which we considered in Chapter 2. This view is, in short, that the company which ignores its stakeholders does so at its peril, and similarly that those which take them into account are more likely to prosper.

Chapter 22 examines the needs of investors and suggests the nature of their information needs; Chapter 23 discusses the needs of employees for accounting information and examines the implications of the Employment Protection Act 1975 in this respect; and Chapter 24 considers the problem of corporate social responsibility and the nature of information which is relevant to this area of accounting responsibility.

# 22 Reporting to investors

## Setting the scene

There is substantial scope for companies to improve the way in which they report their financial performance, analysts and institutional investors believe. This is the conclusion of an extensive survey of city opinion. The research was done by MORI as part of the PriceWaterhouse initiative to encourage companies to pursue a financial reporting model which focuses on prospective cash flows. The survey supports our belief that current financial reporting is unduly focused on historic performance. By contrast, our model envisages companies providing the market with future-oriented information on current anticipated performance over a range of financial and non-financial variables. The research shows that this information will help investors gain insights into the quantum and quality of shareholder value being created.

(Coleman and Eccles, 1999)

## Learning objectives

After studying this chapter you should be able to:

1 Recognize the limitations of current financial reporting procedures from a decision usefulness perspective.

2 Explain the advantages which could accrue from improved long-term disclosures.

3 Discuss the advantages of, and the objections to, the disclosure of company forecasts.

4 Identify the perceived advantages of adopting net realizable value in financial reporting.

5 Discuss the advantages to the investor of quarterly reporting by public companies.

6 Explain what is meant by 'the efficient market hypothesis' and consider its implications for financial reporting.

Businesses everywhere have renewed their focus on the needs of customers. It may be argued that just as successful businesses align the features of their products and services with the needs of those customers so, too, should providers of business reporting. By adopting this view, this chapter concentrates on the information needs of investors to help identify and evaluate ideas for improving financial reporting. As we saw in Chapter 13, the ASB's Statement of Principles argues that the usefulness of information is a function of its relevance and reliability. Users need information that is most relevant for their purposes. They also need information to be as reliable as possible.

This chapter adopts a decision usefulness approach to financial reporting. It draws heavily on the analyses and conclusions of several major studies which have appeared in recent years. These include *Making Corporate Reports Valuable* (The Research Committee of the Institute of Chartered Accountants of Scotland, 1988); *Guidelines for Financial Reporting* (Solomons, 1989); *The Future Shape of Financial Reports* (Arnold *et al.*, 1991); *Improving Business Reporting – A Customer Focus* (American Institute of Certified Public Accountants, 1994); *Report of the CICA Task Force to Review the Recommendations of the AICPA Special Committee on Financial Reporting* (Canadian Institute of Chartered Accountants, 1995); and *Value Reporting Forecast 2000* (PricewaterhouseCoopers, 1999).

## The case for a decision usefulness approach

In Chapter 14 we saw how disclosure requirements have been determined mainly by company law, accounting standards and the Listing Agreement. They have developed in an *ad hoc* fashion with no obvious, overriding rationale for the disclosure of information. Consequently, they are not user-oriented and have severe disadvantages for an investor who is concerned primarily with estimating the dividends and risks associated with an investment. In particular,

1 The present system is essentially backward-looking; it involves the measurement of past performance and current position. Little help is given to the user who wishes to predict future performance.
2 Much emphasis is placed on a single measure of earnings (per share). In an increasingly complex world it is unlikely that any single number can capture the variety of facets which contribute to the changes in an enterprise's worth during a period.
3 It reports measures of performance and position which are based largely on the original or historical costs of resources used by the reporting entity. Little account is taken of the current costs or values of the resources, which are likely to be more relevant in the measurement of efficiency and in the prediction of future performance.

The decision usefulness approach takes the view that financial reporting should provide sufficient quantitative and qualitative information to help investors to make predictions about future performance. It is concerned with long-term disclosure rather than short-term profitability issues. Improved long-term disclosures will have the following advantages:

1 The amount and quality of the information available to the market will be enhanced, which should help the efficiency of the market, and should also improve the market's ability to value the entity concerned.
2 The control of investors over management and their decisions will be improved.
3 Investors, while they will still have to make their own judgements about the past, present and future of the entity, will be provided with a firmer foundation on which to base those judgements.
4 The reputations of entities that take a forward-looking stance are normally enhanced.

# Possible solutions

In this section we consider some suggestions for enabling financial reporting to attain the objective of providing information useful to investors in making predictions about enterprise performance:

1 adopting a forward-looking perspective;
2 reporting high-level operating data;
3 reporting current value information;
4 extending background information;
5 extending interim financial reporting.

## Adopting a forward-looking perspective

The provision of additional forward-looking information is one of the most significant proposals for new information made by the Jenkins Committee (AICPA, 1994) which concluded that financial reports should include the following:

1 information about a company's broad objectives and business strategies used to achieve each broad objective;
2 details of opportunities and risks, but limited to those opportunities and risks that have been identified and considered by management in operating the business – understanding what management thinks about opportunities and risks helps users to understand where management plans to lead a company;
3 management's plans, including critical success factors, i.e. those factors or conditions that must be present for the plans to be successful;
4 a comparison of actual business performance with previously disclosed opportunities, risks and management plans.

The Jenkins Report (AICPA, 1994) does not include a requirement for a forecast in its consideration of forward-looking information. This contrasts with the conclusions of the Research Committee of the ICAS (1988) in *Making Corporate Reports Valuable (MCRV)* which recommends a forecast financial report for the coming year, although this period could be longer if management so decided. Also, MCRV asserts that the major assumptions on which the plan is based should be disclosed. Furthermore, management should provide reasons for the differences between the financial plan disclosed in the previous year's report and the actual results for the year.

It may be argued that the disclosure of company forecasts of future profits or cash flows would be very advantageous to investors. The advantages perceived as attached to the disclosure of company forecasts are as follows:

1 Since investment decisions by management are made in the context of the expectations which they hold of the profitability of future operations, the disclosure of their forecasts would represent the essential information needed by investors. The research conducted by Backer (1970) showed that the procedure employed by security analysts for forecasting profits closely parallels that used internally by companies. Initially, this procedure requires a projection of sales. After making a sales forecast, profit margins are examined, and other significant operating ratios are compiled from published profit and loss accounts. These ratios are adjusted for anticipated changes in sales volume, prices and costs, and are then applied to the sales forecasts to obtain profit forecasts.

2 The disclosure of company forecasts would provide investors with the benefit of management's knowledge of company operations, and its views of the future outlook for such operations.

3 The public disclosure of information relevant to investors' needs might help prevent abnormal returns accruing to privileged individuals having access to inside information.

4 The disclosure of corporate plans would provide investors with a better basis for evaluating managerial performance.

Numerous objections have been made to the proposition that forecasts should be published to investors. The four major objections are as follows:

1 forecasts are uncertain and may mislead investors;
2 forecasts may be manipulated by unscrupulous managers;
3 forecasts are difficult to audit;
4 forecasts made known to competitors may be harmful to the interests of the enterprise, and therefore to those of its investors.

1 It is true, of course, that forecasts are uncertain. This uncertainty stems from the variety of elements incorporated in forecasts which are themselves uncertain. However, this does not render forecasts valueless. Budgetary control implies the necessity of forecasting, as do management decisions regarding production levels, personnel levels, product development and many other factors relating to business life. Clearly, forecasts made and used within the firm by management are of critical importance to the quality of decision making. Such forecasts will be regarded as reliable in this use to the extent that they are carefully prepared. Their quality will be higher than those which are attempted by outsiders. Indeed, it is for this reason that the publication of profit projections has been practised for more than a decade in prospectuses and in circulars issued during the course of mergers and takeovers. It follows that the real question at issue is not whether forecasts are sufficiently reliable in an absolute sense, but whether users of financial reports are likely to find such reports more useful if accompanied by forecasts. As the Trueblood Report stated, 'the important consideration is not the accuracy of management forecasts themselves, but rather the relative accuracy of users' predictions with and without forecasts in financial statements' (AICPA, 1973).

2 It is also true that forecasts may be manipulated by unscrupulous management. However, if management were made accountable by the publication of the results obtained with the forecasts which had been published previously, the need to explain subsequently any material difference between forecasts and results would restrain any tendency to making wild forecasts.

3 It may also be true that forecasts are more difficult to audit than actual results. Auditors have been reluctant to get involved in the audit of forecasts, and the position of auditors as regards forecasts is confused, particularly in the United States where the danger of legal action against auditors is considerably greater than in the United Kingdom. The resistance of the accounting profession to reporting forecasts has diminished since the publication of the City Code and the Institute of Chartered Accountants' statement on the matter.

*The requirement to report publicly was initially accepted with reluctance at the insistence of the Panel. However, when asked if they would report publicly, if it were not for the Panel, an overwhelming number of accountants said 'yes', they would report publicly. Many pointed out that they had been reporting privately on profit forecasts for some time and they felt that public reporting was not that different. (Adelburg, 1976)*

The problem of verifying audits is a very controversial subject. It could be argued that although accountants should have knowledge of forecasting techniques, it does not follow that they should be experts in this field. Moreover, forecasting is not simply a matter of handling techniques: it requires an expert knowledge of the industry and the markets in which the firm is located. Tomkins (1969) has suggested that a solution to this difficulty lies in the accountant obtaining a second opinion on forecasts from individuals other than the company's officials. Experts in the field of business forecasting outside the firm could be employed to provide such second opinions. Consequently, the auditor would not be legally liable for the forecasts and would be responsible merely for verifying the opinions of the experts concerned.

The problem of verification becomes more complex when forecasts covering several years are involved. Forecasts for the year immediately ahead merely provide an extended view of current achievements. Ideally, investors would need to be provided with forecasts covering a longer period. There would seem to be no reason why five-year rolling forecasts should not be adopted as a framework for disclosure, thereby enabling investors to appraise current performance and plans in relation to the firm's attainment of long-term goals. It would be difficult, however, to propose standard procedures which would ensure the required objectivity for audit purposes, for in the face of an increasing time-span there could be a very wide divergence of opinion between management and expert forecasters of the forecasts formulated for disclosure purposes. For this reason, some writers have argued that there is little point in verifying these forecasts (Briston and Fawthrop, 1971).

The ICAS recognizes the problems posed by its advocacy of the use of forecasts. It suggests that it will be necessary to involve non-accountants in what it calls the 'independent assessment teams' which will be responsible for providing assurance on the quality of financial statements. It recognizes that the work of the independent assessor will be more judgemental than that of the present-day auditor. The report produced will need to be longer and more explicit than the present audit report, and tailored to the circumstances of the individual client rather than following a predetermined format.

4 The argument that the disclosure of forecasts to competitors would be harmful to the interests of the enterprise and its shareholders is the same argument which has been advanced for years against the increased disclosure requirements of the Companies Acts, the Stock Exchange and the Statements of Standard Accounting Practice. Forecasts of profits are currently made public during the course of a takeover or merger or issue of shares, when they are thought presumably to do more good than harm. If forecasts were mandatory for all comparable companies, it is difficult to see how an unfair advantage could be gained by a competitor. The only user likely to gain from having such information is the one who is better able to compare and evaluate the prospects of different firms.

## Reporting high-level operating data

*MCRV* concludes that the information which investors need in order to make proper decisions about their involvement with an entity is the same in kind as the information which management need to run it. Similarly, the Jenkins Committee's study indicates that users believe they would benefit by greater access to the high-level operating data and performance measurements management is using to manage the business. One aspect of high-level operating data concerns operating costs.

As we shall see in Part 5, operating costs fall into categories which behave quite differently under changing volumes of business. Variable costs tend to vary in direct proportion to production levels; programmed costs are budgeted annually in corporate plans, for example advertising and research and development costs; long-run fixed costs change little in total with changes in output.

Some knowledge of a company's cost structure is needed by the investor if reliable forecasts are to be made which take account of the impact of changing output levels on profits. The ability of investors to make such forecasts is impeded by the omission in financial reports of information about a company's cost structure. This problem will be examined further in Part 5, where the effects of SSAP 9 'Stocks and Long-Term Contracts' on investment decisions will be discussed.

## Reporting current value information

As we saw in Part 3, most defences of historical cost accounting centre on the reliability of its measures of how funds have been disbursed and thus on its indispensability to the stewardship function. Current values or costs are more relevant to users who wish to evaluate the current performance and position of the business as a basis for making predictions about the future. Consequently, as we saw in Chapter 21, the ASB argues that practice should develop by evolving in the direction of greater use of current values.

According to the Trueblood Report, 'of primary importance for predicting the risk associated with the firm's cash flows (but also for assessing returns) is the degree of flexibility and manoeuvrability that the management possesses in employing its resources'. One alternative way of using a firm's resources is to dispose of them. This alternative may be quantified by using market exit values. Clearly, the more convertible into cash are the firm's resources and the greater the realizable value of these resources, the greater is the degree of flexibility and manoeuvrability that management has over the employment of resources. If the market exit values are small, the alternative uses of resources appear to be more restricted. Consequently, the utilization of resources inside the firm will be highly dependent on the marketability of the specific assets of the enterprise.

*MCRV* strongly advocates the adoption of net realizable value (NRV) in reporting. It argues that NRV has a number of advantages:

1  It is based on values which may be readily observed in the marketplace.
2  It is readily understandable by investors.
3  It removes the need for depreciation calculations.
4  It produces values which are additive because they are all expressed in the same current terms.
5  It provides a useful measure of an entity's liquidity.
6  Its use would improve the comparability of financial statements between entities and between different periods.

## Extending background information

Price Waterhouse's study (Coleman and Eccles, 1999) questioned more than 200 financial analysts and fund managers with the aim of assessing their satisfaction with companies' financial reporting. This report identified an information gap between the needs of analysts and the information provided by companies. Seven measures which the analysts considered valuable were not adequately reported, namely market share, employee productivity, new product development, customer retention, product quality, research and development and intellectual capital.

Both the Jenkins Committee and *MCRV* recommend extending disclosure of the background information about a company so that a better understanding is achieved by users of the business environment. For example, *MCRV* suggests that the following information about the economic environment should be published:

1 *The marketplace.* Every entity requires to have information on various aspects of its market. That information would come mainly from outside the entity. The major divisions are (a) the size of the market, (b) the strength of the market and the position of demand and supply, (c) market share, (d) economic facts likely to affect the market, (e) political factors likely to affect the market, and (f) what major competitors are doing.

2 *Competitive operational statistics.* Information on comparative operational statistics, i.e. comparing the operational statistics of the entity under consideration with information culled from similar statements by its competitors or other entities in similar markets.

## Extending interim financial reporting

Interim financial reports provide financial information for a period of less than one year. In the United Kingdom quoted companies have to deliver a six-monthly report of profitability and financial position to their shareholders. In the United States the disclosure requirement is on a quarterly basis. Interim reports are not audited.

One normative characteristic of the process of reporting to users discussed previously was that of timeliness. The aim of interim reports is to provide users with more timely information about companies so as to alleviate the disadvantages of the significant time lag between annual reports. American experience indicates that a more extensive use of interim reports in the United Kingdom would enhance the predictability of company reports.

According to the Jenkins Committee users in the United States believe strongly that quarterly reporting by public companies should be retained. They provide three main reasons:

1 Quarterly reporting helps users with a longer-term focus. Interest in recent developments is not inconsistent with a longer-term view. It is critical that the user with a longer-term focus detect, on a timely basis, changes in long-term trends. Quarterly reporting helps provide that information.

2 Quarterly reporting provides for an orderly dissemination of reliable information. In its absence investors may base trading decisions on less reliable information, such as rumour.

3 Quarterly reporting reduces problems of trading on inside information. Quarterly reporting provides a vehicle for companies to disseminate information so market participants have equal access to reliable information about a company on which to trade freely.

# The efficient market hypothesis

The efficient market hypothesis supports the case for extending the disclosure of information to investors. The efficient market hypothesis assumes the following:

1 Investors react to new information in such a way as to cause the price of shares traded on the Stock Exchange to change instantaneously. Therefore, an item of information disclosed in a footnote to the financial report will be impounded in the share price just as surely as if it had been included in the main body of the report.

2 The price of shares traded on the Stock Exchange fully reflects all publicly available information.

3 Abnormal returns cannot be earned by investors, that is, no investor can expect to use published information in such a way as to increase the benefits accruing to him/her as against those accruing to other investors. Each investor can expect to earn the return on a security commensurate to its risk class.

The assumptions of the efficient market hypothesis have received considerable support from research findings. These findings show that accounting information does have economic significance in that share prices react to new accounting information. Moreover, research indicates that the Stock Exchange reacts almost immediately to the public release of information. Research also shows that sharp price changes occur on the announcement of new information, but no discernible price movements thereafter, since the adjustment made at that time removes the possibility of future abnormal returns to individual investors. This observed behaviour is consistent with the behaviour of an efficient market.

A further condition required of an efficient market is that it should be able to interpret accounting information correctly. A number of research studies have examined the share price reaction to reported earnings reflecting a change in accounting policy. An interesting example of the market's ability to understand changes in accounting policy is illustrated by Sunder's (1975) research into share price reactions to switches in the basis of stock valuation from FIFO to LIFO and from LIFO to FIFO. The expected results on earnings of these changes were discussed in Chapter 12, and it will be recalled that firms switching from FIFO to LIFO will report lower earnings which will coincide with an improvement in economic earnings resulting from a reduced tax bill. Conversely, firms switching from LIFO to FIFO will report higher earnings as a result of that change and will hope that the market will respond positively to this information, thereby compensating for the negative impact of the increased tax bill that would result from the change. While such changes are not permitted in the United Kingdom, they are allowed in the United States and the American research experience of the impact of changes in accounting policy reflected in stock valuation changes is illuminating. In effect, research evidence shows that firms switching from FIFO to LIFO did not encounter any adverse price reactions from the market. On the contrary, average share prices rose by an average of 5 per cent more than would have been expected, taking account of market movements during the year when the change in accounting policy occurred. Sunder's research also indicated no market reaction to switches from LIFO to FIFO. In effect, it appeared that such an attempt to improve share prices was both fruitless and expensive in the context of the increased tax bill resulting from the change.

Indeed, many other studies have shown results similar to those produced by Sunder, and it may be concluded from these studies that the market does not respond to earnings increases that result from cosmetic changes in accounting policies (Beaver, 1981).

Finally, it does appear that there has been no major readjustment of share prices in the United Kingdom since companies began to publish inflation-adjusted accounts in varying forms several years ago (Brayshaw and Miro, 1985). These findings are consistent with the view that the market made its own assessment of the effects of inflation on company profits, and had already made the necessary adjustments for these effects.

The following inferences may be drawn from research conducted in the area of financial reporting:

1 Where there is controversy over which of two alternative measurements should be reported to external users, and no additional costs are involved in reporting both measurements, the solution to the controversy lies in reporting both measurements. Use could be made of footnotes to the financial report for this purpose, and the market may be left to interpret the importance of such additional information.

2 As there is evidence of a direct relationship between the price of a share and its risk, concern for the ordinary investor is ill-founded. Naive investors are price-takers, and any additional disclosure will be to their advantage. Increased disclosure to sophisticated investors will improve the predictions which they are able to make, and thereby reduce the speculative and destabilizing influences associated with the uncertainties of stock market behaviour. As ordinary investors are likely to be naive investors, and to be price-takers, they have an interest in share prices behaving in an orderly manner.

## The costs of increasing disclosure

So far in this chapter we have considered the benefits of increasing disclosure but not the costs, the most important cost being that of competitive disadvantage. If too much of what is known to the directors and other insiders is made public, the company itself may suffer as a result of competitors and others making use of certain sensitive information. This would clearly be to the detriment of the investors. According to *MCRV* the subset of the internal information has to be carefully tailored so that the maximum useful knowledge is available to the external groups with a right to such knowledge without giving so much that the entity and its owners will be prejudiced.

However, as the Jenkins Report points out, every company that could suffer competitive disadvantage from disclosure could gain competitive advantage from comparable disclosure by competitors. There cannot be competitive disadvantage for one company without one or more others gaining competitive advantage. Assuming it is required, competitors would have access to each other's disclosures. This creates the concept of net competitive disadvantage from disclosure. It would vary from company to company and from time to time, could be positive or negative, and could therefore also be called net competitive advantage from disclosure.

# Summary

The purpose of this chapter is to examine the case for providing investors with financial reports relevant to their needs. The solutions we considered were: adopting a forward-looking perspective, reporting high-level operating data, reporting current value information, extending background information and extending interim financial reporting.

**References**

Adelburg, A H (1976). 'Forecasting and the US dilemma', *Accountancy*, October.

AICPA (1973). *Report of the Study Group on Objectives of Financial Reporting* (The Trueblood Report), American Institute of Certified Public Accountants.

AICPA (1994). *Improving Business Reporting – A Customer Focus* (The Jenkins Report), American Institute of Certified Public Accountants.

Arnold, J, Boyle, P, Carey, A, Cooper, M and Wild, K (1991). *The Future Shape of Financial Reports*, ICAEW.

Backer, M (1970). *Financial Reporting for Security Investment and Credit Decisions*, NAA.

Beaver, W H (1981). *Financial Reporting: An Accounting Revolution*, Prentice Hall.

Brayshaw, R E and Miro, A R O (1985). 'The information content of inflation-adjusted financial statements', *Journal of Business Finance and Accounting*, Summer.

Briston, R J and Fawthrop, R A (1971). 'Accounting principles and investor protection', *Journal of Business Finance*, Summer.

Canadian Institute of Chartered Accountants (1995). *Report of the CICA Task Force to Review the Recommendations of the AICPA Special Committee on Financial Reporting*.

Coleman, I and Eccles, R (1999). *Pursuing value: Reporting Gaps in the United Kingdom*, PricewaterhouseCoopers.

Institute of Chartered Accountants of Scotland, Research Committee (1988). *Making Corporate Reports Valuable*, Kogan Page.

PricewaterhouseCoopers (1999). *Value Reporting Forecast 2000*.

Solomons, D (1989). *Guidelines for Financial Reporting*, ICAEW.

Sunder, S (1975). 'Accounting changes in inventory valuation', *The Accounting Review*, April.

Tomkins, C (1969). 'The development of relevant published accounting reports', *Accountancy*, November.

# Self-assessment questions

1 Why has financial reporting attracted criticism from a decision usefulness perspective?

2 What advantages could accrue from improved long-term disclosures?

3 What are the advantages of publishing company forecasts?

4 Examine the case for adopting net realizable value in financial reporting.

5 Discuss the advantages to the investor of quarterly reporting by public companies.

6 What do the findings of efficient market research show?

# 23 Reporting to employees

## Setting the scene

By challenging its values and reporting on its performance, an organisation can improve the recruitment of high quality employees. The loyalty of existing employees will also be supported by evidence of committment to building a better organisation and by the development of programmes to improve training and other aspects of employee welfare. The corollary of this improved loyalty to the organisation should be increased productivity.

(ISEA, 1999)

## Learning objectives

After studying this chapter you should be able to:

1  Compare the needs of employees with those of investors.

2  Appreciate the advantages and disadvantages of direct reporting to employees.

3  Identify the elements that make up the minimum acceptable settlement.

4  Discuss the problems in estimating the ability to pay.

5  Explain the advantages and disadvantages of collective bargaining.

Traditionally, the focal point of the literature of both accounting and economics has been the needs and the viewpoints of investors. Indeed, the concept of financial management and the theories with which it is associated are founded on the premise that the 'maximization of shareholders' wealth is an appropriate guide for how the firm should act' (Van Horne, 1983). Equally, accounting research which has attempted to assess the importance and relevance of financial reports to decision makers has been confined largely to the decisions of investors and creditors.

The changing social environment has been concerned with the social imbalance between those having wealth and controlling society through the influence of wealth, and those whose political influence in numerical terms has secured the return of governments committed to reforms and the gradual redistribution of wealth.

In effect, this imbalance is reflected in the significance attached to the interests of investors in the literature of accounting and a major part of research in this field. The indications are that the process of redressing this imbalance has been engaged. Developments in reporting to employees in recent years are evidence of progress in recognizing the importance of employees in the activities of business enterprises. These developments have occurred as a result both of changes in social attitudes and changes in the law (Leadley, 1991).

The purpose of this chapter is to analyse the development of financial reporting to employees in the context of their special interests as users of financial information.

## Investor and employee reporting compared

Having already discussed the information needs of investors as users of financial reports, it is interesting to begin the analysis of the information needs of employees by establishing the extent to which they require similar information. The following comparison between the needs of investors and employees may be made:

1 In both cases, it is necessary to focus upon their needs as users rather than upon their wants.

2 The information needs of employees are more complex than those of investors, because employees require additional information on matters of special interest, for example matters of safety. At the same time, the information deemed in Chapter 22 to be relevant to investors is also relevant to employees (Clark and Craig, 1991).

3 In both cases, the disclosure of information has been regulated by law. The Companies Act 1985 prescribes the minimum level of information which should be disclosed to shareholders. The Employment Protection Act 1975 places an obligation on employers to disclose information to trade unions for the purpose of collective bargaining.

4 In both cases, traditional financial reports have limited usefulness. If anything, the timing, presentation and content of corporate financial reports are less relevant to the needs of employees than they are to investors. Thus, these reports do not deal with matters of importance to employees, such as explanations of reductions in the amount of overtime pay and the effects of streamlining the product range.

5 The impact of management decisions falls more obviously and directly on employees than on investors. Shareholders who dislike current management policy have the possibility of selling their shares. Employees do not have such a simple choice, for they may find it difficult to transfer their labour elsewhere.

6 The role of the auditor has been traditionally to protect the interests of share-holders by ensuring that the financial reports present a true and fair view. The presentation of information to employees does not require auditing in the same sense. Reports to employees are devised and presented by management, and consequently may be discredited (Nay, 1991; Cullinan and Knoblett, 1994).

7 One important difference between investors and employees in the area of financial reporting lies in the historical background to the different treatment accorded to these two groups. Financial reporting to investors originated in the nineteenth century, whereas there was very little interest in reporting to employees before 1970.

## Financial reporting to employees

The accountant has been involved in the process of reporting to employees in two distinct ways:

1 direct reporting to employees in the form of employee accounts;
2 reporting as part of the process of collective bargaining.

## Direct reporting

Section 57 of the Industrial Relations Act 1971 imposed a statutory obligation on firms employing more than 350 persons to report directly to employees by means of an annual written statement. When the Industrial Relations Act 1971 was repealed, and the Trade Union and Labour Relations Act 1974 was enacted, neither the latter nor the Trade Union and Labour Relations Amendment Act 1976 re-enacted the obligation to report to employees. At the moment, therefore, there exists no legal obligation of firms to report to employees directly. Nevertheless, the interest in some form of reporting to employees remains very much alive, and the Department of Trade issued in 1976 a preliminary consultative document 'The Aims and Scope of Company Reports', which suggested reinforcing and extending the 'corporate report' proposals for employee reports.

## Scope of employee reports

The purpose of employee reports is to inform employees in the context of a general communicative and consultative philosophy of the corporate environment in which they work. For example, there is a need to inform employees and correct any misunderstanding about the necessity for company profits and for explanations of the manner in which they are applied. Many companies have embarked upon the practice of informing employees about matters of which management believes they should be aware (Cullinan *et al.*, 1994).

The emphasis in employee reports is on making information visually attractive and comprehensible. A general problem is the low level of interest of employees in company affairs, and to overcome apathy, colours, diagrams and cartoons are used. Financial information is shown in the form of bar charts, cakes or other diagrams which are easily understood. In view of employees' interest in the performance of their own units, there is a strong need for segment reporting.

Employee reports are not suitable for the purpose of wage negotiations. It is unlikely, for example, that wage negotiations will occur near the release of year-end financial information.

## Advantages of employee reports

The main aim of reporting directly to employees is to promote goal congruence by explaining how the interests and efforts of employees relate to those of the firm. The intention is to improve communications and the employees' understanding of the manner in which the firm is being managed in the interests of all participants. For example, employees are more likely to accept technological change if direct reporting can create a climate of opinion in which the interests of employees are identified with those of management.

Another aim of reporting directly to employees is to improve public relations. Management realizes that employee reports have effects which extend beyond the firm. Employee reports are read by persons outside the firm, by members of employees' families, and friends. They not only have public relations implications, but also may be helpful in the recruitment of personnel.

## Disadvantages of employee reports

Two major disadvantages affect employee reports. First, as they are prepared by management for employees, they may be perceived by employees as being slanted towards giving employees only what the management wishes them to know. For this reason, employee reports may not be seen by employees as providing them with information directly relevant to their needs. Second, the desire to simplify employee reports so as to make them readily understandable may lead to misleading generalizations.

## Reporting for collective bargaining

In the past, the release of information for collective bargaining purposes has depended on the strengths and abilities of the parties involved in the collective bargaining process. The Employment Protection Act 1975 altered this situation radically by placing a general duty on employers to disclose information for collective bargaining purposes that is both:

1 information without which the trade union representatives would be, to a material extent, impeded in carrying on with such collective bargaining; and
2 information which would be in accordance with good industrial relations practice for the employers to disclose to trade union representatives for the purpose of collective bargaining.

### Three views on disclosure for collective bargaining

The Employment Protection Act 1975 did not specify the information which should be disclosed to trade unions. It was left to the Advisory Conciliation and Arbitration Service to give guidelines on this matter.

The first view on disclosure may be found in the Advisory Conciliation and Arbitration Service's Code of Practice (1977) which, while not more specific than other attempts to specify guidelines for information disclosure, did state that the information disclosed should be relevant to matters under negotiation. The Code of Practice provides a list of 'information relating to the undertaking which could be relevant in certain collective bargaining situations'. The main heads of information listed were pay and benefits, conditions of service, manpower, performance and financial. The Code of Practice stated that 'these examples are not intended to represent a checklist of information that should be provided for all negotiations. Nor are they meant to be an exhaustive list of the types of information, as other items may be relevant in particular negotiations.' The Code of Practice explained restrictions on the general duty to disclose information. These restrictions recognized the sensitive nature of some information, such as cost information on individual products, details of investment plans and details of pricing and marketing. Nevertheless, according to the Code of Practice, it is for the employer to prove that 'substantial injury' to the employer will occur if certain information is disclosed. Furthermore, the cost of providing information should not be disproportionately high in relation to its importance, and the disclosure of information should not be against the national interest. The Code of Practice suggested that a joint arrangement for the disclosure of information for collective bargaining be negotiated, as a means of pre-empting the necessity for employers to prove that disclosure might be substantially injurious.

The second view on disclosure for collective bargaining may be found in a booklet issued by the Confederation of British Industry in 1975 entitled *The Provision of Information to Employees*. This booklet stressed the need for companies to provide employees with 'as much information as is relevant to their needs and wishes and which will assist them to identify with their company, paying due regard to constraints arising out of competitive requirements and confidentiality'. The booklet listed the type of information which could be provided under a number of headings called 'checklists', for example, information about the company as a whole, the organization of the company, finance, competitive situation and productivity, plans and prospects, and information relevant to employment.

The third view on disclosure is to be found in a number of recommended guidelines issued by the Trades Union Congress in a document from 1974 entitled *Industrial Democracy*. This document identified information relating to collective bargaining as including manpower, earnings, costs, sources of revenue, directors' remuneration, performance indicators and the worth of the company.

The main limitations of these three sets of views on information disclosure is that they are in the form of checklists or guidelines giving lists of headings randomly brought together. They do not reflect a well thought-out analysis of the information needs of users. These three views reflect no considered analysis of the normative decision models which those engaged in collective bargaining should use. On the contrary, they reflect very generalized views of beliefs about the information which such users wish to have available.

## A normative theory of pay bargaining information

The construction of a normative theory of financial reporting relevant to pay bargaining between employers and employees and their representatives ought to be based on the criteria suggested by the ASB's Statement of Principles. The information which may be assumed to be most relevant to pay bargaining is related to two factors:

1 the minimum acceptable settlement which is based on considerations of equity, and is made up of a combination of factors including the cost of living, comparability with other industries and value added;
2 the ability to pay, which determines whether the firm is in a position to afford to meet a pay claim without endangering profitability (Cullinan, 1992).

## The minimum acceptable settlement

The elements making up the minimum acceptable settlement may be analysed in more detail.

### The cost of living

The need to take account of expected inflation rather than experienced inflation in assessing changes in the cost of living for pay bargaining purposes has been recognized in recent times when accelerating price rises occurred. Trade union negotiators have been conscious of the need to maintain living standards, and for this reason have attached significance to the maintenance of living standards in real terms. To this end, cost-of-living data has been used in pay bargaining to show that money wages and earnings have failed to keep up with the real cost of living, and that added compensation is required to regain lost ground.

### Comparability

Trade union negotiators make use of two classes of information when engaged in pay bargaining – external and internal wage data. When negotiations are being conducted at a national level, that is, for all the divisions and plant of the same company or industry, external wage data relating to pay conditions existing in other companies or industries is important in establishing pay comparability. When negotiations are being conducted at a plant level, wage data relating to the wage policy of the entire company or industry is important in establishing pay comparability at the plant level. It follows that the process of pay bargaining might be improved considerably if more data on the relative earnings of workers were available, particularly on a company basis.

### Value added

Given the sensitivity attaching to the term 'profit', *The Corporate Report* (Accounting Standards Committee, 1975) suggested that 'the simplest and most immediate way of putting profit into proper perspective *vis-à-vis* the whole enterprise as a collective effort by capital, management and employees is by the presentation of a statement of value added'.

Many companies are introducing value-added concepts into wage incentive schemes in order to improve productivity. The first step is to agree a target for the ratio of wages to value added. If performance exceeds this percentage a bonus will be payable, but if performance falls short of the target there will be no bonus and the deficit will be carried forward to reduce any future bonuses. The process of agreeing on the appropriate percentage which ought to accrue to employees is an important aspect of pay bargaining.

## The ability to pay

The ability of the firm to meet a pay claim is defined as the distributable operating cash flows less the minimum required by those who have provided the capital. This measure signals that the firm:

1 is capable of surviving, and

2 has experienced a change in circumstances relative to the previous period which justifies a change in the level of real wages (Pope and Peel, 1981).

In the context of the firm's ability to pay, the reliability of future cash flow projections becomes very important.

Productivity data is also an important aspect of the definition of the firm's ability to pay. Management may be amenable to arguments that link pay increases to increases in productivity, for pay increases may be absorbed by increased productivity without affecting the firm's pricing policy. The government also tends to favour pay agreements based on productivity increases, for they are more likely to result in non-inflationary pay settlements. One crucial problem revolves around measuring productivity changes. For example, there are classes of employees in respect of whose activity the notion of productivity is difficult to express in numbers. This is true of personnel in research and development departments.

The cost structure of the firm is another factor which affects the firm's ability to pay. If a plant operates at a relatively low break-even point, its ability to pay more will be greater at levels of output which exceed the break-even point. The plant which has a relatively high break-even point will have its ability to pay more restricted by the much longer range of output. The importance of the cost structure is discussed in detail in Part 5.

## Advantage of disclosure in collective bargaining

The main advantage of disclosing information of the type listed above in the collective bargaining process is that it makes that process more rational. According to Morishima (1991), 'when information is provided voluntarily by management . . . unions and employees may develop greater trust in management'.

## Disadvantages of disclosure in collective bargaining

Studies have shown that trade union officials do not understand the information in accounting reports (Hughes and Sale, 1993). However, it may also be suggested that, in itself, this is not an argument against disclosure, but an argument for improving the financial knowledge of trade union negotiators. It may be argued that in certain circumstances management should themselves consider adopting the role of accounting educators since they may benefit if trade union officials are made more fully aware of the financial performance of the company.

A second argument against disclosure is that it may increase the bargaining strength of trade unions to the detriment of the long-term interests of the firm. However, trade unionists are only able to take a long-sighted view in wage negotiations if they are presented with all the relevant information.

A further argument against disclosure is that important information may be revealed during collective bargaining which could be harmful to the firm's negotiating position if leaked outside the firm. It seems, however, that the high level of disclosure which has existed in Germany for many years in this context has not been associated with a problem of breaches in confidentiality.

## Disclosure in collective bargaining and management style

Many of the arguments which revolve around the issue of the disclosure of information in pay bargaining are really issues about management style. It is evident that the successful communication of information during pay bargaining hinges to some extent on management–union relationships. According to the White Paper on *Industrial Democracy* (HMSO, 1978),

> People in industry have different interests, and differ about objectives and how they should be achieved. But part of the conflict is due to poor communication, lack of information and lack of trust. One way to change this is to create a framework for employees and their representatives to join in those corporate decisions which affect them and so encourage them to do so. Where decisions are mutually agreed both sides of industry must then share responsibility for them.

The idea of regularly sharing firm information with labour is in keeping with the European model of 'co-determination' (Ballot, 1992). According to McBarnet *et al.* (1993) labour requests for information disclosure in the UK have increased significantly over the past 15 years.

## Summary

The purpose of this chapter has been to address the problem of reporting to employees as users of financial reports. Traditionally, the interests of investors have been recognized as paramount both in terms of company law and in terms of accounting theory. Changes in the social environment and in political attitudes have begun to emphasize the importance of employees. This process may be seen in the context of the movement towards participation in decision making which has featured largely in the literature of management science, and in the discussion of the concept of industrial democracy which has excited the imagination of progressive elements in western European countries.

The comparison between investors and employees as users of financial reports indicates a similarity of needs for information for decision making. Financial reporting to employees currently occurs at two levels: first, direct reporting by management to employees as part of the process of good staff–employee relations; second, information disclosure in the course of pay bargaining.

It was seen that there exists a need for a normative theory of pay bargaining information, similar in its construction to that required for investors as users, which would be directed to establishing the information which those engaged in pay bargaining negotiations require to make efficient decisions.

**References**

Accounting Standards Committee (1975). *The Corporate Report*, Institute of Chartered Accountants in England and Wales.

Advisory Conciliation and Arbitration Service (1977). *Disclosure of Information to Trade Unions for Collective Bargaining Purposes.*

Ballot, M (1992). *Labour–Management Relations in a Changing Environment*, John Wiley & Sons.

Clark, F and Craig, R (1991). 'Juridical perceptions of the relevance of accounting data in wage fixation', *British Journal of Industrial Relations*, Vol 29, No 3.

Confederation of British Industry (1975). *Guidelines for Action – The Provision of Information to Employees.*

Cullinan, C P (1992). 'The role of accounting information in models of the collective bargaining process'. In *Proceedings of the Twenty-Third Annual Meeting of the Midwest Decision Sciences Institute.*

Cullinan, C P and Knoblett, J A (1994). 'Unionization and accounting policy choices: an empirical examination', *Journal of Accounting and Public Policy*, Spring.

Cullinan, C P, Clark, M W and Knoblett, J A (1994). 'Accounting information and collective bargaining', *Journal of Accounting Literature*, Vol 13.

HMSO (1978). *Industrial Democracy*, White Paper, May.

Hughes, S B and Sale, J T (1993). *The Use of Discounted Cash Flow Techniques in Collective Bargaining Settlement Cost Estimates.* Presented at the 1993 AAA Annual Meeting.

Institute of Social and Ethical Accountability (1999). *Accountability 1000.*

Leadley, K A (1991). 'Employee reporting', *ACCA Students' Newsletter*, February. .

McBarnett, D, Weston, S and Whelan, C (1993). 'Adversary accounting: strategic uses of financial information by capital and labour', *Accounting, Organisations and Society*, January.

Morishima, M (1991). 'Information sharing and firm performance in Japan', *Industrial Relations*, Winter.

Nay, L A (1991). 'The determinants of concession bargaining in the airline industry', *Labour Relations Review*, January.

Pope, P F and Peel, D A (1981). 'The optimal use of information, collective bargaining and the disclosure debate', *Managerial Finance*, Vol 1, No 2.

Trades Union Congress (1974). *Industrial Democracy*, May.

Van Horne, J C (1983). *Financial Management and Policy*, 6th edn, Prentice Hall.

## Self-assessment questions

1  How do the needs of employees for financial information compare with those of investors?

2  What are the advantages and disadvantages of direct reporting to employees?

3  What elements make up the minimum acceptable settlement?

4  What are the problems in estimating ability to pay?

5  What are the advantages and disadvantages of collective bargaining?

# 24 Social accounting

## Setting the scene

The challenge is to create the conditions where social and environmental benefits go hand in hand with competitive advantage. Virtuous but uncompetitive companies will not be part of our future. As important is that competitive, but socially or environmentally destructive companies, must not be part of our future . . . New tools are needed for achieving the positive vision of 'tomorrow's company'; tools that can help organisations and their stakeholders to effectively manage the transition to a more open, inclusive, people-centred approach to success. This need has underpinned the re-emergence of interest in, and the practice of, social and ethical accounting, auditing and reporting.                                        (Gonella *et al.*, 1998)

## Learning objectives

After studying this chapter you should be able to:

1  Discuss three approaches to the concept of social responsibility.
2  Identify six areas in which social objectives may be found.
3  Explain recent trends in corporate social reporting in the UK.
4  Appreciate the implications for accounting of the increasing concern with green issues.

We considered in Chapter 2 the several groups having interests in business organizations, with a view to determining the scope of the accounting problem, defined as the provision of information for making economic decisions having welfare implications. The review of the role of theory in accounting, conducted in Chapter 3, provided justification for approaching the definition of users' information needs by means of a normative specific approach to constructing theories about such users' needs. Accordingly, we were able to discuss the provision of information for shareholders, investors and employees in Chapters 22 and 23 by attempting to stipulate the information which such groups ought to be using in making economic decisions. In effect, we suggested that the needs of investors emphasized financial expectations in line with the hypothesis that investors were primarily concerned with maximizing their own welfare. Equally, we examined the information needs of employees in the same context, and came to the conclusion that such information as they should require related to matters affecting their welfare as a specific group of individuals.

The concept of social accounting raises initial problems of defining not only the users of such information, but their objectives in receiving such information. In effect, the concept of corporate social responsibility, which underlies the debate about social accounting, assumes that there exists a theory about the social role of business firms in modern society. Clearly, not only does such a theory explain the public interest in the role of business in society, but its proponents would seek to monitor and influence the behaviour of firms in accordance with the value judgements on which such a theory might be considered to be founded.

In a very precise sense, the law exists as an institution having the objective of embodying and expressing those value judgements by which behaviour is to be regulated. In accordance with many Acts of Parliament and legal precedents, the accountability of business firms for matters affecting the social good is strictly laid down and enforced. For example, firms are liable at law for various offences in relation to harmful acts, such as allowing the escape of dangerous substances, failing to provide adequate safety precautions for employees, etc. Equally, the law provides very clear rules for the manner in which the accountability of business firms to investors and employees is to be met.

The concept of corporate social responsibility extends beyond notions embodied in current law. Essentially, it represents an emerging debate having its source in political and social theory. In its present state of evolution, there is very real controversy in the following critical areas:

1 the nature of corporate social responsibility;
2 the scope of corporate social responsibility;
3 the manner in which information is required;
4 the greening of accounting.

In this chapter, we examine the problems stipulated above and review the development of social accounting. As we shall see, while there appears to be a great deal of uncertainty about the problems which we have indicated, business firms and governments have already committed themselves to this enlarged concept of business accountability.

## The nature of corporate social responsibility

The concept of social responsibility introduces new dimensions and new problems. First, there is as yet no generally accepted concept of the social responsibility of business enterprises. Almost everyone agrees that they should be socially responsible, though it may be argued that such a view is merely an extension of the universally accepted doctrine that individuals, either singly or in groups, should weigh the impact of their actions on others.

Three approaches to the concept of corporate social responsibility may be distinguished.

The first approach originates in classical economic theory as expressed in the hypothesis that the firm has one and only one objective, which is to maximize profit. By extension, the objective of a corporation should be to maximize shareholders' wealth. It is asserted that in striving to attain this objective within the constraint of the existing legal and ethical framework, business corporations are acting in the best interests of society at large. This classical interpretation of the concept of corporate social responsibility has been advocated by Milton Friedman (1962, p 133) in the following terms:

*There is one and only one social responsibility of business – to use its resources and engage in activities designed to increase its profit, as long as it stays within the rules of the game, which is to say, engages in open and free competition, without decep-tion or fraud. . . . Few trends could so thoroughly undermine the very foundations of our free society as the acceptance by corporate officials of a social responsibility other than to make as much money for their shareholders as possible.*

The second approach developed in the 1970s, and recognizes the significance of social objectives in relation to the maximization of profit. In this view, corporate managers should make decisions which maintain an equitable balance between the claims of shareholders, employees, customers, suppliers and the general public. The corporation represents, therefore, a coalition of interests, and the proper considera-tion of the various interests of this coalition is the only way to ensure that the corporation will attain its long-term profit maximization objective.

This 'stakeholder' approach received much publicity in Britain when it was adopted by the opposition Labour Party in 1996. In the party's draft manifesto for the general election it was described as a 'different economic approach . . . which means opportunities for all – our vision of stakeholder Britain'.

The third view regards profit as a means to an end, and not as an end in itself. In this view, 'the chief executive of a large corporation has the problem of reconciling the demands of employees for more wages and improved benefit plans, customers for lower prices and greater values, shareholders for higher dividends and greater capital appreciation – all within a framework that will be constructive and acceptable to society' (Committee for Economic Development, 1971). Accordingly, organizational decisions should be concerned with the selection of socially responsible alternatives. Instead of seeking to maximize profit generally, the end result should be a satisfac-tory level of profit which is compatible with the attainment of a range of social goals.

The change from the second to the third approach to social responsibility is char-acterized as a move from a concept of the business corporation based on shareholders' interests to one which extends the definition of 'stakeholder'. The former concept views the business enterprise as being concerned with making profits for its shareholders, and treats the claims of other interested groups, such as cus-tomers, employees and the community, as constraints on this objective. The latter concept acknowledges that the business enterprise has a responsibility to all stake-holders, that is, those who stand to gain or lose as a result of the firm's activities.

Second, the acceptance of the third view expressed above that 'organizational deci-sions should be concerned with the selection of socially responsible alternatives' requires clarification of the meaning of 'socially responsible alternatives'. It is evident that unless firms are able to develop clear views of society's preferences and priori-ties, they will be unable to plan activities which will make a social impact, much less report in a meaningful way on their social performance. Therefore, without a precise knowledge of such preferences and priorities, much of the discussion of what is socially desirable must pass for subjective judgements, or at worst pure guesswork.

Third, it has been argued that both from a theoretical standpoint and from the standpoint of welfare economies, it is impossible to make public decisions about the social good. According to Arrow's general impossibility theorem, 'if we exclude the possibility of inter-personal comparisons of utility, then the only method of passing from individual tastes to social preferences which will be satisfactory and which will be defined for a wide range of sets of individual orderings are either imposed or dictated' (Arrow, 1963).

Fourth, at the operational level, there is the problem of the ever-changing nature of the ordering of social preferences, were such ordering ever possible. Social costs, as well as social benefits, are a function of social perception of what is bad and good about business activity. As a result, the nature of corporate social responsibility is not a static concept. Rather, it is concerned with moving targets, many of which are the subject of government action. Such action may take three forms:

1 Legislation which outlaws undesirable social activities. Many examples exist of public concern with undesirable features of business activity, and of legislation to suppress such activities. One early example in the United Kingdom was the legislation relating to child labour in the nineteenth century which was made illegal.
2 Licensing systems may be employed to limit the extent of activities which are useful to society, but present a potential social problem. The licensing of lorries, for example, has been made the subject of certificates of road-worthiness, and attention is now paid to the control of exhaust emission. Thus, licensing may be qualitative as well as quantitative.
3 It has been argued that taxation is a convenient manner of internalizing external social costs of activities having negative effects on society. The objective is to impose taxes on the firm equal in magnitude to the damage sustained by society from the firm's activities. The obvious purpose of such taxes would be to encourage firms to abate the effects of such activities, or alternatively to finance public programmes for controlling these effects. According to some advocates of the taxation approach to dealing with social costs, business firms would be free to choose between abating the social nuisance and avoiding tax, or continuing as before and paying the tax. According to other advocates of this approach, there should be a tariff of taxes designed to encourage firms to locate in areas where their methods of production would do least harm to the environment. Many environmentalists would probably argue, however, that such by-products as pollution do harm wherever they occur, and that suppression through legislation is the only appropriate course of action for society to take.

From the foregoing discussion of the nature of externalities and the role of government in solving social problems, it is apparent that corporate social responsibility is difficult to define. The question may be asked – to what extent should business enterprises be responsible for dealing with all social problems left unsolved by government? Should they concentrate on solving some of these problems? Or should firms merely operate within a strict interpretation of the letter of the law, and if so, would this adherence to the letter of the law frustrate any claim that their behaviour towards externalities could be antisocial?

In the absence of a clear definition of corporate social responsibility by legislation, individual firms must decide for themselves the nature of their social responsibility as a management concept and constraint. The only guidelines available to a firm in this respect are legislation on the one hand and public opinion and pressure on the other. Subject to these constraints, it is evident that corporate social responsibility may be broadly or narrowly defined, and that individual firms have a fair margin of choice as to the standard of corporate social responsibility which they may be willing to accept.

# The scope of corporate social responsibility

Zadek *et al*. (1997) have identified several areas in which corporate social objectives may be found:

1 environmental protection;
2 energy savings;
3 fair business practices;
4 human resources;
5 community involvement;
6 product.

## Environmental protection

This area involves the environmental aspects of production, covering pollution control in the conduct of business operations, prevention or repair of damage to the environment resulting from processing of natural resources and the conservation of natural resources.

Corporate social objectives are to be found in the abatement of the negative external social effects of industrial production, and in adopting more efficient technologies to minimize the use of irreplaceable resources and the production of waste.

## Energy saving

This area covers conservation of energy in the conduct of business operations and increasing the energy efficiency of the company's products.

## Fair business practices

This area concerns the relationship of the company to special interest groups. In particular it deals with the employment and advancement of minorities; the use of clear English in legal terms and conditions with suppliers and customers; and the display of information on its products, etc.

## Human resources

This area concerns the impact of organizational activities on the people who constitute the human resources of the organization. These activities include:

1 recruiting practices;
2 training programmes;
3 experience building job rotation;
4 job enrichment;
5 wage and salary levels;
6 fringe benefit plans;
7 congruence of employee and organizational goals;
8 mutual trust and confidence;
9 job security, stability of workforce, layoff and recall practices;
10 transfer and promotion policies;
11 occupational health.

### Community involvement

This area involves community activities, health-related activities, education and the arts.

### Products

This area concerns the qualitative aspects of the products, for example their utility, life-durability, safety and serviceability, as well as their effect on pollution. Moreover, it includes customer satisfaction, truthfulness in advertising, completeness and clarity of labelling and packaging. Many of these considerations are important already from a marketing point of view. It is clear, however, that the social responsibility aspect of the product contribution extends beyond what is advantageous from a marketing angle.

## Corporate social reporting in the UK

Companies are required by law to disclose the following information:

1 *Fair business practices:* companies with more than 250 employees are required to state the policy regarding the employment, training, career development and promotion of disabled people.

2 *Human resources:*
   (a) For companies which employ 100 or more the Directors' Report is required to state the average number of UK employees and their related remuneration during the year;
   (b) The Health and Safety at Work Act 1974 provides for regulations to be made requiring companies to disclose information about 'arrangements in force for securing the health, safety and welfare at work of employees of the company and its subsidiaries';
   (c) The Directors' Report is required to include action with regard to informing employees, consulting employees, encouraging involvement (e.g. share ownership schemes).

3 *Charitable and political gifts:* these must be disclosed in the Directors' Report.

Several surveys have been undertaken in the UK in order to establish the nature and extent of social disclosures in the annual accounts. Maunders (1982) surveyed the published accounts of 300 large companies for 1981/82. Mirza (1987) examined the annual reports of 131 top companies for 1984/85. Gray (1989) conducted a longitudinal survey of 200 large companies for 1978/87. All three surveys raise the issue of the possible measurement levels that are feasible in relation to social reporting:

1 identification and description of efforts (e.g. general policy statements);
2 physical but non-financial quantification (e.g. employee hours in training); and
3 financial quantification (e.g. expenditure on pollution control).

Most social reporting was found to be of the first type with the exception of human resource information. Gray (1989) found that the trend of mandated disclosure is upward, reflecting an increased response to legislation. No such conclusion could be drawn from the voluntary disclosures, although over 60 per cent of the companies surveyed made voluntary disclosures of some sort.

Maunders (1982) found that the voluntary disclosures by his sample of companies for 1981/82 by categories of information were as follows:

|  | % |
| --- | --- |
| Human resources | 40 |
| Fair business practice | 19 |
| Energy | 15 |
| Community involvement | 12 |
| Product-related | 10 |
| Environmental | 9 |

The largest incidence of voluntary disclosure is in the category of human resources which includes items such as employee training and development. Fair business practice concerns the disclosure by companies of information about women and persons of various ethnic groups in their employment. Mirza (1987) found that 15 per cent of his sample included information about environmental protection including the reporting of activities like treatment of effluent water, following stringent nuclear safety standards, restoration of mining areas and maintenance of trees. However, Gray (1989) showed that there had been no significant increase in environmental and energy disclosures during the five years following the Maunders' survey.

The two categories where voluntary disclosures appear to have shown an upward trend in recent years are 'community involvement' and 'product-related'. According to Gray's (1989) sample, product safety disclosures had increased over the nine years in question and community involvement disclosures had increased to nearly 40 per cent.

Recent surveys show that corporate social and environmental reporting is still, at best, a marginal activity in company practice (C Adams, 1999).

## The greening of accounting

In this section we extend our consideration of the environment as an area in which corporate social objectives may be found. This reflects the growing concern in recent years over natural resource depletion, unacceptably high levels of pollution, global warming, acid rain and deforestation, amongst other issues. The environmental crisis has intensified the debate about social accounting and the role that accounting can play in mitigating or reversing the crisis.

Long-term environmental strategies at national and international level were proposed by the World Commission on Environment and Development in 1987 (the Brundtland Report). The centrepiece of the Report was sustainable development that 'meets the needs of the present without compromising the ability of the future to meet its own needs'. The concept of 'stakeholders' is thus extended to include future generations. Sustainability was at the heart of *Blueprint for a Green Economy* (Pearce *et al.*, 1989). This report, which was commissioned by the Department of the Environment, stresses the need to account for the use of environmental resources and the use of substances which may damage the environment. An effective form of intervention, according to Pearce, was the 'polluter pays principle', which requires those who produce products or services to bear the cost of achieving agreed standards of environmental quality. The report distinguished between two types of capital, namely man-made and natural, and the need to strike a balance between the two to ensure that this generation passed the same value of capital on to future generations.

Man-made capital has been growing very significantly, but this growth has been at the expense of a decline in natural capital.

## Environmental legislation

Growing concern about the environment, and in particular sustainability, has prompted legislation at the national and European level. The Environmental Protection Act 1990 takes the first steps towards piecemeal implementation of the principle that the polluter pays through a system of integrated pollution control. The Act provides for levies on certain categories of companies to fund the regulatory and control bodies which were to enforce it. Controls were to be placed on emissions and industrial processes and there would be more public disclosure on the operations of polluting companies. Of significance for the accounting function is the legal obligation imposed to minimize waste production utilizing what is called the 'best available technology not entailing excessive cost' (BATNEEC) principle.

Developments at the European level are, of course, having an ever increasing influence on UK business practices. Again, the main thrust behind these initiatives has been the issue of sustainability. In 1992, the so-called Fifth Action Plan introduced a long-term strategy together with objectives to be achieved in the medium and short term. This recognizes the finite nature of raw materials and the need to change consumption and behaviour patterns. The aim of the Plan is to promote co-operation between national and local governments, and companies and consumers, in achieving environmental targets in defined areas, for example pollution control, waste reduction and the sustainable use of resources. EU-inspired environmental legislation is set to have an increasingly significant impact on all industrial and commercial activity in the future.

## Challenges facing accountants

Accountants have begun to define the ecological issue as falling within their range of skills. For example, a study by the Chartered Institute of Management Accountants argued that 'the forward-thinking management accountant should be taking an active role in environmental management, as he or she has key skills to apply to the process' (CIMA, 1997).

The basic financial accounting model is an impediment to change because it only records and employs the data which arises from a transaction which generates a price. Prices are only generated when property rights are transferred. The majority of the matters that are of concern in ecology are things over which property rights do not exist. As a result, the basic financial accounting model ignores them (Gray, 1993). Therefore, although there is an active and essential role that accountants can play in the development of sound environmental and reporting procedures, much work must be done to develop more comprehensive reporting systems involving both quantitative and qualitative techniques.

The accountant can make a considerable contribution in developing:

1 financial reporting practice; and
2 environmental management systems.

## Financial reporting practice

Recent accounting research has focused on the demand for data on the environmental performance of an entity and the obligation which accountants have to provide information to shareholders and other users on the costs and benefits involved (Bell and Lehman, 1999). There is also a business case for greater responsibility and accountability. One study has found a positive link between environmental and financial performance, and specifically that over two-thirds of green companies perform better than their non-green counterparts in 1,200 direct comparisons of green and non-green companies (Edwards, 1998).

The United Nations Environment Programme has directed its attention to issues of environmental disclosures. Recommendations have been made for companies to disclose the following (R Adams, 1998):

1  key environmental issues facing the company and plans for addressing these;
2  progress in addressing changes required by future legal requirements;
3  actual and projected levels of environmental expenditure;
4  energy use, material use, emissions and waste disposal routes;
5  financial estimates of savings and benefits flowing from pro-environment efforts;
6  an independent audit statement.

The UK has no formal requirements that organizations should publish statements of their environmental performance. The preference has been to avoid regulated reportings and to encourage companies to experiment with voluntary disclosure. However, UK companies generally give a low priority to the reporting of environmental information. A survey found that only 32 per cent of the top UK companies produced a separate environmental report (KPMG, 1999). Only 14 of these reports included quantifiable targets and only 19 reported on poor performance. The slow response on the part of UK companies towards heightened public concern over environmental issues is unfortunate in view of the fact that external reports are extremely valuable as a means of promoting public accountability, the need for which is central to the emerging green agenda.

The appproach of increasing environmental disclosure is still rooted in conventional accounting measurement. It does not deal with the need to recognize the importance of environmental capital and guard against its depletion. An approach which meets this objective involves the requirements for organizations to calculate and disclose sustainable costs. Sustainable cost can be defined as the amount an organization must spend to put the biosphere at the end of the accounting period back into the state (or its equivalent) that it was in at the beginning of the accounting period (R Adams, 1999). Such a figure would be a notional one, and disclosed as a charge to a company's profit and loss account. Thus, we would be presented with a broad estimate of the extent to which accounting profits had been generated from a sustainable source. This would have the effect of reducing the organization's profit and thus reducing the amount it could distribute to the shareholders – whilst maintaining natural capital. The reader will note the parallel with current value accounting, discussed in Chapter 21.

According to one research study, voluntary disclosure has not been successful, either in terms of its extent or nature, partly because organizations lack experience of social accounting (C Adams, 2000). Guidance is needed on the definition of goals and targets, the measurement of progress made against the targets, the auditing and reporting of performance, the feedback mechanisms. *Accountability 1000* (ISEA, 1999) provides guidance on all these issues. It is private voluntary standard designed for experimentation and to help users innovate their social responsibility and sustainability strategies. It also provides a means by which to evaluate the quality of social reports.

## Environmental management systems

The focus of an environmental management system (EMS) is prevention of environmental damage rather than detection and amelioration after occurrence. This role was identified by the British Environmental Management System Standard, BS 5750 (British Standards Institute, 1994) which states that an EMS should:

1 identify and assess the environmental effects arising from the organization's existing or proposed activities, products or services;
2 identify and assess the environmental affects arising from incidents, accidents and potential emergency situations;
3 identify the relevant regulatory requirements;
4 enable priorities to be identified and pertinent environmental objectives and targets to be set;
5 facilitate planning, control and monitoring, auditing and review activities to ensure both that the policy is complied with, and that it remains relevant;
6 be capable of evolution to suit changing circumstances.

Although implementing an EMS that meets these objectives is a team effort, because expertise in a variety of disciplines is needed, accountants should be in a position to play a major role (Willits and Guitini, 1994). Indeed, many writers view this possible role as being a logical development of the accounting profession in a world where natural resources, as well as monetary capital, are limiting factors (Birkin, 1996).

Environmental issues permeate all aspects of business, from product design to manufacturing and delivery, in all ways that directly impact on the bottom line. When environmental issues are translated into financial terms, they are more likely to be included in the decision-making process. It is suggested that accountants, the primary recipients, analysts and providers of financial information, can play a pivotal role in bringing this about (Bell and Lehman, 1999).

## Adapting management accounting

Management accounting techniques, which we consider in Part 5, will need to be adapted to embrace environmental issues. For example, budgeting can, if properly applied, bring financial discipline into the organization as targets are agreed and managers are held accountable for their performance in achieving them. It should be possible to allocate environmental responsibilities and targets to managers in addition to purely financial goals, with rewards and penalties incorporated (Gannon and Rowell, 1995). Environmental objectives should also be incorporated in investment appraisal techniques if the accountants who apply them are to incorporate the environmental perspective.

## Summary

The concept of corporate social responsibility emerged in the 1960s when changing social values and expectations gave rise to a debate about the role of business in society. This debate focused on the nature of corporate social responsibility, and gave rise to the possibility that this responsibility could be discharged through a method of social accounting. It was argued that such a method of accounting would indicate the nature and the manner of the firm's social contributions or outputs. Corporate social objectives may be found in six areas of enterprise activity. Most social reporting disclosures are descriptive in nature. Although the trend of mandated disclosure in the UK has been upwards in recent years, no such conclusions can be drawn from voluntary disclosures. The recent concern for environmental issues may have a dramatic effect on future corporate environmental and management systems.

## References

Adams, C R (1999). *The Nature and Processes of Corporate Reporting on Ethical Issues*, CIMA.

Adams, C R (2000). 'Ethical reporting: past and future', *Management Accounting*, February.

Adams, R (1998). 'Going green', *The Accountant*, April.

Adams, R (1999). 'Performance indicators for sustainable development', *Accounting and Business*, April.

Arrow, K J (1963). *Social Choice and Individual Values*, Yale University Press.

Bell, F and Lehman, G (1999). 'Recent trends in environment accounting', *Accounting Forum*, June.

Birkin, F (1996). 'Environmental management accounting', *Management Accounting*, February.

British Standards Institute (1994). *BS 5750: Specification for Environmental Management Systems*, BSI.

CIMA (1997). *Environmental Management: the Role of the Management Accountant*, Chartered Institute of Management Accountants.

Committee for Economic Development (1971). *Social Responsibilities of Business Corporations*.

Edwards, D (1998). *The Link Between Company Environmental and Financial Performance*, Earthscan.

Friedman, M (1962). *Capitalism and Freedom*, University of Chicago Press.

Gannon, J and Rowell, S (1995). 'Are accountants ready for the green revolution?', *ACCA Students' Newsletter*, August.

Gonella C, Pilling A and Zadek, J (1998). *Making Values Count*, Association of Certified Accountants.

Gray, R H (1989). *Corporate Social Reporting by UK Companies: a Cross-Sectional and Longitudinal Study*, Draft Working Paper, December.

Gray, R H (1993). *Accounting for the Environment*, Paul Chapman.

Institute of Social and Ethical Accountability (1999). *Accountability 1000*.

KPMG (1999). *International Survey of Environmental Accounting*, 1999.

Maunders, K T (1982). 'Social reporting and the employment report', in Skerratt, L C L and Tonkin, D J (eds) *Financial Reporting 1982–83: A Survey of UK Published Accounts*, The Institute of Chartered Accountants in England and Wales.

Mirza, A M (1987). 'Social reporting by the UK companies', *Business Graduate Journal*, April.

Newell, G E, Kreuze, J G and Newell, S J (1990). 'Accounting for hazardous waste', *Management Accounting* USA, May.

Pearce, D W, Markandya, A and Barbier, E B (1989). *Blueprint for a Green Economy*, Earthscan.

Willits, S D and Guitini, D (1994). 'Helping your company go green', *Management Accounting* (USA), February.

Zadek, S Pruzan, P and Evans, R (1997). *Building Corporate Accountability*, Earthscan.

## Self-assessment questions

1 'There is as yet no generally accepted concept of the social responsibility of business enterprises.' Discuss.

2 What areas in which corporate social objectives may be found were identified by Zadek *et al.*?

3 Examine recent trends in corporate social reporting in the UK.

4 What are the implications for accounting of the increasing concern with green issues?

# PART 5

# Management accounting

Introduction to Part 5

# Introduction to Part 5

Information is vital for the management process and accounting is one of the major information systems within any organization. Therefore, a sound understanding of accounting is essential for managers to fulfil their organizational roles responsibly and competently. This applies in all types of organizations: manufacturing, merchandising (wholesaling and retailing) and service. Although manufacturing firms require a greater quantity and variety of accounting information, most of the management accounting practices discussed in this part are applicable to all organizational settings.

No single management accounting system is suitable for all enterprises, management accounting requirements being contingent upon the particular characteristics of each individual business. However, every system has the following objectives:

1. It must provide reasonably accurate costs of products and services. Cost accounting, a subset of management accounting, focuses on the determination of product or service cost. Cost accounting is essentially a link between financial and management accounting. A business employs a cost accounting system for two reasons:

   (a) It provides managers a means to follow the flow of costs through the company's accounts as the inputs they represent are converted to outputs. Such information is needed for company accounts – the balance sheet stock values and profit and loss statement of cost of goods sold.

   (b) It provides managers with information that is useful for them in carrying out the functions considered below – decision making, planning, and controlling and evaluating performance.

2. It must provide information for making decisions. These decisions may be about acquiring and financing product capacity, determining which products to make, pricing products or services, or determining the best method of delivering finished goods to warehouses.

3. It must provide sufficient useful information to help managers adequately perform their functions of planning, controlling and evaluating performance. Planning is the process of translating the objectives for a business and developing a strategy for achieving them in a systematic manner. Control is the exertion of managerial influence on operations so that they will conform to plans. Essentially, the control process first involves setting performance standards or norms against which actual results are measured. The management accountant helps in determining standards for various quantities, times and costs in all operating areas. Performance is then measured and compared with the standards on a scheduled basis; the management accountant's role is to provide managers with timely, relevant and reliable reports.

Management accountants have been criticized for placing an overemphasis on 1(a) above to the detriment of the other objectives (Johnson and Kaplan, 1987). Where this occurs, financial reporting becomes the driving force for the design of management accounting systems. These organizations may need to expand this database, or to create additional databases, in order to satisfy more fully the needs of internal users. This situation has become more serious since the mid 1980s, following changes in the environment in which many organizations operate. These changes have intensified the criticisms of traditional management accounting practices. In particular,

1 the performance measurements adopted by traditional management accounting may be of limited usefulness in certain circumstances;
2 the internal orientation of management accounting restricts the usefulness of the information provided;
3 the product and service costs which are produced by traditional costing methods could be incorrect and, therefore, misleading for managerial decision making.

As we stressed in Part 1 of the book, the accounting function should reflect the environment at a particular time. It is, therefore, essential to understand how the business environment has changed in recent years.

## World-class manufacturing

The most important recent change in the environment has been the development of 'world-class manufacturing', a phrase first used by Schonberger (1986) as the title of his book. He suggests that the term 'nicely captures the breadth and the essence of the fundamental changes taking place in industrial enterprises'. The term encapsulates the dynamic changes to manufacturing processes brought on by:

1 global competition;
2 advances in advanced manufacturing technology;
3 the adoption of new management philosophies, often developed by the Japanese, e.g. just-in-time and total quality management.

These changes are intended to make radical improvements to the company's competitiveness and to enhance profitability. They involve improving quality, reducing lead times (the time a service or product takes to get through the process), reducing costs and enhancing product flexibility. The aim is to provide total consumer satisfaction. Although these changes have developed under the heading of 'world-class manufacturing' (WCM), it must be stressed that these improvements are not the sole domain of manufacturing industry. They also apply to merchandising and service industries.

WCM introduces a new approach to product quality. This is quite different from the traditional approach because the primary emphasis is placed on resolving problems that cause poor quality, rather than merely detecting it. The purpose is systematically to expose and resolve the root causes of quality problems so that the company can eventually achieve zero defects – or 100 per cent quality. The purpose is not to increase the number of people involved with inspecting and tracing defects but to develop an awareness of quality issues within shop floor operators so that the entire workforce is harnessed to the quest for product perfection. This requires changes to both the design and manufacturing processes so that high quality can be built into the product instead of poor quality being inspected out. The introduction of advanced manufacturing technology with improved use of new machine tools with strict tolerances in manufacturing, and automated inspection not only of the finished product but also of component parts at every stage in the manufacturing cycle, will result in substantial improvements in quality. A style of management aimed at producing high-quality products and services and eliminating waste is called total quality management (TQM).

WCM enhances product flexibility, the ready capability to adapt to new, different and changing requirements. The ability to set up and change production lines quickly increases production flexibility and enables firms to be more responsive to customers' needs. Consumers today are more sophisticated and demand greater variety and customized products and services. Therefore, products need to be more varied, display increasing complexity and have shorter life cycles in virtually all markets. Investment in advanced manufacturing technology (AMT) provides a new flexibility which is of strategic importance. Such systems enable a rapid shift with minimal disruption from one product to another and thus reduce significantly the cost penalty of product diversity. AMT also enables new products and modifications to be introduced more quickly.

Lower costs will result from the changes discussed above. For example, as a result of reduced human involvement with simplified tooling and setting up, and thus the reduction of potential human error, and with the ability to produce tight tolerances, fewer material rejects could be expected. Furthermore, total costs will be reduced by the reduction in labour costs. One of the main motivations for companies investing in robotics is to improve labour productivity and thus save on labour costs. Costs can also be reduced by the introduction of just-in-time (JIT) manufacturing which aims to change the production processes so that stocks which are not immediately required for production are eliminated. JIT will be considered in Chapter 27.

## Growth of the service industry

Service companies provide important benefits to modern economies such as banking, insurance, retailing, health, telecommunications and transportation services. In recent years the service sector has increased in importance. Due partly to the deregulation of many services, increased competition in the service industry has made many managers more conscious of the need to use accounting information for planning, control and decision making. The unique characteristics of service firms necessitate the extension of cost accounting to their peculiar circumstances.

## Implications for management accounting

With changes in business in recent years managements' information needs have significantly expanded in scope and variety. Criticism of management accounting made by some commentators has largely centred on the view that managers, faced with having to make decisions in complex technology-driven situations, are supplied with information by their firm's internal management systems which is inadequate (Bromwich and Bhimani, 1994). The changes in management accounting practices which have been called for by these commentators are briefly considered below.

### New measures of performance needed

Since companies now compete on quality of design, on the performance of the resulting product and on the ability to bring new products to the market quickly, as well as the provision of fast reliable delivery, measures to track performance in these areas are desirable. Over time, the pre-eminence of financial measures may diminish as non-financial measures to account for such factors are developed.

# Strategic management accounting

The internal orientation of traditional accounting information is too narrow for strategic decision making. However, the competitive positioning of business in world markets requires that accountants in management teams adopt a strategic perspective. Similarly, technology cost in highly automated companies is becoming very large and managers in high-tech firms need to take a longer-run perspective in making decisions. Strategic management accounting has developed to assist senior management in taking a genuinely long-term view of their business by providing information which (a) enables them to monitor and control the organization's activities in a manner measurable against the strategy and objectives, and (b) contributes to the strategic decision-making process. Strategic management accounting is considered in Chapter 38.

# Activity-based costing

Traditional systems of product costing were designed for relatively simple, routine manufacturing processes, usually with high labour content. These systems appeared to provide satisfactory information for managers in traditional industries. But the changing environment, and in particular the development of advanced manufacturing technologies, have called into question traditional methods. Activity-based costing (ABC), which has developed to address this problem, is considered in Chapter 27.

This part divides into three sections:

*Section 1: Framework*
This section examines the processes of management and describes traditional cost accounting and its modern version, activity-based costing.

*Section 2: Managerial decision making*
This section examines how the accounting information system facilitates decision making, which is the process of choosing among competing alternatives.

*Section 3: Planning and control*
This section examines the crucial role played by accounting in planning and control. Accounting reports that assist control are called performance reports.

**References**   Bromwich, M and Bhimani, A  (1994). *Management Accounting: Pathway to Progress*, Chartered Institute of Management Accountants.

Johnson, H T and Kaplan, R S  (1987). *Relevance Lost: The Rise and Fall of Management Accounting*, Harvard Business School Press.

Schonberger, R I (1986). *World Class Manufacturing*, New York: Free Press.

# 25 The processes of management

**Setting the scene**

Myths come and go in accounting as in other endeavours of mankind. Accountants, however, should be careful to consider the focus of their efforts to make sure that they are not just following the latest fad that may turn out to be just another myth.

Management accountants should do what their operations colleagues are doing: Go back to the basics and understand your operation. If a management accountant spends time studying the operations of his or her company to understand thoroughly what makes the organization function, then that accountant probably will create a system that helps the managers of that company regardless of whether it includes the latest gimmicks. Solid, relevant information is what managers need, and the accountant who can help managers solve their problems is the accountant who is valuable to the organization. Forget the myths, and concentrate on the fundamentals.

(Böer, 1994)

**Learning objectives**

After studying this chapter you should be able to:

1   Identify the five stages of planning.

2   Demonstrate how the function of organizing coordinates the tasks necessary to achieve strategic goals.

3   Analyse the relationship between control and planning.

4   Discuss the role of communication in obtaining organizational goals.

5   Explain the objectives of motivation.

6   Discuss the role of information in making decisions at three levels – strategic planning, management control and operational control.

There are two conflicting schools of thought regarding the extent to which the firm is in charge of its own destiny. Market theory postulates that the firm is solely at the whim of prevailing economic and social forces, so that successful management depends upon the ability to 'read' the environment. By contrast, planning and control theory asserts that management has control over the firm's future and believes that the firm's destiny may be manipulated and hence planned and controlled. In this view, the quality of managerial planning and control decisions is the key factor for success.

In reality, business organizations normally operate somewhere in between these two extreme views: many elements, such as raw material prices, are completely outside their control; on the other hand some elements, such as the selling price of its product, are determined by the organization itself. One may make a distinction, therefore, between controllable and non-controllable items. It is the function of management to manipulate the controllable items to the firm's best advantage, and to ensure that it is prepared to meet changes in the non-controllable ones, so as to take full advantage of favourable changes and minimize the impact of unfavourable ones. Planning is essential for all the factors which affect the organization, irrespective of whether they are controllable or non-controllable. We may infer from this fact that the greater the degree to which a firm's management reflects the views of control theorists the greater are its chances of success.

Although there are different schools of thought as to what may be understood by the term 'management' and how it should be practised, it is generally accepted that management has five main functions: planning, organizing, controlling, communicating and motivating.

## Planning

Planning is the most basic of all management functions, and the skill with which this function is performed determines the success of all operations. Planning may be defined as the thinking process that precedes action and is directed towards making decisions now with the future in mind. Theoretically, the function of planning is to improve the quality of decision making by a careful consideration of all the relevant factors before a decision is made, and ensuring that decisions conform with a rational strategy by which the firm's future is to be shaped. Planning may be seen as consisting of five stages:

1 Setting organizational objectives.
2 Assessing the environment in which the organization will be operating, by reference to the external factors which are likely to affect its operations. For this purpose, forecasts have to be made which attempt to predict what will happen in the future, with and without policy changes on the part of the planning organization.
3 Assessing existing resources, for management is concerned with making the most efficient use of those scarce resources, often called the four Ms: men, machines, materials and money. This aspect of the planning function involves making an estimate both of external resources which are accessible, and resources already held which are either idle or which might be more efficiently utilized.
4 Determining the strategy for achieving stated objectives by means of an overall plan which specifies strategic goals. Strategic decisions are concerned with establishing the relationship between the firm and its environment.
5 Designing a programme of action to achieve selected strategic goals by means of both long-range programmes and short-range programmes, the latter covering a period of a year or less and containing sets of instructions of the type found in annual budgets.

# Organizing

Organizing involves setting up the administrative structure for implementing strategic decisions. The administrative design area is concerned with establishing the structure and the shape of the firm or organization, and defining responsibilities and lines of authority. It involves a definition of the tasks necessary to achieve strategic goals, determining who is to perform these tasks and assigning responsibility for their performance. The function of organizing is to coordinate these tasks in such a way that the organization is able to work efficiently in fulfilling its objectives. The process of organizing is achieved through departmentalization, by which different specialisms are hived off into separate departments. These departments are linked in a hierarchy, a formal communication structure that enables instructions to be passed downwards and information to be passed upwards to senior management. Figure 5.1 shows a partial organization structure for a firm which is concerned with two main activities – furniture and floor covering.

A manager may be allotted the task of managing the activities in each of these boxes, which then represent executive positions; the lines represent the formal channels of communication between them. The top five boxes represent the five major functions of this firm – marketing, manufacturing, finance, personnel and research and development. For administrative purposes, the firm is organized according to its product categories; therefore, two divisions – furniture and floor covering – are established.

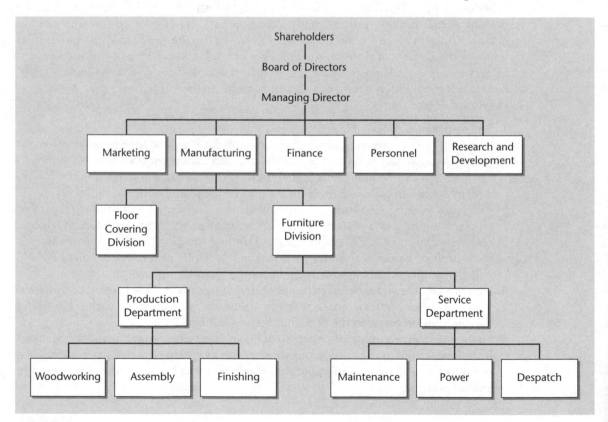

**Figure 5.1**

At the bottom of the pyramid in the figure are the basic organizational units, known as departments; the figure illustrates the six departments belonging to the furniture division. Departments form an occupational classification – in this case they are divided into production and service departments.

A major purpose of any organizational structure is to facilitate the flow of information to and from decision makers. Since management may be said to be the process of converting information into action, organizations should be designed around information flows. Each decision point in this process is a sub-information system having its own elements at input, processor and output. Hence, information networks shape the structure of the organization. The structure of the organization is also used as the basis for data gathering through the use of cost centres, with a manager being responsible for each cost centre.

## Control

The decisions involved in this area stem from two main activities: first, comparing actual performance against that stipulated in the plan, and second, determining whether the plan itself should be modified in the light of this comparison (Figure 5.2).

Control is closely linked to the planning function in that its purpose is to ensure that the firm's activities conform to its plans. It is effected by means of an information feedback system which enables performance to be compared with planned targets. Control is essential to the realization of long-range and short-term plans.

In long-range planning, information feedback enables management to assess what progress has been made towards the realization of the long-range objectives specified in the long-range plan. Additionally, it allows management to review long-range objectives in the light of new circumstances which may have rendered those objectives unrealistic.

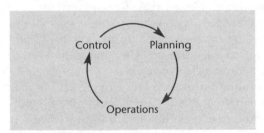

**Figure 5.2**

In practice, by far the greatest emphasis is attached to the control of operations so as to meet the objectives contained in the annual budget which, as we noted earlier, should be seen as part of the long-range plan. Information feedback is an integral part of budgetary control procedures which are intended to be highly sensitive to operational variations on a day-to-day basis. Their aim is to highlight deviations from the budget plan as soon as possible so that remedial action may be taken immediately.

A prerequisite of the successful performance of the control function is an efficient information system which will reveal the need for corrective action at an appropriate time, enabling managers to judge whether their targets are still appropriate as the environment changes month by month and year by year. The control function is closely linked to the planning function by means of a feedback system which provides information on the results of past decisions. Such a system is necessary to the assessment of the quality of the decision-making process and to its improvement, and is illustrated in Figure 5.3.

The feedback system provides the great bulk of analytical information used in the planning process. It provides a means also of evaluating planned objectives. Should, for example, the economic climate change, the efficiency of the organization's operations will depend on the swiftness of its reaction to this change by way of alterations to the planned objectives. The feedback system is also instrumental to the making of control decisions, for it provides a means of continuously assessing current performance against the strategic plan. Decision making in this sense thus involves making day-to-day adjustments to changing conditions in order to map out the most appropriate course of action needed to implement strategic decisions. Thus, information is the lifeblood of any system, and the responsibility for the design of adequate information systems is of paramount concern to management.

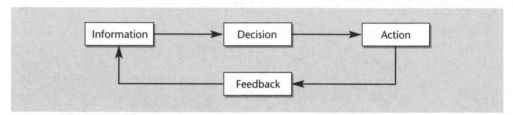

**Figure 5.3**

## Communication

Communication is an exchange of facts, ideas and opinions by two or more persons. The exchange is successful only when actual understanding results. Merely saying is not enough; a receiver of information must understand the message which the sender is trying to communicate. Communication occurs when the former understands what the latter means to convey.

Communication involves linking all the management functions by transmitting information and instructions within the organization. Additionally, the communication process relates the organization to its environment by linking it to suppliers of resources, and to the consumers for whom its products are intended.

In any organization, the specialization of tasks and the consequent division of labour creates a situation in which an unrestricted flow of ideas and facts is necessary if it is to function efficiently. A high degree of communication binds the various members of the organization together, uniting them in the pursuit of organizational goals. Hence, an organization may be viewed not only as a decision-making system, but also as a communication system.

The way in which information is communicated and related to planning and control may be illustrated as in Figure 5.4, which shows how environmental and analytical information is combined in the plans which are designed to meet the organization's objectives. These plans are implemented as resources become inputs which are converted into products and services. The feedback and control systems should function so as to ensure the effectiveness of the plans.

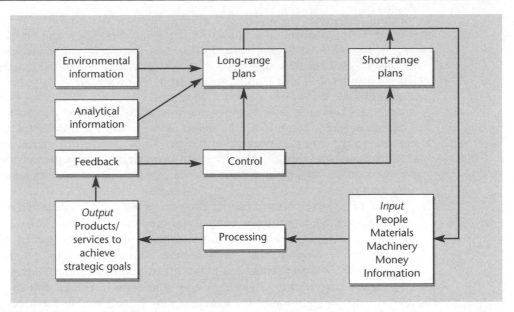

**Figure 5.4**

## Motivation

This involves getting all the members of the organization to pull their full weight, and finding ways in which individual performance may be improved. When we study motivation, we are studying the influences on human beings and what affects their behaviour. For example, when we ask someone to perform a certain task which we know to be within their capability and experience and it is not done satisfactorily, this failure may well be the result of poor motivation rather than lack of ability.

Some motivating factors are related to social needs, and these are influenced by the organization of the work situation. Many studies have examined the effects of these needs, and they illustrate how the size, cohesiveness and motives of the group act as controls on the members' own motives. Hence, the organization should create a situation in which group and individual goals coincide to as great a degree as possible.

## Information and decision making

Decision making has received increasing attention in recent years, and some authorities have argued that management and decision making are synonymous terms. Indeed, there is very little managerial activity which does not involve decision making in some form. Since the quality of information available is crucial to the quality of decision making, an efficient and adequate information system is a prerequisite of managerial success. The hallmark of efficient management may thus be seen in the ability to specify accurately the information needed, and this ability is in itself a function of clear definition of objectives, sound planning and control capability and satisfactory organizational arrangements.

Information is an integrating force which combines organizational resources into a cohesive whole directed towards the realization of organizational objectives. Since information affects the fortunes of an organization in such a fundamental way, it is important that information should be effectively organized and efficiently handled, and this is achieved through what has become known as a management information system. A management information system provides individual managers with the information required for making decisions within their own particular areas of responsibility. It may be likened to the central nervous system of an organism in that it consists of a network of information flows to which each decision may be related. The management accounting information system and the financial accounting information system are two systems within the management information system which tend to be concentrated on financial information. Other information systems are used within a company and these may be of equal importance in management decision making.

Within this information network, decision points may be identified at three levels – strategic planning, management control and operational control (Anthony, 1965, p 24).

Strategic planning involves the determination of corporate objectives and goals, as well as the development of broad policies and strategies by which they may be achieved. This activity relies heavily on information about the environment, and has an irregular pattern. Management control is a lower-level activity which is concerned with the implementation of the strategic plan; it assures that the necessary resources have been obtained, also that they are being used effectively and efficiently. This activity is rhythmic, and follows a weekly, monthly or quarterly pattern. Operational control is the process of ensuring that specific tasks are being carried out effectively and efficiently. It is an activity which focuses on individuals' jobs and transactions, and its tempo is 'real time' (that is, data reported as events occur). Operational control is thus exercised over operating systems, and these include stock records, personnel records, data handling and maintenance records. Examples of the relationship between these levels of activity are illustrated as follows:

| Strategic planning | Management control | Operation control |
|---|---|---|
| Setting marketing policies | Formulating advertising programmes | Controlling the placement of advertisements |
| Setting personnel policies | Planning staff levels | Hiring and controlling staff |

The relationship between these three levels of activities and the information flows is shown in Figure 5.5.

Strategic planning decisions are based upon data derived both from outside and within the system in the form of environmental and analytical information; the latter identifies the organization's strengths and weaknesses, and the former enables it to formulate its strategy.

The constraints imposed upon management control decisions emanate from the strategic decisions incorporated in the strategic plan, and for the purposes of management control decisions these constraints are contained in long- and short-term plans. These plans themselves are broken down into detailed programmes for the various operational subsystems, and into specified information for the purposes of operational control. Hence, management control decisions are based on summarized information which compares the actual performance of cost and profit centres against their planned performance. In order that management should not be inun-

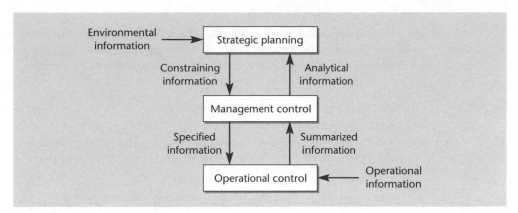

**Figure 5.5**

dated with irrelevant information, reports to management should be in the form of statements of variances from the budget plan, and the reasons why these variances have occurred. Management control exercised in this way is known as management by exception. Management control decisions are thus concerned with investigating variances, and issuing instructions to operating managers on how to deal with them. Alternatively, management may recognize that the variances are inevitable and uncontrollable, and therefore recommend that the strategic plan should be altered to take account of this fact. In such a case, the decision will take the form of a recommendation of an adjustment to the strategic plan.

Operational control decisions are made at the meeting point between specified and operating information associated with the various subsystems. Specified information sets up standards of performance in terms of volume and costs of production and allocated time. Operating information discloses the results in the form of items produced, and production performance in terms of time actually taken. Operational control decisions, unlike management control decisions, are concerned with day-to-day variances occurring in detailed operations, such as the time taken to perform individual tasks.

## Summary

Planning occurs at all management levels, and the success of other management functions depends upon the quality of planning.

Management is also concerned with such functions as organization, control, communication and motivation. Since decision making is a key characteristic of all management functions, decision making has become synonymous with management.

Information is necessary for decision making, and the quality of information will affect the quality of decisions. Hence, an adequate and efficient information system is a prerequisite of managerial success.

Decision making may be classified according to the following areas:

1 strategic planning – which involves the determination of corporate objectives and goals as well as the broad policies and strategies by which they may be achieved;
2 management control – which is concerned with implementing the strategic plans;
3 operational control – which is the process of ensuring that specific tasks are carried out effectively and efficiently.

389

In this part we shall consider the role of accounting as the most important element of a management information system, and we shall also examine the manner in which accounting information assists management in its various functions.

**References**

Anthony, R N (1965). *Planning and Control Systems: A Framework for Analysis*, Harvard Business School.

Böer, G (1994). 'Five modern management accounting myths', *Management Accounting (USA)*, January.

## Self-assessment questions

1 Explain what is meant by 'organizing' as a management function.

2 What is the significance of an 'organizational structure'?

3 What is meant by 'control'?

4 Why is communication viewed as of critical importance in the management process?

5 Discuss motivation in a management context.

6 Discuss the role played by information in management decision making.

7 Explain the different levels of management activity, and comment on their relative importance.

## Problem *(* indicates that a solution is to be found in the Lecturer's Guide)*

1* The Daniels Corporation is a medium-sized company specializing in the leisure industry. The company comprises a hotel, a restaurant, a chauffeur-driven taxi service, a health studio and pool, a coffee shop, a bar and a conference centre. The hotel can accommodate 100 guests and the restaurant 80 places; the taxi service has 10 vehicles; the health studio has 400 members, who use the facilities of the swimming pool, jacuzzi, sauna and multigym; the bar holds 150 people.

*Required:*
(a) What kind of organization structure should be used for the leisure complex?
(b) What type of decision would be taken at the strategic level? Give examples and explain what information would be useful in making the decision and where the information would be obtained.
(c) Specify the management control system which would be needed to run the business. What information would be needed by the managers, and why?
(d) Choose a task at the operational level and write the operational manual for this task.

# 26 Traditional cost accounting

## Setting the scene

Manufacturing cost accounting (cost accounting's rarely used full name) is the third leg of the stool – the other legs being scientific management and the assembly line – on which modern manufacturing industry rests. Without cost accounting, these two could never have become fully effective. It too is American in origin. Developed in the 1920s by General Motors, General Electric, and Western Electric, the new cost accounting, not technology, gave GM and GE the competitive edge that made then worldwide industry leaders. Following World War II, cost accounting became a major US export . . . .

Henry Ford's epigram, 'The customer can have any colour as long as it is black,' has entered American folklore. But few people realize what Ford meant: flexibility costs time and money, and the customer won't pay for it. Even fewer people realize that in the mid-1920s the 'new' cost accounting made it possible for GM to beat Ford by giving customers both colours and annual model changes at no additional cost.

(Drucker, 1990)

## Learning objectives

After studying this chapter you should be able to:

1   Identify the objectives of cost analysis.

2   Describe the elements of cost.

3   Explain the stages involved in the ascertainment of overhead costs applicable to a unit of product (or service).

4   Contrast the accuracy of department and plant-wide overhead rates.

5   Consider the case for a level of activity based on normal capacity.

6   Discuss the limitations of full-cost calculations.

7   Describe five major types of product-costing systems.

Costs represent money measurements of the efforts that an organization has to make to achieve its objectives. Consequently, costs play a very important role in management decision making.

Different costs are used for different types of decision. For example, costs required for the purpose of product costing are analysed as direct costs and indirect costs. Costs that reflect the impact of different activity levels and are relevant to decisions relating to activity volume are presented in the form of fixed costs and variable costs. Accordingly, the various cost terms that are used in accounting, such as direct and indirect costs, fixed and variable costs, sunk costs, differential costs, discretionary and engineered costs, controllable and non-controllable, all have a specific meaning and a specific decision use. These terms will be examined in this chapter and subsequent chapters.

## Objectives of cost analysis

Costs are collected for three major purposes:

1  to assist in the measurement of reported profit;
2  to assist in decision making such as the pricing of products or services;
3  to assist in planning, controlling and evaluating performance.

Costs are accumulated in two forms: in terms of their relationship to a person (responsibility accounting) and in terms of a product or service. Responsibility accounting, which uses costs accumulated in the first form, is directed at the control of costs by associating them with individuals in the management hierarchy. This form of accounting plays a central role in the control of operations, which is dealt with in Chapter 34.

Here we deal with the accumulation of costs in order to calculate full product or service costs: that is, all the manufacturing costs incurred in bringing the product to a marketable state or the full costs of providing a service. One application of full product costs is computing inventory values. Sometimes, non-manufacturing costs such as administrative and marketing costs are added to the full product costs for the purpose of determining the profitability of products and for establishing pricing policies. These product costs are also used in government contracts which seek to establish a 'fair price' by basing the price on total costs.

## The elements of cost

The elements of cost are a classification of the different types of expenditure which can be grouped together under a number of summary headings. For manufacturing industry, the costs can be classified into two major categories, namely, manufacturing and non-manufacturing costs, since these are the costs which are incurred in transforming raw materials into finished products. As regards other industries such as service organizations, this classification is inappropriate, since most service organizations do not manufacture. For these organizations the labels 'direct' and 'indirect' costs should be used.

### Manufacturing costs

These costs comprise three elements:

1  direct material costs;
2  direct labour costs;
3  factory overhead costs.

The term 'direct' cost is applied only to those costs which can be readily identified with the product. Therefore, direct material costs include only those costs which can be directly associated with the finished product. Similarly, if an employee performs a task connected with the making of the product, that employee's wage is considered as a direct labour cost. Direct material and direct labour costs are referred to as prime costs.

In deciding which costs to treat as direct costs, the accountant has to take into consideration the materiality of the item. The expense of determining that some item is a direct cost rather than regarding it as a factory overhead cost may outweigh any benefit attached to such information. Thus, the expense of recording as direct costs such small items as washers, nuts and bolts far outweighs any benefit which may be derived from this exercise.

Factory overhead costs include all the remaining production costs, after direct costs have been determined. They include indirect material costs such as lubricants, and supplies of materials for repairs and maintenance. They also include indirect labour costs such as the salaries and wages of inspectors, timekeepers and workers who do not work on specific products. Factory overhead costs also include other indirect costs such as heat, light, power and the depreciation of factory buildings, plant and equipment.

The manufacturing cost is the total of all direct and indirect costs. It is the cost of manufacture which is recorded as the stock value of the finished product while it is awaiting sale. Upon sale, the manufacturing cost forms part of the cost of sale for the purpose of calculating the trading profit.

## Non-manufacturing costs

These costs are not included in the cost of manufacturing the product, and they are not included, therefore, in the cost of sales. Hence, they are assumed not to attach to the product costs for income measurement purposes. Non-manufacturing costs are 'period' rather than 'product' costs, and they are associated with accounting periods rather than with output. Non-manufacturing costs include administrative and marketing costs. Administrative costs are defined as the costs incurred on executive salaries, head office staff expenses including all clerical and secretarial staff, legal expenses and depreciation on office equipment, furniture, etc. Marketing costs include the activities associated with obtaining orders, such as advertising and selling costs, and activities concerned with fulfilling orders, such as warehousing, packing and delivery.

## Full product costs

The elements of cost involved in the calculation of full product costs for a unit of a product may be summarized by the following ascertained unit costs:

|  | £ |
|---|---|
| Direct material costs | 4 |
| Direct labour costs | 6 |
| Direct cost per unit | 10 |
| Factory overhead costs | 8 |
| Manufacturing cost per unit | |
| Full product cost | 18 |

In calculating full product costs, the accounting problem is to find means of attributing to units of products their appropriate costs for the various decisions which management has to make. The task of calculating the direct material and direct labour costs attributable to individual products is relatively easy. The direct material costs are calculated by ascertaining the quantities of materials used in the product, making due allowance for normal waste, and multiplying the quantity by the raw material purchase price. Similarly, the direct labour costs are obtained by specifying the operations involved in production and the time taken, and multiplying the time factor so derived by the appropriate labour rates. It is in the calculation of total overhead costs per unit that the major accounting problem of cost determination lies.

## Service organizations – service costs

Many accountants now work for service organizations in areas such as hotels and leisure, transport, health services, farming, training, retailing and so on. The emphasis on the composition of costs is significantly different from that in manufacturing organizations with labour comprising a much greater proportion of cost in service organizations than in manufacturing organizations and material costs being greater in manufacturing than in service organizations. Other differences are also present; it is much more difficult to identify the cost with the service delivered. For example, in retailing, most counter staff will be assigned to an area and not a product, whereas in manufacturing the production staff on a food production line will be assigned to a product. Fewer costs can be directly identified with a service than a product and so more will be classified as overheads.

As regards non-manufacturing costs – administration, selling and distribution costs – these also apply to service organizations but will be labelled as administration or selling instead of non-manufacturing.

## The problem of overhead costs

The problem of ascertaining the overhead costs applicable to a unit of product is first and foremost a function of the number of different products which the firm manufactures or the different types of service which an organization provides. When the firm manufactures only one product, or provides only one service, the problem is relatively simple. If, for example, the firm produces 1,000 units of the product, and the overhead costs total £2,000, the total overhead cost per unit is £2. This example could also be applied to some service organizations, e.g. the number of X-rays divided into the cost of the X-ray department of a hospital would result in a cost per X-ray.

Where the firm manufactures more than one product or provides more than one service, however, many problems arise in computing unit (of product or service) overhead costs. We shall discuss these problems in terms of the undermentioned stages in the ascertainment of full product (or service) costs, as follows:

1  the allotment of factory overhead costs to production cost centres;
2  the allotment in turn of the costs of production cost centres to individual products;
3  the selection of an appropriate level of activity for calculating unit product costs. This is necessary because unit costs vary with activity levels, and a choice has to be made as to the activity level which is applicable to future output.

The above stages also apply to a certain extent to service organizations, except that the unit of product is usually tangible in manufacturing and usually intangible in service organizations.

## The allotment of factory overhead costs to production centres

Cost centres are locations with which costs may conveniently be associated for the purpose of product (or service) costing.

Basically, there are two types of cost centres for which costs are accumulated – production and service cost centres. Production cost centres are those actually involved in production, such as machining and assembling departments. 'Production' is used fairly loosely here to represent the area where a product is manufactured or a service provided. For example in the bus industry, direct overheads may be accumulated for a bus route and the depot overheads would be gathered under several service departments within the depot. Service cost centres are those which exist to facilitate production, for example, maintenance, stores and canteen.

The first stage in the allotment of factory overhead costs to production cost centres is to collect and classify factory overhead costs as between indirect material, indirect labour or other identifiable cost headings. The next stage is to allocate these costs, where possible, to production and service cost centres. The term 'cost allocation' has a special meaning, being used to refer to the allotment of whole items of cost to cost centres. For example, the salaries of foremen in charge of individual cost centres may be allocated to those cost centres. Items of costs which cannot be allocated to cost centres must be apportioned. The term 'cost apportionment' means the allotment of proportions only of items of cost to cost centres. For example, the cost of rates cannot be allotted to any particular cost centre and must be apportioned between cost centres.

The third stage is to apportion the costs of the service cost centres to the production cost centres. If we assume that a firm has three service cost centres and two production cost centres, as in Figure 5.6, the apportionment of the service cost centre costs involves selecting appropriate methods for apportioning these costs to the production cost centres.

When the apportionment is completed, the major production cost centres will have accumulated both prime costs and factory overhead costs.

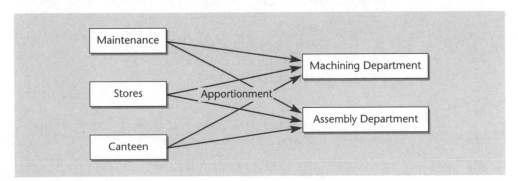

**Figure 5.6**

**Example 1**

The production process of Simplex Ltd is based on a machining department and an assembly department, which are supported by one service department which is a maintenance department. Consider the following cost information:

**Departmental cost data**

| Direct (or allocated overheads) | Total | Machining | Assembly | Maintenance |
|---|---|---|---|---|
| | £ | £ | £ | £ |
| Indirect materials | 15,000 | 8,000 | 5,000 | 2,000 |
| Indirect labour | 6,000 | 4,000 | 1,000 | 1,000 |
| Depreciation of machinery | 7,000 | 2,500 | 4,500 | – |
| **Total direct overhead costs** | 28,000 | 14,500 | 10,500 | 3,000 |
| **Indirect (or unallocated overheads)** | | | | |
| Supervisory salaries | 6,000 | | | |
| Rates | 10,000 | | | |
| **Total overhead factory costs** | 44,000 | | | |

From this information, we may observe that the first stage in the treatment of overhead factory costs has been completed, since those factory overhead costs which may be directly associated with cost centres have already been allotted. In this connection, it should be mentioned that the direct overhead factory costs are said to be direct to the cost centres concerned, but they remain indirect to the units of the product.

The next stage, therefore, is to apportion the indirect overhead factory costs as between the three cost centres. It will be recalled that indirect factory overhead costs are those which cannot be directly associated with any particular cost centres, but are attached to the factory as a whole. Bases are needed, therefore, to apportion them to the three cost centres in question. These bases should reflect the benefits received by the three departments from these costs. For example, since rates are related to the area occupied by the factory, the area occupied by each cost centre may serve as a basis for apportioning rate charges.

Simplex Ltd has adopted the undermentioned bases for the apportionment of indirect factory overhead costs:

| Basis of apportionment | Total | Machining | Assembly | Maintenance |
|---|---|---|---|---|
| Number of employees | 60 | 30 | 20 | 10 |
| Square feet of floor space | 100,000 | 50,000 | 40,000 | 10,000 |
| Maintenance man hours | 2,500 | 1,500 | 1,000 | – |
| Direct labour man hours | 10,000 | 5,000 | 5,000 | – |

Applying these bases to the apportionment of indirect factory overhead costs to the three cost centres, the following distributions are obtained:

## Apportionment of factory overhead costs

| Overhead costs | Basis | Total | Machining | Assembly | Maintenance |
|---|---|---|---|---|---|
| | | £ | £ | £ | £ |
| Indirect materials | Direct | 15,000 | 8,000 | 5,000 | 2,000 |
| Indirect labour | Direct | 6,000 | 4,000 | 1,000 | 1,000 |
| Depreciation of machinery | Direct | 7,000 | 2,500 | 4,500 | – |
| Supervisory salaries | No. of employees | 6,000 | 3,000 | 2,000 | 1,000 |
| Rates | Floor space | 10,000 | 5,000 | 4,000 | 1,000 |
| | | 44,000 | 22,500 | 16,500 | 5,000 |
| Apportionment of maintenance cost centre overheads | Maintenance man hours | – | 3,000 | 2,000 | (5,000) |
| | | 44,000 | 25,500 | 18,500 | – |

We may note from the foregoing example that the final stage in apportioning factory overhead costs to production cost centres was the apportionment of the service cost centre overhead costs. The basis used was the number of maintenance man hours expended in each of the production cost centres. Among other methods commonly used in respect of other service cost centres are the following examples:

| Service cost centres | Basis of apportionment |
|---|---|
| Purchasing | Cost of materials purchased or number of orders placed |
| Stores | Cost of materials used, or the number of stores requisitions |
| Personnel } Canteen } | Number of employees |
| Building maintenance | Space occupied |

The allotment of factory overheads to 'production' cost centres in service organizations follows a similar pattern. Instead of 'Machining' and 'Assembly' we might have 'Paediatrics' and 'ENT Surgery'. The service departments would be very similar in that there could be maintenance, stores (drugs, bedding, clothing, etc.) and a canteen. Other service departments might be 'X-ray', 'blood tests', 'ECG'. The first stage would be as for manufacturing organizations, with overheads being classified by indirect materials, indirect labour and so on. The second stage would be to allocate these costs to direct service and indirect service departments. The third stage would be to apportion the costs of the indirect service cost centres to the direct service cost centres.

## The allotment of production cost centre costs to products

This stage is the second major step in the ascertainment of full product costs. As we mentioned earlier, difficulties arise where production cost centres produce more than one product or service organizations provide more than one service. It is necessary in such cases to establish a method of attributing to each product or service an equitable proportion of the production cost centre's overhead costs. The method to 'recover' or 'absorb' these costs relies on the calculation of an 'overhead rate', which is usually linked to one of three factors in the case of manufacturing organizations:

1  direct labour costs;
2  direct labour hours;
3  machine hours.

The overhead or charge-out rate for service organizations is linked to several factors depending on the organization. For example, a hospital will be linked to patients or patient days. A bus company will be linked to passenger miles.

A prerequisite for the calculation of the 'overhead rate' is the selection of an appropriate base for this purpose.

**Example 2**   Having completed the apportionment of factory overhead costs to the two production cost centres – machining and assembly – the next problem facing Simplex Ltd is to select an appropriate overhead base for apportioning overhead costs to the products manufactured in these two centres. The following information relates to the machining cost centre:

|                      | £      |
|----------------------|--------|
| Direct labour costs  | 5,000  |
| Direct labour hours  | 10,000 |
| Machine hours        | 15,000 |

On the basis of this information, we are able to calculate three different 'overhead rates' for absorbing overhead costs into the full product costs of each unit of the different products manufactured by Simplex Ltd. The calculations are as follows:

*Overhead rate based on direct labour costs*

$$\frac{\text{cost centre overhead costs}}{\text{cost centre direct labour costs}} \times 100$$

$$= \frac{£25,500}{£5,000} \times 100$$

$$= 510\%$$

Thus, for each £1 of direct labour cost which each unit of a product has incurred in the machining cost centre, that unit will also attract £5.10 of the cost centre's overhead costs. Given that the prime costs incurred by Product A in the machining cost centre are:

|                               | £    |
|-------------------------------|------|
| Direct labour costs per unit  | 1.00 |
| Direct material costs per unit| 2.00 |

The full product costs per unit of Product A at the end of processing through the machining department would be:

|  | £ |
|---|---|
| Direct costs as above | 3.00 |
| Factory overhead costs | 5.10 |
|  | 8.10 |

### Overhead rate based on direct labour hours

$$\frac{\text{cost centre overhead costs}}{\text{cost centre direct labour hours}}$$

$$= \frac{£25,500}{10,000}$$

$$= £2.55 \text{ per direct labour hour}$$

Thus, for every hour of direct labour spent on making a unit of a particular product in the machining department, that unit will attract £2.55 of that cost centre's overhead costs. Hence, if Product A needs $2\frac{1}{2}$ direct labour hours, the overhead costs apportioned would be £6.375 per unit.

### Overhead rate based on machine hours

$$\frac{\text{cost centre overhead costs}}{\text{cost centre machine hours}}$$

$$= \frac{£25,500}{15,000}$$

$$= £1.70 \text{ per machine hour}$$

Thus, for every hour which is spent on machining a unit of a product in the machining department, that unit will attract £1.70 of that cost centre's overhead costs. Hence, if product A needs $3\frac{1}{2}$ hours of machining, the overhead costs apportioned would be £5.95 per unit.

The choice of one particular overhead rate as against the others may substantially affect the amount of overhead costs apportioned to a unit of product. Consequently, variations in full product costs may result simply from the manner in which the overhead rate is selected. The 'best' rate to use depends on the particular circumstances facing the firm. The 'direct labour cost' base is easy to use since the necessary information is usually readily available. There may be no relationship, however, between direct labour costs and overhead costs: indeed, most factory overhead costs are incurred on a time basis and are not related to the labour payroll. A further problem resulting from the use of this overhead base is that there will be distortions in the absorption of overhead cost by different products if the rate of pay for similar work is not comparable. The 'direct labour hour' base is usually found to be a better method because most factory overhead costs are more related to time than any other factor. Where, however, there is a greater reliance on machinery rather than on labour, the 'machine hour' base may be the most suitable overhead base for absorbing costs into full-product costs.

## Plant-wide versus department overhead rates of recovery

In our discussion so far, we have examined methods of calculating overhead rates which were related to departmental overhead bases. We took the information for the machining department, for example, as a means of calculating overhead rates for the absorption of its own factory overhead costs into the costs of various products processed in that department. It may be felt that an easier and less extravagant method would be to select an overhead base for use by every department, rather than having different overhead bases used by different departments. The argument in favour of departmental overhead rates is that different departments do not incur the same amount of factory overhead costs, as we have already seen, and do not necessarily use the same number of labour or machine hours, nor do they have the same labour costs. It follows, therefore, that the use of a plant-wide overhead rate will not produce an accurate measure of the departmental costs associated with each unit of product. Departmental overhead rates, by contrast, lead to more accurate measurement, as may be seen from the following example.

**Example 3**  Eastlands Carburettors Ltd manufactures two types of carburettor, Type X and Type Y, both of which are processed in two departments – Department A and Department B. The following cost information is available:

|  | Type X | Type Y |
|---|---|---|
| Direct factory costs per unit | £8 | £8 |
| Direct labour hours |  |  |
| Department A | 4 hours | 1 hour |
| Department B | 1 hour | 4 hours |
| Total hours | 5 hours | 5 hours |

Overhead rates based on direct labour hours are given as follows:

| Overhead rates | Per direct labour hour |
|---|---|
| **Department basis** |  |
| Department A | 6 |
| Department B | 1 |
| **Plant-wide basis** |  |
| Department A | 3 |
| Department B | 3 |

This information enables us to compare the costs per unit which would result from the use of a plant-wide overhead rate as against departmental overhead rates:

**Unit costs using a plant-wide overhead rate**

|  | Type X | Type Y |
|---|---|---|
|  | £ | £ |
| Direct factory costs per unit | 8 | 8 |
| *Add:* Overhead charge per unit |  |  |
| (5 hours at £3.00) | 15 | 15 |
| Manufacturing costs per unit | 23 | 23 |

**Unit costs using departmental overhead rates**

|  | Type X | Type Y |
|---|---|---|
|  | £ | £ |
| Direct factory costs per unit | 8 | 8 |
| *Add*: Overhead charge per unit |  |  |
| Department A (at £6 per hour) | 24 | 6 |
| Department B (at £1 per hour) | 1 | 4 |
| Manufacturing costs per unit | 33 | 18 |

It is noteworthy that:

1 Product X, which spends more processing time in Department A which has the higher overhead rate, is undercosted by £10 when a plant-wide overhead rate is used;

2 Product Y, however, which spends more processing time in Department B, which has the lower overhead rate, is overcosted by £5 when a plant-wide overhead rate is used.

These wide differences highlight the dangers of using cost measurements which do not lead to accurate statements of unit costs. The absorption of factory overhead costs by means of departmental overhead rates rather than a plant-wide overhead rate yields a more accurate measurement of the costs incurred in manufacturing products. Management decisions which require accurate cost measurements for such purposes as pricing policies and production mix decisions would be made incorrectly where a plant-wide rather than departmental rate is employed.

## The selection of an appropriate level of activity

So far we have classified costs into two categories – direct costs and overhead costs. This classification is helpful in understanding how costs are related to products for the purposes of measuring unit costs of production. We mentioned earlier in this chapter that different cost concepts perform different functions. In order to understand the manner in which costs are affected by different levels of activity, we use another classification. This classification requires that costs be categorized into fixed and variable costs, and its purpose is to define how particular items of costs are affected by changes in activity levels.

Fixed costs are those costs which do not vary with changing levels of activity, for example, factory rent, insurance and rates. Variable costs are those costs which do change directly with changes in the level of activity, for example raw material costs and direct labour costs. There are costs, however, which are partly fixed and partly variable, for example, maintenance and repairs of machinery and plant equipment, heat, light and power. These are called semi-variable costs.

The level of activity, therefore, is an economic factor which affects the calculation of the unit cost of output produced. Since fixed costs remain constant as output fluctuates, the greater the output, the lower will be the fixed cost per unit. For example, if fixed costs for the period are £10,000, the fixed cost per unit will depend upon the total number of units produced. If 10,000 units are produced, the fixed cost per unit will be £1; if 5,000 units are produced, the fixed cost per unit will be £2. This problem does not affect the variable costs, for, as we have already noted, variable costs per unit of output remain constant at all levels of activity, assuming always that prices remain stable. For management decision making based on full unit costs, however, the level of activity is an important ingredient which must be taken into account when providing relevant information for such decisions.

The following table illustrates the behaviour of costs as volume changes:

| Units produced | Total fixed costs £ | Total variable costs £ | Total costs £ | Average fixed cost per unit £ | Average variable cost per unit £ | Average total cost per unit £ |
|---|---|---|---|---|---|---|
| 1 | 300 | 100 | 400 | 300 | 100 | 400 |
| 2 | 300 | 200 | 500 | 150 | 100 | 250 |
| 3 | 300 | 300 | 600 | 100 | 100 | 200 |
| 4 | 300 | 400 | 700 | 75 | 100 | 175 |
| 5 | 300 | 500 | 800 | 60 | 100 | 160 |

From the foregoing discussion, we must examine the usefulness of the actual – that is, current – volume of output as a level of activity upon which to base calculations of full unit costs. Current unit costs will fluctuate according to the actual level of activity; here costs are of little use for decisions regarding the future. Thus, pricing decisions require a more stable view of full costs than that provided as a result of fluctuating levels of output. Moreover, cost control implies that full unit costs incurred in one period are compared with those of other periods. Comparisons based on actual levels of output are unreliable because fixed costs per unit will be different where the output levels are different. Even for the purpose of stock valuation, which, as we mentioned, was central to profit measurement, calculations based on actual volume will introduce distortions. Finally, since the calculation of unit costs based on actual volume can be effected only at the end of an accounting period, such unit costs are not relevant to its decision problems, which are more concerned with future than with past costs.

Since actual volume is not a satisfactory basis for calculating a fixed overhead rate which will be useful for the purposes we have mentioned, the following alternative bases may be considered:

1 theoretical capacity, which is the capacity of a particular department to maintain output at a 100 per cent level without interruption;
2 practical capacity, which is the result of making allowances against the theoretical capacity in respect of unavoidable interruptions to output such as time lost for repairs and holidays;
3 expected capacity as a short-run view of capacity, which is determined by immediate expectations of output levels;
4 normal capacity, which is an estimate of output capacity based on a period of time long enough to level out peaks and troughs of cyclical fluctuations.

Normal capacity, as defined above, is the most useful level of activity for the purpose of determining a fixed overhead rate which will be relatively stable over a number of years. It will be appreciated that there is an element of subjectivity in the assessment of normal capacity, and it will lead invariably to some under- or over-absorption of fixed factory overhead costs, depending on whether the actual level of activity is under or over the normal level. We will deal with this problem in Chapter 35. Normal capacity often does provide, however, the most reliable and stable basis for calculating full product costs for decision-making purposes.

## Limitations of full cost calculations

It is clear from the foregoing examination of the problems associated with overhead costs that full product costs cannot be measured with complete accuracy. To some extent, all methods used for apportioning overhead costs are arbitrary, and are based upon assumptions which are subjective to a degree. The 'benefit received' should be the main criterion for apportioning factory overhead costs to cost centres. It is difficult, however, to find bases which are suitable for this purpose. For example, the cost of the factory personnel department may be apportioned to cost centres on the basis of the relative number of their employees, but this base assumes that all employees will benefit equally from the services of this department. This example is, of course, a gross simplification of the general problem of apportioning overhead costs. Labour turnover and the difference in skills between different classes of employees will influence the time and the effort expended by the personnel department.

We have referred already to the element of subjectivity which enters into the selection of the methods of apportioning overhead costs. This is exacerbated by the degree of subjectivity which may be attached to the selection of the level of activity selected from recovering overhead costs. Indeed, two equally competent accountants may arrive at very different product costs simply because their views of what constitutes a 'normal level' of activity may differ. This problem applies similarly to the allotment of administrative costs. The costs of operating the purchasing department cannot be related, for example, to any of the bases which we mentioned.

It is apparent that the main difficulty in computing full product costs stems from the presence of fixed overhead costs. The allotment of these costs to product costs on bases which are arbitrary renders the end result of doubtful accuracy. As we shall see elsewhere in this book, incorrect decisions may arise from the inclusion of fixed costs in product costs. For the purpose of external financial reporting, for example, we argue in Chapter 29 that more useful information may be provided if fixed overhead costs are not absorbed in output, but are treated as period costs. Moreover, their inclusion in product costs may give a misleading view of profit results. It is often claimed that for the purpose of long-range planning, product cost information should reflect total costs. However, as we shall see in Chapter 30, there is a case for directing attention away from a narrowly conceived view of price determination based on markup percentages on costs to the broader implications of cost–volume–profit relationships. As we shall also see, because of the behaviour of fixed and variable costs over different volumes of output, product cost information based on full costs is irrelevant to the problem of control. A distinction has to be made, therefore, between fixed and variable cost information for control purposes.

It follows that the limitations inherent in full-cost computations should be appreciated by all those using such information for decision making. From an accountant's point of view, specific instruction from management should be awaited for the calculation of product costs inclusive of fixed costs. Even then, a clear distinction should be made between fixed and variable cost components.

## Costing systems

Costs are accumulated in costing systems. The development of costing systems reflects the manner in which accounting methods have been adapted to the needs of different forms of activity and technology, and also to the appearance of advanced manufacturing techniques that have been a feature of recent years.

In effect, the objective of costing systems has remained constant in the sense that the accumulation of costs has the ultimate purpose of ascertaining product or service costs. However, the need to render this information relevant for decision making has shifted the emphasis from recording costs *incurred* to costs that *will be incurred* in producing goods and services. The competitive nature of the markets in which goods and services are sold has placed further stress on the efficient management of costs, and this has shifted costing systems to record costs that *should be incurred*.

## Product costing systems

Product costing represents the classical tradition in cost accounting in the manner in which costs are analysed and recorded. Its objective is to allow product costs to be determined as accurately as possible in order to permit efficient management decisions in various areas, for example, in pricing and in seeking to improve the efficiency in use of scarce resources.

The identification of costs with products has focused attention on the identification of costs with products and has relied on the classification of costs as between direct costs and indirect costs. As we have seen, the major problem in determining full product costs is the need to find reliable allocation keys with which to apportion indirect costs to products, thereby accumulating direct costs and indirect costs into 'full product costs'.

The suitability of product costs is also the function of two other criteria:

1 the technology used for providing the goods or services, and
2 the time reference of the cost data itself.

## Cost accounting systems for different technologies

Cost accounting systems allow full product costs to be accumulated in accordance with the type of technology employed. Five major costing systems commonly found are:

1  job order costing;
2  contract costing;
3  process costing;
4  operations costing;
5  service costing.

Job order costing and contract costing share the similarity that the product or contract is undertaken upon receipt of the client's order and is completed in accordance with the client's specifications. Costs are accumulated to the job or contract until it is completed. The essential difference between job order costing and contract costing lies in the time taken to fulfil the order. For this reason, job order costing is found where production is completed in the short term: contract costing is used where completion extends over one or more years. Accordingly, the major accounting problem associated with contract costing systems is the determination of periodic profit. This is because contract costing involves carrying forward substantial work-in-process costs across accounting year ends, until work is delivered to the client in accordance with the terms of the contract. For example, a major road construction contract may take two years to complete, during which only costs are incurred. Hence, at the end of the first year, the question is: can the contractor show a profit if he is not entitled to full payment for the work done in that year?

Process costing is a method of product costing used by manufacturing concerns engaged in the mass production of standardized products. Production is undertaken in anticipation of demand, and hence finished products are stocked until they are sold. Process costing is used in such industries as cement, flour, sugar, cars, oil and chemicals. Product costs are accumulated by reference to a standard quantity of a homogeneous product, expressed in a conventional cost unit, either by quantity, volume or weight, as the case may be.

Operations costing is a form of costing that lies somewhere in between job order costing and process costing. It is found in situations where the technology of production does not rely upon a job order specification, nor is process costing applicable by reason of the homogeneity of the product. In effect, it consists of accumulating product costs by reference to the cost of operations, as such, that batches of slightly dissimilar products undergo.

Service costing is a special application of process costing which is used where services rather than products are supplied: for example, computer services, transport, retailing, health, accountants, solicitors, etc. As mentioned earlier, the particular problems that are involved in setting up service costing systems are:

1  selecting cost units in relation to which the cost of services can be accumulated: for public transport a suitable cost unit might be cost per passenger mile; a hotel might use cost per room per day; a hospital might use cost per patient day, etc;
2  selecting a charge-out rate for services.

Today there is considerable interest in developing more sophisticated costing systems in industries which previously were not particularly concerned about costs. The passenger service industry, the health industry and others have seen radical changes in the approach to costing systems. Many of the principles used for implementing management accounting systems in manufacturing industries are now being applied to service industries and there is significant growth in the development and implementation of these systems. The change in emphasis in some service organizations comes from management requesting information on service costs.

### The time reference of the cost data itself

Two different time references are used with respect to cost data. Cost systems that record invoiced product costs accumulate, in effect, actual costs, defined in accounting as 'historic costs'. These costs are useful for accounting purposes, but have limited usefulness for the control of product costs. The development of the concept of 'standard' or 'predetermined' costs is associated with the concept of cost for control purposes. Standard costs reflect a desire to discover efficient product costs, as a basis for controlling product costs. Standard costs are discussed in Chapter 35.

## Summary

Cost information is required for three main purposes:

1 for the measurement of reported profits;
2 for making decisions;
3 for planning and control.

The type of cost information required may be different in each of these cases. We analyse the nature and the use of various cost measurements in this part.

This chapter has been concerned with the accounting problems involved in the measurement of unit costs of production. The major difficulty in the measurement of full product costs lies in the calculation and assignment of factory overhead costs. The process of assigning factory overhead costs to units of product occurs in the following stages:

1 allotting factory overhead costs to production cost centres and finding appropriate levels of activity for this purpose;
2 allotting the costs of production cost centres to units of product and finding appropriate methods for this purpose.

The emerging area of measuring the unit costs of services was also discussed. The steps used in the determination of unit costs of production could also be applied here.

The use of cost information for planning and control decisions implies that such cost information should reflect the future rather than the past. For this reason, standard costs – which are predetermined costs – are used. They not only reflect expectations about the costs which will be current in the period ahead, but are intended to deal with the uncertainties implicit in decision making.

**Reference** Drucker, P F (1990). 'The emerging theory of manufacturing', *Harvard Business Review*, May–June.

# Self-assessment questions

1 State the three purposes for which costs are collected.

2 Describe the three elements of product costs.

3 What is the significance for product costing of the difference between manufacturing and non-manufacturing costs?

4 What is meant by the term 'full product cost'?

5 What problems are involved in determining factory overhead costs per unit?

6 What methods are commonly used for recovering overhead costs?

7 What are the advantages of departmental rates, as against plant-wide overhead rates?

8 Describe four major types of product costing systems.

# Problems *(\*indicates that a solution is to be found in the Lecturer's Guide)*

1 As the accountant of the Northumberland Engineering Co operating in a very competitive industry by means of special jobs to each customer's requirements, you are required to:
(a) Calculate the (estimated) cost of job enquiry number 876, for which details are given below.
(b) On the basis of your cost figures, indicate the price you feel should be charged to the customer for job 876; or, if you feel unable to do this, indicate what further information you would need in order to arrive at a price.
All calculations should be clearly shown and figures justified.

*Job Enquiry Number 876*
(a) Estimated direct material cost:     £1,000
(b) Estimated direct labour input:

| | Hours | Rate per hour (£) |
|---|---|---|
| Plating department | 81 | 4.00 |
| Welding department | 14 | 3.00 |
| Assembly department | 10 | 2.00 |

(c) Indirect departmental costs:

| | Plating | Welding | Assembly |
|---|---|---|---|
| Total indirect costs: | | | |
| Last year's actual | £20,000 | £8,000 | £4,000 |
| This year's budget | £22,000 | £9,000 | £5,000 |
| (d) Activity levels (labour hours): | | | |
| Last year's actual | 10,000 | 8,000 | 4,000 |
| This year's budget | 9,000 | 10,000 | 4,000 |

2\* Byfokal Product Ltd uses a predetermined overhead rate for the purpose of job order costing. This rate is based on machine hours with regard to the machining department and on direct labour cost with respect to the assembly and finishing department.

The following forecasts have been used to calculate the predetermined overhead rate for these two departments:

| | Machining department | Assembly and finishing department |
|---|---|---|
| Machine hours | 100,000 | 30,000 |
| Direct labour hours | 60,000 | 150,000 |
| Direct labour cost | £500,000 | £1,250,000 |
| Factory overhead costs | £2,500,000 | £2,000,000 |

The job order cost sheet for Job Number 35 showed the following information:

| | Machining department | Assembly and finishing department |
|---|---|---|
| Direct materials used | £3,500 | £1,000 |
| Direct labour cost | £20,000 | £28,000 |
| Direct labour hours | 2,400 | 3,360 |
| Machine hours | 4,000 | 672 |

*Required:*
(a) What is the predetermined overhead rate for each department?
(b) Calculate the total overhead cost for Job 35.

3   The managing director of Marco Fabrication is concerned about the reliability and relevance of the product unit costs which have been used to date for general purposes. Shortly after your appointment as the firm's accountant you are required to write him a report explaining your general approach to the use of cost accounts and in particular the problems of overhead costing. You derive the following information for this purpose:

The company has two producing departments, machining and assembly, and one service department, the canteen. Direct departmental overhead for the coming year is estimated as machining £50,000, assembly £40,000 and canteen £10,000. Details of estimated indirect overhead are as follows:

| | |
|---|---|
| Rates | £1,000 |
| Depreciation | £9,300 |
| Light and power | £600 |

**Departmental data**

| | Kilowatt hours | No of employees | Cost of equipment | Square feet |
|---|---|---|---|---|
| Machining | 600 | 20 | £10,000 | 600 |
| Assembly | 1,100 | 10 | £20,000 | 1,200 |
| Canteen | 300 | 5 | £1,000 | 200 |

| | Estimated direct labour cost | Estimated direct labour hours | Estimated machine hours |
|---|---|---|---|
| Machining | £10,000 | 18,000 | 8,000 |
| Assembly | £15,000 | 12,000 | 20,000 |

The above activity levels are based on what could be attained if produc[...]
capacity. Expected activity for the coming year is estimated to be 70 per cen[...]
and normal activity at 80 per cent.

4   A factory in Norfolk processes turkeys for sale. The production process is classified [...]
    cost centres and the relevant forecast information for each of the cost centres is as follows:

|  | Total £ | Cutting £ | Cooking £ | Canteen £ | Maintenance £ |
|---|---|---|---|---|---|
| Indirect labour | 340,000 | 120,000 | 140,000 | 30,000 | 50,000 |
| Consumables | 82,000 | 24,000 | 32,000 | 20,000 | 6,000 |
| Heating and lighting | 24,000 | | | | |
| Rent and rates | 36,000 | | | | |
| Depreciation | 60,000 | | | | |
| Supervision | 48,000 | | | | |
| Power | 40,000 | | | | |
| | 630,000 | | | | |

The following information is also available:

|  | Total | Cutting | Cooking | Canteen | Maintenance |
|---|---|---|---|---|---|
| Floor space (sq metres) | 60,000 | 20,000 | 24,000 | 6,000 | 10,000 |
| Book value of machinery (£) | 600,000 | 300,000 | 240,000 | 20,000 | 40,000 |
| Number of employees | 160 | 80 | 60 | 10 | 10 |
| Kilowatt hours | 20,000 | 9,000 | 8,000 | 1,000 | 2,000 |
| Direct materials (£) | | 100,000 | 50,000 | | |
| Direct labour (£) | | 50,000 | 42,000 | | |
| Maintenance hours | | 8,000 | 6,000 | | |
| Labour hours | | 12,640 | 8,400 | | |
| Machine hours | | | 15,700 | | |

*Required:*
(a)  An overhead cost statement which clearly shows the bases of apportionment.
(b)  The labour hour overhead absorption rate for the Cutting Department and a machine
     hour overhead rate for the Cooking Department.
(c)  How many alternative methods of overhead absorption might be used in this situation?
     What are the benefits and limitations with regard to using these rates at the company?
(d)  The actual overhead figures for the year were:
         Cutting Department: £310,000; 12,000 labour hours.
         Cooking Department: £312,000; 15,810 machine hours.
     What is the under/over-absorption for each department?

# 27 ABC and JIT

**Setting the scene**

Conventional wisdom having been challenged, new thought emerged: a company should understand its cost drivers – and apply these drivers to the cost of products in proportion to the volume of activity that a product consumes. This powerful thought became popularized under the name activity-based costing (ABC).

Over the last several years, professional literature has been filled with articles on ABC. Of more importance, many companies have adopted activity-based costing methodology. A private survey of Price Waterhouse clients indicates that more than half of American manufacturing companies list ABC as one of their current buzzwords. About one-third of service companies have experimented with the approach. In addition, the technique of activity-based costing is spreading quickly to Pacific Rim and European-based companies.

(Keegan and Eiler, 1994)

**Learning objectives**

After studying this chapter you should be able to:

1   Define activity-based costing (ABC) systems.

2   Explain how ABC systems are developed.

3   Contrast traditional volume-based costing systems with ABC systems.

4   Discuss how ABC systems are used in service organizations.

5   Describe the features of just-in-time (JIT) production systems.

The product costing methods discussed in the previous chapter have been developed and used over the past several decades and were suitable for a particular type of decision environment and a particular type of manufacturing technology. This applies especially to the method by which manufacturing overhead costs are assigned to products. As we saw in the previous chapter the traditional method of costing assigns production overheads to products using volume-based recovery bases. This is acceptable if a large proportion of overheads are volume-related. However, an increasing amount of overhead costs relate to the number of 'transactions' taking place within the factory, e.g. machine set-ups, quality control, material handling, etc. Furthermore, the introduction of new technology and automation results in fixed costs becoming a very high proportion of total costs. In these circumstances the use of overhead rates using, say, labour hours is often unrealistic. Activity-based costing (ABC) has developed to address these issues.

## Developing an ABC system

The basic premise of ABC is that activities consume resources and products consume activities. ABC assumes that it is activities which cause cost, not products. In Chapter 26 we saw how traditional overhead costing first assigns overhead costs to organizational units (e.g. departments) before they are assigned to products. In contrast, an ABC system first traces costs to activity centres and then to products. Activity cost centres are cost accumulations that are associated with a given activity, such as machine usage, inspections and production set-ups. Activity cost centres are assigned to products using cost drivers, which may be the number of production set-ups or the number of inspections involved in each product's manufacture. Although both ABC and the conventional methods finally assign overhead costs to products, ABC uses many cost drivers. Conventional methods typically use only one or two. As a result, it is expected that the ABC method will increase product-costing accuracy.

The steps for developing an ABC system are as follows.

### Step 1: Analyse and define activities

Both service and production activities of an enterprise are identified, a process which decomposes an organization into elemental activities that are understandable and easy to manage. Activities are not necessarily traditional organizational segments such as departments. In some instances, activities may cross department boundaries. In other instances, a department may contain several activities.

### Step 2: Determine the cost driver for each activity

The cost driver is that action or transaction that results in costs being incurred. In many instances the cost driver will be measured in terms of the volume of transactions undertaken. Therefore, if production scheduling cost is driven by the number of production set-ups, then that number would represent the cost drivers for the cost of production scheduling. Examples of activities and cost drivers are given in the following table:

| Activity | Cost driver |
| --- | --- |
| Maintenance | No of breakdowns |
| Quality control | No of inspections |
| Material procurement | No of purchase orders |
| Material handling | No of movements |

### Step 3: Identify activity centres

Activity costs which have the same cost driver are collected in activity centres.

### Step 4: Assign costs to products

The costs of activities in the activity centres are assigned to products/services based on cost drivers.

## Comparison with traditional costing

The following example, which is adapted from the examinations of the Chartered Institute of Management Accountants (CIMA), illustrates the traditional and ABC methods of calculating product costs.

**Example 1**  Having attended a CIMA course on activity-based costing (ABC), you decide to experiment by applying the principles of ABC to the four products currently made and sold by your company. Details of the four products and relevant information are given below for one period:

| Product | A | B | C | D |
|---|---|---|---|---|
| Output in units | 120 | 100 | 80 | 120 |
| Costs per unit (£): | | | | |
|     Direct material | 40 | 50 | 30 | 60 |
|     Direct labour | 28 | 21 | 14 | 21 |
| Machine hours (per unit) | 4 | 3 | 2 | 3 |

The four products are similar and are usually produced in production runs of 20 units and sold in batches of 10 units.

The production overhead is currently absorbed by using a machine hour rate, and the total of the production overhead for the period has been analysed as follows:

| | £ |
|---|---|
| Machine department costs (rent, business rates, depreciation and supervision) | 10,430 |
| Set-up costs | 5,250 |
| Stores receiving | 3,600 |
| Inspection/quality control | 2,100 |
| Materials handling and despatch | 4,620 |
| | 26,000 |

You have ascertained that the 'cost drivers' to be used are as listed below for the overhead costs shown:

| Cost | Cost driver |
|---|---|
| Set-up costs | Number of production runs |
| Stores receiving | Requisitions raised |
| Inspection/quality control | Number of production runs |
| Materials handling and despatch | Orders executed |

The number of requisitions raised on the stores was 20 for each product and the number of orders executed was 42, each order being for a batch of 10 of a product.

*Required:*

1  To calculate the total costs for each product if all overhead costs are absorbed on a machine hour basis.
2  To calculate the total costs for each product, using activity-based costing.
3  To calculate and list the unit product costs from your figures in items 1 and 2 above.

*Solution*

1  Machine hour rate = $\dfrac{\text{total production overheads}}{\text{machine hours}} = \dfrac{£26,000}{1,300} = £20$

**Product costs using machine hour rate**

|  | A £ | B £ | C £ | D £ |
|---|---|---|---|---|
| Prime cost | 68 | 71 | 44 | 81 |
| Overhead (1) | 80 | 60 | 40 | 60 |
| Product cost | 148 | 131 | 84 | 141 |
| Total cost (£) | 17,760 | 13,100 | 6,720 | 16,920 |

2  Activity-based costing

| Cost | £ | Driver | Number | Cost per unit of driver £ |
|---|---|---|---|---|
| Set-ups | 5,250 | Production runs | 21 | 250 |
| Stores receiving | 3,600 | Requisitions | 80 | 45 |
| Inspection/quality | 2,100 | Production runs | 21 | 100 |
| Handling/despatch | 4,620 | Orders | 42 | 110 |

The machine department costs are absorbed on a machine hour basis, viz. £10,430 ÷ 1,300 = £8.02 per machine hour.

| Cost | A £ | B £ | C £ | D £ |
|---|---|---|---|---|
| Prime costs | 8,160 | 7,100 | 3,520 | 9,720 |
| Set-ups | 1,500 | 1,250 | 1,000 | 1,500 |
| Stores receiving | 900 | 900 | 900 | 900 |
| Inspection/quality | 600 | 500 | 400 | 600 |
| Handling/despatch | 1,320 | 1,100 | 880 | 1,320 |
| Machine dept costs | 3,851 | 2,407 | 1,284 | 2,888 |
| Total costs | 16,331 | 13,257 | 7,984 | 16,928 |

3    Comparison of unit product costs

|  | A<br>£ | B<br>£ | C<br>£ | D<br>£ |
|---|---|---|---|---|
| Costs from item 1 | 148.00 | 131.00 | 84.00 | 141.00 |
| Costs from item 2 | 136.09 | 132.57 | 99.80 | 141.07 |
| Difference | (11.91) | 1.57 | 15.80 | 0.07 |

The example shows that ABC does not change the amount of overhead costs incurred; however, it does distribute those costs in a more equitable manner. Traditional cost accounting systems, which presuppose that volume-unrelated resources consumed by a product vary in direct proportion to the quantity of volume-related input consumed, may lead to distorted product costs being reported to management. Non-volume-related factors such as set-up costs are included in the above example. Therefore, the ABC cost assignment better reflects the pattern of overhead consumption and is more accurate. Using only volume-based assumptions can lead to one product subsidizing another. In our example, ABC product costing reveals that the traditional method undercosts item C and overcosts item A. ABC systems reveal that significant resources are consumed by low-volume products and complex production operations. ABC typically shifts a substantial amount of overhead costs from the standard, high-volume products where those costs have been assigned under traditional methods to premium, special-order, low-volume products.

The above example illustrates how ABC provides more visibility on the composition of overheads and cost. Under the traditional system costs are simply collected under the heading of 'total production overheads' and then allocated. The greater segmentation provided by ABC indicates the sources and purpose of resource consumption. This additional detail, together with the gathering of cost-driver information, suggests that management will be provided with valuable feedback which will aid the operational control of their manufacturing processes. Therefore, for performance measurement and control purposes, the information provided by ABC has substantial potential advantages over traditional methods.

## Levels of activity and cost behaviour

Traditionally, cost drivers were viewed only at the unit level: how many hours of labour or machine time does it take to produce a product or render a service? While some costs are unit-level costs that are caused by the production or acquisition of a single unit of product or the delivery of a single unit of service, other costs occur at 'higher' levels of activity. ABC requires costs to be aggregated at these different levels. Only if costs are accumulated on the same level as the activity that generates them can an allocation base be selected that represents a cause/effect relationship between the cost and the cost centre. The 'higher' levels include batch, product and facility levels.

Batch-level activities are those that are performed each time a batch of products is produced, e.g. set-ups, inspections, production scheduling and materials handling. Product-level activities are those that are performed as needed to support the various products produced by a company, e.g. engineering charges, maintenance of equipment and product development. Facility-level activities are those that sustain a factory's general manufacturing process, e.g. plant management, building depreciation and security. Facility-level costs are common to many different activities and products or services and can be assigned to products only on an arbitrary basis. Therefore, facility-level costs theoretically should not be assigned to products at all.

Accountants have traditionally assumed that if costs did not vary with changes in production at the unit level, those costs were fixed rather than variable. In reality, batch, product and facility-level costs are all variable, but these costs vary for reasons other than changes in production volume. Therefore, to determine a valid estimate of product or service cost, costs should be accumulated at each of the higher levels. Since unit, batch and product-level costs are all associated with units of products, these costs can be aggregated to match with the revenues generated by product sales.

Therefore, ABC moves away from the notions of short-term fixed and variable costs and focuses on the variability of costs in the longer term. Advocates of ABC claim that all costs are ultimately variable and can be traced to individual products, thereby enabling more accurate costs to be computed for decision making.

## ABC and service organizations

Although the consideration of ABC so far has focused on manufacturing, ABC can also be useful to service organizations. Since all organizations have activities and output the concepts of ABC can be applied universally. However, there are fundamental differences between manufacturing and service organizations. First, the service sector is less homogeneous than the manufacturing sector. Manufacturing companies tend to perform many of the same types of activities in similar ways, but there is little similarity between the activities of an insurance firm, a hospital, a bank, a retail shop and a government department. Second, output in the service sector is less tangible and, therefore, harder to define. Yet output must be defined so that it can be costed. The intangible nature of service output makes costing more difficult.

*Example 2*  For example, let us consider a hospital. A hospital's product can be defined as a patient's stay and treatment. For the purpose of illustrating the potential of ABC, we will focus on one type of service provided to each patient: daily care. Daily care comprises three activities: hospitalization (admission and discharge), hotel services (accommodation and food) and nursing care. Output is defined as patient days. Traditionally, hospitals have assigned the cost of daily care by using a daily rate (a rate per patient day), which is computed by dividing the annual cost of hospitalization, hotel services and nursing care by the unit's capacity expressed in patient days.

Within each unit (e.g. intensive care unit and obstetrics unit) all patients are charged the same daily rate. However, the traditional method does not take account of the fact that the three activities may be consumed in different proportions by patients. This would imply product diversity and a possible requirement to use more than one activity driver to assign daily care costs accurately to patients. Hansen and Mowen (1995) provide an illustration of a private maternity unit for which the following activity and cost information applies:

| Activity | Annual cost | Cost driver | Annual quantity |
|---|---|---|---|
| Hospitalization and hotel | £1,100,000 | Patient days | 11,000 |
| Nursing care | £1,100,000 | Hours of care | 55,000 |

The activity pool rates are £100 per patient day and £20 per nursing hour.

The traditional approach for charging daily care would produce a rate of £200 per patient day (£2,200,000 ÷ 11,000). Every maternity patient, regardless of type, would pay the daily rate of £200.

However, assume that within the maternity unit there are three levels of increasing severity: normal patients, caesarean patients and patients with complications, and that they have the following annual demands:

| Patient type | Patient days demanded | Nursing hours demanded |
|---|---|---|
| Normal | 8,000 | 30,000 |
| Caesarean | 2,000 | 13,000 |
| Complications | 1,000 | 12,000 |
| | 11,000 | 55,000 |

Using the pool rates for each activity, a different daily rate is produced for each patient which reflects the different demands for nursing services:

| Patient | Daily rate £ |
|---|---|
| Normal | 175[1] |
| Caesarean | 230[2] |
| Complications | 340[3] |

[1] $[(£100 \times 8,000) + (£20 \times 30,000)] \div 8,000$
[2] $[(£100 \times 2,000) + (£20 \times 13,000)] \div 2,000$
[3] $[(£100 \times 1,000) + (£20 \times 12,000)] \div 1,000$

This example illustrates that ABC can produce significant product costing improvements in service organizations that experience product diversity.

## Evaluation of ABC

A company is particularly suited for the use of ABC if:

1 the company produces a wide variety of tailor-made products or services which are targeted at different marketing segments;
2 the company has high overhead costs that are not proportional to the unit volume of individual products;
3 the company has a highly automated production system.

In these circumstances ABC provides a better understanding of the cost of making a product or performing a service. Such insight could result in management decisions about expanding or contracting product variety, raising or reducing prices and entering or leaving a market, e.g. managers may decide to raise selling prices or discontinue production of low-volume speciality output, since that output consumes more resources than high-volume output. Furthermore, as we saw previously, ABC helps to make the behaviour of some costs far more visible, and therefore more controllable, than under traditional accounting methods.

ABC is not a general panacea to costing problems. It is not necessarily appropriate to all businesses. In some cases, especially where a simple product is produced, it may be appropriate to use more traditional methods of cost allocation. Hence, managers have to choose the technique which best suits management's requirements and the organizational environment. In addition, it is now accepted that it is not essential to apply ABC to all costs or to the entire accounting system. ABC can be used alongside a more traditional accounting system.

## Activity-based management

The initial interest in ABC related to product or service costing – how to allocate overhead costs more accurately in order to compute the cost of delivered products or services. More recently, the emphasis on ABC has switched from product costing to improving business management. From a managerial perspective an ABC system offers more than just more accurate cost information. It also provides information about the cost and performance of activities and resources and it can trace costs accurately to cost objects other than products, such as customers and channels of distribution. Knowing the cost of activities, their importance to the organization and how efficiently they are performed allows managers to focus on those activities that might offer opportunities for cost savings. If activities are linked across departments forming cross-functional processes, the model structure of an organization is simplified and powerful information results. This 'process' view of ABC allows management to focus on value-added and non-value-added activities in order to reduce or eliminate those activities that are not adding value but are causing costs to be incurred. Activity-based management is considered further in Chapter 38.

## Just-in-time production systems

Just-in-time (JIT) systems are concerned with reducing production costs by eliminating as far as possible inventories and production delays. Terms that describe just-in-time systems include MIPS (minimum inventory production systems), ZIPS (zero inventory production systems) and MANS (materials as needed systems). JIT systems are, in effect, manufacturing systems with zero inventories and constant production flows. Essentially JIT implies the firm produces only to demand, without the benefit and cost of buffer stocks. Production is dictated by demand and 'pulled' through the system rather than 'pushed'. JIT was developed by Toyota in the 1950s and 1960s and was adopted by other Japanese companies in the 1970s. US companies started adopting it during the 1980s since when it has been adopted by some UK companies.

Traditional manufacturing involves one or more sequential production processes. Raw material stock exists as well as buffer stocks of work in progress and finished goods. An acceptable rate of defects is budgeted and feedback regarding these defective products is provided only at the end of the production period. Plant support services such as quality control or maintenance are usually centrally located within the plant.

JIT systems imply a radical change in the manufacturing environment, since their successful implementation requires an environment concerned with the following:

1  elimination of waste;
2  zero inventories;
3  zero idle production time:
4  constant production rate;
5  balanced capacity:
6  emphasis on zero waste/faulty work;
7  full employee involvement;
8  an emphasis on perfect quality.

These concerns highlight the role of JIT as a management philosophy, not simply a toolbox of techniques. The aim of JIT is the elimination of waste from all parts of the manufacturing process, from product design to product delivery. Thus, JIT aims to eliminate activities which do not add value to the product and to use the minimum amount of material consistent with the market requirements of the product.

The concern with perfect quality implies that things are done correctly the first time. That involves three independent aspects: product design, process design and supplier quality. Design engineers need to establish and maintain close working relationships with customers. The whole production process must be designed with quality in mind. A JIT company will ensure incoming quality not by strict goods-inward inspection procedures but rather by careful selection of a limited number of suppliers with whom a long-term partnership will be established. Bulk deliveries are replaced by small, frequent deliveries from a small number of suppliers who participate in quality assurance programmes. The suppliers are viewed as a vital part of the production team and not an external factor to be treated in a confrontational manner.

Without the full involvement of all employees, the potential benefits of JIT will not be achieved. The implementation of the JIT philosophy requires major cultural change for companies. All employees need to be involved in a process of continued improvement.

As we saw earlier, traditional product costing systems define the objective of costing systems as being concerned with three elements of costs, namely raw materials, direct labour and overhead costs, which are recorded in three separate stock accounts, namely raw materials, work-in-process and finished goods.

The concern with the elimination of inventories implies a radical alteration in the tracking of inventories through inventory accounts, as seen in conventional product costing systems. Consequently, the control of materials focuses on the points of materials utilization, rather than on inventory control. The concern of JIT materials accounting is with the following two aspects of materials control:

1  estimating materials requirements for actual production;
2  eliminating usage variances at the point of usage.

JIT systems also imply radical changes in the tracking of direct labour costs as product costs. Since JIT systems aim to secure constant manufacturing conditions, many of the objectives involved in obtaining direct labour cost information have been superseded. For this reason, JIT direct labour accounting systems are also greatly simplified, and the significance attached to accounting separately for direct labour cost has also decreased. For example, conventional labour utilization and efficiency measures are largely redundant when emphasis is given to constant work flows.

In many industries, the proportion of direct labour costs in total production costs is decreasing. In some companies, the implementation of JIT has seen the introduction of the following methods of accounting for direct labour costs:

1 expensing direct labour at source;

2 recovering direct labour costs in the form of a product overhead rate, thereby eliminating direct labour costs as a separate cost element;

3 retaining direct labour as a separate production cost, but allocating such costs over time.

With the reduced significance of work in progress under JIT, there is less need to carry out detailed allocations of overhead.

In conclusion, JIT allows the use of 'leaner' accounting systems. Furthermore, it accentuates the importance of real-time performance feedback rather than periodic accounting variance reports. Instantaneous feedback permits the immediate identification of problem production areas, allowing corresponding action before entire defective batches of material are produced and cost revenues are incurred. This feedback can be provided by the use of non-financial measures of performance which reflect items like elapsed time, distance moved and space occupied. The role of non-financial measures of performance is discussed further in Chapters 37 and 38.

## Summary

The first part of this chapter reviewed the use of activity-based costing as a means of increasing the accuracy of cost allocation for both manufacturing and service organizations. ABC assumes that it is activities which cause cost, not products. In certain circumstances ABC provides a better understanding of the cost of making a product or performing a service. More recently, the emphasis on ABC has switched from product costing to improving business management. JIT is essentially a management philosophy, not simply a toolbox of techniques. Its use has implications for management accounting systems both in view of the 'leaner systems' which are adopted and the role of non-financial measures of performance.

*References*   Hansen, D R and Mowen, M M (1995). *Cost Management*, South-Western College Publishing.

Keegan, D P and Eiler, R G (1994). 'Let's re-engineer cost accounting', *Management Accounting* (USA), August.

## Self-assessment questions

1 What is activity-based costing? How does it differ from traditional product costing approaches?

2 Describe four general steps in using ABC.

3 What is a cost driver and how is it used? Give some examples of cost drivers.

4 What characteristics of a company would generally indicate that ABC might improve product costing?

5 What is JIT manufacturing? In which ways does JIT manufacturing differ from traditional manufacturing?

6 How does JIT affect accounting systems?

## Problem

1   Redmires Limited had identified the following overhead activities, costs and activity drivers for the coming year:

| Activity | Expected cost £ | Activity driver | Activity capacity |
|---|---|---|---|
| Set-up costs | 60,000 | No of set-ups | 300 |
| Ordering costs | 45,000 | No of orders | 4,500 |
| Machine costs | 90,000 | Machine hours | 18,000 |
| Receiving | 25,000 | No of parts | 50,000 |

Assume for simplicity that each activity corresponds to a process. The following two jobs were completed during the year:

|  | Job 600 | Job 700 |
|---|---|---|
| Direct materials | £750 | £850 |
| Direct labour (50 hours per job) | £600 | £600 |
| Units completed | 100 | 50 |
| No of set-ups | 1 | 1 |
| No of orders | 4 | 2 |
| Machine hours | 20 | 30 |
| Parts used | 20 | 40 |

The company's normal activity is 4,000 direct labour hours.

*Required:*
(a)  Determine the unit cost for each job using direct labour hours to apply overhead.
(b)  Determine the unit cost for each job using the four cost drivers.
(c)  Which method produces the more accurate costs? Why?

# 2 Managerial decision making

# 28 Cost–volume-profit analysis

**Setting the scene**

The purpose of this study is twofold: (1) To understand the effect of cost in response to changing volume of activity, such as sales or production, and (2) To discern the resulting impact of cost on profitability. Thus the variables cost and volume can be manipulated appropriately and changes in profit determined before choosing a level of activity where operations are likely to result in optimal profit.

Cost–volume–profit (CVP) analysis is often called 'break-even' analysis, i.e. determining a level of activity at which an enterprise's total revenues equal total cost. The significance of breaking even stems from the fact that it is an important step forward towards survival and growth. But CVP analysis has much broader applications and its scope extends well beyond the determination of the break-even level of activity.

(Qureshi, 1978)

**Learning objectives**

After studying this chapter you should be able to:

1  Determine the number of units that must be sold to break even or to earn a target profit.

2  Use a cost–volume–profit chart and a profit–volume chart to determine the break-even point and the volume necessary to achieve a target profit.

3  Explain the impact of changing variables on CVP analysis.

4  Calculate and interpret the impact of sales mix considerations in CVP analysis.

5  Discuss the limitations of CVP analysis.


Cost–volume–profit (CVP) analysis is the systematic examination of the inter-relationships between selling prices, sales and production volume, costs, expenses and profits. It is a commonly used tool providing management with useful information for decision making. For example, CVP analysis may be used in setting selling prices, selecting the mix of products to sell, accepting special orders, choosing among alternative marketing strategies and analysing the effects of cost increases or decreases on the profitability of an enterprise.

# Cost analysis and changes in output

The response of cost to a variety of influences is invaluable to management decision making. As we saw in Chapter 26, some costs are constant, or fixed, in a given time-span, whereas other costs vary. Cost–volume–profit analysis focuses on the distinction between 'fixed' and 'variable' costs, with the former being defined for this purpose as the costs which do not change over a range of output, and the latter being those which change directly with output.

CVP analysis requires that the fixed and variable elements be segregated and calculated so that all costs may be divided into simply fixed and variable costs.

One of the most important uses of the distinction between fixed and variable cost lies in the analysis of these costs through different levels of production.

**Example 1** Duofold Ltd produces an article which it sells for £10. Fixed costs of production are £150,000 per year, and variable costs are £4 per unit. The present yearly volume of output is 40,000 units, but could be increased to 50,000.

| Unit sales | 40,000 | | 50,000 | |
|---|---|---|---|---|
| | Total | Unit | Total | Unit |
| | £ | £ | £ | £ |
| Revenue | 400,000 | 10.0 | 500,000 | 10.0 |
| Variable costs | 160,000 ; +4 | 4.0 | 200,000 | 4.0 |
| Contribution margin | 240,000 | 6.0 | 300,000 | 6.0 |
| Fixed costs | 150,000 | 3.8 | 150,000 | 3.0 |
| Net profit | 90,000 | 2.2 | 150,000 | 3.0 |

*Problem:* What will be the effect on total costs of the projected increase in output, and the impact of profit?

The analysis shows that total variable costs increase proportionally with output while unit variable costs are constant. Total fixed costs, however, remain constant at both levels of output so that unit fixed costs fall as output rises and vice versa. It is because unit fixed costs are falling that total unit costs are less for an output of 50,000 units than for one of 40,000 units.

If we assume that selling prices remain unaltered, cost savings themselves will lead to increased profitability. The contribution margin is an important concept in cost-profit analysis. As may be seen from the example above, the contribution margin is calculated by deducting the variable costs from revenue. It is the first stage in calculating the net profit and measures the profit which is available to cover fixed costs. Since fixed costs are incurred irrespective of sales, a firm will make a loss if the contribution margin is insufficient to cover fixed costs. At low levels of output the firm will make a loss because fixed costs are greater than the contribution margin. As output increases, so does the contribution margin which will ultimately equal and then exceed fixed costs. The relation between fixed cost and the contribution margin may be illustrated as in Figure 5.7. The critical point at which the contribution margin is equal to fixed costs is known as the break-even point which indicates that level of output (OA) at which the firm makes zero profits, that is, where total costs are equal to total revenues.

423

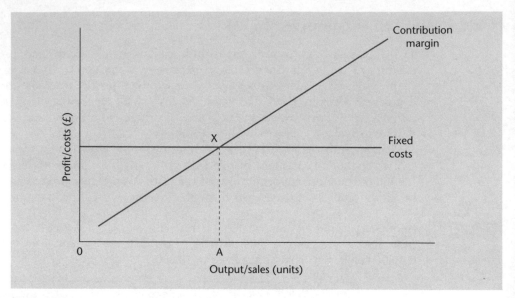

**Figure 5.7**

## Break-even analysis

Break-even analysis focuses on the measurement of the break-even point. Before we attempt any calculations, it is necessary to make certain assumptions about the behaviour of costs and revenues. Thus, we assume that costs and revenue patterns have been reliably determined and that they are linear over the range of output which is being analysed. These assumptions also imply that costs may be resolved without difficulty into fixed and variable costs; that fixed costs will remain constant; that variable costs will vary proportionally with volume of output; and that all other factors will remain constant, that is, that selling prices will remain unchanged, that the methods and the efficiency of production will not be altered and that volume is the only factor affecting costs. It is because these assumptions are difficult to maintain in a 'real life' situation that break-even analysis cannot pretend to be anything but a rough guide. Its real value to management lies in the fact that it highlights the interrelationships between the factors affecting profits, allowing management to make certain assumptions about these factors and seeing the likely effects of changes in these assumptions. Hence, break-even analysis is useful as a management decision model. For example, a small shop selling bathroom fittings, with five employee/owners had achieved sales of £80,000 in its first year of business. The company was making a loss at this sales figure. The sales value necessary to break even was calculated and found to be £160,000. The owners decided that this could not be achieved and closed the business. Had the break-even sales figure been known at the outset, their approach to the business would have been different.

# Calculating the break-even point

There are three methods commonly employed in solving break-even problems:

1 the equation method;
2 the contribution margin method;
3 the graph method.

## The equation method

The relationship between sales, variable and fixed costs and profits may be expressed as an equation:

**sales = variable costs + fixed costs + net profit**

**Example 2**  Take the values given in the previous example, that is, that the unit sale price is £10, variable costs are £4 per unit and fixed costs £150,000 per year.

*Problem 1:* How many units must be produced to break even?

*Analysis:* Let $x$ be the number of units required. Our equation will be:

$$£10x = £4x + £150,000 + £0$$

i.e. $£10x - £4x = £150,000 + £0$

so that

$$x = \frac{£150,000}{6}$$

$$= \underline{\underline{25,000 \text{ units}}}$$

*Problem 2:* Alternatively, the problem may be calculating the sales revenue required to break even.

*Analysis:* Since net profit is zero, our formula remains:

sales = variable costs + fixed costs

Let the unknown level of sales revenue be $x$, and knowing that variable costs are four-tenths of $x$, we can substitute:

$$x = \tfrac{4}{10}x + £150,000$$

$$x - \tfrac{4}{10}x = £150,000$$

$$\tfrac{6}{10}x = £150,000$$

$$\underline{x = £250,000}$$

The break-even sales revenue can be equally derived from the break-even volume of sales (25,000 units at £10 = £250,000), but the calculations are intended to show that the results can be calculated independently.

## The contribution margin method

This method makes use of the variable profit or contribution margin per unit of output which is required to cover fixed costs.

425

**Example 3**

*Problem 1:* On the basis that the unit sale price is £10, that the variable costs are £4 per unit and that fixed costs total £150,000 a year, calculate the break-even volume of sales.

*Analysis:* Let $x$ be the number of units required. We know that the unit contribution margin is the difference between unit sale price and unit variable costs. Our formula is:

$$x = \frac{\text{fixed costs} + \text{net profit}}{\text{unit contribution margin}}$$

$$x = \frac{£150,000 + 0}{(£10 - £4)}$$

$$= \frac{150,000}{6}$$

$$= \underline{\underline{25,000 \text{ units}}}$$

*Problem 2:* Using the same values, calculate the break-even sales revenue.

*Analysis:* In this case, we make use of the contribution margin ratio to calculate the sales revenue required to cover fixed costs. The contribution margin ratio is:

$$\frac{\text{unit contribution margin}}{\text{revenue per unit}}\ \%$$

Our formula may be expressed as follows:

$$x = \frac{\text{fixed costs} + \text{net profit}}{\text{contribution margin ratio}}$$

Substituting the given values we have:

$$x = \frac{150,000 + 0}{60\%}$$

$$= \underline{\underline{£250,000}}$$

Alternatively, the break-even revenue may be found from the following formula:

$$x = \frac{\text{fixed costs} + \text{net profit}}{1 - \dfrac{\text{total variable costs}}{\text{total sales revenue}}}$$

$$\frac{150,000}{1 - \dfrac{\dfrac{160,000}{400,000}}{}}$$

$$= \underline{\underline{£250,000}}$$

It is clear that both the equation method and the contribution margin method can be applied to profit planning by the substitution of the net profit figure, which for the purpose of our analysis of the break-even point we have taken to be zero.

## The graph method

This method involves using what is usually called a break-even chart. This description is not very satisfactory because it gives undue emphasis to the break-even point whereas other points on the graph are just as important.

A break-even chart is easy to compile, but the accuracy of the readings will depend on the accuracy with which the data are plotted. The output or sales in units may be drawn on the horizontal axis and the vertical axis is used to depict money values.

**Example 4**   Using the values given for the previous examples, the stages in compiling the break-even chart are as follows:

1  Using suitable graph paper, draw a horizontal axis to measure total output in units (50,000 units). Draw a vertical axis representing this output at its selling price of £10 per unit (£500,000).
2  Draw the variable-cost curve as a straight line from zero to £200,000 at 50,000 units of output (50,000 at £4).
3  Draw the fixed-cost curve parallel to the variable-cost curve but £150,000 higher, so that total costs including variable costs will be represented by the area below this curve.
4  Insert the total revenue curve from zero to £500,000 at 50,000 units.

Figure 5.8 vividly depicts the relationship between costs, revenues, volume of output and resultant profit. The area between the revenue curve and the variable cost curve represents the contribution to fixed costs and profit at each level of output. The point at which the revenue curve crosses the total cost curve is the break-even point. As output expands from zero, fixed costs are gradually recovered until the break-even point, and thereafter each unit of output contributes to profit.

The excess by which actual sales exceed break-even sales amounts to £250,000, so that sales could be reduced by £250,000 before losses start to be incurred. This excess is known as the margin of safety. The margin of safety ratio is the percentage by which sales revenue may fall before a loss is incurred and is expressed as follows:

$$\text{margin of safety ratio} = \frac{\text{margin of safety revenue}}{\text{actual sales}}$$

Hence, in the example given, the margin of safety ratio is:

$$\frac{£250,000}{£500,000}$$

i.e. 50%

Clearly, the higher the margin of safety ratio, the safer the firm's position.

An alternative way of constructing the break-even chart is as in Figure 5.9. The disadvantage of this form of presentation is that unlike Figure 5.8, it does not emphasize the importance of the contribution margin to fixed costs.

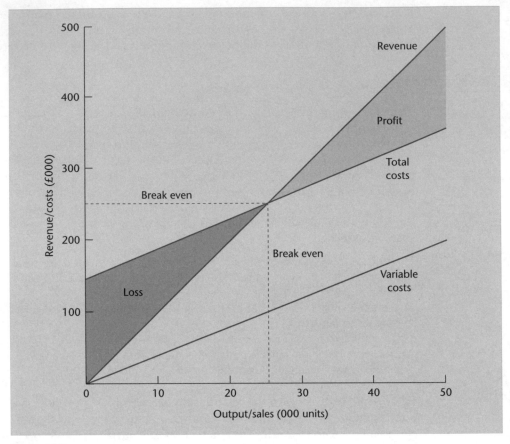

**Figure 5.8**

## The profit–volume chart

The profit–volume chart is a special type of break-even chart. It is concerned with analysing profit and loss at different levels of activity. As in the break-even chart, the horizontal axis is used to measure the volume of output or sales in units, but the vertical axis is employed to measure the profit or loss at any given level of output or sales.

Using the same information as above, Figure 5.10 shows the profit–volume chart. Only three items are needed to plot this chart – the fixed costs, which are £150,000, and which must be recovered before a profit is made, the break-even point, which represents sales of £250,000 necessary to cover fixed costs, and the profit at an assumed level of activity (which in this case is 50,000 units yielding a profit of £150,000).

The profit–volume chart (Figure 5.10) is simply the conventional break-even chart rearranged to show changes in profit or loss which occur through volume changes either of sales or of output. It is less detailed since it does not show separate curves for costs and revenues, but its virtue lies in the fact that it reduces any changes to two key elements – volume and profit. For this reason, the volume–profit chart is useful for illustrating the results of different management decisions.

In so far as the volume–profit chart focuses simply on the relationship between volume and profit, it allows for an extended analysis of this relationship. Thus, the slope of the curve DA indicates the contribution margin ratio, which may be measured by AB/BE or DC/CE – either calculation giving the same results in this case (60 per cent).

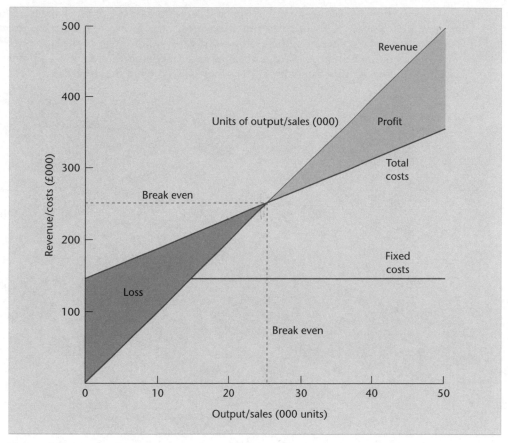

**Figure 5.9**

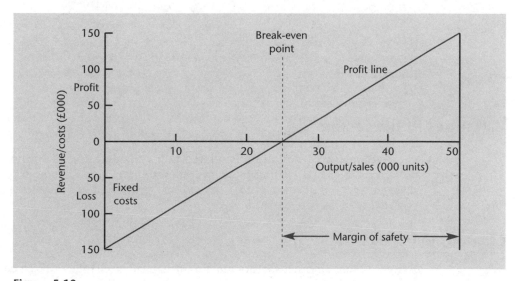

**Figure 5.10**

The slope of the curve DA also indicates the rate at which changes in volume assist in the recovery of fixed costs and affect profit: the greater the slope the greater will be the effect of changes in volume on profits. Equally, the steeper the slope of the profit curve the quicker will the margin of safety be eroded and the break-even point reached as the volume of output or sales falls, as may be seen from the three cases in Figure 5.11.

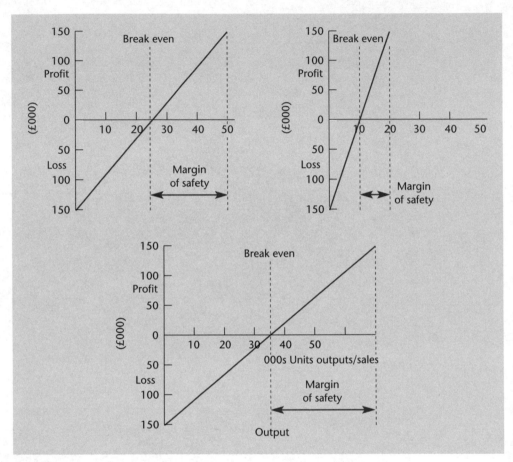

**Figure 5.11**

# Changes in the factors

Cost–volume–profit analysis is related to a consideration of four factors – fixed costs, variable costs, selling price and sales volume. Any change in one or more of these factors will affect profits. Cost–volume–profit analysis enables management to consider the effects of these changes.

## Changes in fixed costs

Assuming that all other factors remain unchanged, a change in fixed costs will affect only the break-even point.

**Example 5** The consequential effect of an increase of £15,000 in head office costs on the break-even level is as follows:

|  | Original | After increase in fixed costs |
|---|---|---|
|  | £ | £ |
| Sales | 500,000 | 500,000 |
| Variable costs | 200,000 | 200,000 |
| Contribution margin | 300,000 | 300,000 |
| Fixed costs | 150,000 | 165,000 |
| Net profit | 150,000 | 135,000 |
| Contribution margin ratio | 60% | 60% |

The new break-even point is:

$$\frac{\text{Fixed costs}}{\text{Unit contribution margin}} = \frac{165,000}{£6} = 27,500 \text{ units}$$

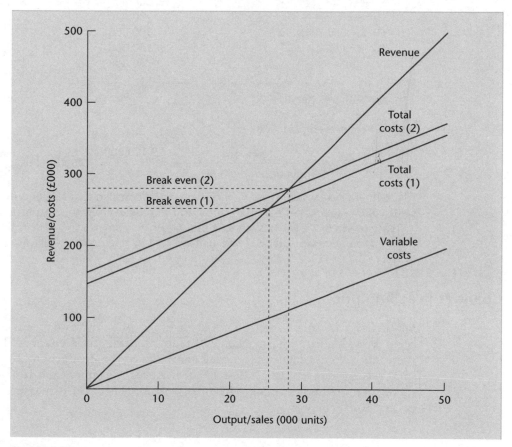

**Figure 5.12**

Hence, a 10 per cent increase in fixed costs has resulted in a 10 per cent increase in the sales volume (and sales revenue) required to break even from 25,000 units (£250,000) to 27,500 units (£275,000). Thus, additional sales of 2,500 units at £10 a unit are required to cover an increase of £15,000 in fixed costs. It should be noted that as the contribution margin ratio has remained constant, the change in fixed costs is the only factor affecting profit. The change may be illustrated as in Figure 5.12.

## Changes in variable costs

A change in variable costs will have the immediate effect of changing the contribution margin ratio, and consequently the break-even point.

**Example 6**  It is decided to improve the quality of a product by incorporating more expensive materials. As a result, variable costs are increased by 10 per cent, and the consequential effects on the break-even level are as follows:

|  | Original | After increase in variable costs |
|---|---|---|
|  | £ | £ |
| Sales | 500,000 | 500,000 |
| Variable costs | 200,000 | 220,000 |
| Contribution margin | 300,000 | 280,000 |
| Fixed costs | 150,000 | 150,000 |
| Net profit | 150,000 | 130,000 |
| Contribution margin ratio | 60% | 56% |

The new break-even point will be:

$$\frac{\text{fixed costs}}{\text{contribution margin per unit}} = \frac{£150,000}{5.6} = 26,786 \text{ units.}$$

Note that whereas a 10 per cent increase in fixed costs led to a 10 per cent increase in the sales volume (and sales revenue) required to break even in this instance, a 10 per cent increase in variable costs has led to a proportionately smaller increase in the sales volume required to break even, that is, 1,786 units or 7.14 per cent. We may illustrate the change as in Figure 5.13.

## Changes in selling price

Successful profit planning through changes in selling prices depends upon management knowing how the market will react to these price changes. If the price is reduced, will customers buy greater quantities of the product so as to increase the total revenue derived from sales? In other words, it is important to know the effect upon total revenue of changes in selling prices. This effect is measured through the price elasticity of demand.

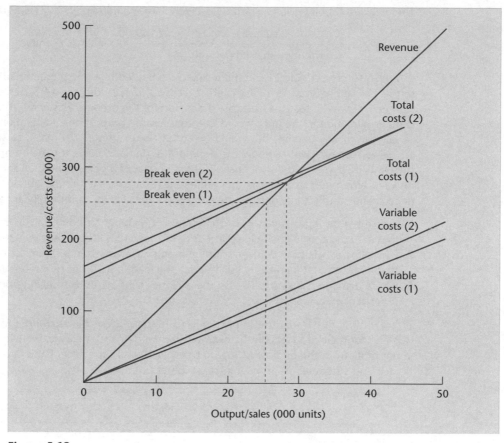

**Figure 5.13**

**Example 7**    Let us assume that a 10 per cent increase in selling price will lead to a 10 per cent reduction in the volume of sales. Assuming all other factors remain constant, the result of the price change will be as follows:

|  | Original | After increase in variable costs | |
|---|---|---|---|
| Sales in units | 50,000 | 45,000 | |
| Sales revenue | £500,000 | £495,000 | (45,000 @ £11) |
| Variable costs | 200,000 | 180,000 | (45,000 @ £4) |
| Contribution margin | 300,000 | 315,000 | |
| Fixed costs | 150,000 | 150,000 | |
| Net profit | 150,000 | 165,000 | |
| | | | |
| Contribution margin ratio | 60% | 63.6% | |

The break-even point will, as a result, be lowered from 25,000 units to 21,429 units as follows:

$$\frac{\text{fixed costs}}{\text{contribution margin per unit}} = \frac{£150,000}{£7} = 21,429 \text{ units}$$

Thus, a 10 per cent increase in the selling price has led to a much greater adjustment in the sales volume required to break even, that is, 3,571/25,000 or 14.3 per cent. We have assumed, however, that the elasticity of demand for the product was unity, that is, that a percentage alteration in the price would lead to the same proportionate alteration in the volume of sales. In most situations this would be an unreal assumption to make, so that it becomes crucial to management to know the slope of the demand curve for the commodity, that is, the elasticity of demand if their analysis of the impact of a price change on the net profit is to be valid. We may compare the three different results that would be obtained by the same price change under three different demand conditions for the commodity as follows:

1  where the demand is *elastic*, i.e. elasticity is greater than unity: in this case we assume that a 10 per cent increase in selling price will lead to a 20 per cent reduction in sales;
2  where the elasticity of demand is unity: in this case we assume, as in the example above, that a 10 per cent increase in selling price will lead to a 10 per cent reduction in sales;
3  where demand is inelastic: we assume a 10 per cent increase in selling price will lead to a 5 per cent reduction in sales.

This example illustrates the importance to management of knowing the nature of the demand for their products. In the example, where demand is elastic, we witness a sharp fall in net profit from the original £150,000 to £130,000. On the other hand, a unitary or inelastic demand schedule results in an increase in net profit.

|  | Elastic | Unity | Inelastic |
|---|---|---|---|
| Sales units | 40,000 | 45,000 | 47,500 |
| Sales revenue (£11) | £440,000 | £495,000 | £522,500 |
| Variable costs (£4) | 160,000 | 180,000 | 190,000 |
| Contribution margin | 280,000 | 315,000 | 332,500 |
| Fixed costs | 150,000 | 150,000 | 150,000 |
| Net profit | £130,000 | £165,000 | £182,500 |

# The sales mix

We mentioned at the beginning of this chapter that CVP analysis is important to short-term profit planning, and that it is helpful also to the solution of other types of managerial problems. One such problem is that of selecting the best sales mix. So far in our discussion, we have assumed that the firm had only one product so that profit planning involved a consideration of only four factors, that is, fixed and variable costs, selling price and sales volume. Most firms, however, either produce or sell more than one product and management has to decide in what combination these products ought to be made or sold. It may be possible, for example, that by altering the existing sales mix by selling proportionately more of the product which has the highest contribution margin, the overall contribution margin and the break-even point may be improved.

**Example 8**  Assume that Maximix Ltd has data concerning the three products which it markets as follows:

| Product | A | B | C | Total |
|---|---|---|---|---|
| | £ | £ | £ | £ |
| Sales | 100,000 | 100,000 | 50,000 | 250,000 |
| Variable costs | 50,000 | 30,000 | 20,000 | 100,000 |
| Contribution margin | 50,000 | 70,000 | 30,000 | 150,000 |
| Fixed costs | | | | 150,000 |
| Net profit | | | | Nil |
| | | | | |
| Contribution margin ratio | 50% | 70% | 60% | 60% |

If the firm could switch its sales so as to sell more of product B, which has a higher contribution margin ratio than the other two, it would succeed in improving its profitability. At the present moment, the firm is just breaking even. Let us assume that it maintains the present total sales of £250,000, but that the sales mix is altered as shown below:

| Product | A | B | C | Total |
|---|---|---|---|---|
| | £ | £ | £ | £ |
| Sales | 50,000 | 175,000 | 25,000 | 250,000 |
| Variable costs | 25,000 | 52,500 | 10,000 | 87,500 |
| Contribution margin | 25,000 | 122,500 | 15,000 | 162,500 |
| Fixed costs | | | | 150,000 |
| Net profit | | | | 12,500 |
| | | | | |
| Contribution margin ratio | 50% | 70% | 60% | 65% |

Hence the new product mix has raised the contribution margin ratio by 5 per cent, leading to a profit of £12,500 and a lowering of the break-even point from £250,000 to £230,769 as follows:

$$\frac{\text{Fixed costs}}{\text{Contribution margin ratio}} = \frac{£150,000}{65\%} = £230,769$$

The effect of the change in the product mix may be depicted graphically as in Figure 5.14.

## Cost–volume–profit analysis: some limitations

CVP analysis, though it is a very useful tool for decision making, is based upon certain assumptions which can rarely be completely realized in practice. Hence the fragility of these assumptions places limits on the reliability of CVP analysis as a tool in decision making. For example, it is assumed that fixed costs are constant, and that both the variable cost and the revenue curves are linear over the relevant volume of output. It is also assumed that volume is the only factor affecting costs, and that the price both of cost factors and of the product produced or sold remains unaffected by changes in the volume of output.

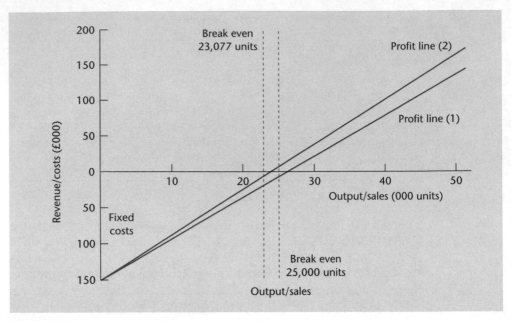

**Figure 5.14**

All these assumptions may be challenged. Fixed costs may not remain constant over the entire output range considered in the analysis, that being particularly true if the volume range considered is fairly extensive. Fixed costs may indeed be constant over a band of output, but may then rise sharply and remain constant for another stage, as shown in Figure 5.15.

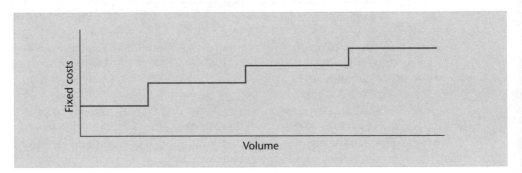

**Figure 5.15**

Equally doubtful is the assumption that the variable cost curve is linear so that variable costs change in direct proportion to changes in volume. As demand for input factors increase so will their price, with the effect that the variable-cost curve is likely to increase proportionately faster as volume of output expands.

To overcome these limitations, and to retain the usefulness of CVP analysis, it is necessary to limit the volume range to be examined so that the behaviour of both fixed and variable costs may be more accurately determined. The basic assumption that the cost–volume relationship is a linear relationship is realistic only over narrow ranges of output which is called the relevant range.

As regards the revenue curve, to increase sales it may be necessary to reduce price, so that a straight line is not an accurate portrayal of the behaviour of sales. Therefore, computations are often needed at several price levels – several total-revenue curves are needed instead of just one.

Finally, the break-even chart presents an extremely simplified picture of cost–revenue–volume relationships. Each of these three is subject to outside influences as well as to the influence of the other two. Above all, the break-even analysis should be viewed as a guide to decision making, not a substitute for judgement and common sense.

Despite its limitations, the real usefulness of CVP is that it enriches the understanding of the relationship between costs, volume and prices as factors affecting profit, enabling management to make assumptions which will assist the decision-making process in the short-run planning period.

## Long-term variable costs

In the previous chapter we saw that activity-based costing moves away from the notions of short-term fixed and variable costs and focuses on the variability of costs in the longer term. It is appropriate to regard fixed costs as long-term variable costs because fixed costs are not fixed forever. Companies can, over the long term, through managerial decisions lay off supervisors and sell plant and equipment items. Where companies have become less focused on production and sales volumes as cost drivers, they will begin to recognize that 'fixed costs' exist only under a short-term reporting period perspective.

## Summary

In the short run, the firm's output is fixed, so that its freedom of action is limited in this respect. Given this condition, short-range decision making considers the most desirable action to take to achieve a planned profit. Cost–volume–profit analysis (CVP) has an important role to play in short-run decision making by providing an insight into the relationships between costs, volume of output, revenue and profit. In particular, CVP analysis highlights the significance of the distinction between fixed and variable costs and the behaviour of these two types of costs through changes in the volume of output.

CVP analysis makes an important contribution to short-run decision making by providing an understanding of the conditions required to break even. It does not assist in the discovery of the conditions required to maximize profits, in sharp contrast to economic theory which pays particular attention to this aspect of profit planning. Its advantage to management is that it is a method which is operationally useful. Moreover, it deals with the most important consideration – the avoidance of losses. In this sense, CVP analysis reflects the assumption of risk analysis that decision makers are risk-averse.

CVP analysis has limitations as a result of the assumptions that it incorporates. Many of these assumptions may be challenged, for example, the linearity of the behaviour of costs and revenues over a range of output. Although some of the criticism of CVP analysis may be partially refuted, its real usefulness lies in the manner in which it enriches the understanding of the relationship between cost, volume of output and revenue for decision-making purposes in the short run, thereby assisting management in the making of short-run decisions.

Reference    Qureshi, M A (1978). *Analysing Business Strategy: The Uses of Cost–Volume–Profit Analysis*, CIMA.

## Self-assessment questions

1 Explain what is meant by CVP analysis.

2 Describe how CVP analysis is used in profit planning.

3 What is the significance of the break-even point?

4 Describe various ways in which the break-even point may be calculated.

5 What is a profit–volume chart?

6 List a number of possible ways in which short-term profitability may be improved.

7 What difficulties are implied in using CVP analysis for short-term decision making?

## Problems  (* indicates that a solution is to be found in the Lecturer's Guide)

1    The Carbon Ink Company's profit statement for the preceding year is presented below. Except as noted, the cost and sales relationship for the coming year is expected to follow the same pattern as in the preceding year.

|  | £ |
| --- | --- |
| Sales (2,000,000 bottles at £0.25) | 500,000 |
| Variable costs | 300,000 |
| Fixed costs | 100,000 |
| Total costs | 400,000 |
| Profit | 100,000 |

*Required:*
(a)  What is the break-even point in sales value and units?
(b)  An extension to the factory will add £50,000 to the fixed costs and increase production capacity by 60 per cent. How many bottles would have to be sold after the extension to break even?
(c)  The management of the company feels that it should earn at least £10,000 on the new investment. What sales volume is required to enable the company to maintain existing profits and earn the minimum required on the new investment?
(d)  If the factory operates at full capacity after extension, what profit will be earned?
(e)  What are the weaknesses in the use of break-even analysis?

2*   An accountant and an economist were having an argument. The economist accused the accountant of using a naive, over-simplified model of cost–volume–profit relationships by assuming linear patterns in variable costs. Since costs do not behave in this simplistic way, the accountant, argued the economist, should be more realistic in his assumptions.

The accountant countered by saying that the economist was just as bad, if not worse, because most economic models ignore variations in fixed costs. Although the accountant agreed that in the long run all costs are variable, a firm had to make decisions in the short run in order to survive. And, argued the accountant, in the short run some costs are definitely fixed.

The economist was becoming somewhat agitated and accused the accountant of not using a dynamic analysis for solving business problems. The economist claimed, for example, that the static nature of cost–volume–profit analysis often produced misleading information. The accountant thought this a case of the pot calling the kettle black, and accused the economist of using unrealistic models which never exist in practice.

*Required:*
Both the accountant and the economist turn to you for support; what would be your reply? Use the case below to illustrate your answer.

The Malplaquet Company cans fresh orange juice. The company's budget at 80 per cent capacity for 20X0 was as follows:

|  | £ |
|---|---|
| Sales | 250,000 |
| Cost of oranges and other materials used | 60,000 |
| Cost of cans | 30,000 |
| Direct labour | 60,000 |
| Manufacturing expenses: | |
| Fixed | 20,000 |
| Variable | 30,000 |
| Administration, selling and other indirect expenses: | |
| Fixed | 10,800 |
| Variable | 8,000 |

The directors of the company anticipate the following in costs during 20X1:

| | |
|---|---|
| Price of oranges and other materials used | 5% increase |
| Price of cans | No change |
| Rates for direct labour | 10% increase |
| Manufacturing expenses: fixed | £800 decrease |
| Administration, selling and other indirect expenses: | |
| Fixed | No change |

Manufacturing variable expenses will maintain the same ratio to wages paid, and administration, selling and other indirect variable expenses will vary only with quantity sold.

In 20X1 sales quantity and selling price are expected to remain constant.

3    The Brown Fox motel is owned and run by Billy Fisher. Fisher, a professional footballer, could earn £24,000 per annum as a full-time player, but prefers to play on a part-time basis (for £12,000) and run the motel.

The motel has 60 available rooms which are charged out at £30 per day. The variable costs of operation of the motel amount to £8 per room rental per day. This includes cleaning, laundry, coffee, tea, etc.

The fixed costs per annum are:

| | |
|---|---|
| Reception/office staff | £65,000 |
| Repairs/maintenance | £39,000 |
| Depreciation | £75,000 |
| Miscellaneous | £23,600 |

439

Fisher complains that business is not as good from October to March as it is from April to September, as illustrated below:

| | April–<br>September | October–<br>March |
|---|---|---|
| Potential rentals | | |
| (60 × 26 × 7) | 10,920 | 10,920 |
| Rooms rented | 8,736 | 6,552 |

*Required:*
(a) Prepare a contribution break-even chart of the data for each six-month period, illustrating the margin of safety.
(b) Calculate the number of rooms per period which must be rented in order to break even.
(c) Calculate the number of rooms which would have to be rented to break even if the room charges were reduced from £30 to £25 from October to March.
(d) Assuming that it is impossible to cover the fixed costs during November and February, regardless of the price per room, should the motel be closed during these months? What would be the financial and non-financial effects of the closure?
(e) What are the limitations of using break-even analysis in short-term decision making? Illustrate by reference to the Brown Fox motel.

4* The Bolton Haulage company is a small to medium-sized removals firm with ten large removal vans. Following the deregulation of passenger transport, the owner of the business proposes to diversify into passenger transport using eight mini buses. The diversification will lead to greater use of the servicing facilities and the pool of drivers employed.

It is proposed to operate minibuses on four existing routes which were bid for by the company, and have now been awarded by the Passenger Transport Authority. The mini-buses will also be available for private hire.

The company currently only prepares six-monthly accounts. The owner believes this is insufficient to run the proposed business.

The current expense headings (taken from the financial accounts) are: drivers' wages; fuel and oil; repairs and maintenance; servicing (three months or 20,000 miles); motor tax; insurance; mechanics' wages; depreciation of vehicles; rent and rates; electricity; and tyres.

A manager is currently responsible for running the removals business, and a transport manager is to be appointed to run the minibus side of the business. In addition to these staff, there is the owner of the business, and a general staff to cash-up, provide refreshments, clean the buses, etc. Their offices are on the same site as the garage.

*Required:*
(a) Design a draft operating cost statement to facilitate control of the removal vans and the minibuses. Justify your format and classification of expenses and the purpose and objectives of reporting such information.
(b) Design a draft management accounting information statement which will assist management in assessing the efficiency and effectiveness of both segments of the business.
(c) How will the statement meet the twin objectives of measuring efficiency and effectiveness?

# CHAPTER

# 29 Marginal costing

## Setting the scene

One of the most progressive phases in the history of management accountancy – in the sense of distinguishing it from other sectors of the profession – was that in which marginal costing came to the fore.

It was, and remains, perfectly reasonable in financial accounts to use techniques of apportionment and absorption, so as to arrive at figures suitable for valuing stocks, and analysing profits by product.

What the marginal costers pointed out, however, was that such an approach did not reflect how profits are actually earned. In the real world, products make contributions (sales minus variable costs) to a pool from which fixed costs are defrayed. If, in aggregate, contribution exceeds fixed costs, the company makes a profit; if not, it makes a loss.

(Allen, 1993)

## Learning objectives

After studying this chapter you should be able to:

1 Explain the differences between marginal and absorption costing.

2 Prepare the profit statements based on a marginal costing approach.

3 Discuss the advantages of a marginal costing approach over absorption costing.

Marginal costing is an invaluable management accounting tool used to provide management with information about cost, volume and profit relationships in a form that is easy to understand. The key advantage of marginal costing is that it facilitates decision making, cost management and profit planning. Like the cost–volume–profit relationships considered in the previous chapter, marginal costing stresses the difference between fixed and marginal manufacturing costs. This distinction is critical for many decision and control models that are used in management accounting. However, for financial reporting to external users the conventional method of product costing based on full or absorption costing is required under generally accepted accounting principles.

## e case for marginal costing for stock valuation

As we saw in Part 2, periodic profit measurement and the matching principle constitute the core of financial accounting. According to SSAP 2 'Disclosure of Accounting Policies', 'revenues and costs are matched with one another so far as their relationship can be established or justifiably assumed'.

## Different methods of matching

The logic behind the matching principle springs from a desire to provide a rule which will secure uniformity in the preparation of profit and loss accounts. Investors require uniformity in accounting practices if they are to be able to evaluate the performance of one firm against another. The development of accounting standards represents an attempt at ensuring these comparisons can be made. However, no set formula has been prescribed for valuing stock, particularly work-in-progress and finished goods, so that there is a great deal of flexibility in the valuation of stocks. Terms such as 'at cost or net realizable value' and 'should include a proportion of factory overhead' are loose enough to allow significant variations in companies' methods. As far as the matching principle is concerned the problem is to develop suitable methods for matching costs to revenues. Two such methods have been developed: product costing and period costing.

## Product costing

Accountants long ago recognized the product itself as a convenient vehicle for matching costs with revenues. Product costing involves attaching all costs, whether direct or overhead costs, to the product. In measuring the cost of goods produced and sold to be matched against revenues from sales, product costing requires the inclusion of those manufacturing costs which are incurred irrespective of production. Thus, costs such as rent, insurance and rates which are incurred on a time basis rather than on the rate of production are recovered against the units produced.

The proponents of product costing as the only method of matching costs to revenues argue that all manufacturing costs are product costs, and that there is no such thing as a period cost because 'ideally all costs incurred should be viewed as absolutely clinging to definite items of goods sold or services rendered. . . . The ideal is to match costs incurred with the efforts attributable to or significantly related to such costs' (Paton and Littleton, 1940). They argue, therefore, that manufacturing costs are incurred solely to make possible the creation of a product.

## Period costing

Period costing recognizes that certain costs are incurred on a time basis, and that the benefit derived from these costs is not affected by the actual level of production during a period of time. Since rent, insurance and salaries are items which are incurred on a time basis, their deteriorating effect on a firm's cash resources are not halted by the lack of revenue.

Period costing is a method of costing which conflicts with the traditional view of costing expressed by product costing, and has given rise to the marginal costing controversy. The issue between the two schools of thought revolves round the question of whether fixed manufacturing costs, that is those costs incurred irrespective of production, should be charged as the costs of the product or charged against the revenue of the period. According to the supporters of product costing, who employ absorption or full costing, all manufacturing costs should be absorbed by the product. Marginal costing assigns only the marginal costs, that is the costs which vary with the level of production, to the products, and fixed manufacturing costs are written off each year as period costs.

One advantage of marginal costing over absorption costing which is often advanced by its advocates is its superiority for management decision making. Because the distinction between fixed and marginal costs is 'built into' the accounting system, it assists profit planning, product pricing and control. However, the controversy which surrounds marginal costing is whether or not it should be used for external reporting. The advocates of absorption costing argue that figures prepared on a marginal costing basis for the use of management should be adjusted to an absorption costing basis before they are released to external users.

Both management and investors are concerned primarily with the future outcome of present decisions. Accountants who advocate the use of absorption costing for external financial statements deprive investors of a useful analytical device and make the task of interpreting the results more difficult.

Marginal costing emphasizes the behaviour of fixed and variable costs, which is of utmost importance to investors. Marginal costing helps to predict cash flows in relation to volume changes; the isolation of fixed costs in the profit statement permits more accurate forecasts of claims on cash in meeting current outlays on fixed expenses. Marginal costing also helps to correlate fluctuations in cash flows with fluctuations in sales volume.

We argued earlier that management should not receive the credit for increasing the net worth of business before the critical event has occurred, and we conceded that in almost every case, the sale was the critical event. Since profit should vary with a company's performance (which really means accomplishing the critical event) where profit is related to sales, it is logical that there should be a direct relationship between the two. Marginal costing should therefore be used in these cases. Absorption costing, being based on the product concept, does not provide this relationship between profit and sales, because under this method, profit variation is partly related to production.

Marginal costing also permits more accurate profit forecasts because net profit will have a direct relationship with sales, instead of confusing the picture with the impact of the two activities of producing and selling.

## The treatment of overheads

SSAP 9 'Stocks and Long-Term Contracts' restated the traditional accounting view that the aim should be to match costs and revenues 'in the year in which revenue arises rather than the year in which cost is incurred', cost being defined for this purpose as including 'all related overheads, even though some of these may accrue on a time basis'.

## Absorption and marginal costing compared

**Example 1**  Let us assume the following basic data:

| | |
|---|---|
| Total sales and production over 4 years (500 units per year) | 2,000 units |
| Direct material costs per unit | £1 |
| Direct labour costs per unit | £1 |
| Marginal overhead costs per unit | £0.5 |
| Fixed overhead costs | £1,000 p.a. |
| Sales price per unit | £6 |

Let us further assume that the volume of sales and of production are constant in time. The volume of production, sales and the level of stocks in units are as follows:

| Year | 1 | 2 | 3 | 4 | Total |
|---|---|---|---|---|---|
| Opening stock (units) | 40 | 40 | 40 | 40 | 40 |
| Production (units) | 500 | 500 | 500 | 500 | 2,000 |
| Sales (units) | 500 | 500 | 500 | 500 | 2,000 |
| Closing stock (units) | 40 | 40 | 40 | 40 | 40 |

The results under the two forms of costing would appear as follows:

| Year | 1 | 2 | 3 | 4 | Total |
|---|---|---|---|---|---|
| **Marginal costing** | £ | £ | £ | £ | £ |
| Sales | 3,000 | 3,000 | 3,000 | 3,000 | 12,000 |
| Cost of goods produced | 1,250 | 1,250 | 1,250 | 1,250 | 5,000 |
| *Add:* Opening stock | 100 | 100 | 100 | 100 | 100 |
| Available for sale | 1,350 | 1,350 | 1,350 | 1,350 | 5,100 |
| *Less:* Closing stock | 100 | 100 | 100 | 100 | 100 |
| Cost of goods sold | 1,250 | 1,250 | 1,250 | 1,250 | 5,000 |
| Contribution margin | 1,750 | 1,750 | 1,750 | 1,750 | 7,000 |
| Fixed overheads | 1,000 | 1,000 | 1,000 | 1,000 | 4,000 |
| Net profit | 750 | 750 | 750 | 750 | 3,000 |
| | | | | | |
| **Absorption costing** | | | | | |
| Sales | 3,000 | 3,000 | 3,000 | 3,000 | 12,000 |
| Cost of goods produced | 2,250 | 2,250 | 2,250 | 2,250 | 9,000 |
| *Add:* Opening stock | 180 | 180 | 180 | 180 | 180 |
| Available for sale | 2,430 | 2,430 | 2,430 | 2,430 | 9,180 |
| *Less:* Closing stock | 180 | 180 | 180 | 180 | 180 |
| Cost of goods sold | 2,250 | 2,250 | 2,250 | 2,250 | 9,000 |
| Net profit | 750 | 750 | 750 | 750 | 3,000 |

The above example illustrates the effects on profits of using absorption and marginal costing methods for a firm in which everything stayed exactly the same in four consecutive years. Therefore, sales and levels of production are constant in each period and both opening and closing stocks remain unchanged. Under these conditions profit figures for each year remain the same under both methods of calculating profit.

In reality, the effect on production of shortages of materials, or the effect on sales of credit squeezes and changes in indirect taxation, will distort the relationship between sales and production and stock levels act as buffers. Stock levels, therefore, are not stable; they are in fact very volatile. Moreover, modern methods of production require a constant rate of production, not only to maintain the efficiency of operations but also to prevent layoffs and so assist in the preservation of good industrial relations. Flexible stock level standards are normally established for the purpose of planning for a reasonably uniform level of production.

We shall now examine the different results obtained under marginal and absorption costing under the following circumstances:

1  where sales fluctuate but production remains constant;
2  where sales are constant but production fluctuates.

# Results where sales fluctuate but production is constant

As soon as the rate of sales begins to differ from the rate of production the use of different methods of allocating overheads to costs of production starts to affect profit calculations.

**Example 2**  Let us take the figures given in the earlier example, but keeping the level of production constant against varying levels of sales as follows:

| Year | 1 | 2 | 3 | 4 | Total |
|---|---|---|---|---|---|
| Opening stock (units) | 40 | 140 | 340 | 240 | 40 |
| Production (units) | 500 | 500 | 500 | 500 | 2,000 |
| Sales (units) | 400 | 300 | 600 | 700 | 2,000 |
| Closing stock (units) | 140 | 340 | 240 | 40 | 40 |

The results under the two methods of costing would appear as follows:

| Year | 1 | 2 | 3 | 4 | Total |
|---|---|---|---|---|---|
| **Marginal costing** | £ | £ | £ | £ | £ |
| Sales | 2,400 | 1,800 | 3,600 | 4,200 | 12,000 |
| Cost of goods produced | 1,250 | 1,250 | 1,250 | 1,250 | 5,000 |
| *Add:* Opening stock | 100 | 350 | 850 | 600 | 100 |
| Available for sale | 1,350 | 1,600 | 2,100 | 1,850 | 5,100 |
| *Less:* Closing stock | 350 | 850 | 600 | 100 | 100 |
| Cost of goods sold | 1,000 | 750 | 1,500 | 1,750 | 5,000 |
| Contribution margin | 1,400 | 1,050 | 2,100 | 2,450 | 7,000 |
| Fixed overheads | 1,000 | 1,000 | 1,000 | 1,000 | 4,000 |
| Net profit | 400 | 50 | 1,100 | 1,450 | 3,000 |
| | | | | | |
| **Absorption costing** | | | | | |
| Sales | 2,400 | 1,800 | 3,600 | 4,200 | 12,000 |
| Cost of goods produced | 2,250 | 2,250 | 2,250 | 2,250 | 9,000 |
| *Add:* Opening stock | 180 | 630 | 1,530 | 1,080 | 180 |
| Available for sale | 2,430 | 2,880 | 3,780 | 3,330 | 9,180 |
| *Less:* Closing stock | 630 | 1,530 | 1,080 | 180 | 180 |
| Cost of goods sold | 1,800 | 1,350 | 2,700 | 3,150 | 9,000 |
| Net profit | 600 | 450 | 900 | 1,050 | 3,000 |

It becomes evident why there is a controversy between the two schools of thought as regards the measurement of profit for the purpose of financial reporting for under the circumstances outlined above wide differences appear in net profit figures. These differences may be illustrated graphically in Figure 5.16, and it may be seen that the profit profile fluctuates more widely when overheads are excluded, as they are under marginal costing, than when they are included as under absorption costing.

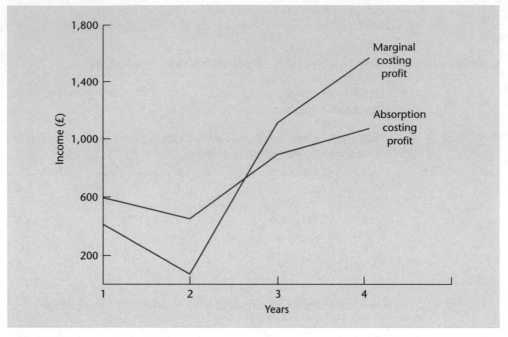

**Figure 5.16**

## Results where sales are constant but production fluctuates

**Example 3**    Let us now keep the figures for sales constant, and compare results under the two methods of costing when levels of production vary.

| Year | 1 | 2 | 3 | 4 | Total |
|---|---|---|---|---|---|
| Opening stock (units) | 40 | 140 | 340 | 240 | 40 |
| Production (units) | 600 | 700 | 400 | 300 | 2,000 |
| Sales (units) | 500 | 500 | 500 | 500 | 2,000 |
| Closing stock (units) | 140 | 340 | 240 | 40 | 40 |

The results under the two methods would be calculated as follows:

| Year | 1 | 2 | 3 | 4 | Total |
|---|---|---|---|---|---|
| **Marginal costing** | £ | £ | £ | £ | £ |
| Sales | 3,000 | 3,000 | 3,000 | 3,000 | 12,000 |
| Cost of goods produced | 1,500 | 1,750 | 1,000 | 750 | 5,000 |
| *Add:* Opening stock | 100 | 350 | 850 | 600 | 100 |
| Available for sale | 1,600 | 2,100 | 1,850 | 1,350 | 5,100 |
| *Less:* Closing stock | 350 | 850 | 600 | 100 | 100 |
| Cost of goods sold | 1,250 | 1,250 | 1,250 | 1,250 | 5,000 |
| Contribution margin | 1,750 | 1,750 | 1,750 | 1,750 | 7,000 |
| Fixed overheads | 1,000 | 1,000 | 1,000 | 1,000 | 4,000 |
| Net profit | 750 | 750 | 750 | 750 | 3,000 |

| Year | 1 | 2 | 3 | 4 | Tot. |
|---|---|---|---|---|---|
| **Absorption costing** | £ | £ | £ | £ | £ |
| Sales | 3,000 | 3,000 | 3,000 | 3,000 | 12,000 |
| Cost of goods produced | 2,700 | 3,150 | 1,800 | 1,350 | 9,000 |
| *Add:* Opening stock | 180 | 630 | 1,530 | 1,080 | 180 |
| Available for sale | 2,880 | 3,780 | 3,330 | 2,430 | 9,180 |
| *Less:* Closing stock | 630 | 1,530 | 1,080 | 180 | 180 |
| Cost of goods sold | 2,250 | 2,250 | 2,250 | 2,250 | 9,000 |
| Over- (or under-) absorbed overhead | 200 | 400 | (200) | (400) | – |
| Total cost of goods sold | 2,050 | 1,850 | 2,450 | 2,650 | 9,000 |
| Net profit | 950 | 1,150 | 550 | 350 | 3,000 |

In order to simplify the calculations under the absorption costing method we have assumed a normal level of production of 500 units a year. Since total fixed cost is £1,000 per year, a recovery rate of £2 per unit is used. We have assumed, also, that selling prices and costs remain unchanged over the four years. By using a normal overhead rate for recovering fixed overhead, the value of opening and closing stock per unit remains constant at £4.50 (£2.50 marginal + £2 fixed). In the first two years the normal output level is exceeded by 100 and 200 units respectively, with shortfalls in the last two years. The cost of goods sold is adjusted by the over- or under-recovery of fixed overhead resulting from those differences in deriving profit under absorption costing.

In this example, where sales have remained constant but production has fluctuated, we note that profit results obtained under marginal costing remain constant, but those based on absorption costing show wide fluctuation – £1,150 in year 2 and £350 in year 4.

## Marginal and absorption costing: their impact on profit summarized

The various examples we have considered enable the following generalizations to be made on the impact on profit of these two different methods of costing:

1 where sales and production levels are constant through time, profit is the same under the two methods;
2 where production remains constant but sales fluctuate, profit rises or falls with the level of sales, assuming that costs and prices remain constant, but the fluctuations in net profit figures are greater with marginal costing than with absorption costing;
3 where sales are constant but production fluctuates, marginal costing provides for constant profit, whereas under absorption costing, profit fluctuates;
4 where production exceeds sales, profit is higher under absorption costing than under marginal costing, since the absorption of fixed overheads into closing stock increases their value thereby reducing the cost of goods sold;
5 where sales exceed production, profit is higher under marginal costing. The fixed costs, which previously were part of stock values, are now charged against revenue under absorption costing. Therefore, under absorption costing the value of fixed costs charged against revenue is greater than that incurred for the period.

## The marginal costing controversy

We have seen in this chapter how profit may be affected by the manner in which costs are matched against revenues, so that the selection of one accounting procedure rather than another may, according to prevailing circumstances, affect the outcome of profit plans. Advocates of marginal costing base their case on the superiority of this method for planning and control purposes. It does so by clarifying the relationship between costs, volume and profit by identifying the contribution margin, that is the excess of sales revenue over marginal costs of production, linking profit to the level of sales which is the most critical event affecting a firm's financial performance.

The arguments in favour of providing marginal costing information for assisting decision making by external users are overwhelming. Some opponents of marginal costing assert that it is incorrect to suggest that information which is useful for management decision making is relevant for all business purposes, although it is difficult to accept the contention that marginal costing information may be helpful to management but not to external users, for both management and investors are faced with the same task, that is, decision making.

Some accountants have been concerned by the fluctuations which are imported in profit measurement by the exclusion of fixed costs, and to secure a certain stability in profit, advocate the retention of the absorption costing method of valuing stocks. A further controversy arises from the effects of marginal costing on the balance sheet of omitting fixed factory overheads from stock values. The real argument on this issue is whether the balance sheet should show stocks at actual cost or at a value to the current period of the resources transferred from the period just ended. Marginal costing is said to have a 'profit and loss account emphasis', whereas absorption costing is said to have a 'balance sheet emphasis'.

The absorption costing method allows overheads to be carried into the next period, thus enabling a manipulation of the profit figure. By carrying forward overheads, profits are increased. Moreover if the stock value falls, profits will fall, resulting in a strong temptation to keep the stock figure increasing as this will almost always lead to an increase in profits.

## Marginal costing and ABC

The development of activity-based costing has provided support for the product concept. As we saw in Chapter 27, ABC aims to allocate all costs to products, including those that occur at the 'higher' levels. However, because some of these costs (e.g. facility-level costs) can only be allocated on an arbitrary basis, they should not be assigned to products at all. In the short term they remain period costs which are incurred on a time basis.

## Summary

Accountants are more likely to agree on the nature of measurement if they agree on the purpose of accounting. If the central purpose of accounting is to make possible the periodic matching of costs and revenues, and if the matching principle is the 'nucleus of accounting theory', then clearly the absorption costers are correct in their view. But if, as we argue in this book, the prime objective of accounting is to provide information which is useful for decision making, then the case for marginal costing is very strong.

**References**     Allen, D (1993). 'A picture paints a thousand words', *Management Accounting* (UK), September.

Paton, W A and Littleton, A C (1940). *An Introduction to Corporate Accounting Standards*, Monograph 3, AAA.

## Self-assessment questions

1  What do you understand by marginal costing?

2  Explain the treatment of overhead costs under absorption costing and marginal costing.

3  Discuss the different profit results that are obtained using absorption costing and marginal costing under the following circumstances:
   (a)  where sales fluctuate but production remains constant;
   (b)  where sales are constant but production fluctuates.

## Problems

1  Computer Limited was formed three years ago to produce a single product, the 'Mini'. The directors are receiving the financial results of the first three years presented by the company accountant, and are concerned with the decline in profits in the year 20X2 despite a substantial increase in sales.
   Summarized results are shown below:

|  | 20X0 | 20X1 | 20X2 |
|---|---|---|---|
| Production: Budget (units) | 1,000 | 1,000 | 1,000 |
|     Actual (units) | 900 | 1,100 | 800 |
| Sales (units) | 800 | 800 | 1,000 |
| Selling price per unit | £80 | £80 | £80 |
| Marginal production cost per unit | £10 | £10 | £10 |
| Fixed production overheads | £40,000 | £40,000 | £40,000 |
| Fixed selling and administrative overheads | £20,000 | £20,000 | £20,000 |
| Net profit | nil | £8,000 | £2,000 |

Fixed overheads are absorbed on the basis of budgeted annual production. Under- or over-absorbed overheads are charged to cost of goods sold.

*Required:*
(a)  Prepare a statement showing the profit figures derived by the company accountant.
(b)  Prepare profit and loss accounts using a marginal costing approach.
(c)  Reconcile the profits calculated in parts (a) and (b) above.
(d)  Explain the rationale behind the approaches adopted in parts (a) and (b).

2  The Sherwood Co Ltd is a single-product manufacturing company, which uses a marginal costing system for internal management purposes. The year-end external reports are converted to absorption costs. Variances are charged to the cost of goods sold.

The following data refers to the years ended 31 December 20X0 and 20X1:

|  | 20X0 | 20X1 |
|---|---|---|
|  | £ | £ |
| Sale price per unit | 80 | 90 |
| Standard marginal costs per unit: |  |  |
| Direct materials | 21 | 23 |
| Direct labour | 19 | 22 |
| Marginal factory overheads | 8 | 10 |
| Marginal selling and administrative expenses | 2 | 3 |
| Fixed factory overheads | 170,000 | 180,000 |
|  | Units | Units |
| Opening stocks | 1,500 | 2,000 |
| Closing stocks | 2,000 | 1,500 |
| Sales | 20,000 | 25,000 |

The normal volume used for the purpose of absorption costing is 28,000 units in both years.

*Required:*

(a)  Prepare profit and loss accounts for the year ended 31 December 20X1 on a marginal costing and on an absorption costing basis.

(b)  Discuss any differences which you may find between these two profit and loss accounts.

(c)  State what advantages and disadvantages attach to the marginal costing approach for internal management purposes.

# 30 Pricing

## Setting the scene

In command economies, central control leads to the use of cost base methods of pricing. In market economies, price is a function of supply, demand and competition; many command economies are currently transforming into market economies. Business people and their management accountants are having to move pricing away from cost based methods towards market pricing.

Of the various factors influencing marketing decisions, price (in connection with volume) is the only one directly generating revenue; all other items give rise to cost, although non-price considerations are increasingly taking precedence in competing.

In setting prices, a systematic approach is necessary. This entails knowing the market, the customer, the competition and then setting pricing objectives, based on an understanding of economic theory and after carrying out pricing research. Pricing policy can then be formulated.                                    (Claret and Phadke, 1995)

## Learning objectives

After studying this chapter you should be able to:

1  Explain the nature of the pricing problem.

2  Understand pricing theory in economics.

3  Describe full-cost pricing and show how it differs from conversion-cost pricing.

4  Explain return on investment pricing.

5  Discuss the advantages of marginal-cost pricing.

6  Explain target pricing.

It is generally assumed that capitalist enterprises are sales-led, and that the ability to sell under competitive conditions is a critical success factor on which the production process is significantly dependent.

One of the key factors in selling products under competitive market conditions is product pricing. The significance of pricing goes much beyond the simple question of determining product profitability. The complex set of notions that are involved in pricing have their fundamental roots in the strategic decisions that are concerned with capital investment, as well as those that relate to the immediacy of current operating profitability.

If a firm develops a pricing policy that affects its position in the market, it is evident that such a policy has long-term implications, for in the long term, any change in the volume of demand for products will affect the capital budgeting.

Equally, pricing policy has a direct influence on market demand, and, given cost–volume–profit relationships discussed in Chapter 28, current profitability also will be directly affected.

The purpose of this chapter is to discuss these problems, with particular reference to the costing approach to pricing with which traditionally accountants have been concerned.

## The nature of the pricing problem

The firm's long-term survival depends on its ability to sell its products at prices that will cover costs as well as providing a profit margin that will ensure a reasonable rate of return to investors. This simple statement of the pricing problem suggests that it is sufficient for accountants to accurately measure costs, and then add a profit margin that will provide the return on capital that investors expect.

The truth is that the pricing problem is much more complex than simply estimating costs. In the short term, the firm's cost structure will determine whether a given price will produce a profit or a loss at product unit level, but total profit may be affected also by changes in consumer demand, and the firm's business environment. Competition and economic policies that affect the aggregate level of demand frequently are more significant to the pricing problem than the firm's total costs per unit. Moreover, a variety of circumstances call for different pricing policies, implying alternative cost concepts and cost measurements.

Pricing is only one of the ways through which the firm can influence the demand for its products. For example, sales can be expanded by advertising, increasing the sales force, improving the selling style, and improving product presentation, as well as by lowering price. In effect, altering pricing policy may not necessarily be the best way of expanding sales and improving total profits. Equally, a fall in demand for a product may be remedied by improvements in selling methods rather than increasing its price competitiveness. Therefore, in focusing on the pricing problem, we are focusing on only one of the factors that may influence the level of sales.

Recent years have seen a remarkable shift in the relative importance of long-term rather than short-term considerations in developing pricing policies. Whereas traditional approaches to pricing utilized by US and European enterprises have involved pricing by reference essentially to short-run cost analysis, Japanese enterprises have categorized pricing policies as a long-term, rather than a short-term, problem. In this regard, the concept of 'target pricing' involves deliberately determining prices in the context of long-range planning, and forcing down planned production costs to targeted costs.

## The nature of pricing theories

Two distinct influences are seen at play in various pricing theories: first, the influence of classical economic theory that is concerned with guidelines for finding the best or optimal price; second, the influence of business traditions of conservatism and sound management, that looks to costs as setting a minimum level in price determination.

In sharp contrast to classical economists, business people and accountants have been less concerned with finding the best price than with establishing a price that covers an agreed measure of costs and provides a sufficient profit. Hence, pricing is part of both long-range and budgetary planning.

# Pricing theory in economics

Classical theorists hold that the firm should determine the optimum price, which is that price that will maximize the firm's profits. From their point of view, the price which maximizes profits implies the most efficient use of the economic resources held by the firm. Furthermore, such a pricing policy is necessary if capitalist enterprise is to reflect correctly the tenets of classical philosophy of capitalism, that is, that the objective of the firm is to maximize the returns accruing to the owner of its capital. The efficient allocation of resources through the economy is secured by the assumption that every owner of capital will seek to maximize the return on invested capital. Accordingly, scarce economic resources will be distributed between competing ends in a manner which will produce the greatest national wealth.

The price which maximizes profits is found at that level of sales where the addition to total revenue resulting from the sale of the last unit (the marginal revenue) is equal to the addition to total costs resulting from the production of that last unit (marginal cost).

It is clear that economic theory imposes very exacting conditions on the analysis of the optimum price, and in particular makes demands for information which are extremely difficult to meet. Classical theorists argue, nevertheless, that this principle is a useful guide to profit maximization.

**Example 1**

Let us assume that a firm producing Widgets in large numbers has sufficient knowledge of the revenue and cost schedules at different volume levels associated with different selling prices. The accountant is able to produce the following data:

| Selling price per unit | No of units which may be sold | Total sales revenue | Total variable costs | Fixed costs | Profit (loss) |
|---|---|---|---|---|---|
| £ | | £ | £ | £ | £ |
| 30 | 100,000 | 3,000,000 | 1,800,000 | 800,000 | 400,000 |
| 32 | 90,000 | 2,880,000 | 1,620,000 | 800,000 | 460,000 |
| 34 | 80,000 | 2,720,000 | 1,440,000 | 800,000 | 480,000 |
| 36 | 70,000 | 2,520,000 | 1,260,000 | 800,000 | 460,000 |
| 38 | 60,000 | 2,280,000 | 1,080,000 | 800,000 | 400,000 |
| 40 | 50,000 | 2,000,000 | 900,000 | 800,000 | 300,000 |

It is clear that the price of £34 a unit yields the maximum profit, and that is the price which the firm should establish. At this price, marginal revenue equals marginal costs.

The limitations of the classical theorists' approach arise from the failure to appreciate the many practical problems with which managers are faced. In particular, it is extremely difficult to estimate the exact shape of the demand curve, that is, how much will be sold at any particular price.

There are further reasons for doubting the assumptions of classical theory. It is not only myopic in ignoring the information problem completely, but it assumes that the volume of sales is solely a function of price. As we mentioned earlier, expenditure on sales promotion may well affect the demand curve without the need to adjust the price of the product.

Economic theory makes an important contribution to pricing theory, despite the criticisms we have just mentioned, because it draws attention to the factors which are relevant to the pricing decision, in particular the importance of the interaction of revenue and cost information for deciding upon a 'good' price, and draws attention to those cost elements relevant to such a price. It has most certainly encouraged the idea of marginal cost pricing, and the formulation of flexible pricing strategies.

## Cost-based pricing theories

Business people have for long been aware that pricing a product is one of the most important and complicated problems which they have to face. In attempting to resolve this problem, and in trying to find some general guidelines by which to establish a sound pricing policy, they are in agreement that cost is one of the factors which must be taken into account. Consistently selling below full costs will lead to insolvency, while if the firm is to survive it must try to sell at prices which will not only cover costs but yield a sufficient profit. No hard and fast rules may be laid down since each firm's product and market situations have features which themselves may be unique.

The influence of costs on pricing decisions varies according to circumstances. Where firms are under contract to supply on a cost-plus basis, their costs are all-important in deciding the contract price. In other situations, for example a liquidation sale, costs are irrelevant because the prices at which the goods are sold are not related to their costs. Normally, the importance of the firm's costs lies somewhere between these two extremes.

The relevance of costs to pricing decisions is influenced also by the firm's drive to meet certain objectives, for example, earning a specified rate of return, increasing its share of the market, or penetrating a new market. Moreover, the firm's relative marketing strength in a particular market may be a more dominant influence on pricing than its costs. Thus, a firm may be so strong as to be a price-maker, so that it is able to fix a price which other producers will have to follow. Conversely, a firm may be a price-taker, that is, its position in the market is so weak that it cannot influence the price.

In general, cost-based pricing theories are concerned with two elements of price. The first is the relevant costs which should be included in the price, and the second is the profit margin which must be added to reach the price. The profit margin will reflect a degree of caution about the likely reactions of customers or the nearness of a substitute if the firm is contemplating improving its profitability. Its relationship with near competitors may affect the firm's views on the size of its profit margin. Price cutting through the reduction of profit margins may lead to a price war, and profit margins may be safeguarded and increased by means of trading agreements. Some of these agreements in restraint of trade, which were really agreements in restraint of competition, are now illegal.

Cost-based pricing theories have a moral quality which economic theory does not reflect. In the sense that cost-based pricing reflects the notion that a cost-plus formula is 'fair', it reflects that medieval notion of a 'just price' which was such an important part of the teaching of such men as St Thomas Aquinas, and which still dominates our own conception of fair trading. It is incorrect to suggest, as does economic theory, that business theories and the actions of business people may be divorced from the rules of morality by which their behaviour as individuals is affected. It is evident that business people are concerned with finding a 'fair' price, and that this 'fair price' is one which on the one hand will cover their own costs and on the other will contain that measure of reward the buyer will regard as reasonable. In this sense, cost-based pricing theories do reflect the interaction of demand and supply, but unlike economic theory, do so in a way which reflects behavioural realities.

Cost-based pricing theories present themselves in two distinct forms:

1 cost-based pricing relying on budgeted costs;
2 target pricing relying on target costs.

## Cost-based pricing and budgeted costs

### Full-cost pricing

This theory requires that all the costs both fixed and marginal of bringing the product to the market be included in the selling price. Once the full costs have been established, it suffices to add the agreed profit margin.

*Example 2*  High Speed Castings Ltd produces two castings, Type A and Type B. The total unit costs are as follows:

|  | Type A | Type B |
|---|---|---|
|  | £ | £ |
| Direct materials | 4 | 12 |
| Direct labour | 6 | 4 |
| Factory overheads: |  |  |
| Variable | 6 | 3 |
| Fixed | 4 | 1 |
| **Total manufacturing costs** | 20 | 20 |
| Marketing and administrative costs: |  |  |
| Variable | 2 | 3 |
| Fixed | 4 | 3 |
| **Full costs per unit** | 26 | 26 |

To calculate the selling price under this method, we simply add the required profit margin, as follows:

|  | £ | £ |
|---|---|---|
| Full costs per unit | 26 | 26 |
| *Add:* Markup (50% on costs) | 13 | 13 |
| **Selling price** | 39 | 39 |

Full-cost pricing appears on the surface to be an easy method. By ignoring demand considerations completely and concentrating on costs, it avoids one of the major problem areas of pricing. Nevertheless, there are problems in calculating full costs which are not easy to resolve. By and large, one may assume that the calculation of unit marginal costs presents no serious measurement difficulties. By contrast, the assignment of fixed costs to units of output is an extremely complex matter.

### Indirect costs and full-cost pricing

Many factory, administrative and marketing costs cannot be identified clearly with a particular cost centre. Furthermore, there is the problem of selecting an appropriate basis for assigning them to individual products. Under full-cost pricing, this problem is critical to the determination of the selling price.

Consider the previous example of High Speed Castings Ltd and let us assume that the demand for Product B is buoyant whereas the demand for Product A is slack. In these circumstances, it may be a good idea to transfer a higher proportion of fixed costs to Product B, and so enable the price of Product A to be lowered to encourage more sales. By introducing such considerations to the problem of the allocation of fixed costs in multiproduct firms, one is introducing a new principle to full-cost pricing, that is, the ability of the market to accept costs. Consequently, one is moving away from the essence of full-cost pricing.

### Fixed costs and volume changes

The impact of changes in the sales volume upon unit fixed costs leads to a circular discussion, because price changes affect the volume of sales which in turn affects unit fixed costs which finally open up the possibility of further price changes. Since full-cost pricing implies flexible pricing in this sense, it is difficult to see its usefulness to those business people who instead of wanting a 'safe' price are looking for an aggressive price which will encourage the expansion of sales. Hence, they will tend to select a price which will be below full costs and look to the expanded volume of sales to cover total costs ultimately. It is in the nature of things that until such people are satisfied with their market position, price will always be below full costs. This is explainable in terms of the wish of business people to achieve market as well as profit objectives.

The following table shows the relationship of fixed costs and volume changes. Given that the percentage markup remains constant, there is a range of selling prices which will cover costs at a particular volume of sales:

| No of units (thousands) | 100 | 200 | 300 | 400 | 500 |
|---|---|---|---|---|---|
| Variable cost per unit | £4.00 | £4.00 | £4.00 | £4.00 | £4.00 |
| Fixed cost per unit | 2.00 | 1.00 | 0.67 | 0.50 | 0.40 |
| Full cost per unit | 6.00 | 5.00 | 4.67 | 4.50 | 4.40 |
| 10% Markup | 0.60 | 0.50 | 0.47 | 0.45 | 0.44 |
| Selling price | 6.60 | 5.50 | 5.14 | 4.95 | 4.84 |

It is also interesting to note the resulting aggregate profits which these different prices produce.

| No of units (thousands) | 100 | 200 | 300 | 400 | 500 |
|---|---|---|---|---|---|
| Selling price | £6.60 | £5.50 | £5.14 | £4.95 | £4.84 |
| Profit per unit (at 10%) | 0.60 | 0.50 | 0.47 | 0.45 | 0.44 |
| Aggregate profit (£000) | 60.00 | 100.00 | 141.00 | 180.00 | 220.00 |

Clearly, faced with these production possibilities, management would wish to pursue an aggressive pricing policy which would place the highest aggregate profits within the firm's reach. As explained above, full-cost pricing would stand in the way of such a pricing policy because of the decreasing nature of fixed costs per unit as output expands. A stage will be reached, of course, when the firm has reached the limit of production under existing capacity. In other words, a point exists where the firm must stabilize production or incur further capital expenditure on the expansion of productive capacity. This would involve the firm in a capital investment decision and a complete reconsideration of its pricing policy.

The price which the firm would wish to establish under full-cost pricing, therefore, is that price which will not only be the best price from the point of view of profit, but one which is related to the best output capacity which the firm can maintain. It is for this reason that a 'normal volume' of output must be established so that the firm may decide the appropriate full costs which are to form the basis of the price. This is a most important consideration, for customers do not like frequent price changes.

Another factor which will also have an effect is that of a consistent reduction in the activity level caused by a long recession. Generally organizations use the 'normal' level of activity to calculate overhead recovery rates for inclusion in product pricing. Where the normal activity level will not be achieved in the short term (that is, two to three years), at what level should the activity be set? Should it be set at current forecast activity level, which will result in higher absorption rates and therefore prices in a market where pressure on prices is likely to lead to a fall and not an increase? Or should the target level be retained, in which case there will be a built-in under-absorption of overheads?

## Full-cost pricing and the markup percentage

Having gone through the complicated process of ascertaining the full cost per unit, one moves to the final problem of determining the markup percentage which, when added to full costs, will yield the price.

We have already mentioned that there are a number of influences which bear upon the size of the percentage markup. First, there is the notion of the 'fair price', and business people will argue strongly that such-and-such a percentage is a 'fair profit' for a given trade. There is a connection between the rate of turnover and the markup percentage; for example, it is quite normal to expect jewellers to impose a higher markup percentage on their goods than butchers. Second, the markup is influenced by the elasticity of demand for the product, and market conditions generally. Third, as we have already mentioned, the markup is influenced by the nature of the firm's long-term strategy. Fourth, although business people argue that they seek a reasonable profit, it is evident that they mean the highest profit which they can 'reasonably' make. Finally, there is evidence also in the pricing policies of large firms, and particularly state corporations, that the need to generate capital to finance expensive capital projects influences the profit markup, and hence the price.

## Conversion-cost pricing

Unlike full-cost pricing, conversion-cost pricing takes into account only the costs incurred by the firm in converting raw materials and semi-finished goods into finished products. One of the limitations of full-cost pricing is that where the firm is selling two products which require different degrees of effort to convert to marketable state, no distinction is drawn between them.

Conversion-cost pricing, therefore, excludes direct materials and may be calculated easily from the example given on page 455 which is repeated below.

|  | Product A | | Product B | |
|---|---|---|---|---|
|  | £ | £ | £ | £ |
| Direct materials |  | 4 |  | 12 |
| **Conversion costs:** |  |  |  |  |
| Direct labour | 6 |  | 4 |  |
| Factory overheads | 10 |  | 4 |  |
|  |  | 16 |  | 8 |
| Total factory costs |  | 20 |  | 20 |

Under full-cost pricing, both products were priced at £39 as follows:

|  | Product A | Product B |
|---|---|---|
|  | £ | £ |
| Total factory costs | 20 | 20 |
| Selling and administrative costs | 6 | 6 |
| Full costs | 26 | 26 |
| Markup at 50% | 13 | 13 |
| Selling price | 39 | 39 |

The objective of conversion-cost pricing is to provide a pricing policy which will relate the cost or effort required by the firm to convert raw material into a marketable product to the selling price of the product. From the foregoing example, it is evident that Product A takes twice the effort to produce (£16) as Product B (£8). Hence, the firm should wish to formulate a pricing policy which will encourage the expansion of Product B, two units of which may be produced for the same production effort as one of Product A. This may be achieved by conversion-cost pricing, which will establish a lower price for Product B than for Product A. Under conversion-cost pricing, the markup is calculated on the conversion costs, as shown below.

It will be recalled from Chapter 28 that in selecting an appropriate sales mix from a profit planning point of view, the firm is attempting to plan production in such a way as to have that mix of product which will produce the best aggregate profit situation. Conversion-cost pricing will assist the firm which is faced with such a problem. If the demand for Product B were such that the firm could switch entirely to that product, the firm would simply cease manufacturing Product A. It is owing to the fact that the firm is compelled to produce both products because demand is limited that the sales-mix problem arises. It is equally for this reason that conversion-cost pricing is useful in such situations.

|  | Product A | Product B |
|---|---|---|
|  | £ | £ |
| **Conversion costs:** |  |  |
| Direct labour | 6 | 4 |
| Factory overheads | 10 | 4 |
|  | 16 | 8 |
| Markup at 100% | 16 | 8 |
|  | 32 | 16 |
| **Other costs:** |  |  |
| Direct materials | 4 | 12 |
| Selling and administrative costs | 6 | 6 |
| Selling price | 42 | 34 |

## Return-on-investment pricing

The cost-based pricing theories which we have examined so far focus on costs of production. Although such costs will include depreciation, they exclude any consideration of the capital employed by the firm. The firm has profit expectations, of course, and these are stated in terms of a percentage markup on costs of production. Return-on-investment pricing attempts to link the markup to the capital employed, and so set a price which includes a return on capital employed. Research has shown that many firms have pricing policies which reflect a target rate of return. The formula used is as follows:

$$\text{Selling price} = \frac{\text{total costs} + (\text{desired \% return on capital employed})}{\text{volume of output}}$$

*Example 3*  Let us assume that High Speed Castings Ltd, which produces the two products Type A and Type B, has a 'normal' output of Product A amounting to 20,000 units a year. Let us assume also that the capital employed by the firm is £1.5 million, of which £1 million is employed in the production of Product A. The desired rate of return which the firm has imposed on all its capital investment decisions is 20 per cent. Accordingly, the firm seeks a profit markup which reflects this objective. The selling price may be calculated as follows:

|  | Product A |
|---|---|
|  | £ |
| Total costs of production (20,000 × £26) | 520,000 |
| Desired return on capital employed (20% of £1 m) | 200,000 |
| Expected sales revenue | 720,000 |
| Selling price per unit (£720,000 ÷ 20,000) | £36 |

The attraction of this method of establishing a markup to costs is that it relates the problem of pricing to financial objectives and criteria, and integrates pricing decisions with the firm's overall planning objectives. It is clearly superior from a rational point of view to simply deciding upon a percentage markup on the basis of what is considered to be 'fair'. At the same time, return-on-investment pricing has all the tendencies to rigidity which are the features of full-cost pricing policies.

Since pricing decisions are generally short-run in nature, their effects on long-range objectives require that these objectives be considered. A firm which has a long-range target rate of return may find that, in attempting to apply such a target to short-run pricing policies, it may be forced from the market by competition. Thus, the firm may be compelled to price below its target rate of return to retain its share of the market, and thereby ensure the attainment of its long-range objectives in the broad sense.

Return-on-investment pricing may, in practice, invert the relationship of costs to price, in that costs are tailored to fit selling policies. This means that more complete knowledge of the market is possessed, for example the likely size of the market and its sensitivity to quality and packaging. In these circumstances, a firm may ensure that a specific rate of return on investment is obtained by selling a commodity at a price not exceeding a predetermined cost.

## Marginal-cost pricing

Sometimes referred to as the contribution method of pricing, this method of pricing is related to the ideas which we discussed in Chapter 28. No one seriously disputes that in the long term a firm's pricing policy must cover full costs, whether these are interpreted as full production costs or the replacement of the capital invested, as well as providing an acceptable margin of profit. As we saw earlier, this is the main argument put forward by the supporters of full-cost pricing. For short-term decisions, however, no one can doubt the usefulness of marginal-cost pricing.

There are many situations in which a price which covers variable cost but not full costs will nevertheless make a contribution to profits. Thus, if a firm has spare capacity and has covered its fixed costs at the price set for its regular customers, and no further sales can be made to this market, the firm may attempt to reach another market by selling the article at a lower price with a slight alteration to the product presentation. Price discrimination, as this practice is known, enables the firm to sell the same product in different markets at different prices. The firm's total profits will be much greater as a result. This aspect of imperfect competition is commonly treated in economics textbooks. Similarly, where the firm is facing a fall in demand for its product due to a temporary market recession with the result that it is operating at a loss, any sales at a price which is above marginal costs will contribute to the recovery of fixed costs.

Marginal-cost pricing enables the firm to pursue special marketing policies, such as the penetration of a new market, or the development of an export market, by imposing upon the home market a price which recovers fixed costs so as to permit sales at marginal costs in the new market. Marginal-cost pricing is useful, therefore, because it indicates the lowest limit for a price decision. For example, the variable costs of the two products of High Speed Castings Ltd are as follows:

| | Product A | Product B |
|---|---|---|
| | £ | £ |
| Direct materials | 4 | 12 |
| Direct labour | 6 | 4 |
| Variable factory overheads | 6 | 3 |
| Variable selling and administrative overheads | 2 | 3 |
| **Minimum price** – variable costs | 18 | 22 |

Although marginal-cost pricing is useful for dealing with temporary market difficulties or for exploiting new marketing strategies, there may be a danger that marginal-cost pricing becomes the established method of pricing. The firm should therefore try to evolve both long-term and short-term pricing strategies, and return to a long-term pricing strategy once the short-term situation has been cleared.

In this section we have discussed the advantages of marginal-cost pricing for short-term situations. It also has advantages for the long term. Full-cost pricing, as we have already suggested, may inhibit the firm from developing sales and production strategies which management considers to be desirable from a profit planning point of view. Marginal-cost pricing takes account of the relationship between price, volume and costs, and in this sense it enables better profit planning decisions to be made.

## Going-rate pricing

Where the price for a product is determined by the market, so that the firm is faced with a 'going rate', the major problem for the firm is how much to produce. In these situations, the volume produced is determined by the firm's costs and its profit planned accordingly. The classic examples where firms are faced with the going rate are the various commodity markets. Producers try to solve the price uncertainty by selling in the 'future markets', that is, contracting now to supply say in three months' time at an agreed price.

## Target pricing and target costs

Until recently, the development of cost-based pricing theories has assumed that product cost measurements were needed as the starting point from which to build up prices by adding required profit margins. Accountants have been concerned with improving the accuracy of cost measurements. In this regard, a significant innovation of this century was the shift from historic to standard costs. This enabled cost measurements to be predetermined by the anticipation of changes in cost elements in the annual budgeting process.

As indicated earlier, the concept of target pricing is a radical development that seeks to improve price competitiveness by imposing a target price in the long-range product planning process. The objective of target pricing is to seek the required profit margin through product cost economies. Hence, target costs are used to attempt to compress costs principally by searching for ways of improving resource utilization and thereby reducing costs.

By making costs rely on selling prices rather than making selling prices depend on costs, a certainty can be introduced into the pricing decision that all costs incurred during production are necessary. Unnecessary costs should be eliminated without reducing value. One way to do this is to eliminate those activities that do not add value to the final production service.

## Summary

Pricing decisions form an integral part of the firm's planning process, and are related directly to its objectives. The nature of the firm's product, the market situation and the firm's short-term and long-term objectives are all factors relevant to pricing decisions.

Pricing policies must be examined in terms of the particular objectives which they seek to achieve, and we have already said that occasions may arise where a short-term objective requires a policy which would be unacceptable in the long term. Numerous examples may be given of business objectives which require their own tailor-made pricing policies. The introduction of a new product may require a 'skimming price policy', that is, setting a high price initially and lowering the price as the product gains acceptance and popularity and permits the firm to expand the scale of production, so reducing its costs. Ballpoint pens, nylons and television sets have all undergone this process. 'Penetration price policies', on the other hand, have been a popular way of entering a foreign market and call for low prices to encourage rapid acceptance of the product.

For all these reasons, the only general rule that can be laid down is that unit costs provide a means of determining the lowest limit of an acceptable short-term price, while in the long term the price should cover all costs and provide the margin of profit required by management.

*Reference*   Claret, J and Phadke, P D (1995). 'Pricing – a challenge to management accounting', *Management Accounting* (UK), October.

## Self-assessment questions

1 Review briefly some of the business objectives involved in pricing policies.

2 Discuss briefly the objective of pricing policy in classical economic theory.

3 Explain the nature of cost-based pricing policies.

4 What do you understand by 'full-cost' pricing?

5 What kind of accounting information do you consider to be relevant to making full-cost pricing decisions?

6 Comment on the statement that 'since prices are determined by supply and demand factors, accounting data is irrelevant in determining a firm's pricing policy'.

7 Explain what is implied by:
   (a) conversion-cost pricing;
   (b) return-on-investment pricing.

8 What do you understand by 'marginal cost' pricing? In what circumstances do you consider this method of pricing useful to pricing decisions?

9 Explain the objectives of target pricing.

10 Consider the view that long-term factors are more significant than short-term ones in determining pricing policies.

## Problems

1 Schlutz and Co Ltd manufactures a product which it distributes through its own branches in England and Wales. The managing director was recently approached by McTosh and Co Ltd, a Glasgow-based company interested in obtaining sole distributor rights in Scotland. McTosh proposes to purchase the product from Schlutz at a price of £32.50 and to offer it for sale to retailers in Scotland at £42.50 and would pay the transport charges to Scotland averaging £3.50 per unit. No commission would be payable to McTosh on these sales. Schlutz and Co undertook to consider this offer. Given the undermentioned information (a) to (f), would you advise Schlutz and Co to accept the offer?

(a) The products now sold to retailers in England and Wales at a price of £44 inclusive of delivery charges.
(b) Sales commissions paid to retailers are computed at 5 per cent of sales.
(c) Transport costs average £1.50 per unit.
(d) Other selling and administrative costs are regarded as fixed and amount to £4.50 per unit.
(e) Manufacturing costs amount to £29.50 per unit as follows:

| | |
|---|---|
| Materials | £18.70 |
| Labour | 3.00 |
| Variable overheads | 3.30 |
| Fixed overheads | 4.50 |
| | £29.50 |

(f) Manufacturing capacity is adequate to handle the increased volume which is estimated to amount to 1,000 units a month, but fixed factory overheads would probably increase by £1,500 a month.

2 A standard unit of the Whitmore Manufacturing Company contains the following marginal costs:

| | Per unit |
|---|---|
| Direct materials | £5.60 |
| Direct labour cost | 1.50 |
| Variable factory overhead | 0.40 |
| | £7.50 |

Fixed factory overhead is budgeted at £280,000 for a normal sales volume of 400,000 units. Factory capacity is 500,000 units. Distribution and administrative expenses are budgeted at £180,000.

Capital employed is considered to consist of 50 per cent of net sales for current assets and £450,000 for fixed assets.

Additional analysis indicates:

(a) Direct material prices will increase £0.40 per unit.
(b) An unfavourable direct labour variance of approximately 6 per cent has been experienced for the past two years.
(c) Customers' discounts average to about 2 per cent of the gross sales price.

*Required:*

Determine a sales price which will yield 16 per cent return on capital employed.

# 31 Short-run tactical decisions

## Setting the scene

The concept of relevant costs for decisions is a pervasive one in accounting and economics. Simply stated, the relevant-cost approach requires that, for any decision, the cost which will change *as a result of the decision*, i.e. costs which are variable relative to the decision, should be compared with the revenues which will be earned *as a result of that decision*. Costs which will not alter, i.e. costs which are fixed relative to that decision, are not a relevant consideration in the incremental approach.

Where incremental revenue exceeds incremental cost it is recommended that the proposed course of action be followed as it will increase the wealth of the organisation. Conversely, where there is an excess of incremental cost over incremental revenue it is recommended that the proposed course of action be rejected.                                                 (Kennedy, 1995)

## Learning objectives

After studying this chapter you should be able to:

1   Define and explain the concept of relevant costs.

2   Discuss the importance of the contribution margin in short-run decision making.

3   Explain how opportunity costs affect decision making.

4   Identify business situations in which relevant costing is appropriate.

5   Explain the importance of qualitative factors in using the relevant costing decision model.

6   Discuss the role of limiting factors in short-term decision making.

7   Use linear programming to find the optimal solution to a problem of constrained resources.

We discussed in Chapter 28 the importance of the relationship between cost and volume of output for profit planning purposes. Cost behaviour is a crucial element in profit planning, but a knowledge of the behaviour of future costs is equally important for a whole range of other decisions which management has to make.

We may divide the accountant's task of providing information as to costs for decision making into two parts. First, when planning the volume of output in the short term, the accountant has to provide information as to the behaviour of fixed and variable costs over the planned range of output. Second, for a number of 'special decisions' relating to alternative courses of action, such as the acceptance or rejection of a special order, s/he has to provide cost information which will guide management towards making the best, that is the most profitable, decisions.

The analysis of special decisions not only requires costs that are relevant to these decisions, but focuses on the size of the contribution margin that is associated with different alternatives. The usefulness of the contribution margin is not limited to one-off special decisions, but is applied also to handling problems resulting from limiting factors that exist as on-going problems.

The purpose of this chapter is to examine the nature of relevant costs, and the importance of the contribution margin in these areas of decision making.

## The nature of relevant costs

The nature of the costs which are relevant for short-run tactical decisions will depend on the type of decision problem for which they are required. We shall examine several different types of decision problems, and in this way ascertain the type of cost information which ought to be supplied by the accountant. In general, however, the relevant costs have two important characteristics:

1 They are future costs, that is, they are costs not yet incurred. This is a most important point, for it is easy to fall into the error of believing that costs which have already been incurred must be recovered. Past costs, that is sunk costs, are irrelevant costs: their only usefulness is the extent to which they may help the accountant to estimate the trend of future costs.

**Example 1**  Excelsior Ltd has spent £5,000 on developing a new process. A revised estimate of further expenditure required to complete the development work shows an increase of 20 per cent on the original total estimate of £10,000. The cost which is relevant to the decision to continue with the development work is £7,000, that is, the future cost which will be incurred, and not the new estimate of total costs of £12,000. Hence, the costs already incurred are irrelevant to the decision to be made concerning the completion of the development work.

2 Relevant costs are differential costs. Not all future costs are relevant costs: differential costs will be different under the alternative courses of action under examination.

**Example 2**  John Brown has decided to go to the cinema, and he is considering whether to go by bus or by car. The price of the cinema ticket is not a relevant cost, for it is not affected by the manner in which he travels to the cinema. Likewise, since cars tend to depreciate over time, the additional mileage on the car is also not a relevant cost. Although Brown's decision on his mode of travel will be influenced by his individual preference, the relevant cost is the cost difference between the cost of using the car, that is, petrol and parking, and going by bus. This cost difference is the differential cost.

From the foregoing examples, it might appear that only variable costs will be relevant costs, and that fixed costs cannot be relevant costs, since by definition they are not susceptible to change. The examples show that not all variable costs are relevant costs, for this depends on whether in the circumstances under review they are also differential costs.

In the long term, of course, fixed costs do become variable costs, so that in decisions affecting the long term, fixed costs may be differential costs and so will become relevant costs.

For short-run tactical decisions, however, it is possible, as we shall see, for fixed costs to be relevant costs. Thus, if a decision affects the short-run activity level, requiring further capital expenditure, the extra fixed costs so incurred will be relevant costs as regards that decision.

## The importance of the contribution margin

Usually, short-run tactical decisions are aimed at making the best use of existing facilities. The contribution margin is an important concept in this analysis. It is defined as the excess of the revenue of any activity over its relevant costs, which is available as a contribution towards fixed costs and profits. Profits, of course, will not be made until all fixed costs have been covered, but under certain circumstances the expectation of a contribution margin will be sufficient to justify a particular decision.

One decision problem with which business people are frequently faced is the acceptance of a special order, which may be a large order at a price below the usual selling price, and sometimes below total manufacturing costs.

**Example 3**  Minnies Kurt Ltd manufactures a garment which is sold under the trade name of Withitog. Its total productive capacity is 100,000 units in the current period, and actual production is running at 80 per cent of productive capacity. The product sells at £1.00 per unit, and the firm's costs of production are as follows:

| | |
|---|---|
| Fixed costs | £25,000 |
| Variable costs | £0.50 per unit |

The firm receives a special order for 10,000 Withitogs from a mail order firm, subject to the firm agreeing to sell the product at £0.60 per unit. The managing director is reluctant to accept the order because the selling price is well below the manufacturing costs, which he has calculated as follows:

Fixed costs per unit (allocated over 90,000 units)

$$\frac{£25,000}{90,000}$$ £0.28

| | |
|---|---|
| Variable costs per unit | 0.50 |
| Total manufacturing costs per unit | £0.78 |

The contribution margin approach to the solution of this decision problem leads to a different conclusion. The revenue per unit is £0.60, and the relevant costs associated with the decision are the variable costs of production only, that is £0.50 per unit. Hence, there is a unit contribution margin of £0.10 per unit, and on that basis, the firm should accept the special order. The fixed costs are not relevant costs for two reasons: first they are sunk costs, that is they are not future costs, and second they are not affected by the decision to accept the special order, that is they are not differential costs.

The result of accepting the special order on the firm's total profit may be seen from the calculations below.

It is clear, therefore, that it is advantageous to the firm to accept the special order, since overall profits will be improved by £1,000, which is the amount of the contribution margin resulting from the acceptance of that order.

It is evident, too, that the widespread belief that all costs should be covered may influence business people in considering special offers. Absorption costing is useful in determining the full costs of production, but leads to erroneous conclusions if indiscriminately applied.

|  | Without the special order | | With the special order | | Contribution margin |
|---|---|---|---|---|---|
|  | (80,000 units) | | (90,000 units) | | – |
| Sales revenue: | £ | £ | £ | £ | £ |
| 80,000 units @ £1.00 |  | 80,000 |  | 80,000 |  |
| 10,000 units @ £0.60 |  | – |  | 6,000 |  |
|  |  | 80,000 |  | 86,000 | 6,000 |
| Manufacturing costs: |  |  |  |  |  |
| Fixed costs | 25,000 |  | 25,000 |  | – |
| Variable costs @ |  |  |  |  |  |
| £0.50 per unit | 40,000 |  | 45,000 |  |  |
|  |  | 65,000 |  | 70,000 | 5,000 |
| Net profit |  | £15,000 |  | £16,000 | £1,000 |

**Example 4** Speedo Engineering Ltd manufactures an electrical component widely used in the motor industry. It is currently producing 5,000 units selling at £10 a unit. Its total productive capacity is 8,000 units, and budgeted costs at different levels of output have been estimated as follows:

| Output (units) | 5,000 | 6,000 | 7,000 | 8,000 |
|---|---|---|---|---|
| Variable costs | £30,000 | £36,000 | £42,000 | £48,000 |
| Fixed costs | 10,000 | 10,000 | 10,000 | 10,000 |
| Total costs | £40,000 | £46,000 | £52,000 | £58,000 |
| Total costs per unit | £8.00 | £7.67 | £7.43 | £7.25 |

The firm receives three offers for three lots of 1,000 units at selling prices of £8, £7 and £6.50 per unit respectively. Should these offers be accepted or rejected?

The unit costs of production under the absorption costing method may be calculated and compared with the respective offers, as shown below:

| Output (units) | 6,000 | 7,000 | 8,000 |
|---|---|---|---|
| Total costs per unit | £7.67 | £7.43 | £7.25 |
| Selling price per unit | 8.00 | 7.00 | 6.50 |
| Profit (loss) per unit | £0.33 | £(0.43) | £(0.75) |

From these calculations one might deduce that the firm should accept the order at £8 per unit, which will produce a profit of £0.33 per unit, but should reject the other two offers of £7 and £6.50 since they would result in losses.

An examination of the relevant costs leads to a different conclusion. The fixed costs are not relevant costs, since they will be incurred irrespective of the level of output. By comparing the relevant costs with the three offers, we may calculate the differential profits thus:

| Output (units) | 6,000 | 7,000 | 8,000 |
|---|---|---|---|
| Differential units | 1,000 | 1,000 | 1,000 |
| Differential selling price | £8.00 | £7.00 | £6.50 |
| Differential unit cost | 6.00 | 6.00 | 6.00 |
| Differential profit per unit | 2.00 | 1.00 | 0.50 |
| Differential total profit | £2,000 | £1,000 | £500 |

These figures illustrate the misleading effect of using absorption costing methods for decision making, and the necessity for using the relevant cost analysis. Using this latter method, it is clear that all three offers should be accepted, for in each case they provide a contribution margin towards fixed costs and profits.

# Opportunity costs

Opportunity costs are not recorded in the accounting process, and although they are favoured by economists as appropriate costs for decision making, they are difficult to identify and to measure in practice. Hence, accountants prefer to record and use more objective measures of costs, such as past costs or budgeted future costs, as guidelines for decision making. There are a number of decision problems, however, in which the only relevant cost is the opportunity cost. The opportunity cost may be defined as the value of the next best opportunity forgone, or of the net cash inflow lost as a result of preferring one alternative rather than the next best one. In cases where it is clear that only the opportunity cost will assist in making the decisions, the accountant is often able to attempt its measurement.

**Example 5**  The Nationwide Investment Corporation Ltd seeks to invest £1 million. It has selected two investment projects for consideration: project A which is estimated to produce an annual return of 15 per cent, and project B which is expected to yield 20 per cent annually.

On the basis of these facts it is clear that the Corporation will select project B. The additional gain resulting from that decision may only be measured in terms of the opportunity costs of sacrificing project A, as follows:

| | |
|---|---|
| Estimated annual return from project B | £200,000 |
| *Less:* Opportunity cost (the sacrifice of the estimated annual returns from project A) | 150,000 |
| **Advantage of project B** | **£50,000** |

The opportunity cost is always a relevant cost concept when the problem facing the firm is a problem of choice: the measure of the cost of the decision is the loss sustained by losing the opportunity of the second best alternative. It is the opportunity cost which must be taken into account in calculating the advantage of choosing one alternative rather than the other.

The use of the opportunity cost concept is illustrated in the following situations:

1 dropping a product line;
2 selling or further processing a semi-manufactured product;
3 operate or lease;
4 make or buy a product.

# Dropping a product line

Invariably, the reason for wishing to drop a product line is that it is unprofitable, or it is less profitable than another product line to which the firm could switch resources.

**Example 6**  Mechanical Toys Ltd manufactures three products, whose contributions to total profits for the year just ended are:

| Products | A | | B | | C | | Total | |
|---|---|---|---|---|---|---|---|---|
| | £ | | £ | | £ | | £ | |
| Sales | 200,000 | | 100,000 | | 150,000 | | 450,000 | |
| Variable costs | 100,000 | | 70,000 | | 80,000 | | 250,000 | |
| Contributions | 100,000 | (50%) | 30,000 | (30%) | 70,000 | (47%) | 200,000 | (44%) |
| Fixed costs | 60,000 | | 40,000 | | 50,000 | | 150,000 | |
| Net profit (loss) | 40,000 | | (10,000) | | 20,000 | | 50,000 | |

The company is considering dropping product B as it is showing a loss. By dropping product B, fixed costs could be reduced by £10,000, though the remaining balance of fixed costs of £30,000 being overhead fixed costs allocated to the product would have to be reallocated to products A and C.

The only choice facing the company is to continue or to cease making product B, and the financial consequences of that choice may be shown as follows:

|  | Keep product B | Drop product B |
|---|---|---|
|  | £ | £ |
| Sales | 450,000 | 350,000 |
| Variable costs | 250,000 | 180,000 |
| Contribution | 200,000 | 170,000 |
| Fixed costs | 150,000 | 140,000 |
| Net profit | 50,000 | 30,000 |

It is clear that although an overall loss appears to result from producing product B, the contribution which product B makes to the firm's fixed costs would be lost if the decision were made to drop product B. The net cost of dropping product B would be £20,000, that is, the contribution margin less the fixed costs of £10,000 incurred solely as a consequence of its production.

Expressed in terms of opportunity cost analysis, the company has the choice between a profit of £50,000 associated with a decision to keep product B, and a profit of £30,000 associated with a decision to drop product B. Clearly, it cannot have both: hence the cost of selecting the profit of £50,000 is the sacrifice of the opportunity of the alternative profit of £30,000. Hence, the opportunity cost of the decision to keep product B is £30,000, and the advantage of this decision over the alternative of dropping product B is £20,000.

There may be other alternatives open to the firm, of course, besides the two alternatives which we have discussed, such as replacing product B by a more profitable product. In such a case, all the available alternatives must be examined and their outcomes accurately estimated if the best decision is to be made.

# Selling or further processing

On occasions, it is possible for a firm to bring a product to its semi-finished state and then sell it, rather than proceed to complete the production process and sell the finished article.

**Example 7** Product A, which cost £4.80 per unit to produce, is sold as a refined petroleum product at £8 a unit. It could be put through a further processing stage after which it may be sold for £12 a unit. The costs associated with the further processing stage are estimated at £2 per unit.

The outcome of the two alternatives facing the firm, to sell or to further process the product, may be stated in the following terms:

|  | To sell | To process further |
|---|---|---|
| Revenues associated with the decision | £8.0 | £4 |
| Costs associated with the decision | 4.8 | 2 |
| Differential profit per unit | £3.2 | £2 |

It is clear that if the firm decides to sell rather than to process further, it will lose the additional profit of £2 per unit. Hence, the opportunity cost of the decision to sell is £2 and the advantage of selling over further processing is £1.20.

## Operate or lease

The decision as to whether to operate or lease assets is another example of the importance of opportunity costs for decision making.

**Example 8**
Betashoes Ltd owns a desirable freehold in Puddingford High Street, which it uses as a selling outlet. The Managing Director receives an offer to lease the property to a local company willing to pay an annual rent of £30,000. The net contribution of the selling outlet in Puddingford to the group profits of Betashoes Ltd is £40,000, after deducting the expenses attributable to it. The information which is relevant to the decision to continue to use the selling outlet may be set out as under:

| | |
|---|---|
| Contribution to group profits | £40,000 |
| Opportunity cost (rent) | £30,000 |
| Net advantage of operating | £10,000 |

In the absence of other factors which may induce Betashoes to sell the site, the offer to lease the premises should be rejected and Betashoes should continue to use them as a selling outlet.

## Make or buy

It is quite common for firms to subcontract the making of components to specialist firms. This practice does increase their dependence on outside suppliers and reduce to some extent their control on the quality of the components. The opportunity cost approach to this type of decision enables the firm to consider the advantages which could be obtained from alternative uses of the productive capacity released as the result of subcontracting the making of components.

**Example 9**
Highperformance Motors Ltd specializes in the manufacture of sports cars, making some of the components which are required and buying others. Alparts Ltd offers to supply a part currently made by Highperformance Motors Ltd at a price of £7. The costs incurred by Highperformance Motors in making the part are as follows:

| | |
|---|---|
| Variable costs | £4 |
| Traceable fixed costs | 2 |
| Allocated fixed costs | 3 |
| **Total unit costs** | **£9** |

Let us assume for the moment that the productive capacity released as a result of accepting the offer will remain idle. On the basis of a monthly production of 5,000 units a month, the relevant monthly costs, that is, those which would be affected by the decision to buy the units, are as follows:

| | |
|---|---|
| Variable costs | £20,000 |
| Traceable fixed costs | 10,000 |
| Relevant costs | 30,000 |
| Cost of buying | 35,000 |
| **Advantage in making** | **£5,000** |

The allocated fixed costs are irrelevant to the decision since they are not affected, and will continue to be incurred by Highperformance Motors irrespective of whether the parts are made or bought. Since the relevant costs of making are less than the costs of buying, the firm should reject the offer and continue to make the parts.

Let us now consider the possibility that if the firm accepted the offer, the productive capacity released as a result will not remain idle, and will be used to extend the production line of motor cars. It is calculated that an additional four cars a month could be produced, leading to an increase in profits of £10,000. The opportunity costs of not accepting the offer, therefore, amount to £10,000. Hence, the information which is now relevant to the decision as to making or buying the part is as under:

| | |
|---|---|
| **Cost of making** | |
| Relevant manufacturing costs | £30,000 |
| Opportunity cost | 10,000 |
| | 40,000 |
| **Cost of buying** | 35,000 |
| **Advantage of buying** | **£5,000** |

The introduction of the opportunity cost of not accepting the offer has altered the nature of the decision completely, and reversed the previous conclusion that it was advantageous to make the part.

## Decision making in the face of limiting factors

In the examples examined so far, a course of action has been selected on the basis of seeking the most profitable result. Business enterprises are limited in the pursuit of profit by the fact that they have limited resources at their disposal, so that quite apart from the limitation on the quantities of any product which the market will buy at a given price, the firm has its own constraints on the volume of output. Hence at a given price, which may be well above costs of production, the firm may be unable to increase its overall profit owing simply to its inability to increase its output.

The limiting factors which affect the level of production may arise out of shortages of labour, material, equipment and factory space to mention but a few obvious examples. Faced with limiting factors of whatever nature, the firm will wish to obtain the maximum profit from the use of the resources available; and, in making decisions about the allocation of its resources between competing alternatives, management will be guided by the relative contribution margin which they offer. Since the firm will be faced with limiting factors, however, the contribution margins must not be calculated in terms of units of product sold which fail to reflect constraints on the total volume of output, but should be related to the unit of quantity of the most limited factor. A simple example will serve to explain this point.

**Example 10** Multiproduct Ltd manufactures three products about which is derived the following data:

| Product | Machine hours required per unit of product | Contribution margin per unit | Contribution margin per machine hour |
|---|---|---|---|
| A | 3 hours | £9 | £3.0 |
| B | 2 hours | £7 | £3.5 |
| C | 1 hour | £5 | £5.0 |

The three products can be made by the same machine, and on the basis of this information, it is evident that product C is the most profitable product, yielding a contribution of £5 per machine hour, as against product A, which shows the smallest contribution per machine hour. Hence, in deciding how to use the limiting factor the firm should concentrate on the production of product C, rather than products A and B. If there were no limits to the market demand for product C, then there would be no problem in deciding which product to produce – it would be product C alone.

Firms undertake the manufacture of different products because the market demand for any one product is limited, so that they seek to find that product mix which will be the most profitable. Let us assume that the maximum weekly demand for the three products and the total machine capacity necessary to meet this demand are as follows:

| Product | Maximum demand in units | Machine hours equivalents |
|---|---|---|
| A | 100 | 300 |
| B | 100 | 200 |
| C | 100 | 100 |
| | | 600 |

Machine capacity is limited to 450 hours per week, so that the most profitable product mix is a function of both machine capacity and market demand. The following product mix would maximize profits:

| Product | Output units | Machine hours | Contribution per machine hour | Total contribution |
|---|---|---|---|---|
| C | 100 | 100 | £5.0 | £500 |
| B | 100 | 200 | £3.5 | £700 |
| A | 50 | 150 | £3.0 | £450 |
| | | 450 | | £1,650 |

This product mix reflects the order of priority in allocating machine use to the products with the highest contribution margin per hour. Product C receives the highest priority, then product B, and lastly product A. If machine hours were further limited to 300 hours, the firm would cease to make product A.

# Linear programming and decision making

Linear programming is a mathematical technique which seeks to make the best use of a firm's limited resources to meet chosen objectives, which in accounting terms may take the form of the maximization of profits or the minimization of costs. In those situations, for example, where a manufacturer has a limited plant capacity, the level and cost of output will be determined by such capacity.

**Example 11**  Blackamoor Steels Ltd manufactures two high-quality steel products in respect of which the following information is available:

|  | Product A £ | Product B £ |
|---|---|---|
| Selling price per unit | 30 | 20 |
| Variable costs per unit | 15 | 10 |
| Contribution margin | 15 | 10 |

Milling and grinding machines are used in the manufacturing process, and the total machine hours necessary to produce one unit of each product are:

|  | Product A | Product B |
|---|---|---|
| Milling | 5 hours | $1\frac{1}{2}$ hours |
| Grinding | 2 | 2 |
|  | 7 | $3\frac{1}{2}$ |

Both products are in great demand, and the only constraint on expanding output is machine capacity. The total machine hours available per month are:

Milling (3 machines at 200 hours a month)    600 hours
Grinding (2 machines at 200 hours a month)   400 hours

On the basis of the facts given above, the problem facing management is to ascertain that combination of output of products A and B which will maximize the total contribution margin to overheads and profits. The problem is similar to the example discussed in the previous section (see p 474). At first glance, it would appear that the firm should maximize the production of product A since that product yields the highest unit contribution margin. Analysed in terms of the machine capacity limit, the total number of units of either product A or product B which could be manufactured is as follows:

Product A    600 hours ÷ 5 hours = 120 units
Product B    400 hours ÷ 2 hours = 200 units

These output limits are derived in the case of product A by the fact that output is limited to the capacity of the milling machines, for product A requires five hours of milling as against only two hours of grinding. Product B, however, is limited in output by the capacity of the grinding machines of which it requires two hours per unit, as against one and a half hours of milling time.

By relating the calculation of the contribution margin to the machine capacity limits, the total contribution to overhead costs and profits which will be obtained by the production of *either* A or B is as follows:

| | |
|---|---|
| Product A | 120 units × £15 = £1,800 |
| Product B | 200 units × £10 = £2,000 |

It follows, therefore, that given the option of making either product A or product B the firm should concentrate on the making of product B.

The approach to the solution of this problem under linear programming consists, first, of formulating the problem in simple algebraic terms. There are two aspects to the problem, the first being the wish to maximize profits and the second being the need to recognize the production limits. The two aspects may be stated algebraically as follows:

1 The objective is to maximize the contribution to fixed overheads and profit. This objective is called the objective function, and may be expressed thus:

$$\text{Maximize } C = 15A + 10B$$

where C is the total contribution and A and B are the total number of units of the two products which must be manufactured to maximize the total contribution. This equation is subject to the limits that:

$$A \geq 0$$
$$B \geq 0$$

for it is not possible to produce negative quantities of either A or B.

2 The constraints on production arising from the machine capacity limits of the milling department (600 hours) and of the grinding department (400 hours) may also be expressed in algebraic terms as follows:

$$5A + 1\tfrac{1}{2}B \leq 600$$
$$2A + 2B \leq 400$$

The first inequality states that the total number of hours used on milling must be equal to or less than 600 hours; the second inequality states that the total hours used on grinding machines must be equal to or less than 400 hours.

The problem may now be summarized in the form:

$$\text{Maximize } C = 15A + 10B$$

subject to the constraints:

$$5A + 1\tfrac{1}{2}B \leq 600$$
$$2A + 2B \leq 400$$
$$A \geq 0$$
$$B \geq 0$$

It is possible to solve the problem by means of a graph (Figure 5.17) showing the manufacturing possibilities for the two departments, as given in the following data:

| | |
|---|---|
| **Milling department:** | |
| Product A | 600 ÷ 5 = 120 units |
| or  Product B | 600 ÷ 1½ = 400 units |
| **Grinding department:** | |
| Product A | 400 ÷ 2 = 200 units |
| or  Product B | 400 ÷ 2 = 200 units |

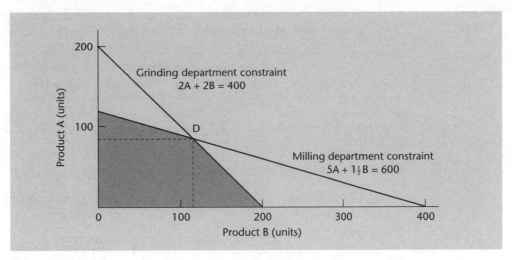

**Figure 5.17**

The shaded region in Figure 5.17 contains all the combinations of products A and B which are feasible solutions to the problem, hence its name – the feasibility region. The optimal solution, that is, the product combination of A and B which is the best of all the feasible solutions, lies at the intersection of the lines at point D, and may be read off as 85 units of A and 115 of B. It will be observed that the optimal solution lies on a tangent which is the furthest away from the point of origin. The graphical method of solving the problem is susceptible to error unless carefully plotted, and a more reliable answer may be obtained by solving the problem mathematically.

The optimal combination of products A and B may be found by solving the simultaneous equation given above, that is,

$$1 \quad 5A + 1\tfrac{1}{2}B = 600$$
$$2 \quad 2A + 2B = 400$$

The solution is obtained by multiplying (1) by 4 and (2) by 3 to give us the value of A, as follows:

$$
\begin{aligned}
20A + 6B &= 2{,}400 \\
-\quad 6A + 6B &= 1{,}200 \\
\hline
14A \qquad\ &= 1{,}200 \\
A \qquad\ &= 8\tfrac{5}{7}
\end{aligned}
$$

Since we are concerned only with completed units of A, the optimal production of product A is 85 units. The optimal number of units of B may be calculated by inserting the known value of A into the equation, as follows:

$$
\begin{aligned}
(6 \times 85) + 6B &= 1{,}200 \\
\text{i.e.} \quad 510 + 6B &= 1{,}200 \\
6B &= 1{,}200 - 510 \\
B &= 115
\end{aligned}
$$

Hence, the optimal combination of products A and B is 85 units and 115 units respectively, in terms of the limited machine capacity which will be utilized as follows:

| | Milling department (hours) | Grinding department (hours) |
|---|---|---|
| Product A – 85 units | 425 (85 × 5) | 170 (85 × 2) |
| Product B – 115 units | 172.5 (115 × 1½) | 230 (115 × 2) |
| Total hours used | 597.5 | 400 |
| Total hours available | 600 | 400 |

The optimal combination will produce a total contribution to overheads and profits of £2,425 as follows:

| | | |
|---|---|---|
| Product A | 85 units of £15 = | 1,275 |
| Product B | 115 units of £10 = | 1,150 |
| | | £2,425 |

We may verify that this combination of products is the optimal one in terms of profits and available machine capacity, as follows:

1 Altering the product combination from 85 units of A and 115 units of B to 84 units of A and 116 units of B, which would affect machine use as follows:

| | Milling department (hours) | Grinding department (hours) |
|---|---|---|
| Product A – 84 units | 420 (84 × 5) | 168 (84 × 2) |
| Product B – 116 units | 174 (116 × 1½) | 232 (116 × 2) |
| Total hours used | 594 | 400 |
| Total hours available | 600 | 400 |

Hence, this combination is as efficient in the utilization of the grinding department but less efficient in the utilization of the milling machines. It is also less profitable, yielding a contribution of only £2,420 as against £2,425 as follows:

| | | |
|---|---|---|
| Product A | 84 units at £15 = | 1,260 |
| Product B | 116 units at £10 = | 1,160 |
| | | £2,420 |

2 Altering the product combination from 85 units of A and 115 units of B to 86 units of A and 113 units of B, which would affect machine use as follows:

| | Milling department (hours) | Grinding department (hours) |
|---|---|---|
| Product A – 86 units | 430 (86 × 5) | 172 (86 × 2) |
| Product B – 113 units | 169½ (113 × 1½) | 226 (113 × 2) |
| Total hours used | 599½ | 398 |
| Total hours available | 600 | 400 |

Hence, whereas this combination is more efficient in the use of the milling machines than the optimal combination, it is less efficient in the use of the grinding machinery. Moreover, to keep within the capacity limits of the milling department we have had to forgo the production of two units of product B to expand the manufacture of product A by one unit. The consequential contribution to profits is also only £2,420 as against the optimal contribution of £2,425, which may be calculated as follows:

| | | |
|---|---|---|
| Product A | 86 units of £15 = | 1,290 |
| Product B | 113 units of £10 = | 1,130 |
| | | £2,420 |

It is noteworthy, also, that the linear programming approach to the best product combination mix gives a solution which is more profitable than the one which relates the contribution margin to the machine capacity limits, which we discussed on page 475, and which suggested that only product B should be made so that 200 units of B would be manufactured to yield a contribution of £2,000.

We have so far discussed only simple cases involving at the maximum only two resource constraints. In real life, a firm may be faced with more than two constraints, but mathematical techniques exist for coping with larger numbers of limits. The Simplex Method, for example, which is based on matrix algebra, may be employed in such cases and it is ideally suited for solutions using a computer.

## Summary

In addition to providing information for short-run decision-making purposes, the accountant also often has to provide information for a number of short-run tactical decisions such as dropping a product line or choosing between selling or further processing a semi-manufactured product. As in other areas of accounting, cost information plays an important role in short-run tactical decisions. The costs which are relevant for such decisions are future differential costs.

Although opportunity costs are not recorded in the accounting process, there are a number of decision problems where opportunity costs are the only relevant costs. Opportunity costs may be defined as the value of the next best opportunity forgone, or of the net cash inflow lost as a result of preferring one alternative rather than the next best one.

Limits placed on resources have to be recognized in decision making. Product-mix decisions illustrate the nature of this problem and the manner in which the best use of limited resources may be made. In this connection, linear programming affords a useful technique for maximizing profits or minimizing costs in the face of constraints on resources.

**References**     Kennedy, A (1995). 'Activity-based management and short-term relevant cost: clash or complement?', *Management Accounting* (UK), June.

## Self-assessment questions

1  Define the nature of relevant costs.

2  State what you understand by the following terms:
   (a) future costs,
   (b) sunk costs,
   (c) differential costs.

3  Give examples of future, sunk and differential costs, and state the conditions required for such costs to be relevant costs.

4  Define the contribution margin.

5  What do you understand by 'opportunity costs'? Are opportunity costs also relevant costs?

6  Name four major classes of special decisions, and review the impact of these decisions on the enterprise in the short and the long term.

7  Explain how opportunity costs may be relevant costs in the four major classes of special decisions referred to in (6) above.

8  Define a limiting factor, and give four examples of limiting factors.

9  Explain how the contribution margin may be applied to decision making in the face of a limiting factor.

10  What do you understand by linear programming? Explain the usefulness of this method in decision making.

1 Heating Products Ltd has a division which manufactures radiators. The standard radiator is the Radwarm, but the company also produces radiators to customers' specification. Such radiators are described in the firm as Specials. The forecast results of the division for the year ending 31 December 20X0 are shown below:

| | Radwarm | Specials | Total |
|---|---|---|---|
| | £ | £ | £ |
| Sales | 50,000 | 100,000 | 150,000 |
| Materials | 16,000 | 20,000 | 36,000 |
| Labour | 18,000 | 40,000 | 58,000 |
| Depreciation | 7,200 | 12,600 | 19,800 |
| Power | 800 | 1,400 | 2,200 |
| Rent | 2,000 | 12,000 | 14,000 |
| Heat and light | 200 | 1,200 | 1,400 |
| Miscellaneous costs | 1,800 | 800 | 2,600 |
| | 46,000 | 88,000 | 134,000 |
| Net profit | 4,000 | 12,000 | 16,000 |

The expenses have been arrived at as follows:

(a) Depreciation is calculated on the book value of machinery used during production of each of the two groups of products.
(b) Rent is based on the space occupied in the division by each of the product lines. The building housing this division is rented at £14,000 p.a. on a ten-year lease.
(c) Heat and light for the building are apportioned on the basis of area occupied by the two groups of products.
(d) All other costs are traced directly to the product lines.

The divisional manager has received an order to supply 1,000 Special radiators. To accommodate this order, the division would have to switch half of its Radwarm production capacity. The customer has offered a price of £70 per radiator for these Specials and each radiator would take £20 of materials and £36 of labour.

A special press would need to be purchased for this order at a price of £4,000. There would be no further use for this once this order is finished and it would be discarded.

*Required:*
(a) Calculate
   (i) the differential cost of the special order;
   (ii) the full cost of the order; and
   (iii) the opportunity cost of accepting this order.
(b) Write a report explaining whether Heating Products Ltd should accept the special order.

2 It is three months since William Wright was appointed accountant at Broomhill Manufacturing Company. During this period he has become increasingly dissatisfied with the company's accounting system. In particular, overheads are not analysed into fixed and variable elements. Wright believes that profit planning requires an understanding of the characteristics of cost and their behaviour at different operating levels. He resolved to write to the managing director and explain his new approach. To support his case Wright searched for examples which could be used to illustrate his arguments. One such example is given below.

*Example*

The profit and loss account for 31 December 20X0, Wright believed, could be improved for making the predictions implied in the profit planning process. This showed the following results:

|  | £ |
|---|---|
| Sales revenue | 100,000 |
| Cost of sales: | |
| Materials | 15,000 |
| Labour | 20,000 |
| Factory overheads | 20,000 |
|  | 55,000 |
| Gross margin | 45,000 |
| Selling and administrative expenses | 35,000 |
| Net profit | 10,000 |

Wright estimated that fixed factory overheads amounted to £5,000 and fixed selling and administrative expenses to £25,000.

The accountant of Broomhill Manufacturing, previous to Wright's appointment, had analysed the results for 20X0 by product groups and this had led the managing director to consider eliminating Product B, a loss-making product. The analysis by product is given below:

|  | A | B | C |
|---|---|---|---|
|  | £ | £ | £ |
| Sales revenue | 60,000 | 15,000 | 25,000 |
| Cost of sales: | | | |
| Materials | 10,000 | 2,000 | 3,000 |
| Labour | 11,000 | 4,000 | 5,000 |
| Factory overheads | 11,000 | 4,000 | 5,000 |
|  | 32,000 | 10,000 | 13,000 |
| Gross margin | 28,000 | 5,000 | 12,000 |
| Selling and administrative expenses | 20,000 | 8,000 | 7,000 |
|  | 8,000 | (3,000) | 5,000 |

Factory overheads were allocated to products at a rate of 100 per cent direct labour cost. Wright estimated that fixed factory overhead elements of the assigned costs were as follows:

    A   £3,000
    B   £1,000
    C   £1,000

Selling and administrative expenses had been assigned to products on an arbitrary basis. Wright estimated the fixed elements as below:

    A   £15,000
    B   £6,000
    C   £4,000

*Required:*

To what extent is Wright justified in seeking a reappraisal of the situation?

3* The Appleton Apparel Company manufactures and sells three types of outer-wear, a Basic, a Standard and a Superior waxed jacket.
   The forecasts for the forthcoming year are as follows:

|  | Basic £ | Standard £ | Superior £ |
|---|---|---|---|
| Selling price | 56 | 120 | 225 |
| Direct materials | 20 | 40 | 100 |
| Direct wages | 16 | 30 | 40 |
| Variable overheads | 16 | 30 | 40 |
| Fixed overheads (apportioned) | 8 | 15 | 20 |
| Sales (units) | 3,000 | 2,000 | 1,500 |

The material price per metre varies according to each coat but the usage (4 metres per coat) is the same. Employees are paid at a rate of £2 per labour hour. The fixed overheads for the period are £84,000.
   At the same time as the forecasts were completed a competitor in the same industry increased the wage rates to its employees and some Appleton Apparel employees secured jobs at the other company. This resulted in the workforce of Appleton Apparel falling by approximately 30 per cent. The total labour hours now stands at 60,000 hours.

*Required:*
(a) Prepare an income statement, using the original forecast, which provides meaningful accounting information to management.
(b) Given the reduction in labour hours, which product(s) should the company concentrate on? Calculate the net profit resulting from your suggestion.
(c) A comparable product could be imported. The buying-in prices for the three products are £62, £110 and £175 for the Basic, Standard and Superior respectively. What would be your advice?
(d) What other factors should be taken into consideration?

4 An electronics company produces many types of expensive components. A recent contract for a batch of components (KRS) was priced by the company's accountant. Although the company is short of work, the accountant has advised the managing director that the contract should not be accepted because it will result in a loss, as follows:

| Contract: KRS | £ | £ |
|---|---|---|
| Contract price | | 100,000 |
| *Less:* | | |
| Materials | 65,000 | |
| Labour | 49,000 | |
| Depreciation | 10,000 | |
| Variable overheads | 6,000 | |
| Fixed overhead allocation | 20,000 | 150,000 |
| Loss | | (50,000) |

The following additional information is available:

£10,000 of material, for which there is no other use, is already in stock. If the contract does not go ahead, it will be disposed of at a cost of £1,000. A contract has been agreed for £5,000 worth of stock. The balance of the stock will also need to be purchased.

Labour costs include an allocation of supervisor's costs of £20,000. If the contract is not accepted, some of the workforce will be made redundant at a cost of £10,000.

It has just been realized that the machinery for the contract needs some modification at a cost of £3,000. If the machinery is not used in the contract it will be sold for £5,000.

The contract will take 3,600 direct labour hours.

*Required:*
(a) Should the contract be accepted or rejected? Justify your inclusion or exclusion of costs and state what other factors should be taken into account.
(b) Before a final decision is made, the company receives a new order for its products. The following information is available:

| Per unit | £ |
| --- | --- |
| Selling price | 100 |
| Direct materials | 45 |
| Direct labour | 20 |
| Allocated fixed costs | 10 |
| Variable cost | 15 |

To make one unit takes five labour hours.

The company does not have the labour hours available to complete contract KRS and accept the new order. Should contract KRS or the new order be accepted? Explain your reasons and give supporting figures.

(c) 'Decision making is not concerned solely with costs and revenues.' Give some examples of non-financial considerations that may be taken into account when making various types of decision.

# 32 Capital investment decisions

## Setting the scene

It needs to be stressed that the very features of the traditional accounting model, which make it appropriate as a basis for measuring short-term performance, make it totally *inappropriate* as a basis for making decisions affecting long-term financial health. Financial managers are concerned, not with the static concept of *whether or not* a profit can be declared on the basis of a selected convection of capital maintenance, but with the dynamic one of *whether enough* wealth will be created to justify the commitment of funds necessary to support the aspirations of the enterprise. Specifically, their quantifications of their team's judgements are likely to be expressed in terms of projected cashflows, discounted at the cost of capital.                              (Allen, 1992)

## Learning objectives

After studying this chapter you should be able to:

1 Explain what is meant by a capital investment decision and why it is important.
2 Compute the payback period and accounting rate of return for a proposed investment and explain their role in capital investment decisions.
3 Compute the present value of future cash flows.
4 Use net present value analysis to determine whether an investment is acceptable.
5 Use the internal rate of return to assess the acceptability of an investment.
6 Explain the impact of inflation on the capital investment decision.
7 Appreciate the problem of high-tech investments.

Probably the most significant factor affecting the level of profitability in a business is the quality of managerial decisions affecting the commitment of the firm's resources to new investments within the firm. The reasons which render such strategic decisions so important may be listed as follows:

1 They involve the commitment of substantial sums of money.
2 This commitment is made for a long period of time, and the element of uncertainty is therefore much greater than in the case of decisions whose effects are limited to a short period of time.

3 Once made, capital investment decisions are almost impossible to reverse should they appear subsequently to have been wrongly made.

4 Occasionally, the success or the failure of a firm may depend upon a single decision. In all cases, the future profitability of the firm will be affected by the decision.

5 Not only is capital expenditure policy of major importance to a firm, but it is of great significance to an industry as well as to the national economy.

## Types of capital investment decisions

A capital investment may be defined as an investment which yields returns during several future time periods, and may be contrasted with other types of investments which yield all their return in the current time period. Capital investment decisions may concern the following:

1 The acquisition or replacement of long-lived assets, such as buildings and plant.

2 The investment of funds into another firm from which revenues will flow.

3 A special project which will affect the firm's future earning capacity, such as a research project or an advertising campaign.

4 The extension of the range of activities of the firm involving a capital outlay, such as a new production line or indeed a new product.

Capital investment decisions encompass two aspects of long-range profitability: first, estimating the future net increases in cash inflows or net savings in cash outlays which will result from the investment; and second, calculating the total cash outlays required to effect the investment.

## The analysis of capital investment proposals

In the analysis of capital investment proposals, many of the important facts are uncertain, so that the first problem is to reduce the area of uncertainty before a decision is made. The second problem is to ensure that all known facts are correctly assessed and quantified. Both known and uncertain facts are estimated in cash terms, and methods of capital investment appraisal focus on cash flows.

The selection of investment projects is always a question of considering which of several competing alternatives is the best from the firm's point of view. By quantifying the cash inflows and the cash outlays which are involved in the various alternatives, a decision may be made by selecting that alternative which is preferred by the firm.

*Example 1* Wall Street Finance Ltd is offered the opportunity of selecting two investments, each of which will yield £500,000 yearly. Investment A requires a total cash outlay of £5,000,000 – hence it promises a rate of return of 10 per cent. Investment B requires a total cash outlay of £50,000,000 – and therefore offers a rate of return of 1 per cent per annum. The firm would prefer investment A. However, if the firm has a minimum acceptable rate of return of 15 per cent, neither project would be acceptable.

We may conclude, therefore, that there are three major factor[s] investment decisions:

1 The net amount of the investment required, expressed as the needed to support the project during its entire life.
2 The net returns on the investment, expressed as the future [cash] inflows. These may be actual cash flows, or cash savings.
3 The rate of return on investment, expressed as a percentage. The determination of the lowest acceptable rate of return on investment will be influenced by a number of factors, among which are the firm's rate of return on its other investment opportunities and the cost of capital to the firm.

## The relevant cash flows

Before we proceed to examine the methods of selecting investment projects, let us briefly define the meaning of the terms which we shall be employing.

## Net investment outlays

These consist of initial investment outlays required to establish the project, and the subsequent investment outlays which are envisaged at the outset, and are distinguishable from operating cash outlays. Thus, initial investment outlays may compromise expenditure on equipment, installation costs, training, working capital, etc. Subsequent investment outlays may include 'second stage' developments, plant extensions, etc. The analysis of a capital project is in terms of net cash costs to the firm, so that where tax credits are allowable, these credits must be deducted from the total cash costs to obtain the relevant cash outlay.

## Net cash inflows

These are the operating cash flows associated with the investment over the period of its useful life. They are calculated after deducting operating cash expenditure and taxation. Since there may be year-to-year variation in the profile of these net cash flows, and since their periodic pattern is largely guesswork, they are the most difficult cash flows to quantify.

All cash flow calculations are made on the basis of the estimated useful life of the investment, which is defined as the time interval that is expected to elapse between the time of acquisition or commencement and the time at which the combined forces of obsolescence and deterioration will justify the retirement of the asset or project. The useful life of the investment may be shortened by market changes which will diminish its earnings.

## ethods of appraising capital investments

The more commonly used methods of evaluating capital investment proposals are:

1 the payback period.
2 the accounting rate of return.
3 the discounted cash flow techniques, of which there are two main forms:
   (a) the net present value method (NPV);
   (b) the internal rate of return (IRR).

## The payback period

This method attempts to forecast how long it will take for the expected net cash inflows to *pay back* the net investment outlays. The payback period is calculated as follows:

$$\text{payback period (years)} = \frac{\text{net investment outlays}}{\text{average net cash inflows}}$$

**Example 2**  Northend Engineering Co Ltd is considering the acquisition of machinery which will considerably reduce labour costs. The following are the relevant facts:

| | |
|---|---:|
| Net investment outlays | £200,000 |
| Estimated annual cash savings (after tax) | 60,000 |
| Estimated useful life | 5 years |
| Salvage value | nil |

The payback period is as follows:

$$\frac{£200,000}{60,000} \quad \text{i.e. } 3\tfrac{1}{3} \text{ years}$$

The payback method has the advantage of simplicity. By advocating the selection of projects by reference only to the speed with which investment outlays are recovered, it recommends the acceptance of only the safest projects. It is a method which emphasizes liquidity rather than profitability, and its limitations may be stated to be as follows:

1 It lays stress on the payback period rather than the useful life of the investment, and ignores the cash flows beyond the payback period. Hence, it focuses on breaking even rather than on profitability.
2 It ignores the time profile of the net cash inflows, and any time pattern in the net investment outlays. Any salvage value would also be ignored. This method, therefore, treats all cash flows through time as having the same value, so that in the example given, the value of £200,000 invested now is equated with £200,000 of net cash inflows over $3\tfrac{1}{3}$ years.

These problems may be illustrated as follows.

**Example 3** Multiplexed Ltd is considering four different investment projects each costing £20,000. The following information relates to these projects:

| Project No. | 1 | 2 | 3 | 4 |
|---|---|---|---|---|
| | £ | £ | £ | £ |
| Initial investment outlay | 20,000 | 20,000 | 20,000 | 20,000 |
| Cash inflows | | | | |
| Year 1 | 9,000 | 11,000 | 3,000 | 10,000 |
| Year 2 | 11,000 | 9,000 | 6,000 | 6,000 |
| Year 3 | – | – | 8,000 | 4,000 |
| Year 4 | – | – | 10,000 | 4,000 |
| Year 5 | – | – | 10,000 | 3,000 |
| Payback period (years) | 2 | 2 | $3\frac{1}{3}$ | 3 |

A crude application of the payback method would select projects 1 or 2 but would be unable to decide between these two projects.

# The accounting rate of return

The accounting rate of return method seeks to express the average estimated yearly net inflows as a percentage of the net investment outlays. As, however, it is possible to recover depreciation from the yearly net inflows, the formula is expressed as follows:

$$R = \frac{C - D}{I}$$

where
$R$ = the accounting rate of return
$C$ = average yearly net inflows
$D$ = depreciation
$I$ = net investment outlays

Substituting the figures given in our example on p 488, the accounting rate of return would be calculated as follows:

$$R = \frac{£60,000 - £40,000}{£200,000} \times 100\%$$

$$= 10\%$$

It may be argued, however, that the recovery of depreciation over the useful life of the investment reduces the value of the net investment outlays through time. Assuming an average recovery through depreciation at the rate of £40,000 per year, the average net investment over the estimated useful life of five years is £100,000, calculated by using the arithmetic mean method as follows:

$$\text{Average lifetime investment} = \frac{£200,000}{2}$$

$$= £100,000$$

The average lifetime investment may be calculated graphically as shown in Figure 5.18.

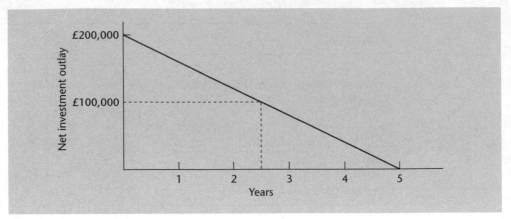

**Figure 5.18**

In the light of this argument, the accounting rate of return on investment should express the annual net cash inflows as a percentage of the average annual net investment outlays, so that, substituting the values given in our example, the average return on investment is:

$$R = \frac{£60,000 - £40,000}{£100,000} \times 100\%$$

$$= 20\%$$

This method of evaluating investment projects overcomes the disadvantage of the payback method in that it attempts to calculate the profitability of the various projects under study. Its main disadvantage is that it fails to consider the changing value of money through time, and treats the value of £1 in the future as equal to £1 invested today. Moreover, it ignores also the differences which may occur through time in the rate of net cash inflows. In both these senses, it suffers from the same defects as the payback method. Furthermore, there is a lack of agreement about a single method of calculating the accounting rate of return.

## Discounted cash flows

The methods of investment appraisal we have just examined are generally regarded as producing misleading results. The DCF method has gained widespread acceptance, for it recognizes that the value of money is subject to a time preference, that is, that £1 today is preferred to £1 in the future unless the delay in receiving £1 in the future is compensated by an interest factor. This interest factor is expressed as a discount rate.

In simple terms, the DCF method attempts to evaluate an investment proposal by comparing the net cash flows accruing over the life of the investment at their present value with the value of funds about to be invested. Thus, by comparing like with like it is possible to calculate the rate of return on the investment in a realistic manner.

To find the present equivalent value of £1 receivable one year hence, one applies the rate of interest to discount that £1 to its present value. This is the same thing as asking 'what sum of money invested today at the rate of interest would increase in value to £1 a year hence?'

**Example 4**  Given that the rate of interest is 10 per cent per annum the following calculations may be made:

£1 invested now at 10 per cent will amount to £1.10 in a year. Conversely, the value of £1.10 a year's hence is worth £1 now if the rate of interest is 10 per cent.

Using this principle, discount tables may be constructed for the value of £1 over several time periods ahead by compounding the interest rate through time, i.e. £1.00 invested for 1 year at 10 per cent will be worth £1.10 at the year end, £1.10 then reinvested for another year at 10 per cent will be worth £1.10 + 0.11 = £1.21 at the end of the second year.

**Example 5**  The value of £1 at the end of 1 year at 10% is £1+.10 $=$ £1.1
The value of £1 at the end of 2 years at 10% is $(£1.1)^2 =$ £1.21
The value of £1 at the end of 3 years at 10% is $(£1.1)^3 =$ £1.331
The value of £1 at the end of 4 years at 10% is $(£1.1)^4 =$ £1.464
The value of £1 at the end of 5 years at 10% is $(£1.1)^5 =$ £1.611

Conversely, the present value of £1 receivable at a future date is as follows:

$$£1 \text{ receivable in 1 years' time is } \frac{£1}{1.1} = £0.9091$$

$$£1 \text{ receivable in 2 years' time is } \frac{£1}{1.21} = £0.8264$$

$$£1 \text{ receivable in 3 years' time is } \frac{£1}{1.331} = £0.7513$$

$$£1 \text{ receivable in 4 years' time is } \frac{£1}{1.464} = £0.6831$$

$$£1 \text{ receivable in 5 years' time is } \frac{£1}{1.611} = £0.6208$$

The value of money is, therefore, directly affected by time, and the rate of interest is the method which is used to express the time value of money. Compound interest tables and discount tables are available which show the value of money at different interest rates over a number of years, so that in actual practice, it is a simple matter to apply the DCF method to the evaluation of an investment.

## The net present value

This method is based on an assumed minimum rate of return. Ideally, this rate should be the average cost of capital to the firm (see p 496) and it is this rate which would be used to discount the net cash inflows to their present value. The net investment outlays are subtracted from the present value of the net cash inflows leaving a residual figure, which is the net present value. A decision is made in favour of a project if the

NPV is a positive amount. This method may likewise be applied to the comparison of one project with another when considering mutually exclusive investments.

The rule may be stated as follows:

Accept the project if:

$$\frac{a_1}{(1+i)^1} + \frac{a_2}{(1+i)^2} + \dots + \frac{a_n}{(1+i)^n} > A$$

where  $A$ is the initial project cost
 $a$ are the net annual cash inflows
 $i$ is the cost of capital
 $n$ is the expected life of the project

**Example 6**  Corween Ltd is considering a project which has a life of five years and which will produce an annual inflow of £1,000. The investment outlay is £3,000 and the required rate of return is 10 per cent.

| Year | Inflow | Discount factor (at 10%) | Present value of inflow |
|---|---|---|---|
| 1 | £1,000 | 0.9091 | £909.1 |
| 2 | £1,000 | 0.8264 | £826.4 |
| 3 | £1,000 | 0.7513 | £751.3 |
| 4 | £1,000 | 0.6831 | £683.1 |
| 5 | £1,000 | 0.6208 | £620.8 |
| Present value of net inflows | | | £3,790.7 |
| Cost of investment outlay | | | £3,000.0 |
| Net present value of the project | | | £790.7 |

Since the net present value of the cash inflows ($a$) is greater than the present value of the cash outlay ($A$), the project should be accepted.

## The internal rate of return

This method requires us to calculate that rate of interest which used in discounting will reduce the net present value of a project to zero. This enables us to compare the internal rate of return (IRR) with the required rate.

The rule may be stated as follows:

Accept the project if:

$$A = \frac{a_1}{(1+r)} + \frac{a_2}{(1+r)^2} + \dots + \frac{a_n}{(1+r)^n}$$

and $r > i$
where  $A$ is the initial project cost
 $a$ are the net annual cash inflows
 $r$ is the solution discount rate
 $i$ is the required rate of return

**Example 7**  Let us return to the example given above and assume that Corween Ltd applies the internal rate of return analysis to the project under consideration. The analysis would be as follows:

| Year | Inflow | Discount factor at 19% | Present value at 19% | Discount factor at 20% | Present value at 20% |
|---|---|---|---|---|---|
| | £ | | £ | | £ |
| 1 | 1,000 | 0.8403 | 840.3 | 0.8333 | 833.3 |
| 2 | 1,000 | 0.7062 | 706.2 | 0.6944 | 694.4 |
| 3 | 1,000 | 0.5934 | 593.4 | 0.5787 | 578.7 |
| 4 | 1,000 | 0.4987 | 498.7 | 0.4823 | 482.3 |
| 5 | 1,000 | 0.4190 | 419.0 | 0.4019 | 401.9 |
| Present value of net inflow | | | 3,057.6 | | 2,990.6 |
| Cost of investment outlay | | | 3,000.0 | | 3,000.0 |
| Net present value of the project | | | + 57.6 | | − 9.4 |

We can see that the IRR is almost 20 per cent. (It is often possible to approximate the true rate more closely by assuming a linear relationship and interpolating between the two nearest points.) The ascertainment of the IRR at 20 per cent enables us to compare the IRR with the required rate of return on investment by the company.

## Net present value and internal rate of return compared

When dealing with simple investment appraisal projects, that is, those involving a once-and-for-all investment outlay followed by a stream of cash inflows, both the NPV and the IRR methods produce the same YES or NO decisions.

But the advantage of the NPV method is the simplicity with which the results are stated. Our example shows that with the NPV method, the expected results are expressed in terms of pounds which directly reflect the increased wealth position. The internal rate of return, on the other hand, produces a result which is shown as a percentage, and this result has to be compared with a minimum required rate of return before a decision may be made.

**Example 8**  Norwell Industries Ltd is studying two projects, each of which requires a net investment outlay of £3,000. Both have a useful life of five years, and the estimated profile of the net cash inflows is:

| End of year | Project A | Project B |
|---|---|---|
| | £ | £ |
| 1 | 500 | 2,000 |
| 2 | 1,000 | 1,500 |
| 3 | 1,500 | 1,500 |
| 4 | 2,000 | 1,000 |
| 5 | 2,000 | 500 |
| | £7,000 | £6,500 |

The desired minimum rate of return is 10 per cent.

493

### Analysis – net present value

The present value of the two projects may be calculated by using the desired minimum rate of return as a discount factor.

| End of Year | Discount factor 10% | Project A | Present value | Project B | Present value |
|---|---|---|---|---|---|
| | | £ | £ | £ | £ |
| 1 | 0.9091 | 500 | 454.6 | 2,000 | 1,818.2 |
| 2 | 0.8264 | 1,000 | 826.4 | 1,500 | 1,239.6 |
| 3 | 0.7153 | 1,500 | 1,073.0 | 1,500 | 1,073.0 |
| 4 | 0.6831 | 2,000 | 1,366.2 | 1,000 | 683.1 |
| 5 | 0.6208 | 2,000 | 1,241.6 | 500 | 310.4 |
| Present value of total cash inflows | | | £4,961.8 | | £5,124.3 |
| *Less*: Net investment outlay | | | £3,000.0 | | £3,000.0 |
| Net present value | | | £1,961.8 | | £2,124.3 |

Both projects are acceptable to the firm, and if a choice has to be made between them, Project B would be selected since it produces the highest net present value of the two. The time profile of the net cash inflows is seen to be a determining influence on the result, for although the total cash inflows before discounting are higher with Project A, the cash flows associated with Project B are concentrated in the earlier years and, when discounted, have a higher net present value than A's.

### Analysis – the internal rate of return

Taking the net cash inflows estimated for Project A, the rate which will discount the net cash inflows to £3,000 is found once again by trial and error. Using discount tables, we establish in this way that the discount rate is between 28 per cent and 29 per cent, as follows:

| Cash inflows | Discount factor at 29% | Present value at 29% | Discount factor at 28% | Present value at 28% |
|---|---|---|---|---|
| £ | | £ | | £ |
| 500 | 0.7752 | 387.7 | 0.7813 | 390.7 |
| 1,000 | 0.6009 | 600.9 | 0.6104 | 610.4 |
| 1,500 | 0.4658 | 698.7 | 0.4768 | 715.2 |
| 2,000 | 0.3611 | 722.2 | 0.3725 | 745.0 |
| 2,000 | 0.2799 | 559.8 | 0.2910 | 582.0 |
| | | £2,969.3 | | £3,043.3 |
| Original investment outlay | | £3,000.0 | | £3,000.0 |
| | | – 30.7 | | + 43.3 |

Using the same approach, the IRR from Project B may be calculated as 39 per cent.

The crucial test upon which the final acceptance of a project depends is whether or not the IRR compares favourably with the required rate of return. If the required rate of return is 20 per cent then both projects qualify.

One of the problems of comparing rates of return on projects is that direct comparisons between two percentages are meaningless unless referred to the initial outlays, so that their true dimensions may be perceived. This problem should never be lost sight of when using IRR percentages.

With more complicated investment problems, for example those which require that cash surpluses be set aside to meet an obligation arising at the end of the project's life, both methods assume that those cash surpluses are reinvested at the appropriate rate of return. Thus, where a loan has been raised to finance the project,* the IRR method envisages that the cash surpluses will be reinvested at the IRR discounting rate, whereas the NPV method envisages that they will be reinvested at the minimum acceptable rate of return used in that method. Thus, the advantage of the NPV method is that it makes more realistic assumptions about reinvestment opportunities.

More complex problems arise when applying the IRR method to investment projects which do not have the simple pattern of cash flows of the above examples, but we regard these problems as beyond the scope of this text.

## Taxation and other factors

In order that DCF calculations should lead to correct results, it is important that all factors affecting the calculations of cash flows should be taken into account. The most important of these factors is, of course, taxation. Indeed, we have assumed from the outset that the cash flow figures were net after tax. Apart from the direct effects of taxation, we should also adjust our figures for indirect aspects of taxation, such as investment grants, and the reader will recall that in calculating the net investment outlay, any recoveries in the form of investment incentives must be deducted from the amount brought into the DCF calculation. The effects of these incentives vary from project to project.

## The cost of capital

The evaluation of an investment project by DCF analysis requires a firm to calculate its cost of capital. This is true in selecting the discount rate for appraisal by means of the net present value method, or for establishing the acceptability of the internal rate of return.

A full discussion of the concept of the 'cost of capital' is beyond the scope of this book; indeed, the subject is perhaps the most difficult and controversial topic in the whole theory of finance. Our discussion will be a very elementary one so as to provide the reader with some understanding of investment planning.

The first problem in discussing the cost of capital lies in different meanings which the term has acquired. From a lender's point of view, the cost of capital represents the cost to them of lending money which may be equated to the return they could have obtained by investing in a similar project having similar risks. This concept of the cost of capital is founded on its 'opportunity cost'. The opportunity cost approach to the assessment of the cost of capital is one which a firm must always consider when evaluating an investment project. A firm may find, for example, that investing funds outside the firm may produce higher returns than an internal project. The main obstacle to a more widespread use of the opportunity cost concept is that of identifying investments of equal risks and hence measuring the opportunity cost.

---

* The simplifying assumption which we are making for the purpose of illustrating the point is that the firm's finances are linked to specific investment projects, which in reality is not perhaps the case.

Another concept in use is the actual cost incurred by a firm in borrowing money. A firm may obtain funds in a variety of ways, and each way has a different cost attached to it. Thus, a firm may issue shares and will pay a dividend on those shares, which must represent the cost of raising funds in that way. It may also borrow by the issue of debentures or by bank or other methods, and in these cases interest is payable. The fact that the firm may have raised its finance in several different ways makes it more realistic to use the 'average cost of capital' which is based on an analysis of its capital structure.

**Example 9**  The Keystone Corp Ltd has a capital structure distributed as to 80 per cent share capital and 20 per cent loan capital. The dividend rate is 10 per cent and the interest payable on the loan capital is 8 per cent. Calculate the average cost of capital.

| Source of funds | Proportion of total funds % | Cost of capital % | Product |
|---|---|---|---|
| Share capital | 80 | 10 | £800 |
| Loan capital | 20 | 8 | 160 |
| | 100 | | £960 |

The weighted average cost of capital is:

$$\frac{960}{100} = 9.6\%$$

The average cost of capital so calculated would in the case of this firm represent the minimum acceptable rate of return.

## Gearing and the cost of capital

It will be recalled from Part 2 that the distribution of a firm's capital structure as between share capital (equity capital) and fixed-interest stock (preference shares and debentures) is known as the gearing. A firm which is highly geared has a higher ratio of fixed-interest stock to equity capital. By changing its gearing, a firm may alter its average cost of capital.

**Example 10**  The firm in the above example increases its gearing by raising the proportion of loan capital from 20 per cent to 40 per cent. Its average cost of capital, as a result, is reduced to 9.2 per cent:

| Source of funds | Proportion of total funds % | Cost of capital % | Product |
|---|---|---|---|
| Share capital | 60 | 10 | £600 |
| Loan capital | 40 | 8 | 320 |
| | 100 | | £920 |

The average cost of capital is

$$\frac{920}{100} = 9.2\%$$

It should be noted that financial theorists have argued that it is due only to the influence of a corporation tax system which allows loan interest as a tax deductible expense that gearing is of any significance.

Financial planning requires a firm to give very serious consideration to its capital structure and to its gearing. Very complex issues are involved in planning an appropriate capital structure. Circumstances may make it advantageous to attempt to increase the proportion of loan capital, that is increase the gearing, such as the tax deductibility of loan interest which we have already mentioned. There is an upper limit to debt finance, however, for not only are there obvious dangers in the presence of large fixed-interest charges against corporate income, but there are practical limits to the amount of funds which may be borrowed for long-term purposes.

## Investment appraisal and inflation

As the cash flows associated with a particular project may span a considerable period of time, it is evident that the level of inflation during that time will affect considerably the profitability of the project. We pointed out in Chapter 26 that estimates of future events should take inflation into account, and in Part 3 the distinction between general price level and specific price changes was discussed. We indicated the need to adjust cash flow forecasts for specific price changes which would affect the enterprise, so as to maintain its operating capability. Accordingly, it is the inflating cost of specific items which are to be taken into account in investment appraisal. The cost of these specific items will exhibit different rates of change, as will the prices of the products containing elements of the specific items of costs. In effect, the existence of a lag between increases in cost and increases in prices may considerably reduce the profitability of a project under conditions of inflation. As the rate of inflation increases, so this problem becomes more acute. For this reason, firms entering into fixed-price contracts extending over a long period of time should arrange for cost-escalation clauses to mitigate the impact of inflation.

The most appropriate method of incorporating the effects of inflation into DCF calculations is to adjust cash flow forecasts for specific price increases. Such adjusted cash flows are then discounted by the monetary cost of capital.

*Example 11* In the earlier example (p 492), Corween Ltd had annual net cash flows of £1,000 for a period of five years, and the discount rate was given as 10 per cent. It may now be assumed that the annual net cash flows were derived as follows:

|  | £ | £ |
|---|---|---|
| Cash inflows from sales |  | 5,000 |
| Cash outflows: |  |  |
| Materials | 3,000 |  |
| Labour | 1,000 |  |
|  |  | 4,000 |
| Annual net cash flow |  | 1,000 |

The impact of inflation is considered in the following terms:

1 Sales revenues are expected to be adjusted for price changes at the rate of 15 per cent per annum. The adjustment to the annual expected cash inflows from sales is shown below.
2 Material costs are expected to increase at the rate of 18 per cent per annum. The adjustment for this increase is also shown below.
3 Labour costs are expected to increase at the rate of 10 per cent per annum. The adjustment is also shown below.

| | Annual rate of change | Year 1 | Year 2 | Year 3 | Year 4 | Year 5 |
|---|---|---|---|---|---|---|
| | % | £ | £ | £ | £ | £ |
| Sales revenue | 15 | 5,750 | 6,613 | 7,605 | 8,746 | 10,058 |
| Materials | 18 | 3,540 | 4,177 | 4,929 | 5,816 | 6,863 |
| Labour | 10 | 1,100 | 1,210 | 1,331 | 1,464 | 1,610 |
| | | 4,640 | 5,387 | 6,260 | 7,280 | 8,473 |
| Net cash flows (adjusted) | | 1,110 | 1,226 | 1,345 | 1,466 | 1,585 |

These annual expected future net cash flows may now be discounted at the appropriate discount rate. For simplicity, if it is assumed that the discount rate is 10 per cent, these annual net cash flows have a present value of £5,017, as follows:

| Year | Net cash flow | Discount factor at 10% | Present value |
|---|---|---|---|
| | £ | % | £ |
| 1 | 1,110 | 0.9091 | 1,009 |
| 2 | 1,226 | 0.8264 | 1,013 |
| 3 | 1,345 | 0.7513 | 1,010 |
| 4 | 1,466 | 0.6831 | 1,001 |
| 5 | 1,585 | 0.6208 | 984 |
| | | | 5,017 |
| Less: Initial investment outlay | | | 3,000 |
| Net present value of the project | | | 2,017 |

The foregoing example shows the manner in which inflation adds a new dimension to the problem of calculating present values. More calculations are involved, and the degree of uncertainty is increased. Many accountants feel that, under conditions of rapid and high inflation, the task of forecasting cash flows over the lifetime of a project covering several years seems somewhat academic. Research has shown that the most popular method of investment appraisal is the payback method, which emphasizes the rate of recovery of investment outlays. During periods of inflation, the payback method places emphasis on projects which have shorter payback periods.

# High-tech investments

Many of the long-term strategic effects of investing in advanced manufacturing technology (AMT) in a technologically competitive and changing production environment are simply not known or are very difficult to identify. As such, strategic considerations do not readily lend themselves to traditional capital investment appraisal. In many situations, strategic positioning becomes an overriding consideration. For example, should a competitor adopt AMT that enables it to offer greater product heterogeneity, more customized service, greater product liability and shorter lead time, there is little doubt that a firm's own discounted cash flow assumptions regarding such an investment will be of limited value. If it does not adopt the technology it will cease to be a player in the marketplace.

A second item of consideration in regard to high-tech investments is that such projects are not free-standing, i.e. many high-tech investments are interrelated, integrated parts of a whole and should not be viewed as individual projects. Many benefits will invariably appear in a different department from that where the investment is made. As they were not forecast or quantified, when they do occur, possibly one or two years after the initial costs were incurred, they will appear as an unplanned variance which will not be attributed to the project.

Third, operating qualitative benefits may outweigh quantitative factors in advanced technology investment decisions. These intangibles are numerous. Beyond its quantifiable labour savings, AMT, for example, may lead to improved design and

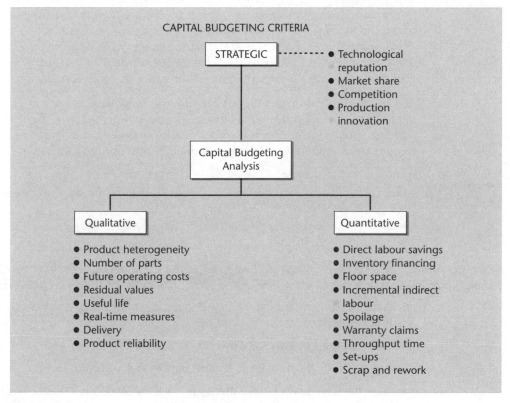

**Figure 5.19**

fewer product parts. The former would improve revenues and the latter production costs and product reliability. While these numbers are very difficult to quantify, they are probably more material then the actual labour cost savings.

Following Chalos (1992) quantitative and qualitative capital investment decisions are summarized in Figure 5.19. Once the numbers indicate whether or not an investment is worth while, qualitative factors should be addressed, in conjunction with the strategic implications for the firm.

## Summary

Preparing the capital expenditure plan is part of the long-range planning process. The quality of managerial decisions committing the firm's resources to new investments is probably the most significant factor affecting the level of future profitability.

Capital investment decisions encompass two aspects of the long-range profit plan – first, estimating the future net increases in cash inflows or net savings in cash outlays which will result from an investment; second, calculating the total cash outlays required to carry out an investment.

There are three well-known techniques for appraising investment proposals from a financial viewpoint:

1 *the payback method*, which emphasizes the length of time required to recoup the investment outlay;
2 *the accounting rate of return*, which seeks to express the average estimated yearly net inflows as a percentage of the net investment outlays for the purpose of assessing the profitability of a proposed investment;
3 *discounted cash flow methods*, which attempt to evaluate an investment proposal by comparing the present value of the net cash inflows accruing over the life of the investment with the present value of the funds to be invested.

Discounted cash flow techniques provide the most useful procedures for evaluating capital investment proposals. They comprise two methods – the net present value and the internal rate of return. Both methods take into account the time value of money, unlike the other methods mentioned which ignore this factor.

**References**   Allen, D (1992). 'The cost of capital: the criterion for sound financial management', *Management Accounting* (UK), December.

Chalos, P (1992). *Managing Cost in Today's Manufacturing Environment*, Prentice Hall.

## Self-assessment questions

1 What do you understand by capital investment decisions? State briefly the reason for their importance.

2 Give four examples of capital investment decisions.

3 Explain briefly the type of information used in making capital investment decisions.

4 State the three major factors affecting capital investment decisions.

5  What are the advantages and disadvantages associated with the payback period?

6  Do you consider the accounting rate of return method to be more useful than the payback period in evaluating capital investment?

7  Explain briefly the discounted cash flow method, and discuss its advantages and disadvantages when applied to investment appraisal.

8  Compare and contrast present value and internal rate of return methods.

9  What is the significance of the cost of capital in investment appraisal?

10 Suggest possible ways in which inflation may be taken into account in making capital investment decisions.


## Problems  *(\* indicates that a solution is to be found in the Lecturer's Guide)*

1  The purchase of a machine is contemplated and the relevant facts concerning two possible choices are as follows:

|  | Machine A | Machine B |
| --- | --- | --- |
| Capital expenditure required | £50,000 | £60,000 |
| Estimated life – years | 3 | 4 |
| Residual value | nil | nil |
| Cash flow after taxation – | | |
| constant each year at | £25,000 | £24,000 |

*2 year exact .*   *2 - 2000 12,000*

Assume a rate of interest of 10 per cent for which the reciprocals are:   *2 . 5 mongh .*

|  |  |  |  |
| --- | --- | --- | --- |
| Year 1 | 0.9091 | Year 2 | 0.8264 |
| Year 3 | 0.7513 | Year 4 | 0.6830 |

*Required:*
Set out calculations illustrating and comparing the following methods of evaluating the return from these investments:

(a)  payback period;
(b)  accounting rate of return;   *171. ov*
(c)  discounted cash flow.

Comment on the results.

2  Jazz Ltd is considering replacing three of its record-pressing machines with one machine which has just come on to the market. The three existing machines are two years old and cost £1,500 each. They are being depreciated on a straight-line basis over twelve years. It was expected that their final scrap value would be £600 each. Their replacement is being considered because a fault has developed in their operation which can only be corrected at a total cost of £5,000 for the three machines. The current second-hand market value of the machines is £1,000 each.

501

The annual operating costs of the existing and new machines are as follows:

**Existing machines: costs per machine**

|  |  | £ |
|---|---|---|
| Materials |  | 60,000 |
| Labour: one operator at 1800 hours |  | 1,350 |
| Variable expenses |  | 925 |
| Maintenance (excluding exceptional items) |  | 2,000 |
| Fixed expenses: |  |  |
| Depreciation | 75 |  |
| Fixed overheads absorbed | 2,700 | 2,775 |

**New machine**

|  |  | £ |
|---|---|---|
| Materials |  | 162,000 |
| Labour: two operators at 1,500 hours | 3,000 |  |
| one assistant at 1,500 hours | 900 | 3,900 |
| Variable expenses |  | 2,275 |
| Maintenance |  | 4,500 |
| Fixed expenses: |  |  |
| Depreciation | 9,550 |  |
| Fixed overheads absorbed | 7,800 | 17,350 |

The new machine's estimated life is 10 years and it will cost £100,000.
The company's cost of capital is 10 per cent.

*Required:*
(a) Advise the management of Jazz Ltd on the most profitable course of action to undertake.
(b) Comment on the method you have used and the other factors which might influence the decision.

3 Barry has invented an electronic executive toy which can be activated to emit various noises on selection of one of six buttons. The toy is pocket-sized and it is anticipated that it will retail for £10. Barry is keen to exploit the toy and with the help of his business partner, Bryn, they consider the following possibilities:

(i) Sell the exclusive rights to the game to a major toy manufacturer for £110,000.
(ii) Sell the rights to the manufacturer for £10,000 but receive an annual payment of £35,000 for the next five years (the payment being made at the end of each year).
(iii) Set up a manufacturing and selling operation. The best estimates for the next five years are:
 – Initial capital expenditure: £30,000.
 – Residual value at the end of year 5: £5,000.
 – Net working capital required to start up: £10,000.

| Year | Sales (units) | Sale price/ unit | Variable costs/unit | Fixed costs p.a.* |
|---|---|---|---|---|
| 1 | 20,000 | £10 | £8 | £45,000 |
| 2 | 40,000 | £10 | £8 | £45,000 |
| 3 | 100,000 | £10 | £8 | £45,000 |
| 4 | 60,000 | £10 | £8 | £45,000 |
| 5 | 40,000 | £10 | £8 | £45,000 |

* *Note:* Including depreciation of £5,000 p.a.

*Required:*
(a) Evaluate the proposals, given that the required rate of return is 20 per cent, and recommend the optimum proposal. Justify the reasons for your selection.
(b) What factors would influence your choice of a required rate of return?
(c) Would you advise the use of the cash payback method? Justify your answer with appropriate calculations.

4* David and Ruth are the joint owners of Whirlow Farm with an average turnover of £180,000.
    The annual proposed target rate of return is 15 per cent. Ruth has recently attended the local agricultural show and seen the latest models in tractors. She believes that their current tractor should be replaced by a new one so that operating costs will be reduced. The details are as follows:

– The tractor is eight years old and has a net book value of £9,500. It cost £19,100 when new and has been depreciated at £1,200 per annum. The tractor could be disposed of for £2,100 to Neil, the local second-hand machinery dealer.
– The new tractor will cost £38,000 and will last for seven years. It will have a residual value of £6,500 at the end of the period.
– The maintenance costs of the new machine will increase by £3,000 for the first two years; and then reduce by £400 for the remaining five years.
– In addition, the operating costs will reduce by £6,000 per annum.

David believes that there is nothing to be gained from replacing the current tractor and he produces the following schedule to support his view:

| | £ |
|---|---|
| Cost of new tractor | 38,000 |
| Net increase in maintenance costs | |
| (2 years × £3,000 less 5 years × £400) | 4,000 |
| Loss on old machine £9,500 – £2,100 | 7,400 |
| | 49,400 |
| Savings (7 years × £6,000) | 42,000 |
| Loss on investment | (7,400) |

*Required:*
(a) Using discount tables calculate the net benefit (or cost) at the target rate of return if the old machine is sold and a new one purchased. Advise Ruth on whether they should proceed with the investment and discuss any other factors which should be borne in mind.
(b) Comment on the part played by the following factors in a decision of this kind: (i) book value of old equipment; (ii) cost of new equipment; (iii) gain or loss on disposal of old equipment; (iv) disposal value of old equipment; (v) disposal value of new equipment.
(c) Critically evaluate the schedule prepared by David.

# 3 Planning and control

# 33 Budgeting for planning and control

**Setting the scene**

While some proposed management accounting techniques seem to be little used in practice, this cannot be said of budgeting. Surveys have shown that 99% of all companies in Europe operate formal budgeting systems. Most management accountants spend a considerable amount of time preparing, revising and monitoring budgets and most organisations have clear and well proven budgeting routines.

(Kennedy and Dugdale, 1999)

**Learning objectives**

After studying this chapter you should be able to:

1  Explain how strategic planning relates to budgeting.

2  Identify the budgets that make up the overall budget.

3  Prepare operating budgets for a manufacturing enterprise.

4  Describe zero-based budgeting.

5  Appreciate the difference between traditional budgeting and activity-based budgeting.

The process of budgeting focuses on the short term, normally one year, and provides an expression of the steps which management must take in the current period if it is to fulfil organizational objectives. However, many organizations prepare three-year budgets, with a detailed budget covering the first year, and a summarized one covering each of the following two years. The focus of this chapter is on the preparation of the budget for the first year.

## Objectives of budgeting

Long-range planning involves the selection of the mission statement (i.e. the reason for the organization being in business) and the determination of a suitable plan for attaining its objectives. Budgets are the quantitative expressions of these plans stated in either physical or financial terms or both. Therefore, the long-range plan is the guide for preparing the annual budgets and defines actions that need to be taken now in order to move towards long-term objectives. Indeed, the budget represents the first one-year span of the long-range budget. Budgeting is part of the management control process discussed in Chapter 25.

The reader will recall that one important feature of planning is the coordination of the various activities of an enterprise, and of its departments, so that they are harmonized in the overall task of realizing corporate objectives. For example, if the marketing function were to increase sales massively over a short period of time, the manufacturing function would have to increase output substantially – probably through the use of costly overtime labour, or by buying goods from an outside supplier at high prices. Conversely, excessive production may force the marketing function to sell at unrealistically low prices in order to avoid excessive investment in stock. The function of budgeting is to coordinate the various activities of an organization in order to achieve company rather than divisional or departmental objectives. Therefore it is necessary to establish objectives for each section of the organization which are in harmony with the organization as a whole.

As a plan of action, budgets can be used to control by comparing actual outcomes as they happen with the planned outcomes. If the actual differs significantly from the planned, actions can be taken to put the plan back on track if necessary.

## The need for flexibility

Because business conditions are always changing, it is necessary to view the budgeting process as a guide to future action, rather than a rigid plan which must be followed irrespective of changing circumstances. The latter approach may place the manager in a straitjacket in which he or she is forced to take decisions which are not in accordance with company objectives. For example, a departmental manager may find, due to changing conditions, that he has not spent all of his budget on a particular item. In order to spend all his budget allowance, so as to prevent the possibility of a cut in his allowance next year, he may squander funds which could have been put to better use in other sections of the organization. This used to be the case in government organizations, in that if money was not spent, the next year's budget would be reduced regardless of whether the money was needed that year. Towards the end of the government financial year, many managers would ensure that any expense heading which was underspent was spent by the year end.

More importantly, management must plan for changing business conditions, in order that appropriate action may be taken to deal with changes that may occur should any of the assumptions underlying plans be affected by such changes. This implies that contingency plans should be available to deal with changes which were unforeseen at the time when the budget was originally prepared.

Some firms relate their planning budgets to changing conditions by means of a rolling budget which is prepared every quarter, but for one year ahead. At the end of each quarter the plans for the next three quarters are revised, if this is necessary, and a fourth quarter is added. By this process the budgets are kept continually up-to-date.

Flexibility is also required if budgetary control is to be effective. Indeed the type of budget which may be suitable for planning may be inappropriate for control purposes. Therefore, budgets should be established for control purposes which reflect operating conditions which may be different from those envisaged in the planning stages. This is essential if individual managers are to be held responsible only for those deviations over which they have control. Such a requirement is called for by the use of a responsibility accounting system, which is discussed in Chapter 34.

# The organization of budgeting

The budgeting process itself requires careful organization. In large firms, budgeting is often in the hands of a budgeting committee which acts through the budget officer whose function it is to coordinate and control the budgeting process for the whole organization. Departmental budget estimates are requested from divisional managers, who in their turn collate this information from estimates submitted to them by their own departmental managers. Hence, budget estimates are based on information which flows upwards through the organization to the budget committee. The budget committee is responsible for coordinating this information, and resolving any differences in consultations with the managers involved. The final budget proposal is presented to the board of directors for its final approval.

# Steps in budgeting

The first stage of a budgeting exercise is the determination of the 'key' factors or constraints which impose overall limits to the budget plan. Among these factors are the productive capacity of the plant, the finances available to the firm, and, of course, the market conditions which impose a total limit on the output the firm is able to sell. Normally from a management point of view, the critical question is 'what is the firm able to sell in the budget period?', and this question summarizes all the limits to the budget plan. It is for this reason that the sales budget is at once the starting point and the fulcrum of the budgeting process.

Figure 5.20 illustrates how the various resources and activities of an enterprise are coordinated. A similar exercise would be carried out in a non-manufacturing organization or service organization. The areas which would not feature in some service organizations would be finished goods stock budget, material usage budget, raw materials budget and materials purchases budget. It is necessary to adapt the budget process to the industry and type of organization. For example in the health service, each service (acute, maternity, diagnostic and paramedic, etc.) would prepare an expense budget based on staff and the forecast of patients to be treated. Some materials costs would be incurred (drugs, bed sheets, etc.) but the major expense would be salaries. Next, the service costs would be accumulated into an expenditure budget while concurrently the money available to run the service would be cascading from the DoH downwards towards the area health authorities and then down to the hospitals. Ultimately a master budget would be prepared and submitted to the governing body.

The arrows indicate the flow of relevant information. Once the level of sales is established, selling and distribution cost may be ascertained. The production budget itself is determined by the sales forecast, the desired level of stock of finished goods and plant capacity. From the production budget may be estimated the production costs, and the cost schedules for materials, labour and overheads.

In addition, the budgeting process for capital expenditure reflects decisions taken in developing the long-range plan. The capital expenditure budget is concerned with expenditure during the budget period on the maintenance and improvement of the existing productive capacity. Associated with this budget are research and development costs for improving methods of production and product improvement as well.

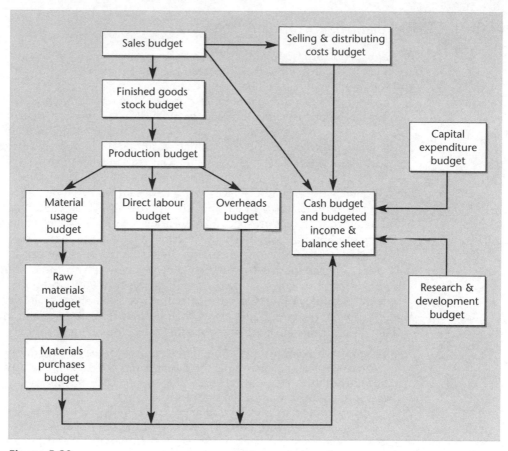

**Figure 5.20**

From a financing point of view, the cash surplus or deficits arising out of the overall budget are revealed by the cash budget which incorporates all cash revenues and cash expenditures. This enables the firm to arrange its financial needs accordingly.

Finally, the projected results in terms of the overall net profit and the changes in the structure of the firm's assets and liabilities are expressed in the budgeted profit and loss account and the budgeted balance sheet at the end of the budget period.

This description of the manner in which the budget coordinates the various activities of the firm is a simplified one. Budgetary planning is an activity which is of critical importance to the firm, and the problems involved are often complex and difficult ones to resolve. A firm's sales policy, for example, cannot be considered in isolation from its pricing policy and its cost structure. The firm's planned costs in relation to the required output may be too high to reach the profit target. If this should be the case, pricing and advertising policies may require further scrutiny, both planned and development costs may have to be reduced, and the final product itself may have to be modified. The role of the budget committee is, therefore, a very important one: not only has it to harmonize all the divisional budgets into an overall planning framework, but it has to deal with the numerous adjustments which may have to be made if the overall budget fails to meet some of the firm's stated objectives. Hence, the role of the budget committee is not only important in a practical sense: it affects important and sensitive areas of policy making and management.

## Forecasting sales

A major problem in budgeting is forecasting sales, for many factors affecting sales are outside the firm's control, for example the behaviour of the firm's competitors and the future economic climate.

The importance of an accurate sales forecast cannot be overemphasized. If the sales forecast is too optimistic, the firm may be induced to expand its capital expenditure programme and incur costs which may not be recoverable at a later date. In the meantime the production target may be set too high, resulting in the pile-up of stock of finished goods, which in itself has important financial consequences. Moreover, an optimistic sales forecast may disguise a deteriorating sales position, so that the necessary economies are not made which would produce a satisfactory profit. If, on the other hand, the sales forecast is pessimistic, the firm will miss the opportunity of larger current profit and may be misled as to its future prospects. The firm may, as a result, not undertake the necessary capital expenditure which would place it in a good position to exploit the market.

The sales forecast is the initial step in preparing the sales budget. It consists of not only analysing the market for the firm's products, but also forecasting the levels of sales at different prices. Hence, the study of the firm's pricing policy is an integral aspect of sales forecasting. Once the sales forecast is completed, the sales budget may be derived from the target sales established both as regards price and sales volume.

There are various methods of forecasting sales, for example:

1 *The salesforce composite method.* This method places responsibility upon individual salespeople for developing their own sales forecasts. The advantage of this method is that if participative budgeting is to be encouraged, the sales staff should assist in the preparation of the sales forecast.
2 *The analysis of market and industry factors.* This method recognizes the importance of factors not within the knowledge of the salesforce, such as forecasts of the gross national product, personal incomes, employment and price levels, etc. The salespeople's estimates are modified by the information so obtained.
3 *Statistical analysis of fluctuations through time.* Sales are generally affected by four basic factors: growth trends, business cycle fluctuations, seasonal fluctuations and irregular variations in demand. A time series analysis of sales is a statistical method of separating and analysing the historical evidence of the behaviour of sales to identify these several effects and their impact on sales. The results of this analysis are applied to the sales forecast, and are means of testing the quality of the forecast.
4 *Mathematical techniques for sales forecasting.* Of recent years, mathematical techniques have been applied to the study of the relationship between economic trends and a firm's sales pattern through time, to arrive at a projection of future sales. These techniques usually involve the use of computers. One such technique is known as exponential smoothing, which is really a prediction of future sales based on current and historical sales data, weighted so as to give a greater importance to the latest incoming information.

## An illustration of the budgeting process

Once the sales forecast is known, a firm may begin to prepare the budget. We believe that the reader will obtain a better understanding of budgeting if we work through a simple example. In the following example, we focus on the technical problems of budget construction, and we assume that the problem of changing price levels is not present. This assumption allows us to treat asset values as remaining constant.

**Example 1**  The Edco Manufacturing Co Ltd manufactures two products, A and B.

A formal planning system had been introduced some time ago as a means of steering the company into more profitable levels of operation. Considerable progress had already been made in streamlining production and reducing costs. The budgeting process normally began in October, prior to the end of the accounting year on 31 December.

### The Edco Manufacturing Co Ltd
### Forecast results for the year ending 31 December 20X0

**Profit and loss account**

|  | £ |
|---|---:|
| Sales | 135,000 |
| Cost of goods sold | 80,000 |
| Gross margin | 55,000 |
| Selling and administrative expenses | 25,000 |
| Profit before tax | 30,000 |
| Tax at 40% | 12,000 |
| Profit after tax | 18,000 |

**Balance sheet**

|  | Cost £ | Depreciation £ | £ |
|---|---:|---:|---:|
| **Fixed assets** | | | |
| Plant and machinery | 250,000 | 30,000 | 220,000 |
| **Current assets** | | | |
| Stocks: | | | |
| Raw materials | | 1,650 | |
| Finished goods | | 6,025 | |
| | | 7,675 | |
| Debtors | | 20,000 | |
| Cash | | 5,325 | |
| | | 33,000 | |
| *Less:* Creditors: amounts falling due within one year | | | |
| Creditors | 5,000 | | |
| Tax | 12,000 | | |
| | | 17,000 | |
| Net current assets | | | 16,000 |
| Total assets *less* current liabilities | | | 236,000 |
| **Capital and reserves** | | | |
| Called-up share capital | | | 210,000 |
| Profit and loss account | | | 26,000 |
| | | | 236,000 |

The expected results for the current year ending on 31 December 20X0 were as shown above. From these forecast results, the expected performance for the current year may be calculated as follows:

$$\text{return on shareholders' equity: } \frac{£18,000}{£236,000} = 7.6\%$$

$$\text{return on capital employed: } \frac{£30,000}{£236,000} = 12.7\%$$

The following additional information was obtained for the purpose of preparing the budget for the year ending 31 December 20X1.

## The sales forecast

|  | Product A | Product B |
|---|---|---|
| Expected selling price per unit | £11 | £14 |
| Sales volume forecast |  |  |
| 1st quarter | 1,500 units | 2,000 units |
| 2nd quarter | 1,000 | 2,000 |
| 3rd quarter | 1,000 | 2,000 |
| 4th quarter | 1,500 | 2,000 |
| Total for the year | 5,000 | 8,000 |

## Factory costs forecast

Two departments are concerned with production: the preparation department and the machining department. The following analysis relates to the production of these departments:

### 1 Direct costs

|  | Direct labour required per unit of product (in labour hours) | | Departmental wage rate | Direct labour cost per unit of output | |
|---|---|---|---|---|---|
|  | A | B |  | A | B |
| Preparation department | $\frac{1}{5}$ | $\frac{1}{2}$ | £2 per hour | £0.40 | £1.00 |
| Machining department | $\frac{1}{2}$ | $\frac{1}{2}$ | £2 per hour | £1.00 | £1.00 |
|  |  |  |  | £1.40 | £2.00 |

### 2 Raw material requirement forecast

The standard quantities of the two raw materials, X and Y, which should be used in the manufacture of the two products, and the prices of these raw materials have been estimated as follows:

**Standard quantities:**
Raw material X – 2 units for each unit of product A
Raw material Y – 3 units for each unit of product B

**Estimated costs:**
Raw material X – £0.50 for each unit of X
Raw material Y – £0.30 for each unit of Y

## 3 Overhead costs

Factory overheads are classified into fixed and variable costs. The fixed overhead costs are deemed to be incurred in equal amounts quarterly for the purpose of allocation, whereas the variable overheads vary according to the level of production. The following estimates are available:

| | |
|---|---|
| Fixed overheads: | |
| Depreciation | £10,000 per annum |
| Rates and insurances | 4,000 |
| Supervisory salaries | 6,000 |
| | £20,000 |

**Variable overheads**

| | Cost per unit of output | |
|---|---|---|
| | A | B |
| | £ | £ |
| Indirect labour | | |
| Indirect material | | |
| Repairs and maintenance | £0.50 | £1.00 |
| Power | | |

Using activity-based costing, some of the fixed and variable overheads may be allocated on the basis of cost drivers, as mentioned in Chapter 27, instead of on the basis of cost per unit, or cost per labour hour.

## Stock forecasts

### Finished goods

Product A – estimated opening stock:   750 units
Product B – estimated opening stock:   1,000 units

It was planned that the closing stock level at the end of each quarter should be maintained at a level equal to half the expected sales for the next quarter for both products.

For the purposes of calculating the expected profit, the closing stock is to be valued on a variable costing basis, as follows:

| | A | B |
|---|---|---|
| Raw materials | £1.00 | £0.90 |
| Direct labour | 1.40 | 2.00 |
| Variable overheads | 0.50 | 1.00 |
| **Total variable costs per unit** | £2.90 | £3.90 |

### Raw materials

Raw material X – estimated opening stock: 1,500 units
Raw material Y: 3,000 units

## Administrative and selling costs forecast

|  | £ | £ |
|---|---:|---:|
| **1 Administrative costs** | | |
| Office salaries | 18,000 | |
| Stationery | 1,000 | |
| Other | 1,000 | |
|  |  | 20,000 |
| **2 Selling costs** | | |
| Salaries | 15,000 | |
| Advertising | 5,000 | |
|  |  | 20,000 |
| **Total** |  | 40,000 |

## Cash flow forecast

### 1 Sales receipts
50 per cent of sales received in cash during month of sales
50 per cent of sales received in cash in the following month

### 2 Cash expenditure
(a) *Production costs:* Direct labour, direct materials and variable overheads paid in the month in which incurred. Fixed overheads paid in equal amounts quarterly.
(b) *Administrative and selling costs:* Paid in equal amounts quarterly.
(c) *Other costs:* Tax outstanding amounting to £12,000 will be paid off in equal instalments quarterly over the year.

*Capital expenditure:* Expenditure on the acquisition assets is planned as follows:

|  | £ |
|---|---:|
| 1st quarter | 10,000 |
| 2nd quarter | 15,000 |
| 3rd quarter | 8,000 |
| 4th quarter | 20,000 |
|  | 53,000 |

## Sundry creditors balance
The amount outstanding to sundry creditors will remain at a constant amount of £5,000 throughout the year.

# Preparing the budget for the year ending 31 December 20X1

The task of preparing the overall budget involves a sequence of steps:

Step 1 The sales budget
2 The production budget
3 The direct materials usage budget
4 The materials purchases budget
5 The budgeted direct labour costs
6 The overhead costs budget
7 The closing stock budget
8 The selling and administrative costs budget
9 The capital expenditure budget
10 The cost of goods sold budget
11 The cash budget
12 The budgeted profit and loss account
13 The budgeted balance sheet

## Step 1 The sales budget

The sales budget is prepared from the sales forecast as follows:

| | 1st quarter | 2nd quarter | 3rd quarter | 4th quarter | Total |
|---|---|---|---|---|---|
| **Units** | | | | | |
| Product A | 1,500 | 1,000 | 1,000 | 1,500 | 5,000 |
| Product B | 2,000 | 2,000 | 2,000 | 2,000 | 8,000 |
| **Value** | | | | | |
| Product A (£11) | £16,500 | £11,000 | £11,000 | £16,500 | £55,000 |
| Product B (£14) | 28,000 | 28,000 | 28,000 | 28,000 | 112,000 |
| | £44,500 | £39,000 | £39,000 | £44,500 | £167,000 |

## Step 2 The production budget

The production budget is designed to plan the resources required to produce the output envisaged by the sales forecast. A precondition for an agreement as to the size of the sales budget is the adequacy of the productive capacity of the plant to provide the required output. If existing capacity is inadequate, decisions will have to be made as to the advisability of introducing overtime working, of subcontracting production, or of hiring or purchasing additional plant and equipment. If, on the other hand, the sales forecast falls short of productive capacity, sales promotion schemes may be considered as a means of closing or reducing the gap. With the tendency of business people to use stock levels as buffers to insulate an efficient rate of production from variations in sales, the production budget is also dependent upon the planned levels of closing stock.

Using the information given in our example, the following production budget may be prepared:

| | 1st quarter | 2nd quarter | 3rd quarter | 4th quarter | Year |
|---|---|---|---|---|---|
| **Product A** | | | | | |
| Desired closing stock (units) | 500 | 500 | 750 | 750 | 750 |
| *Add:* Sales | 1,500 | 1,000 | 1,000 | 1,500 | 5,000 |
| Total required | 2,000 | 1,500 | 1,750 | 2,250 | 5,750 |
| *Less:* Opening stock | 750 | 500 | 500 | 750 | 750 |
| **Production required** | 1,250 | 1,000 | 1,250 | 1,500 | 5,000 |
| | | | | | |
| **Product B** | | | | | |
| Desired closing stock (units) | 1,000 | 1,000 | 1,000 | 1,000 | 1,000 |
| *Add:* Sales | 2,000 | 2,000 | 2,000 | 2,000 | 8,000 |
| Total required | 3,000 | 3,000 | 3,000 | 3,000 | 9,000 |
| *Less:* Opening stock | 1,000 | 1,000 | 1,000 | 1,000 | 1,000 |
| **Production required** | 2,000 | 2,000 | 2,000 | 2,000 | 8,000 |

## Step 3  The direct materials usage budget

The rate of usage of raw materials is known, so that the direct materials usage may be budgeted by multiplying the usage rate by the production required.

| | 1st quarter | 2nd quarter | 3rd quarter | 4th quarter | Year |
|---|---|---|---|---|---|
| Material X (2 units for A) | 2,500 | 2,000 | 2,500 | 3,000 | 10,000 |
| Material Y (3 units for B | 6,000 | 6,000 | 6,000 | 6,000 | 24,000 |

## Step 4  The materials purchase budget

The purpose of this budget is to determine both the quantities and the values of raw material purchases necessary to meet the production levels stipulated in the production budget. The information required for this budget is found in the direct materials usage budget, stock forecasts and raw materials purchase prices.

| | 1st quarter | 2nd quarter | 3rd quarter | 4th quarter | Year |
|---|---|---|---|---|---|
| **Raw material X** | | | | | |
| Desired closing stock | 1,000 | 1,000 | 1,500 | 1,500 | 1,500 |
| *Add:* Material usage (Step 3) | 2,500 | 2,000 | 2,500 | 3,000 | 10,000 |
| Total required | 3,500 | 3,000 | 4,000 | 4,500 | 11,500 |
| *Less:* Opening stock | 1,500 | 1,000 | 1,000 | 1,500 | 1,500 |
| Purchases required (units) | 2,000 | 2,000 | 3,000 | 3,000 | 10,000 |
| Price per unit | £0.50 | £0.50 | £0.50 | £0.50 | £0.50 |
| Total purchases (value) | £1,000 | £1,000 | £1,500 | £1,500 | £5,000 |

| | 1st quarter | 2nd quarter | 3rd quarter | 4th quarter | Year |
|---|---|---|---|---|---|
| **Raw material Y** | | | | | |
| Desired closing stock | 3,000 | 3,000 | 3,000 | 3,000 | 3,000 |
| *Add:* Material usage (Step 3) | 6,000 | 6,000 | 6,000 | 6,000 | 24,000 |
| Total required | 9,000 | 9,000 | 9,000 | 9,000 | 27,000 |
| *Less:* Opening stock | 3,000 | 3,000 | 3,000 | 3,000 | 3,000 |
| Purchases required (units) | 6,000 | 6,000 | 6,000 | 6,000 | 24,000 |
| Price per unit | £0.30 | £0.30 | £0.30 | £0.30 | £0.30 |
| Total purchases (value) | £1,800 | £1,800 | £1,800 | £1,800 | £7,200 |
| | | | | | |
| Total purchases (value) | £2,800 | £2,800 | £3,300 | £3,300 | £12,200 |

## Step 5 Budgeted direct labour costs

This budget is based upon calculations of the labour requirements necessary to produce the planned output. The direct labour costs are computed by multiplying the labour requirements by the forecast of wage rates payable during the budget period.

| | 1st quarter | 2nd quarter | 3rd quarter | 4th quarter | Year |
|---|---|---|---|---|---|
| **Production** (Step 2 – units) | | | | | |
| Product A | 1,250 | 1,000 | 1,250 | 1,500 | 5,000 |
| Product B | 2,000 | 2,000 | 2,000 | 2,000 | 8,000 |
| | | | | | |
| **Labour hours** | | | | | |
| Preparation department | | | | | |
| Product A ($\frac{1}{5}$) | 250 | 200 | 250 | 300 | 1,000 |
| Product B ($\frac{1}{2}$) | 1,000 | 1,000 | 1,000 | 1,000 | 4,000 |
| Total | 1,250 | 1,200 | 1,250 | 1,300 | 5,000 |
| | | | | | |
| Machining department | | | | | |
| Product A ($\frac{1}{2}$) | 625 | 500 | 625 | 750 | 2,500 |
| Product B ($\frac{1}{2}$) | 1,000 | 1,000 | 1,000 | 1,000 | 4,000 |
| Total | 1,625 | 1,500 | 1,625 | 1,750 | 6,500 |
| | | | | | |
| **Direct labour costs** | | | | | |
| Preparation department | | | | | |
| Labour hours | 1,250 | 1,200 | 1,250 | 1,300 | 5,000 |
| Wage rate/hour | £2 | £2 | £2 | £2 | £2 |
| Direct labour cost | £2,500 | £2,400 | £2,500 | £2,600 | £10,000 |
| | | | | | |
| Machining department | | | | | |
| Labour hours | 1,625 | 1,500 | 1,625 | 1,750 | 6,500 |
| Wage rate/hour | £2 | £2 | £2 | £2 | £2 |
| Direct labour cost | £3,250 | £3,000 | £3,250 | £3,500 | £13,000 |
| **Total direct labour cost** | £5,750 | £5,400 | £5,750 | £6,100 | £23,000 |

## Step 6  The overhead costs budget

Having disposed of the direct costs of production in the form of materials and direct labour, we now come to the preparation of the estimates of the overhead costs of production. These costs are divided into the two categories mentioned earlier. We are told that the fixed overheads are incurred in equal amounts quarterly, and we may calculate the total variable costs per quarter by multiplying the expected variable costs per unit by the planned quarterly output.

|  | 1st quarter | 2nd quarter | 3rd quarter | 4th quarter | Year |
|---|---|---|---|---|---|
| **Production** (Step 2) | | | | | |
| Product A (units) | 1,250 | 1,000 | 1,250 | 1,500 | 5,000 |
| Product B (units) | 2,000 | 2,000 | 2,000 | 2,000 | 8,000 |
| **Variable costs** | | | | | |
| Product A (£0.50 per unit) | £625 | £500 | £625 | £750 | £2,500 |
| Product B (£1.00 per unit) | 2,000 | 2,000 | 2,000 | 2,000 | 8,000 |
| Total | 2,625 | 2,500 | 2,625 | 2,750 | 10,500 |
| **Fixed costs** | | | | | |
| Depreciation | 2,500 | 2,500 | 2,500 | 2,500 | 10,000 |
| Rates and insurance | 1,000 | 1,000 | 1,000 | 1,000 | 4,000 |
| Supervisory salaries | 1,500 | 1,500 | 1,500 | 1,500 | 6,000 |
| Total | 5,000 | 5,000 | 5,000 | 5,000 | 20,000 |
| **Total overhead costs** | £7,625 | £7,500 | £7,625 | £7,750 | £30,500 |

## Step 7  The closing stock budget

The closing stock budget consists of an estimate of the value of planned closing stock of raw materials and planned stocks of finished goods. It is arrived at by calculating the budgeted unit cost of stock and multiplying the result by the planned stock level.

### 1  Budgeted closing raw material stock

| Raw material | X | Y | |
|---|---|---|---|
| Closing stock (units) | 1,500 | 3,000 | |
| Cost per unit | £0.50 | £0.30 | |
| **Value of closing stock** | £750 | £900 | |
| Total | | | £1,650 |

### 2  Budgeted finished goods stock

We are told that the accountant values the stock of finished goods on a variable costing basis, and that the unit cost of Products A and B has been calculated to be £2.90 and £3.90 respectively. These values are applied to the budgeted closing stock figures as follows:

| Product | A | B | |
|---|---|---|---|
| Closing stock (units) | 750 | 1,000 | |
| Cost per unit | £2.90 | £3.90 | |
| **Value of closing stock** | 2,175 | 3,900 | |
| **Total** | | | £6,075 |

## Step 8  The selling and administrative expenses budget

| | | |
|---|---|---|
| **Selling expenses** | | |
| Salaries | £15,000 | |
| Advertising | 5,000 | £20,000 |
| **Administrative expenses** | | |
| Office salaries | 18,000 | |
| Stationery | 1,000 | |
| Other expenses | 1,000 | 20,000 |
| **Total** | | £40,000 |

## Step 9  The capital expenditure budget

We devoted Chapter 32 to a discussion of capital budgeting as an aspect of long-range planning. The annual capital expenditure budget must be seen, therefore, as a one-year slice of the long-term capital budget. The purpose of the annual capital expenditure is to make provision in the current budget for the planned capital expenditure in the current year. This information has been provided as follows:

| **Capital expenditure** | |
|---|---|
| 1st quarter | £10,000 |
| 2nd quarter | 15,000 |
| 3rd quarter | 8,000 |
| 4th quarter | 20,000 |
| **Total for the year** | £53,000 |

## Step 10  The cost of goods sold budget

The reader will recall that all the previous budgets mentioned have dealt with the various aspects of the production process, in unit and value terms, including the expenses associated with selling and administration and the valuation of closing stock. The purpose of this budget is to bring all these items together to arrive at an estimate of the cost of the goods sold. This estimate will be used in the budgeted profit and loss account. It is compiled as follows:

| | |
|---|---:|
| Opening raw materials stock (balance sheet 31.12.20X0) | £1,650 |
| *Add:* Materials purchases (Step 4) | 12,200 |
| Raw materials available for production | 13,850 |
| *Less:* Planned closing stock of raw materials (Step 7) | 1,650 |
| Cost of raw materials to be used in production | 12,200 |
| Cost of direct labour (Step 5) | 23,000 |
| Factory overhead costs (Step 6) | 30,500 |
| Cost of goods to be manufactured | 65,700 |
| *Add:* Opening stock of finished goods (balance sheet 31.12.20X0) | 6,025 |
| | 71,725 |
| *Less:* Planned closing stock of finished goods | 6,075 |
| **Budgeted cost of goods sold** | **£65,650** |

## Step 11 The cash budget

The cash budget consists of the estimates of cash receipts and cash payments arising from the planned levels of activities and use of resources which are considered in the various budgets we have examined. The cash budget is a complete survey of the financial implication of expenditure plans of both a current and a capital nature during the year. Moreover, by comparing the anticipated outflows of cash with the expected inflows, the cash budget enables management to anticipate any deficits so that the necessary financing arrangements may be made, and to decide upon a policy for placing any cash surpluses.

As its name implies, the cash budget deals only with 'cash' flows – it excludes expenses of a non-cash nature, such as depreciation. The cash budget is one of the last budgets to be prepared because it depends upon the other budgets which form part of the budgeting process.

Note that the cash budget is planned through time: the time profile of cash receipts and cash payments is critical to the analysis of a firm's cash needs at any given point of time.

In practice, determining the level of cash which is required at any point in time may not be an easy matter. The dilemma of cash management lies in the conflict of liquidity with profitability. If a firm holds too little cash in relation to its financial obligations, a liquidity crisis may occur and may lead to the collapse of the business. On the other hand, if a firm holds too much cash it is losing the opportunity to employ that cash profitably in its activities. Idle cash balances usually earn very little profit for the firm. A reasonable balance must be found, therefore, between the financial objectives of maintaining a degree of liquidity and of minimizing the level of unproductive assets. The problem of ascertaining optimal balances of physical stocks has for long attracted the attention of operational researchers, and certain of the ideas which they have developed may have applicability as regards the holding of optimal cash balances. Such techniques include just-in-time (JIT) stock purchase systems, developing supply chains, where there is a direct link between suppliers and purchasers so that stock needs are known almost immediately. Boots Company installed a computer system costing £75 million which saves £400 million per annum on stocks. It does this by linking the sales system to the stock system to the resupply system so that only the relevant amount of stock is resupplied.

| | 1st quarter | 2nd quarter | 3rd quarter | 4th quarter | Total |
|---|---|---|---|---|---|
| | £ | £ | £ | £ | £ |
| Opening cash balance | 5,325 | 10,900 | 11,450 | 15,275 | 5,325 |
| **Receipts** | | | | | |
| Debtors (balance sheet) | 20,000 | – | – | – | 20,000 |
| 50% of current sales (Step 1) | 22,250 | 19,500 | 19,500 | 22,250 | 83,500 |
| 50% of previous quarter (Step 1) | – | 22,250 | 19,500 | 19,500 | 61,250 |
| Total receipts | 42,250 | 41,750 | 39,000 | 41,750 | 164,750 |
| Total cash available | 47,575 | 52,650 | 50,450 | 57,025 | 170,075 |
| **Payments** | | | | | |
| Purchases (Step 4) | 2,800 | 2,800 | 3,300 | 3,300 | 12,200 |
| Direct labour (Step 5) | 5,750 | 5,400 | 5,750 | 6,100 | 23,000 |
| Factory overheads (Step 6) (excluding depreciation) | 5,125 | 5,000 | 5,125 | 5,250 | 20,500 |
| Selling and administrative expenses (Step 8) | 10,000 | 10,000 | 10,000 | 10,000 | 40,000 |
| Capital expenditure (Step 9) | 10,000 | 15,000 | 8,000 | 20,000 | 53,000 |
| Tax (balance sheet) | 3,000 | 3,000 | 3,000 | 3,000 | 12,000 |
| Total payments | 36,675 | 41,200 | 35,175 | 47,650 | 160,700 |
| **Closing cash balances** | 10,900 | 11,450 | 15,275 | 9,375 | 9,375 |

The effects of inflation on business enterprises are manifested in a growth in monetary terms, which may be in some direct relationship with the rate of inflation, while at the same time undergoing no growth at all in real terms, or even shrinking in profitability and value. The financing problem resulting from the monetary growth associated with inflation lies in the need to finance higher levels of stocks and debtors. If a firm is unable to finance the higher level of working capital required from adjustments to its prices and sales revenues, it must either borrow or reduce its level of activity. In effect, the rapid inflation which business firms experienced in the 1970s caused severe liquidity problems and many cases of insolvency.

The problems of cash budgeting under conditions of inflation require that special attention be given to the timing of cash inflows and outflows, which should be adjusted for changes in specific price changes affecting the firm. In this connection, adjustments to budget figures for changes in the general purchasing power of money will not reflect the impact of inflationary changes as they affect individual firms.

Among the special problems associated with budgeting under conditions of inflation is the loss of purchasing power exhibited by holdings of net monetary assets. This implies that losses in the value of net monetary items should be minimized in a manner consistent with the overall objectives of the firm by the reduction of holdings of net monetary assets. In effect, particular attention should be given to cash and debtor balances, and the impact of changes in selling prices on cash inflows should be carefully monitored. At the same time, gains resulting from the impact of inflation on creditor balances should encourage more aggressive borrowing policies.

## Step 12  The budgeted profit and loss account

The purpose of the budgeted profit and loss account is to summarize and integrate all the operating budgets so as to measure the end result on the firm's profit.

|  | £ |
|---|---|
| Sales (Step 1) | 167,000 |
| Cost of goods sold (Step 10) | 65,650 |
| Gross profit | 101,350 |
| Selling and administrative expenses (Step 8) | 40,000 |
| Net profit before tax | 61,350 |
| Tax (40%) | 24,540 |
| Net profit after tax | 36,810 |

## Step 13  The budgeted balance sheet

The final stage is the projection of the budgeted results on the firm's financial position at the end of the year. The following balance sheet reflects the changes in the composition of assets and liabilities as a result of the planned activities:

**Budget balance sheet as at 31 December 20X1**

| Fixed assets | Cost | Depreciation | |
|---|---|---|---|
|  | £ | £ | £ |
| Plant and machinery | 303,000 | 40,000 | 263,000 |
| **Current assets** | | | |
| Stocks | | | |
|    Raw materials | 1,650 | | |
|    Finished goods | 6,075 | | |
| | | 7,725 | |
| Debtors | | 22,250 | |
| Cash | | 9,375 | |
| | | 39,350 | |
| *Less:* Creditors: amounts falling due within one year | | | |
|    Creditors | 5,000 | | |
|    Tax | 24,540 | | |
| | | 29,540 | |
| Net current assets | | | 9,810 |
| Total assets *less* current liabilities | | | 272,810 |
| **Capital and reserves** | | | |
| Called-up share capital | | | 210,000 |
| Profit and loss account | | | 62,810 |
| | | | 272,810 |

# Evaluating the budget proposals

As a means of comparing the planned performance for the coming year with the results of the current year, the planned performance may be interpreted as follows:

Return on shareholders' equity: £36,810 ÷ £272,810 = 13.5% (previous 7.6%)

Return on capital employed: £61,350 ÷ £272,810 = 22.5% (previous 12.7%)

It is evident, therefore, that the firm is expected to make considerable improvements in the forthcoming period. If the budgeted results are considered to be satisfactory, the final stage is a recommendation that the budget proposal be accepted by the board of directors as its policy, and as conforming with its view of the future.

# Budgeting systems

In this section we consider briefly three budget approaches: (1) zero-based budgeting; (2) feed-forward control; and (3) flexible budgeting.

## Zero-based budgeting

The traditional approach to budgeting is the incremental approach which starts with the previous year's budget and adds or subtracts from that budget to reflect changing assumptions for the coming year. For example, if the previous year's budget expenditures for a department were £1 million, the department might request a 5 per cent increase (£50,000) to provide the same level of service for the coming year. The typical justification for increased expenditures is the increased cost of inputs (labour and materials, and so on). Any inefficiencies in the previous year's budget tend to be perpetuated by this almost automatic acceptance of that document as the starting point of the new plan.

One method developed to overcome the shortcomings of the incremental budgeting approach is zero-based budgeting, by which all levels of management start from zero and estimate the resource requirements to fund the year's activities. Managers must defend their budget levels at the beginning of each year. This, unlike the incremental budgeting approach, the zero-based approach requires past budget decisions to be re-evaluated each year. Thus resource requirements are more likely to be adjusted to changing business conditions.

## Feed-forward control

Feedback systems aim to highlight deviations from the budget plan as soon as possible so that remedial action may be taken. A feed-forward system differs from a feedback system in that it seeks to anticipate, and thereby to avoid, deviations between actual and desired outputs. The aim is to improve forecasting procedures. Therefore, once effective forecasting procedures have been established, the significant comparisons are no longer between planned and actual costs, but between forecasts, as follows:

1 *Latest forecast vs previous forecast.* This comparison becomes the prime action mover, and leads to the following questions:

(a) Why has the forecast changed?
(b) How does the latest forecast affect the net cash flow?
(c) What actions should be taken to improve the situation?

2 *Actual vs previous forecast.* This comparison leads to the following questions being asked:
(a) Was the previous forecast effective as regards identifying the events now facing the firm?
(b) If not, why was the previous forecast wrong?
(c) Are the errors in forecasting due to excessive pessimism or optimism, and can these errors be corrected?

## Flexible budgeting

So far, we have discussed functional budgets and cash budgets. Another type of budget which takes into account changes in the volume of activity is the flexible budget. Most budgets assume a certain level of activity and this level of activity is used in the preparation of the budget. For example, in the Edco Manufacturing case above it was assumed that 1,250 units of output would be produced in the first quarter. However, actual production might be greater or less than 1,250 units. To compare the actual costs of, say, 1,300 units with the budgeted costs of 1,250 units would render the comparison meaningless. In a situation where the actual production was greater than budget, this would tend to show overspends on variable costs as these costs would increase with activity, but the budgeted value of these costs would remain at the 1,250 units level. Conversely, if no production was produced, then the financial report would show a saving on the variable costs as these would be set at the 1,250 units level, whereas the actual costs would be zero.

To overcome this conflict in reporting, flexible budgets are prepared which reflect the changes in production levels by flexing the variable costs per unit by the actual activity levels. These are then compared with the actual costs and a meaningful variance is calculated. Any fixed costs are isolated in the report and shown separately. Flexible budgets are considered further in Chapter 35.

## Activity-based budgeting

We saw in Chapter 27 that the initial interest in activity-based costing (ABC) related to product or service costing, but that an ABC system offers more than just accurate product-cost information. It also provides information about the cost and performance of activities and resources. Activity-based management (ABM) is a term which has developed from the early approaches to ABC, and is designed to denote much wider use of the concept by management than just for product costing. It becomes useful to organizations which have undertaken ABC for the product costing. ABM is based on the premise that since people are involved in activities, and activities consume resources, the control of activities allows the control of costs at their sources. Activity-based budgeting (ABB) is an important element of ABM. It is a planning and budgetary tool which provides an understanding of the linkages between the drivers behind the activities. ABB defines the activities underlying the financial figures in each function and uses the level of activity to determine how much resource should be allocated, how well it is managed and how to explain variances from budget.

Traditional budgeting systems tend to view the organization vertically in functional blocks of cost and focus on resources bought by function or department. Most cost reports typically show wages, salaries, rent and so on by department in line with the functional organization structure. These reports reveal little about how the resources are being used to add value to the customer, what drives the level of resources required and whether the right amount of resources is in place. Alternatively, a business can be viewed as a series of linked activities which ultimately add value to the customer. In adopting this view, ABM helps management to understand the activities, their cost and how they link together to form a simple chain of value-creating activities for a business. In doing so, ABM focuses on activity outputs rather than resource inputs.

ABB provides the foundation for a more effective control of overhead. We saw in Chapter 27 that ABC product costs give enhanced visibility to the components of overhead, providing greater segmentation and one which indicates the sources and purpose of resource consumption. This additional detail, together with the gathering of cost-driver information, provides management with valuable feedback which will aid the operational control of their manufacturing processes. Example 2 below indicates the type of report which can be produced where ABB is in use. This activity-based budget report directs attention at the use of resources in the overhead area. It shows differences from budget for both expenditure and cost-driver levels. It highlights areas for investigation (Innes and Mitchell, 1993).

| Example 2 | **Budget report** | | | | | | |
|---|---|---|---|---|---|---|---|
| **Cost** | **Budget cost driver** | | **£000** | **Actual cost driver** | **£000** | **Variance £000** |
| Purchasing | 1,000 | Orders | 25 | 1,100 | 28 | 3U |
| Set-ups | 50 | Set-ups | 200 | 40 | 205 | 5U |
| Handling | 400 | Movements | 100 | 500 | 145 | 45U |
| Inspection | 500 | Inspections | 70 | 550 | 83 | 13U |
| | | | 395 | | 461 | 66U |

In view of the fact that activities are linked across departments forming cross-functional processes, ABB permits managers to recognize the horizontal flow of products, services and activities through an organization by focusing attention on the organization as a whole. ABB ensures that there is an optimum allocation of scarce resources across the business. For example, consider the case of a conflict between two departments of a firm, the purchasing and warehouse functions. The purchasing department was buying from a supplier which delivered weekly, and the warehouse section held high staff levels solely to cater for this event. Although the change to smaller daily deliveries caused an increase in purchase prices, it eased the workload on staff in the warehouse and provided overall a substantial cost saving to the company.

In providing an understanding of the costs of activities, their importance to the organization and how efficiently they are performed, ABM allows managers to focus on those activities that might offer opportunities for cost savings. The process view of organizations allows management to focus on value-added and non-value-added activities that are not adding value, but are causing costs to be incurred. These issues will be considered further in Chapter 38.

## Summary

Budgetary planning is an activity which should be seen as being concerned with the implementation of a yearly segment of the long-range plan. The budget expresses this plan in financial terms in the light of current conditions.

We have seen that the process of budgeting can be applied to any organization, such as retailing, local government, health service, leisure, banking, insurance and farming, to name but a few. Some steps (finished goods stock) may be omitted but the process is fundamentally the same. Budget plans may be evaluated by means of financial ratios such as the return of shareholders' equity and the return on capital employed.

Activity-based budgeting directs cost control to the course of overhead costs (the activities) rather than their consequences (the production).

**References**   Innes, J and Mitchell, F (1993). *Overhead Cost*, Academic Press.

Kennedy, A and Dugdale D (1999). 'Getting the most from budgeting', *Management Accounting* (UK), February.

## Self-assessment questions

1 Outline the series of steps that are implied in orderly budgeting.

2 Discuss the importance of the sales forecast.

3 State the various methods used for forecasting sales.

4 Examine the relationship between the sales budget and the production budget.

5 Comment on the significance of the cash budget.

6 Describe (a) zero-based budgeting; (b) feed-forward control; and (c) flexible budgeting.

7 How does an activity-based budgeting system differ from a traditional system?

## Problems   *(* indicates that a solution is to be found in the Lecturer's Guide)*

1   Dafa Ltd is a trading company dealing in a single product. It is preparing its annual budget for the twelve months ending 30 June 20X1. So far, the following budgets have been prepared:

|  | July–<br>Sept | Oct–<br>Dec | Jan–<br>Mar | April–<br>June |
|---|---|---|---|---|
| **Sales** (at £3 per unit) | 15,000 | 18,000 | 21,000 | 12,000 |
| **Purchases** (at £2 per unit) | 12,000 | 14,000 | 10,000 | 8,000 |
| **Sundry expenses** |  |  |  |  |
| Distribution | 500 | 800 | 1,100 | 200 |
| Administration | 1,000 | 1,000 | 1,000 | 1,000 |
| Depreciation | 500 | 500 | 500 | 500 |
|  | 2,000 | 2,300 | 2,600 | 1,700 |

*Notes:*
(a) Sales are made on one month's credit. It may be assumed that debtors outstanding on sales at the end of each quarter are equivalent to one-third of sales in that quarter, and that this is received the following quarter.
(b) All purchases are for cash. No credit is received.
(c) Distribution and administration expenses are paid in cash as incurred.
(d) The company has no expenses apart from those given.
(e) Opening balances at 1 July 20X0 are:

| | |
|---|---|
| Debtors | £3,000 |
| Cash | £2,000 |
| Stock | 1,000 units |

*Required:*
Complete Dafa Ltd's annual budget by preparing:
(a) a debtors' budget
(b) a cash budget, *and*
(c) a stock budget to show the number of units in stock at the end of each quarter.

**2**  A small private company, after several years of unprofitable trading, was taken over by a new management on 31 December.

The accounts for the following year were summarized thus:

| | £ |
|---|---:|
| Direct materials | 78,000 |
| Direct wages | 31,200 |
| Variable overheads | 15,600 |
| Fixed overheads | 30,000 |
| Profit | 1,200 |
| Sales | 156,000 |

The balance sheet as at the end of the first twelve months of trading was as follows:

| | £ | £ | £ |
|---|---:|---:|---:|
| **Fixed assets** | | | 24,000 |
| **Current assets** | | | |
| Stocks | | 26,000 | |
| Debtors | | 26,000 | |
| | | 52,000 | |
| *Less:* Creditors: amounts falling due within one year | | | |
| Bank overdraft | 26,500 | | |
| Creditors | 19,500 | | |
| | | 46,000 | |
| Net current assets | | | 6,000 |
| Total assets *less* current liabilities | | | 30,000 |
| **Capital and reserves** | | | |
| Called-up share capital | | | 40,000 |
| Profit and loss account | | | (10,000) |
| | | | 30,000 |

The budgeted sales for the second year of trading are as follows:

| | £ |
|---|---|
| 1st quarter | 42,000 |
| 2nd quarter | 45,000 |
| 3rd quarter | 48,000 |
| 4th quarter | 51,000 |

It is anticipated that the ratios of material consumption, direct wages and variable overheads to sales are unlikely to change; that the fixed overheads (incurred evenly during the year) will remain at £30,000 per annum; and that creditors can be held at three months' direct material usage. Both stocks and debtors can be maintained at two months' sales.

Bank interest and depreciation, the latter at 10 per cent per annum on fixed assets, are included in the overheads.

*Required:*
Prepare quarterly budgets for the second year of operation to indicate to management:

(a) Whether the results are likely to be satisfactory.
(b) Whether the overdraft facilities (which are normally limited to £25,000) are sufficient, or whether further capital must be introduced.

**3\*** Jones is considering whether to open up his own wholesaling business. He makes the following estimates about the first six months' trading:

| | | |
|---|---|---|
| (a) | *Sales on credit* | – For first two months £50,000 per month. |
| | | – Thereafter £80,000 per month. |
| | | – One month's credit allowed to customers. |
| (b) | *Gross margin* | – The cost of goods bought for resale is expected to be 75 per cent of the selling price. |
| (c) | *Closing stock* | – £75,000. |
| (d) | *Purchases creditors at end* | – £50,000. |
| (e) | *Wages and salaries* | – Paid for period £40,000. |
| | | – Owing at end of period £2,500. |
| (f) | *Warehouse expenses* | – Cash paid for rent, rates, lighting, heating, etc. £50,000. |
| | | – In addition £5,500 of warehouse expenses will be owing at end of six months. |
| | | – Of the cash paid, however, £3,500 will be rent and rates paid in advance. |
| (g) | *Furniture, fixtures and fittings* | – Amounting to £50,000 to be purchased on opening of business and will be subject to 10 per cent p.a. depreciation. |
| (h) | *Delivery vehicles* | – Three vans costing £2,000 each will be purchased at once and will be subject to 25 per cent p.a. depreciation. |
| (i) | *Loan interest* | – Long-term loans can be raised at an interest rate of 10 per cent p.a. |
| (j) | *Jones* | – Expects to draw from the business accounts his own 'wages' at a rate of £300 per month. |

*Required:*
(a) A budgeted cash account for the period on the basis of the above information (see part (c) below).
(b) Budgeted profit and loss account for the period and balance sheet as at the end on the basis of the above information (see part (c) below).
(c) Advise Jones as to how much capital should be introduced initially into the business. Jones, however, has only £50,000 available as capital. Complete the accounts on the assumption that he accepts your advice.
(d) Jones asks you whether the business appears to be a worthwhile one. Give a *brief* reply to this question.

4   The Astra leisure complex is a medium-sized company specializing in the leisure industry. The complex comprises a swimming pool, a diving pool, a leisure pool, a sauna, a sports hall (suitable for basketball, five-a-side football, etc.) and a conference hall. The complex also has a bar and a restaurant.
    The managing director of the business, who has been recently appointed, is surprised to discover that there is no budgeting system at the complex.

*Required:*
(a) List five main reasons why a formal system of budgeting should be introduced.
(b) Identify which functional budgets will be required. For each functional budget named, propose which member of the organization should be responsible for its preparation and justify your choice. Draw an organization chart to illustrate your answer.
(c) Explain how computer applications could be used to advantage in the proposed budgeting system.

5*  Rutland Furnishings Company is a small carpet and upholstery cleaning business with both commercial and domestic customers.
    The balance sheet of the company at 31 October 20X0 was:

| | | £ |
|---|---|---|
| **Fixed assets** (NBV) | | |
| Freehold premises | | 32,000 |
| Fixtures, fittings, equipment | | 4,000 |
| Motor vehicles | | 12,000 |
| | | 48,000 |
| **Current assets** | | |
| Stock | 3,200 | |
| Debtors | 20,000 | |
| | 23,200 | |
| **Current liabilities** | | |
| Creditors | 4,000 | |
| Bank overdraft | 8,200 | 12,200 |
| Net working capital | | |
| | | 11,000 |
| | | £59,000 |
| **Capital** | | £59,000 |

The company allows credit to its commercial customers but domestic customers are expected to pay cash. On the basis of past performance, the company expects sales in the coming six months to be:

| November | December | January | February | March | April |
|----------|----------|---------|----------|--------|--------|
| £16,000 | £16,000 | £20,000 | £40,000 | £12,000 | £12,000 |

The proportions of cash and credit sales are usually:

| Month of sale | Cash sales (%) | Credit sales (%) |
|---------------|----------------|------------------|
| November | 30 | 70 |
| December | 45 | 55 |
| All other months | 20 | 80 |

Customers who are on extended credit normally pay in the month following sale. The company's invoice price is made up of 55 per cent wages, 25 per cent materials and 20 per cent profit. Wages are paid in the month incurred.

Half the materials purchased each month are subject to a 3 per cent cash discount for immediate payment and it is company policy to take advantage of this discount. The firm pays the remainder of the purchases, without discount, in the month after purchase. Goods are normally purchased in the month they are sold except December when owing to a supplier's shut-down, half December's goods are purchased in November.

Expenditure on petrol and other expenses is £2,600 per month. Additionally, the fixtures, equipment and motor vehicles are depreciated at 25 per cent per annum on a reducing balance basis.

*Required:*
(a) Prepare a cash budget for the six months November to April.
(b) Prepare a profit and loss statement for the same period.
(c) Prepare a balance sheet at 30 April 20X1.
(d) The company proposes to purchase a new industrial cleaner costing £10,000 in January. Given the overdraft facility is £9,500, what action should the management take?

# 34 Organizing for control

*Setting the scene*

As organisations grow in size and complexity, top management find themselves unable to make all the decisions. In such circumstances authority for certain types of decision-making is delegated to subordinate managers and decentralisation takes place. Total decentralisation could occur whereby a division operated in complete autonomy. Of course, such a situation is unlikely. Certain types of decisions invariably are retained by central management. Decentralisation improves local decision-making, flexibility, motivation and training for divisional management. At the same time it relieves central management of making lower level, routine decisions. Therefore, if properly organised and controlled, it makes the enterprise as a whole more efficient.

(Kam-por, 1994)

*Learning objectives*

After studying this chapter you should be able to:

1  Understand the relationship between planning and control.

2  Appreciate why firms choose to decentralize.

3  Identify the differences among the three types of responsibility centre.

4  Explain the role of transfer pricing in a decentralized firm.

5  Discuss the methods of setting transfer prices.

6  Compare and explain return on investment and residual profit.

## The integration of planning and control

We mentioned in Chapter 25 that control may be related to planning by defining the purpose of control as being to ensure that the organization's activities conform with its plans. Control is itself an activity, therefore, and it should and does affect every aspect of the organization. We may depict the control cycle in the form of a generalized model as shown in Figure 5.21.

The control cycle illustrated in Figure 5.21 shows that the origin of control is in the objectives of the organization from which plans are developed. These plans, as we saw in Section 2, consist of both long-range and annual plans. The control cycle integrates both the long-range and the annual plan. Information feedback enables actual

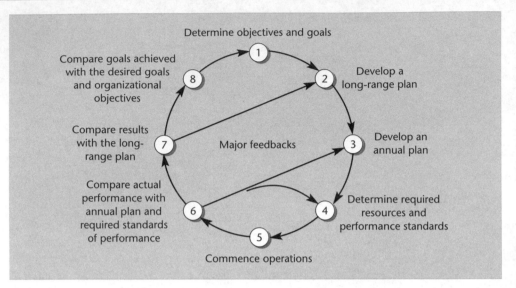

**Figure 5.21**

performance to be compared with the planned performance required by the annual plan, thus enabling management to control operations and the resources allocated to those operations. At the end of the year, the results may be compared with those envisaged in terms of the long-range plans, thereby providing information feedback for the purposes of reviewing the long-range plan. Finally, the control process allows achievements to be compared with the organization's desired objectives, thereby enabling new goals and new objectives to be formulated. Recently, as we saw in Chapter 33, control has been developed into feed-forward and feedback control. Feedback control is concerned with comparing actual figures against budget and highlighting variances to provide feedback. It allows corrective action to be taken in order to ensure that the variance is minimized in the future. With feed-forward control, the actual figures are extrapolated into the future and these figures are compared against the future budget figures, in order to forecast any future deviations from the plan. This system of control enables problem areas to be identified earlier and, therefore, solved quicker.

The control model illustrates the multidimensional nature of the control process, and the coincidence of the control process with the planning processes. It is this coincidence which allows the planning and the control process to be integrated into one model which is focused on organizational objectives and the goals derived from those objectives. Overall control is concerned with measuring progress towards the realization of organizational objectives and the strategic goals defined in the strategic plan. This aspect of control is exercised by top management. Using the terminology adopted in Chapter 25, management control is a subordinate activity concerned with the efficient use of resources committed to the realization of organizational goals. Finally, operational control is concerned with ensuring that the tasks defined in the operational plan are carried out effectively. Specific performance standards are attached to these tasks, and information feedback allows actual performance to be compared with the required performance.

From the foregoing, it follows that control standards are designed in the planning process. They are used as indices by which the effectiveness and the result of organizational activities are to be assessed, for they provide the basis by which actual and planned

performance are to be compared. Moreover, since organizational
the planning process, plans themselves also constitute performance

There remains, however, a perceptible distinction between pla
the sense in which we consider these terms in this text. A plan refl
and the means of achieving stipulated goals during a specified peri
to be useful for control purposes as well, it should reflect adequ
which those expectations and those means are subject to organ
Hence, it should provide the basis for the system of responsibility a ......ing which
requires a clear definition of the controllable elements at every level of responsibility.

## Responsibility accounting

Control depends on the existence of an organizational framework which will define
the responsibility for securing the performance of individual tasks. This is achieved
by establishing responsibility centres throughout the organization, and defining the
responsibilities of managers accordingly.

A responsibility centre may be defined as a segment of the organization where an
individual manager is held responsible for the segment's performance.

The nature of the organizational framework and the kinds of responsibility centres
established will depend partly on the size of the organization and partly on the style
of management adopted.

As organizations grow, top management faces two continuing problems:

1 how to divide activities and responsibilities;
2 how to coordinate subunits.

Inevitably, authority for decision making has to be allocated to various managers, and
as soon as this occurs the result is the decentralization of the decision-making process.
In essence, therefore, decentralization is the process of granting the freedom to make
decisions to subordinate managers. In theory, there are two extreme states: total decentralization, meaning a minimum of constraint or control on managers and a maximum
of the freedom to make decisions even at the lowest level of the management hierarchy,
and total centralization, implying the maximum of constraint or control on managers
and the minimum freedom to make independent decisions. In practice, total centralization and total decentralization rarely occur. Total centralization is not feasible because
it is impossible for top management to attend to all the decisions which are required to
be made. Equally, total decentralization is rarely found because the degree of freedom
which it implies would result in an organizational structure consisting of a collection of
completely separate units all aiming at their own individual goals. The extent to which
an organization will be decentralized depends upon the philosophy of its top management, and the benefits and costs associated with decentralization.

Having decided to decentralize to a greater or lesser extent, the problem of control
nevertheless remains. It may be resolved by establishing new responsibility centres
called 'divisions'. These divisions may take the form of profit or investment centres.
We shall consider these responsibility centres later in this chapter.

The problem of controlling divisional operations is more complex than that of controlling a single activity within an organization. Where decision making is centralized,
for example, it is possible to establish expense centres and to control their activities by
means of budgetary control. Some of these expense centres may be cost centres, which
are smaller segments of activity or areas of responsibility in respect of which costs are

533

accumulated. Control may be exercised, therefore, by means of information feedback about the level of costs arising from the activities of these responsibility centres. Indeed, cost control has been the traditional means of securing the control of operations, although, as we shall see later, the failure to recognize behavioural factors affecting performance has implications for the effectiveness of cost control. Where decision making is decentralized, however, the control of divisional performance is made more difficult for a number of reasons. The range of decisions over which divisional managers have authority is much more extensive. Thus, they may have authority over the determination of the pricing of products, make-or-buy decisions and some investment decisions. The problem goes beyond the control of costs, therefore, to the control of profits and to ensuring that there is a high degree of goal congruence between the various divisions and the organization's top management.

Our analysis of the problem of control through responsibility accounting should recognize the problems created by the degree of centralization and decentralization of authority. The first category of responsibility centre which we shall examine, namely expense centres, is appropriate to highly centralized organizations or units. The second and third categories of responsibility centres, namely profit and investment centres, are appropriate to those organizations where the authority for decision making has been decentralized to some extent, and where the problem of control is necessarily more complex. We deal with the behavioural aspects of control which such a degree of centralization creates in Chapter 37. For the time being, we focus attention on the accounting problems stemming from the establishment of these various types of responsibility centres.

## Expense centres

An expense centre may be defined as a responsibility centre in which the manager has no control over revenue but is able to control expenditure. It will be recalled that in Chapter 26 we drew a distinction between the accumulation of costs for product costing purposes and that for control purposes. In product costing, we noted that costs are first allocated and apportioned to service departments and production departments; next, that service department costs are apportioned to the production departments; finally, overhead recovery rates are computed to enable overhead costs to be absorbed into product costs. Since the production departments are the focal points on which the process of cost accumulation converges, these departments are known as 'cost centres'.

From the foregoing, we may distinguish an expense centre from a cost centre. An expense centre is a department which incurs expenditure. It provides a service to the departments which are making the product or providing the service. For example, the maintenance department would be an expense centre as it incurs expenses in maintaining machinery to produce the product. A cost centre is a production department in which product costs are accumulated. The term 'production' is used loosely here to mean any department through which a product or service passes.

As we stated earlier, a prerequisite for an effective responsibility accounting system is the establishment of an organizational framework which will define the formal relationships which link the different executive roles in the organization. Levels of responsibility may be delineated for foremen, departmental managers, works managers and upwards to director level. Figure 5.22 is an organizational chart applied to a centralized organization and shows that the three foremen are responsible to the manager of department B, who in turn reports to the works manager. The works manager is responsible to the board.

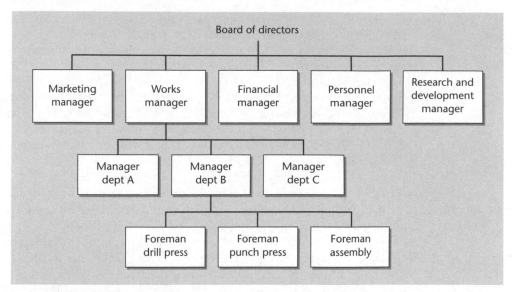

**Figure 5.22**

An important facet of a comprehensive planning and control programme is a system of performance reports incorporating comparisons of actual performance against planned performance for individual responsibility centres throughout the enterprise. These reports provide a means of instituting responsibility accounting, which is a method of cost control in which the costs of responsibility centres are identified with individual managers who are given authority over such costs and responsibility for them. The nature of the relationship existing between various levels of management and the flow of information between these levels may be illustrated as in Figure 5.23.

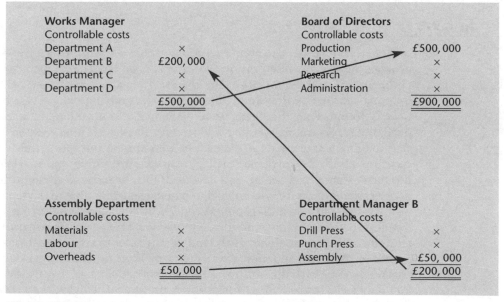

**Figure 5.23**

Responsibility budgets deal only with the costs for which each manager is to be held responsible, and their performance as managers is evaluated by reference to the success with which they have managed their own area of responsibility. It is important, therefore, to make a distinction between those costs which are under the control of a particular manager and those for which other managers are responsible. For example, the foreman of the assembly department may be responsible for the amount of direct labour used, but he will certainly not be responsible for the wage rate which is paid to these workers. This is determined by collective bargaining and is outside his sphere of influence. In assessing managerial performance under systems of responsibility accounting, managers should not be held responsible for costs which are outside their control. An inference which may be drawn from our diagram is that the higher one ascends the pyramid of control, the greater is the proportion of total costs which is defined as controllable costs: at board of directors level all costs are by definition controllable as the board is ultimately responsible for all costs.

There are conflicting views as to whether non-controllable costs should be included in performance reports. One view is that, if they are included, managers will be informed of all the costs affecting their departments. Their inclusion also enables department managers to appreciate the size and the costs of the organizational support upon which their department depends. If non-controllable costs are included in performance reports, they should be distinguished from the costs which fall within the manager's responsibility, that is, those costs which are defined as controllable.

Managers in charge of expense centres have the responsibility for seeing that the expenditure incurred by their departments should not exceed the limits contained in the budgeted expenditure. Clearly, their ability to control expenditure will be an important consideration in the evaluation of their effectiveness as managers. It follows, therefore, that the use of budgets for evaluating the performance of managers has implications for the manner in which budgets are organized. We discuss this problem in the next chapter.

## Profit centres

In recent years, there has been a tendency for organizations to grow in size, and the problem of control which this growth has created has encouraged the devolution of authority in large organizations by the creation of organizational structures based upon the concept of 'divisions'. The rationale underlying this process of decentralization is founded on the belief that divisionalization enhances overall corporate profitability. Several reasons are adduced for this belief. First, responsibility for decision making is transferred to executives who are 'on the spot', and who are directly concerned with the particular problems of manufacturing and marketing divisional products. Hence, they are able to devote all their energies to these problems, whereas under systems of centralized control, top management is able to devote less time to the problems of individual divisions. Second, it is considered that the greater degree of freedom enjoyed by divisional executives increases their motivation towards the attainment of organizational goals, and in particular the profit goal. Third, the opportunity which divisionalization affords of using accounting information to measure the contribution of each division towards the profit goal, also reveals areas of weakness and may suggest possibilities for profit improvement. Finally, the decentralization of the decision-making process provides a training ground for managers as they progress successively through the organization to higher levels of responsibility.

Conventional accounting measurements of performance, such as the return on capital employed, may serve a useful purpose in evaluating the financial performance of individual divisions, where they are completely independent of each other. Where, however, the activities of individual divisions are interrelated, so that the output of one division provides a substantial part of the input of another division, the usefulness of conventional accounting measurements of financial performance is less clear. Under these circumstances, there is a need to establish a price for transferring these so-called intermediate products between the divisions, and this price will clearly affect their profits.

## Transfer pricing

From the foregoing, it is clear that the use of profit centres for the control of divisional performance may give rise to the problem of determining the price at which the product of one profit centre should be transferred to another profit centre. The transfer price is critically important to the profit of both centres, being at once revenue to the selling centre and cost to the buying centre. The evaluation of managerial performance based on the size of the divisional profit requires that the transfer price should be so calculated as to reflect accurately the value added to the product by the selling centre. If it is set too high, it will reflect too favourably upon the selling centre and too unfavourably upon the buying centre, and vice versa. Hence, financial results may be heavily biased by the prices adopted for the transfer of intermediate goods. Defects in the transfer price mechanism may frequently invalidate the conclusions which divisional profit figures might seem to suggest. In such cases, these figures may not merely fail to produce the right decisions: they may actively promote wrong ones.

In Chapter 30, we examined pricing as a means of regulating the exchange of the firm's products with the outside world. In this chapter, we examine transfer pricing as a method of controlling the activities of profit centres within the firm. Hence, we see that the distinction between pricing and transfer pricing lies in their different purposes.

Transfer prices should satisfy the following three criteria:

1 They should promote goal congruence within the organization by harmonizing the interest of individual divisions with the interest of the organization as a whole, by preventing divisional managers from optimizing divisional profits by policies which are harmful to the rest of the organization.
2 They should make possible reliable assessments of divisional performance for the following purposes:
   (a) making predictions for decision-making purposes;
   (b) appraising managerial performance;
   (c) evaluating the divisional contribution to corporate profits.
3 They should ensure that the autonomy of the individual divisions is respected, and that their profits are not dependent upon the actions of other divisions.

## Transfer pricing methods

There are three main methods for establishing transfer prices:

1 market-based transfer pricing;
2 cost-based transfer pricing;
3 negotiated pricing.

## Market-based transfer pricing

Where external markets do exist for the selling centre's products, it is preferable to use market prices rather than cost-based prices. This is because market price is a better guide to the value added to products than a cost-based price which incorporates a profit element. If the external market is competitive and divisional interdependence is minimal, the market price generally leads to optimal decisions within the organization, that is, decisions which satisfy the three criteria stipulated above. Where market prices can be used with a large measure of success, the divisions are effectively separate business entities.

When using market prices, it is essential that the transfer price should be no higher than the buying centre would have to pay on the market. Otherwise, it is evident that an imbalance will be created between the interests of the selling and the buying centres. The existence of an independent market price imposes an upper limit to the transfer price, for given that the selling centre is able to sell at that price, the buying centre should be compelled to buy internally rather than to purchase from external suppliers.

A number of problems arise from the use of the market price as the basis for the transfer price. Thus, changes in supply may lead to large price changes, and the recognition of these changes will cause large variations in the transfer price. As a result, a degree of instability will be introduced in the control mechanism. Further problems are associated with the weight which should be attached to different market price rulings during the transfer period, and to such other factors affecting market prices, such as quantity discounts, area and trade channel differentials, transportation and delivery allowances and service factors. The market price also reflects the result of a bargain, and a reconciliation between what one has to accept to effect a sale, and what one has to pay to effect a purchase. The effects of relative bargaining positions on the market price have implications for the transfer price selected – should it favour the selling or the buying division?

Hence the determination of a fair market price for establishing a viable transfer pricing system which will satisfy the three criteria which have been stipulated calls for a solution to the various problems mentioned above. In many cases, the solution may be arrived at only by an independent arbitrator. This process immediately undermines the third criterion – the preservation of the autonomy of individual divisions – and results in the establishment of a negotiated price.

## Cost-based transfer pricing

In many cases, the transfer of products between profit centres involves intermediate goods in respect of which an external market does not exist. In such cases, it is necessary to use cost-based transfer prices.

A common problem which may arise in employing cost-based transfer prices is that they may conceal inefficiencies in the activities of the selling centre. It is essential, therefore, that the transfer price should be based on standard costs rather than actual costs. As we shall see in the following chapter, the standard cost represents what an item should cost to produce rather than what it does cost, that is it excludes inefficiencies which have arisen in production. Hence, the use of standard costs prevents inefficiencies which have occurred in one profit centre from being transferred to another profit centre.

As we mentioned in Chapter 30, there are different kinds of cost-based prices. Two commonly used cost-related prices are full-cost and marginal-cost prices.

## Full-cost transfer pricing

The major disadvantage of using full cost, or rather full cost plus a profit percentage, as a transfer price is that this method may encourage managers to make decisions which are not in the interest of the firm as a whole.

**Example 1**  The following data relates to profit centre A which sells to profit centre B at full cost plus a profit percentage:

| Profit centre | A | B | |
| --- | --- | --- | --- |
| | £ | £ | £ |
| Variable costs | 10 | 30 + 10 | |
| Fixed costs | 10 | 10 | |
| Markup (50%) | 10 | 25 | |
| Total unit cost | 30 | 75 | |

Profit centre B treats the input of £30 from profit centre A as a variable cost. Hence, before profit centre B is able to have a contribution margin (defined, it will be remembered, as the excess of sales revenue over variable costs which contributes to fixed costs and profits), it must be able to sell its own output at £40 a unit. It is clear, however, that as far as the firm as a whole is concerned, total variable costs per unit are only £20. Given that both profit centres have spare capacity, it is in the firm's interest that profit centre B should produce and sell if it can obtain a price of £20 or over per unit for its output. If it regards £40 as its minimum acceptable price, the firm will lose the benefit of a contribution margin which otherwise it would have had.

In addition to the limitations of full-cost transfer pricing illustrated by the previous example, the use of full costs as a basis for transfer pricing may import a rigidity in an organization which contradicts the rationale for establishing profit centres. Managers should be able to control all the determinants of profits (selling price, volume, fixed and variable costs) if they are to be held responsible for profits. Thus, in the example given above, the manager of profit centre A may feel that its output is constrained by the obligation to sell to profit centre B at a transfer price of £30 a unit. Furthermore, its production is also dependent upon the sales volume attained by profit centre B. This volume may be too low to enable profit centre A to achieve a satisfactory profit, and the manager of that profit centre may well wish to sell its output outside the firm, if that is possible, at varying prices.

Therefore, the rigidity imposed on a firm by virtue of the inflexibility of an agreed full-cost transfer pricing system does not provide a sound basis for the delegation of decisions to profit centres.

## Marginal-cost transfer pricing

Transfer prices based upon marginal cost are designed to overcome some of the problems stemming from the use of full-cost measurement. Thus, in the above example, profit centre A would have transferred to profit centre B at a unit price of £10. In the short run, when both profit centres have surplus capacity, this would enable centre B to adopt a more realistic pricing policy to the benefit of the organization as a whole. Such a decision, however, applies only in special circumstances. In the long run, transfer prices based upon variable costs are of little value for the purpose of performance evaluation, for they result in a loss to the selling division, and would impair the degree of motivation which is one of the reasons for decentralizing.

As we saw in Chapter 30, pricing policies should be based on differential costs and revenues of the company as a whole in order that better profit planning decisions may be made. This implies that decisions about the output volume of divisions cannot be determined independently, thereby undermining the autonomy of individual divisions.

### Negotiated pricing

Whatever method the firm adopts for determining transfer prices, it is evident that some form of negotiated price must be agreed between the managers of profit centres if the transfer pricing system is to operate satisfactorily. It is assumed that independent negotiations between managers will produce results which are beneficial to the firm as a whole, and that the resolution of conflicts of interests will not reflect any bias in favour of any particular groups. These assumptions are probably questionable for a number of reasons. First, transfer price negotiations are very time-consuming, and may lead to a diversion of managerial interest from their own work as they get more involved in the negotiations. Second, conflicts which undoubtedly will occur may lead to recriminations and the involvement of top management as arbitrators may be required.

### The advantages of transfer pricing

The various transfer pricing systems we have examined seem fraught with problems and drawbacks. Nevertheless, these difficulties should be weighed against the advantages which may be derived from setting up profit centres. Equally, these difficulties do not amount to a substantial case for abandoning the practice of assigning transfer prices to interdivisional products. Some value must be found and attached to each element of input and output for the purpose of effective organizational control. Without some form of transfer pricing, the whole structure of intradepartmental analysis and control would collapse.

Very few aids for planning and control are perfect. This is certainly true of transfer pricing. It should be recognized that no available transfer pricing system is likely to serve all the purposes for which it is needed. The limitations found present in any transfer pricing system should be recognized, and any results obtained should be interpreted in the full knowledge of those limitations.

## Investment centres

Investment centres represent the ultimate stage in the decentralization of the decision-making process. Divisional managers are made responsible not only for cost goals (expense centres) and profit contribution goals (profit centres), but also for elements of the capital invested in the division.

Investment centres extend the principles underlying profit centres by associating divisional profits with the capital invested in the divisions. The criterion most commonly employed for assessing the financial performance of investment centres is the return on capital employed (ROCE). It is a comprehensive measure of financial performance which enables comparisons to be made between companies and divisions for the purpose of evaluating the efficiency with which assets are utilized. The ROCE is calculated as follows:

$$ROCE = \frac{\text{net profit before interest and tax}}{\text{average capital invested}} \times 100$$

This formula may be extended so as to incorporate the ratio of net profit to sales, and the ratio of sales to capital employed (the rate of asset turnover).

$$ROCE = \frac{\text{NP PBIT}}{\text{sales}} \times \frac{\text{sales}}{\text{average capital invested}} \times 100$$

The expanded formula is useful for focusing attention on the important elements which affect the ROCE. It implies that profitability may be improved in the following ways:

1 by increasing the volume of sales;
2 by reducing total assets;
3 by reducing costs;
4 by improving the profit markup, for example by raising selling prices or improving the product mix.

The asset turnover will be improved by 1 and 2 and the profit margin by 3 and 4.

**Example 2**    The following table compares the sales, profit and capital employed for three divisions of a large organization. Their profit contribution is £50,000 in each case.

|  | Division A | Division B | Division C |
|---|---|---|---|
| Sales | £500,000 | £500,000 | £1,000,000 |
| Net profit PBIT | £50,000 | £50,000 | £50,000 |
| Capital employed | £250,000 | £500,000 | £500,000 |
| Return on sales | 10% | 10% | 5% |
| Asset turnover | 2 | 1 | 2 |
| ROCE | 20% | 10% | 10% |

It is clear that Division A has the most effective financial performance since its ROCE of 20 per cent is higher than the ROCE of the other two divisions. Division B's return on sales, that is its profit margin, is equal to that of Division A, but its asset turnover is half as high as A's, implying that it employs twice as much capital as A to earn the same profit. This position indicates either that sales could be improved or that excessive capital is being carried by Division B, and that an investigation of asset use may reveal that plant and stocks could perhaps be reduced. Division C has the same ROCE as Division B. Its margin on sales, however, is inferior to that of both other divisions, thereby indicating that selling prices may be too low or that operating costs may be too high.

The foregoing example shows that an ROCE analysis may isolate factors requiring investigation. These factors are illustrated in Figure 5.24.

## Problems associated with ROCE measurements of performance

Three major problems arise as a result of employing ROCE measures for assessing divisional performance. They stem from the following factors:

1 the measurement of profit and capital employed;
2 the appropriation of costs and assets as between divisions;
3 the limitations inherent in ROCE.

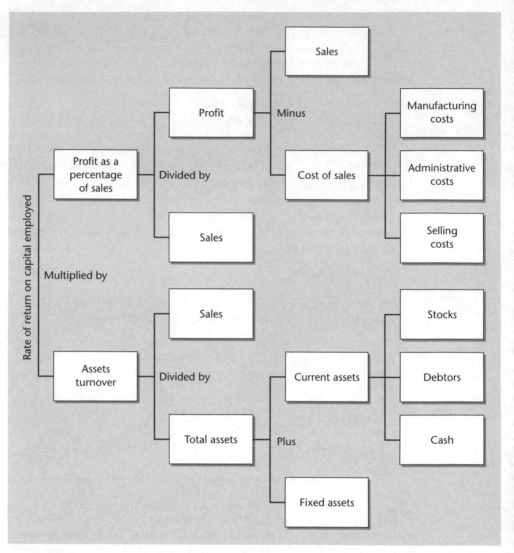

**Figure 5.24**

## The measurement of profit and capital employed

The use of ROCE measures of performance for comparing the performance of similar divisions requires measurements of profit and capital employed which are free from any accounting bias. Thus, uniform accounting procedures should be established for valuing stock, and charging against profit such costs as depreciation, research and development and advertising costs. If comparisons are to be meaningful, the effect of price level changes should also be eliminated from accounting measurements. Moreover, profit and capital employed as measured by conventional accounting methods tend to reflect a much better rate of return than is the case. The valuation of assets on a historical cost basis means that the assets forming the capital investment base are a composite from different monetary dimensions. It follows that the same problem applies to the measurement of costs applied to current revenues for profit calculation.

In order to overcome these problems, therefore, current operating revenues should be associated with the current costs of earning them, and the current value of the assets comprising the capital employed in current operations.

## The appropriation of costs and assets as between divisions

In circumstances where factory buildings, production facilities, office, canteen and other facilities are shared by more than one division, the problem arises of apportioning the costs of these facilities and the value of the investment which they represent. In any event, certain facilities will invariably be conducted by the organization on behalf of all the divisions, and apportionments may have to be made in respect of such items as head-office costs, management and technical services, etc.

The problem of finding suitable bases for apportioning such costs and assets as between several divisions bears a strong resemblance to that of apportioning factory overheads to product costs, which we examined in Chapter 26. As we saw, such appointments tend to be arbitrary, and seldom are the methods selected entirely immune from criticism.

There is a strong case for avoiding apportionments, whether of costs or of assets, for the purpose of ROCE calculations. In accordance with our definition of responsibility accounting, the evaluation of performance should recognize only those elements which are under the divisional manager's control. The incorporation of non-controllable items with controllable ones in performance reports is admissible for information purposes, so long as they are distinguished from each other, and the fundamental principles enshrined in responsibility accounting are maintained. It follows that the divisional reporting statement should schedule the financial information in terms of controllable and non-controllable expenses and possibly controllable and non-controllable assets and liabilities.

## Limitations inherent in ROCE

The main disadvantage of ROCE measures of performance is that they contain a conceptual weakness. This stems from the fact that different investment centres will have different ROCE measurements. Thus, the ROCE for the whole organization may be 10 per cent, whereas the various investment centres may have ROCEs ranging from under 10 per cent to over 10 per cent. The manager of an investment centre enjoying a ROCE of 15 per cent will be unwilling to consider any project offering a rate of return on investment of less than 15 per cent, even though it offers a rate of return of over 10 per cent. This is because the evaluation of his own performance will be made in terms of the current ROCE for his own investment centre. Hence, the use of ROCE for the evaluation of divisional performance may well motivate divisional managers to act in a way inconsistent with the financial objectives of the organization as a whole.

It was to deal with this difficulty that the General Electric Company introduced the residual-profit method of performance appraisal in the 1950s. Under this method, the performance of investment centres is evaluated by the residual profit after charging an appropriate amount calculated by reference to the rate of return on investment being earned by different types of assets. Because the residual profit is an absolute figure and not a ratio, a division which is trying to improve its residual-profit figure will undertake investment programmes even where the expected rate of return is less than the current ROCE.

**Example 3**  The net assets (total assets – current liabilities) of a division are valued at £1,000. The company has decided that a return of 10 per cent on these net assets is an appropriate target. The division's profit statement for the current year is given below:

| | |
|---|---:|
| Revenue | £1,000 |
| *Less:* Costs | 700 |
| | 300 |
| *Less:* Taxes | 150 |
| Profit after taxes | 150 |
| Capital charge (10%) | 100 |
| Residual profit | £50 |

If the manager of this division were evaluated on the ROCE basis, s/he would not invest in a project which produced a return of below 30 per cent, i.e.

$$\frac{£300}{£1,000} \times 100$$

However, if s/he were evaluated on residual profit s/he would invest in a project which gives a return above 10 per cent because this would increase residual income. This action would be beneficial to the company.

## Summary

Control and planning are integrated processes which affect every aspect of organizational activity, including the determination of objectives and the development of long-range and short-range plans. The comparison of actual performance with the goals stipulated in these plans discloses the extent to which they have been attained.

Responsibility accounting underpins the control process, and requires the establishment of responsibility centres throughout an organization. A responsibility centre is a segment of an organization where an individual manager is held responsible for the segment's performance.

Responsibility centres may take three forms:

1 expense centres in which the manager has no control over revenue but is able to control expenditure;
2 profit centres where the manager has control over both revenue and costs;
3 investment centres where the manager has responsibility not only for revenues and costs but also for the capital invested.

The control problem is made more complex by the size of business organizations and the occurrence of transactions between various divisions of such organizations. In order that divisional performance should be accurately assessed for control purposes, transfer prices should be established which will be useful in this respect. If transfer pricing systems are to operate satisfactorily, some form of negotiated pricing must be agreed by divisional managers. Investment centres pose additional problems as regards the assessment of financial performance. The ROCE is a comprehensive measure of performance, but its limitations should be understood.

**Reference**  Kam-por, Y (1994). 'The influence of divisionalisation on an effective internal accounting system', *ACCA Students' Newsletter*, June.

# Self-assessment questions

1 State what you understand by 'control'.

2 Examine the nature of the control process.

3 What is meant by 'responsibility accounting'?

4 What is the difference between an 'expense centre' and a 'cost centre'?

5 Discuss the significance of the distinction between 'controllable' and 'non- controllable' costs.

6 What is meant by a profit centre? Give some examples of organizational segments that would be able to function as profit centres.

7 State what criteria are relevant for evaluating transfer pricing policies.

8 Review three main methods used for establishing transfer prices.

9 What is meant by an 'investment centre'? Identify types of organizational segments that would be able to function as investment centres.

10 'ROCE is a comprehensive measure of performance, but its limitations should be understood.' Discuss this statement.

# Problems *(\* indicates that a solution is to be found in the Lecturer's Guide)*

1 Electrical Products Company consists of four operating divisions. Divisional managers are granted considerable discretion in setting employment, sales and production policies. For some time the Chairman, Ronald Jackson, has been concerned with the method of evaluating divisional performance. On 1 June 20X0, he wrote the following letter to Miles French, a management consultant:

Dear Mr French

We have been trying to develop a system which will provide an incentive to our division managers and act as a basis for evaluating their effectiveness. Originally we used profit as an index for evaluation. Then we realized that, in order to be meaningful, profit should be related to another index such as profits of prior periods. After giving the matter much thought I have now become convinced that only a composite index, as shown below, will give equal weights to the three principal objectives of a division.

**Composite index for evaluating division performance**

| Objective | Criterion | Last year | This year | % change |
|-----------|-----------|-----------|-----------|----------|
| Minimize capital | Capital turnover | 1.5 | 1.7 | +13 |
| Profitability | Return on sales | 10.0% | 9.0% | −10 |
| Growth | Share of market | 15.0% | 15.6% | +4 |
|  | Net composite change |  |  | +7% |

I propose to offer each division manager a bonus of £200 for each one per cent increase in the composite index. I aim to present this proposal to the board at the October meeting, and, if approved, start the system next year.

Please let me have an evaluation of this plan in writing.

Yours sincerely,
Ronald Jackson.

*Required:* Assuming you are the consultant, write a letter to Mr Jackson evaluating the proposal.

545

**2\*** The Akroid Corporation Ltd is a divisionalized enterprise manufacturing specialized equipment for the construction industry. Division A makes one of the basic components – the Spikron – which is used by Division B in the manufacture of the Akroid Scraper, which is then sold as a final product. Division B absorbs about three-quarters of the total output of Division A. The Spikron has other applications, and Division A has been selling the remaining 25 per cent of its output to outside firms. The annual output of Spikrons is 16,000 units. The Spikron is transferred at £350 to Division B, and is sold at £400 to outside firms.

The following costs are associated with the Spikron produced in Division A:

| | £ |
|---|---|
| Variable costs at £300 per unit | 4,800,000 |
| Fixed costs | 200,000 |
| Total costs | 5,000,000 |

A German company makes a similar product to the Spikron, which could be adapted for integration into the Akroid Scraper, and has offered to supply Division B with the adapted product at a cost of £320 per unit.

The manager of Division B wishes to buy the German product as this will substantially reduce his costs, and make his own product more competitive on the market. The manager of Division A argues that he would not be able to expand his sales of the Spikron to outside firms, and that, as a result, the profitability of his division would be seriously affected.

*Required:*
Discuss the implications of the German offer from the point of view of the Akroid Corporation Ltd and of both divisions.

# 35 Standard costs and variance analysis

**Setting the scene**

Cost control can only come from comparing actual cost incurred with some pre-conceived idea of how much costs should be. The comparison can be with similar costs of a previous period, but the usefulness of that is limited. Previous costs will not reflect expected price increases, improved methods of production, different output levels and so on. It is also possible that past and present costs both reflect inefficiencies so that they are not revealed by the comparison. Much more effective control can be exercised by comparing actual cost with a standard cost taking into account expected inflation, levels of output, and objective assessments of reasonable efficiency levels.

It should not be assumed that standard costing is a useful technique to be applied to ALL costs in ALL organisations. It is likely that standard costing will be most usefully employed in mass production process costing type industries.                    (Smith, 1990)

**Learning objectives**

After studying this chapter you should be able to:

1   Explain why standard cost systems are adopted.

2   Describe the basic concepts underlying variance analysis and explain when variances should be investigated.

3   Calculate materials and labour variances and explain how they are used for control.

4   Describe the purpose of flexible budgeting.

5   Calculate variable and fixed overhead variances and explain their meanings.

6   Calculate and explain the variances which are applied to the analysis of sales.

7   Discuss the limitations of standard costing.

We turn now to a consideration of an important method of establishing standards of performance by the use of standard costs. The difficulty about using data recorded in the financial accounting system for planning purposes is that it relates to the past and although managers are interested in the results of previous decisions, they are primarily concerned with decisions which will affect the future.

For control purposes, historical costs are of little use. Particularly in times of inflation, past experience will not inform management whether an operation, a job or a department costs too much. Indeed, what management wishes to know is not what costs were in the past but what they ought to be in the present. Once it has been determined what these costs ought to be, actual costs can be compared with them and any difference analysed.

Standard costing has been evolved as a method to meet this need. It relies upon predetermined costs which are agreed as representing acceptable costs under specified operating conditions.

## Standard costs and budgeted costs

The principal differences between standard costs and budgeted costs lie in their scope. Whilst both are concerned with laying down cost limits for control purposes, budget costs impose total limits to costs for the firm as a whole, for departments or for functions for the budget period, whereas standard costs are attached to products and to individual manufacturing operations or processes. For example, the production department's budget for the period ahead may envisage a total production of 100,000 units at a cost of £10 a unit, so that the production department will be allocated an expenditure ceiling of £1 million. The unit cost of £10 will have been based upon the established standard costs relating to material usage and price, labour usage and labour costs as well as allocated overhead costs. Standard costs are revised when it is clear that they have ceased to be realistic in terms of current costs.

The relationship between budgeted costs and standard costs is clear: the setting of standard costs as performance standards for control purposes implies that they must be used as a basis for drawing up budget statements and calculating budget costs, for otherwise there can be no confidence in their use as a basis against which actual performance may be measured.

## Applications of standard costing

Standard costing is a useful method of control in a number of ways. First, the process of evaluating performance by determining how efficiently current operations are being carried out may be facilitated by the process of management by exception. Very often the problem facing management is the time lost in sifting large masses of feedback information and in deciding what information is significant and relevant to the control problem. Management by exception overcomes this problem by highlighting only the important control information, that is the variances between the standard set and the actual result. This process allows management to focus attention on important problems so that maximum energy may be devoted to correcting situations which are falling out of control.

Second, a standard costing system may lead to cost reductions. The installation of such a system demands a reappraisal of current production methods as it necessitates the standardization of practices. This examination often leads to an improvement in the methods employed which is reflected in a reduction of the cost of the product. One example of cost reductions through increased efficiency may be seen in the simplification of the clerical procedures relating to stock control. All similar items of stock may be recorded in the accounts at a uniform price; this eliminates the need which arises under historical costing for recalculating a new unit price whenever a purchase of stock is made at a different price.

Third, standard costs are used as a basis for determining selling prices. Standard costs represent what the product should cost, and are a much better guide for pricing decisions than historical costs which may contain purchasing and production inefficiencies which cannot be recouped in competitive markets.

Finally, perhaps the most important benefit which may be derived from a standard costing system is the atmosphere of cost consciousness fostered among executives and foremen. Each individual is aware that the costs and output for which s/he is responsible are being measured, and that s/he will be called on to take whatever action is necessary should large variances occur. If the philosophy of top management is positive and supportive, standard costing may work as an incentive to individuals to act in the best interest of the firm. Moreover, a standard costing system which allows subordinates to participate in setting the standards fosters a knowledge of costing down to shop floor level, and assists in decision making at all levels. Thus, if there should occur spoilt work necessitating a decision from the foreman in charge on whether to scrap or rectify the part involved, a knowledge of costs will enable him to make the best decision.

## Setting cost standards

To be effective for the purpose of cost control, standard costs should reflect attainable standards of cost performance. This means that the process of setting standard costs is of critical importance if a standard costing system is to be effective as a means of cost control.

Setting standard costs implies:

1 establishing procedures for setting standards with respect to the price at which resources are acquired and their usage. This suggests the employment of specialist engineers and consultants for determining relative levels of cost efficiency that should be within the firm's reach;
2 establishing procedures for allowing participation by cost centre managers in setting attainable standards. This suggests that there may be resistance to cost standards that are too harshly set, in the form of negative reactions by personnel.

Cost standards are set for all categories of costs and for all cost centres. Setting cost standards for direct costs, such as direct material and direct labour costs, focuses upon price and usage as the two key cost components.

Setting cost standards for indirect costs is relatively more difficult since there is no direct output against which standard costs can be set. This problem is resolved by a surrogate measure of output in respect to which overhead costs can be related.

Overhead costs are considered to vary with activity levels, which are expressed in standardized measures, such as standard labour hour, standard machine hour or standard labour cost.

Further problems associated with standard overhead costs are as follows:

1 an appropriate overhead rate must be selected for allocating standard variable and standard fixed costs per unit;
2 in the case of fixed overhead costs, the overhead rate selected must be calculated by reference to a standard activity level for the budget period.

# Setting standard costs for direct material and direct labour

Setting standard costs for direct material and direct labour involves two aspects:

1. quantifying an efficient input of resources;
2. acquiring that input at the best price.

## Standard direct material costs

The quantity of raw material required for a standard unit is determined by engineers. The standard quantity should include an appropriate allowance for normal wastage in production.

Responsibility for purchasing rests with the purchasing department. The standard price should reflect the best price that the purchasing department can obtain, and be the price expected to be paid during the budget period.

## Standard direct labour costs

Before standard labour costs can be set, operatives have to be graded according to standardized categories of skills. Labour time standards are set by time and motion study engineers. The standard wage rates are those that are expected to be paid during the budget period.

# Variance analysis for direct costs

The control of direct costs through variance analysis is based on two principles:

1. *Management by exception.* Actual expenditure is assumed to be in line with standard costs, unless this is contradicted by information showing that variances are occurring between the budget allowance, based on standard costs, and actual expenditure being recorded in the financial accounts through the process of recording invoices.
2. *Accounting responsibility.* Responsibility for the control of costs is located with the manager having the responsibility for cost centre costs.

The first sign that standard costs are not being respected is the appearance of a *budget variance* on direct material or direct labour. A budget variance is defined as *a difference between the budget allowance for the output achieved and actual spending on the output achieved.* It requires further analysis before its causal factors may be identified, investigated and, if possible, corrected.

The analysis of the budget variance necessitates splitting up the budget variance into the two components of standard costs, namely the quantity standard and the price standard. As a result, it is possible to attribute the problem to the occurrence of excessive usage or excessive price, or both.

Variances fall into two categories:

1. *Unfavourable variances* that arise when the standard allowance is exceeded by actual expenditure.
2. *Favourable variances* that are due to actual expenditure being less than the standard allowance.

Clearly, management will be more immediately concerned with possible inefficiencies arising as a result of *unfavourable* variances. *Favourable variances* may arise out of fortuitous events occurring in the firm's favour, for example, a fall in market prices for raw materials. However, favourable variances may also indicate that standards should be adjusted upwards to reflect actual performance more accurately. The truth remains that, under ideal conditions, favourable or unfavourable variances should not occur if standards have been correctly set.

## Direct material variances

The analysis of the direct material variance begins by identifying the direct material budget variance. The material budget variance is t*he difference between the actual expenditure and budgeted expenditure*. It provides a measure of the overall difference that has to be investigated. It is composed of two elements:

1 *price variance* that explains the proportion of the budget variance that is caused by paying more or less than the standard price for actual purchase;
2 *usage variance* that explains the proportion of the budget variance that is due to using more or less material in production than the standard quantity.

The principle of accounting responsibility means that responsibility for the price variances is laid on the purchasing department, whereas responsibility for the usage variance lies with the manager of the appropriate production cost centre.

| Example 1 | Ragon Ltd is a small manufacturing company making a product known as Platron. It has a standard costing system, and standard direct material costs per unit of Platron have been set for the budget year 20X1 as follows: |

Standard material quantity per unit      3 kilos
Standard price per kilo      £0.50

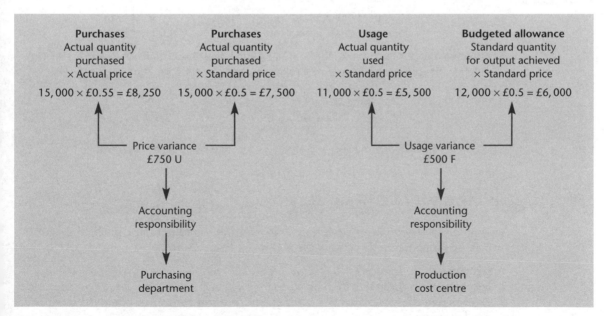

Figure 5.25  Analysis of direct material variances

During the month of January 20X1, 4,000 units of Platron were produced. This was the budgeted output volume. The following information was obtained by the costing department:

| | |
|---|---|
| Quantity used during January | 11,000 kilos |
| Quantity purchased during January | 15,000 kilos |
| Budgeted expenditure for January | £6,000 |
| Actual expenditure for January | £8,250 |

The analysis of the direct material budget variance into its two components is as shown in Figure 5.25.

It should be noted that the effects of the price variance have been magnified due to excessive purchasing over usage. Responsibility for the price variance falls on the purchasing department, which may well have acted rationally and in the best interests of the firm in stocking up in anticipation of rising prices. By contrast, responsibility for the usage variance falls entirely on production cost centres.

## Direct labour variances

The analysis of the direct labour variance begins by determining the *direct labour budget variance* defined as *the difference between the actual payroll and the standard labour cost of actual production*. The major difference between the analysis of direct material and direct labour variances is in the stocking of direct materials in excess of usage. The terminology is slightly different, though the same meaning is retained. The notion of price is expressed in the labour wage rate; and the notion of usage is stated in labour efficiency. Accordingly, once the direct labour budget variance has been calculated, it is split into *the direct labour wage rate variance and the direct labour efficiency variance.*

**Example 2**   Standard costs established by Ragon Ltd for the 20X1 budget year were as follows:

| | |
|---|---|
| Standard direct labour hour per unit | 0.25 hour |
| Standard direct labour rate per unit | £4.00 per hour |

The actual output for the month of January 20X1 was 4,000 units of Platron. This corresponded to the budgeted volume. The following additional information is given:

| | |
|---|---|
| Actual hours | 900 |
| Actual expenditure | £3,690 |

The direct labour budget variance is analysed into its two components, as shown in Figure 5.26.

## Setting standards for overhead costs

Setting standard overhead costs poses more difficult and complex problems than the setting of standard direct costs in the following respects:

1  setting cost standards;
2  selecting an overhead rate for both standard fixed and variable overhead cost allocation;
3  determining the standard volume for the purpose of recovering standard fixed overhead costs.

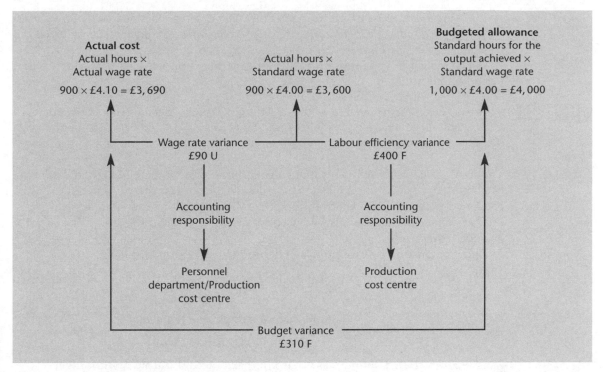

**Figure 5.26  Analysis of direct labour variances**

## Setting cost standards

The setting of efficient cost standards for overheads requires ensuring that the resources classified as fixed and variable overheads have been acquired by means of efficient purchasing, and that the usage of these resources corresponds to an efficient utilization.

Efficient purchasing implies that the responsible departments will have secured resources at the best price, and that the budget allowance is a spending level that reflects such purchasing. In this respect, the budget allowance for fixed and variable overheads has a component element that is similar to the standard price and standard wage rate used for setting standard direct material and direct labour costs.

The budget allowance also has another component that assumes that there will be an efficient usage made of variable and fixed costs. This implies that such costs will support a standard level of activity. Therefore, setting efficient usage levels for variable overheads consists in finding what type of activity provokes variations in variable overheads, and then attempting to impose expenditure limits on variable overheads with respect to activity. For example, if the simplifying assumption is made that machine repair and maintenance costs vary with machine hours, the problem is not simply to ensure that repair charges are the best obtainable, but that in relation to machine hours, repairs themselves are not excessive but reflect good machine usage.

## Selecting a standard overhead rate

The difficulty in establishing an appropriate level of activity in relation to variable and fixed costs lies in that overhead costs are not directly related to output expressed as units of product. As discussed earlier in Chapter 26, an overhead rate has to be selected for the purposes of allocating standard variable and fixed overheads to products.

The most convenient overhead rate is the *standard hour* defined as *a unit of measurement representing the quantity of any product or service which can be produced or performed in one hour by any process, machine or operative.*

The standard hour is not a measure of time but a measure of performance in a period of one hour.

**Example 3**

If the estimated time required to write 200 letters is 20 hours, a standard hour represents 10 letters. Similarly, if 48 units of product A can be produced in 12 hours, a standard hour of that product represents 4 units.

The standard hour not only constitutes a convenient base for establishing standard overhead rates, but can also be applied to all types of cost centres where it is useful to have a common measure through which the output of diverse products can be expressed.

The standard hour may also be used to develop overhead rates both for variable and fixed overheads.

Three production control ratios are derived from the standard hour:

1 *The efficiency ratio* that measures the efficiency of direct labour and is expressed as follows:

$$\text{Efficiency ratio} = \frac{\text{Standard hours of production achieved}}{\text{Actual direct working hours}} \times 100$$

2 *The production volume ratio* that compares actual output with budget and is expressed as follows:

$$\text{Production volume ratio} = \frac{\text{Standard hours of production achieved}}{\text{Budgeted standard hours}} \times 100$$

3 *The capacity ratio* that compares actual hours with budgeted hours and is expressed as follows:

$$\text{Capacity ratio} = \frac{\text{Actual hours worked}}{\text{Budgeted hours}}$$

**Example 4**

Tafel Ltd manufactures tables and chairs. It is estimated that two hours are required for one table and 1 hour for one chair. In March, 20X0, actual production was 50 tables and 150 chairs. Budgeted production for the period was 40 tables and 160 chairs. Actual hours worked were 230 and actual output in terms of standard hours was:

| | |
|---|---|
| Tables: 50 units x 2 hours per unit = | 100 hours |
| Chairs: 150 units x 1 hour per unit = | 150 hours |
| | 250 standard hours |

Budgeted production in terms of standard hours was:

| | |
|---|---|
| Tables: 40 units x 2 hours per unit = | 80 hours |
| Chairs: 160 units x 1 hour per unit = | 160 hours |
| | 240 standard hours |

$$\text{Efficiency ratio} = \frac{250}{230} \times 100 = 108.7\%$$

$$\text{Production volume ratio} = \frac{250}{240} \times 100 = 104.2\%$$

$$\text{Capacity ratio} = \frac{230}{240} \times 100 = 95.8\%$$

These results may be checked as follows:

$$\text{Production volume ratio} = \text{Capacity ratio} \times \text{Efficiency ratio}$$

$$104.2\% = \frac{230}{240} \times \frac{250}{230}$$

## Determining the standard volume for fixed overhead cost recovery

Variable overhead costs vary directly with output. Hence, if the output is expressed in standard hours, variable overheads will be applied to actual output in accordance with the predetermined rate.

Fixed costs, however, do not vary with output. Hence, a normal or standard output must be budgeted to enable a fixed overhead rate to be calculated. The standard fixed overhead rate will be applied to the number of standard hours fixed in the budget.

The term *fixed budgeting* refers to budgets prepared on the basis of a standard output for the purposes of establishing budget allowances throughout the firm. Under fixed budgeting, standard fixed overheads will be over- or under-applied whenever actual output is greater or less than the standard output, giving rise to favourable or unfavourable volume variances.

Firms will need always to plan their financing requirements on the assumption that they will attain the budgeted output level. In this sense, the financial budget will always be a *fixed budget*. The disadvantage of using the fixed budget for control purposes lies in the inability to control costs under fluctuating output conditions.

## Flexible budgeting

Flexible budgeting is intended to overcome the difficulties posed by fixed budgeting for controlling overhead costs. Flexible budgeting does not replace fixed budgeting for planning the financing requirement purposes. It only replaces fixed budgeting for control. The particular difficulties that make fixed budgeting redundant for control are:

1 overhead allowances are budgeted in respect of only one output volume, namely the standard output;
2 fixed overheads will generally be under- or over-applied, but responsibility for volume variances cannot be attributed to cost centre managers, since they are not responsible for output variations.

## le budget allowances

Flexible budgeting allows fluctuations in output levels to be taken into account for cost control purposes by means of flexible budget allowances.

**Example 5**  Jobin Ltd is a small manufacturing company that has a budgetary planning and control system based on the fixed budgeting principle. The fixed budgeted overhead allowance for assembly cost centre A is £20,000 for a period during which the standard output was represented by 5,000 standard hours. The budgeted allowance was calculated as follows:

|  | £ |
|---|---|
| Indirect material | 5,000 |
| Indirect labour | 2,500 |
| Repairs and maintenance | 5,000 |
| Insurance | 1,500 |
| Rates | 3,000 |
| Depreciation | 3,000 |
|  | £20,000 |

The overhead costs per unit are:

$$£20,000 \div 5,000 = £4$$

The firm has experienced severe fluctuations in demand for its products over several months. As a result, actual costs have diverged significantly from budget allowances. It has now decided to introduce flexible budgeting making it possible to match any given actual output with a corresponding budget allowance. During the month of June, actual activity level of cost centre A was 4,000 standard hours, for which the following flexible budget allowance was calculated:

|  | Total variable costs | Fixed costs | Total budget allowance |
|---|---|---|---|
|  | £ | £ | £ |
| Indirect material | 4,000 |  | 4,000 |
| Indirect labour | 2,000 |  | 2,000 |
| Repairs and maintenance | 2,400 | 2,000 | 4,400 |
| Insurance | 800 | 500 | 1,300 |
| Rates |  | 3,000 | 3,000 |
| Depreciation |  | 3,000 | 3,000 |
|  | 9,200 | 8,500 | 17,700 |

Flexible budgeting improves the control of overhead costs by establishing a flexible budget allowance for each output level, once that output is known. In effect, cost centres are allowed to incur overhead costs at a predetermined standard rate. Control is applied routinely for each management reporting period, usually monthly, when the flexible overhead allowance for the actual output achieved is calculated.

| **Example 6** | Jobin Ltd has a fixed financial budget providing for a monthly output of 5,0(
basis, each cost centre has been given a monthly budget allowance correspon
termined standard costs per unit. Jobin Ltd uses flexible budgeting for cost c
the month of June, actual output was 4,500 units. Actual overhead costs incurr
to £19,150. The following overhead cost control report was prepared. |

|  | (1) | (2) | (3) | (4) Variation from | (5) Variation from |
|---|---|---|---|---|---|
|  | Actual cost of production | Total budget allowance | Original budget | original budget | budget allowance |
| Units produced | 4,500 | 4,500 | 5,000 | (1) – (3) | (1) – (2) |
| Indirect materials | £4,700 | £4,500 | £5,000 | £300F | £200U |
| Indirect labour | 2,400 | 2,250 | 2,500 | 100F | 150U |
| Repairs and maintenance | 4,600 | 4,700 | 5,000 | 400F | 100F |
| Insurance | 1,450 | 1,400 | 1,500 | 50F | 50U |
| Rates | 3,000 | 3,000 | 3,000 | – | – |
| Depreciation | 3,000 | 3,000 | 3,000 | – | – |
|  | £19,150 | £18,850 | £20,000 | £850F | £300U |

## Variance analysis for overhead costs

The analysis of overhead cost variances fall into two parts:

1 the analysis of variable overhead costs;
2 the analysis of fixed overhead costs.

## Variable overhead cost variance

The analysis of the variable overhead cost variance begins by identifying the variable overhead budget variance, which is *the difference between the actual expenditure and budgeted expenditure*. It provides a measure of the overall difference that has to be investigated. It is composed of two elements:

1 *Expenditure variance* that explains the proportion of the budget variance that is caused by differences in the price paid for services charged as overhead costs. It is calculated as follows:

**Expenditure variance = actual overheads – (actual hours ×
standard variable overhead rate)**

2 *Efficiency variance* that explains the proportion of the budget variance that is due to difference in the usage of services charged as overhead costs. It is calculated as follows:

**Efficiency variance = (actual hours – standard hours of actual production) ×
standard variable overhead rate**

**Example 7**

Scat Ltd has an assembly cost centre that is budgeted for an output of 5,000 standard hours. The following information is given with respect to October 20X0:

| | | |
|---|---|---|
| (a) | actual hours worked | 4,800 |
| (b) | variable costs incurred | £11,600 |
| (c) | standard variable overhead rate per standard hour | £2.3 |

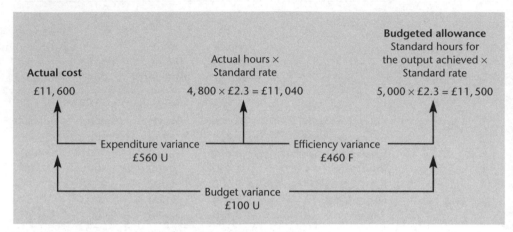

**Figure 5.27  Analysis of variable overhead variances**

The expenditure and efficiency variances are calculated as shown in Figure 5.27.

## Fixed overhead cost variances

Fixed overhead cost variances fall into two types:

1 *Expenditure variances*, calculated as follows:

**Fixed overhead cost expenditure variance = actual fixed overheads – budgeted fixed overhead costs**

2 *Volume variances*, calculated as follows:

**Fixed overhead cost volume variance = budgeted fixed overheads – (standard fixed overhead rate × standard hours in the output achieved)**

**Example 8**

Refer to example above, where the assembly department is budgeted for an output of 5,000 standard hours and actual hours worked were 4,800. The following fixed overhead cost information is given with respect to October 20X0:

| | | £ |
|---|---|---|
| (a) | actual fixed overhead costs | 6,200 |
| (b) | budgeted fixed overhead costs | 6,000 |
| (c) | standard fixed overhead rate per standard hour | 1.7 |

The expenditure and volume variances are calculated in Figure 5.28.

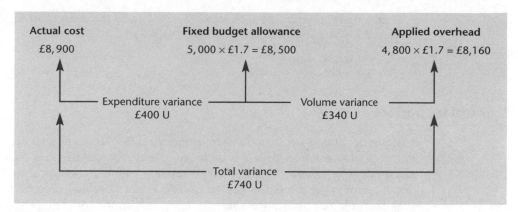

**Figure 5.28 Analysis of fixed overhead variances under fixed budgeting**

The analysis of fixed overhead cost variances will be different under fixed budgeting and flexible budgeting cost control systems with respect to the volume variance. As mentioned earlier, the use of fixed budgeting will lead to the appearance of a fixed overhead cost volume variance, since the fixed overhead rate used for recovering fixed overheads will have been determined on the basis of a fixed output level. Under flexible budgeting, however, the fixed overhead cost volume variance disappears, and there is only an expenditure variance. The reader should note that the under- and over-absorption of overheads which we discussed in Chapter 26 results in expenditure and volume variances.

## Sales variance analysis and the control of revenue

In general terms, the procedures appropriate for the control of revenue are similar to those applied to the control of costs, and may be summarized as follows:

1 the establishment of a sales plan;
2 the prompt determination and reporting of variances between actual and planned performance;
3 the investigation and analysis of variances so as to ascertain their causes and those responsible for them;
4 The implementation of appropriate corrective action.

The determination of the sales plan has both long-range and budgetary aspects. Long-range planning will be concerned with establishing revenue objectives and goals, from which may be derived specific sales targets and prices for the budget planning period. Since the level of demand for most products exhibits a seasonal pattern, the annual sales plan should be divided into smaller periods so as to make possible a system of responsibility accounting based on a meaningful comparison of actual and planned performance.

So far, we have discussed the control of revenue in terms of analysing the difference between actual and planned sales. It should be apparent, however, that management is not really so much concerned about sales themselves as the profit from sales. It is for this reason that sales variance analysis has been developed to measure the effects on profits of variances between actual sales and planned sales, and not the effect of such variances merely on revenue.

Three different variances are commonly applied to the analysis of sales:

1 sales price variance;
2 sales volume variance;
3 sales mix variance.

## Sales price variance

It is quite common for actual selling prices to differ from the planned selling price. Numerous factors may be responsible for sales price variances, such as the need to adjust prices to meet competition, or to provide a new marketing strategy. By far the largest factor is the discretion allowed to individual sales managers to adjust prices to meet particular circumstances, such as price reductions for slightly spoiled goods or to secure the goodwill of a client.

The sales price variance is an ordinary price variance of the type we have already discussed. It may be calculated from the following formula:

**Sales price variance = units sold**
**× (actual contribution per unit less the standard contribution)**

It indicates, therefore, the total effect on profit of differences between set prices and the prices at which goods were actually sold.

## Sales volume variance

This variance discloses the effect on profits of differences between the planned sales volume and the actual volume of sales. It is calculated as follows:

**Sales volume variance = standard contribution per unit**
**× (actual number of units sold – budgeted units of sales)**

## Sales mix variance

A change in the product mix may change the profitability of the total mix if the contribution margin of the different products is different. In these circumstances, changes in the product mix will lead to a variance between planned and actual profits. The dimension of this variance may be computed as follows:

**Sales mix variance = standard contribution per unit of each product**
**× (actual quantities of units sold**
**– actual total sales of units in budgeted mix proportions)**

### Example of all three variances

The following data relate to products X and Y sold by Biproducts Ltd during the quarter ended 31 December 20X0:

**Budgeted sales:**
  X 5,000 units at £10 (standard contribution margin £4)
  Y 5,000 units at £5 (standard contribution margin £2)

**Actual sales:**
X 4,000 units for £44,000 (i.e. £11 per unit)
Y 8,000 units for £32,000 (i.e. £4 per unit)

These data may be tabulated as follows:

| | (a) Actual contribution | (b) Actual quantity | (c) Standard contribution margin | (d) (b) × (c) Value | (e) Actual quantity in standard proportions | (f) Standard contribution margin | (g) (e) × (f) Value | (h) Budgeted margin |
|---|---|---|---|---|---|---|---|---|
| | £ | Units | £ | £ | Units | £ | £ | £ |
| X | 20,000 | 4,000 | 4 | 16,000 | 6,000 | 4 | 24,000 | 20,000 |
| Y | 8,000 | 8,000 | 2 | 16,000 | 6,000 | 2 | 12,000 | 10,000 |
| | 28,000 | 12,000 | | 32,000 | 12,000 | | 36,000 | 30,000 |

*Notes:*
1  Column (a) is derived from the following formula:

actual contribution
= actual sales less (actual units × standard cost)
= £44,000 – (4,000 × £6)
= £20,000

2  Column (e) is derived by taking total actual sales of 12,000 units and applying the budgeted mix proportions. According to the budget, 50 per cent of X and 50 per cent of Y should be sold. Total sales were 12,000 units, which expressed in budgeted mix proportions amount to 6,000 units of X and 6,000 units of Y.

The variances which may be extracted from these data are as follows:

*Sales price variance*
X  = units sold × (actual contribution per unit less standard contribution)
= column (a) – column (d)
= £28,000 – £32,000
= £4,000 U

The sales price variance is unfavourable to the extent of £4,000 because 3,000 units of Y were sold at a price which was £1 lower than the standard, while only 1,000 units of X were sold at a price which was £1 higher than the standard price.

*Sales volume variance*
X  = standard contribution per unit ×
(actual number of units sold less budgeted units of sales)
= column (g) – column (h)
= £36,000 – £30,000
= £6,000 F

This variance reflects the fact that 12,000 units were actually sold as against a budgeted volume of only 10,000 units. Its value is the contribution which the extra 2,000 units would have brought if they were at standard price and mix.

### Sales mix variance

= (standard contribution per unit of each product × the actual quantities of units sold) − (standard contribution per unit of each product × actual total sales in budgeted mix proportions)

= column (d) − column (g)

= £32,000 − £36,000

= £4,000 U

This variance discloses the reduction in budgeted profits caused by selling a greater proportion of units having a lower contribution margin than the standard.

## Responsibility for variances

Under responsibility accounting only those costs incurred by a responsibility centre over which it can exercise control may be used as a basis for evaluation. In variance analysis it is necessary that the precise cause of a variance be determined and that the cause be traced to the individual responsible. It is the function of the individual in charge of each responsibility centre to act promptly upon reports of variances within his or her control. Variances are not ends in themselves. Rather, they raise the questions: 'Why did the variance occur? What must be done to eliminate them?' Obviously the importance of these questions depends on the significance of the deviations. We see how the significance of a variance is determined in the next section.

The material usage and labour efficiency variances respectively reveal that the quantities of material and labour used in production are either more or less than planned, depending on whether the variances are unfavourable or favourable. If more material is being used than planned, the cause may lie elsewhere than in the production department, for example in the purchase of inferior materials by the purchasing department. The fault may lie in the production department and may be found to be attributable to careless supervision, or the use of untrained staff, or faulty machines. An unfavourable labour efficiency variance may be due to poor control by the foreman, bad labour relations, health factors, production delays, inferior tools and badly trained staff. Again, the responsibility for the variance should be located. For example, if due to badly trained staff, this may be caused by inefficiency on the part of the personnel department, but if, on the other hand, the variance is caused by the economic conditions prevailing at the time which had produced a shortage of specialized labour, the variance is considered to be uncontrollable. Some of the variances may be interrelated. For example, if cheaper materials are purchased, this will result in a favourable materials price variance. It may also result in an adverse material usage variance because if the quality of the material is poor; this may then lead to an adverse labour efficiency variance. Conversely, the use of higher grade labour may cause an adverse labour rate variance but may cause a favourable materials usage variance and a favourable labour efficiency variance. Finally, an adverse (or favourable) labour efficiency variance will affect the variable overhead efficiency variance and the fixed overhead efficiency variance.

Price and wage rate variances may not be controllable by the firm, and this is particularly true of raw material prices and wages agreed nationally with trade unions. On the other hand, variances may occur in the negotiation of contracts for materials which are the responsibility of the purchasing department. The purchasing department controls prices by getting several quotations, taking advantage of economic lots and securing cash discounts. Inefficiency in these areas will reveal unfavourable variances for which that department should be held responsible.

With regard to overhead variances, spending variances are usually the responsibility of the department head, because they are usually controllable by him/her. The volume variance is not normally controllable by the departmental manager; it is usually the responsibility of the sales department or production control.

## The investigation of variances

Managerial time is too valuable to be wasted on the unnecessary checking of performance. When standard costs are properly established, they provide an automatic means of highlighting performance variances upon which management may concentrate their attention. Thus, the investigation of variance is concerned only with exceptional variances and not those which are minor deviations from the established standards.

The investigation of a variance is a three-stage process consisting of:

1  an investigation to determine whether the variance is significant;
2  if it proves to be significant, an investigation into its causes;
3  if the variance can be corrected, action is taken to ensure that it will not occur in the future.

The determination of the significance of a variance in itself may be problematic. If its definition is left to managerial judgement and experience, inconsistencies may arise in the treatment of different variances solely by reason of behavioural factors affecting a manager's judgement of a situation. Thus, pressure of work in itself may lead the manager to perceive the significance of a variance as less important than it really is. Moreover, there is unlikely to be complete agreement between different managers about the investigation of borderline cases.

It is necessary, also, to distinguish 'chance' or 'random' variances from significant variances requiring investigation. By viewing the standard as an arithmetical mean about which fluctuations will occur, it is possible to eliminate random variances from significant variances. Experience of the investigation of variances shows that random variances are inherent in standard costing systems. Such variances assume the shape of a 'normal distribution' about the standard, and they are not controllable. It follows that a statistical control chart may be utilized to enable a manager to determine whether a variance is significant or not. It will define the limits within which random or normal variances occur, so that those variances which fall outside these limits may be assumed to be abnormal and, therefore, significant variances.

Statistical control charts have been used for many years for the purpose of quality control, but it is only recently that this technique has been applied to the control of standard cost variances. Statistical control charts permit the elimination of random variances while providing a high probability that non-random variances will be revealed.

The use of statistical control charts requires that upper and lower limits of random variance tolerance be laid down with precision. Setting these limits requires an analysis of the pattern of sample variances, and the standard deviation of the sample may be used to determine the acceptable limits of tolerance. These limits are illustrated in Figure 5.29.

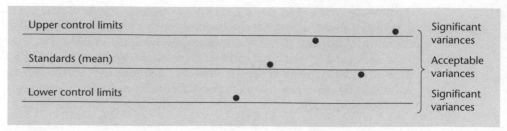

**Figure 5.29**

# Limitations of standard costing

Standard costing was developed to meet the needs of a traditional manufacturing environment. In a 'world-class manufacturing' environment the use of standard costs for performance evaluation has been questioned.

Firms that advocate continuous improvement may find that the use of standards acts as a demotivating agent because they represent a ceiling for employees' improvement efforts. In other words, once the standard performance is reached, there will be no incentive to improve the process any further. Standard costing, therefore, tends to reflect the status quo. In pursuit of continuous improvement, standard costs can be replaced by target costs. The former represents what ought to be achieved as far as current circumstances are concerned, whilst the latter represents what must be achieved to enjoy competitive advantage. Alternatively, standard costs can be replaced by actual costs as efficiency targets. Actual costs are tracked from period to period in the expectation of continuous cost reduction. Under this approach, last period's actual cost becomes this period's standard.

Standard costing encourages those responsible for the achievement of standards to produce favourable variances. But the pressure to meet standards may create dysfunctional behaviour. The reporting of material price variances my be inappropriate where firms have just-in-time purchasing techniques. For example, purchasing officers may acquire materials of low quality, or in large lots, in order to produce a favourable materials price variance. As a consequence, scrap, the number of defective units and the amount of rework activity may increase, or raw material stocks may be excessive. These outcomes run contrary to the objectives of total quality control and zero stocks. JIT companies will wish to focus on performance measures which emphasize quality and reliability rather than material price variances which direct attention away from these key factors. Similarly, efficiency variances may encourage workers to produce more than needed to achieve targeted efficiency levels or to avoid an unfavourable volume variance. But producing more product than needed is diametrically opposed to the JIT goal of zero stocks. In a JIT environment idle workers (in the short run) are not necessarily viewed as bad; keeping workers active by over-producing can be much more costly than the labour services cost.

In an advanced manufacturing environment it is necessary to supplement standard cost information with non-financial measures for guiding operational performance. Non-financial measures such as lead time, number of line stops, and number of units scrapped are used in place of cost information for day-to-day decisions because the non-financial data can be supplied much faster than can accounting data, which must be first translated into £s and then summarized. Therefore, conventional accounting data are much better suited for the longer term and overall performance summaries of an operation, whilst non-financial information can provide more timely and focused performance information. This applies particularly to computer-controlled manufacturing equipment with its immediate contemporaneous information feedback to the production manager. The control cycle is generally more effective with this non-monetary data than converting production data in monetary units at intervals for inclusion in periodic variance reports.

## Summary

Standard costing underlies most business activities. The cost of a product must be ascertained prior to production for pricing and control purposes. Standard costing may also lead to cost reductions. Perhaps the most important benefit which results from a standard costing system is the atmosphere of cost consciousness fostered among managers.

Standard cost data are compared with actual cost data for the purpose of ascertaining variances. Such variances are normally broken down into two basic components – quantity variances and price variances. The control of overhead costs as distinct from direct costs requires a method which takes into account the possibility of changes in the level of production during the planning period. Flexible budgeting affords such a method, and provides for each department a series of budget allowance schedules for various volume levels within the normal range of operations.

The ascertainment of variances is only the first stage in assessing results. Variances should be analysed in depth in order to establish whether they are significant, whether they are controllable and if so where responsibility lies. At the same time, the analysis of variances enables established standards to be validated and methods for establishing standards in the future to be improved.

*Reference*   Smith, R (1990). 'Standard setting – objectives and limitations', ACCA *Students' Newsletter*, June.

## Self-assessment questions

1 Distinguish standard costs and budgeted costs.

2 State some applications of standard costing.

3 Examine the problems of setting cost standards.

4 Explain what is meant by a budget variance.

5 What is the formula for calculating:
   (a) direct material price variance,
   (b) direct material usage variance,
   (c) wage rate variance,
   (d) labour efficiency variance?

6 What problems are involved in setting overhead cost standards?

7 Distinguish between fixed and flexible budgeting.

**8** What is the formula for calculating:
  (a) variable overhead expenditure variance,
  (b) variable overhead efficiency variance,
  (c) fixed overhead expenditure variance,
  (d) fixed overhead volume variance?

**9** State three variances that can be applied to the analysis of sales.

**10** Comment briefly on the problems that are implied in the investigation of variances.

## Problems *(* indicates that a solution is to be found in the Lecturer's Guide)*

**1** For March 20X0 the master budget and actual results for Dept A of a firm were as follows:

|  | Master budget | Actual |
|---|---|---|
| Output – Units A | 600 | 500 |
| Units B | 400 | 500 |
|  | £ | £ |
| Costs: Materials | 13,200 | 13,300 |
| Direct labour | 7,000 | 8,400 |
| Machining | 9,600 | 9,450 |
| Overhead costs | 4,400 | 4,400 |
|  | 34,200 | 35,550 |

The master budget was constructed on the following production specifications:

(a) Material required per unit – A, 4 kg; B, 5 kg.
(b) Direct labour hours required per unit – A, 1 hour; B, 2 hours.
(c) Machining costs include a variable element of £4 per machine hour. Machining time required per unit – A, 0.5 hours; B, 0.25 hours.
(d) Overhead costs include a variable element of £1 per direct labour hour worked.

*Required:*
(a) Construct a flexible budget for the actual output and show any variances.
(b) If it is known that in fact 1,400 direct labour hours were worked in March, what further information about the direct labour variance can be given?

**2*** The Vitrox Manufacturing Co Ltd is a single-product company and employs a standard absorption costing system. The standard cost per unit is calculated as follows:

|  | £ |
|---|---|
| Direct labour 4 hours at £3.00 | 12.00 |
| Direct materials 10 kg at £1.00 | 10.00 |
| Overhead | 10.00 |
| Total standard cost per unit | 32.00 |

The standard volume of output is 10,000 units per month. The variable overhead cost component is £1.00 per standard direct labour hour.

The following information is available for the month of December 20X0:

| | £ |
|---|---|
| Units completed | 8,000 |
| Direct materials used 83,000 kg at £1.05 | 87,150 |
| Direct labour hours recorded 33,000 hours at £3.10 | 102,300 |
| Variable overhead costs incurred | 32,500 |
| Fixed overhead costs incurred | 65,000 |

*Required:*
(a) Analyse the following variances:
   – direct material variances;
   – direct labour variances;
   – variable overhead variances;
   – fixed overhead variances.
(b) Explain possible reasons for the appearance of these variances.

3  K Kiely makes and sells apple tarts which are sold in packs of ten. The company operates a standard costing system and the standard cost of a box of apple tarts is as follows:

| Direct materials | 2 kg at £1 per kilo |
|---|---|
| Direct labour | 2 hours at £2.20 per hour |
| Variable production overheads | £1 per direct labour hour |

The actual figures for the month of October were:

| Production | 8,200 boxes |
|---|---|
| Direct materials | |
| Opening stock | 1,000 kg |
| Closing stock | 2,500 kg |
| Purchases | 9,000 kg at 98p per kg |
| | 12,000 kg at 86p per kg |
| Direct labour | 15,800 hours costing £36,340 |
| Variable production overheads | £14,250 |

The company operates a standard marginal costing system.

*Required:*
(a) Calculate the variances for materials, labour and variable overheads in a form which would be useful to management.
(b) Comment on the purpose of variances.
(c) On being presented with the statement of variances, K Kiely offers the following reasons as to why they have arisen:
   (i)  Although we used experienced employees, they were less efficient.
   (ii) The standard wastage allowance which was set for the apples was significantly exceeded.

(iii) The projected increase in the labour rate of 4 per cent, turned out to be 2 per cent.

(iv) The increased quantities of apples purchased. Because the market had a surplus, the buyer was able to negotiate a substantial discount in price.

(v) The excessive electricity costs (included in the variable overheads) caused by cooking the tarts for longer than usual, resulted in the expense being higher than forecast.

Match the variance to the reasons and consider whether the explanation is acceptable.

# 36 The control of managed costs

## Setting the scene

The question is, 'What is the most effective way of controlling period costs?' The answer is through exactly the same techniques as are used for direct material and direct labour, that is, changing the design specifications of the job description to eliminate inefficiency, redundant, and unnecessary work elements. The difference is that cost analysts and administrators make the design changes rather than engineers and buyers. . . .

In any cost control or reduction activity, the one fundamental fact that must be kept in mind is that all costs are results, not causes. Costs can be reduced or eliminated only by attacking their causes. Simply firing people to attack the salary expense line is likely to by offset by increases in overtime premiums and temporary help lines, in addition to separation expenses.                                                                    (Byrum, 1990)

## Learning objectives

After studying this chapter you should be able to:

1   Appreciate the nature of managed costs.

2   Describe two methods for controlling managed costs.

3   Indicate the main problems in controlling administrative costs.

4   Discuss the main issues concerned with the control of marketing costs.

Traditionally, accountants have been concerned with the control of manufacturing costs, where clear-cut input–output relationships may be established. Accordingly, such costs suggest an engineering approach to cost control and they are described as engineered costs. Standard costing typically represents the development of cost control techniques in this regard.

In recent years, the growing significance of non-manufacturing costs has underlined the importance of developing effective methods of cost control for such costs. The major obstacle that has been encountered lies in the absence of clear-cut input–output relationships. In this chapter, we review some of the methods that are applied in the control of managed costs.

## The nature of managed costs

Essentially, managed costs are non-manufacturing costs. Their level is determined at the discretion of management, and for this reason, they are often referred to as 'discretionary costs'.

There are four major categories of managed costs:

1 Administrative costs, incurred in providing the administrative structure. Unlike engineered costs, they are not strictly defined in terms of short-term output, and for this reason, they are considered as relatively fixed. Administrative costs include not only management salaries, but also costs associated with the provision of a host of administrative, accounting and secretarial services.

2 Research and development costs, incurred in developing new products and processes. Research and development is in the nature of capital investment, and for this reason is related to long-term planning. There are two reasons why research and development costs are difficult to control:

   (a) Given the speculative nature of research, and the uncertainty of a return from expenditure invested in research, research spending is no indicator of the effectiveness of a research department or as a means of evaluating a research project.

   (b) There is a long lead time between incurring costs and obtaining results, even when research is successful.

3 Marketing costs, incurred in maintaining and increasing market share for the firm's products and services. Marketing costs include a variety of costs, such as advertising, market research, selling, warehousing, distribution, etc. Some of these costs, such as advertising, that are concerned with introducing new products or extending market share are in the nature of capital expenditure: others, such as selling costs, are in the nature of operating expenditure. These costs may be difficult to control for the following reasons:

   (a) Some costs, such as advertising, are acknowledged to have an impact on sales, but the relationship between cost and benefit is not easily ascertainable. Furthermore, the long-term and short-term nature of these benefits cannot be measured with accuracy.

   (b) Other costs may be susceptible to input–output analysis, for example, warehousing costs, but most of them, such as salespeople's salaries and sales administration costs, lack accurate performance measurement standards.

4 Training costs, incurred in the development and improvement of staff, include costs of courses, training department salaries, the loss of production time, etc. These costs are difficult to control as there are very few measures of their success.

In service organizations the discretionary costs are significantly greater. For example, in the health service the inputs to the process (salaries and expenses) can be measured, the outputs (patients) are more difficult; additionally, there are no profit figures to provide a relative measure. Attempts have been made recently to measure the outputs in terms of waiting lists but there is a long way to go before these measures equate to the accuracy of the standard costs.

## The control of managed costs

The discretionary nature of managed costs implies that budgeted volume of spending is not analysed in terms of expected output. None the less, despite the difficulties of applying an input–output analysis to discretionary costs, there are implicit assumptions as to the volume and especially to the quality of the activity and services that such costs are expected to provide. In effect, the benefits associated with managed costs are both qualitative and quantitative.

Two main methods that have been developed for controlling managed costs are:

1 Work study measurements, that are in the nature of work engineering studies in which tasks are analysed in terms of workloads, techniques used and number of people required to perform the work efficiently. Work study measurements rely on establishing key control factors to apply to particular activities. Examples of control factors are:

| Activity | Control factor |
|---|---|
| Purchasing | Number of orders placed |
| Typing | Number of letters typed |
| Receipting cheques | Number of cheques received |

Work study measurements are more suitable for controlling routine costs. They are not useful for controlling non-routine activities that characterize management and specialist functions, in which qualitative factors are critical to success.

2 Budgetary controls which treat discretionary costs are controlled in terms of departmental spending budgets. This approach to the control of discretionary costs is an application of the methods used to control variable and fixed overhead manufacturing costs discussed in Chapter 35.

The key to the control of discretionary costs lies in spending budgets relying on the principle of responsibility accounting. The initial problem to be resolved is whether such costs are variable costs or fixed costs for budgeting purposes.

A marginal-costing approach to the development of departmental budgets rests on the assumption that there is a cost–volume relationship in which costs rise directly with the volume of activity, and that the relationship is quantifiable.

A fixed-cost approach to the development of departmental budgets treats discretionary costs as fixed during the budget period. This approach more correctly reflects the assumptions made by large organizations that existing organizational structures, with which discretionary costs are typically associated, are not changed in the short term, even if they are reviewed from time to time.

## The control of administrative costs

These costs are relatively fixed in the short run irrespective of short-term changes in the level of business activity. As yet the stricter costing procedures applied to manufacturing activities have not been applied generally to administrative activities. Management would certainly argue that administrative functions are not susceptible to work study methods. Nevertheless, certain tasks such as clerical ones are susceptible to work study, and some organizations have attempted to establish standards of efficiency by which to determine staff requirements. Examples of some of the control factors employed were quoted earlier, namely:

| Activity | Control factor |
| --- | --- |
| Purchasing | Number of orders placed |
| Typing | Number of letters typed |
| Receipting cheques | Number of cheques received |

Generally, administrative services are rendered indirectly to many different departments, and it is practically impossible to establish input–output relationships which would enable overall evaluations to be made. Hence, the control of administrative costs is one of the most difficult areas of management control.

To some extent, budgets can assist in exercising control over administrative costs. The budgetary control of such costs requires that accounting responsibility be clearly identified with particular managers. Financial requirements must be submitted as budget requests by individual managers, and should be scrutinized, modified as necessary and incorporated subsequently into an overall administrative budget. The administrative budget becomes the standard against which expenditure is to be assessed.

The difficulty in using this method of controlling administrative costs lies in determining whether the initial budget is reasonable for the proposed level of activity, for there is no way of establishing an acceptable standard of administrative expenditure in relation to particular activity levels. Hence, decisions regarding administrative cost budgets must be based largely on executive judgement and experience.

## The control of research and development costs

There are two main reasons why research and development costs are difficult to control. First, since there is little connection between research costs and their benefits, research spending is no indicator of the effectiveness of a research department, or indeed of a research project. Second, there is a long lead time between costs incurred and benefits received.

Research and development is an activity directly related to long-range planning. The effectiveness of research and development expenditure may be assessed only in relation to the attainment of goals specified in the long-range plan. These goals should be selected by top management as crucial areas to which major research effort should be directed. In this connection, research expenditure should be concentrated on specific projects which form part of the research effort in a particular area. The control of such expenditure may be exercised by reference to the progress made towards the completion of such projects.

## The control of marketing costs

Marketing costs have become significant elements in total costs, owing to the rising burden of such costs as advertising and market development. It follows that attention should be directed towards developing the most efficient cost control methods in this area to provide marketing managers with information which will enable them to make the best decisions from the firm's point of view.

Marketing costs cover a wide range of activities, including obtaining sales orders, warehousing and distribution, handling returns and after-sales service. They may be analysed on three different bases – the nature of the cost, the function performed and the appropriate sector of the firm's business, as follows:

1 *Classification as to costs*
Salespeople's salaries and commission
Travelling
Advertising

2 *Classification as to function*
Selling
Advertising
Transportation
Credit collection
Warehousing
Invoicing

3 *Classification as to business sector*
Territory
Product
Marketing channels
Operating divisions
Customers

The analysis of marketing costs is helpful in providing information which is useful for a number of purposes, such as:

- determining the profitability of sales territories;
- evaluating the profitability of product lines;
- setting selling prices;
- evaluating salespeople's performance;
- determining the importance of individual customers;
- analysing order size profitability.

It is evident from the description of the range of decisions for which information is required that the analysis of marketing costs is concerned essentially with profitability, which is a function both of revenue control and cost control.

## Determining the profitability of sales territories

Most marketing activities are organized on a territorial basis. As a first stage in the analysis of territorial profitability, it is necessary to distinguish direct and indirect marketing costs. Direct costs are those incurred in respect of a territory: indirect costs are those incurred for all the various sales territories. Direct costs will be controllable by territorial sales managers: indirect costs are beyond their control. Nevertheless, despite difficulties in effecting accurate apportionments of indirect costs, such apportionments serve the useful purpose of providing regional managers with information on the back-up services which support their own activities and should be made, provided that they are distinguished from controllable items on reports.

Table 5.1 shows how the analysis of the profitability of sales territories may be made. Its purpose is to locate territories where weaknesses and problems exist. Once they have been located, prompt and intelligent managerial action is required, which may include such decisions as an increase in the number of salespeople operating in the area, or an improvement of the services provided. It will be recalled that the existence of a contribution margin warrants the continuance of operations in the short run even though conventional calculations indicate a loss.

**Table 5.1  Profit analysis by territories**

| | Territory 1 | Territory 2 | Territory 3 | Total |
|---|---|---|---|---|
| Sales | £500,000 | £300,000 | £100,000 | £900,000 |
| **Direct costs by territories** | | | | |
| Cost of goods sold | 250,000 | 160,000 | 40,000 | 450,000 |
| Transport and outside warehousing | 30,000 | 20,000 | 10,000 | 60,000 |
| Regional office expenses | 50,000 | 30,000 | 20,000 | 100,000 |
| Salesforce's expenses | 25,000 | 15,000 | 6,000 | 46,000 |
| Other regional expenses | 15,000 | 10,000 | 5,000 | 30,000 |
| Total direct cost by territories | 370,000 | 235,000 | 81,000 | 686,000 |
| Contribution to headquarters' overheads and profit | 130,000 | 65,000 | 19,000 | 214,000 |
| **Indirect costs** | | | | |
| Central administration | 50,000 | 22,000 | 8,000 | 80,000 |
| Central warehousing | 20,000 | 8,000 | 2,000 | 30,000 |
| Advertising | 30,000 | 15,000 | 5,000 | 50,000 |
| Total indirect costs | 100,000 | 45,000 | 15,000 | 160,000 |
| Net profit | 30,000 | 20,000 | 4,000 | 54,000 |
| Percentage of net profit | 56% | 37% | 7% | 100% |
| Percentage of sales | 56% | 33% | 11% | 100% |
| Contribution/sales % | 26% | 22% | 19% | 24% |

## Determining the profitability of products

The analysis of the profitability of different products is useful to management in a number of ways. It indicates not only the relative profitability of different products, but also areas of strength and weakness which should be noted in the development of corporate strategy. The application of techniques such as contribtion margin analysis may assist in deciding whether or not to drop a product line. Pricing decisions may also be based on profitability analysis.

The selection of appropriate bases for determining profitability is problematical, as it is for other management purposes which require the apportionment of indirect costs.

Table 5.2 below shows how the analysis may be conducted. It indicates that product C is the least profitable product in the product range, for although it makes a contribution of £78,000 to fixed expenses and profit, a net loss of £28,000 is associated with its manufacture. Hence, the analysis implies that action should be taken to improve its profitability in the future.

## Controlling marketing costs

Marketing costs may be classified into order-getting and order-filling costs. The former are associated with such activities as advertising, sales promotion and other selling functions: the latter are incurred after the order has been obtained, and cover such costs as packing, delivering, invoicing and warehousing finished products.

Table 5.2 Profitability analysis by product

| | Product | | | |
| | A | B | C | Total |
|---|---|---|---|---|
| Sales | £350,000 | £300,000 | £250,000 | £900,000 |
| Variable costs of goods sold | 90,000 | 85,000 | 125,000 | 300,000 |
| Gross contribution | 260,000 | 215,000 | 125,000 | 600,000 |
| **Variable marketing costs** | | | | |
| Transport and warehousing | 15,000 | 12,000 | 13,000 | 40,000 |
| Office expenses | 30,000 | 30,000 | 20,000 | 80,000 |
| Salesforce's salaries | 20,000 | 15,000 | 10,000 | 45,000 |
| Other expenses | 6,000 | 5,000 | 4,000 | 15,000 |
| Total variable marketing expenses | 71,000 | 62,000 | 47,000 | 180,000 |
| Contribution to fixed expenses and profit | 189,000 | 153,000 | 78,000 | 420,000 |
| **Fixed expenses** | | | | |
| Manufacturing | 55,000 | 50,000 | 45,000 | 150,000 |
| Administration | 30,000 | 25,000 | 25,000 | 80,000 |
| Marketing | 50,000 | 50,000 | 36,000 | 136,000 |
| Total fixed costs | 135,000 | 125,000 | 106,000 | 366,000 |
| Net profit (loss) | £54,000 | £28,000 | £(28,000) | £54,000 |
| Contribution/Sales % | 54% | 51% | 31% | 47% |

## Order-getting costs

The effectiveness of such costs may only be satisfactorily assessed by relating them to sales revenue. Many factors which affect sales, however, are outside the control of the sales department, and for this reason it is difficult to establish standards of performance which are relevant to the problem of maintaining and increasing the effectiveness of order-getting activities. Budgetary control may be used to determine the limits of expenditure but it is not possible to use such budgetary control methods as flexible budgeting in respect of some items, particularly advertising. Flexible budgeting is designed to control expenditure through changing levels of activity: advertising is incurred in order to increase the level of activity. It would be nonsense, therefore, to attempt to apply flexible budgeting to the control of advertising expenditure.

The search for suitable methods of controlling order-getting costs continues. Objective measures may be too limited in their scope to be useful. Firms are using such objective measures as selling costs per order, selling costs per call, or calls per day to control selling costs. These measures should be used with care, for they do not necessarily reflect difficulties in selling to different markets at different times.

Advertising costs, in particular, involve such a large financial commitment that it is necessary that the effectiveness of such costs should be assessed. Market research departments are better equipped than accountants to assess the effectiveness of advertising, since its effects go beyond the expansion of immediate sales.

## Order-filling costs

It is comparatively easier to control order-filling costs than order-getting costs, since order-filling costs are associated with internal procedures. These procedures are of a standard form and of a repetitive nature making them susceptible to standard control methods: the costs of invoicing, packaging and despatching can be controlled by reference to such objective standards as number of invoices dealt with, number and size of packages, etc. Moreover, unlike order-getting costs, flexible budgeting may be applied to the control of order-filling costs.

**Example**

Bloxwich Ltd has a sales budget which envisages the sales of 100,000 units of its product in the current year. Budgeted delivery costs are based on standard delivery costs of £1 per unit. If only 80,000 units were sold and delivered by the end of the year at a cost of £90,000, it would be evident that the unfavourable delivery costs variance of £10,000 would require investigation.

## Summary

There are two main cost classifications – manufacturing and non-manufacturing costs. Non-manufacturing costs may be subdivided into three categories – administrative, research and development and marketing costs. These costs are frequently referred to as 'managed' or 'discretionary costs' since they are incurred at the discretion of management.

The difficulty of controlling managed costs is created by the absence of a method for determining appropriate cost levels since it is not possible to relate accurately and in financial terms the benefits associated with such costs. Moreover, it is not possible to determine whether a change in managed costs represents an improvement in performance. For example, providing product specifications are maintained, a reduction in manufacturing costs represents an improvement in performance. No such inference may be drawn from a reduction in managed costs.

In view of the rising proportion of managed costs as a percentage of total costs, the analysis and control of such costs is important and means should be found of overcoming the problems caused by the inability to establish rigorous standards.

**Reference**

Byrum, A J (1990). 'The right way to control period expense', *Management Accounting* (UK), September.

## Self-assessment questions

1 What do you understand by managed costs?

2 Explain the problems implied in the control of managed costs.

3 Examine the process of budgetary control as applied to managed costs.

4 Discuss the problems associated with the control of administrative costs.

5 Review the problems of controlling research and development costs.

6 Indicate some of the considerations implied in the control of marketing costs.

7 Review three bases on which marketing costs may be analysed.

# 37 Behavioural aspects of performance evaluation

## Setting the scene

Do management accounting and control systems benefit organisations? Nobel Laureate Herbert Simon and his colleagues, among others, say they do. Such systems, they believe, play three roles: score-keeping, attention-directing and problem-solving. Robert Simons, writing in the March 1992 *CA Magazine* concurs. Management accounting, he says, consists of 'identification, measurement, accumulation, preparation, interpretation, and the communication of information that helps executives in filling organisational objectives'. In fact, most writers agree that financial controls, such as budgeting systems, aid in planning, co-ordinating and controlling any organisation's complex flow of interrelated activities, and in motivating workers. But research also suggests there is a dark side to management accounting, that the system can do more harm than good.

(Mackintosh, 1994)

## Learning objectives

After studying this chapter you should be able to:

1 Explain what is meant by 'management style'.

2 Contrast 'Theory X' with 'Theory Y'.

3 Describe possible management reactions to budgets.

4 Identify three possible levels of cost performance.

5 Define 'management by objectives'.

6 Explain what is meant by 'contingency theory'.

Traditionally, accountants have followed economists in assuming the main organizational problem to be the maximization of profits and the optimization of resource allocation to this end. Consequently, accountants have tended to regard organizations in purely technical terms, subjecting human resources to the same analysis as that applied to other economic resources in the search for maximizing productivity and profits.

For more than two decades, social progress, political change and the internationalization of corporate organizations have created a strong awareness of the uniqueness of human resources, and in particular, of the way in which the behaviour of both management and workers affects the realization of organizational objectives. Both management and workers are recognized as having variable performance patterns depending directly on management styles and organizational culture. Much of the early work in this area was concerned with managerial performance evaluation, and the reaction of workers to management style and organizational culture, and was in the literature of accounting. Recently, the success of Japanese organizations that is seen as a function of organizational culture has prompted more research into the influence of culture on business performance.

In this chapter, we review briefly some of these developments.

## Managerial style and organization culture

According to Horngren and Foster (1987) managerial style is 'the set of behaviours exhibited by key managers in an organization'. This is interpreted as a tendency to authoritarian as against participative management styles in relation to decision making and the context in which performance is evaluated.

Again, according to these authors, organization culture is 'the set of beliefs and values shared by members of the organization'. This is interpreted as relating to prevalent interpersonal relationships and other significant constraints on social behaviour.

The considerable success of Japanese industry has underlined the importance of culture as a key success factor, and points to a definition of this concept in an organizational setting that arguably is much broader than the definition adopted by Horngren and Foster. In effect, culture may be deemed to determine the manner in which both workers and management interact, and also the manner in which management decisions are made. Accordingly, management style may be viewed as subsumed in the concept of organization culture.

Much of the international comparison of the relative success of business organizations made currently tends to find substantial cause for disparity precisely in different national cultures as they find their expression in business enterprises. How far this may be substantiated as against the weight of other success factors may be questioned. Nevertheless, the existence of the belief is in itself symptomatic of the importance attached to culture.

There is considerable controversy in the debate regarding the deterministic influence of culture as an organisational success factor. Moreover, culture is not transmissible in the peculiar way in which it is associated with national traits. For these reasons, we shall concern ourselves with the traditional accounting concern of evaluating management performance, as expressed in the literature of the English-speaking nations.

## The objectives of performance evaluation

The objectives of performance evaluation may be stated as follows:

1 to assess how effectively the responsibilities assigned to managers have been carried out;
2 to identify areas where corrective actions should be taken;
3 to ensure that managers are motivated towards organizational goals;
4 to enable comparisons to be made between the performance of different sectors of an organization, to discover areas where improvements may be made.

In our analysis of the process of control, we have so far discussed two important pre-requisites for performance evaluation:

1 identifying areas of responsibility over which individual managers exercise control (responsibility accounting), and
2 the setting of standards of performance to be used as yardsticks for the evaluation of performance.

In this chapter, we address ourselves to some of the behavioural problems of budgets as measures for evaluating performance.

## Leadership styles and the problem of control

There is a tendency for firms to expect desired results merely from the use of appropriate techniques, thereby failing to recognize that success in organizational control depends upon the actions of responsible individuals and their appreciation of the importance of sound interpersonal relationships. The manner in which the budgeting process is viewed depends on the leadership style adopted by management. McGregor has characterized the two extremes of management styles as 'Theory X' and 'Theory Y' (McGregor, 1960). According to McGregor, these extreme views are conditioned by the manager's view of man.

### Theory X

The Theory X view of man, as summarized below, is supportive of an authoritarian leadership style:

1 Management is responsible for organizing the elements of productive enterprise – money, materials, equipment and people – in activities directed to economic ends.
2 As regards people, management is concerned with directing their efforts, motivating and controlling their actions, and modifying behaviour to fit the needs of the organization.
3 Without this active intervention by management, people would be passive – and even resistant – to organizational needs. Therefore, they must be persuaded, rewarded, punished, controlled. In short, their activities must be directed, and therein lies the function of management. This view is often summed up by the assertion that management consists of getting things done through other people.

### Theory Y

By contrast, Theory Y is supportive of a more democratic and participative leadership style:

1 Management is responsible for organizing the elements of productive enterprise – money, materials, equipment and people – in activities directed to economic ends.
2 People are not by nature passive or resistant to organizational needs. They appear to have become so as a result of negative experiences of organizational needs.
3 The motivation, the potential for development, the capacity for assuming responsibility, the readiness to direct behaviour towards organizational goals are all present in people. Management does not put these qualities in people. It is the responsibility of management to make it possible for people to recognize and develop these human characteristics.

4  The essential task of management is to arrange organizational conditions and methods of operation so that people can achieve their own goals best by directing their efforts towards organizational objectives.

There is evidence that the Theory X leadership style is widely prevalent and is clearly operational. Those who prefer the assumptions of Theory Y claim that the Theory X leadership style has a human cost in the frustration and the lack of personal development which result from its application to people. The trend in behavioural research suggests that benefits may be derived from leadership and organizations based on the assumptions of Theory Y. These assumptions recognize, in particular, that the basic motivating forces affecting people at work include biological, egoistic and social factors.

As people, employees at whatever organizational level have certain needs which condition their own objectives. They are seeking *compensation* for their efforts to enable them to provide some desired standard of life for themselves and their families. They need outlets for their physical and intellectual energies which provide both *stimulation* and *satisfaction*. They seek *self-realization* in a sense of their own worth and usefulness. They are pursuing further *growth* and greater *personal effectiveness*. They seek the *recognition* of their fellows, whether their organizational equals, superiors or subordinates. They appreciate their *identification* with a worthwhile and successful undertaking.

In order to maximize employees' contribution to organizational activities, it follows that these personal needs and goals should be capable of realization in the tasks in which they are employed. An awareness of the nature of personal needs, therefore, is an important aspect of control.

# The effects of budgets on people

Research suggests that there is a great deal of mistrust of the entire budgetary process at the supervisory level (Argyris, 1953). There is a tendency for traditional budgets to provide the following responses.

## Reactions to pressure

The evaluation of a manager's performance in terms of the departmental budget is one of the few elements in performance appraisal which is based on concrete standards. There is little room for manipulation or escape if results are not going to turn out as expected in the budget. If budget pressure becomes too great, it may lead to mistrust, to hostility and eventually to poorer performance levels as reaction sets in against budgetary control.

The problem of distinguishing between controllable and non-controllable costs is an important cause of tension among managers. The task of the manager of a department or expense centre, for example, is to attain goals with the minimum cost. One of the initial difficulties which arises in evaluating performance applies to all levels of management, namely, the treatment of factors beyond their control. This problem is aggravated when the responsibility for an activity is shared by two or more individuals or functions. Labour inefficiency, for example, may be due to excessive machine breakdowns (maintenance function), inferior materials (purchasing function), defective materials (inspection function) or poor-calibre personnel (personnel function).

Establishing standards of performance in itself is not an easy task. It demands the clear definition of goals and responsibilities, the delegation of authority, the use of satisfactory surrogates for the activities concerned, effective communication of information and an understanding of the psychology of human motivation.

## Overemphasis on the short run

One of the dangers facing organizations which evaluate the effectiveness of managers in profit terms is that too much emphasis is given to achieving short-term profitability, and measures taken to improve short-term profitability may be detrimental to the organization's long-term prospects. Short-term increases in profits gained at the expense of reductions in research and development and the failure to maintain adequate standards of maintenance are two examples of short-term cost savings which are detrimental to the firm in the long term.

## Poor-quality decision making by top management

Excessive reliance on the profit performance of divisions may also affect the quality of decisions made by top management. If the managerial competence of divisional managers is assessed solely on the basis of the profit performance of their respective divisions, serious errors of judgement may result. Moreover, if profit results are used as part of an early-warning system, action may be taken by top management which may not be warranted. Therefore, although profit budgets are indispensable for planning purposes, great care should be taken in utilizing them for control purposes. The attainment of profit targets is dependent on many factors, some of which are entirely outside the control of a divisional manager. The uncertainty attached to profit forecasts, in particular, limits the usefulness of profit targets for the evaluation of the performance of a divisional manager. The process of formulating the divisional profit forecast also introduces bias in the evaluation of performance. Divisional profit targets are usually based on the divisional manager's forecast of future events. Therefore, it is the ability to forecast the future successfully, rather than the ability to manage successfully, which forms the basis on which that manager's performance is evaluated. This consideration also affects the validity of comparisons between the performance of different divisions. For example, it is easier to determine an attainable profit goal for a division whose major constraint is productive capacity, where sales are limited only by output, than for a division which sells in a highly competitive market.

Another problem arising from the use of profit budgets in evaluating divisional performance stems from the fact that an annual budget covers too short a period in which to obtain a realistic picture of managerial performance. The effects of decisions in some instances may take several years before being reflected in profit performance. Thus, the decision to introduce a new product is one of several decisions whose impacts on divisional profits take some years before they are fully realized. The more complex and innovative the division the longer will be the time period necessary for the evaluation of performance. In the light of these considerations, the use of an annual profit result may give a completely inaccurate view of divisional performance.

## Poor communication

Where a Theory X style of management exists, negative attitudes may be generated against organizational goals which may lead to faked budget results and the unwillingness to transmit information. Managers will feel that their own survival justifies these tactics.

The prevalence of negative behaviour in an organization which practises management by domination may be aggravated by the response of top management, when it is realized that information which is needed for decision making is not transmitted. Their immediate reaction may be to impose even tighter controls, which will reinforce the negative attitudes held by subordinate managers leading to the transmission of even less accurate and useful information. The progressive tightening of the managerial reins may well result, therefore, in a progressive deterioration of the information flow.

The communication of information is of central importance to the processes of planning and control, as it provides the link between various levels of management and the various decision points. Any reluctance on the part of subordinate managers to communicate information is a serious impediment to the efficiency with which planning and control decisions are made. It is not a sufficient condition for success that an organization should have accounting control systems and that it should have stipulated standards of performance. These control methods will not operate successfully and standards of performance will not be attained if the style of management adopted fails to secure a high degree of motivation and goal congruence within the organization.

## Departmental self-centredness

The budget process which involves defining areas of responsibility, measuring and comparing performance accordingly, concentrates the manager's entire attention on his/her own department. The tendency to departmental self-centredness which is thus encouraged obscures the important relationships between departments, so that interdepartmental dependencies may be ignored or overlooked in the quest for optimizing departmental results. Consequently, economies which would result from greater interdepartmental collaboration may be lost to the organization.

## The stifling of initiative

The planning and control aspects of budgeting may be overemphasized within an organization with the result that opportunities for the exercise of personal initiative may be excluded. Budgets which appear to be straitjackets discourage managers from deviating from budget stipulations even when circumstances indicate that individual action should be taken.

## Bias in budgeting

In the last analysis, the process of setting budget targets may be said to be a matter of making subjective judgements, and, as a result, bias may inevitably be found in the budgeting process in a conscious or unconscious form. Managers may inflate costs and reduce revenue expectations when setting budget targets, thereby ensuring that they are more readily achievable. In this way, the introduction of conscious bias is a deliberate means of ensuring that their performance as managers will be highly evaluated.

The introduction of bias into estimates that find their way into budget standards typifies the behavioural responses of individuals to organizational pressures. Take the example of a salesman threatened with the possibility of redundancy as a result of falling sales. In such circumstances, he may well find it to his advantage to make optimistic forecasts of sales expectations in his area. By contrast, he may make pessimistic forecasts of achievable sales if his bonus and his performance are evaluated in terms of the extent to which he improves upon the budget target.

The presence of bias in setting budget targets may be met either through the process of counter-biasing, which leads to gamesmanship in budgeting, or by reducing ignorance of fears about the objectives of the firm in relation to personnel. The reduction of conflict between the firm's objectives and the objectives of managers and personnel is discussed later in this chapter, in the context of the system known as management by objectives.

## Budget information and performance evaluation

According to Hopwood (1974), budget information may be used in three different ways for the purposes of assessing managerial performance, as follows:

1 Budget-constrained evaluation, where the manager's performance is primarily evaluated on the basis of the ability to continually meet budget targets on the short-term basis.
2 Profit-conscious evaluation, where the manager's performance is evaluated on the basis of the ability to increase the general effectiveness of the operations of his/her unit in relation to the long-term objectives of the firm. In this case, budget information will be used with a degree of flexibility.
3 Non-accounting evaluation, where budget information plays a relatively small part in the evaluation of the manager's performance.

A summary of the effects of these different styles of managerial evaluation on managerial behaviour is given below:

|  | Budget-constrained | Profit-conscious | Non-accounting |
|---|---|---|---|
| Involvement with costs | High | High | Low |
| Job-related tension | High | Medium | Medium |
| Manipulation of accounting reports | Extensive | Little | Little |
| Relations with supervisor | Poor | Good | Good |
| Relations with colleagues | Poor | Good | Good |

## The need for several measures of performance

While the use of standard costs and variable budgets plays an important role in the control of activities and in the evaluation of performance, undue attention to cost control tends to diminish the importance of other goals. For example, a factory manager is expected to maintain a high level of productive efficiency, to maintain the quality of the product, to meet production schedules on time, to minimize expenses and to maintain satisfactory relations with employees.

The evaluation of performance therefore requires both quantitative and qualitative measures of performance. It is evident that some organizational and departmental goals may conflict, such as for example the need to minimize costs and to maintain product quality. Emphasis on specific goals will therefore mean that other goals may not be attained. The objectives of performance evaluation, which we have stipulated, require a balanced view of performance covering the various areas of managerial responsibility. If management uses only conventional measurement of revenues, expenses, profit, cost variances and output, it is possible that short-run economic gains may be achieved at the expense of long-run goals. The failure to appreciate the impact of control techniques on individuals responsible for organizational activities may adversely affect employee morale, loyalty, trust and motivation.

## The importance of participation

The active participation by managers in the planning process not only enhances their personal sense of involvement in the organization, but improves the efficiency of the planning process. Moreover, such participation establishes a common understanding of purpose, and promotes the acceptance of organizational objectives and goals at all levels. Likewise, the control process is aided by the active participation of managers in the investigation of variances, the evaluation and selection of appropriate solutions and the development of related policies.

The degree of effort expended by members of an organization in attempting to achieve designated goals is particularly dependent upon their personal aspiration level. The aspiration level may be defined as that level of future performance in a familiar task which individuals explicitly undertake knowing their past performance level. For example, a manager's aspiration level as regards costs is the spending level which s/he accepts as realistic and with which s/he will strive to comply. Hence, we may identify three potential levels of cost performance:

1 the budgeted level;
2 the aspiration level;
3 the actual level.

Since the aspiration level is the real inner goal acceptable to the manager, the purpose of participation is to bring the aspiration level in harmony with the budgeted level (or vice versa). Clearly, a budgeted level significantly at variance with the aspiration level will have a negative effect on managerial behaviour.

It follows that managers should be motivated and not pressurized into achieving their budgetary goals. This may be achieved by recognizing the importance of aspiration levels in the planning stage and the timely communication of results as a basis for improving performance, where necessary. The purpose of participation in the control process is, therefore, to motivate managers and to generate in each participant the desire to accomplish or even improve his/her level of performance.

# Management by objectives

From the foregoing discussion of the problem of controlling the activities of an organization and evaluating managerial performance, it follows that several conditions must be satisfied if the accounting function is to play a useful role.

1 Divisional and departmental goals must be clearly identified and defined, and appropriate measurements selected by which to express them and evaluate managerial performance. Where objectives are too vague or too ambiguous to be susceptible to clear definition in conventional terms, surrogates should be sought which will enable them to be defined and measured.
2 There should be participation by all levels of management in the control process, thereby ensuring good communication between supervisor and subordinate.
3 A style of management is required which pays particular attention to the human element in organizations, and in so doing provides an environment conducive to the employment of all resources.

The aim of management by objectives is to provide a framework for administering a control system which embraces the above-mentioned three conditions. By translating organizational objectives and goals in such a way that they become the personal objectives and goals of all management personnel, whether they be divisional or departmental managers, management by objectives seeks to create a high degree of goal congruence within an organization. The unity of personal and organizational objectives encourages managers to take actions which are in the best interest of the organization.

Some organizational goals are too remote from individual managers, and therefore have little significance for them, for example, goals relating to the return on capital employed or overall growth targets envisaged in the long-range plan. Management by objectives seeks to establish personal targets at all levels as a means of overcoming this problem. By relating personal goals to department and divisional goals and thence to organizational goals, an integration is achieved between them which may be depicted as follows:

Personal goals → Divisional goals → Organizational goals

Management by objectives involves the following processes:

1 The review of long-term and short-term organizational objectives and goals.
2 The revision, if necessary, of the organizational structure. An organizational chart is required to illustrate the titles, duties and the relationships between managers.
3 Standards of performance necessary to fulfil key tasks are set by individual job holders in agreement with their immediate supervisors. Unless job holders participate in setting performance standards, they will not feel committed to them. The standards of performance which result from systems of management by objectives are not 'ideal', nor are they minimum acceptable levels of performance. They indicate what are agreed to be 'satisfactory' levels of performance. As far as possible, they should be expressed in quantitative terms.

Management controls are operated so that supervisors do not act as watchdogs but rather as sources of help and guidance to their subordinates. A divisional profit goal in this sense is not only a target for the divisional manager, for it may also act as a means whereby top management may help to solve divisional problems should they become apparent through the failure to reach a stipulated figure.

4 Results are measured against goals. An important aspect of this stage is the use of periodic performance appraisal interviews, in which supervisor and subordinate jointly discuss results and consider their implications for the future. The performance appraisal interview is essentially a discussion between manager and subordinate about objectives and their achievement. Performance appraisal should evaluate managers not merely in terms of current performance as expressed in tangible results; it should also enable their performance as managers, their personal qualifications and character and their potential for advancement to be assessed. It is an integral part of the process of managing by results by which both parties to the interview assess their efficiency as managers. The managers assess their own role as tutors to the subordinates; the subordinates consider their role in supporting the managers.

5 Long- and short-term organizational goals are reviewed in the light of current performance.

These stages in management by objectives are illustrated in Figure 5.30.

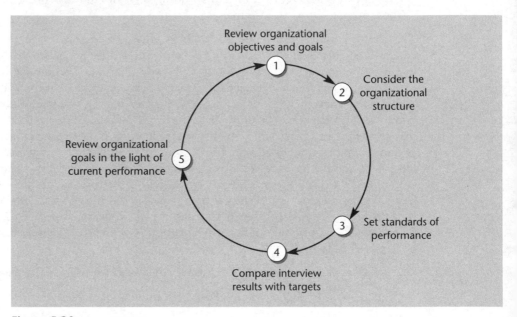

**Figure 5.30**

## Organization theory

Some of the assumptions upon which we have so far relied have been necessary for the purpose of facilitating the examination of the basic aspects of accounting for planning and control. If an accounting system is to be effective in providing information for planning and control purposes, it should be capable of adapting to organizational and environmental factors peculiar to individual enterprises. Different enterprises may require different methods of control, depending on the internal and external influences affecting their own activities. Hence, some of our assumptions may be more applicable to some organizations than to others. In this respect, organization theory attempts to provide a framework for understanding the influences which bear upon organizations and is important, therefore, for clarifying issues of importance to the accountant.

# Approaches to organization theory

By regarding the organization as a logical and rational process, the classical approach focuses in some detail on the organizing function of management. Hence, the classical theory is concerned with the structure of organizations and the determination of the tasks necessary to attain organizational objectives. By contrast, the human relations approach stresses people rather than structures, their motives and behaviour rather than the activities which need to be harnessed for achieving organizational goals. This approach originated in the Hawthorne experiments of the 1920s, which revealed that social and human factors in work situations were often more important than physical factors in affecting productivity. The human relations theory asserts that since the most important factors are individual needs and wants, the structure of organizations should be geared to individuals rather than the individual being geared to the structure.

Finally, there has developed the contingency approach which starts with the premise that there is no single organizational design that is best in all situations. According to this approach, there are four factors or forces of particular significance in the design of an organizational structure: forces in the manager; forces in the environment; forces in the task; and forces in the subordinates.

1 *Forces in the manager.* This refers to factors relating to the personalities of managers and their influence on the design of the organizational structure. Managers tend to perceive organizational problems in a unique way, which is a function of background, knowledge, experience and values. These factors shape organizational decisions in such areas as strategy, organizational structure and style of management. Accordingly, organizations do not have objectives – only people have objectives. In this analysis, these objectives will differ from manager to manager.

2 *Forces in the environment.* Some studies suggest that the most effective pattern of organizational structure is that which enables the organization to adjust to the requirements of its environment (Burns and Stalker, 1961). These studies indicate that organizations with less formal structures are best able to cope with uncertain and heterogeneous environmental conditions. Conversely, highly structured organizations will be more effective in stable environmental conditions. Hence, bureaucratic structures, as implied in classical theory, are more appropriate to stable conditions, whereas more democratic structures are required to enable organizations to adapt to a changing environment.

3 *Forces in the task.* Empirical studies indicate that technology has an important impact on the design of an organizational structure. For example, Woodward (1965) has found that organizational structures varied according to the technology involved. According to Woodward, fewer managers are required under systems of unit production than under systems of mass production. The technology associated with unit production systems may also require relatively higher levels of operative skill, and there is evidence to suggest that skilled workers feel more involved in their jobs and are more anxious for an opportunity to participate in decision making relating to their jobs than unskilled workers. This makes it possible to delegate more authority to lower levels in an organization and has important implications for devising schemes based on 'management by objectives'.

4 *Forces in the subordinates.* This refers to the psychological needs such as the subordinate's desire for a measure of independence, for the acquisition of skills and the motivation for assuming responsibility. The desire to participate in decision making is not uniform among employees, and as implied earlier it is much stronger among skilled workers and employees with a professional background than it is among unskilled workers. Hence, organizations employing relatively more skilled than unskilled employees will be faced with a greater desire for a democratic structure.

## Agency theory

According to Antle (1989), agency models are highly stylized logical tools for discovering basic relationships. They extend the traditional intellectual boundaries of accounting by assuming that its problems have psychological, sociological, economic and political dimensions. Heretofore, these problems have been recognized to some extent in articles dealing with the behavioural aspects of performance evaluation, which have been discussed earlier in this chapter.

Specifically, agency theory re-examines extant basic assumptions about human behaviour in organizations, by considering behaviour in terms of a model in which actors are acting out a principal and agent relationship. This relationship grants the agent delegated powers to act on behalf of the principal.

Agency theory is claimed to be particularly relevant when focusing on financial reports generated by agents whose performance is in part evaluated on the basis of those reports. If the choice of accounting method rests with the agents, as is normally the case in so far as management information systems are concerned, agency theory assumes that the information reported through these systems will reflect management preferences over what is reported.

E O Williamson's seminal work on the existence of managerial discretion as highly significant in organizational decision making brought new light on the manner in which personal interests influenced decisions. Williamson's thesis conflicted with the traditional view assumed in accounting theory that the interests of shareholders and managers are joined in the maximization of shareholders' wealth. Agency theory addresses the problem of information reporting for assessing managerial behaviour where management holds private information and does not communicate it, or communicates only the information that it wants to communicate.

From the foregoing, it is evident that agency theory considerably extends the debate over the assessment of managerial performance. It shifts this debate from one in which performance is seen as a reactive problem to be examined in the light of managerial styles to the much wider issue of the vested interests that exist in organizations and that are not adequately recognized in extant theories of the firm.

## Summary

The budget process alone is not sufficient to maintain adequate management control. Too often, organizations tend to expect results from budgetary control and fail to recognize its behavioural implications. As a result, pressures are created leading to mistrust, hostility and actions detrimental to the long-term prospects of an organization. It follows that accountants should work more closely with behavioural scientists and that they should learn more about the behavioural implications of organizational control.

Participation schemes may be introduced into organizations with due consideration for the psychological problems entailed. One such scheme is management by objectives. Management by objectives differs from the conventional budgetary control theory in that it enables the precepts of Theory Y to be put into practice by creating an environment which allows employees to develop as individuals and to exercise responsibility through self-control. Self-control is found to induce stronger work motivation, for by giving individual managers greater freedom of action, it affords them in greater measure the satisfaction and pleasure which a sense of accomplishment confers.

Being concerned with the provision of information for planning and control, the accountant should find a knowledge of organization theory particularly useful in understanding the internal and external influences which affect the nature of organizational activities and the environment in which decisions are made. These influences have implications for the design of control systems, and the significance of contingency theory lies in the identification of their sources.

New considerations in the assessment of managerial behaviour have been inspired by protagonists of agency theory, which looks at the impact of discretionary managerial behaviour on management information.

**References**

Antle, R (1989). 'Commentary on intellectual boundaries in accounting research', *Accounting Horizons*, June 1989.

Argyris, C (1953). 'Human problems with budgets', *Harvard Business Review*, January–February.

Burns, T and Stalker, G M (1961). *The Management of Innovation*, Tavistock Publications.

Hopwood, A (1974). *Accounting and Human Behaviour*, Accountancy Age Books.

Horngren, C T and Foster, G (1987). *Cost Accounting: A Managerial Emphasis*, 6th edn, Prentice Hall.

McGregor, D M (1960). *The Human Side of the Enterprise*, McGraw-Hill.

Mackintosh, N B (1994). *CA Magazine*, September.

Williamson, E O (1964). *The Economics of Discretionary Behaviour: Managerial Objectives in a Theory of the Firm*, Prentice Hall.

Woodward, J (1965). *Industrial Organization: Theory and Practice*, Oxford University Press.

# Self-assessment questions

1 State what you understand by 'managerial style'.

2 What is meant by 'organization culture'?

3 List the objectives of performance evaluation.

4 Explain 'Theory X'.

5 Contrast 'Theory X' with 'Theory Y'.

6 Comment on possible managerial reactions to budgets.

7 Describe three possible levels of cost performance.

8 Define 'management by objectives'.

9 What do you understand by 'contingency theory'?

1* The following extract is taken from a conversation between the chairman of Westway Engineering Company and James Brown, accountant, on the day Brown took up his appointment with the company.

*Chairman*: 'We apply a system of payment by results to foremen as well as to operatives. For each department, budgeted allowances are set for the expenditure which should be incurred over varying levels of output. The greater the saving on budgeted expenditure for a department, the greater the bonus received by the foreman concerned. For example, this report shows how the bonus the foreman of our assembly department had built up suffered a severe jolt last month.'

He hands the following report to Brown.

**Westway Engineering Company – Assembly Department**
**Foreman: W Rodgers**

|  | Budget allowance | Actual | For month (Over) under budget | Year to date (Over) under budget |
|---|---|---|---|---|
|  | £ | £ | £ | £ |
| Direct material | 4,000 | 5,000 | (1,000) | (3,000) |
| Direct labour | 10,000 | 12,000 | (2,000) | (3,500) |
| Indirect labour | 5,000 | 4,500 | 500 | 1,000 |
| Indirect material | 2,000 | 1,700 | 300 | (1,000) |
| Power | 6,000 | 6,500 | (500) | (2,000) |
| Maintenance | 7,000 | 10,000 | (3,000) | 4,000 |
| Depreciation | 5,000 | 4,000 | 1,000 | 2,000 |
| Insurance | 100 | 80 | 20 | 500 |
| General expense | 10,000 | 8,500 | 1,500 | 4,500 |
|  |  |  | (3,180) | 2,500 |

*Chairman*: 'Since the new accounting system was installed a year ago, there appears to have been a general deterioration in morale. The relations between a number of staff certainly need improving. Two months ago an error was made on an order, and the goods were returned for correction, a process which cost £700. None of the departmental foremen were prepared to accept the cost of the error, which was finally charged to general factory loss. Because of the incident two foremen stopped talking to each other.'

*Required:*
Discuss what improvements should be made in the accounting system in operation at Westway's.

# 38 Strategic dimensions

**Setting the scene**

The defining characteristic of strategic management accounting is its external emphasis. Another way of describing this is its emphasis on the market, hence the notion of
strategic management accounting as market-orientated, or even market-driven,
accounting. Within this emphasis, there are three focuses: competitors, customers and,
linking them, products. Strategic management accounting seeks to produce a range of
information about these three focuses.                              (Roslender et al., 1998)

**Learning objectives**

After studying this chapter you should be able to:

1   Contrast the stance of the strategist with that of the traditional management
    accountant.

2   Understand the scope of strategic planning.

3   Discuss the objectives of activity analysis.

4   Describe competitor analysis.

5   Explain 'market-led accounting'.

6   Appreciate the role of non-financial measures of performance.

We explained in the introduction to this part that management accounting has
attracted criticism on the grounds that its focus is too narrow and inward-
looking. Most accounting textbooks assume that virtually all the information
produced by the management accountant originates from internal costs. Admittedly,
this information is important in the context of operational planning and control.
However, if this is the only information which is produced then managers will tend
to concentrate mainly on operational issues rather than on overall policy and the
direction of the organization (Clarke, 1995). Such behaviour by managers will affect
the competitive situation of their businesses. Recent changes in the environment
necessitate the adoption of a strategic perspective if businesses are to survive and
prosper. This has important implications for management accountants if they are to
assist the strategic process. Unlike the traditional management accountant, the strategist is outward-looking and concerned with competitive market forces.

## Objectives of strategic planning

In Chapter 25 we saw that strategic planning is a systematic attempt to influence the medium- and long-term future of the entity and to manage change. It involves the determination of corporate objectives and goals as well as the development of broad policies and strategies by which they may be achieved. Its main objective is to enable the business to develop and sustain a competitive advantage in its chosen marketplace so that it can earn a super profit (i.e. above normal rate of return) in this area of its operations. Porter (1985) argues that rather than being an out-growth of one's own company products and markets, strategic planning has to be viewed primarily in the context of the industrial competitive situation. The critical features in the strategic position are the rivalry between the existing competitors, seen in the context of possible new entrants to the industry and the barriers to their entry, the possibility of substitute products or the power of suppliers to influence strategies and the power of the customers to influence strategic change. The thrust of competitive strategy formulation is to identify the competitive advantage that the business holds and to build on that, denying any existing or potential competition the opportunity to meet it. Therefore, strategic planning relies heavily on information about the environment. To be successful it is necessary for the management team to adopt the following postures:

1 To remain sensitive to the needs and demands of clients and customers. Within this context, market research, market segmentation and customer targeting are now accepted as essential inputs to the process of strategic analysis. Such inputs permit the enterprise to remain close to its customers.

2 To identify the forces which shape competitive rivalry within a business sector. The company can only set objectives and strategies in the context of the firm's position relative to its key competitors. Products (goods and services) can be viewed as a bundle of attributes or characteristics which are on offer to potential customers. These characteristics become crucial to the formulation of the firm's strategies and include a variety of elements such as price, quality, performance and after-sales service.

3 To understand the nature and interaction between the various environmental forces which can bring pressure to bear on industry, enterprise or agency alike. This requires environmental scanning which involves monitoring of the environment for technological developments, population trends and changing social and political attitudes.

4 To adopt a strategic perspective to internal data. In addition to the increased focus on external information, it is necessary to take a strategic view of internal information.

The difference between a strategic and traditional approach to cost categorization is illustrated by Richardson (1988) in Figure 5.31. Accountants have traditionally been concerned with the operational matters illustrated in the top right-hand quadrant. A comprehensive view embraces strategic and tangible and intangible items and requires accountants to extend their horizons. They must embrace new skills and cooperate much more with general management, corporate strategists, marketing and product development.

|  | **Strategic** | **Operational** |
|---|---|---|
| **Tangible** | Debt charges<br>New plants<br>Market development<br>Product development | Labour<br>Materials<br>Energy<br>Supplies<br>Contract services |
| **Intangible** | Poor product positioning<br>Technological obsolescence<br>Poor location of facilities | Poor quality<br>Absenteeism<br>Labour turnover<br>Low morale<br>Lost output<br>Late delivery |

**Figure 5.31**

To be successful, world-class enterprises stress the following:

1 activity analysis;
2 customer profitability and analysis;
3 competitor analysis;
4 market-led accounting;
5 development of non-financial measures of performance.

# Activity analysis

Porter (1985) suggests that firms can be viewed as a flow of activities performed to provide products or services to customers. Above-average performance can be achieved if you can successfully manipulate and enhance two key variables: the distinctiveness of your products and your organization's level of costs. These two variables are important because Porter focuses on the ability of activities to add value. The best performing companies in any industry are those which add value either cheaply or distinctively.

We saw in Chapter 27 that ABC, from a managerial perspective, offers more than just more accurate cost information. It also provides information about the cost and performance of activities and resources. If activities are linked across departments forming cross-functional processes, the model structure of an organization is simplified and powerful information results. Activity-based management (ABM) focuses on the activities incurred during the production/performance processes as the way to improve the value received by a customer and the resulting profit achieved by providing this value. This process view of ABM enables management to judge each activity as value-added or non-value-added.

Value-added activities contribute something that is worthwhile to the enterprise and its customers. Such activities are essential to the enterprise's success. Where an activity increases the worth of a product or service to the customer, the customer is willing to pay for that activity and it is, therefore, value added. For example, physically distributing your product faster than anyone else will add value if your customers are prepared to pay over and above the extra costs of providing quicker service. Also, you might try to add distinctiveness to your basic product with product features, superior customer service or clever advertising. In the latter case, the differences will have to add value in the sense that your customer must be willing to pay a premium price over and above the added cost of providing the unique difference embodied in your product.

Non-value-added activities represent waste; these activities can be reduced or eliminated without decreasing the enterprise's ability to compete and meet customer demands. Armed with a list of non-value-added activities, the organization can create teams to find innovative ways to eliminate, reduce, or re-engineer those activities. One of the costliest things a company can do is to invest in equipment and people to make non-value-added activities more efficient. The objective is to eliminate them altogether or subject them to a major overhaul, not to make them more efficient.

Inspection of incoming raw materials is a non-value-added activity that can be eliminated without diminishing the value received by the enterprise if its customers do not value inspection; they value high quality. If a supplier of raw materials makes a commitment to supply high-quality materials, then inspection is no longer required, and buying testing equipment and hiring more people to inspect the incoming raw materials would waste time and money. Non-value-adding activities are not necessary for a firm to remain in business. Thus, the challenge of activity analysis is to find ways to produce the goods or services without using any of these activities.

## Customer profitability analysis

In increasingly competitive markets, it is critical to know customer, market and channel of distribution profitability as well as product profitability. Companies need to be able to quantify and present the implications of the trading relationship so that they can add real value to commercial decisions. Such an approach should answer key questions which conventional accounting fails to address questions such as:

1　Does selling to company X meet our profitability criteria? Can it ever? If so, how?
2　Which customer or market segment generates our greatest profit contribution? How best can we protect it?
3　What are the maximum discounts or after-sales servicing packages that we are prepared to allow in the next round of negotiations?
4　Do our largest accounts earn us reasonable contributions, or are the advantages of volume offset by the costs of promotional activity, distribution and discounts?
5　Should we drop a customer or customer group?

Whereas product costs are generally determined from manufacturing costs, customer costs are often determined from the distribution, marketing and sales costs that are incurred after the product is manufactured. These post-manufacturing costs are considered period costs for generally accepted accounting principles. As a result, conventional management reporting practice will sometimes follow financial reporting requirements and avoid allocating these costs. For decision-making purposes, activity-based approaches may be used to assign post-manufacturing costs to customers. Allocating these costs reflects the different ways in which customers consume resources. For example, one customer may frequently call on a company's technical support because they have no in-house technical staff. Another customer may not require such support because they have an in-house staff. Differences such as these have an overall impact on the profitability of serving different customers. The table below lists examples of other activities for which customers may have different resource demands.

| Activity | High-cost customer | Low-cost customer |
|---|---|---|
| Stock-carrying requirements | Customer requires safety stocks close to their plants | Customer does not require safety stocks |
| Post-sales technical support | Customer requires specialized training to use product | Customer provides their own in-house training to use product |
| Promotional support | Customer requires promotional displays | Customer requires no promotional displays |
| Credit taken | Customer pays accounts in 90 days | Customer pays accounts in 15 days |

**Example 1**    Simon Electronics employs a staff of technical support personnel whose cost is determined to be £300,000. During the year, the technical support staff estimate they will receive 600 requests for technical assistance from customers. Simon Electronics has hundreds of customers generating total revenues of £1,200,000 and a gross profit of £400,000. Assume that customers X, Y and Z each purchase a single piece of test equipment from Simon Electronics for a price of £3,000. The cost of goods sold for each piece of equipment is £2,000. Customer X requires no technical assistance because it employs in-house technical staff. Customer Y made one technical request to the technical centre, while Customer Z made five requests to the centre. A customer report for these three customers is shown below.

**Simon Electronics**
**Partial customer profitability report**

| | X<br>£ | Y<br>£ | Z<br>£ | Total<br>£ |
|---|---|---|---|---|
| Sales | 3,000 | 3,000 | 3,000 | 1,200,000 |
| Cost of goods sold | 2,000 | 2,000 | 2,000 | 800,000 |
| Gross profit | 1,000 | 1,000 | 1,000 | 400,000 |
| Technical support* | 0 | 500 | 2,500 | 300,000 |
| Profit (loss) | 1,000 | 500 | (1,500) | 100,000 |

* £300,000 ÷ 600 requests = £500 per request.

Customer profitability can be seen to vary by the amount of technical support resources used by the customer. Simon Electronics could use this information to adjust its customer strategies. For example, Simon Electronics could drop Customer Z, or they could price technical services as a separate product.

Without accurate customer profitability information, a company may make strategic errors. For example, if Simon Electronics did not assign the technical support costs to customers according to their use of this activity, there would be no way to price services to customers to reflect differences in service levels. Failing to price differences in service levels provides incentives for customers to use what appear to be 'free' services and impose the cost on other customers.

According to Howell and Soucy (1990), who argue that customer profitability is as critical as product profitability,

*Few companies have management information that provides managers with a clear understanding of which customers and markets are profitable. As services (sales, general and administrative costs) become a more significant part of companies' competitive advantage and cost structure, the management tools must respond.*

## Competitor analysis

A competitive analysis starts with identifying competitors and potential competitors. There are two very different ways of identifying current competitors. The first takes the perspective of the customer who must make choices among competitors. In this case, substitute products can be relevant competitors. For example, rice and pastas are very real competitors to the makers of granulated potato buds which are used by institutions and restaurants for making mashed potatoes. Competitors are grouped according to the degree to which they compete for a buyer's choice. The second type of identification approach attempts to place competitors into strategic groups on the basis of their competitive strategy. The concept of a strategic group provides a very different approach towards understanding the competitive structure of an industry. A strategic group is a group of firms that:

1 over time pursue similar competitive strategies (e.g. the use of the same distribution channel and heavy advertising);
2 have similar characteristics (e.g. size, aggressiveness);
3 have similar assets and skills (e.g. quality, image).

The conceptualization of strategic groups can make the process of competitor analysis more manageable. Numerous industries contain many more competitors than can be analysed individually. Often it is simply not feasible to consider thirty competitors to say nothing of hundreds. Reducing this set to a small number of strategic groups makes the analysis compact, feasible and more useable. Further, little strategic content and insight will be lost in most cases, because firms in a strategic group will be affected by, and react to, industry developments in similar ways. Thus, in projecting future strategies of competitors, the concept of strategic groups can be helpful.

After competitors are identified the focus shifts to attempting to understand them and their strategy. What are the competitors' objectives? What strategies are being pursued by competitors and how successful are they? What are the competitors' strengths and weaknesses? The identification and evaluating of competitors' strengths and weaknesses is at the very heart of a well-developed competitive strategy. Competitive strengths and weaknesses are based upon the existence or absence of assets or skills. Thus, an asset such as a well-known name or prime location could represent a strength, as could a skill, such as the ability to develop a strong promotional programme. Conversely, the absence of an asset or skill can represent a weakness. It involves finding answers to questions such as 'Why are successful businesses successful?' and 'What are the key customer motivations?' It also involves an examination of competitors' innovative ability and financial, management and marketing skills.

Competitor analysis enables competitors' moves to be anticipated, thereby allowing an enterprise both to plan to the defence of its territory and to prepare for opportunities that result from competitors' mistakes and weaknesses. According to Bromwich and Bhimani (1989),

> *The need to consider the firm's comparative advantages relative to competitors and the benefits for which customers are willing to pay and their costs is the main theme of strategic management accounting. Providing the relevant accounting information configured in a way in which it can be used for strategy is thought by many commentators to be a major contemporary challenge to accountants.*

## Accounting for market-led design

According to Hiromoto (1988), Japanese companies tend to use their management control systems to support their manufacturing strategies. He found that a more direct link existed between management accounting practices and corporate goals in Japanese concerns than in their Western counterparts. Japanese companies use accounting systems more to motivate employees to act in accordance with long-term manufacturing strategies than to provide senior managers with precise and essentially short-term data on costs, variances and profits. Hiromoto claims that Japanese accounting plays a more of an 'influencing' role than an 'information' role in the managerial process.

When estimating the cost of new products, for example, many Japanese companies do not rely on prevailing engineering standards. Instead, they establish target costs derived from estimates of a competitive market price. These target costs are usually well below those currently achievable by the firm. Managers are then set benchmarks to measure their progress towards meeting the target cost objectives by means of design and technology improvements. This amounts to a market-led approach whereby operating costs and efficiencies are designed to achieve a desired state of competitiveness.

A good example of market-led accounting practice is provided by Hiromoto's (1988) description of design practices at the Daihatsu Motor Company. The process begins when a product development manager instructs the functional departments to submit the features and performance specification that they believe the car should include.

The next stage is cost estimation. However, management does not simply present the development specification to the accountants to determine what it should cost to build the car based on existing engineering standards. Instead, Daihatsu establishes a target selling price, based on what it believes the market will accept, and specifies a target profit margin that reflects the company's strategic plans and financial projections. The difference between these two figures represents the allowable cost per car.

Throughout the design process, which usually lasts for three years, the design engineers frequently liaise with staff from other functional areas (purchasing, shop floor, sales, etc.) who will implement the final design. As the process unfolds, the participants compare estimated costs with the targets. The variances are fed back to the product developers, and the cycle repeats: design proposals, cost estimates, variance calculations, value engineering analysis to include desired features at the lowest possible cost. The cycle ends with the approval of the final design that meets the target cost.

The market-led philosophy at Daihatsu and other Japanese companies helps to explain why standard costing systems are used less extensively in Japan than in Britain. Standard costs reflect an engineering-led approach where the goal is to minimize variances within existing technological constraints. Market-driven management, on the other hand, emphasizes doing whatever is necessary to achieve a desired performance level under market conditions. How efficiently a company should be able to make a product is less important to the Japanese than how efficiently it must be able to build it for marketplace success.

Hiromoto highlights a central principle that seems to guide management accounting in Japan – accounting practices are subservient to corporate strategy and not independent of it.

## Non-financial measures of performance

In recent years, world-class manufacturing companies have introduced dramatic changes to their manufacturing processes. These changes are intended to make radical improvements in the companies' competetiveness by improving quality, reducing lead times, reducing costs and enhancing production flexibility. With world-class manufacturing companies, other performance measures can become of at least equal importance to the financial results, a situation which applies particularly to the company's operational staff. The day-to-day control of the manufacturing and distribution operations is often better handled with non-financial measures. These include lead time, set-up time, number of line stops, number of units scrapped, deviation from scheduled production and delivery performance.

Non-financial measures provide fast feedback. With world-class manufacturing it is important to be able to detect and resolve problems as they occur, not wait for several days while reports are produced. Many problems can be detected on the spot by the operators if they are provided with training and equipment that enables them to monitor quality, rate of flow, set-up time, etc. Performance measurement reports, based on non-financial measures, may be provided daily, twice daily, or as required.

## Summary

Management accounting is criticized on the grounds that its focus is too narrow and inward-looking. Advocates of change suggest that management accounting should broaden its range of relevant information to include data on the environment in which the company operates and on its competitors. This emerging discipline is referred to as strategic management accounting. In this chapter we have introduced activity analysis, customer profitability analysis, competitor analysis, market-led accounting and the development of non-financial measures of performance.

**References**

Bromwich, M and Bhimani, A (1989). *Management Accounting: Pathways to Progress*, Chartered Institute of Management Accountants.

Clarke, P J (1995). 'The old and the new in management accounting', *Management Accounting*, June.

Hiromoto, T (1988). 'Another hidden edge: Japanese management accounting', *Harvard Business Review*, July–August.

Howell, R A and Soucy, S R (1990). 'Customer profitability – as critical as product profitability', *Management Accounting* (USA), October.

Porter, M E (1985). *Competitive Advantage: Creating and Sustaining Superior Performance*, New York: The Free Press.

Richardson, R R (1988). *Cost Containment*, New York: The Free Press.

Roslender, R, Hart, S and Ghosh, J (1998). 'Strategic management accounting: refocusing the agenda', *Management Accounting* (UK), December.

## Self-assessment questions

1 Contrast the objectives of the strategist with those of the traditional management accountant.

2 Identify the four postures which are necessary for strategic planning to be successful.

3 Define value-added and non-value-added. Give examples of each.

4 What kinds of questions does profitability analysis address?

5 Describe in general terms the steps taken in competitor analysis.

6 Explain what is meant by 'market-led accounting'.

7 Identify four non-financial measures of importance. Why are they important?

# Solutions to self-assessment questions and problems

## Chapter 1 Scope of accounting

### Answers to self-assessment questions

1 Early definitions of accounting described the activities of accountants and focused on the importance of individual concepts (e.g. matching). More recent definitions have concerned the needs of users of financial reports and their role in making economic decisions. These definitions have been extended into the social welfare arena and described accounting information in terms of the costs and benefits to society as a whole.

2 Stewardship accounting is concerned with accountability, i.e. reports by stewards to owners of wealth on how they have managed that wealth. Financial accounting addresses the role of financial reports in the economic decisions of shareholders and potential shareholders. Management accounting assists management in the planning and control of organizations. Unlike financial accounting, which reports on past events, management accounting is forward-looking. Social accounting widens the scope of accounting by considering the social effects of business decisions as well as their economic effects. It has arisen partly from the increasing attention which is being given to environmental problems over recent years.

3 The usefulness of the concepts upon which financial reporting is based has been questioned. Traditional management accounting techniques, it has been argued, are not suitable in fully technology-driven situations. Accounting concepts of growth and profit are too narrow because they fail to address important social issues.

4 A standard-setting board aimed at developing a conceptual framework for external financial reporting has been established. New management accounting systems have emerged and social accounting issues are being increasingly debated.

## Chapter 2 Accounting as an information system

### Answers to self-assessment questions

1 Shareholders and investors are concerned with the value of their investment (or proposed investment) and the income they expect to derive from their holding. Management requires information for planning, control and decision-making purposes. Employees require information about the performance of their unit and how this contributes to the performance of the firm as a whole. Also, they require information for collective bargaining purposes. Governments use accounting information in making decisions about the economy. Creditors are concerned with whether or not an organization is creditworthy, i.e. will it be able to meet its financial obligations? The local community is concerned with job prospects and environmental issues.

2 Accounting information affects the allocation of resources. It is important that such information is relevant and reliable so that users' decisions do not result in a misallocation of resources. Also, the financial statements of different companies must be comparable.

## Chapter 3  The role of accounting theory

### Answers to self-assessment questions

1 Theories are generalizations which serve to organize otherwise meaningless masses of data, and which establish significant relationships in respect of such data. They are concerned with explanation. Empirical theories assist in making predictions.

2 Accounting theories assist accounting policy makers in their deliberations on recommendations on accounting practice. Accounting policy makers have the responsibility of responding to the needs of users of accounting information.

3 Elements are directly related to the measurement of performance and financial status of an entity and include assets, liabilities, capital, revenue, expenses, profit and transactions. Concepts determine the rules which are applied to accounting procedures. Procedures are the various activities concerned with processing transactions.

4 Descriptive theories are concerned with what accountants do and, therefore, describe current practice. Normative approaches prescribe what should be.

5 The welfare approach is an extension of the decision-making approach and considers the effects of decision-making on social welfare. For example, the supply of information to one group of users may have implications for the welfare of other groups. According to the welfare approach these effects should be taken into account.

## Chapter 4  Financial accounting statements

### Answers to self-assessment questions

1 To report the profit performance of a business for a specific period of time.

2 It lists the assets owed by a business, the liabilities owed to others and the accumulated investment of its owners at a specified date.

3 The profit for a period is added to the owners' opening capital.

4 Fixed assets are used in the business and not intended for resale. Current assets are expected to be transformed into cash in the near future. Current liabilities are the amounts owing by the business which will fall due for payment within one year. Working capital is the difference between current assets and current liabilities.

5 Cost refers to original cost, i.e. the cost at which the asset was purchased. Depreciation is the apportionment to expense of the original cost of the asset over its productive life. Net book value is derived by deducting accumulated depreciation from the cost of an asset.

6 Profit is derived by matching a period's sales revenue with the expenses incurred in earning those revenues. A cash flow statement shows what cash has been generated by a business's operations and where the cash has gone.

7 Net cash flow from operating activities, returns on investment and servicing of finance, tax paid, capital expenditure, financing activities and increase/decrease in cash.

# Chapter 5  Financial accounting concepts

## Answer to self-assessment question

1 The role of so-called accounting concepts is to provide the ground rules for preparing financial reports. These concepts are discussed in the text.

## Solutions to problems

1

(a) Assuming the company will not incur any significant costs relating to this contract, it seems reasonable in the light of the matching concept to take the advances into account when calculating profit. However, if there is a possibility that the payments represent a figure which is in excess of the total fee due, then prudence suggests that the firm makes an appropriate allowance (presumably in the form of a provision). Any payments received in advance of work carried out should certainly not be taken as profit immediately. The aim is, so far as possible, to ensure that revenue is shown in the period in which it is earned and matched by the expenses relating to it.

(b) (i) If advances are discretionary, little difference should be made to their treatment. Such a system may be a better indicator that payments match work actually done.

   (ii) Consultat Inc should certainly make allowance for possible guarantee work. Again, the matching convention is particularly relevant since work we have to do later may be directly related to the income we are currently receiving. Instead of taking all the payments as profit, the prudent course is to set up a provision to cover the potential cost. However, if in our experience these claims are unusual or immaterial, it would be more usual to take the profit but note in the accounts the possibility of having to carry out guarantee work (a contingent claim).

2

(a) It might be argued that prudence would suggest that we should write down the machine to £30,000. However, it will often be the case that the resale value of an asset is less than its book value and it is not usual to write the asset down. The justification for this lies with the matching convention. The aim of depreciation is to match the cost of the asset to its use and not a temporary market value which is only of relevance if the asset is actually sold. In this case, it seems this is not so. Therefore, it is consistent with the conventions to maintain the asset at its existing written-down value.

(b) This is a different case because there is no intention to continue using the asset and its only value to the company is the value it can realize. Since the asset is to be sold forthwith and we know the price, prudence dictates that we should write the asset down to £15,000. It might even be argued that since there is £10,000 interest to be paid in the next year the true value of the asset is actually £5,000. This would, however, seem to be taking prudence too far and, in any case, the interest will be payable whatever happens to the asset.

# Chapter 6  Financial accounting standards

## Answers to self-assessment questions

1 See text. Standards are concerned either with how information might be presented, what information ought to be presented or how assets might be valued (e.g. stocks, depreciation). The general aim is to achieve a greater level of consistency along with more reliable accounting data. But it should be remembered that the need to produce a 'true and fair view' overrides any specific standard.

2 SSAP 2 identified four particular accounting concepts (going concern, accruals, consistency and prudence) stating that 'their use is presumed unless otherwise stated'.

SSAP 2 defines these concepts in a way similar to the conventions discussed in Chapter 5. It might be noted that the accruals concept is in fact consistent with both the accruals and matching conventions described in Chapter 5.

3 An accounting base is a way of expressing or applying concepts in practice. SSAP 2 lists examples of cases where different bases might be applied such as depreciation, stock valuation, hire-purchase arrangements, translation of foreign currency and others. Since there are many ways of applying concepts in practice there must be more bases than concepts.

## Chapter 7  The generation of financial accounting data

### Answer to self-assessment question

1 See text for examples of source documents. Source documents effectively start the accounting process. They also act as evidence when accounting records are verified by auditors.

### Solutions to problems

**1**

(a) *Purchase day book*. Debit fixed assets (plant and equipment), credit trade creditors control.
(b) *Cash book*. Debit trade creditors control, credit bank (or, rather unlikely, cash).
(c) *Cash book*. Debit sundry expenses (bank charges account), credit bank.
(d) *Cash book*. Debit bank, credit trade debtors control.
(e) *Sales day book*. Debit trade debtors control, credit sales.
(f) *Sales day book* (or sales returns book). Debit sales, credit debtors control.

**2**

| | | | |
|---|---|---|---|
| 1 April | *Purchase day book* | | |
| | Debit plant and equipment | £400 | |
| | Credit creditors control | | £400 |
| 2 April | *Purchase day book* | | |
| | Debit purchases | £700 | |
| | Credit creditors control | | £700 |
| 4 April | *Cash book* | | |
| | Debit Bank | £50 | |
| | Credit debtors control | | £50 |
| | Debit creditors control | £250 | |
| | Credit bank | | £250 |
| 5 April | *Purchase day book* | | |
| | Debit purchases | £800 | |
| | Credit creditors control | | £800 |
| 6 April | *Sales day book* | | |
| | Debit debtors control | £98 | |
| | Credit sales | | £98 |
| 7 April | *Cash book* | | |
| | Debit bank | £70 | |
| | Credit debtors control | | £70 |
| 8 April | *Purchase day book* | | |
| | Debit rates expense account | £500 | |
| | Credit creditors control | | £500 |
| 9 April | *Cash book* | | |
| | Debit bank | £700 | |
| | Credit cash | | £700 |

# Chapter 8  Data processing and double-entry bookkeeping

## Solutions to problems

### 1

| | Capital | + | Liabilities | = | Assets |
|---|---|---|---|---|---|
| | £ | | £ | | £ |
| (a) | 20,000 | | | | 20,000 |
| (b) | | | 5,000 | | 5,000 |
| (c) | (1,000) | | | | (1,000) |
| (d) | | | 10,000 | | 10,000 |
| (e) | | | | | 15,000 |
| | | | | | (15,000) |
| (f) | 2,000 | | | | 2,000 |
| (g) | (1,000) | | | | (1,000) |
| | 20,000 | | 15,000 | | 35,000 |

### 2

| | Accounting effects | |
|---|---|---|
| Transaction | Balance sheet | P&L a/c |
| | £ | £ |
| Cash sales £400 | 400 | 400 |
| Cash purchases £75 | 75(75) | |
| Received from trade debtor £35 | 35(35) | |
| Equipment purchased on credit terms £345 | 345(345) | |
| Invoice received for repairs to machinery £67 | (67) | (67) |
| Wages paid £78 | (78) | (78) |
| Payment of rent due last month £90 | 90(90) | |
| Equipment sold as scrap £20 (book value £10) | 20(10) | 10 |
| Loan received £600 | 600(600) | |
| Bank interest charged £49 | (49) | 49 |

### 3

| Cash book | | | Bank account | | |
|---|---|---|---|---|---|
| Ref | | £ | Ref | | £ |
| (A) | Capital | 10,000 | (1) | Rent | 200 |
| (14) | Debtors | 50 | (7) | Motor expenses | 10 |
| | | | (8) | Entertaining | 20 |
| | | | (10) | Entertaining | 30 |
| | | | (11) | Wages | 70 |
| | | | (12) | Creditors | 1,000 |
| | | | (13) | Creditors | 150 |
| | | | | Bal c/d | 8,570 |
| | | 10,050 | | | 10,050 |
| | Bal b/d | 8,570 | | | |

## Sales account

|  |  | £ | Ref |  | £ |
|---|---|---|---|---|---|
|  |  |  | (5) | Debtors | 50 |
|  | Bal c/d | 110 | (9) | Debtors | 60 |
|  |  | 110 |  |  | 110 |
|  |  |  |  | Bal b/d | 110 |

## Rent and rates account

| Ref |  | £ |  |  | £ |
|---|---|---|---|---|---|
| (1) | Cash book | 200 |  | Bal c/d | 200 |
|  | Bal b/d | 200 |  |  |  |

## Fixed asset (equipment) account

| Ref |  | £ |  |  | £ |
|---|---|---|---|---|---|
| (2) | Trade creditors | 1,000 |  | Bal c/d | 1,000 |
|  | Bal b/d | 1,000 |  |  |  |

## Sundry office supplies account

| Ref |  | £ |  |  | £ |
|---|---|---|---|---|---|
| (3) | Creditors | 150 |  | Bal c/d | 150 |
|  | Bal b/d | 150 |  |  |  |

## Capital account

|  |  | £ | Ref |  | £ |
|---|---|---|---|---|---|
|  | Bal c/d | 12,000 | (A) | Cash book | 10,000 |
|  |  |  | (6) | Fixed asset (motor) | 2,000 |
|  |  | 12,000 |  |  | 12,000 |
|  |  |  |  | Bal b/d | 12,000 |

## Debtors account

| Ref |  | £ | Ref |  | £ |
|---|---|---|---|---|---|
| (5) | Sales | 50 | (14) | Cash book | 50 |
| (9) | Sales | 60 |  | Bal c/d | 60 |
|  |  | 110 |  |  | 110 |
|  | Bal b/d | 60 |  |  |  |

## Wages account

| Ref |  | £ |  |  | £ |
|---|---|---|---|---|---|
| (11) | Cash book | 70 |  | Bal c/d | 70 |
|  | Bal b/d | 70 |  |  |  |

### Fixed asset (motors) account

| Ref | | £ | | £ |
|-----|--------|-------|----------|-------|
| (6) | Capital | 2,000 | Bal c/d | 2,000 |
| | Bal b/d | 2,000 | | |

### Entertaining account

| Ref | | £ | | £ |
|-----|-----------|-----|----------|-----|
| (8) | Cash book | 20 | Bal c/d | 50 |
| (10) | Cash book | 30 | | |
| | | 50 | | 50 |
| | Bal b/d | 50 | | |

### Motor expenses account

| Ref | | £ | | £ |
|-----|-----------|-----|----------|-----|
| (7) | Cash book | 10 | Bal c/d | 10 |
| | Bal b/d | 10 | | |

### Trade creditors account

| Ref | | £ | Ref | | £ |
|------|-----------|-------|-----|----------------------|-------|
| (12) | Cash book | 1,000 | (2) | Fixed asset equipment | 1,000 |
| (13) | Cash book | 150 | (3) | Office supplies | 150 |
| | | 1,150 | | | 1,150 |

### Bill Cashing Trial balance

| | Dr £ | Cr £ |
|---|---|---|
| Cash book | 8,570 | |
| Rent and rates | 200 | |
| Fixed assets (equipment) | 1,000 | |
| Office supplies | 150 | |
| Fixed asset (motors) | 2,000 | |
| Capital account | | 12,000 |
| Entertaining | 50 | |
| Motor expenses | 10 | |
| Debtors | 60 | |
| Sales | | 110 |
| Wages | 70 | |
| | 12,110 | 12,110 |

**4**

| AB Ltd Journal | | Dr £ | Cr £ |
|---|---|---|---|
| (a) | Stationery | 100 | |
| | Suspense | | 100 |
| (b) | Sales account | 36 | |
| | Suspense | | 36 |
| (c) | Cash account | 60 | |
| | Suspense | | 60 |
| (d) | Sales ledger control | 175 | |
| | Suspense | | 250 |
| | Purchase ledger control | 75 | |
| (e) | Stock | | 2,250 |
| | Suspense | 2,250 | |
| (f) | Discounts allowed | 650 | |
| | Suspense | | 650 |
| (g) | Discounts received | | 521 |
| | Suspense | 521 | |
| (h) | Cash at bank | | 20 |
| | Suspense | 20 | |

**AB Ltd Suspense account**

| | £ | | £ |
|---|---|---|---|
| Stock account | 2,250 | Balance from trial balance | 1,695 |
| Discounts received | 521 | Stationery account | 100 |
| Bank account | 20 | Sales account | 36 |
| | | Cash account | 60 |
| | | Sales ledger control | 175 |
| | | Purchase ledger control | 75 |
| | | Discounts allowed | 650 |
| | 2,791 | | 2,791 |

**6**

**Cash account**

| | | £ | | | £ |
|---|---|---|---|---|---|
| (1) | Capital | 4,000 | (2) | Purchases | 1,130 |
| (10) | Victor | 190 | (3) | Wages | 13 |
| | | | (3) | Sundry expenses | 2 |
| | | | (7) | Fixtures and fittings | 350 |
| | | | (8) | Wages | 38 |
| | | | (9) | Drawings | 80 |
| | | | (11) | Rent | 500 |
| | | 4,190 | | | 2,113 |
| | | | | Balance c/d | 2,077 |
| | | 4,190 | | | 4,190 |
| | Balance b/d | 2,077 | | | |

**Capital account**

| | | £ | | | | £ |
|---|---|---|---|---|---|---|
| Balance c/d | | 5,750 | (1) | Cash | | 4,000 |
| | | | (1) | Motor car | | 1,750 |
| | | 5,750 | | | | 5,750 |
| | | | | Balance b/d | | 5,750 |

**Motor account**

| | | £ | | | £ |
|---|---|---|---|---|---|
| (1) | Capital | 1,750 | Balance c/d | | 1,750 |
| | Balance b/d | 1,750 | | | |

**Purchases account**

| | | £ | | | £ |
|---|---|---|---|---|---|
| (2) | Cash account | 1,130 | Balance c/d | | 1,215 |
| (6) | William | 85 | | | |
| | | 1,215 | | | 1,215 |
| | Balance b/d | 1,215 | | | |

**Wages account**

| | | £ | | | £ |
|---|---|---|---|---|---|
| (3) | Cash | 13 | Balance | | 51 |
| (8) | Cash | 38 | | | |
| | | 51 | | | 51 |
| | Balance b/d | 51 | | | |

**Sundry expenses account**

| | | £ | | | £ |
|---|---|---|---|---|---|
| (3) | Cash | 2 | Balance c/d | | 2 |
| | | 2 | | | 2 |
| | Balance b/d | 2 | | | |

**Sales account**

| | | £ | | | £ |
|---|---|---|---|---|---|
| Balance c/d | | 430 | (4) | Victor | 190 |
| | | | (5) | Susan | 240 |
| | | 430 | | | 430 |
| | | | | Balance b/d | 430 |

**Victor's account**

| | | £ | | | £ |
|---|---|---|---|---|---|
| (4) | Sales | 190 | (10) | Cash | 190 |

**Susan's account**

| | | £ | | £ |
|---|---|---|---|---|
| (5) | Sales | 240 | Balance c/d | 240 |
| | Balance b/d | 240 | | |

**Rent account**

| | | £ | | £ |
|---|---|---|---|---|
| (11) | Cash | 500 | Balance c/d | 500 |
| | Balance b/d | 500 | | |

**William's account**

| | £ | | | £ |
|---|---|---|---|---|
| Balance c/d | 85 | (6) | Purchases | 85 |
| | | | Balance b/d | 85 |

**Fixtures and fittings account**

| | | £ | | £ |
|---|---|---|---|---|
| (7) | Cash | 350 | Balance c/d | 350 |
| | Balance b/d | 350 | | |

**Drawings account**

| | | £ | | £ |
|---|---|---|---|---|
| (9) | Cash | 80 | Balance c/d | 80 |
| | Balance b/d | 80 | | |

**Trial balance as at 31 June 20X0**

| | Dr £ | Cr £ |
|---|---|---|
| Cash | 2,077 | |
| Capital | | 5,750 |
| Motor car | 1,750 | |
| Purchases | 1,215 | |
| Wages | 51 | |
| Sundry expenses | 2 | |
| Sales | | 430 |
| Susan | 240 | |
| Rent | 500 | |
| William | | 85 |
| Fixtures and fittings | 350 | |
| Drawings | 80 | |
| | 6,265 | 6,265 |

## 7

### Cash account

| | | £ | | | £ |
|---|---|---|---|---|---|
| (1) | Loan | 10,000 | (2) | Purchases | 6,000 |
| (3) | Sales | 8,000 | (4) | Bicycle | 140 |
| (7) | Cash | 4,200 | (5) | Rent | 240 |
| (8) | Capital | 2,000 | (6) | Creditors | 3,000 |
| | | | (9) | Electricity | 180 |
| | | | (10) | Drawings | 240 |
| | | | | Balance c/d | 14,400 |
| | | 24,200 | | | 24,200 |
| | Balance b/d | 14,400 | | | |

### Loan account

| | | £ | | | £ |
|---|---|---|---|---|---|
| | Balance c/d | 10,000 | (1) | Cash | 10,000 |
| | | 10,000 | | Balance b/d | 10,000 |

### Sales account

| | | £ | | | £ |
|---|---|---|---|---|---|
| | Balance c/d | 15,600 | (3) | Cash | 8,000 |
| | | | (7) | Debtors | 7,600 |
| | | 15,600 | | | 15,600 |
| | | | | Balance b/d | 15,600 |

### Purchases account

| | | £ | | £ |
|---|---|---|---|---|
| (2) | Cash | 6,000 | Balance c/d | 10,000 |
| (6) | Creditors | 4,000 | | |
| | | 10,000 | | 10,000 |
| | Balance b/d | 10,000 | | |

### Bicycle account

| | | £ | | £ |
|---|---|---|---|---|
| (4) | Cash | 140 | Balance c/d | 140 |
| | Balance b/d | 140 | | |

### Rent account

| | | £ | | £ |
|---|---|---|---|---|
| (5) | Cash | 240 | Balance c/d | 240 |
| | Balance b/d | 240 | | |

### Creditors account

| | | £ | | | £ |
|---|---|---|---|---|---|
| (6) | Cash | 3,000 | (6) | Purchases | 4,000 |
| | Balance b/d | 1,000 | | | |
| | | 4,000 | | | 4,000 |
| | | | | Balance b/d | 1,000 |

### Debtors account

| | | £ | | | £ |
|---|---|---|---|---|---|
| (7) | Sales | 7,600 | (7) | Cash | 4,200 |
| | | | | Balance b/d | 3,400 |
| | | 7,600 | | | 7,600 |
| | Balance b/d | 3,400 | | | |

### Capital account

| | | £ | | | £ |
|---|---|---|---|---|---|
| | Balance c/d | 2,000 | (8) | Cash | 2,000 |
| | | | | Balance b/d | 2,000 |

### Electricity account

| | | £ | | | £ |
|---|---|---|---|---|---|
| (9) | Cash | 180 | | Balance c/d | 180 |
| | Balance b/d | 180 | | | |

### Drawings account

| | | £ | | | £ |
|---|---|---|---|---|---|
| (10) | Cash | 240 | | Balance c/d | 240 |
| | Balance b/d | 240 | | | |

### Trial balance as at 31 March 20X0

| | Dr £ | Cr £ |
|---|---|---|
| Cash | 14,400 | |
| Loan – father | | 10,000 |
| Sales | | 15,600 |
| Purchases | 10,000 | |
| Bicycle | 140 | |
| Rent | 240 | |
| Creditors | | 1,000 |
| Debtors | 3,400 | |
| Capital | | 2,000 |
| Electricity | 180 | |
| Drawings | 240 | |
| | 28,600 | 28,600 |

## Chapter 9 Double-entry bookkeeping and periodic measurement

### Answer to self-assessment question

1 The most significant conventions are:
  (i)  Accruals. Clearly it is most important that a proper matching of revenue and expense is achieved. This can be illustrated by accruals, prepayments, depreciation, the carrying forward of stock values, deferred expenditure such as research and development and many other examples.
  (ii)  Going concern. If the company is on the verge of liquidation, many values may need modification.
  (iii)  Prudence. This implies that profits are not recognized until they are realized by external sale. Similarly, expected losses, such as the situation where realizable value is less than cost, will be recognized immediately.
  (iv)  Related to prudence, assets will be valued at original cost. Clearly this has a 'knock-on' effect for revenue and expenses.
  (v)  Consistency. The same methods will generally be used each year in valuation and recognition of profits/expenses. Thus changes in depreciation policy or stock valuation would not normally take place and if they did, the effect of the change on profit would need to be noted in the accounts.

### Solutions to problems

**1**

**Cost of goods sold**

|  | £ |
|---|---|
| Opening stock | 10,000 |
| *Plus:* Purchases | 40,000 |
|  | 50,000 |
| *Less:* Closing stock | 15,000 |
| Cost of sales | 35,000 |

**2**

**Rent and rates account**

| | | £ | | | £ |
|---|---|---|---|---|---|
| 2.7.X0 | Rent to 24.6.X0 | 400 | 1.7.X0 | Rent owing b/d | 400 |
| 2.7.X0 | Rates to 30.9.X0 | 300 | 1.7.X0 | Rates owing b/d | 150 |
| 10.10.X0 | Rates to 31.3.X1 | 300 | | | |
| 10.10.X0 | Rent to 29.9.X0 | 400 | | | |
| 4.1.X1 | Rent to 25.12.X0 | 400 | | | |
| 6.4.X1 | Rates to 30.9.X1 | 300 | | | |
| 6.4.X1 | Rent to 25.3.X1 | 400 | 30.6.X1 | Rent owing c/d | 150 |
| 30.6.X1 | Rates prepaid c/d | 400 | | Profit and loss account | 2,200 |
| | | 2,900 | | | 2,900 |

Note that brought forward and carried forward figures have been estimated on the basis of whole months outstanding rather than accurately to the nearest day. The latter could, of course, be done but the charge to the profit and loss account should still stand at £2,000, i.e. rent of £1,600 and rates of £600.

4

**Rent payable account**

| | | £ | | | £ |
|---|---|---|---|---|---|
| 31 Dec | Balance b/d | 300 | 31 Dec | Profit and loss account | 400 |
| 31 | Balance c/d | 100 | | | |
| | | 400 | | | 400 |
| | | | 1 Jan | Balance b/d | 100 |

**Telephone account**

| | | £ | | | £ |
|---|---|---|---|---|---|
| 31 Dec | Balance b/d | 60 | 31 Dec | Profit and loss account | 80 |
| 31 | Balance c/d | 20 | | | |
| | | 80 | | | 80 |
| | | | 1 Jan | Balance b/d | 20 |

**Rates account**

| | | £ | | | £ |
|---|---|---|---|---|---|
| 31 Dec | Balance b/d | 400 | 31 Dec | Profit and loss account | 300 |
| | | | | Balance c/d | 100 |
| | | 400 | | | 400 |
| 1 Jan | Balance b/d | 100 | | | |

**Insurance account**

| | | £ | | | £ |
|---|---|---|---|---|---|
| 31 Dec | Balance b/d | 100 | 31 Dec | Profit and loss account | 75 |
| | | | 31 | Balance c/d | 25 |
| | | 100 | | | 100 |
| 1 Jan | Balance b/d | 25 | | | |

**Electricity account**

| | | £ | | | £ |
|---|---|---|---|---|---|
| 31 Dec | Balance b/d | 80 | 31 Dec | Profit and loss account | 96 |
| 31 | Balance c/d | 16 | | | |
| | | 96 | | | 96 |
| | | | 1 Jan | Balance b/d | 16 |

**Rents receivable account**

| | | £ | | | £ |
|---|---|---|---|---|---|
| 31 Dec | Profit and loss account | 400 | 31 Dec | Balance b/d | 500 |
| 31 | Balance c/d | 100 | | | |
| | | 500 | | | 500 |
| | | | 1 Jan | Balance b/d | 100 |

Commission receivable account

| | £ | | | £ |
|---|---|---|---|---|
| 31 Dec  Profit and loss account | 500 | 31 Dec | Balance b/d | 300 |
| | | 31 | Balance c/d | 200 |
| | 500 | | | 500 |
| 1 Jan  Balance b/d | 200 | | | |

## Chapter 10  Losses in asset values and periodic measurement

### Answers to self-assessment questions

1 Clearly the overriding issue when deciding on a depreciation policy is the provision of a true and fair view within the constraints of accounting standards and company law. It should be noted that the usefulness of any depreciation charge will be limited by the more general accounting system in use, and even then it is based on a number of assumptions of varying reliability.

2 Having defined fixed assets, the standard describes depreciation as 'the measure of the wearing out, consumption or other reduction in the useful economic life of a fixed asset, whether arising from use, effluxion of time or obsolescence . . . '.

FRS 15 requires that fixed assets be depreciated and that the profit and loss account and balance sheet must be consistent. It prohibits the setting of depreciation directly to reserves.

Its main thrust is to achieve realism (given the constraints that might be imposed by the more general accounting systems adopted). It requires a consistent approach, year by year, unless it can be shown that a change is desirable for the purpose of realism.

Land should not be depreciated unless it is depleted by, for example, extraction of minerals, but buildings are no different from other fixed assets.

*Disclosure:*
1 depreciation methods used;
2 useful economic lives or depreciation rates used;
3 total depreciation charged for the period;
4 gross amount of depreciable assets and related accumulated depreciation.

Any material changes in the method of depreciation should also be disclosed along with the reason for the change. Revaluations should be disclosed.

### Solutions to problems

1
(a) *Straight-line depreciation*

$$r = \frac{c - rv}{n} \left( \frac{\text{cost} - \text{residual value}}{\text{life in years}} \right)$$

i.e. $\dfrac{£48,000 + £2,000 - £4,000}{8} = £5,750 \text{ p.a}$

provision for 20X0 = £5,750

accumulated depreciation end 20X1 = £11,500 (at end of 8 years = £46,000)

(b) *Reducing balance*

$$r = 1 - n\sqrt{\frac{rv}{c}}$$

i.e. $1 - 8\sqrt{\dfrac{4,000}{50,000}} = 1 - 0.73 = 27\%$

| | Opening NBV | Provision (@ 27%) | Accumulated depreciation |
|---|---|---|---|
| 19X9 | £50,000 | £13,500 | £13,500 |
| 20X0 | £36,500 | £9,855 | £23,355 |

**2**
*Relevant cost*

| | £ | |
|---|---|---|
| Invoice price | 142,600 | (Note: the cost related to the |
| Transportation | 2,000 | old machine has been written off) |
| Installation | 3,400 | |
| | 148,000 | |

Estimated life 8 years, salvage value zero.

(a) Straight-line depreciation produces an annual charge of:

£148,000/8 = £18,500.

There is a problem in calculating a rate for reducing balance depreciation here, because applying the normal formula to a salvage value of zero would produce a rate of 1 (i.e. 100% depreciation). One way around this would be to use a salvage value and accept that this would eventually need to be written off. If we arbitrarily use 1,000 we end up with:

$$1 - 8\sqrt{\frac{1,000}{148,000}} = 0.46, \text{ i.e. } 46\%$$

This raises some interesting issues concerning the general realism of reducing balance depreciation.

(b) FRS 15 states that where it is considered necessary to revise the estimated life of an asset 'usually . . . there will be no material distortion of future results or financial position if the net book amount is written off over the revised remaining useful economic life.' It goes on to recommend that any material distortions should be recognized in accordance with SSAP 6 'Extraordinary Items and Prior Year Adjustments'.

In this case we are faced with a choice between:

(i) Adjustment which is not really material.
NBV end of year 20X0 = £148,000 – (£18,500 × 2) = £111,000.
New estimate of life means 10 years remain;
thus new charge = £11,100 p.a.

(ii) Adjustment which is regarded as material.

$$\text{New charge from acquisition } \frac{£148,000}{12} = £12,333.$$

New accumulated depreciation end of 20X0 = £24,666. Thus a prior year adjustment of £12,334 (i.e. reducing accumulated depreciation) with a charge of £12,333 for year 20X1 would be made.

## 3
### Plant and machinery at cost

| | | | | |
|---|---|---|---|---|
| B/d | 7,500 | (4) | £500 | Asset realization disposal |
| (3) | 1,000 | | | |

### Depreciation of plant and machinery

| | | | |
|---|---|---|---|
| (4) Asset realization disposal | £200 | B/d | £3,000  (1) |

### Motor vehicles at cost

| | | | | |
|---|---|---|---|---|
| B/d | £3,500 | (5) | £750 | Asset realization disposal |

### Asset realization account

| | | £ | | | £ | |
|---|---|---|---|---|---|---|
| (4) | Plant at cost | 500 | (4) | 325 | | Proceeds |
| | P&L (surplus on disposal) | 25 | (4) | 200 | | Depreciation |
| | | 525 | | 525 | | |
| (5) | Motors at cost | 750 | (5) | 400 | | Proceeds |
| | | | (5) | 300 | | Depreciation |
| | | | | 50 | | P&L (loss on disposal) |
| | | 750 | | 750 | | |

### Depreciation of motor vehicles

| | | | |
|---|---|---|---|
| (5) Disposal | £300 | B/d | £1,400  (2) |

## 5
### (a)
### Bad and doubtful debts account

| | £ | | £ |
|---|---|---|---|
| 19X9 | | 19X9 | |
| 31.3 | | 31.3 | |
| Balance c/d | 500 | P&L b&d debts | 500 |
| 20X0 | | 20X0 | |
| (Bad debt w/o) | | b/d | 500 |
| Debtors control | 250 | | |
| Balance c/d | 625 | P&L b&d debts | 375 |
| | 875 | | 875 |
| 20X1 | | 20X1 | |
| (Bad debt w/o) | | b/d | 625 |
| Debtors control | 270 | | |
| Balance c/d | 400 | P&L b&d debts | 45 |
| | 670 | | 670 |

(b)

| | £ |
|---|---|
| P&L 19X9 Bad and doubtful debts | 500 |
| P&L 20X0 Bad and doubtful debts | 375 |
| P&L 20X1 Bad and doubtful debts | 45 |

## 6

(a) (i) **Straight-line method**

| | £ |
|---|---|
| Cost | 7,000,000 |
| *Less*: Expected residual value | 1,500,000 |
| | 5,500,000 |
| Depreciation per annum | 1,375,000 |

| Annual charge | £ |
|---|---|
| Year to 31 January 19X8 | 1,375,000 |
| Year to 31 January 19X9 | 1,375,000 |
| Year to 31 January 20X0 | 1,375,000 |
| Year to 31 January 20X1 (balance) | 1,675,000 |
| Actual depreciation (£7,000,000 – £1,200,000) | 5,800,000 |

(ii) **Flying hours logged method**

| | £ |
|---|---|
| Cost | 7,000,000 |
| *Less*: Expected residual value | 1,500,000 |
| Expected depreciation | 5,500,000 |
| Expected flying hours | 10,000 |
| Depreciation per flying hour | 550 |

| Annual charge | |
|---|---|
| Year to 31 January 19X8 (3,000 × £550) | 1,650,000 |
| Year to 31 January 19X9 (2,800 × £550) | 1,540,000 |
| Year to 31 January 20X0 (2,300 × £550) | 1,265,000 |
| Year to 31 January 20X1 (balance) | 1,345,000 |
| Actual depreciation (£7,000,000 – £1,200,000) | 5,800,000 |

(b)

**Flying hours logged method**
**Aircraft account**

| 20X0 | | £ | 20X0 | | £ |
|---|---|---|---|---|---|
| Feb 1 | Balance b/f | 7,000,000 | June | Assets disposals | 7,000,000 |

**Provision for depreciation – aircraft**

| 20X0 | | £ | 20X0 | | £ |
|---|---|---|---|---|---|
| June | Assets disposals | 4,455,000 | Feb 1 | Balance b/f | 4,455,000 |

**Assets disposals account**

| 20X0 | | £ | 20X0 | | £ |
|---|---|---|---|---|---|
| June | Aircraft | 7,000,000 | June | Provision for depreciation | 4,455,000 |
| | | | | Bank | 1,200,000 |
| | | | 20X1 | | |
| | | | Jan 31 | Profit and loss | 1,345,000 |
| | | 7,000,000 | | | 7,000,000 |

**Straight-line method**

**Aircraft account**

| 20X0 | | £ | 20X0 | | £ |
|---|---|---|---|---|---|
| Feb 1 | Balance b/f | 7,000,000 | June | Assets disposals | 7,000,000 |

**Provision for depreciation – aircraft**

| 20X0 | | £ | 20X0 | | £ |
|---|---|---|---|---|---|
| June | Assets disposals | 4,125,000 | Feb 1 | Balance b/f | 4,125,000 |

**Assets disposals account**

| 20X0 | | £ | 20X0 | | £ |
|---|---|---|---|---|---|
| June | Aircraft | 7,000,000 | June | Provision for depreciation | 4,125,000 |
| | | | | Bank | 1,200,000 |
| | | | 20X1 | | |
| | | | Jan 31 | Profit and loss | 1,675,000 |
| | | 7,000,000 | | | 7,000,000 |

**7**

**Asset account**

| | £ | | £ |
|---|---|---|---|
| Balance at 1 Jan 20X0 | 8,000 | Balance at 31 Dec 20X0 | 8,800 |
| Modification | 800 | | |
| | 8,800 | | 8,800 |

**Provision for depreciation account**

| | £ | | £ |
|---|---|---|---|
| Balance at 31 Dec 20X0 | 4,320 | Balance at 1 Jan 20X0 | 3,200 |
| | | Depreciation for 20X0 (W1) | 1,120 |
| | 4,320 | | 4,320 |

**Profit and loss account**

| | £ |
|---|---|
| Depreciation | 1,120 |
| Maintenance and replacements (W2) | 750 |

**Workings:**

1  The net book value of the asset is to be written off over the remaining useful life which is a further five years.

| | £ |
|---|---|
| Asset (cost) | 8,800 |
| Depreciation to date | 3,200 |
| | 5,600 |
| Depreciation $\frac{1}{5}$ | 1,120 |

2  The £500 for renewal has been charged to profit and loss account as it would appear to have no connection with the improvements which extend the useful life.

# Chapter 11  Preparing a profit and loss account and a balance sheet

**Solutions to problems**

**1**

(a)  Adjustments to profit:

|  |  | £ |
|---|---|---|
| (i) | Cr profit | 100 |
|  | Dr bank | 100 |
| (ii) | Dr profit | 210 |
|  | Cr debtors | 100 |
|  | Cr provision | 110 |
| (iii) | Dr Fixed assets | 500 |
|  | Cr P&L | 500 |
|  | Dr P&L | 50 |
|  | Cr Prov. Depn. | 50 |
| (iv) | Cr Stock | 250 |
|  | Dr P&L | 250 |
| (v) | Cr cash | 40 |
|  | Dr P&L | 40 |

Net effect is profit increased by £50 and now stands at £2,100.

(b)

|  | £ |  | £ | £ |
|---|---|---|---|---|
| Capital account | 10,000 | Plant cost | 8,500 |  |
| Profit for the year | 2,100 | Depreciation | 2,050 | 6,450 |
|  | 12,100 | Vehicle cost | 3,000 |  |
|  |  | Depreciation | 1,000 | 2,000 |
| Creditors and provisions | 5,000 | Stock |  | 6,750 |
| Bank overdraft | 900 | Debtors | 3,100 |  |
|  |  | Provision | 310 | 2,790 |
|  |  | Cash |  | 10 |
|  | 18,000 |  |  | 18,000 |

**2**

|  | £ | £ |
|---|---|---|
| Sales |  | 50,000 |
| Purchases | 30,000 |  |
| Stock 1 Apr 20X0 | 35,000 |  |
| Admin expenses | 5,000 |  |
| Selling expenses | 5,000 |  |
| Trade creditors |  | 27,000 |
| Bank overdraft |  | 32,000 |
| Trade debtors | 55,000 |  |
| Debentures |  | 50,000 |
| Plant and machinery at cost | 80,000 |  |
| Depreciation of plant and machinery |  | 30,000 |
| Fixtures at cost | 40,000 |  |
| Depreciation of fixtures |  | 10,000 |
| Capital account 1 Apr 20X0 |  | 51,000 |
|  | 250,000 | 250,000 |

## John Reeve Profit and loss account

|  | £ | £ |
|---|---|---|
| Sales |  | 50,000 |
| Opening stock | 35,000 |  |
| Purchases | 30,000 |  |
|  | 65,000 |  |
| Closing stock | 40,000 | 25,000 |
| Gross Profit |  | 25,000 |
|  |  |  |
| *Less:* |  |  |
| Administration expenses | 5,000 |  |
| Selling expenses | 5,000 |  |
| Depreciation of plant | 16,000 |  |
| Depreciation of fixtures | 8,000 | 34,000 |
| Loss for year |  | (9,000) |

## John Reeve Balance sheet

|  | £ |
|---|---|
| Capital account b/f | 51,000 |
| Loss for year | 9,000 |
|  | 42,000 |
| Debentures | 50,000 |
|  | 92,000 |

| Represented by: | Cost | Depr | NBV |
|---|---|---|---|
|  | £ | £ | £ |
| Plant and machinery | 80,000 | 46,000 | 34,000 |
| Fixtures | 40,000 | 18,000 | 22,000 |
|  | 120,000 | 64,000 | 56,000 |

| Current assets |  |  |
|---|---|---|
| Stock | 40,000 |  |
| Debtors | 55,000 |  |
|  | 95,000 |  |

| Current liabilities |  |  |
|---|---|---|
| Creditors | 27,000 |  |
| Bank overdraft | 32,000 |  |
|  | 59,000 |  |
| Net current assets |  | 36,000 |
|  |  | 92,000 |

**4**

Matt Spode Profit and loss account for year ended 31 December 20X0

| | £ | £ |
|---|---:|---:|
| Sales | | 157,240 |
| Opening stock | 19,250 | |
| Purchases | 92,400 | |
| | 111,650 | |
| Closing stock | 22,400 | |
| Cost of sales | | 89,250 |
| Gross profit | | 67,990 |
| Motor expenses | 7,300 | |
| Rates | 2,300 | |
| Wages and salaries (42,000 + 1,200) | 43,200 | |
| Insurance (2,000 − 900) | 1,100 | |
| Sundry expenses | 16,200 | |
| Bad debts written off | 800 | |
| Increased provision for doubtful debts (1,200 − 560) | 640 | |
| Depreciation motors (30,000 − 8,200) × 0.25 | 5,450 | |
| Depreciation fixtures and fittings (6,500 × 0.1) | 650 | |
| Loan interest | 2,000 | 79,640 |
| Net loss | | (11,650) |

Matt Spode Balance sheet as at 31 December 20X0

| | £ |
|---|---:|
| Capital b/f | 112,000 |
| Loss for year | 11,650 |
| | 100,350 |
| Drawings | 9,600 |
| Capital carried forward | 90,750 |
| Long-term loan | 20,000 |
| | 110,750 |

Represented by:

| Fixed assets | Cost | Depr | NBV |
|---|---:|---:|---:|
| Premises | 64,000 | – | 64,000 |
| Motors | 30,000 | 13,650 | 16,350 |
| Fixtures and fittings | 6,500 | 1,750 | 4,750 |
| | 100,500 | 15,400 | 85,100 |

| | £ | £ | £ |
|---|---:|---:|---:|
| Current assets | | | |
| Stock | | 22,400 | |
| Debtors | 17,200 | | |
| *Less:* Provision | 1,200 | 16,000 | |
| Prepayments | | 900 | |
| Cash at bank and in hand | | 4,550 | |
| | | 43,850 | |

|  | £ | £ |
|---|---|---|
| **Current liabilities** | | |
| Trade creditors | 15,000 | |
| Accrued wages | 1,200 | |
| Accrued interest | 2,000 | |
| | 18,200 | |
| Net current assets | | 25,650 |
| | | 110,750 |

## 5

### A Merchant Profit and loss account year ended 31 December 20X0

|  | £ | £ | Notes |
|---|---|---|---|
| Gross profit | | 27,000 | |
| *Less:* Expenses | | | |
| Selling and distribution | 4,500 | | |
| Depreciation motors | 4,000 | | |
| Rates and insurance | 5,000 | | (1) |
| Office salaries | 3,000 | | |
| Office expenses | 1,250 | | |
| Bad debts written off | 500 | | |
| Increased provision for doubtful debts | 100 | | (2) |
| Discounts received and allowed (net) | (1,500) | 16,850 | |
| | | 10,150 | |

1 Prepayment of £1,000 re 3 months' rates to March.
2 Required provision 5% of £52,000 = £2,600. Provision brought forward £2,500.

### A Merchant Balance sheet as at 31 December 20X0

|  | £ |
|---|---|
| Capital account. A Merchant | |
| Balance brought forward | 90,000 |
| Introduced | 1,500 |
| Profit for year | 10,150 |
| | 101,650 |
| Drawings | 8,000 |
| | 93,650 |

| Represented by:<br>Fixed assets | Cost<br>£ | Depr<br>£ | NBV<br>£ |
|---|---|---|---|
| Freehold premises | 30,000 | 30,000 | |
| Motor vehicles | 20,000 | 8,000 | 12,000 |
| | 50,000 | 8,000 | 42,000 |

|  | £ | £ | £ |
|---|---|---|---|
| **Current assets** |  |  |  |
| Stock |  | 23,600 |  |
| Debtors | 53,000 |  | (3) |
| *Less:* Provision | 2,600 | 50,400 |  |
| Bank balance |  | 8,750 |  |
|  |  | 82,750 |  |
|  |  |  |  |
| **Current liabilities** |  |  |  |
| Creditors |  | 31,100 |  |
|  |  |  | 51,650 |
|  |  |  | 93,650 |

(3) Includes prepayment of £1,000 re rates.

6
Movement in cash and bank
    Closing    £(50)    Opening   £(450)
Increase     £400
**Other assets/liabilities**

| **Closing** £ | **Opening** £ |
|---|---|
| 3,300 | 2,600 |
| 5,100 | 4,500 |
| (1,900) | (1,450) |
| (2,500) | (4,000) |
| 4,000 | 1,650 |

|  | £ |  |
|---|---|---|
| Drawings 200 × 52 = | 10,400 | cash |
| Insurance for private house | 100 |  |
| Furniture for private house | 600 |  |
|  | 11,100 |  |
| *Less:* Payment of business expenses |  |  |
| from private account | 3,100 |  |
| Net | 8,000 |  |

| Profit for year = | 2,750 | Increase in assets |
|---|---|---|
|  | 8,000 | Drawings |
|  | (2,000) | Depr of shop |
|  | (600) | Depr of fittings, etc. |
|  | 8,150 |  |

Financial position at 31 December 20X0

| Fixed assets | Cost £ | Depr £ | NBV £ | Notes |
|---|---|---|---|---|
| Shop | 40,000 | 10,000 | 30,000 | (1) |
| Fittings and fixtures | 6,000 | 3,000 | 3,000 | (2) |
| | 46,000 | 13,000 | 33,000 | |

| Current assets | | | |
|---|---|---|---|
| Stock | 3,300 | | |
| Debtors | 5,100 | | |
| Cash | 250 | | |
| | 8,650 | | |

| Current liabilities | | | |
|---|---|---|---|
| Creditors | 1,900 | | |
| Overdraft | 300 | | |
| | 2,200 | | |
| Net current assets | | 6,450 | |
| | | 39,450 | |
| Capital account | | 36,950 | (3) |
| Loan from Mrs Jackson | | 2,500 | |
| | | 39,450 | |

1  Depreciation 5 years @ 5% × 40,000
2  Depreciation 5 years @ 10% × 3,000
3  Balancing figure

8

| | £ | £ | Notes |
|---|---|---|---|
| Sales | | 105,190 | (1) |
| Opening stock | 24,000 | | |
| Purchases | 67,940 | | (2) |
| | 91,940 | | |
| Closing stock | 29,000 | | |
| | | 62,940 | |
| | | 42,250 | |
| Expenses | | | |
| General | 7,630 | | (3) |
| Depreciation f, f & f | 300 | | |
| Depreciation motor van | 1,700 | | |
| Loss on disposal of motor vehicle | 900 | 10,530 | |
| | | 31,720 | |

### Realization of motor vehicles

| | £ | | £ |
|---|---|---|---|
| Cost | 5,625 | Depreciation | 1,125 |
| | | Proceeds | 3,600 |
| | | Loss on disposal | 900 |
| | 5,625 | | 5,625 |

1  Bankings £98,740 plus increase in debtors £450 plus takings not banked £6,000.
2  Bank payments £57,180 plus increase in creditors £10,760.
3  Bank payments £6,720 plus £1,500 cash payments, less reduction in amount owing.

### Balance sheet

| Fixed assets (net) | £ | £ | Notes |
|---|---|---|---|
| Motor van | | 6,800 | |
| Furniture, etc. | | 5,700 | |
| | | 12,500 | |
| **Current assets** | | | |
| Stock | 29,000 | | |
| Debtors | 1,250 | | |
| Bank | 27,140 | | |
| Cash | 350 | | |
| | 57,740 | | |
| **Current liabilities** | | | |
| Creditors | 18,400 | | |
| Accrued expenses | 730 | | |
| | 19,130 | | |
| | | 38,610 | |
| | | 51,110 | |
| **Snailsby capital account** | | | |
| Balance brought forward | | 30,470 | (4) |
| Profit for year | | 30,540 | |
| | | 61,010 | |
| Drawings | | 9,900 | (5) |
| | | 51,110 | |

4  Balancing figure derived from working backwards from balance sheet total.
5  Bank drawings £5,400 plus cash drawings £4,500.

## 9
### Cash book

| | £ | | £ |
|---|---|---|---|
| Balance | 12,600 | Discharged cheque | 70 |
| Dividend received | 340 | Bank charges, etc. | 60 |
| | | Trade subscription | 15 |
| | | Balance c/d | 12,795 |
| | 12,940 | | 12,940 |

### Bank reconciliation

| | £ |
|---|---|
| Balance per statement | 13,500 |
| *Add:* Uncleared lodgement | 230 |
| | 13,730 |
| *Less:* Unpresented cheques | 935 |
| | 12,795 |

## 11
### Tim Russell
### Profit and loss account for the year ended 31 December 20X0

| | £ | £ |
|---|---|---|
| Sales | | 105,560 |
| **Cost of sales** | | |
| Stock at 1 Jan 20X0 | 7,154 | |
| Purchases | 71,812 | |
| | 78,966 | |
| Closing stock | 8,221 | 70,745 |
| Gross profit | | 34,815 |
| | | |
| **Expenses** | | |
| Salaries and wages | 7,576 | |
| Rent, rates and insurance | 5,760 | |
| Discounts allowed | 1,206 | |
| Carriage | 2,000 | |
| Postage and stationery | 1,213 | |
| Advertising | 2,029 | |
| Bad debts | 1,234 | |
| Depreciation | 4,870 | |
| Discounts received | (684) | 25,204 |
| Net profit | | 9,611 |

Balance sheet as at 31 December 20X0

| | Cost | Depreciation | Net book value |
|---|---|---|---|
| | £ | £ | £ |
| **Fixed assets** | | | |
| Equipment | 48,700 | 26,520 | 22,180 |
| **Current assets** | | | |
| Stock | | 8,221 | |
| Debtors | | 13,170 | |
| Prepaid expenses | | 213 | |
| Cash at bank | | 3,054 | |
| Cash in hand | | 312 | |
| | | 24,970 | |
| **Current liabilities** | | | |
| Creditors | | 11,640 | |
| Accruals | | 177 | |
| | | 11,817 | 13,153 |
| Net current assets | | | 35,333 |
| **Capital account** | | | |
| Balance c/d | | | 31,653 |
| Profit for year | | | 9,611 |
| | | | 41,264 |
| Drawings | | | 5,931 |
| | | | 35,333 |

# Chapter 12  Reporting recorded assets and liabilities

## Answer to self-assessment question

1 The difficulty in accounting for research and development expenditure arises from the question as to how much of the expenditure might be interpreted as being of a capital nature and how much is really of a revenue nature. This is often so unclear that it is not possible to make an objective judgement. SSAP 13 states that the position is dominated by the concepts of accruals and prudence: 'It is a corollary of the prudence concept that expenditure should be written off in the period in which it arises unless its relationship to the revenue of a future period can be established with reasonable certainty'. As a result, pure research is viewed as being of a revenue nature because there is often little certainty as to its relationship with future revenue. (It should, however, be noted that this may be more of a measurement problem than one of principle.) Similarly, it is felt that applied research will be difficult to assess and this is to be treated as revenue. As in all cases of allocating costs to differing periods, this is an area of great difficulty so far as accounting treatment is concerned. It may well be possible to make a realistic assessment of the revenue/capital content of all three categories, but it is difficult to see how this could ever be verifiable. This being so, it is easy to see why FASB Statement No 2 takes the form that it does. It removes the problems of verification and subjectivity (at one level) but at the same time it may give an unrealistic picture and even discourage R&D expenditure.

## Solutions to problems

### 2

(a) The price paid for McMaltby was £120,000.

| | £ | £ |
|---|---|---|
| Price paid | | 120,000 |
| **Fixed assets** | | |
| Premises | 60,000 | |
| Plant | 25,000 | |
| **Current assets** | | |
| 32,000 + 5,000 – 3,000 | 34,000 | |
| | 119,000 | |
| *Less:* Current liabilities | 15,000 | |
| | | 104,000 |
| Goodwill | | 16,000 |

(b) FRS 10 states that goodwill should be capitalized and written off over a period of time.

(c)

| | £ | £ |
|---|---|---|
| Share capital | | 250,000 |
| Reserves | | 95,000 |
| | | 345,000 |
| Debentures and loan | | 186,000 |
| | | 531,000 |
| Goodwill | | 16,000 |
| Tangible fixed assets | | |
| 295,000 + 85,000 | | 380,000 |
| Current assets | | |
| 221,000 + 34,000 – 20,000 | 235,000 | |
| Current liabilities | | |
| 85,000 + 15,000 | (100,000) | |
| | | 135,000 |
| | | 531,000 |

### 3

| | 19X8 | 19X9 |
|---|---|---|
| Gross profit margin | 5,655/18,850 = 30% | 7,722/25,740 = 30% |

**Debtors account**

| | £ | | £ |
|---|---|---|---|
| Balance b/f | 5,130 | Balance c/f | 6,050 |
| Sales | 31,000 | Cash received | 30,080 |
| | 36,130 | | 36,130 |

### Creditors account

|  | £ |  | £ |
|---|---|---|---|
| Balance c/f | 1,870 | Balance b/f | 1,790 |
| Payments | 22,220 | Purchases | 22,300 |
|  | 24,090 |  | 24,090 |

Gross profit is a constant 30% of sales, therefore gross profit for 20X0 = 30% × £31,000 = £9,300.

|  | £ | £ |
|---|---|---|
| Sales |  | 31,000 |
| Opening stock | 1,400 |  |
| Purchases | 22,300 |  |
|  | 23,700 |  |
| Closing stock | 2,000 |  |
| Cost of sales |  | 21,700 |
| Gross profit |  | 9,300 |

Closing stock is calculated by working back from the gross profit figure and forward from opening stock/purchases.

**5**

(a)

**Stock account** (units)

| **19X8** |  | **19X8** |  |
|---|---|---|---|
| B/f | 0 | Sales | 12,000 |
| Purchases | 15,000 | C/f | 3,000 |
|  | 15,000 |  | 15,000 |

| **19X9** |  | **19X9** |  |
|---|---|---|---|
| B/f | 3,000 | Sales | 15,000 |
| Purchases | 15,500 | C/f | 3,500 |
|  | 18,500 |  | 18,500 |

| **20X0** |  | **20X0** |  |
|---|---|---|---|
| B/f | 3,500 | Sales | 18,000 |
| Purchases | 16,500 | C/f | 2,000 |
|  | 20,000 |  | 20,000 |

(b)  Value of year-end stocks using FIFO:

| 19X8 | 3,000 units @ £30 = | £90,000 |
|---|---|---|
| 19X9 | 3,500 units @ £37 = | £129,500 |
| 20X0 | 2,000 units @ £45 = | £90,000 |

Value of year end stocks using LIFO:

| 19X8 | 3,000 units @ £22 = | £66,000 |
|---|---|---|
| 19X9 | 3,000 units @ £22 = | £66,000 |
|  | 500 units @ £32 = | £16,000 |
|  |  | £82,000 |
| 20X0 | 2,000 units @ £22 = | £44,000 |

Value of stock using weighted average:

| 19X8 | Units | | Value £ |
|---|---|---|---|
| B/f | 0 | | 0 |
| Purchased | 15,000 | | 388,000 |
| | 15,000 | $\left(\dfrac{3,000}{15,000} \times (A)\right)$ | (A) 388,000 |
| Closing stock 19X8 | 3,000 | | 77,600 |
| 19X9 Purchases | 15,500 | | 528,000 |
| | 18,500 | $\left(\dfrac{3,500}{18,500} \times (B)\right)$ | (B) 605,600 |
| Closing stock 19X9 | 3,500 | | 114,573 |
| 20X0 Purchases | 16,500 | | 698,500 |
| | 20,000 | $\left(\dfrac{2,000}{20,000} \times (C)\right)$ | (C) 813,073 |
| Closing stock 20X0 | 2,000 | | 81,307 |

(c)

## Profit and loss account

| | FIFO £ | | LIFO £ | | AVCO £ | |
|---|---|---|---|---|---|---|
| 19X8 Sales | | 600,000 | | 600,000 | | 600,000 |
| Purchases | 388,000 | | 388,000 | | 388,000 | |
| Cl. stock | 90,000 | | 66,000 | | 77,600 | |
| | | 298,000 | | 322,000 | | 310,400 |
| Gross profit | | 302,000 | | 278,000 | | 289,600 |
| 19X9 Sales | | 900,000 | | 900,000 | | 900,000 |
| Op. stock | 90,000 | | 66,000 | | 77,600 | |
| Purchases | 528,000 | | 528,000 | | 528,000 | |
| Cl. stock | (129,500) | | (82,000) | | (114,573) | |
| | | 488,500 | | 512,000 | | 491,027 |
| Gross profit | | 411,500 | | 388,000 | | 408,973 |
| 20X0 Sales | | 1,170,000 | | 1,170,000 | | 1,170,000 |
| Op. stock | 129,500 | | 82,000 | | 114,573 | |
| Purchases | 698,500 | | 698,500 | | 698,500 | |
| Cl. stock | (90,000) | | (44,000) | | (81,307) | |
| | | 738,000 | | 736,500 | | 731,766 |
| Gross profit | | 432,000 | | 433,500 | | 438,234 |

(d) It is difficult to say which method of stock valuation is 'most appropriate'. SSAP 9 implies that the use of base stocks or LIFO will generally be inappropriate. It may well be that the use of LIFO produces a more realistic cost of sales figure since stock consumed approximates more closely to replacement cost. However, this is really part of a much bigger issue covered in later chapters. Generally speaking, both LIFO and AVCO will tend to undervalue stocks in the balance sheet.

## 6

SSAP 9 covers the treatment of long-term contracts and the taking of profit during the period of the contract. It states that 'there can be no attributable profit until the outcome of a contract can reasonably be foreseen'.

Accrued profit is normally taken as:

$$[\text{Total contract price} - (\text{costs to date} + \text{estimated costs to completion})] \times \frac{\text{work certified}}{\text{total contract price}}$$

In this case, cost to date =

|  | £ | £ |
|---|---|---|
| Materials from store | 42,000 | |
| *Less:* Stock | 970 | |
| | | 41,030 |
| Wages | | 39,820 |
| Expenses | | 12,130 |
| Direct materials | | 4,910 |
| Depreciation of plant | | 342 |
| | | 98,232 |

The treatment of overheads depends on whether they are directly attributable to the project or merely an arbitrary allocation of general expenses.

In the case in question we have no indication of the estimated costs to completion, but it would seem that half the project has been completed (£100,000 grossed up to reflect 20% retention).

Assuming future costs to be consistent with past costs would produce a profit to date of:

|  | £ | £ |
|---|---|---|
| | | 125,000 |
| *Less:* | 98,232 | |
| Direct o/h | 790 | |
| | | 99,022 |
| | | 25,978 |

How much of this profit would be taken depends on assessments of guarantee costs, etc., as well as the likelihood of future costs remaining at the same levels as past costs. The figure calculated above would, effectively, represent the maximum profit that might be taken at this stage.

## 7

| | £ | £ |
|---|---:|---:|
| **Costs to date** | | |
| Wages | | 60,000 |
| Materials | 42,500 | |
| Stock | 1,250 | 41,250 |
| Sundries | | 4,000 |
| HO charges (deemed directly attributable to contract) | | 5,500 |
| Plant: Cost | 17,500 | |
| Disposal | (1,500) | |
| | 16,000 | |
| Estimated residual value | 4,500 | 11,500 |
| | | 122,250 |

| | £ | £ |
|---|---:|---:|
| **Future costs** | | |
| Wages | | 52,800 |
| Materials | 1,250 | |
| | 35,000 | 36,250 |
| Sundries | | 1,800 |
| Plant b/f | 4,500 | |
| Additions | 6,500 | |
| | 11,000 | |
| Residual | 3,750 | 7,250 |
| Contingencies | | 3,500 |
| | | 101,600 |

Attributable profit =

[Total contract price − (Costs to date +

$$\text{Estimated costs to completion})] \times \frac{\text{Work certified to date}}{\text{Total contract price}}$$

Work certified to date = £125,000
(i.e. 100,000 grossed up for 20% retention)
Thus accrued profit =

$$[250,000 - (122,250 + 101,600)] \times \frac{125,000}{250,000}$$

$$= 26,150 \times 0.5 = £13,075$$

**Summarized contract account**

| | £ | | £ | £ |
|---|---:|---|---:|---:|
| Costs to date | 122,250 | Payments rec'd | | 100,000 |
| | | Contract debtor c/d | | |
| Profit and loss account | 13,075 | certified | 25,000 | |
| | | uncertified | 10,325 | |
| | | | | 35,325 |
| | 135,325 | | | 135,325 |

## Chapter 13  Companies: their nature and regulation

### Answers to self-assessment questions

1 Share capital represents a stake in the ownership of a company. The holders of ordinary shares are not guaranteed a dividend. When profits are low they may get no return at all. Loan capital carries a fixed rate of interest. This is an annual commitment which has to be met each year regardless of whether the company has made any profits and before any of the shareholders become entitled to any dividends.

2 Gearing is the relationship between 'risk' capital (i.e. ordinary shares) and fixed return funding. Ordinary shareholders will do well in a profitable year, but a poor year may result in no dividend being paid after the fixed charges have been met.

3 When a company sells its shares, it may ask a price in excess of the nominal value of those shares. This excess is known as the share premium and must be transferred to a special account.

4 According to the 'true and fair view' criterion, financial statements should contain sufficient information in quality and quantity to satisfy the reasonable expectations of the readers to whom they are addressed. Readers will expect such statements to comply with accounting standards.

5 The Financial Reporting Council gives guidance to the ASB on priorities, work programme and issues of public concern, and acts as an instrument for promoting good accounting practice.

   The ASB issues accounting standards.

   The FRRP examines accounts in cases where departures from standard accounting practice have occured.

   The UITF assists the ASB in areas where conflicts are likely to develop between Companies Act provisions and an accounting standard.

6 Accounting regulations in the UK are influenced by the EU and IASC.

7 The aim of a conceptual framework is to allow standards to develop in a coherent manner. Also it acts as a vehicle for evaluating current standards. Financial position information – concerning economic resources, financial structure, solvency and liquidity – is provided by the balance sheet. Performance comprises return on resources and embraces profit and loss account information. Financial adaptability consists of the ability of an enterprise to alter its cash flows so that it can respond to unexpected events and opportunities.

8 Qualitative characteristics make the information provided in financial statements useful to users.

9 'Relevance' means relevance to decision making. 'Reliability' means that information is free from material errors or bias. Relevant information has the ability to influence the decisions of users. Reliable information can be depended upon by the users.

# Chapter 14 Published financial statements

## Solutions to problems

**2**

(a) By issuing ordinary shares, the company becomes less highly geared, i.e. less risky so far as those dealing with the company are concerned. There will also be a lower level of variation in returns to shareholders. However, the cost of issuing shares is high (especially for a PLC) and, unless this issue takes the form of a rights issue, the current shareholders' stake in the company (and their control) will be diluted. However, because the company is already highly geared, this may be a preferred alternative.

(b) 50,000 preference shares would lead to a greater variation (and risk) to the holders of ordinary shares. Also 8% may not be a particularly attractive return for this degree of risk. Advantages are that it would (a) reduce the company's gearing and provide greater financial flexibility, (b) not dilute the ordinary shareholders' control, (c) be less risky in terms of cash outflows than a loan.

   It should be remembered that dividends on preference shares are not tax-deductible.

(c) The additional loan would increase gearing and thereby the existing shareholders' risk. However, debenture interest is tax-deductible and this may turn out to be the company's cheapest source of funds. Finance theory would suggest that there is a trade-off between tax benefit and the costs of gearing arising out of increased risk for shareholders. There will be an optimal capital structure for every company, but identifying it may be very difficult.

**3**

### Huby Haulage Ltd Profit and loss account

|  | £ | £ |
|---|---:|---:|
| Sales |  | 365,000 |
| Repairs to property | 22,000 |  |
| Wages (60 + 15) | 75,000 |  |
| Salaries (20 + 25) | 45,000 |  |
| Drivers' subsistence | 6,150 |  |
| Depreciation of vehicles | 62,500 |  |
| Parts and consumables (70 − 18) | 52,000 |  |
| Licences and insurance (20 − 4) | 16,000 |  |
| Administrative expenses | 12,000 |  |
| Debenture interest | 5,000 | 295,650 |
| Net profit |  | 69,350 |

## Huby Haulage Ltd Appropriation account

|                                  | £      |
|----------------------------------|--------|
| Trading profit                   | 69,350 |
| Corporation tax                  | 22,400 |
|                                  | 46,950 |
| Proposed dividend                | 20,000 |
| Retained profit                  | 26,950 |
| Profit brought forward           | 70,000 |
| Retained profit carried forward  | 96,950 |

## Huby Haulage Ltd Balance sheet as at 31 December 20X0

|                                  | £       |
|----------------------------------|---------|
| £1 ordinary shares fully paid    | 200,000 |
| Profit and loss account          | 96,950  |
| Shareholders' equity             | 296,950 |
| 10% Debenture                    | 50,000  |
|                                  | 346,950 |

Represented by:

| Fixed assets      | Cost    | Depr    | NBV     |
|-------------------|---------|---------|---------|
|                   | £       | £       | £       |
| Freehold property | 165,000 |         | 165,000 |
| Motor vehicles    | 360,000 | 172,500 | 187,500 |
|                   | 525,000 | 172,500 | 352,500 |

| Current assets                 | £      |
|--------------------------------|--------|
| Stocks of parts, etc.          | 18,000 |
| Prepaid insurance and licences | 4,000  |
| Bank and cash                  | 20,000 |
|                                | 42,000 |

| Current liabilities         | £      |         |
|-----------------------------|--------|---------|
| Drivers' subsistence owing  | 150    |         |
| Taxation                    | 22,400 |         |
| Proposed dividend           | 20,000 |         |
| Accrued interest            | 5,000  |         |
|                             | 47,550 |         |
| Net current liabilities     |        | (5,550) |
|                             |        | 346,950 |

**4**

**Nether Edge plc Profit and loss account for the year ending 31 December 20X0**

|  | £000 | Notes |
|---|---|---|
| Turnover | 2,400 | (1) |
| Cost of sales (Workings 1) | (800) | |
| Gross profit | 1,600 | |
| Distribution costs (200 + 680) | (880) | |
| Administrative expenses (300 + 80 + 40) | (420) | |
| Operating profit | 300 | (2) |
| Other income | 30 | (3) |
| Interest payable and similar charges | (10) | (4) |
| Profit on ordinary activities before taxation | 320 | |
| Tax on profit on ordinary activities | (100) | (5) |
| Profit for the financial year | 220 | |
| Dividends paid and proposed | (70) | (6) |
|  | 150 | |
| Earnings per share | 39p | (7) |

**Nether Edge plc Balance sheet as at 31 December 20X0**

|  | £000 | Notes |
|---|---|---|
| **Fixed assets** | | |
| Tangible assets | 120 | (8) |
| Investments | 140 | (9) |
|  | 260 | |
| **Current assets** | | |
| Stock | 600 | |
| Debtors | 558 | (10) |
| Cash | 118 | |
|  | 1,276 | |
| **Creditors** | | |
| Amounts falling due within one year | (326) | (11) |
| Net current assets | 950 | |
| Total assets less current liabilities | 1,210 | |
| **Creditors** | | |
| Amounts falling due after more than one year | (180) | (12) |
|  | 1,030 | |
| **Capital and reserves** | | |
| Called-up share capital | 560 | |
| Share premium account | 140 | |
| Profit and loss account (180 + 150) | 330 | |
|  | 1,030 | |

| Notes | | £000 |
|---|---|---:|
| (1) | Turnover | |

Turnover represents the amount received, net of VAT, for goods sold during the year.

(2) Operating profit
Operating profit is stated after charging:

| | | £000 |
|---|---|---:|
| | Depreciation | 80 |
| | Directors' emoluments | 110 |
| | Hire charges for distribution activities | 680 |
| | Auditors' remuneration | 40 |

(3) Other income
Other income arising from trade investments     30

(4) Interest
Interest payable on debenture stock     10

(5) Taxation
Taxation on the profit for the year:
UK corporation tax at 30%     100

(6) Dividends

| | | £000 |
|---|---|---:|
| | Ordinary – interim 2.5p per share | 14 |
| |      – proposed final 10p per share | 56 |
| | | 70 |

(7) Earnings per share
The calculation is based on 560,000 ordinary shares of £1 each in issue during the year.

(8) Tangible fixed assets

| | | | £000 |
|---|---|---:|---:|
| | Furniture and fittings at cost | | 400 |
| | *Less:* Accumulated depreciation to 31 Jan 19X9 | £200 | |
| |     Depreciation for the year | 80 | 280 |
| | | | 120 |

(9) Investments
Shares at cost in respect of investments listed on a recognized stock exchange (market value £170,000)

(10) Debtors

| | | | £000 |
|---|---|---:|---:|
| | Trade | 360 | |
| | Prepaid expenses | 140 | 500 |
| | Amount falling due within one year | | 58 |
| | | | 558 |

(11) Creditors: Amounts falling due within one year

| | | £000 |
|---|---|---:|
| | Trade creditors | 120 |
| | Taxation | 100 |
| | Accruals | 50 |
| | Proposed dividend | 56 |
| | | 326 |

(12) Creditors: Amounts falling due after more than one year

| | | £000 |
|---|---|---:|
| | Debenture loans | 100 |
| | Deferred taxation | 80 |
| | | 180 |

Workings

1    Cost of sales

| | |
|---|---:|
| Opening stock | 400 |
| Purchases | 1,000 |
| | 1,400 |
| *Less:* Closing stock | 600 |
| Cost of sales | 800 |

## Chapter 15  Cash flow statements

### Solutions to problems

**1**
**South Ltd**
**Cash flow statement for the year ended 31 December 20X0**

| | £000 | £000 |
|---|---:|---:|
| Net cash inflow from operating activities | | 5,035 |
| Returns on investments and servicing of finance | | |
|    Interest received | | 2,290 |
| Corporation tax paid | | (2,460) |
| Capital expenditure | | |
|    Payments to acquire intangible fixed assets | (150) | |
|    Payments to acquire tangible fixed assets | (2,540) | |
|    Receipts from sales of tangible fixed assets | 96 | |
| Net cash outflow from capital expenditure | | (2,594) |
| | | 2,271 |
| Dividends paid | | (1,570) |
| | | 701 |
| Financing | | |
|    Issue of ordinary share capital | 400 | |
|    Expenses paid in connection with share issues | (10) | |
| Net cash inflow from financing | | 390 |
| Increase in cash and cash equivalents | | 1,091 |

| Notes to the cash flow statement | £000 |
|---|---:|
| 1  Reconciliation of operating profit to net cash inflow from operating activities | |
|    Operating profit | 4,100 |
|    Depreciation charges | 1,080 |
|    Loss on sale of tangible fixed assets | 20 |
|    Increase in working capital | (165) |
| | 5,035 |

2
**Walkley Ltd**
**Cash flow statement for the year ended 31 December 20X1**

|  | £000 | £000 |
|---|---|---|
| Net cash inflow from operating activities |  | 912 |
| Corporation tax paid |  | (470) |
| Payments to acquire fixed assets | (1,200) |  |
| Receipts from sales of fixed assets | 41 |  |
| Net cash outflow from capital expenditure |  | (1,159) |
|  |  | (717) |
| Dividends paid |  | (230) |
|  |  | (947) |
| Financing |  |  |
| Issue of share capital | 300 |  |
| Issue of loan capital | 65 |  |
| Repayment of loans | (235) |  |
| Net cash inflow from financing |  | 130 |
| Decrease in cash |  | (817) |

**Notes to the cash flow statement**

|  | £000 |
|---|---|
| 1 Reconciliation of operating profit to net cash inflow from operating activities |  |
| Operating profit | 1,195 |
| Depreciation charges | 401 |
| Loss on sale of fixed assets | 4 |
| Increase in stocks | (640) |
| Increase in debtors | (37) |
| Decrease in creditors | (11) |
| Net cash inflow from operating activities | 912 |

4
**Zepf and Co Ltd**
**Cash flow statement for the year ended 31 December 20X1**

|  | £000 | £000 |
|---|---|---|
| Net cash inflow from operating activities |  | 204 |
| Corporation tax paid |  | (60) |
| Capital expenditure |  |  |
| Payments to acquire fixed assets | (460) |  |
| Receipts from sale of fixed assets | 6 |  |
| Net cash outflow from capital expenditure |  | (454) |
|  |  | (310) |
| Dividends paid |  | (16) |
|  |  | (326) |
| Financing |  |  |
| Issue of debenture loan |  | 60 |
| Decrease in cash |  | (266) |

Notes to the cash flow statement

|  | £000 |
|---|---|
| 1 Reconciliation of operating profit to net cash inflow from operating activities | |
| Operating profit | 180 |
| Depreciation charges | 68 |
| Loss on sale of fixed assets | 10 |
| Increase in stocks | (30) |
| Increase in debtors | (72) |
| Increase in creditors | 48 |
| Net cash inflow from operating activities | 204 |

## Chapter 16 Interpreting and comparing financial reports

### Solutions to problems

**1**

(a) Current ratio = $\dfrac{\text{Current assets}}{\text{Current liabilities}}$

We need first to define what we mean by 'current assets' and 'current liabilities'. For this exercise current assets are relatively straightforward being shown at book values. However, should current liabilities include taxation and dividends? We shall make the (reasonable) assumption that taxation will be payable in a short time, and the more heroic assumption that the same applies to dividends. However, this highlights a difficulty in this type of analysis because every approach we adopt will produce a potentially misleading position. If we exclude tax and dividends, we produce a misleading ratio in that we are hiding the fact that these amounts are payable, thereby producing a higher ratio than might otherwise be the case. If we include tax and dividends, we might also produce a misleading picture, since these liabilities will not appear throughout the year. On balance, it is probably better to include tax and dividends in current liabilities, but this is an interesting point for discussion and may help in educating students about the difficulties that are inherent in ratio analysis.

| 20X2 | 20X1 |
|---|---|
| $\dfrac{635 + 425 + 40}{496 + 15 + 52 + 30}$ | $\dfrac{600 + 410 + 55}{493 + 17 + 43 + 25}$ |
| = 1.85:1 | = 1.84:1 |

(b) The acid test ratio is one where definitions (and interpretation) can be extremely difficult. The traditional definition has been that of the current ratio but with stock being deducted from the numerator. However, it should be recognized that, for many types of business, the ratio will be rather meaningless. This is most obvious in the case of the cash retailer with a rapid stock turnover, e.g. a good retailer such as a supermarket. In companies like this, the 'currentness' of stock will match that of trade creditors and it is thus difficult in the extreme to justify the use of the traditionally defined acid test ratio. Clearly, supermarkets represent a special case, but the general principle raised should be remembered when attempting to interpret such a ratio.

If we assume in this case that it is reasonable to exclude stocks and still derive a meaningful ratio, we would arrive at the following:

$$\begin{array}{cc}
\textbf{20X2} & \textbf{20X1} \\
\dfrac{425 + 40}{496 + 15 + 52 + 30} & \dfrac{410 + 55}{493 + 17 + 43 + 25} \\
= 0.78:1 & = 0.80:1
\end{array}$$

(c) The major difficulty in calculating average stock turnover is that we do not know what 'average stock' is. We are forced into an assumption that (opening stock + closing stock) ÷ 2 is a reasonable approximation, but it should be remembered that seasonal patterns of sales and/or upturns/downturns in sales during the period around the year end would seriously affect the reliability of this approximation. Allowing for this we find stock turnover of:

$$\begin{array}{ccc}
& \textbf{20X2} & \textbf{20X1} \\
\text{Cost of sales} & \dfrac{600,000}{(635,000 + 600,000) \div 2} & \dfrac{550,000}{(600,000 + 520,000) \div 2} \\
& = 0.97 \text{ times} & = 0.98 \text{ times}
\end{array}$$

i.e. less than once a year.

(d) As with stock turnover, we lack information concerning the average level of debtors and are thus forced to adopt an approximation. Often the simplest solution (i.e. using the closing debtors) is adopted, although in this case we will use an average based on opening and closing debtors. However, it should be remembered that year-end debtors are most closely related to sales in the period immediately preceding the year end. The correct way to assess days' sales in debtors would be to work back through the sales day book, but it is recognized that this course will, generally, be unavailable.

Our approximation will thus be:

$$\dfrac{(\text{opening} + \text{closing debtors}) \div 2 \times 360}{\text{sales}}$$

$$\begin{array}{cc}
\textbf{20X2} & \textbf{20X1} \\
\dfrac{(425 + 410) \times 180}{1,000} & \dfrac{(410 + 440) \times 180}{900} \\
= 150 \text{ days} & = 170 \text{ days}
\end{array}$$

(e) As a measure of gearing, the shareholders' equity ratio is much less problematical than the ratios that have gone before. It simply expresses shareholders' equity as a percentage of assets. One minor difficulty is whether we should use gross assets or net assets. Both are useful measures which convey slightly different information. We will use gross assets as our measure here.

$$\begin{array}{cc}
\textbf{20X2} & \textbf{20X1} \\
\dfrac{(600 + 125 + 532) \times 100}{2,050} & \dfrac{(600 + 125 + 512) \times 100}{2,015} \\
= 61.3\% & = 61.4\%
\end{array}$$

(f) The return on capital employed ratio also requires some definition as there are a number of alternatives. However, it is generally accepted that the most useful definition is that of net profit before interest and tax divided by net capital, i.e. shareholders' equity plus any other long-term sources of finance (debentures, long-term loans, etc.).

| 20X2 | 20X1 |
|---|---|
| $\dfrac{100}{600 + 125 + 532 + 200}$ | $\dfrac{75}{600 + 125 + 512 + 200}$ |
| $= 6.86\%$ | $= 5.2\%$ |

It should, however, be noted that we have included the closing profit and loss account balances in our denominator and it might be argued that either the opening figure or some estimate of an average for the year might be more meaningful.

(g) Earnings per share is a more straightforward ratio to define since this is described in FRS 14 which states that 'earnings per share . . . should be calculated and disclosed on a comparable basis . . . so far as this is possible'. It is defined as:

> *The profit in pence attributable to each equity share base on the consolidated profit of the period after tax and after deducting minority interests, preference dividends and extraordinary items, divided by the number of equity shares in issue and ranking for dividend in respect of the period.*

| 20X2 | 20X1 |
|---|---|
| $\dfrac{50}{600} \times 100$ | $\dfrac{37.5}{600} \times 100$ |
| $= 8.33\text{p}$ | $= 6.25\text{p}$ |

It is very difficult to assess the liquidity position of the company in any useful sort of way apart from saying that its position as regards current asset type ratios is much the same in 20X2 as it was in 20X1, as is its gearing position. Whether it is in a strong or weak position is impossible to say without access to much more information.

3 Since Jack and Jill appear to be very similar, we are in a position to attempt a comparison through the use of accounting ratios.

**Profitability**

Return on capital:

| Jack | Jill |
|---|---|
| $\dfrac{8,640}{108,000}$ | $\dfrac{7,700}{30,800}$ |
| $= 8\%$ | $= 25\%$ |

Although the companies are supposed to be similar, Jill is operating on 28.5% of the capital of Jack. This may imply either that Jack is much less efficient in the use of assets than Jill or that Jack's and Jill's assets were acquired at different times and that interpretation is hampered through the use of historic cost accounting data. This can be further emphasized by calculating the turnover of capital, i.e. sales ÷ net capital employed:

| Jack | Jill |
|---|---|
| $\dfrac{144,000}{108,000}$ | $\dfrac{140,000}{30,800}$ |
| $= 1.33$ times | $= 4.55$ times |

It is difficult to imagine that one business could make so much better use of its assets if they are indeed similar. It is, of course, possible for a business to be more capital-intensive than another similar business but we would expect this to show up in an improved net profit margin.

|                | Jack    | Jill    |
|----------------|---------|---------|
|                | 8,640   | 7,770   |
|                | 144,000 | 140,000 |
|                | = 6%    | = 5.5%  |

This would not appear to be significant enough to explain the difference in capital usage.

**Liquidity ratios**

If we now turn to the liquidity position of each company we find:

Current ratio:

$$\frac{\text{Jack}}{32 + 28.8 + 8.95} \qquad \frac{\text{Jill}}{4.8 + 11.2 + 11.36}$$
$$\frac{}{15.5} \qquad\qquad \frac{}{30.4}$$
$$= 4.5{:}1 \qquad\qquad = 0.9{:}1$$

Jack is clearly far more liquid than Jill and it is probably safe to suggest that Jack may not be controlling current assets sufficiently well. Jill may be slightly under-capitalized. However, if we consider the position with stocks excluded, we find:

$$\frac{\text{Jack}}{28.8 + 8.95} \qquad \frac{\text{Jill}}{11.2 + 11.36}$$
$$\frac{}{15.5} \qquad\qquad \frac{}{30.4}$$
$$= 2.4{:}1 \qquad\qquad = 0.74{:}1$$

If we assume that, in this case, stocks are not readily convertible into cash, we see that Jack still has very high coverage of creditors whilst Jill cannot cover creditors with short-term assets. There are potential problems here for Jill, but this might simply reflect an extremely effective use of resources and, since this is a sole trader, the proprietor may be in a position to solve the problems should they arise. Jack, on the other hand, carries far more stock than Jill and is also carrying far more non-productive short-term assets.

**Stock turnover**

Assuming opening and closing stock ÷ 2 as a reasonable approximation for average stocks, we find:

|                              | Jack              | Jill             |
|------------------------------|-------------------|------------------|
| Cost of sales × 2            | $120 \times 2$    | $120 \times 2$   |
| Opening + closing stock      | $28 + 32$         | $3.2 + 4.8$      |
|                              | = 4 times         | = 30 times       |

Clearly, this is an enormous difference. It seems that Jill operates in an entirely different way from Jack. However, is it possible to operate one business effectively with so little stock? Might it not be possible to reduce stock holdings for the other company as well? A similar result is found for days' sales in debtors:

$$\frac{\text{Jack}}{28.8 \times 365} \qquad \frac{\text{Jill}}{11.2 \times 365}$$
$$\frac{}{144} \qquad\qquad \frac{}{140}$$
$$= 73 \text{ days} \qquad\qquad = 29.2 \text{ days}$$

Again, Jill seems to be using assets much more efficiently.

It is possible to calculate many more ratios but the picture remains the same. Jack uses assets far less effectively than Jill (assuming their valuation to be on the same basis). But, at the same time, Jack would seem to be a more stable, safer, business than Jill.

However, it is not really possible to draw more significant conclusions than this without more information about the proprietors' circumstances. It would certainly make a difference if these were limited companies, as Jill's capital does not even cover long-term assets, an indication of overtrading.

**4**

(a)

|  | Us | Them |
| --- | --- | --- |
| Return on net assets | 11.2% | 11.5% |
| Sales/net assets | 0.67 times | 1.14 times |
| Sales/fixed assets | 0.73 times | 1.33 times |
| Net profit/sales | 16.8% | 10.04% |
| Gross profit/sales | 33.9% | 24.0% |
| Current ratio | 1.35:1 | 1.57:1 |
| 'Acid test' ratio | 0.87:1 | 0.81:1 |
| Debtor period | 106 days | 60 days |
| Creditor period | 126 days | 60 days |
| Stock turnover | 4.0 times | 5.1 times |

(b)

Improve utilization of fixed assets; dispose of surplus assets. Reduce prices to improve sales volume, asset utilization, stock turnover. Examine purchasing policy. Improve liquidity through actions to reduce and control stocks, debtors, creditors.

(c)

Different asset ages. Different accounting bases. Comparison with entire sector needed. Different stages in business cycle. Policy differences. Seasonal distortions.

# Chapter 17 Financial accounting for groups of companies

## Solutions to problems

**1** First we assume that the consolidation falls under the acquisition provisions rather than merger accounting provisions as set out in FRS 6.

**Workings**
Goodwill

|  | Paid £000 | Acquired £000 |
|---|---|---|
| Purchase price | 962 | |
| $\frac{2}{3}$ shares (600) | | 400 |
| $\frac{2}{3}$ reserves (312) | | 208 |
| | 962 | 608 |
| | 608 | |
| Goodwill | 354 | |

**Profit and loss**

|  | £000 |
|---|---|
| Macro | 4,050 |
| Post ac | 652 |
| Micro $\frac{2}{3}$ res (702 – 312) | 260 |
| $\frac{2}{3}$ profit (144) | 96 |
| Unrealized profit on inter-company sales | |
| $208 \times 33\frac{1}{3}/133\frac{1}{3}$ | (52) |
| | 5,006 |
| Minority interest $\frac{1}{3} \times (1,446)$ | 482 |
| Stocks 1,244 + 514 – 52 | 1,706 |
| Debtors 2,048 + 390 | 2,438 |
| Bank 960 + 46 + 17 | 1,023 |
| Creditors 2,825 + 634 | 3,459 |
| Tax 315 + 60 | 375 |
| Fixed assets 5,121 + 1,230 | 6,351 |

**Macro group consolidated balance sheet 20X0**

|  | £000 | £000 |
|---|---|---|
| Fixed assets | | 6,351 |
| Goodwill | | 354 |
| **Current assets** | | |
| Stocks | 1,706 | |
| Trade debtors | 2,438 | |
| Cash at bank | 1,023 | |
| | 5,167 | |
| Trade creditors | (3,459) | |
| Taxation | (375) | |
| Net current assets c/f | | 1,333 |

|  | £000 | £000 |
|---|---|---|
| Net current assets b/f |  | 1,333 |
|  |  | 8,038 |
| *Less:* Debenture loan |  | 750 |
|  |  | 7,288 |
| Share capital |  | 1,800 |
| Reserves |  | 5,006 |
| Minority interest |  | 482 |
|  |  | 7,288 |

## 2
**Workings (in 000s)**
Goodwill

|  | Paid £ | Acquired £ |
|---|---|---|
| Shares in S | 12,000 |  |
| $\frac{2}{3}$ Shares |  | 10,000 |
| $\frac{2}{3}$ P&L at acquisition |  | 2,666.667 |
|  | 12,000 | 12,666.667 |
|  |  | 12,000 |
|  |  | 666.667 |

|  |  |
|---|---|
| Minority interest |  |
| $\frac{1}{3}$ of 19,250 | 6,416.667 |
| P&L |  |
| Balance b/f | 10,000 |
| Profit for year (from P&L a/c) | 1,166.667 |
|  | 11,166.667 |
| Stocks 7,100 + 6,600 − 1,000* | 12,700 |
| Trade debtors 8,000 + 4,000 | 12,000 |
| Cash 3,400 + 2,400 | 5,800 |
| Trade creditors 12,000 + 10,250 | 22,250 |
| Fixed assets 40,000 + 20,000 | 60,000 |
| *unrealized profit |  |

### Consolidated profit and loss account

|  | £ | Notes |
|---|---|---|
| Turnover (300.8 + 150.5 − 15) | 436,300.000 |  |
| Cost of sales (116.9 + 59.4 − 15 + 1) | 162,300.000 | (1) |
| Gross profit | 274,000.000 |  |
| Expenses | 269,000.000 |  |
|  | 5,000.000 |  |
| Taxation | 3,500.000 |  |
|  | 1,500.000 |  |
| Dividend paid to minority | 250.000 |  |
| Retained profit | 1,250.000 |  |
| Minority interest in profit | 83.333 | (2) |
| Group profit for year | 1,166.667 |  |

**Notes**

(1) Holding company cost of sales + subsidiary company's cost of sales less inter-company sales plus unrealized profit in stock.

(2) $\frac{1}{3}$ of £250.000.

**Consolidated balance sheet**

|  | £000 | £000 |
|---|---|---|
| Tangible fixed assets |  | 60,000 |
| Shares in non-group companies |  | 3,000 |
|  |  | 63,000 |
| Stocks | 12,700 |  |
| Debtors | 12,000 |  |
| Cash | 5,800 |  |
|  | 30,500 |  |
| Trade creditors | (22,250) |  |
| Net current assets |  | 8,250 |
|  |  | 71,250 |
| *Less:* Debenture loan |  | (23,000) |
|  |  | 48,250 |
| Share capital |  | 30,000 |
| Capital reserve arising on consolidation |  | 667 |
| Profit and loss account |  | 11,167 |
| Minority interest |  | 6,416 |
|  |  | 48,250 |

**3**

**Workings**

**Goodwill**

| | Growing $\frac{2}{3}$ Paid £000 | Declining 80% Acquired £000 |
|---|---|---|
| Growing | 140 | |
| $\frac{2}{3}$ shares | | 100 |
| $\frac{2}{3}$ reserves | | 30 |
| Declining | 32 | |
| 80% shares | | 40 |
| 80% reserves | | – |
| | 172 | 170 |
| | 170 | |
| Goodwill on consolidation | 2 | |

**Profit and loss account**

|  | £000 |  |
|---|---|---|
|  | £000 |  |
| Expanding | 350 |  |
| Growing $\frac{2}{3} \times 60$ | 40 |  |
| Declining 80% × (15) | (12) |  |
| Unrealized profit in stock | (0.6) |  |
|  | 377.40 |  |
| Stocks 63 + 83 + 28 − 0.6 + 2 | 175.4 | (Stock in transit 2) |
| Debtors 60 + 36 + 15 | 111 |  |
| Cash 10 + 7 + 2 + 1 | 20 | (Cash in transit 1) |
| Fixed assets 525 + 210 + 60 | 795 |  |
| Creditors 120 + 68 + 46 | 234 |  |
| **Minority interest** |  |  |
| Growing $\frac{1}{3} \times 255$ | 85 |  |
| Declining 20% × 35 | 7 |  |
|  | 92 |  |

**Reconciliation of group balances**

|  | £000 |
|---|---|
| Expanding shows growing debtor | 24 |
| Growing shows expanding creditor | 22 |
| *Add:* Stock in transit | 2 |
|  | 24 |
| Expanding shows declining debtor | 16 |
| Declining shows expanding creditor | 16 |
| Growing shows declining debtor | 9 |
| *Less:* Cash in transit | 1 |
|  | 8 |
| Declining shows growing creditor | 8 |

**Expanding group consolidated balance sheet**

|  | £000 | £000 |
|---|---|---|
| Tangible fixed assets |  | 795 |
| Goodwill on consolidation |  | 2 |
|  |  | 797 |
| Stock | 175.4 |  |
| Debtors | 111 |  |
| Cash | 20 |  |
|  | 306.4 |  |
| Trade creditors | (234) |  |
| Net current assets |  | 72.4 |
|  |  | 869.4 |
| Called-up share capital |  | 400 |
| Profit and loss |  | 377.4 |
| Minority interests |  | 92 |
|  |  | 869.4 |

# Chapter 18  Understanding consolidated financial statements

## Solutions to problems

### 1
#### (i)  Subsidiary treatment

|  | Paid £000 | Acquired £000 |
|---|---|---|
| Goodwill | 2,000 | |
| 50% shares | | 500 |
| 50% reserves (1.9m) | | 950 |
| | 2,000 | 1,450 |
| | 1,450 | |
| Goodwill | 550 | |
| | | |
| Minority interest | | |
| 50% × 3,000 | 1,500 | |

| | |
|---|---|
| Tangible fixed assets | 6,500 + 4,000 = 10,500 |
| Current assets | 3,500 + 3,000 =  6,500 |
| Current liabilities | 4,550 + 2,500 =  7,050 |
| Debentures | 2,000 + 1,500 =  3,500 |

### Royal Group profit and loss account

| | £000 | R | B | Adj |
|---|---|---|---|---|
| Operating profit | 1,600 | 1,100 | 500 | |
| Taxation | (590) | (433) | (200) | 43 Tax credit |
| Profit after tax | 1,010 | | | |
| Minority share of profit | 150 | 50% × 300 | | |
| | 860 | | | |
| Dividends paid | 300 | | | |
| | 560 | | | |
| Balance b/f | 2,940 | 3,450 – 510 | | |
| Carried forward | 3,500 | | | |

### Royal Group balance sheet

| | £000 | £000 |
|---|---|---|
| Tangible fixed assets | | 10,500 |
| Goodwill | | 550 |
| Current assets | 6,500 | |
| Current liabilities | (7,050) | |
| Net current assets | | (550) |
| | | 10,500 |
| Debentures | | (3,500) |
| | | 7,000 |

|  | £000 | £000 |
|---|---|---|
| Share capital | | 2,000 |
| Reserves | | 3,500 |
| Minority interest | | 1,500 |
| | | 7,000 |

### (ii) Associate company treatment (equity)
#### Royal Plc profit and loss account

|  |  | £000 |  |
|---|---|---|---|
| Operating profit before tax | | 1,100 | |
| Share of profit of associate | | 250 | |
| | | 1,350 | |
| Taxation Royal | 390 | | |
| Share of associate's tax | 100 | 490 | |
| Profit after tax | | 860 | |
| Dividends paid | | 300 | |
| | | 560 | |
| Write-off of goodwill | | 550 | (see working above) |
| Retained profit | | 10 | |
| Retained profit b/f | | 2,940 | (see above) |
| Carried forward | | 2,950 | |

### Balance sheet

|  |  | £000 |  |
|---|---|---|---|
| Tangible fixed assets | | 6,500 | |
| Investment in associate | | 1,500 | (50% net assets) |
| | | 8,000 | |
| Current assets | 3,500 | | |
| Current liabilities | (4,550) | | |
| Net current assets | | (1,050) | |
| | | 6,950 | |
| Debenture | | 2,000 | |
| | | 4,950 | |
| Share capital | | 2,000 | |
| Reserves | | 2,950 | |
| | | 4,950 | |

### (iii) *Investment approach*

In this case the accounting statements as shown for Royal in the question would be unchanged. There would, however, be a note to the accounts showing the valuation of Butler at the accounting date as £2,050,000. The profit on the disposal would be taken in 20X1. In this case, it is clear that Royal did not invest in Butler with the intention of achieving long-term control since Butler was disposed of shortly after the accounting date. SSAP 14, para 2, states that 'the objective of group accounts . . . is to give a true and fair view of the profit and loss and of the state of affairs of the group'. Similarly in para 22 the statement says 'a subsidiary should be excluded from consolidation if . . . control is intended to be temporary'.

The statement then specifies valuation of the investment as the lower of cost or net realizable value and its inclusion in the balance sheet as a current asset.

There is little doubt that the investment approach provides the most reliable information in this case.

## 2
**Workings**
Value of shares acquired in Sition

| | | | | |
|---|---|---|---|---|
| 95% of 10,000 | | 9,500 | | |
| Consideration | book | | agreed | prop |
| Shares 9,500 × 8/10 | 7,600 | | 14,440 | 91% |
| Loan stock 9,500 × 1.5/10 | 1,425 | | 1,425 | 9% |
| | 9,025 | | | |
| Reserve arising on consolidation | | 475 | | |
| Goodwill in books of Sition | | 1,000 | | |
| Write-off at 20% p.a. | | 200 | | |
| Profit before tax reduced by | 200 | | | |
| P&L reduced by | 200 | | | |
| Goodwill reduced by | 200 | | | |
| Minority interest | | | | |
| 5% of 14,450 | 722.5 | | | |

### (1) Expo plc Consolidated profit and loss account

| | | |
|---|---|---|
| | | £000 |
| Turnover | 21,350 | |
| Profit before tax | 4,350 | (3,250 + 1,100) |
| Taxation | 620 | |
| | 3,730 | |
| Dividends | 1,200 | |
| | 2,530 | |
| Due to minority | 53.5 | |
| Retained profit | 2,476.5 | |
| Statement of retained earnings | | |

| | Group | Minority |
|---|---|---|
| Balance brought forward | 7,101 | 169 |
| Retained profit for year | 2,476.5 | 53.5 |
| | 9,577.5 | 222.5 |

Expo plc Consolidated balance sheet

|  | £000 |
|---|---|
| Fixed assets | 28,850 |
| Goodwill | 800 |
| Current assets | 10,200 |
| Current liabilities | (6,050) |
|  | 33,800 |
|  |  |
| £1 ordinary shares | 21,600 |
| Capital reserve on consolidation | 475 |
| Profit and loss | 9,577.5 |
| Minority interest | 722.5 |
| 15% loan stock | 1,425 |
|  | 33,800 |

(2) This requires coverage of the capitalization of pre-acquisition profits and the calculation of goodwill. Students should be aware of the fundamental differences in approach that allow for the alternative treatment of reserves. This also requires appreciation of 'fair' or agreed values compared with book.

(3) The third part of the question should produce an analysis of the information content of the two alternatives. It should include reference to the inconsistency produced by valuing the acquired companies at agreed value whilst the holding company is at historic cost.

# Chapter 19  Capital, value, income

## Answers to self-assessment questions

1 Accountants define capital by reference to the financial investment made in the enterprise by the owner(s). This financial investment consists of the personal capital that the owner(s) invested in the firm at the time of its creation, and the subsequent investments made, either in the form of further injections of personal capital or in the form of retained profits. The accounting value of the enterprise capital is shown in the capital account, and represents an eventual liability by the firm to repay the owner(s) on winding up the firm.

2 Economists define capital by reference to assets. In this sense, economic capital is the source of future income or profits when actively committed to business operations. Accordingly, economists define the capital of the business in terms of the assets found on the balance sheet, whereas accountants define capital in terms of the financial investment made by its owners and shown on the balance sheet as an equity by the owners in the assets of the business. In accounting, the capital of the business is interpreted as its net worth to the owners.

3 The concept of capital maintenance finds its significance in the measurement of business income or profit. Essentially, it is a criterion which evaluates income as a periodic surplus available for distribution. The strict condition imposed by the capital maintenance concept is that periodic income should be measured by reference to the value of the capital at the beginning and at the end of the year. If the value of the capital at the end of the year is larger than at the beginning (no further injections of capital having been made), the difference is income and it is available for distribution. This concept is linked to Hicks's definition of personal income as being that amount which a person may consume during a period, and as a result not be worse off at the end of the period than at the beginning.

4 Five concepts of capital maintenance are discussed in the literature:

(a) The money amount concept, which refers capital maintenance to the need to maintain the monetary value of the shareholders' equity constant.

(b) The investment purchasing power concept, which is based on the notion of economic income defined as being the present value of future cash flows generated by the firm's assets. Accordingly, the maintenance of capital is assured when the opening and closing value of the shareholders' equity based on this value remains constant.

(c) The financial capital concept, which requires that capital maintenance be assured by maintaining the financial value of shareholders' equity constant through adjustments to the historical cost of assets for changes in the value of money.

(d) The operating capability concept, which requires that the productive (operating) capacity of the firm should be maintained by making adequate provision for replacing asset values exhausted in the course of operations. This concept of capital maintenance is the main pillar supporting the case for replacement cost accounting.

(e) The disposable wealth concept, which suggests that the maintenance of capital should be viewed from the perspective of the realizable value of assets. It is based on the proprietorship theory of the firm, and views capital from the strict viewpoint of the owners of the business.

5 The general consensus is that the operating capability concept of capital maintenance is the most appropriate both for corporate shareholders and managers. It has been the major theoretical support for the use of replacement costs in measuring business income. From a management viewpoint, it ensures that the operating capability is maintained by providing for the replacement of assets as they are used in operating, and avoids the problem of excessive distributions to shareholders. From the viewpoint of corporate shareholders, some may argue that either the disposable wealth or the financial capital concept may be more relevant in making sell-or-buy decisions. However, the majority opinion has supported the relevance of the operating capability concept for shareholders' decision making.

6 Accountants measure business income on a periodic basis by identifying the revenues of the period and the expenses of the period. Hence, the measurement of business income results from a process of accruing revenues and expenses to an accounting period, and matching expenses with the revenues that they have produced. It should be noted that the principle of prudence requires losses to be recognized as soon as they are considered to have occurred. Consequently, some of the expenses charged against the revenues of a period are considered as expenses of the period rather than expenses of earning the revenues of that period.

7 Income measurement is relevant to the following decisions:

(a) for evaluating business efficiency in terms of profitability;

(b) for making investment decisions on the basis of the expected future cash flows resulting from different alternatives;

(c) for evaluating managerial performance both by reference to the effectiveness of managerial decisions and as stewards of business capital;

(d) as a basis on which annual income tax declarations may be made to the Inland Revenue. The tax authorities generally accept accounting conventions used in measuring business profits when preparing tax assessments;

(e) as a guide to creditworthiness, on the principle that if a business is profitable it is able to pay its debts;

(f) as a guide to socio-economic decisions, for example, in wage-bargaining situations where the ability of the firm to afford bonuses and pay increases may depend upon current profits;

(g) as a guide to dividend policy, for, generally, the ability to pay dividends depends upon the existence of profits, either current or past profits that may justify such dividends.

8 The meaning of 'value' has been the subject of considerable debate in the literature of economics. It finds its significance in the context in which it is used. Value has been associated with the notion of usefulness or utility. In that context, major problems have been encountered in measuring value in terms of utility. Another aspect is the notion of 'worth', which may be linked with the notion of capital. Capital is an economic and accounting concept of considerable significance. The notion of 'value' is also used as a measurement base. In this sense, one may refer to cost value, market value, etc. The terms value, capital and income form part of a complex of theoretical concepts concerning economic and accounting income.

9 The term 'valuation' refers to the measurement base by which value is determined. Commonly, value is established by reference to money as an exchange standard. In this sense, both economics and accounting utilize money value as a measurement base. Acquisition or input values, defined as historic cost, and realization or output values, defined as market values, also illustrate other approaches to valuation. These valuation bases are found in the measurement of accounting income. The 'present value' concept is an attempt to value on the basis of the current value of future expected cash flows. This notion of value is used in the measurement of economic income.

10 From the foregoing, it is evident that the use of different valuation bases in the measurement of capital and income will produce different conclusions or results. This may be seen from alternative valuations implied in different notions of capital maintenance, that result in different measurements of capital and income. The significance of these different values lies, therefore, in the problem of selecting the most relevant values for decision making.

## Chapter 20  Accounting and economic concepts of income and value

### Answers to self-assessment questions

1 The basis of valuation in accounting is historical cost. Underlying this convention is the assumption that the money measurement standard is stable through time. Given that this assumption is in practice false, its use leads to serious distortions in the measurement of income when the value of money changes through time. These distortions result from the fact that the historical cost of items charged as expenses is less than their current replacement cost. Consequently, historic cost profit is overstated, leading to excessive taxation on profit and the possibility of excessive distributions. Accordingly, the firm may be unable to finance the replacement cost of assets, and to maintain its operating capability.

2 The historic cost convention likewise leads to balance sheet valuation of assets being understated by reference to their current replacement cost. Asset values being understated, it follows that the value of the firm is itself understated. Conversely, liabilities that have been expressed at their historical cost will be exaggerated in real terms at a rate corresponding to the rate of monetary inflation. These distortions are aggravated in direct proportion as the time gap lengthens between the entry date and the current year.

3 The modifications to historic cost accounting that need to be made to improve the quality of information for financial reporting are to be found in the selection of appropriate methods for correcting the instability of the money value measurement standard. Under conditions of zero price changes, historic cost accounting does not, of itself, distort the measurement of income or balance sheet values. It is only when price levels change that distortions appear. The translation of historic cost values into their current values is a problem that has been much discussed. Several different concepts and methods have been proposed, including indexing to assure constant purchasing power, and using current replacement costs.

4 The significance of the realization convention lies in the timing of the recognition of changes in values for the purpose of income measurement and balance sheet presentations. In effect, in accordance with the realization convention changes in value are not recorded until they have crystallized through a transaction. Accountants justify their attachment to the realization convention because a realized transaction assures an objective and verifiable measure of a change in value, and also because a sale is the most decisive and significant event in the chain of transactions that make up business activity. None the less, the use of the realization convention may occasionally lead to absurd results.

5 The essential differences between the accounting and the economic approaches to income measurement stem from the transaction-based approach used in accounting to measure a historic result, and the economic approach that attempts to provide guidelines for consumption decisions. The transaction approach identifies revenues and expense transactions as relevant to the measurement of periodic income in an operational context. This implies that transactions that have an income-earning objective are segregated from those that are in the nature of investment. The latter are shown as balance sheet values. Accordingly, the measurement of accounting income is a matter of preparing a periodic profit and loss account of operating transactions. The economic approach looks to changes in balance sheet values as affording a method of measuring periodic income. It does not require, as does the accounting approach, that changes in values be realized.

6 Hicks defined individual income as the amount that a man can consume during a period and still remain as well off at the end of the period as he was at the beginning. This definition links the measurement of income to the valuation of capital or wealth. It expresses income as limiting consumption to the maximum that may be consumed without eating into capital. Hicks's definition of income poses a measurement problem, since it requires an individual to estimate what can be consumed between two different points in time. The 'ex-ante' approach to economic income is really the only one that is relevant to the stream of consumption decisions that are made between two points in time. This requires the individual to have information about the year-end situation from the perspective of the beginning of the year.

7 Alexander extended Hicks's definition of individual income to the statement of business income. According to Alexander, the definition of the income of a company is the amount that it may distribute to shareholders during a period and still be as well off at the end of the year as it was at the beginning. Alexander's definition suffers from the same measurement problems as those that affect Hicks's concept of individual income, namely, the inability to estimate with certainty the situation at year end from the perspective of the situation at the beginning of the year.

8 In economics, income and value are closely related in the measurement of economic income, since income is a result of changes in value between two points in time. The economic concept of income treats asset values of all kinds as representing expected future receipts. They are discounted to their present value to give in aggregate terms a valuation of present well-offness, or capital. It is the change in the perception of the value of future expected net receipts between two points in time that affords a measure of disposable income.

9 The 'ex-ante' approach to the measurement of economic income implies that income is measured from the standpoint of the beginning of the period by comparing the present situation with the situation at the end of the period. Since income is used as a guide to consumption in economics, the 'ex-ante' approach is fraught with uncertainty, since it relies extensively on forecasting. The 'ex-post' approach is historic in nature since the measurement of income is effected at the end of the period, rather than at the beginning of the period.

10 The major problems that are to be found in applying economic concepts of income and value to accounting measurements lie in the measurement problems implied in making the necessary forecasts of future expected receipts. These forecasts are information requirements both for asset valuations and for the measurement of periodic income. Many would agree that economic concepts provide valuations that are more relevant for decision making, but they also recognize the difficulties of providing the degree of objectivity that accountants seek. As noted, accountants seek objectivity in the notion of verifiability. This is obtained through transaction-based information.

## Chapter 21 Accounting for changing prices

### Answers to self-assessment questions

1 One of the major criteria of the quality of any form of data is that it should not have a fluctuating meaning, that is, a value that is unstable. Accounting data are transaction-based, and measured in terms of the money value established at the date of transaction. The application of historic cost accounting under conditions of price level changes means, in effect, that goods and services recorded as acquisition costs will be valued in terms of their exchange rate against money at the date of the transaction. Under conditions of inflation, for example, the purchasing power of money over goods and services decreases through time. The result is that exactly similar goods and services acquired at different dates are represented as items of different accounting value. Thus, being unable to portray in a reliable manner the goods and services that are being recorded, the recording process registers misleading data.

2 Current purchasing power accounting involves correcting for changes in the purchasing power of money over goods and services by reference to general price level changes. For accounting purposes, it does not involve altering the money value of recorded transactions, but, for the purposes of financial reporting only, restating the historical money values at the date of transaction to their current money values at the end of the accounting period. In effect, current purchasing power accounting means dealing with the instability of the money measurement standard by adjusting data to a common transaction date, assumed as the accounting year end.

   Current purchasing power accounting, known as constant dollar accounting in the USA, was introduced in the United Kingdom by SSAP 7, later withdrawn. It recommended the use of the Retail Price Index for converting historical costs into current purchasing power equivalent at year end.

3 The method used to convert historic cost profit into current purchasing power profit relies on adjusting the figures shown on the profit and loss account to the current purchasing power at the year end. This is effected by using the general index of price level changes across the year. Thus, if the index is 100 at the beginning of the year, and the index is 130 at the end of the year, the adjustment requires all values to be stated at the year-end index value.

   Essentially, the problem lies in selecting the appropriate conversion factor to convert individual items to the year-end index value. This means that such items as sales, purchases and expenses running across the year have to be converted upwards by reference to the index at transaction date and the index at year-end date. Some items, such as depreciation, may relate to depreciable assets existing at the beginning of the year. In this case, the adjustment will correspond to the change in the index across the full year.

4 The method used to restate a historic cost balance sheet into current purchasing power involves restating all balance sheet items to their year-end index value. Non-monetary items are not treated as suffering purchasing power gains or losses, and hold their value in real

terms. Hence, under current purchasing power accounting, these items are restated up to the year-end index value. The problem essentially lies in identifying the index value at the entry date of these items. For example, fixed assets existing at the beginning of the year and the accumulated depreciation thereon has to be converted up to the year-end index value from the year-beginning index value. Other assets, such as stocks acquired across the year, have to be up-valued from the index at acquisition date to year-end index value.

Monetary item balances established as closing balances are treated as having appeared at year-end index values and, therefore, do not require an upward adjustment.

5  The objectives of current value accounting lie in the reconciliation of the desirable aspects of economic concepts of income and value with conventional accounting concepts based on historic cost measurements. In this way, current value accounting seeks to provide a concept of income for financial reporting purposes that satisfies criteria of relevance and feasibility. Replacement cost and realizable value accounting are different forms of current value accounting.

6  Replacement cost accounting deals with two components of profits:

(a)  current operating profits, resulting from operating activities, which involves matching current revenues with the current cost of earning those revenues;

(b)  calculating holding gains or losses, that result from holding assets rather than from operating activities.

The distinction is important, since it it acknowledged that businesses are able to derive income either in the form of realized (operating) profits, or from increased asset value (holding gains) resulting from asset management decisions. These two aspects are recognized in the concept of economic income, but are not recognized in the conventional accounting concept of business income.

7  The value to the business criterion used in connection with current value accounting defines the value to the business of an asset as the maximum loss that the business would suffer if it were deprived of that asset. In most cases, that value would be the replacement cost of the asset.

## Solutions to problems

### 1 Vitex plc Calculation of the purchasing power gain or loss on monetary items

| | HC | | Factor | CPP | |
|---|---|---|---|---|---|
| | £ | £ | | £ | £ |
| Opening capital contributed | | 150,000 | 120/100 | | 180,000 |
| *Add:* Sales | | 200,000 | 120/120 | | 200,000 |
| | | 350,000 | | | 380,000 |
| | | | | | |
| *Less:* | | | | | |
| Purchases of equipment | 40,000 | | 120/100 | 48,000 | |
| Purchase of goods | | | | | |
| (i) index at 100 | 88,000 | | 120/100 | 105,600 | |
| (ii) index at 110 | 90,000 | | 120/110 | 98,182 | |
| Expenses | 32,000 | | 120/110* | 34,909 | |
| | | 250,000 | | | 286,691 |
| | | 100,000 | | | 93,309 |

*Based on the average index value for the year

| | | £ |
|---|---|---|
| Net current monetary items at 31 December 20X0 | | 100,000 |
| Adjusted monetary items at 31 December 20X0 | | 93,309 |
| Purchasing power gain | | 6,691 |

In addition, the purchasing power gain on the long-term balance due on equipment is:

| | | |
|---|---|---|
| £50,000 × 120/100 = | 60,000 | |
| less sum due | 50,000 | |
| | | 10,000 |

**Profit and loss account for the year ended 31 December 20X0**

| | HC | | Factor | CPP |
|---|---|---|---|---|
| | £000 | | | £000 |
| Sales | 200 | | 120/120 | 200 |
| *Less:* Cost of sales | 120 | | see below | 140.5 |
| Gross profit | 80 | | | 59.5 |
| *Less:* Expenses | | 32 | 120/110 | (34.9) |
| Depreciation | | 9 | 120/100 | (10.8) |
| | | 41 | | |
| | | 39 | | 13.8 |

| | £ |
|---|---|
| Cost of sales comprises £88,000 bought at index 100, CPP equivalent = | 105,600 |
| Cost of sales comprises £32,000 bought at index 110, CPP equivalent = | 34,909 |
| | 140,509 |

**Balance sheet as at 31 December 20X0**

| | HC | Factor | CPP | |
|---|---|---|---|---|
| | £000 | | £000 | |
| Fixed assets | | | | |
| Equipment (cost) | 90 | 120/100 | | 108.0 |
| *Less:* Acc dep | 9 | 120/100 | | 10.8 |
| | 81 | | | 97.2 |
| Current assets | | | | |
| Stocks | 58 | 120/110 | 63.3 | |
| Trade debtors | 36 | 120/120 | 36 | |
| Bank | 81 | 120/120 | 81 | |
| | 175 | | 180.3 | |
| *Less:* Creditors | | | | |
| Amounts due within one year | | | | |
| Trade creditors | 17 | 120/120 | 17 | |
| | | 158 | | 163.3 |

| | HC £000 | Factor | CPP £000 | |
|---|---|---|---|---|
| Total assets *less* current liabilities | 239 | | | 260.5 |
| *Less:* Creditors | | | | |
| Amounts due after one year | 50 | 120/120 | | 50 |
| | 189 | | | 210.5 |
| Capital and reserves | | | | |
| Issued share capital | 150 | 120/100 | | 180.0 |
| Profit and loss account | 39 | – | | 13.8 |
| | | 189 | | |
| Accumulated purchasing power gain | | *Note 1* | | 16.7 |
| | | | | 210.5 |

| | | | |
|---|---|---|---|
| *Note 1* | The accumulated purchasing power gain is made up of: | £000 | |
| | Purchasing power gain on monetary items | 6.7 | |
| | Purchasing power gain on long-term liability | 10.0 | |
| | | | 16.7 |

## Chapter 22 Reporting to investors

### Answers to self-assessment questions

1 The text suggests the main reasons: the present system is backward-looking, much emphasis is placed on a single measure of earnings and historical cost is used.

2 The efficiency of the market will be helped, the control of investors over managers will be improved, investors will have more useful information and the reputations of forward-looking entities will be improved.

3 It will assist investors in forming their own forecasts, management's view of the future outlook will be disclosed, it will help prevent abnormal returns and it will provide investors with a better basis for evaluating managerial performance.

4 *MCRV* argues that NRV is market-based, is readily understandable, removes the need for depreciation, produces additive numbers, improves comparability and improves liquidity information.

5 Quarterly reporting helps users with a longer-term focus, provides reliable information and reduces inside information problems.

6 The findings of efficient market research show (i) financial accounting information does have economic significance in that share prices react to new information, (ii) the market does not respond to earnings increases that result from cosmetic changes in accounting policies.

# Chapter 23  Reporting to employees

## Answers to self-assessment questions

1 See the seven points identified in the text.

2 The advantages of employee reports are that they should promote goal congruence if properly used. The intention is to improve communications and the employee's understanding of his role in the firm. Also, they foster public relations.

3 The minimum acceptable settlement comprises the following elements: (i) the cost of living, (ii) comparability and (iii) value added. See text for discussion.

4 The ability to pay is defined in the text as the distributable operating cash flows less the minimum required by those who have provided the capital. Problems arise from estimating cash flow projections. See the text for discussion. Other important factors are productivity data and the cost structure of the firm.

5 See the text which deals with a discussion of relevant issues.

# Chapter 24  Social accounting

## Answers to self-assessment questions

1 Three approaches to corporate social responsibilities are distinguished in the text: (i) the classic economic theory objective of profit maximization, (ii) the significance of social objectives in relation to profit maximization and (iii) the view that the firm should seek a satisfactory level of profit which is compatible with the attainment of a range of social goals.

2 Six areas are discussed in the text: environmental protection, energy saving, fair business practices, human resources, community involvement and product.

3 The text examines three surveys undertaken to establish the nature and extent of social responsibility disclosures in the annual accounts of companies. The surveys show that the trend of mandated disclosure is upward, reflecting an increased response to legislation. No such conclusion could be drawn from voluntary disclosures, although two areas, community involvement and product, indicate an upward trend of disclosure.

4 The implications of the increasing concern for green issues are considered in the text.

# Chapter 25  The processes of management

## Answers to self-assessment questions

1 Organizing involves setting up the administrative structure for implementing strategic decisions. It involves defining the tasks necessary to achieve strategic goals, determining who is to perform these tasks and assigning responsibility for their performance. The function of organizing is to coordinate these tasks in such a way that the organization is able to work efficiently in fulfilling its objectives.

2 The significance of the organizational structure lies in the manner in which tasks are structured in terms of different specialisms and areas of responsibility. A major purpose of any organizational structure is to facilitate the flow of information to and from decision makers. Management may be considered as a process of converting information into action. Hence, the organizational structure should be designed around information flows.

3 The term 'control' may be defined in a broad or in a narrow way. In a broad way, no distinction is made between planning and control. More narrowly, control may be defined as closely linked to planning in that its purpose is to ensure that the firm's activities conform to plans. It is effected by means of an information feedback system which enables performance to be compared with planned targets.

4 Communication involves linking all the management functions by transmitting information and instructions within the organization. Additionally, communication relates the organization to its environment by linking it to the suppliers of resources and to the consumers for whom its products are intended. A high degree of communication throughout the organization binds its various members together, uniting them in the pursuit of organizational objectives. Hence, an organization may be viewed not only as a decision-making system, but also as a communication system.

5 Motivation involves getting all members of an organization to work together and to put their maximum efforts into the realization of organizational objectives by improving their personal performance. The purpose of motivation is to increase the level of congruence between the personal objectives of individual members of the organization and the objectives that the organization as a whole seeks to attain.

6 Information is the integrating force that combines organizational resources into a cohesive whole directed towards the realization of organizational objectives. Since the quality of information available is crucial to the quality of decision making, an efficient and adequate information system is a prerequisite of managerial success. A management information system provides individual managers with the information they require for making decisions within their own areas of responsibility. It consists of a network of information flows to which each decision is related.

7 Different levels of management activity may be related to the three major areas of decision making, namely, strategic planning, management control and operational control. Strategic planning involves the determination of corporate objectives and goals, and developing broad policies by which they may be achieved. Management control is concerned with the implementation of the strategic plan, ensuring that the necessary resources have been obtained and that they are being used efficiently and effectively. Operational control is the process of ensuring that specific tasks are being carried out efficiently and effectively. It focuses on individual tasks.

## Chapter 26 Traditional cost accounting

### Answers to self-assessment questions

1 Costs are collected for the following four purposes:

(a) To assist in planning decisions, such as the determination of which products to manufacture, the quantities that should be produced and the prices at which they should be sold.

(b) To assist in the control of operations by maintaining and improving the efficiency with which resources are employed.

(c) To assist in the measurement of reported profits.

(d) To assist in the collective bargaining process.

2 The three elements of product costs comprise:

    (a) Direct material costs, that is, the material costs that can be directly associated with the finished product.

    (b) Direct labour costs, that is, the wages of workers directly associated with a particular finished product.

    (c) Factory overhead costs that include all the remaining manufacturing costs, after the direct costs have been determined. They include indirect materials, such as supplies of materials, indirect labour, such as the salary of inspectors, and cleaners, heat, light, power and depreciation of factory buildings, plant and equipment.

3 Manufacturing costs consist of the costs of transforming raw materials into finished products, namely direct materials, direct labour and factory overhead costs. Non-manufacturing costs comprise selling, administrative and financial costs that are not incurred in the manufacturing process. Consequently, the cost of sales is computed by reference to manufacturing costs only. Non-manufacturing costs are treated as 'period' costs and not 'product costs', and are expensed out against periodic profit.

4 The term 'full product cost' refers to the method of determining product cost per unit by calculating the total unit factory costs. The direct material costs are calculated by reference to the quantities of materials used per unit of the product and the materials' purchase price. The direct labour costs per unit are calculated by the labour time taken to complete the operations involved in making the product and the appropriate wage rates of the operative involved. Full product costing requires that factory overhead costs be apportioned to each unit of the product. This is effected by means of a factory overhead rate that is an allocation key.

5 The problems involved in accounting for overhead costs are found where factories produce more than one product. In this case, the ascertainment of full product costs per unit means that factory unit costs have to be apportioned to the units of the different products. Since factory overhead costs are collected by departments, problems are involved in apportioning such costs to unit of a particular product, as follows:

    (a) the allotment of factory overhead costs to production cost centres;

    (b) the allotment of production cost centre costs to individual products.

The presence of fixed overhead costs means also that the choice of an appropriate level of activity is critical to correctly apportioning overhead costs at the unit level.

6 Once factory overhead costs have been allotted to production cost centres, the recovery of such costs is effected by charging out (apportioning) them to units of the product through an overhead rate (sometimes known as an overhead allocation key). Three overhead rates commonly used are:

    (a) overhead rate based on direct labour costs per unit of the product;

    (b) overhead rate based on direct labour hours per unit of the product;

    (c) overhead rate based on machine hours per unit of the product.

7 The adoption of a plant-wide overhead rate means that all factory departments use the same overhead rate for allocating overhead costs. In effect, regardless of the specific nature of the operations needed for their manufacture, unit costs of the different products will include factory overhead costs charged out on the same basis. Thus, if one product is machine-intensive and another product is labour-intensive in the use of factory resources, the use of a plant-wide rate based on machine hours will load up factory overhead costs disproportionately on the product that is machine-intensive.

    More accurate and reliable measurements of full product costs per unit will be obtained where departments select an overhead rate that more correctly reflects the predominant nature of the resource used in each department. This will be very important as regards establishing reliable product pricing policies.

663

8 Four major types of product costing systems are:

  (a)  job order costing;
  (b)  contract costing;
  (c)  process costing;
  (d)  service costing.

Job order costing and contract costing are similar in that production is undertaken on the receipt of the client's order and to that client's specifications. The difference between these two systems lies essentially in that contract costing is used in the case of contracts that take more than one accounting period to complete. Costs are accumulated per job order or per contract.

Process costing is a method of product costing used by manufacturing companies engaged in the mass production of standardized products. Production is undertaken in anticipation of market demand, and finished products are stocked until they are sold. Product costs are accumulated by reference to a standard quantity of the product, expressed in terms of quantity, volume or weight, as the case may be.

Service costing is a special application of process costing used where services rather than products are supplied. Particular problems involve the selection of cost units in relation to which costs can be accumulated, and the selection of charging rates for services.

## Solutions to problems

### 1

(a)  Estimated cost of job enquiry number 876.

|  | £ | £ |
|---|---|---|
| Direct material |  | 1,000 |
| Direct labour |  |  |
|   Plating | 324 |  |
|   Welding | 42 |  |
|   Assembly | 20 | 386 |
|  |  |  |
| Indirect departmental costs* |  |  |
|   Plating | 197.6 |  |
|   Welding | 12.6 |  |
|   Assembly | 12.5 | 222.7 |
|   Total cost |  | 1,608.7 |

*Based on this year's budgeted rates per hour
  Plating £22,000/9,000 = £2.44
  Welding £9,000/10,000 = £0.90
  Assembly £5,000/4,000 = £1.25

(b)  If the customer accepts the estimated price, that is what should be charged for the completed job. The £1,608.70 calculated above is the cost of the job, which will be a starting point in the determination of the ultimate price, which will be set after considering factors such as the amount of spare capacity which the firm has, market conditions, alternative work which may be available and the attractiveness of doing work for this particular customer. From the information given, there is no way in which a price for the work can be estimated, but three considerations may be:

1 as an absolute minimum, assuming that there is spare capacity and that the indirect costs are all fixed, a price of £1,386 would recover all the incremental costs which are expected and would maximize the probability of getting the work, but it would result in no contribution being made;

2 the overhead cost in the Plating Department might be recalculated, since budgeted hours are less than last year's actual hours, this resulting in an increased overhead absorption rate which causes job costs to rise. If last year's actual hours are used, the rate per hour reduces to £2.20 (£22,000/10,000) in the Plating Department, which will reduce the charge to the job by 81 × (£2.44 − £2.20) = £19.44 and prevent a drop in activity from generating cost increases which cause further drops in activity;

3 in the long run, for all costs to be recovered and a profit to be made, the total costs of all the jobs undertaken have to be covered. For this job, therefore, long-run profitability would require a price in excess of £1,608.70.

## 3 Departmental overheads with capacity production

|  | Machining £ | Assembly £ | Canteen £ |
|---|---|---|---|
| Allocated overheads | 50,000 | 40,000 | 10,000 |
| Apportioned overheads |  |  |  |
| Rates (area) | 300 | 600 | 100 |
| Depreciation (equipment cost) | 3,000 | 6,000 | 300 |
| Light and power (Kw hours) | 180 | 330 | 90 |
|  | 53,480 | 46,930 | 10,490 |
|  |  |  | (10,490) |
| Re-apportionment of canteen costs |  |  |  |
| (No of employees) | 6,993 | 3,497 |  |
|  | 60,473 | 50,427 |  |
| Rate per hour |  |  |  |
| Machine (8,000) | £7.56 |  |  |
| Labour (12,000) |  | £4.20 |  |

Using normal capacity as an absorption base yields the following charge-out rates:

|  | | |
|---|---|---|
| Total cost | £60,473 | £50,427 |
| Normal hours, rate per hour |  |  |
| Machine (6,400) | £9.45 | – |
| Labour (9,600) | – | £5.25 |

With expected activity as a base:

|  | | |
|---|---|---|
| Total cost | £60,473 | £50,427 |
| Expected hours, rate per hour |  |  |
| Machine (5,600) | £10.80 | – |
| Labour (8,400) | – | £6.00 |

The above adjustments could have been calculated thus:

Machining rate per hour (capacity base) £7.56/0.8
= Normal capacity rate per hour, £9.45 × 0.8/0.7
= Budgeted rate per hour, £10.80.

*Report*

The above analysis demonstrates the difficulties involved in the use of overhead absorption rates:

(i) They are based on a subjective apportionment of cost over production centres (the 'benefit' principle).

(ii) No analysis of the cost by behaviour takes place.

(iii) The choice of activity level influences the charge-out rate quite substantially.

(iv) The determination of unit costs for 'general purposes' is not an adequate justification. It is not clear for example why overhead costs should be charged to products in parallel with production taking place.

(v) By setting an inappropriate overhead rate product cost can be distorted and poor decisions may result. If using expected hours as an absorption base a high overhead rate is the result, and this, if incorporated into a pricing decision may lead to overpricing and loss of orders.

**4**

**(a)**

| Expense (basis) | Total | Cutting | Cooking | Canteen | Maintenance |
|---|---|---|---|---|---|
| Indirect labour (given) | 340,000 | 120,000 | 140,000 | 30,000 | 50,000 |
| Consumables (given) | 82,000 | 24,000 | 32,000 | 20,000 | 6,000 |
| Heating and lighting (area) | 24,000 | 8,000 | 9,600 | 2,400 | 4,000 |
| Rent and rates (area) | 36,000 | 12,000 | 14,400 | 3,600 | 6,000 |
| Depreciation (capital values) | 60,000 | 30,000 | 24,000 | 2,000 | 4,000 |
| Supervision (number of employees) | 48,000 | 24,000 | 18,000 | 3,000 | 3,000 |
| Power (kWh) | 40,000 | 18,000 | 16,000 | 2,000 | 4,000 |
| | 630,000 | 236,000 | 254,000 | 63,000 | 77,000 |
| Canteen (number of employees) | | 33,600 | 25,200 | (63,000) | 4,200 |
| Maintenance (maintenance hours) | | | | | 81,200 |
| | | 46,400 | 34,800 | – | (81,200) |
| | 630,000 | 316,000 | 314,000 | – | – |

**(b)**

| Labour hours | 12,640 | |
|---|---|---|
| | = £25/direct labour hour | |
| Machine hours | 15,700 | |
| | = £20/machine hour | |

**(c)**

**Direct materials cost percentage**

This method is best used when the price of materials is constant and there is a direct relationship between the materials and labour costs incurred to manufacture the product. Consider the following example:

| | Job A £ | Job B £ | Budget £ |
|---|---|---|---|
| Materials | 250 | 100 | 150,000 |
| Labour | 100 | 100 | 92,000 |

The overheads charged to a job will be distorted. Job A is charged with a greater proportion of overheads than Job B even though the labour costs were the same.

**Direct wages cost percentage**

This method is best used when the wages rates are the same throughout the company and the same for each job.

**Prime cost percentage rate**

This method combines the faults of the direct materials cost percentage and the direct labour cost percentage rates.

Labour hours method could have been used in the cooking department. But on the basis of the labour hours and machine hours for this department it is obviously machine-intensive and, therefore, machine hours should be used.

(d)
The under/over-absorption figures are:

|  | Cutting | Cooking |
|---|---|---|
| Actual overheads | £310,000 | £312,000 |
| Absorbed overheads | 12,000 | 15,810 |
|  | × £25 | × £20 |
|  | = £300,000 | = £316,200 |
|  | = £10,000 under-absorbed | £4,200 over-absorbed |

# Chapter 27  ABC and JIT

## Answers to self-assessment questions

1  ABC assumes that it is activities which cause costs, not products. Cost drivers are used to assign overheads. Traditional product costing assigns production overheads to products using volume-based recovery bases.

2  Activities are analysed and defined. The cost driver for each activity is determined. Activity centres are identified. Costs are assigned to products.

3  A cost driver is the action or transaction that results in costs being incurred. It is related to an activity, e.g. the number of purchase orders drives material procurement costs.

4  Where the company (i) has overhead costs that are not proportional to the unit volume of individual products; (ii) has a highly automated production system; (iii) produces a wide variety of tailor-made products or services.

5  JIT aims to reduce costs by eliminating inventories and production delays. These costs are 'accepted' by traditional manufacturing.

6  JIT results in 'leaner' accounting systems.

## Solution to problem

1
(a)  Overhead rate = £220,000/4,000 = £55 per DLH

|  | Job 600 £ | Job 700 £ |
|---|---|---|
| Direct materials | 750 | 850 |
| Direct labour | 600 | 600 |
| Overhead* | 2,750 | 2,750 |
| Total cost | 4,100 | 4,200 |
| Units | 100 | 50 |
| Unit cost | £41 | £84 |

*Overhead assigned = £55 × 50 hrs = £2,750

(b)  Pool rates
Set-up:           £60,000/300 = £200 per set-up
Ordering:         £45,000/4,500 = £10 per order
Machine costs:    £90,000/18,000 = £5 per machine
Receiving:        £25,000/50,000 = £0.50 per part

|  | Job 600 £ | Job 700 £ |  |
|---|---|---|---|
| Direct materials | 750 | 850 | |
| Direct labour | 600 | 600 | |
| Overhead | | | |
| Set-ups | 200 | 200 | (£200 × 1; £200 × 1) |
| Ordering | 40 | 20 | (£10 × 4; £10 × 2) |
| Machine costs | 100 | 150 | (£5 × 20; £5 × 30) |
| Receiving | 10 | 20 | (£0.50 × 20; £0.50 × 40) |
| Total costs | 1,700 | 1,840 | |
| Units | 100 | 50 | |
| Unit cost | £17 | £36.80 | |

(c)  In a firm with product diversity and significant non-unit overhead costs, multiple rates using unit and non-unit drivers produce better cost assignments because the demands of the products for overhead activities are more fully considered. Specifically, there are three non-unit activities, causing £130,000 out of the £220,000 of overhead costs. These non-unit costs should be assigned using non-unit cost drivers.

## Chapter 28  Cost–volume–profit analysis

### Answers to self-assessment questions

1  Cost–volume–profit (CVP) analysis lies at the centre of short-term profit planning because of its wider application to a series of decision problems. In examining the relationship between costs and volume of output, CVP analysis is helpful in establishing an optimal volume of output in relation to costs that will maximize short-term profit. Likewise, it is helpful in determining a pricing strategy. CVP analysis is also relevant to the selection of the best sales mix, by selecting the most profitable combination of different products having regard to their cost and prices.

2  CVP analysis is widely used in profit planning because it focuses on the distinction between fixed and variable costs in analysing the consequence of changes in activity levels. Fixed costs are costs that are fixed or constant regardless of the volume of output. Consequently, there is implied a minimum level of output to cover fixed costs. Failure to reach this level will result in an accounting loss. Variable costs are costs that vary directly with the volume of output. The firm's cost structure analysed as between fixed and variable costs will determine its profitability at given levels of output, and reveal the consequence of changes in levels of output on profits.

3  Given the firm's cost structure, analysed as between fixed and variable costs, and the revenue associated with a given pricing policy, the break-even point signifies that level of activity at which the total revenues generated just cover total costs, producing a zero profit zero loss result.

4  Three methods are commonly used to calculate the break-even point. These are:

(a) the equation method in which the break-even point is found either in terms of the volume of output or volume of revenue through the following equation:

sales = variable costs + fixed cost + zero profit

(b) the contribution margin method that makes use of the contribution margin per unit of output to determine the number of units of output or the sales revenues required to reach the break-even level. For example, to calculate the break-even volume of output, the formula is:

$$x = \frac{\text{fixed costs} + \text{zero profit}}{\text{unit contribution margin}}$$

(c) the graph method, using a break-even chart, in which the revenue and the cost structure, analysed in terms of total costs made up of fixed and variable costs, is plotted to indicate the break-even point.

5  The profit–volume chart is a special type of break-even chart that is concerned with analysing profit and loss at different levels of activity. As in the case of the conventional break-even chart, the horizontal axis is used to measure the volume of output or sales in units, but the vertical axis is employed to measure the profit or loss at any given level. It represents a profit line at different levels with the break-even point indicated on the profit line.

6  Given that short-term profitability is dependent on four factors – fixed costs, variable costs, selling prices and sales volume – improvements in profitability may result from changes in any one of these factors. These changes may be analysed through the break-even chart. Thus, changes in fixed costs and variable costs will affect the break-even point differently, as will changes in selling prices and sales volumes.

7  The main limitations in using CVP lie in the assumptions upon which the analysis is based. These include the assumption that fixed costs are constant, and that both the variable cost and the revenue curves are linear over the relevant volume of output. It is also assumed that volume is the only factor affecting costs, and that the price both of the cost factors and of the product itself remain unaffected by changes in the volume of output. To overcome these limitations, it is necessary to limit the volume range to be examined, so that the behaviour of costs and revenue over the relevant range may be more reliably determined.

Despite its limitations, the real usefulness of CVP analysis is that it enriches the understanding of the relationship between costs, volume and profits, enabling management to make assumptions that will assist in the management of short-term profitability.

## Solutions to problems

1

|  | Per unit (£) | % |
|---|---|---|
| Selling price | 0.25 | 100 |
| Variable cost | 0.15 | 60 |
| Contribution | 0.10 | 40 |

(a)  £100,000/0.4                     = £250,000 sales value
                                        = 1m units

(b)  FC now £150,000
     break-even £150,000/0.1          = 1.5m bottles

(c)  Required profit £110,000

$$\frac{£100,000 + £110,000}{0.4} \qquad = £525,000$$

(d)  2,000,000 × 1.6     = 3,200,000 bottles
 3.2m × 0.10p – £150,000  = £170,000 profit

(e)  (i)   Assumption of cost linearity.
 (ii)  Difficulty in defining relevant range.
 (iii) Difficulty in separating cost into component parts.
 (iv) Assumption that all other variables remain constant – production methods, price levels, production efficiency.
 (v)  With multiple products, assumption of constant product mix.

**3**
(a)

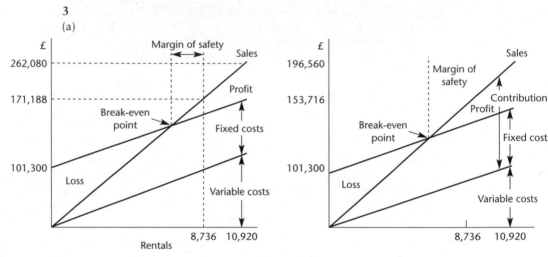

| Workings | | £ | | £ |
|---|---|---|---|---|
| Sales | 8,736 × £30 = | 262,080 | 6,552 × £30 = | 196,560 |
| Variable costs | 8,736 × £8 = | 69,888 | 6,552 × £8 = | 52,416 |
| Contribution | | 192,192 | | 144,144 |
| Fixed costs | | | | |
| $\left(\dfrac{65,000 + 39,000 + 75,000}{+ \ 23,600}\right) \div 2$ | | 101,300 | | 101,300 |
| Net profit | | 90,892 | | 42,844 |

(b)  $\dfrac{\text{Fixed costs}}{\text{Contribution/rooms}}$

 $= \dfrac{£101,300}{£22} \quad = 4,605 \text{ rentals}$

  = 177 per week
  = 25/day
  = 42% of capacity

(c)  $= \dfrac{£101,300}{£17} \quad = 5,959$

  = 229/week
  = 33/day
  = 55% of capacity

(d) The financial factors which would need to be taken into account should the hotel be closed for two months are:

- No saving on depreciation.
- There may be a saving on reception staff if they are employed on monthly contract.
- There would be some savings on repairs and maintenance and miscellanies.

The non-financial factors would be customer goodwill, loss of staff goodwill and, possibly, motivation.

An alternative strategy would entail reducing fixed and variable costs whilst attempting to increase the number of rooms booked.

(e) The limitations of break-even analysis are:

- The problem of classifying costs into fixed and variable.
- The assumption that costs and revenues behave in a linear fashion.
- The assumption that fixed costs will remain fixed.

These three limitations are all applicable here.

# Chapter 29 Marginal costing

## Answers to self-assessment questions

1 Marginal costing is a method of costing that records only variable costs for product costing. The analysis of costs as between fixed costs and variable costs identifies such costs in terms of their behaviour in relation to changes in activity levels. Fixed costs are those that are constant, irrespective of the level of activity, whereas variable costs are those that vary directly in terms of the activity level. Accordingly, marginal costing ignores fixed costs in determining product costs, and uses only variable cost information for that purpose.

2 Overhead costs are defined as indirect product costs that require to be allocated to product costs by an appropriate allocation key. The distinction between direct and indirect costs is used for product costing purposes under both absorption and marginal costing. The distinction between fixed costs and variable costs is used only for the purpose of analysing cost behaviour through different levels of activity. Absorption costing ignores this consideration in addressing the problem of product costing. Marginal costing considers that fixed costs should not be included as product costs. Therefore, absorption costing will include, under full product costs, direct and overhead costs, both fixed and variable, whereas marginal costing will include under product costs only variable direct and overhead costs.

3 Different profit results will be obtained using absorption costing and marginal costing whenever stock levels vary as a result of differences between sales levels and production levels. Given that the major difference between absorption costing and marginal costing is the valuation of stocks, either appearing as cost of sales in the year of sales, or carried forward to the following year as stocks, it follows that:

(a) where sales fluctuate but production remains constant, reported profits will be higher under marginal costing whenever stocks are reduced to support a volume of sales greater than the volume of production;

(b) where sales are constant but production fluctuates, reported profits will be higher under marginal costing whenever stocks are reduced because the volume of production is insufficient to meet the sales volume requirement.

## Solutions to problems

**1**

(a)

| | 20X0 £ | 20X1 £ | 20X2 £ |
|---|---|---|---|
| Sales revenue | 64,000 | 64,000 | 80,000 |
| cost of sales* | (40,000) | (40,000) | (50,000) |
| | 24,000 | 24,000 | 30,000 |
| (Under-) over-absorption | (4,000) | 4,000 | (8,000) |
| | 20,000 | 28,000 | 22,000 |
| Fixed selling and admin | 20,000 | 20,000 | 20,000 |
| Profit | – | 8,000 | 2,000 |

* Unit production cost £10 VAR + £40 Fixed = £50.

(b)  Contribution/unit = £70.

| | | | |
|---|---|---|---|
| Sales revenue | 64,000 | 64,000 | 80,000 |
| VAR costs | 8,000 | 8,000 | 10,000 |
| Contribution | 56,000 | 56,000 | 70,000 |
| Fixed units | 60,000 | 60,000 | 60,000 |
| Profit/(loss) | (4,000) | (4,000) | 10,000 |

(c)

| | | | |
|---|---|---|---|
| (i)   Absorption profit per (a) | £– | £8,000 | £2,000 |
| (ii)  Difference in stock levels (units) CS-OS | + 100 | + 300 | – 200 |
| (iii) Fixed production overload cost/unit | £40 | £40 | £40 |
| (iv) Additional MC charge (Credit) to profit | £4,000 | £12,000 | £(8,000) |
| (v)  Marginal costing profit (i)–(ii) | £(4,000) | £(4,000) | £10,000 |

(d)  In part (a) an absorption costing approach is used. Fixed production overhead costs are unitized and charged to products on the 'cost attach' principle, any eventual over- or under-recovery of these overhead costs being written off at the end of the year in the profit and loss account. This method, when production exceeds sales, results in the carrying forward in stock valuation of a proportion of the fixed production overhead costs, which in a marginal costing system would be written off. A marginal costing system would treat all fixed costs as period costs, writing them off in the period of incurrence. Thus, when stocks are rising absorption costing will report higher profits, while when sales are in excess of production marginal costing profits will be higher. Over the life of a business, or over a period in which opening and closing stock levels are identical, both methods will yield the same profit figure.

**2**

(a)

| | | 20X0 | | 20X1 |
|---|---|---|---|---|
| Selling price | | £80 | | £90 |
| Variable production cost | | 48 | | 55 |
| Variable selling/admin cost | | 2 | | 3 |
| Contribution | | 30 | | 32 |
| Fixed overhead absorption rate/unit | | | | |
| | 170,000 | | 180,000 | |
| | 28,000 | £6.07 | 28,000 | £6.43 |
| Absorption unit cost | | £54.07 | | £61.43 |

**Marginal costing**

|  | 20X0 £ |
|---|---|
| Sales 20,000 × £80 | 1,600,000 |
| Variable cost 20,000 × £50 | 1,000,000 |
| Contribution | 600,000 |
| Fixed factory overheads | 170,000 |
|  | 430,000 |

|  | 20X1 £ |
|---|---|
| Sales 25,000 × £90 | 2,250,000 |
| Variable cost (2,000 × £51) + (23,000 × £58)* | 1,436,000 |
|  | 814,000 |
| Fixed factory overheads | 180,000 |
| Profit | 634,000 |

Closing stock valuation 1,500 × £55 = £82,500

*OS brought forward in 20X1 will be sold in 20X1 at 20X1 level of variable selling costs (£3).

**Note**

In the following calculations, computations are based on unrounded unit costs.

**Absorption costing**

|  |  | 20X0 |
|---|---|---|
|  | £ | £ |
| Sales revenue |  | 1,600,00 |
| Opening stock 1,500 × £54.07* | 81,105 |  |
| Production cost 20,500 × £54.07 | 1,108,435 |  |
|  | 1,189,540 |  |
| Closing stock 2,000 × £54.07 | 108,140 |  |
| Costs of sales |  | 1,081,428 |
|  |  | 518,573 |
| Under-absorption 7,500 × £6.07 |  | 45,536 |
| Selling and admin costs |  | 473,036 |
|  |  | 40,000 |
| Profit |  | 433,036 |

\* Assumption that OS in 20X0 is valued as per 19 × 5 standard costs.

|  |  | 20X1 |
|---|---|---|
|  | £ | £ |
| Sales revenue |  | 2,250,000 |
| Opening stock (b/f) | 108,143 |  |
| Production cost 24,500 × £61.43 | 1,505,000 |  |
|  | 1,613,143 |  |
| Closing stock 1,500 × £61.43 | 92,143 |  |
| Cost of sales |  | 1,521,000 |
|  |  | 729,000 |
| Under-absorption 3,500 × £6.43 |  | 22,500 |
|  |  | 706,500 |
| Selling and admin costs |  | 75,000 |
| Profit |  | 631,500 |

|  |  | £ | 20X1 £ |
|---|---|---|---|
| **(b) Reconciliation** | | | |
| 20X0 | Marginal profit | | 430,000 |
| | *Add:* Fixed overhead | | |
| | C/F in stock increase | | |
| | 500 × £6.07 | | 3,036 |
| | Absorption profit | | 433,000 |
| 20X1 | Marginal profit | | 634,000 |
| | Fixed overhead B/F in | | |
| | absorption OS | | |
| | 2,000 × £6.07 | 12,143 | |
| | Fixed overhead C/F in | | |
| | absorption CS | | |
| | 1,500 × £6.43 | 9,643 | |
| | Reduction in absorption profit | | 2,500 |
| | Absorption profit | | 631,500 |

The differences in profit figures are caused by the different treatments of fixed production overheads, which are all written off as period costs in marginal costing systems, while a proportion is carried forward in stock valuation in absorption costing systems. The above reconciliation shows why the profit figures differ.

(c) **Advantages and disadvantages of marginal costing**

| Advantages | Disadvantages |
|---|---|
| Useful information for decision making being based on cost behaviour. | Not in accordance with SSAP 9. |
| Removes the effect of stock level changes on profit. | May be less useful for long-term pricing or contract pricing on a cost-plus basis. |
| Avoids inclusion of fixed overheads in unmarketable stock valuations. | May lead to less attention being accorded to fixed cost – possibly the most significant area of cost. |
| More prudent. | |
| Gives less ambiguous contribution figure rather than product profits with multi-product production. | |

# Chapter 30 Pricing

## Answers to self-assessment questions

1 Profits are a function of two elements, namely revenues and costs. Profitability may be improved, all things being equal, if sales revenues can be increased through price changes. It follows that a firm's relationship with the market for its products and services is intimately linked in one important respect to its pricing policy. Therefore, management needs to formulate a pricing strategy that takes into account the likely effect of price changes on the market's demand for its products. As a result, it will be able to plan a level of activity that,

given the firm's cost structure, will produce the required profit. Pricing may be viewed as having both short-term and long-range implications. Any alteration in the level of demand for the firm's products resulting from its pricing policy will also affect its capital budgeting programme. Thus, both short-term and long-range objectives are involved in the making of pricing policies.

2   Classical economic theory holds that the objective of pricing policy is to establish the optimal price, which is that price that will maximize the firm's profits. The optimal price is found where the addition to total revenue resulting from the sale of the last unit is equal to the contribution to total costs resulting from the production of that unit. The objective of profit maximization through the search for the optimal price is a strict condition that ensures the most efficient use of economic resources by the firm. Consequently, in a market economy, optimal pricing by all firms will lead to the most efficient allocation of resources between competing firms.

3   Cost-based pricing policies rely on product cost information for determining the selling price. They are concerned with two elements of price: first, that relevant costs should be recovered in setting the price; second, that a reasonable profit margin should be added to relevant costs in arriving at the price. Cost-based pricing policies do not aim at determining the optimal price. Rather, they reflect a practical and prudent approach to price, in which the first objective of price is to ensure that product costs are covered, thereby avoiding losses and allowing for the survival of the firm. Cost-based pricing policies also contain a moral view of what is a 'normal' profit. They are not concerned in a practical way with finding out that price that will maximize profit, but rather that price that will reflect what the market is able and willing to bear, taking into account a reasonable profit for the firm and its shareholders.

4   'Full-cost' pricing reflects a cost-based approach to pricing that requires that all product costs be covered in setting the selling price. Once full costs have been determined, the required profit margin is added to establish the selling price.

5   Accounting information relevant to making full-cost pricing decisions consists of all costs involved in bringing the product to the market. They comprise total manufacturing costs, consisting of direct and overhead production costs, to which are added marketing and administrative costs. Full product costs appear on first sight as relatively easy to determine. This is true in so far as direct costs are concerned. However, indirect costs, in the form of factory, administrative and marketing costs, have to be allocated to products. For this purpose, allocation keys have to be devised that produce satisfactory indirect cost allocation. In particular, such allocations should not produce biasing in the selling price of different products.

  A further problem stems from the nature of fixed costs in relation to levels of output. Fixed costs are fixed in aggregate terms, but are variable in relation to unit of the product. This means that as volume rises, fixed costs allocated to products decrease. Variable costs per unit remain constant. Hence, the variability of fixed costs at the unit level is a significant factor for pricing.

6   The statement that 'since prices are determined by supply and demand factors, accounting data is irrelevant in determining a firm's pricing policy' has some substance of truth in market situations where all firms are price-takers. This implies that there is a perfect market and that, as a result of perfect competition, individual firms compete as to costs. In this analysis, accounting data with respect to costs will be a key factor in providing the firm with knowledge of its own costs, and implicitly, where it is operating under efficiency conditions, with knowledge of the costs of competitors.

  Where markets are imperfect, it is evident that firms may not necessarily be price-takers, but may be price-makers. In this case, accounting data will be significant in determining a firm's pricing policy.

7  Conversion-cost pricing takes into account only the costs incurred by the firm in converting raw materials and semi-finished goods into finished goods. It has to do with one of the limitations of full-cost pricing that makes no difference between two products that require different degrees of effort to convert them into a marketable condition. In effect, conversion pricing excludes direct material costs, providing a pricing policy that refers pricing to the internal efforts made in converting raw materials into finished goods.

Return-on-investment pricing attempts to link the markup on costs with a desired return on invested capital in establishing pricing policies. The formula used is as follows:

$$\text{selling price} = \frac{\text{total costs} + (\text{desired percentage return on capital} \times \text{capital employed})}{\text{volume of output}}$$

The attraction of this method is that it relates the problem of pricing to financial objectives, and integrates pricing decisions with the firm's overall planning objectives.

8  'Marginal-cost' pricing is a method of cost-based pricing that defines product costs only in terms of variable costs. Unlike full or absorption costing, this method of costing excludes fixed costs from product costs. This results in product costs that are comparatively lower than under full costing. Consequently, cost of sales and stock values are understated by reference to full-product costing. Fixed costs are treated as period costs, and are charged against profits. This method of pricing is useful for developing aggressive sales policies, and in special marketing situations, for example, in expanding into export markets, and in introducing new products.

9  Target pricing is a recent innovation in the development of pricing theory. It is associated with the concept of target costing. This method of costing seeks to constrain product costs by imposing costs targets as desired cost objectives prior to introducing and producing products. Consequently, target pricing involves setting predetermined prices as targets for pricing policies that will meet targeted cost of production objectives as well as a profit requirement.

10  Pricing policies very significantly determine the firm's relationship with the market for its products and services. In the short term, pricing will affect the demand for those products, and thus directly impact on the firm's sales revenues. Since pricing affects the volume of demand, it is evident that the firm's long-term position in the market will be affected by its pricing policies. As a consequence of regulating the volume of demand, decisions relating to total production capacity will be affected by demand considerations. However, Western industrialized countries have hitherto tended to regard pricing as having emphatically short-term considerations. Setting pricing policies with long-term considerations predominantly in view has been contrary to this viewpoint. None the less, Japanese firms have developed alternative approaches that consider that long-term factors are more significant than short-term ones in determining pricing policies.

## Solutions to problems

**1**

If the McTosh offer is accepted the financial effect will be:

|  | Per unit £ |
|---|---|
| Price to McTosh | 32.5 |
| Manufacturing costs (variable) | (25) |
| Incremental overheads | (1.5) |
| Incremental benefit | 6.0 |
| Profit increase | 6,000 |

The effect of selling to Scotland at the price anticipated by McTosh would be:

|  | £ | Per unit £ |
|---|---|---|
| Price |  | 42.5 |
| Variable costs |  |  |
| Manufacturing | 25 |  |
| Transport | 3.5 |  |
|  |  | 28.50 |
|  |  | 14.0 |
| Incremental fixed costs |  | 1.5 |
| Incremental benefit |  | 12.5 |
| Profit increase |  | £12,500 |

If the price and terms set in Scotland were identical to those in England, the effect would be:

|  | £ | Per unit £ |
|---|---|---|
| Price |  | 44.0 |
| Variable costs |  |  |
| Manufacturing | 25.0 |  |
| Transport | 3.5 |  |
| Commission | 2.2 |  |
| Incremental PC | 1.5 |  |
|  |  | 32.2 |
|  |  | 11.8 |
| Profit increase |  | £11,800 |

Thus the offer should not be accepted, preferable options being:

(i) Schultz sells its production in Scotland on its own account, but on the McTosh terms re price and commission, resulting in a £12,500 incremental profit.

(ii) Sell to Scotland on its existing price/commission terms. The profit thus generated is £700 less than that at (i) above, being (a) an extra £1.50 per unit revenue + (b) an additional cost of £2.20 in commission = 70p per unit incremental cost × 1,000 sales units.

**2**

This is an awkward question, since the sales price, which is what the question asks for, is required in order to calculate the capital employed figure, yet one of the requirements which must be satisfied by the sales price is that it must 'yield a 16 per cent return on capital employed', and 'capital employed is considered to consist of 50 per cent of net sales for current assets'.

The problem can be solved by the use of simple algebra, where:

p = profit
a = required net selling price

and (1) profit is a function of sales revenue less total costs

(2) 16 per cent return on capital employed is calculated by dividing profit by capital employed.

From (1) above:

p = sales revenue − variable costs − fixed costs
p = 400,000a − (400,000 × 8) − 460,000 (Note 1)
p = 400,000a − 3,660,000

From (2) above:

$$0.16 = \frac{400,000a - 3,660,000}{0.5(400,000a) + 450,000}$$

$$400,000a - 3,660,000 = 32,000a + 72,000$$
$$368,000a = 3,732,000$$
$$a = £10.14$$

The net selling price is £10.14 per unit, giving a gross selling price, before discount, of £10.14/0.98 = £10.35.

Note 1:

|  | £ |  |
|---|---|---|
| DM | 6.00 | |
| DL | 1.60 | (£1.50 × 1.06) |
| VFO | 0.40 | |
|  | 8.00 | |

Proof:

| Calculation of profit | | £ |
|---|---|---|
| Contribution | 400,000 × £2.14 | 856,000 |
| Fixed costs | | 460,000 |
| Profit | | 396,000 |

Calculation of return on capital employed:

$$ROCE = \frac{396,000}{450,000 + (0.5\,(400,000 \times 10.14))} = 0.16$$

The above calculations assume sales to be constant at 400,000 units.

## Chapter 31  Short-run tactical decisions

### Answers to self-assessment questions

1 Relevant costs are costs useful for making short-term tactical decisions involving alternative courses of action. Relevant costs have two important characteristics:

(a) they are future costs, that is, they are costs that have not yet been incurred;
(b) they are differential costs, that is, they are different according to the decision alternatives being considered.

2 Future costs are costs that have not yet been incurred. They will be incurred as the direct result of a decision now being taken. Sunk costs are costs that have been incurred in the past. They cannot be affected by a decision now being taken. Differential costs are future costs that will differ according to the alternatives being considered for decision making.

3 An example of future costs would be costs that will be incurred as the result of continuing a project, rather than abandoning the project. Costs that have been incurred in the acquisition of fixed assets would be regarded as sunk costs, once those assets have been purchased. Differential costs are future costs that will differ according to the alternative selected. For example, where a decision is being considered either to continue or to abandon a project, the costs associated with the decision to complete the project, rather than abandon the project, are differential costs.

4   In the analysis of special decisions, the contribution margin is the excess of the revenue of any activity over its relevant costs, which is available to make a contribution to fixed costs and profits. Commonly, the contribution margin is the excess of revenue over variable costs.

5   Opportunity costs are not recorded in accounting. This is a cost concept found in economic analysis that is relevant to decision making. Opportunity costs only exist at a time when a decision has to be taken. They are defined as the value of the next best opportunity forgone, or the net cash-inflow lost as a result of preferring one alternative rather than the next best one. Opportunity costs are particularly useful for making special decisions, where choice is involved.

6   Four major classes of special decisions are the following:

   (a)   dropping a product line;
   (b)   selling or further processing a semi-manufactured product;
   (c)   operating or leasing an asset;
   (d)   making or buying a product.

   A decision to drop a product line involves considerations that may be extended to a series of decisions of a similar nature, such as closing a branch, a division, or any area of organizational activity where revenues and costs are involved. These decisions have both short- and long-range consequences, affecting the contribution margin that such activities are considered to be making towards overall profits.

   A decision to sell or further process is also a decision that has short- and long-range consequences, affecting the contribution margin that is involved by a decision to extend an activity, thereby choosing to further process rather than to sell at a given cut-off point.

   Similarly, decisions to operate or to use an asset in a different context are decisions of a tactical nature having both short-term and long-range consequences with respect to the structure of business activity.

   Finally, decisions to make or not to make a product and rather obtain it by purchasing is a tactical decision having also short-term and long-range consequences with respect to the structure of business activity.

7   The significance of opportunity costs analysis to the four main categories of special decisions lies in clarifying the impact on overall profits of selecting one alternative rather than the other. The best alternative is that which is the most advantageous by comparison to the next best one. The comparative advantage of selecting the best decision is calculated by taking into account as an opportunity cost the benefits forgone by not choosing the next best alternative.

8   Business enterprises are limited in the pursuit of profit by the fact that they have limited resources and also limited opportunities and face constraints in maximizing profits. Limiting factors may arise from shortages of labour, materials, equipment, productive capacity and a variety of other constraints.

9   The significance of a contribution margin analysis in the face of limiting factors lies in the clarification of the impact of choice on the contribution to overall profits that results from the selection of one alternative as against another alternative, where limiting factors play a determining role.

   The contribution margin analysis focuses on the contribution to organizational profits that results from a particular activity, rather than a limited view of sector profits involved in the activity itself. The contribution margin indicates that, even though a particular activity may not be profitable in a full cost accounting analysis, its contribution margin to organizational profits is a more meaningful measure of its profitability. In effect, closing a loss-making activity that makes none the less a positive contribution margin will result in an overall loss of profits.

By integrating the impact of limiting factors on the contribution margin, and expressing the contribution margin in relation to the limited factor, the contribution margin analysis allows optimal choice decisions to be made as between mutually exclusive alternatives.

10 Linear programming is a mathematical technique that seeks to make the best use of a firm's limited resources to meet chosen objectives. In accounting terms, this means maximizing profits or minimizing costs. In the face of limited plant capacity, the level and cost of output will be determined by such capacity. Linear programming allows the analysis of the choice that has to be made with respect to the possibility of applying the available capacity to one or other of the products, or a combination of both. The problem of profit maximization under such conditions under linear programming involves stating the problem in simple algebraic terms that have two aspects: first, an objective function to maximize profit; second, the recognition of the production constraint. This formulation of the choice problem pinpoints the relative output volume of each product that will maximize overall profits.

## Solutions to problems

### 1

(a)  (i) The differential cost of the order.

|  | Radwarm costs £ | Specials cost £ | Differential cost £ |
|---|---|---|---|
| Materials | (8,000) | 20,000 | 12,000 |
| Labour | (9,000) | 36,000 | 27,000 |
| Special press write-off | – | 4,000 | 4,000 |
| Power | (400) | 1,400 (1) | 1,000 |
|  | (17,400) | 61,400 | 44,000 |

**Note (1)** To determine the power bill for Specials it is necessary to know how many units of production are represented by the existing power budget. It has been assumed that the existing budget is based on the production of 1,000 Specials, a doubling of production therefore causing the power bill to double. It is clearly not logical to assume that by halving the output of Radwarms the power saving on that product will exactly match the power required to produce 1,000 Specials.

(ii)  The full cost of the order

|  | £ |
|---|---|
| Materials | 20,000 |
| Labour | 36,000 |
| Special press write-off | 4,000 |
| Depreciation | 3,600 |
| Power | 1,400 |
| Rent | 1,000 |
| Heat and light | 100 |
| Miscellaneous | 900 |
|  | 67,000 |

**Note** Because we are not aware of the quantities involved, some of the figures produced above look unusual. For example, the apportioned heat and light charge for the new order of 1,000 units is £100, while the cost for the existing (assumed) budgeted quantity of 1,000 is £1,200.

(iii) The opportunity cost of the order

|  | £ | £ |
|---|---|---|
| Radwarm |  |  |
| Sales revenue |  | 50,000 |
| Variable costs: |  |  |
| Materials | 16,000 |  |
| Labour | 18,000 |  |
| Power | 800 | 34,800 |
| Lost contribution |  | 15,200 |

The opportunity cost of the order is therefore the loss of contribution of (£15,200/2) = £7,600 which would result from the transfer of half of the Radwarm production capacity to Specials.

(b)

To: Divisional manager　　　　　　　　　　　　　　　　　　Ref: Special order
From: Management accountant

From the above figures it can be seen that the differential cost associated with the production of the Specials is £44,000. For the order to be accepted, additional working capital and plant financing would be required of up to this amount. If the differential costs are matched with the differential revenue from the order of £70,000 – £25,000 = £45,000, it can be seen that the new order is marginally worthwhile, generating a contribution gain of £1,000 (Note 2). This may not be a sufficiently attractive financial proposition. There may, however, be additional sound reasons for undertaking the work, such as that the customer is valued, and should not be turned away, or that the order represents an introduction to some new technology, and can be used as a springboard from which to obtain further work with other customers at higher prices, or that although £70 is a poor price now, in time, with productivity improvements, costs will fall so that £70 may be acceptable.

|  |  | £ |
|---|---|---|
| Note 2 | This can also be calculated as: |  |
|  | Contribution gain from new order | 8,600 |
|  | Contribution loss from reduction |  |
|  | in Radwarm sales | 7,600 |
|  | Net gain | 1,000 |

In the above analysis the arguments depend upon the assumption that the current price is £100 per unit.

## 2

Using a marginal costing approach, eliminate common fixed costs from the analysis of product profitability.

|  | A £K | B £K | C £K | Total £K |
|---|---|---|---|---|
| Sales revenue | 60 | 15 | 25 | 100 |
| Variable costs |  |  |  |  |
| Materials | 10 | 2 | 3 | 15 |
| Labour | 11 | 4 | 5 | 20 |
| Overheads | 8 | 3 | 4 | 15 |
| Selling and admin. | 5 | 2 | 3 | 10 |
| Total variable cost | 34 | 11 | 15 | 60 |
| Contribution | 26 | 4 | 10 | 40 |
| Fixed costs |  |  |  |  |
| Overheads |  |  |  | 5 |
| Selling and admin. |  |  |  | 25 |
| Profit |  |  |  | 10 |

Thus, all products make a contribution towards the common fixed cost pool, and in the absence of any reason for discontinuance which does not show up on this short-term financial analysis, all the products should be produced.

4

(a) Focus on the future costs and revenues and ignore the past (sunk) costs and revenues. Following this approach the following relevant costs can be identified:

(i) Materials:
 - Value of materials in stock (£10,000) is a sunk cost which should be ignored.
 - Disposal costs of stock will be incurred in the future and therefore are relevant to the decision.
 - The agreed contract for £5,000 is a future cost and therefore should be included.
 The balance of the stock is £65,000 – £5,000 – £10,000 = £50,000.
(ii) 
 - Allocated supervision costs of £20,000 should be ignored as it is a fixed cost which will be incurred regardless of whether the contract is entered into or not.
 - The cost of redundancy is a future cost, or in this case a saving if the contract goes ahead.
(iii) Depreciation should be ignored as it will be charged regardless of whether any work is carried out.
(iv) Variable overheads will be incurred as the costs vary with the contract.
(v) Fixed overhead allocation of £20,000 is another cost which will be incurred regardless of whether any sales are made or work carried out.
(vi) The modification of the machinery is a relevant cost and therefore it should be included. The opportunity cost of £5,000, resulting from the machinery being used on the contract instead of being sold, is also a relevant cost.

The full figures are:

| | £ | |
|---|---|---|
| Materials | 50,000 | Cost (balance) |
| | 5,000 | Cost |
| | (1,000) | Saving |
| Labour | (10,000) | Saving |
| Variable overheads | 6,000 | Cost |
| Machinery | 3,000 | Cost |
| | 5,000 | Opportunity costs |
| Net cost | 58,000 | |

The contract should proceed as it will generate a contribution of £42,000 towards fixed costs and profit.

Several other factors need to be borne in mind, such as whether there are other contracts which might be more profitable. What will be the effect on existing customers? Will discounts on materials be lost when the company purchases smaller quantities? Will the employees be demotivated by potential short-time working?

(b) The special contract will take up 3,600 direct labour hours and will displace the large new order. It is important to calculate the opportunity cost if the special order is pursued.

The limiting factor in this situation is direct labour hours. Therefore, the contribution for both the special order and the new order need to be calculated per labour hour:

$$\text{Special order } \frac{£42,000}{3,600} = £11.67/\text{labour hour}$$

$$\text{New order } \frac{£20}{5} = £4/\text{labour hour}$$

From a financial perspective, the special order should be accepted and the large new order should be rejected. However, if the large new order is from an existing customer, what will be the consequences of rejecting their order? Will the special order lead to further business? Why is the contribution on the large new order so low? This and other information will need to be evaluated before a decision is made.

(c) Non-financial factors which may be taken into account under various decision-making alternatives are as follows:

(i) *Make or buy.* Will the quality of the product be the same? Is the supplier reliable? Will the price fluctuate? Can the supplier keep the delivery schedules? What will happen to the existing labour? Is the order significant to the supplier?

(ii) *Dropping a product or department.* Are the products interdependent? Is there a suitable replacement? Will the costs be truly variable, particularly wages? What will be the customers' reaction? Will goodwill be lost?

(iii) *Limiting factors.* If products are lost because of a reduction in labour hours, will customers complain? Will the limiting factor change?

## Chapter 32 Capital investment decisions

### Answers to self-assessment questions

1 Capital investment decisions fall in the category of long-range planning. They are concerned with maintaining and enlarging the firm's assets, and therefore affect directly the firm's future profitability. The reasons which render such decisions of major importance are the following:

(a) usually, they involve substantial money outlays;

(b) the funds are committed for a long period of time, and are exposed to the higher level of risk that is involved in long-range decisions;

(c) once made, investment decisions are generally irreversible, if they should appear to have been ill-founded;

(d) occasionally, the firm's entire future may depend on a single major capital investment decision;

(e) such decisions are not only major ones for the firm, but they may be of great significance to an industry and to the economy.

2 Four common examples of capital investment decisions are:

(a) the acquisition or replacement of long-lived assets, such as buildings or plant;

(b) the investment of funds into another form of revenue-creating activity, such as a financial stake in another company;

(c) a special project, which will affect the firm's future earnings, such as a research project;

(d) the extension of the firm's range of activities, for example, a new production line or a new product line.

3 Capital investment decisions mostly focus on two aspects of long-range profitability, namely:

(a) estimating the future net increases in cash inflows or net savings in cash outlays that will result from the investment;

(b) calculating the total cash outlay required to undertake the investment.

Although such decisions are analysed in cash flow terms, it is evident that the range of information required for making the cash flow forecasts implied will cover all factors, both external and internal to the firm that will bear on such forecasts.

4 The three major factors affecting capital investment decisions are:

(a) the net amount of the investment required, expressed as the total cash outlay needed to support the project during its entire life;

(b) the net returns on the investment, expressed as the future expected net cash inflows. These may be actual cash flows or cash savings;

(c) the rate of return on investment, expressed as a percentage. The determination of the lowest acceptable rate of return will be affected by a number of factors, among which are the firm's rate of return on other investment opportunities and the firm's cost of capital.

5 The payback method is an attempt to forecast the time it will take for the expected net cash inflows to pay back the investment outlay. The payback method has the advantage of simplicity, and by selecting the alternative that most quickly repays the investment outlay, it recommends the selection of the safest projects.

However, the payback ignores the cash flows beyond the payback period. Hence, it ignores the overall profitability of the project, and emphasizes its liquidity. Moreover, the time pattern of cash inflows and outflows is also ignored, thereby treating cash flow through time as having a constant value.

6 The accounting rate of return method seeks to express the average estimated yearly net inflows as a percentage of the net investment outlays. This method overcomes the disadvantage of the payback method in that it attempts to calculate the profitability of projects. Its main disadvantage is that it also ignores the time pattern of cash inflows and outflows, and in this sense, suffers from the same defect as the payback method.

7 The discounted cash flow (DCF) method attempts to evaluate an investment by comparing the net cash flows accruing over the life of the investment at their present value, against the net cash outlay, also calculated at its present value. Thus, by comparing like with like, this method makes possible the calculation of the rate of return on an investment in a realistic manner.

As compared to the payback and the accounting rate of return methods, the DCF method is much more demanding with respect to information. For example, the time profile of cash inflows and outlays is an important information requirement, as are other factors such as the impact of taxation and the cost of capital, in the analysis of investment decisions. The sensitivity of the DCF method to forecasting errors is a significant factor in using this method.

8 The present value method and the internal rate of return method both use discounted cash flows in the analysis of investment decisions. The net present value method assumes a minimum rate of return in discounting forecasted cash inflows and cash outflows to their present value. This minimum rate of return is the firm's cost of capital. Using this rate of return in the present value calculation of cash inflows and outflows results in either a positive or negative difference between these cash inflows that determines their relative acceptability. Alternatives having negative net present values are rejected.

By contrast, the internal rate of return method does not assume a rate of return, but requires the expected rate of return on an investment to be calculated. This is the rate of return that will reduce the net present value of cash inflows to zero, after taking into account the net cash outlays. Accordingly, the selection of investment projects is effected by comparing the resulting rate of return with the firm's required rate of return.

In effect, both methods produce the same 'yes' or 'no' decisions. The advantage of the present value method is its simplicity and its insistence on investment alternatives satisfying the minimum expected rate of return, which is the cost of capital.

9 The cost of capital has been extensively discussed in the financial literature. Its basic assumption is that there is a cost involved in financing investment projects. One interpretation of this cost is in the nature of the opportunity cost of applying funds to an investment project. In this sense, the cost of capital is the cost of financing a project in terms of the return that could be obtained by investing in a similar project having similar

risks. Another interpretation, which is more usually discussed in the literature, is that the firm has to meet the expectations of shareholders and lenders by providing them with a return on the funds invested in the firm. This involves estimating the cost of capital of a particular firm in terms of its capital structure. The cost of capital will be very much affected by the gearing (leverage), representing the proportion of interest-bearing capital to the total long-term capital.

In the latter sense, the cost of capital imposes a strict requirement on firms to finance only those investment projects that meet the firm's own bottom line with respect to the return that it has to ensure to its own investors, be they shareholders or lenders. In effect, this criterion resides in a more refined notion of profitability.

10   The impact of inflation is an important consideration in assessing investment decisions due to the manner in which inflation erodes the purchasing power of cash, on which investment decisions are based. Hence, inflation affects critically forecasts of investment profitability.

Several methods are available for dealing with inflation. For example, it is possible to incorporate cost-escalation estimates into cash flow forecasts. A commonly used method of correcting DCF calculation is to adjust cash flow forecasts for specific price increases. Such adjusted cash flows are then discounted by the monetary cost of capital.

## Solutions to problems

1

|  | Machine A | Machine B |
|---|---|---|
| (a)  Payback period | 2 years | 2.5 years |
| (b)  Accounting rate of return | | |
| Depreciation | £50,000/3 | £60,000/4 |
| | £16,667 | £15,000 |

$$ARR = \frac{\text{average cash flow} - \text{depreciation}}{\text{average investment}}$$

|  | Machine A | Machine B |
|---|---|---|
| | £25,000 − 16,667 | £24,000 − 15,000 |
| | £50,000/2 | £60,000/2 |
| | 33.3% | 30% |

(c)  Discounted cash flow

| | Machine A | | Machine B | |
|---|---|---|---|---|
| Year | Cash flow | Discounted | Cash flow | Discounted |
| | £ | £ | £ | £ |
| 0 | (50,000) | (50,000) | (60,000) | (60,000) |
| 1 | 25,000 | 22,728 | 24,000 | 21,818 |
| 2 | 25,000 | 20,660 | 24,000 | 19,834 |
| 3 | 25,000 | 18,782 | 24,000 | 18,031 |
| 4 | – | – | 24,000 | 16,392 |
| | | 12,170 | | 16,075 |

From the above calculations it can be seen that machine A has the shorter payback period, but the method of calculating the payback period ignores the time value of money and ignores any cash flows occurring after the payback period.

Machine A also has a marginally higher accounting rate of return, but this measure of profitability is also compromised by considering all cash flows to be of equal significance no matter where in the life cycle of the machine they occur. Thus, machine A would have an identical ARR to that calculated above should all of its £75,000 lifetime cash inflow be concentrated into year 3.

The DCF figures, which incorporate adjustments to take account of the time value of money, show that machine B is the more attractive, yielding, in present-day money, a cash fund of £16,075, which is £3,905 more than that generated by machine A. The figures are not strictly comparable, however, since machine A yields its cash surplus one year before machine B, and to produce a true comparison it would be necessary to know what return would be made on the available funds yielded by machine A in year 4.

2
(a)

| Year | | | Existing machine | | |
|---|---|---|---|---|---|
| | | Scrap | Fault correction | Operating costs | Total |
| | | £ | £ | £ | £ |
| 0 | | – | 5,000 | – | 5,000 |
| 1 | | – | – | 192,825 | 192,825 |
| 2 | | – | – | 192,825 | 192,825 |
| 3 | | – | – | 192,825 | 192,825 |
| 4 | | – | – | 192,825 | 192,825 |
| 5 | | – | – | 192,825 | 192,825 |
| 6 | | – | – | 192,825 | 192,825 |
| 7 | | – | – | 192,825 | 192,825 |
| 8 | | – | – | 192,825 | 192,825 |
| 9 | | – | – | 192,825 | 192,825 |
| 10 | | (1,800) | – | 192,825 | 191,025 |

| Year | Net | Operating | New machine Total | Existing | Difference | DCF |
|---|---|---|---|---|---|---|
| | £ | £ | £ | £ | £ | £ |
| 0 | 97,000 | – | 97,000 | 5,000 | (92,000) | (92,000) |
| 1 | – | 172,675 | 172,675 | 192,825 | 20,150 | 18,318 |
| 2 | – | 172,675 | 172,675 | 192,825 | 20,150 | 16,652 |
| 3 | – | 172,675 | 172,675 | 192,825 | 20,150 | 15,138 |
| 4 | – | 172,675 | 172,675 | 192,825 | 20,150 | 13,762 |
| 5 | – | 172,675 | 172,675 | 192,825 | 20,150 | 12,511 |
| 6 | – | 172,675 | 172,675 | 192,825 | 20,150 | 11,374 |
| 7 | – | 172,675 | 172,675 | 192,825 | 20,150 | 10,334 |
| 8 | – | 172,675 | 172,675 | 192,825 | 20,150 | 9,400 |
| 9 | – | 172,675 | 172,675 | 192,825 | 20,150 | 8,545 |
| 10 | – | 172,675 | 172,675 | 191,025 | 18,353 | 7,075 |
| | | | | | | 31,109 |

The most profitable course of action to take would be to purchase the new machine, raising the net present value to the organization by £31,109.

(b) In coming to the above conclusion the discounted cash flow method has been used in order to calculate the discounted values of the cash flow differences between the two proposals over the ten-year period. An assessment of the profitability of the proposals cannot be made since there are no revenue figures.

In addition to considering the relative cash flows, the following should be considered in relation to the decision:

(a)  reliability of the forecasts regarding future costs, lifespans and cost of capital;
(b)  desirability of any change upon labour requirements;
(c)  effect of any change upon labour requirements;
(d)  improvements in quality caused by the new machine.

**3**

(a) (i)  NPV = £110,000

(ii)

| Year | Discount factor | NPV |
|---|---|---|
| 0 | – | £10,000 |
| 1 | 0.833 | |
| 2 | 0.694 | |
| 3 | 0.579 | |
| 4 | 0.482 | |
| 5 | 0.402 | |
| | 2.99 × 35,000 | 104,650 |
| | | £114,650 |

(iii)

| Year | | Cash flow | Discount factor | NPV |
|---|---|---|---|---|
| 0 | £30,000 + £10,000 = | £(40,000) | 1.00 | (40,000) |
| 1 | Note (1) | – | 0.833 | |
| 2 | | 40,000 | 0.694 | 27,760 |
| 3 | | 160,000 | 0.579 | 92,640 |
| 4 | | 80,000 | 0.482 | 38,560 |
| 5 | | 40,000 | 0.402 | 22,110 |
| | £10,000 + £5,000 | 15,000 | | |
| | | | | £141,070 |

**Note (1)**

| Units | SP | VC | Fixed costs | Depreciation |
|---|---|---|---|---|

$20,000 \times (10 - 8) = 40,000 - (45,000 - 5,000)$

Based on NPV the optimum plan is (iii), as it results in the highest NPV. However, the choice would depend on Barry's attitude to risk; proposal (i) is low-risk whilst proposal (iii) is very high-risk.

(b) The choice of a required rate of return is sometimes based on the weighted average cost of capital. This comprises the return on shares, both ordinary and preference, from stocks, reserves and so on. The calculation is quite sophisticated and complicated. Therefore, companies tend to use surrogate measures such as the overdraft rate charged to the company of the average risk-free rate of return, plus a reward for the risk of running the business. Some companies appear to choose a figure almost at random (e.g. 20%).

(c) Using cash payback as the basis of assessment, the figures would be as follows:
(i) and (ii) Immediate as cash payback is not a practical measure.

(iii) YR  0    (£40,000)
      1        –
      2     27,760    2 yrs 1.6 months
            12,240
      3     92,640

## Chapter 33 Budgeting for planning and control

### Answers to self-assessment questions

1 The first stage in budgeting is the determination of the key factors or constraints that impose overall limits to the budget plan. These include market conditions, productive capacity and the financing available. Once the sales budget is determined, it is possible to determine the production budget, taking into account the level of stock required to be maintained and the volume of production needed. The various production department budgets may then be prepared from the basis of the estimated costs involved in the output required. The overall financial needs are calculated in terms of a cash budget. This will represent the total finance needed to support all budgeted expenditure, including selling and distribution expenses, the production expenses, the capital expenditure budgeted for the period as well as the research and development budget. The overall budget will be expressed in terms of a budgeted profit and loss account and a budgeted balance sheet at the end of the budget period.

2 A major problem in budgeting is forecasting sales, for many factors affecting sales are outside the firm's control. The importance of an accurate sales forecast cannot be over-emphasized. If the sales forecast is too optimistic, the firm will commit itself to excessive expenditure, both on current production and on capital expenditure, which will result in excessive production and excessive production capacity. If the sales forecast is too pessimistic, the firm will underproduce and miss the opportunity of realizing sales, and the profits involved in the lost sales.

3 There are four commonly used methods for forecasting sales:

(a) The salesforce composite method, which places the responsibility on individual sales representatives for developing their own sales forecasts. These are aggregated into an overall sales forecast.

(b) The analysis of market and industry factors, which recognizes the importance of factors that are not within the knowledge of sales representatives. They include statistical information relating to gross national product, personal income, employment figures, etc. This information is used to modify the internal forecasts developed by sales representatives.

(c) Statistical analysis of business trends and fluctuations, such as growth trends, business cycle fluctuations, seasonal fluctuations and irregular variations in demand. This analysis is applied to validating the sales forecast.

(d) Sales forecasting using mathematical models that have been developed in recent years to establish relationships between economic trends and a firm's sales forecast.

4 The sales forecast is the determining factor for planning the level of activity that the firm will wish to adopt as a target for developing the sales budget. The sales budget will dictate the volume of production required to meet the budgeted sales volume. The essential feature of the relationship between the sales budget and the production budget is the command position occupied by the sales budget. In a market economy, firms are generally sales-led in terms of budget planning. The importance of the production budget lies in the analysis of production costs. The production budget may be regarded as implementing the sales budget, and stating its implications in terms of the budgeted cost of sales, where goods are costed on the basis of factory cost of production.

5 The cash budget projects the cash flows arising from the planned activities for the budget period. It provides a forecasted profile of these cash flows across the budget period. It is a vital management planning tool, for it addresses the critical problem of cash flow management, both in terms of planned expenditure and the financing of such expenditure.

6 (a) Managers start from zero in estimating future budgets.
   (b) Comparisons are made between forecasts.
   (c) Flexible budgets take account of changes in the volume of activity.

7 ABB focuses on activities rather than on the functional organization structure.

## Solutions to problems

### 1

(a) Debtors' budget

| Quarter | July–Sept £ | Oct–Dec £ | Jan–March £ | April–June £ | Year £ |
|---|---|---|---|---|---|
| Sales per month | 5,000 | 6,000 | 7,000 | 4,000 | |
| Month end debtors | 5,000 | 6,000 | 7,000 | 4,000 | 4,000 |

(b) Cash budget

| | July–Sept | Oct–Dec | Jan–March | April–June | Year |
|---|---|---|---|---|---|
| balance b/f | 2,000 | 1,500 | 2,700 | 10,600 | 2,000 |
| Receipts | | | | | |
| from sales* | 13,000 | 17,000 | 20,000 | 15,000 | 65,000 |
| | 15,000 | 18,500 | 22,700 | 25,600 | 67,000 |
| Payments | | | | | |
| Purchases | 12,000 | 14,000 | 10,000 | 8,000 | 44,000 |
| Expenses | 1,500 | 1,800 | 2,100 | 1,200 | 6,600 |
| Balance c/f | 1,500 | 2,700 | 10,600 | 16,400 | 16,400 |
| | 15,000 | 18,500 | 22,700 | 25,600 | 67,000 |

*Note Cash receipts in any quarter will equal sales for months 1 and 2 of that quarter plus receipts from the debtors at the end of the previous quarter, as follows:

| | £ | £ | £ | £ |
|---|---|---|---|---|
| From debtors | 3,000 | 5,000 | 6,000 | 7,000 |
| From sales in qtr | 10,000 | 12,000 | 14,000 | 8,000 |
| | 13,000 | 17,000 | 20,000 | 15,000 |

(c) Stock budget

| | units | units | units | units | units |
|---|---|---|---|---|---|
| Opening stock | 1,000 | 2,000 | 3,000 | 1,000 | 1,000 |
| Purchases | 6,000 | 7,000 | 5,000 | 4,000 | 22,000 |
| | 7,000 | 9,000 | 8,000 | 5,000 | 23,000 |
| Units sold | 5,000 | 6,000 | 7,000 | 4,000 | 22,000 |
| Closing stock | 2,000 | 3,000 | 1,000 | 1,000 | 1,000 |

### 2

**Profit statement**

| Quarter | 1 £ | 2 £ | 3 £ | 4 £ |
|---|---|---|---|---|
| Sales | 42,000 | 45,000 | 48,000 | 51,000 |
| *Less:* | | | | |
| Direct materials (50%) | 21,000 | 22,500 | 24,000 | 25,500 |
| Direct wages (20%) | 8,400 | 9,000 | 9,600 | 10,200 |
| Variable overheads (10%) | 4,200 | 4,500 | 4,800 | 5,100 |
| | 8,400 | 9,000 | 9,600 | 10,200 |

**Balance sheet**

| Quarter | 1 | 2 | 3 | 4 |
|---|---|---|---|---|
| | £ | £ | £ | £ |
| Fixed assets | 23,400 | 22,800 | 22,200 | 21,600 |
| Current assets | | | | |
| Stocks | 28,000 | 30,000 | 32,000 | 34,000 |
| Debtors | 28,000 | 30,000 | 32,000 | 34,000 |
| Total assets | 79,400 | 82,800 | 86,200 | 89,600 |
| Current liabilities | | | | |
| Bank overdraft | 27,500 | 27,900 | 27,700 | 26,900 |
| Creditors | 21,000 | 22,500 | 24,000 | 25,500 |
| Total assets *less* current liabilities | 30,900 | 32,400 | 34,500 | 37,200 |
| Capital and reserves | | | | |
| Share capital | 40,000 | 40,000 | 40,000 | 40,000 |
| Profit and loss account | 9,100 | 7,600 | 5,500 | 2,800 |
| | 30,900 | 32,400 | 34,500 | 37,200 |

**Cash flow budget**

| Quarter | 1 | 2 | 3 | 4 |
|---|---|---|---|---|
| | £ | £ | £ | £ |
| Opening cash balance | (26,500) | (27,500) | (27,900) | (27,700) |
| Inflows from customers | 40,000 | 43,000 | 46,000 | 49,000 |
| Outflows | | | | |
| Paid suppliers | 21,500 | 23,000 | 24,500 | 26,000 |
| Wages | 8,400 | 9,000 | 9,600 | 10,200 |
| Variable overheads | 4,200 | 4,500 | 4,800 | 5,100 |
| Fixed overheads | | | | |
| Depreciation | 6,900 | 6,900 | 6,900 | 6,900 |
| | 41,000 | 43,400 | 45,800 | 48,200 |
| Net cash flow | (1,000) | (400) | 200 | 800 |
| Closing cash balance | (27,500) | (27,900) | (27,700) | (26,900) |

| | £ | £ | £ | £ |
|---|---|---|---|---|
| Opening debtors | 26,000 | 28,000 | 30,000 | 32,000 |
| *Add:* Sales | 42,000 | 45,000 | 48,000 | 51,000 |
| *Less:* Closing debtors | 28,000 | 30,000 | 32,000 | 34,000 |
| From customers | 40,000 | 43,000 | 46,000 | 49,000 |

| | £ | £ | £ | £ |
|---|---|---|---|---|
| Cost of sales | 21,000 | 22,500 | 24,000 | 25,500 |
| *Add:* Closing stock | 28,000 | 30,000 | 32,000 | 34,000 |
| *Less:* Opening stock | 26,000 | 28,000 | 30,000 | 32,000 |
| Purchases | 23,000 | 24,500 | 26,000 | 27,500 |

| | £ | £ | £ | £ |
|---|---|---|---|---|
| Opening creditors | 19,500 | 21,000 | 22,500 | 24,000 |
| *Add:* Purchases | 23,000 | 24,500 | 26,000 | 27,500 |
| *Less:* Closing creditors | 21,000 | 22,500 | 24,000 | 25,500 |
| Paid to suppliers | 21,500 | 23,000 | 24,500 | 26,000 |

**4**

(a) (i)   To assist the planning of the organization through the setting of objectives and goals.

(ii)   To control the organization via setting plans and comparing the actual figures against them.

(iii)   To coordinate the various departments and functions within the organization.

(iv)   To motivate managers to achieve the budget, and thereby the organization's objectives.

(v)   To communicate the plans of the organization to the various parts of the organization.

(b)   The organization can be classified by profit centre as well as by functional area. The profit centres are likely to follow the current organization structure, that is, swimming pool manager, diving pool manager, conference hall manager and so on. The functional budgets for this type of organization are: sales, purchases, labour and overheads. Each manager would be expected to prepare the figures for their particular area of responsibility.

The chart below is a proposed organization chart for the leisure complex, with each manager responsible for the staff, expenses and income in their area of responsibility.

(c)

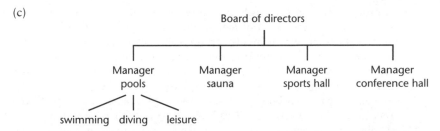

There are many software programs available for the preparation of budgets. These programs can be developed on spreadsheet software or can be run on a spreadsheet such as Lotus, Supercalc, Excel, etc.

## Chapter 34  Organizing for control

### Answers to self-assessment questions

1   The purpose of 'control' lies in ensuring that the organization's activities conform with its plans. Control, therefore, is an activity affecting every aspect of the organization. The terms planning and control are frequently joined together in expressing the nature of their relationship.

2   The control process may be seen as a cycle that shows the origin of control in the objectives of the organization from which plans are developed. These plans include long-range and annual plans. The control cycle integrates both the long-range and the annual plan. Information feedback enables actual performance to be compared with planned performance, thus enabling management to control operations and the resources allocated to those operations. The control process allows achievements to be compared with the organization's desired objectives, thereby enabling new goals and new objectives to be formulated.

3   'Responsibility accounting' defines managerial responsibility in terms of an organizational framework in which responsibility centres are established, and individual managers appointed to manage such centres are made responsible for the centre's performance. There are different kinds of responsibility centres, that depend partly on the size of the organization and partly on the style of management adopted.

4   An 'expense centre' may be defined as a responsibility centre in which the manager has no control over revenues, but is able to control expenditure. By contrast, a 'cost centre' is a production department in which costs are accumulated. Accordingly, the manager of a cost centre is responsible for the costs incurred in that department. An expense centre may be distinguished from a cost centre in that the former is a department that incurs expenditure, whereas the latter is a production department that incurs costs.

5   The distinction between 'controllable' and 'non-controllable' costs is significant for the purposes of responsibility accounting. Managers should only be held responsible for the costs that fall under their control. These are defined as 'controllable costs'. Costs over which they have no control are defined as 'uncontrollable costs'. Where systems of responsibility accounting have been installed, managers are not held responsible for 'uncontrollable costs', that is, costs over which they have no control. For example, a departmental manager would be held responsible for costs incurred in his/her department. S/he would not be held responsible for costs transferred into that department from another department as work-in-process.

6   A profit centre is a responsibility centre that involves a responsibility for profit. It represents a much higher level of management responsibility than expense centres and cost centres. In particular, it involves responsibility for factors affecting profit, namely revenues and expenses. It follows that a profit centre is a responsibility centre presenting specific features. First, it is generally a large responsibility centre, that includes subordinate responsibility centres, such as expense centres and cost centres. Second, given that management responsibility includes revenues, it follows that a profit centre must include revenue-producing activities. Third, given the broad nature of management responsibility involved, profit centres imply the existence of an organizational structure that allows the degree of centralized decision making that gives profit centre managers the necessary freedom of activity implied in the notion of running a segment of the organization as a business. Typical examples of profit centres are factories operating as profit centres, product and service divisions, and in large organizations, subsidiary companies that are managed as profit centres.

7   Large enterprises that have organizational structures that are decentralized and divisionalized face particular problems in planning, controlling and evaluating profit centres where intra-company trading occurs. This will occur in the following circumstances:
    (a) where profit centres trade with the external markets as well as with each other with respect to finished products and services;
    (b) where profit centres trade with each other in respect of intermediary products. This occurs where the activities of profit centres are interrelated, so that the output of one profit centre provides a substantial part of the input to another profit centre.

The purpose of transfer prices is to provide a price mechanism that allows trading between profit centres to take place, thereby permitting them to function as profit centres. Accordingly, transfer prices provide the profit centre that sells an output in the form of measurable revenue. Equally, it provides the buying profit centre with an input cost that would reflect efficient buying prices.

The availability of an efficient transfer pricing mechanism is of critical importance to the evaluation of profit centre performance in decentralized and divisionalized corporations.

Transfer prices should satisfy the following three criteria:
    (a) they should promote goal congruence within the organization by harmonizing the interests of individual divisions with the interests of the organization as a whole;

(b) they should make possible reliable assessments of divisional performance for the following purposes:
  (i) making predictions for decision making;
  (ii) appraising managerial performance;
  (iii) evaluating divisional contributions to corporate profits.
(c) they should ensure the autonomy of individual divisions is respected and profits are not dependent on the actions of other divisions.

8 Three main methods are used for establishing transfer prices, namely:
  (a) market-based transfer pricing,
  (b) cost-based transfer pricing,
  (c) negotiated transfer pricing.

Market-based transfer pricing applies where external markets exist for the goods that are traded between profit centres. If the external markets are competitive, and divisional interdependence is minimal, market-based transfer pricing satisfies the required conditions for an effective transfer pricing mechanism.

Cost-based transfer pricing overcomes difficulties associated with the absence of market prices, for example, when intermediary goods are transferred between profit centres. Two commonly used cost-related prices are full-cost and variable cost prices.

Cost-based transfer prices can be simply at cost, in which case, the transferring profit centre simply recovers its costs and makes no profit, or at cost-plus, in which case, the required profit markup is added to costs. Cost-based transfer prices pose a number of problems in actual practice.

Negotiated transfer pricing results from negotiations between profit centre managers. Given that their performance as managers is at stake, it is evident that this method will lead to disputes requiring arbitration.

9 Investment centres represent the ultimate stage in the decentralization of organizational decision making. Usually found in autonomous divisions and subsidiary companies, investment centres have managerial responsibility not only for cost goals (expense centres) and for profit contribution (profit centres), but also for invested capital. They extend the principle underlying profit centres by evaluating investment centre profits with the capital invested in the centre. The evaluation of investment centre performance implies selecting performance criteria that would apply to wholly autonomous enterprises.

10 The criterion most commonly applied for assessing the financial performance of investment centres is the return on capital employed (ROCE). It is a comprehensive measure of performance that enables comparisons to be made between companies and divisions for the purpose of evaluating the efficiency with which assets are utilized. It is calculated as follows:

$$\text{ROCE} = \frac{\text{net profit before interest and tax}}{\text{average capital invested}} \times 100$$

Some limitations are inherent in using ROCE for the assessing of investment centre performance. They stem from the measurement of profit and capital employed, the appropriation of costs and assets as between divisions, and some conceptual weaknesses affect ROCE. In particular, it is normal for different investment centres to have ROCEs that are different and that reflect the particular conditions affecting their particular sectors of business. Managers of investment centres having naturally lower ROCE than other investment centres will feel disadvantaged when evaluated on the basis of ROCE. This may well affect their behaviour.

## Solutions to problems

**1**
To: Mr Jackson
From: Management Consultant

Dear Mr Jackson
EVALUATION OF DIVISIONAL PERFORMANCE

I have studied your proposals for the evaluation of the effectiveness of your divisional managers and the linking of their rewards with this evaluation. My comments are as follows:

(1) Any system of targets will influence the behaviour of those for whom the targets are set, indeed this is the purpose of the target setting exercise. Your composite index will avoid the problems associated with a single target, which is that desirable behaviour which does not have an immediate effect upon the target set will be much reduced. Your weighted targets do have problems, though. The weightings are subjective – are equal weights for the three objectives really in accord with the priorities of your business? Furthermore, change to the various criteria may not be equally easy to achieve, so that managers concentrate on improving the performance criteria which are easy to improve, and neglect those which are more difficult. Thus organizational 'improvement' effort becomes distorted. Finally, there may be conflict between achieving the different objectives, for example, by reducing volume a higher price in the market may be achieved, but the improved profit margin may be countered by a reduction in the rate of capital turnover.

(2) There has to be a recognition that there may be a difference between managerial performance and divisional performance, and it may be inappropriate to reward managers for divisional performance improvements for which they are not responsible. To take the opposite as an example, it would clearly be inequitable to withhold a bonus from the manager of a division where growth, profitability and capital turnover are decreasing when the manager may be operating in a fiercely competitive market which is experiencing import penetration and a trade depression. In the particular situation, while in absolute terms the performance may be poor, in reality the management may be doing a superb job with the resources which they have available to them.

(3) It is necessary to ensure that the managers have control over the areas on which they are being assessed. To assess on capital turnover implies that capital acquisition decisions are taken by the managers, and not at Head Office. If the latter case holds, the managers may justifiably complain that it is unfair to be assessed on the use of a capital base over which they have little influence, and which is not the one which they would have chosen.

(4) It might be better to assess each of your divisions separately, looking at their environments and their strengths and weaknesses, and then to produce, working with divisional managements, a statement of objectives for each of the divisions. This 'customized' statement of objectives may be more effective in promoting the kind of performance and decision making which is in the best interests of the division and of the company, at that particular time.

(5) In your assessment of effectiveness you might use a 'pyramid of ratios' approach, so that instead of simply looking at capital turnover, you look at particular components of this figure which may cause concern, such as the relationship between sales and, say, stocks. Greater emphasis may well be placed on non-financial factors when assessing performance, and you might consider looking at areas such as quality of production/service, which can be assessed by indicators such as number of customer complaints, length of order to delivery time and amount of repeat business generated.

(6) Your bonus of £200 for each 1 per cent improvement in the composite index seems a little arbitrary. It might be better to tie the bonus in more closely with the amount of savings made – say, as a percentage. This principle would require modification in the situation in which the management of a particular division is performing a holding operation in a hostile market, however, for in that case reduced losses rather than savings may be the mark of sound management.

I hope that you find these comments helpful, and shall be pleased to discuss them with you at any time prior to your October board meeting.

Signed

Management Accountant

## Chapter 35  Standard costs and variance analysis

### Answers to self-assessment questions

1  The principal difference between budgeted and standard costs lies in their scope. Budgeted costs impose total cost limits for the firm as a whole, for departments or for functions for the budget period. Standard costs impose total cost limits in respect of units of products. The relationship between budgeted costs and standard costs lies in the fact that the setting of standard costs as performance standards for control purposes at the product level implies that they must be used as a basis for calculating budgeted costs at the firm or departmental level, as the case may be.

2  There are several important applications of standard costing. First, it allows the evaluation of performance through the process of management by exception by highlighting only the variances between the standard cost set and the actual cost performance achieved. Second, a standard costing system may lead to cost reductions, since it involves a reappraisal of current production methods in the search for increased cost efficiency. Third, standard costs may be used for price setting, since they represent what products should cost. Hence, they are a better guide to selling prices than historic costs. Four, standard costing systems create an atmosphere of cost consciousness among managers.

3  The setting of standard costs involves problems in the following respects:
   (a) establishing procedures for setting standards with respect to the price at which resources are acquired and in the manner in which they are utilized;
   (b) establishing procedures for allowing participation by cost centre managers in setting attainable cost standards.

   Particular problems exist in relation to setting cost standards for overheads, since there is no direct measurement of output against which they can be set. Hence, it is necessary to establish surrogate measures of output to which overhead costs can be related. As regards fixed overhead costs, it is necessary that there should be established a standard level of activity for the budget period.

4  A budget variance is defined as a difference between the budget allowance for the output achieved and the actual spending on the output achieved. Total expenditure budgeted for that output will have been calculated by reference to the standard costs per unit of the product multiplied by the number of units budgeted as the total output for the period. The actual expenditure recorded may reveal that budget allowances have been exceeded by actual expenditure, and will appear as an *unfavourable budget variance*. On the other hand, the actual expenditure may turn out to be less than the budget allowance, giving rise to a *favourable budget variance*.

The appearance of a budget variance allows for the process of management by exception by indicating the necessity to take corrective action to bring performance back to the standard performance set. Where the budget variance is considered to be significant, it must be investigated whether it be a favourable or an unfavourable budget variance. A favourable budget variance may be an indication that the standards need to be revised: an unfavourable budget variance may indicate that the desired performance is not being achieved.

The analysis of budget variances involves establishing which cost elements are involved, and then determining by reference to the analysis of standard costs whether the variance is due to price or to usage factors.

5 The formula for calculating the direct material price variance is:

actual quantity purchased × (standard unit price – actual unit price)

The formula for calculating the direct material usage variance is:

standard unit price × (standard quantity for the output achieved – actual quantity used)

The formula for calculating the wage rate variance is:

actual hours × (standard wage rate – actual wage rate)

The formula for calculating the labour efficiency variance is:

standard wage rate × (standard hours for the output achieved – actual hours).

6 Problems exist in setting overhead cost standards in the three important areas, namely setting cost standards, selecting a standard overhead rate and determining the standard volume for fixed overhead cost recovery.

The setting of cost standards implies that resources have been acquired at the best price, and that they have been used in the most efficient manner. The problem of setting efficient usage levels supposes that these costs will support a standard level of activity. Since overhead costs are not directly related to products, the problem is selecting a measurement of activity that can be used as a surrogate for the output expressed as product volume.

The selection of a standard overhead rate by which to allocate (recover) overhead costs to units of products depends on determining what measurement of activity should be used. In effect, this problem is resolved by using the concept of the standard hour, defined as *a unit of measurement representing the quantity of any product or service which can be produced or performed in one hour by any process, machine or operative.* It is not a measure of time, but a measure of performance in a period of one hour.

Fixed overhead costs, unlike variable overhead costs, do not vary with output. For this reason, the allocation (recovery) of fixed overheads to units of products requires that a normal (standard) output be budgeted as a reference base by which to calculate a fixed overhead rate. Should there be a volume variance, that is, a difference between actual and budgeted output level, there will necessarily be either an over-recovery or under-recovery of fixed overhead costs, according as to whether actual output is greater or less than the standard output.

7 Fixed budgeting refers to the setting of budgets on the basis of a standard output for the purpose of establishing budget allowances throughout the firm. With fixed budgeting, standard fixed overhead costs will be over-applied (over-recovery) or under-applied (under-recovery) whenever actual output is greater or less than the standard output. These conditions manifest themselves as favourable or unfavourable volume variances.

Fixed budgets are useful for determining the financing requirement for the budget period, since they indicate that there is a target output volume that the firm aims to achieve, and for which finance is needed. The disadvantage of using fixed budgets for control purposes as well lies in the fact that where actual volume does not match exactly with the planned (standard) volume, there will always be a fixed overhead cost volume variance.

The objective of developing flexible budgets is precisely to overcome the problem caused by fixed budgets, when actual and standard volume differ. Flexible budgeting is used only for controlling performance. It involves recalculating the budget allowance for the actual volume of output achieved. Hence, fixed overhead volume variances are eliminated as regards the analysis of performance. This means, in effect, that managers are not made responsible for variances in activity levels for which they are not responsible.

8   The formula for calculating the variable overhead expenditure variance is:

actual overheads − (actual hours × standard variable overhead rate)

The formula for calculating the variable overhead efficiency variance is:

standard variable overhead rate × (actual hours − standard hours)

The formula for calculating the fixed overhead expenditure variance is:

actual fixed overheads − budgeted fixed overheads

The formula for calculating the fixed overhead volume variance is:

budgeted fixed overheads − (standard fixed overhead rate × standard hours in the output achieved)

9   The three variances that can be applied to the analysis of sales are:

(a)  Sales price variance that indicates the effect on profits of the difference between set prices and prices at which goods were actually sold. It is calculated as follows:

number of units sold × (actual contribution per unit − standard contribution per unit)

(b)  Sales volume variance that indicates the effect on profits of the difference between the planned and the actual sales volume. It is calculated as follows:

standard contribution per unit × (actual units sold − budgeted units of sales)

(c)  Sales mix variance indicates the change in total profitability that is due to changes in the mix of products sold, where these products have differing contribution margins. It is calculated as follows:

standard contribution per unit of each product × (actual quantities of units sold − actual total sales in budgeted mix proportions).

10  Standard costing allows the application of the concept of management by exception, which focuses managerial attention on variances between planned and actual performance as they appear. Therefore, the investigation of variances is concerned only with exceptional variances, that is, those regarded as being sufficiently significant to require investigation. Accordingly, the investigation of variances is a three-stage process consisting of:

(a)  determining whether the variance is significant;
(b)  if significant, determining its causes;
(c)  if it can be corrected, taking action to prevent its recurrence.

## Solutions to problems

**1**

(a) The master budget totals and actuals do not permit a breakdown of costs into those relating to A or to B, therefore total variances by cost element will be calculated.

| | Fixed budget | | Flexed budget | | Actual | | Variance |
|---|---|---|---|---|---|---|---|
| | A | B | A | B | A | B | |
| Units | 600 | 400 | 500 | 500 | 500 | 500 | |
| Materials | 13,200 | | 13,500 | | 13,300 | | 200(F) |
| Labour | 7,000 | | 7,500 | | 8,400 | | 900(U) |
| Machining | | | | | | | |
| – Var | 1,600 | | 1,500 | | | | |
| – Fixed | 8,000 | | 8,000 | | 9,450 | | 50 (F) |
| Overheads | | | | | | | |
| – Var | 1,400 | | 1,500 | | | | |
| – Fixed | 3,000 | | 3,000 | | 4,400 | | 100(F) |
| | 34,200 | | 35,000 | | 35,550 | | 550(U) |

Note: The std variable cost/unit of input is:
Material    £13,200/4,400 = £3/kg
Labour      £7,000/1,400 = £5/direct labour hour
Machining           = £4/m/c hour
Overheads         = £1/direct labour hour

(b) 1,400 hours worked.

| | | | | |
|---|---|---|---|---|
| Actual labour cost | 8,400 | Rate variance | £1,400 | (U) |
| Actual hours at std | | | | |
| 1,400 × £5 | 7,000 | Efficiency variance | £500 | (F) |
| Std cost of output | 7,500 | | £900 | (U) |

**3**

(a) **Materials variances**

| | | £ | |
|---|---|---|---|
| Actual materials purchased at actual price: | | | |
| 9,000 kg × 98p/kg | = | 8,820 | |
| 12,000 kg × 86p/kg | = | 10,320 | |
| | | £19,140 | |
| *Less:* actual materials at standard price: | | | |
| 21,000 kg × £1 | = | £21,000 | |
| Price variance | | £1,860 | (F) |
| Actual usage at standard price: | | | |
| 19,500 kg × £1 | = | £19,500 | |
| *Less:* actual production at standard price cost/unit: | | | |
| 8,200 × £2 | = | £16,400 | |
| Usage variance | | £3,100 | (U) |

**Direct labour variances**

| | | | |
|---|---|---|---|
| Actual hours at actual rate | = | £36,340 | |
| *Less:* actual hours × standard rate: | | | |
| 15,800 × £2.20 | = | £34,760 | |
| Rate variance | | £1,580 | (U) |
| *Less:* actual production at standard labour cost/unit | | | |
| 8,200 × 2 × £2.20 | = | £36,080 | |
| Efficiency variance | | £1,320 | (F) |

|  |  | £ |  |
|---|---|---|---|
| **Variable overhead variances** |  |  |  |
| Actual expenditure | = | £14,250 |  |
| *Less:* actual hours × standard rate |  |  |  |
| 15,800 × £1 | = | £15,800 |  |
| Expenditure variance |  | £1,550 | (F) |
| *Less:* actual production × standard cost/unit |  |  |  |
| 8,200 × £2 | = | £16,400 |  |
| Efficiency variance |  | £600 | (F) |

(b) The purpose of variances is to provide feedback to management very quickly. The price variance on materials needs to be reported to the buyer; hence the calculation of the price variance is based on materials purchased, not used.

The production manager would receive feedback on materials usage and labour efficiency. The rate variance is the responsibility of the personnel manager.

It should be noted that some variances may be interrelated: for example, the materials price variance may have resulted from the purchase of cheaper and poorer quality materials. This would lead to more waste and an unfavourable materials usage variance.

The unfavourable labour rate variance may have been caused by employing a higher grade of labour. This was reflected in the favourable labour efficiency variance.

(c) (i) The labour efficiency variance was favourable indicating that labour usage was efficient; therefore, the explanation is unacceptable.

(ii) The materials usage variance was unfavourable, indicating there was a higher level of waste than expected; therefore, the explanation is acceptable.

(iii) The labour rate was unfavourable which shows that the explanation is unacceptable. Labour was paid a higher rate than standard.

(iv) A discount on materials price would be reflected in a favourable variance, supporting the explanation.

(v) The variable overhead expenditure variance was favourable, indicating a saving on overheads and not on additional expense as suggested by the explanation.

# Chapter 36 The control of managed costs

## Answers to self-assessment questions

1 Essentially, managed costs are non-manufacturing costs. Their level is determined at the discretion of managers, rather than by strict requirements defined by manufacturing operations. They are often referred to as 'discretionary costs'.

2 The problems involved in the control of managed costs arise from the fact that unlike engineered costs, they cannot be strictly defined in terms of short-term output. Administrative costs, for example, are considered as relatively fixed. Research and development costs are related to long-term planning, and may be difficult to control by reason of the speculative nature of research. In effect, managed costs involve expenditure (inputs) without necessarily giving rise to results (outputs) that may be difficult to evaluate objectively.

3 Budgetary control is a method of controlling managed costs in terms of departmental spending budgets, relying on the principle of responsibility accounting. Two different methods are the marginal-costing approach and the fixed-cost approach. Under the marginal-costing approach, the development of department budgets assumes a cost–volume relationship, in which costs vary directly with activity volume and the relationship is quantifiable. The fixed-cost approach treats managed costs as fixed during the budget period,

and not susceptible to variation in the short term. In this approach, control is focused on the spending variance.

4 Administrative costs refer to the costs associated with management activities and the various tasks involved in those activities. Management activities concerned with decision making are generally viewed as discretionary, and the tasks involved are of a non-routine and non-repetitive nature. Moreover, although cost inputs are often quite substantial in terms of salaries and other expenses, there is no measurable output that can be evaluated objectively. None the less, there are whole categories of lower-level activities that are found in the administrative function that may be exposed to some measure of control. These are routine tasks that are repetitive and routine, and can be controlled in terms of work study measurements.

Generally, administrative costs are controlled in terms of spending budgets, and actual spending is reviewed in terms of budget allowances.

5 There are two main reasons why research and development costs are difficult to control. First, there is little connection between the costs committed and the benefits obtained. Second, there is usually a long lead-time between costs incurred and any ultimate result obtained.

Research and development expenditure is an activity related to long-range planning, and the effectiveness of a research and development programme can only be assessed in terms of specified long-range goals. The control of research and development costs committed to a particular programme may be controlled in terms of progress made towards completion.

6 Marketing costs have become a significant cost element, owing to the costly nature of advertising and marketing. The development of the most efficient cost control methods in this is a most important consideration. This requires the analysis of all the activities involved in marketing, ranging from obtaining orders, warehousing and distribution, to handling returns and after-sales service. These activities may be analysed on three different bases: the nature of the costs involved, the functions performed, and the appropriate sector of the firm's activity.

7 The three bases on which marketing costs may be analysed, namely, cost classification, functional classification and sectorial classification, involve the following:

(a) Cost classification, which is concerned with analysing costs as to their nature, for example, salespeople's salaries and commission, travelling expenses, and advertising.
(b) Functional classification, which involves analysing costs classified as to nature in the context of particular functions, for example, selling, advertising, transportation, credit collection, warehousing and invoicing. In this way, it is possible to assess the burden of particular cost categories in different functions.
(c) Sectorial classification, which involves analysing different sectors in which costs are committed in terms of particular functions, for example, sectors such as different territories, different products, different divisions, different customers, etc.

The end-purpose of such analyses is to provide the firm with analysed information permitting some form of evaluation of cost performance in relation to such goals as profitability and other indices of marketing performance.

## Chapter 37  Behavioural aspects of performance evaluation

**Answers to self-assessment questions**

1   Managerial style is said to be the 'set of behaviours exhibited by key managers in an organization' (Horngren and Foster). This means, in effect, that it is representative of the manner in which key managers relate to their subordinates and personnel throughout the organization. In this sense, two distinct and contrasting managerial styles are those that tend towards authoritative as against participative management styles.

2   Organization culture is said to be the 'set of beliefs and values that are shared by members of an organization'. It describes the prevalent interpersonal relationships that exist in an organization, and the constraints that exist as regards social behaviour. Much has been discussed about the importance of organizational culture of recent years, in particular in referring to the success of Japanese businesses. In this debate, organizational culture is deemed to determine the manner in which management and workers interact, and also the manner in which management decisions are made. Hence, managerial style may be viewed as subsumed in the concept of organizational culture.

3   The objectives of performance evaluation may be listed as follows:

   (a)  to assess how effectively managers have performed the tasks to which they were assigned;
   (b)  to identify where corrective actions should be taken;
   (c)  to ensure that managers are motivated towards organizational goals;
   (d)  to enable comparisons to be made between different sectors of an organization, and to discover where improvements may be made.

4   Theory X was defined by McGregor (1960) as a leadership style adopted by management. In effect, Theory X is a 'managerial style' that indicates an authoritarian style of management. It is based on a view of people in organizations that reflects the following sentiments:

   (a)  Management is responsible for organizing the elements of production.
   (b)  Management is responsible for directing the efforts of people, for motivating and controlling their actions, and modifying their behaviour to fit the needs of the organization.
   (c)  Management consists of getting things done through people. Without active intervention by management, people would be passive and even resistant to change. Their activities must be directed by management, by the means of persuasion, reward, punishment and on-going control.

5   By contrast to Theory X, Theory Y is a more modern view of management, the view that business firms should reflect the ideals of social democracy found in society evidenced in a willingness of managers to allow subordinates to participate in decision making.

   Although both Theory X and Theory Y agree that the role of management is to manage, they differ markedly as regards their view of people in organizations. According to Theory Y, for example, people are not passive nor indeed resistant to change. It is the attitude of management that produces these reactions. The qualities that good management seeks, namely motivation, development potential, capacity for assuming responsibility, and the readiness to work for the realization of corporate goals already exist in people: they need only be brought out. According to Theory Y, the essential task of management is to arrange organizational conditions and methods of operation that will allow people to realize their own goals in the attainment of organizational objectives.

6 Managers may react negatively to budgets prepared in a traditional manner, that is, where the style of management reflects Theory X. The reaction to excessive budget pressure may lead to mistrust, hostility and eventually to poorer performance. There may be an over-emphasis on short-term performance at the expense of the long term. Excessive emphasis on profit performance may tend to limit the ability of top management to correctly evaluate the all-round managerial qualities of their subordinates.

Among other negative reactions may be an unwillingness to communicate information, a stifling of initiative and biasing in preparing departmental budget information, where the style of management is authoritarian.

Proponents of participative budgeting argue that these negative reactions can be prevented, by altering management styles and creating conditions that allow managers to participate in setting attainable budgets.

7 Proponents of participative budgeting argue that the active participation of management in the budgeting process makes it possible to envisage three levels of cost performance. First, there is the budgeted level, which is decided as the planned level of cost performance. Second, managers will have their own aspiration level, defined as that level of future performance in a familiar task which individual managers explicitly undertake knowing their own past performance level. Hence, the aspiration level as regards costs is the spending level that managers regard as realistic. Third, the actual cost performance is that performance that is currently being achieved.

8 Management by objectives is a management concept that seeks to translate organizational objectives and goals in such a way that they become the personal objectives and goals of all management personnel. The aim is to create a high degree of goal congruence between organizational objectives and personal objectives throughout the organization and so encourage managers to take actions that are in the best interests of the organization.

9 Contingency theory is an approach to organization theory that starts with the premise that no single organizational design is the best in all situations. Contingency theory defines four factors as being of particular significance in the design of an organizational structure, as follows:

(a) Forces in the manager. These are factors relating to the personalities of managers. Contingency theory states that organizations do not have objectives, only people have objectives. Hence, these objectives will vary from manager to manager.

(b) Forces in the environment. Contingency theory argues that the most effective organizational structures are those that enable the organization to adjust to environmental requirements.

(c) Forces in the task. Contingency theory argues also that technology has an important impact on the design of organizational structures.

(d) Forces in subordinates. Organizations employing relatively more skilled than unskilled personnel will be faced with a greater desire for democratic structure.

# Chapter 38  Strategic dimensions

## Answers to self-assessment questions

1 The strategist is outward-looking and concerned with competitive market forces. The traditional management accountant is inward-looking and concerned with internal costs.

2 To remain sensitive to the needs and demands of clients and customers. To identify the forces which shape competitive rivalry. To understand environmental forces. To adopt a strategic perspective to internal data.

3 Value-added activities contribute something that is worthwhile to the enterprise and its customers, e.g. distinctive product features, superior customer service. Non-value-added activities can be reduced or eliminated without decreasing the enterprise's ability to compete and meet customers' demands, e.g. inspection of incoming materials.

4 All questions concerning the profitability of customers and customer groups, e.g. 'Which customer or group generates our greatest profit contribution?'

5 Identify competitors and potential competitors. Identify substitute products. Place competitors into strategic groups. Analyse competitors and their strategy.

6 A competitive market price is estimated in the first instance from which is derived a target cost.

7 Lead time, set-up time, number of line stops and number of units scrapped. Non-financial measures provide fast feedback.

# Index